Lecture Notes in Artificial Intelligence   6943

Subseries of Lecture Notes in Computer Science

Abdelhamid Bouchachia (Ed.)

Adaptive and Intelligent Systems

Second International Conference, ICAIS 2011
Klagenfurt, Austria, September 6-8, 2011
Proceedings

 Springer

Series Editors

Randy Goebel, University of Alberta, Edmonton, Canada
Jörg Siekmann, University of Saarland, Saarbrücken, Germany
Wolfgang Wahlster, DFKI and University of Saarland, Saarbrücken, Germany

Volume Editor

Abdelhamid Bouchachia
University of Klagenfurt
Department of Informatics-Systems
Universitätsstr. 65-67, 9020 Klagenfurt, Austria
E-mail: hamid@isys.uni-klu.ac.at

ISSN 0302-9743 e-ISSN 1611-3349
ISBN 978-3-642-23856-7 e-ISBN 978-3-642-23857-4
DOI 10.1007/978-3-642-23857-4
Springer Heidelberg Dordrecht London New York

Library of Congress Control Number: 2011935600

CR Subject Classification (1998): I.2, H.4, H.2, I.4, I.5, F.1

LNCS Sublibrary: SL 7 – Artificial Intelligence

Typesetting: Camera-ready by author, data conversion by Scientific Publishing Services, Chennai, India

Printed on acid-free paper

Springer is part of Springer Science+Business Media (www.springer.com)

Preface

Adaptation plays a central role in dynamically changing systems. It is about the ability of the system to "responsively" self-adjust upon change in the surrounding environment. Like living creatures that have evolved over millions of years developing ecological systems due to their self-adaptation and fitness capacity to the dynamic environment, systems undergo similar cycles to improve or at least not weaken their performance when internal or external changes take place. Internal or endogenous change bears on the physical structure of the system (hardware and/or software components) due mainly to faults, knowledge inconsistency, etc. It requires a certain number of adaptivity features such as flexible deployment, self-testing, self-healing and self-correction. Extraneous change touches on the environment implication such as the operational mode or regime, non-stationarity of input, new knowledge facts, the need to cooperate with other systems, etc. These two classes of change shed light on the research avenues in smart and autonomous systems.

To meet the challenges of these systems, a sustainable effort needs to be developed: (1) adequate operational structures involving notions like self-healing, self-testing, reconfiguration, etc.; (2) appropriate design concepts encompassing self-x properties (self-organization, self-monitoring, etc.) to allow for autonomy and optimal behavior in the (dynamically changing) environment; (3) efficient computational algorithms targetting dynamic setting, life-long learning, evolving and adaptive behavior and structure. For this three-fold development direction, various design and computational models stemming from machine learning, statistics, metaphors of nature inspired from biological and cognitive plausibility, etc. can be of central relevance.

Due to its versatility, online adaptation is involved in various research areas which are covered by the International Conference on Adaptive and Intelligent Systems (ICAIS): neural networks, data mining, pattern recognition, computational intelligence, smart and agent-based systems, distributed systems, ubiquitous environments, Internet, system engineering, hardware, etc. The ICAIS conference strives to sharpen its focus on issues related to online adaptation and learning in dynamically evolving environments and to expand the understanding of all these inter-related concepts.

ICAIS is a biennial event. After the very successful ICAIS 2009, the conference witnessed another success and become more attractive this year. The number and quality of the papers substantially increased. ICAIS 2011 received about 72 submissions from 24 countries around the world (Algeria, Austria, Bangladesh, Belgium, Bulgaria, Chile, China, Croatia, Egypt, Estonia, France, Germany, India, Indonesia, Iran, Italy, Japan, Romania, Poland, Serbia, Sweden, Tunisia, Turkey, UK), which underwent a rigorous and tough peer-review process. All papers were refereed by, at least, two independent referees, most by three reviewers. Based on the referees' reports, the Program Committee selected 36 full papers.

ICAIS 2011 was enhanced by four keynote speeches given by internationally renowned researchers, presenting insights and ideas in the research areas covered by the conference. The rest of program featured interesting sessions. As we worked hard to make ICAIS 2011 an enticing and informative event.

This volume and the whole conference are of course the result of team effort. My thanks go to the local organizers, particularly to Annette Lippitsch and Markus Künstner, to Saliha Dali, the Steering Committee, the Publicity Chair and especially the Program Committee members and the reviewers for their cooperation in the shaping of the conference and running the refereeing process. I highly appreciate the hard work and timely feedback of the referees who did an excellent job. I would like to thank all the authors and participants for their interest in ICAIS 2011. Thank you for your time and effort in preparing and submitting your papers and your patience throughout the long process. Your work is the backbone of this conference.

The support of the University of Klagenfurt and the Department of Informatics-Systems was crucial in making this event happen. I also thank the technical sponsors, IEEE Computational Society and the International Neural Networks Society for their trust in ICAIS, and Springer for enabling the publication of this volume.

July 2011   Abdelhamid Bouchachia

Organization

ICAIS 2011 was organized by the department of Informatics-Systeme, Alps-Adria University of Klagenfurt, Austria.

Conference Committee

Conference Chair

Abdelhamid Bouchachia   Universität Klagenfurt, Austria

Steering Committee

Nikola Kasabov	Auckland University, New Zealand
Nicolò Cesa-Bianchi	University of Milan, Italy
Djamel Ziou	University of Sherbrooke, Canada
Plamen Angelov	University of Lancaster, UK
Hani Hagras	University of Essex, UK
Witold Pedrycz	University of Edmonton, Canada
Janusz Kacprzyk	Polish Academy of Sciences, Poland

Program Committee

A. Bouchachia (Chair)	Universität Klagenfurt, Austria
P. Angelov	University of Lancaster, UK
F. Buarque	Universidade de Pernambuco, Brazil
U. Bodendorfer	Universität Linz, Austria
N. Bouguila	Concordia University, Canada
M. Butz	University of Würzburg, Germany
H. Camargo	Federal University of Sao Carlos, Brazil
A. de Carvalho	University of Sao Paulo, Brazil
B. Cukic	West Virginia University, USA
H. Hagras	Essex University, UK
B. Hammer	University of Osnabrück, Germany
A. Hassanien	Cairo University, Egypt
S. Hassas	Université Claude Bernard-Lyon, France
H. He	University of Rhode Island, USA
E. Huellermeier	Philipps-Universität Marburg, Germany
F. Klawonn	Ostfalia University of Applied Sciences, Germany
M. Koeppen	Kyushu Institute of Technology, Japan
L. Kurgan	University of Alberta, Canada
Y. Li	Brunel University, UK

A. Lofti	Nottingham University, UK
E. Lughofer	Universität Linz, Austria
C. Marsala	Université Pierre et Marie Curie, France
M. Sayed Mouchaweh	Université de Reims, France
F. Neumann	University of Adelaide, Australia
M. Paprzycki	Polish Academy of Sciences, Poland
W. Pedrycz	University of Alberta, Canada
D. Sanchez	University of Granada, Spain
V. Snasel	Technical University of Ostrava, Czech Republic
G. Spezzano	Italian National Research Council, Italy
A. Tsymbal	Siemens AG, Germany
D. Ziou	University of Sherbrooke, Canada

Additional Reviewers

M. Prossegger (Austria)
F. Armetta (France)
S. Aknine (France)
N. Ghali (Egypt)

Local Organizing Committee

M. Prossegger	Carinthia University of Applied Sciences, Austria (Publicity Chair)
A. Lippitsch	Universität Klagenfurt, Austria
M. Kuenstner	Universität Klagenfurt, Austria

Technical Sponsoring Institutions

Alps Adria University of Klagenfurt
IEEE Computational Intelligence Society
International Neural Networks Society

Table of Contents

Adaptive System Architecture

Intelligent System Engineering

Data Mining and Pattern Recognition

Intelligent Agents

Computational Intelligence

The Game-Theoretic Approach to Machine Learning and Adaptation

Nicolò Cesa-Bianchi

Chair for Information Sciences, University of Milano, Italy
nicolo.cesa-bianchi@unimi.it

The design of artificial systems able to learn and adapt has been one of the main goals of Artificial Intelligence since its very beginning. To this end, statistical modeling has proven to be a tool of extraordinary effectiveness. In some cases, however, statistics is not the most adequate language for analyzing the interaction between a learning agent and an ever-changing environment. Indeed, a research thread, emerged in parallel with statistical learning, views this interaction as a repeated game between agent and environment. This different approach allows to analyze, in a rigorous framework, predictive models without any statistical assumptions. In this talk we will trace the roots of the game-theoretic approach in learning theory and describe some of the key results.

A. Bouchachia (Ed.): ICAIS 2011, LNAI 6943, p. 1, 2011.

Exploration and Exploitation in Online Learning

Peter Auer

Chair for Information Technology, University of Leoben, Austria
auer@unileoben.ac.at

Online learning does not distinguish between a training and an evaluation phase of learning, but considers learning as an ongoing process, such that learning algorithms need to perform and make predictions while they learn. After reviewing the online learning model and some algorithms, I will consider variants of the model where only partial information is revealed to the learner, in particular the bandit problem and reinforcement learning. The uncertainty of the learner caused by receiving only partial information, leads to an exploration-exploitation dilemma: is further information needed, or can the available information already be exploited? I will discuss how optimism in the face of uncertainty can address this dilemma in many cases.

A. Bouchachia (Ed.): ICAIS 2011, LNAI 6943, p. 2, 2011.
© Springer-Verlag Berlin Heidelberg 2011

Towards Online Adaptive Ambient Intelligent Environments for Multiple Occupants

Hani Hagras

School of Computer Science and Electronic Engineering, University of Essex, UK
hani@essex.ac.uk

Adaptation is a relationship between a system and its environment where change is provoked to facilitate the survival of the system in the environment. Biological systems exhibit different types of adaptation so as to regulate themselves and change their structure as they interact with the environment.

The dynamic and ad-hoc nature of Ambient Intelligent Environments (AIEs) means that the environment has to adapt to changing operating conditions and user changing preferences and behaviours and to enable more efficient and effective operation while avoiding any system failure. Thus there is a need to provide autonomous intelligent adaptive techniques which should be able to create models which could be evolved and adapted online in a life learning mode. These models need to be transparent and easy to be read and interpreted via the normal user to enable the user to better analyze the system and its performance. These intelligent systems should allow to control the environment on the user behalf and to his satisfaction to perform given tasks. The intelligent approaches used should have low computational overheads to effectively operate on the embedded hardware platforms present in the everyday environments which have small memory and processor capabilities. These models need to be transparent and easy to be ready and interpreted via the normal user to enable the user to better analyze the system and its performance. This task based system could be used to control the environment on the user behalf and to his satisfaction to perform given tasks. In addition, the intelligent approaches should allow for real-time data mining of the user data and create on-the-fly updateable models of the user preferences that could be executed over the pervasive network. Moreover, there is a need to provide an adaptive life-long learning mechanism that will allow the system to adapt to the changing environmental and user preferences over short and long term intervals. There is a need also to provide robust mechanisms that will allow handling the varying and unpredictable conditions associated with the dynamic environment and user preferences.

This talk will present novel adaptation strategies that will allow the environments to adapt to the uncertainties associated with the changes in the environments characteristics, context as well as changes in the user(s) preferences in AIEs. The talk will present new general type-2 fuzzy logic systems that could be used to model and handle the uncertainties associated with these environments where we will present real world experiments from the Essex iSpace real world AIE.

A. Bouchachia (Ed.): ICAIS 2011, LNAI 6943, p. 3, 2011.

The Evolution of Evolutionary Computation

Xin Yao

School of Computer Science at the University of Birmingham, UK
x.yao@cs.bham.ac.uk

Evolutionary computation has enjoyed an incredible growth in recent years. This talk will highlight a few recent examples in evolutionary computation in terms of its applications, including data-driven modelling using the evolutionary approach in materials engineering, dynamic route optimisation for salting trucks, multi-objective design of hardware and software, neural network ensemble learning for pattern classification, and online ensemble learning in the presence of concept drifts. The primary objective of this talk is to illustrate novel applications of various evolutionary computation techniques, rather than to go into depth on any of the examples. However, I would be delighted to go into the depth on any of the topics if there is an interest.

A. Bouchachia (Ed.): ICAIS 2011, LNAI 6943, p. 4, 2011.
© Springer-Verlag Berlin Heidelberg 2011

Online Identification of the System Order with ANARX Structure

Sven Nõmm* and Juri Belikov**

Institute of Cybernetics at Tallinn University of Technology,
Akadeemia tee 21, 12618 Tallinn, Estonia
{sven,jbelikov}@cc.ioc.ee

Abstract. Online training of neural networks based Additive Nonlinear Autoregressive exogenous models constitutes main subject of present research. Main accent is made on determining order of the identified model by increasing number of sub-neural networks corresponding to the model order.

Keywords: NN-ANARX model, online identification.

1 Introduction

Online identification of the neural networks based (NN) Additive Nonlinear Autoregressive eXogenous (ANARX) models with emphasis on determination of the model order, constitutes main contribution of present paper. The ANARX structure was proposed in [1] as a subclass of a more general Nonlinear Autoregressive eXogenous (NARX) models class, by restricting coupling of different time instances. Namely in ANARX models different time instances are always separated. Such restriction guarantees that unlike its parent NARX, ANARX models always admit classical state-space realization [1] and always linearizable by dynamic output feedback [2]. Those two properties have a crucial importance for further modeling and control synthesis. NN-ANARX models have lower number of weights compared to the NN-NARX models of the same order what leads to the reduced computational complexity during network training and simulation. While restriction on coupling of different time instances may seem too restrictive, it was demonstrated that NN-ANARX provide sufficient accuracy for practical applications [3] and can be used in such applications like modeling of backing up motion of a truck-trailer [4] or gesture recognition of the right hand of operating surgeon [5].

A more formal approach to compare the quality of identified NN-ANARX and NN-ANARX models of the same system was proposed in [6]. The structure of the NN-ANARX model is the parallel connection of sub-neural networks of

---

* This research was supported by the Estonian Science Foundation ETF through the state funding project SF0140018s08 and research grant ETF 8365.
** Partially supported by the Estonian Science Foundation ETF through the research grant 8738.

A. Bouchachia (Ed.): ICAIS 2011, LNAI 6943, pp. 5–15, 2011.

the same structure where each sub-NN corresponds to the certain time shift, obviously order of the model corresponds to the number of sub neural-networks. Such structure inspires the idea to determine model order online.

The main goal of the research is to investigate possibility to determine the order of NN-ANARX model online. In addition to the mean square error which is usually used as qualitative characteristic of the identified NN-model, combined omni-directional cross-correlation validation procedure (ODCCF), proposed in [7] and adopted for NN-model comparison in [6], is employed. The idea itself was formulated for the validation of nonlinear systems in [8], and [9].

Present paper is organized as follows. Problem statement and mathematical tools are presented in Section 2. Proposed technique is described in Section 3. Section 4 presents simulation results. Discussion of the obtained results and limitations constitutes Section 5. Concluding remarks are drawn in the last section.

2 Mathematical Tools

The NARX models are usually represented by high order difference equation

$$y(t+n) = f\big(y(t), y(t+1), \ldots, y(t+n-1), u(t), u(t+1), \ldots u(m)\big), \quad (1)$$

where $m < n$, $u(t)$ and $y(t)$ denote system input and output respectively and the function f is a smooth nonlinear function. Its subclass ANARX was defined in [1] as follows

$$y(t+n) = f_1\big(y(t), u(t)\big) + f_2\big(y(t+1), u(t+1)\big) + \ldots$$
$$+ f_n\big(y(t+n-1), u(t+n-1)\big), \quad (2)$$

where $f_1, f_2, \ldots, f_n$ are nonlinear smooth functions. It can be clearly seen that in ANARX different time instances are separated.

2.1 NN-ANARX

NN-ANARX models are the neural networks implementation of the ANARX [1]. Usually NN-ANARX models are described by the following difference equation

$$y(t+n) = \sum_{i=1}^{n}\sum_{k=1}^{m} c_{i,k}\phi_i\big(w_{i,k}^1 y(t+i-1) + w_{i,k}^2 u(t+i-1)\big), \quad (3)$$

where $u(t)$ and $y(t)$ denote system input and output respectively and ϕ_i are the saturation type smooth nonlinear functions, c_k and $w_{i,k}^j$ are the synaptic weights. Or in a more compact form

$$y(t+n) = \sum_{i=1}^{n} C_i\phi_i(W_i z(t+i-1)), \quad (4)$$

where, $z(t) := [y(t), u(t)]^T$, C_i and W_i are $1 \times m$ and $m \times 2$ dimensional matrices, respectively. While in general functions ϕ_i can all be different in the framework

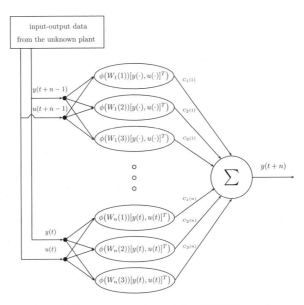

Fig. 1. NN representation of the ANARX model

of present research we assume that $\phi_1 = \phi_2 = \ldots = \phi_n$ therefore all the sub-NNs involved would have exactly the same structure. Schematic diagram of the NN corresponding to the ANARX structure (4) is presented in Figure 1.

It may be easily seen that NN-ANARX model has a fewer number of weights compared to the NN-NARX model of the same order. Note that in a similar manner single-input single-output ANARX may be defined for the multi-input multi-output case [10].

2.2   Correlation Based Test

In order to make this paper self-sufficient the main idea of correlation based test will be presented here [8] and [9]. Next, we will follow the notation proposed in [6]. Let $\{\gamma(t), t = 1, \ldots, N\}$ and $\{\eta(t), t = 1, \ldots, N\}$ denote two arbitrary data sequences (usually $\eta(t)$ represent independent variable and $\gamma(t)$ - dependent variable). The normalized sequences $\{\gamma'(t)\}$ and $\{\eta'(t)\}$ with removed mean level are defined as follows:

$$\gamma'(t) = \gamma(t) - \frac{1}{N} \sum_{t=1}^{N} \gamma(t), \tag{5}$$

$$\eta'(t) = \eta(t) - \frac{1}{N} \sum_{t=1}^{N} \eta(t). \tag{6}$$

Denote by $\alpha(t)$ and $\beta(t)$ sequences whose elements are absolute values of the sequences $\{\gamma'(t)\}$ and $\{\eta'(t)\}$, respectively.

$$\alpha(t) = |\eta'(t)|,$$

$$\beta(t) = |\gamma'(t)|.$$

Finally, normalize those sequences again by removing mean level

$$\alpha'(t) = \alpha(t) - \frac{1}{N} \sum_{t=1}^{N} \alpha(t), \tag{7}$$

$$\beta'(t) = \beta(t) - \frac{1}{N} \sum_{t=1}^{N} \beta(t). \tag{8}$$

If an NN-based model is valid, the residuals should be reduced to white noise consequently if a NN is invalid there should be significant correlation between residuals and delayed inputs, delayed outputs and delayed residuals. Unlike to linear case there are four types of nonlinear associations. In order to detect those four types of associations between residuals and delayed residuals, delayed outputs and delayed inputs one should compute values of so called *Omni-Directional Cross- Correlation Functions* here and after ODCCF's.

– **Type 1:** The amplitude of the dependent variable varies as the amplitude of the independent variable varies.

$$r_{\beta'\alpha'}(\tau) = \frac{\sum\limits_{t=\tau+1}^{N} \alpha'(t)\beta'(t-\tau)}{\left[\left(\sum\limits_{t=1}^{N} \alpha'^2(t)\right)\left(\sum\limits_{t=1}^{N} \beta'^2(t)\right)\right]^{1/2}}, \tag{9}$$

– **Type 2:** The amplitude and the sign of the dependent variable varies as the amplitude of the independent variable varies.

$$r_{\beta'\gamma'}(\tau) = \frac{\sum\limits_{t=\tau+1}^{N} \gamma'(t)\beta'(t-\tau)}{\left[\left(\sum\limits_{t=1}^{N} \gamma'^2(t)\right)\left(\sum\limits_{t=1}^{N} \beta'^2(t)\right)\right]^{1/2}}, \tag{10}$$

– **Type 3:** The amplitude and the sign of the dependent variable varies as the amplitude and the sign of the independent variable varies.

$$r_{\eta'\gamma'}(\tau) = \frac{\sum\limits_{t=\tau+1}^{N} \gamma'(t)\eta'(t-\tau)}{\left[\left(\sum\limits_{t=1}^{N} \gamma'^2(t)\right)\left(\sum\limits_{t=1}^{N} \eta'^2(t)\right)\right]^{1/2}}, \tag{11}$$

– **Type 4:** The amplitude of the dependent variable varies as the amplitude and the sign of the independent variable varies.

$$
r_{\eta'\alpha'}(\tau) = \frac{\displaystyle\sum_{t=\tau+1}^{N} \alpha'(t)\eta'(t-\tau)}{\left[\left(\displaystyle\sum_{t=1}^{N} \alpha'^2(t)\right)\left(\displaystyle\sum_{t=1}^{N} \eta'^2(t)\right)\right]^{1/2}}. \tag{12}
$$

In (9) - (12) τ denotes the time delay. If the values of $r_{\beta'\alpha'}(\tau)$, $r_{\beta'\gamma'}(\tau)$, $r_{\eta'\alpha'}(\tau)$, and $r_{\eta'\alpha'}(\tau)$ belong to the confidence interval, correlations between residuals and delayed residuals, delayed outputs and delayed inputs are insignificant and therefore identified NN is valid. The values of ODCCF's should be found for the following pairs

– residuals and delayed outputs,
– residuals and delayed inputs,
– residuals and delayed residuals.

In [7] validity analysis is based on the values of so-called *combined* ODCCF's. Instead of analyzing all the values of $r_{\beta'\alpha'}(\tau)$, $r_{\beta'\gamma'}(\tau)$, $r_{\eta'\alpha'}(\tau)$, and $r_{\eta'\alpha'}(\tau)$ combined ODCCF's are defined for each time delay τ as the maximum of absolute values of $r_{\beta'\alpha'}(\tau)$, $r_{\beta'\gamma'}(\tau)$, $r_{\eta'\alpha'}(\tau)$ and $r_{\eta'\alpha'}(\tau)$. In [7] the values of the combined ODCCF's are computed for the time delays τ in range between 1 and 20 and confidence interval of 95%. While such approach is suitable for model validation, it provides less information for comparison purposes therefore in the framework of present studies all the values of $r_{\beta'\alpha'}(\tau)$, $r_{\beta'\gamma'}(\tau)$, $r_{\eta'\alpha'}(\tau)$ are analyzed. Since correlation test based validation procedure was not developed to compare quality of two identified models the following technique was proposed in [6] to convert results of correlation test to the value of certain qualitative parameter. If one model is valid and the other is not, then the valid model declared to be winner. If the both models are valid or not, then the following qualitative parameter Q is proposed. Let $\bar{r}_{xy}$ denote the mean computed for the sequence of correlation coefficients $r_{xy}(\tau)$, $\tau = 2 \ldots 2n$ (where n -order of the model) computed according to (9-12)

$$
\bar{r}_{xy} = \sum_{1=2}^{\tau} (|r_{xy}(\tau)|), \tag{13}
$$

where x and y may represent either the normalized sequences of inputs, outputs or residuals, with or without removed mean level (5)-(8). Next, compute the average of the means of the correlation coefficients (9) - (12).

$$
\Xi_{\varphi\psi} = \frac{1}{4}\left(\bar{r}_{\beta'\alpha'} + \bar{r}_{\beta'\gamma'} + \bar{r}_{\eta'\gamma'} + \bar{r}_{\eta'\alpha'}\right), \tag{14}
$$

where φ and ψ may denote the sequences of residuals, outputs or inputs. Finally, define Q as follows

$$
Q = \frac{1}{3}\left(\Xi_{\epsilon\epsilon} + \Xi_{\epsilon u} + \Xi_{\epsilon y}\right) \tag{15}
$$

The value of the parameter Q is the mean of the means of the means of cross correlation coefficients computed for three pairs of sequences (residuals vs. delayed residuals, inputs, outputs), for each nonlinearity type and for each $\tau = 2, \ldots, 2n$. Obviously, lower values of Q indicate better model quality.

3   The Algorithm

This section provides information about the basic steps of the algorithm together with explanatory comments.

Step 1. Preprocessing stage: collecting all required information about modeled process such as input-output data, etc.

Step 2. Initialization. Here, one has to choose the maximum number of iterations (the order of the models in the last set), the number of models in the training set confidence level, and the number of time delays τ [1] and all other parameters necessary for the NN training and validation.

Step 3. If this is not the first iteration increase the order of the identified model.

Step 4. Train all neural networks using the training parameter values specified on **Steps 2-3**.

Step 5. Validation: compute mean square error and qualitative parameter Q (15).

Step 6. If the goal[2] is reached, then go to **Step 7**, otherwise execute again all **Steps 2-6**. Roughly speaking if all the values of combined ODCCF's are in the confidence interval (Q is small enough) and mean square error is low enough, then the goal is reached.

Step 7. End of the Algorithm.

The presented above algorithm is represented schematically in Fig. 2.

4   Simulation Results

In order to illustrate the proposed algorithm, let us consider the following real-life and academic examples. While usually one have no information about the order of the system, in the framework of present research information about the order of modeled system allows to judge the ability of the proposed algorithm to determine model order adequately. Since the training results in many cases depend on initial conditions, each system was identified by 10 NN-models of the same structure.

---

[1] In the frameworks of present studies the values of the combined ODCCF's were computed for $\tau = 2, \ldots, 2n$, where n is the model order.

[2] As a first step of our research we decided to select the maximum number of iterations as a stop criterion, which equals to $2n + 1$. However, in the future research we are planning to replace this condition and introduce an alternative one, which allows to avoid unnecessary computations and makes the whole process faster and more precise.

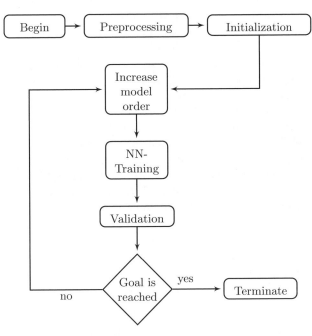

Fig. 2. The algorithm

Example 1. The model of a liquid level system of interconnected tanks [11] is represented by the following input-output equation

$$
\begin{aligned}
y(t+3) =\ & 0.43y(t+2) + 0.681y(t+1) - 0.149y(t) + 0.396u(t+2) \\
& + 0.014u(t+1) - 0.071u(t) - 0.351y(t+2)u(t+2) \\
& - 0.03y^2(t+1) - 0.135y(t+1)u(t+1) - 0.027y^3(t+1) \\
& - 0.108y^2(t+1)u(t+1) - 0.099u^3(t+1)
\end{aligned}
\tag{16}
$$

We treat this the 3-rd order system as our unknown plan. Note, that (16) does not have ANARX structure. In order to obtain the input-output data, system (16) was simulated with uniformly distributed pseudo-random numbers and the obtained data set was divided into two parts. The first part contained the data required for training neural network and the second part was considered as a validation set. Logarithmic sigmoid hidden layer activation functions (17)

$$
\phi_i = \text{logsig}(x) = \frac{1}{1+e^{-x}}, \quad \text{for} \quad i = 1, \ldots, n
\tag{17}
$$

were used for identification of the model. Since neural network representing ANARX model has the restricted connectivity structure, Levenberg-Marquardt (LM) training algorithm was chosen to perform the training of the model. In [12] it was shown that LM algorithm is much more efficient compared to other techniques when the network contains no more than a few hundred weights. Also, in that case, the convergence rate of LM algorithm is much higher and the feed-forward neural network trained by this algorithm can better model the nonlinearity [13]. In fact, for some real life applications the order of the system may become too large and as a result LM algorithm, which works fine for the small number of connections, will be too slow. Since computing time plays a very important role in the most applications, this algorithm has to be replaced by faster algorithm such as back-propagation or its modifications. Confidence level of 90% was chosen for cross-correlation validation procedure. Next, according to the algorithm presented in Section 3, we iteratively increased the order of the identified model. In most cases the values of the qualitative parameter Q and mean square error were small enough already for the models of orders 3 (4 in the worst cases). Note that for the majority of models alls the values of combined ODCCF's fall into the confidence interval. In order to study convergence, the algorithm was forced to continue for the models of order up to 7. Performance of the qualitative parameter Q can be seen in Figure 3 on the left (a).

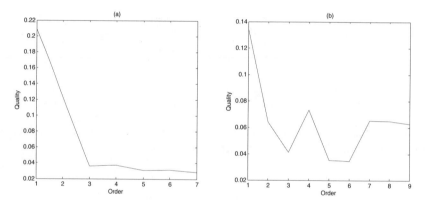

Fig. 3. Performance of the qualitative parameter Q

Evolution of the qualitative parameters Q (15) for each of 10 models is depicted in Figure 4, left sub-figure. It can be clearly seen that once algorithm reaches the order of the initial model majority of qualitative parameters are low enough. Also all the values of the combined ODCFF's fall in to the confidence interval. The similar behavior was observed for other systems belonging to ANARX class.

Example 2. Consider the following input-output academic equation which does not possess the ANARX structure

$$y(t+4) = \sin\left(y(t+3)u(t+2) - y(t+2) + u(t+3)^3\right)$$
$$+ \cos\left(y(t)^2 u(t+3) - \sin(y(t+2))\cos(u(t+1)^3)\right)$$
$$- \cos(\sin(u(t)y(t+2) - y(t+3)u(t))) \quad (18)$$

The identification and validation procedures rely on the same technique as was used in the previous example also training and validation parameters are the

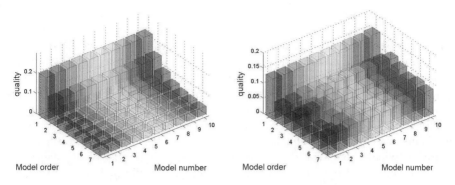

Fig. 4. Evolution of the qualitative parameters Q

same. Figure 3 (b) on the right depicts the behavior of the qualitative parameter for one NN-ANARX model and Figure 4 right sub-figure represents behavior of the qualitative parameters of all 10 models. It can be clearly seen that the algorithm does not converge. While some models of order lower than initial system are valid and obviously accurate enough, it can be seen that in some cases (model nr. 10) increasing model order up to 7 did not lead to valid and accurate model. If ANARX system is modeled by NN-ANARX structure, one can conclude that except some rear occasions proposed algorithm converges to the model with order either smaller or equal to the initial system. However, this is not the case for NARX systems.

5 Discussion

In addition to the two examples presented above, number of other academic and real life systems were modeled by NN-ANARX structure. In those cases when the nature of the modeled system is similar to ANARX structure (from the behavioral point of view) the proposed algorithm converges, and therefore can be used to determine the correct order of the model. Obviously, some exceptions exist. This results coincide with conclusions provided in [6]. On the other side modeling of the NARX systems by NN-ANARX model did not lead such accurate results. Cases when the algorithm converges did not constitute more than 25% of the all experiments. In certain cases the algorithm converges to the models of order higher than original (modeled system). Such behavior of the algorithm can be interpreted in many different ways. Most obvious explanation is that some systems simply can not be modeled by NN with restricted connectivity, and fully connected NN-NARX is required.

Another possible explanation is that in those cases when model by its nature differs form the ANARX the algorithm becomes more sensitive to the initial values of the weights generated randomly. Obviously, more studies are required to tackle those questions. When the algorithm shows good convergence one can relay on the obtained results. If the algorithm does not converge, it is a clear signal to employ more complicated model.

6 Conclusions

Present paper employs one of the main structural properties of the NN-ANARX structure to determine the order of the identified model online. Namely number of layers of the ANARX type neural network corresponds to the model order. Therefore, if the performance criteria were not met one just have to add one more layer and perform training again. Number of numerical simulations has demonstrated that proposed algorithm demonstrate robust performance when modeling systems which behavior is similar to ANARX. Modeling systems with more complicated behavior did not lead to robust performance of the algorithm, but still can be used with certain precautions. In Section 4 it was shown the practical application of the proposed algorithm for determining the correct order of the model. On one hand the method works well if the training data originates from the plant which has so-called ANARX nature. On the other hand sometimes this algorithm gives the correct results for NARX type of the models as well. Thus, the development of an additional criteria for distinguishing the type of the input data makes one of the subjects of our future research. Another direction of future research will be spanned around implementing proposed technique into closed loop control system.

References

1. Kotta, Ü., Chowdhury, F., Nõmm, S.: On realizability of neural networks-based input-output models in the classical state space form. Automatica 42(6),1211–1216 (2006)
2. Pothin, R., Kotta, Ü., Moog, C.: Output feedback linearization of nonlinear discrete-time systems. In: Proc. of the IFAC Conf. on Control System Design, Bratislava, pp. 174–179 (2000)
3. Petlenkov, E., Nõmm, S., Kotta, Ü.: Neural Networks based ANARX structure for identification and model based control. In: Proc: 9th International Conference on Control Automation Robotics & Vision (ICARCV 2006), Singapore, pp. 2284–2288 (2006)
4. Belikov, J., Petlenkov, E., Nõmm, S.: Application of Neural Networks based ANARX structure to backing up control of a truck-trailer. In: Proceedings of the 6th IFAC Symposium on Intelligent Autonomous Vehicles IAV 2007, Touluse, France (2007)
5. Nõmm, S., Petlenkov, E., Vain, J., Yoshimitsu, K., Ohnuma, K., Sadahiro, T., Miyawaki, F.: Nn-based anarx model of the surgeon's hand for the motion recognition. In: Proceedings of the 4th COE Workshop on Human Adaptive Mechatronics (HAM), pp. 19–24. Tokyo Denki University, Tokyo (2007)
6. Nomm, S., Kotta, Ü.: Comparison of Neural Networks-based ANARX and NARX Models by application of correlation tests. In: 2011 International Joint Conference on Neural Networks, San Jose, California (2011)
7. Zhang, L.F., Zhu, Q.M., Longden, A.: A Correlation-Test-Based Validation Procedure for Identified Neural Networks. IEEE Transactions on Neural Networks 20(1), 1–13 (2009)
8. Zhu, Q.M., Zhang, L.F., Longden, A.: Development of omni-directional correlation functions for nonlinear model validation. Automatica 43, 1519–1531 (2007)

9. Zhang, L.F., Zhu, Q.M., Longden, A.: A set of novel correlation test for nonlinear system variables. International Journal of Systems and Science 38(1), 47–60 (2007)
10. Petlenkov, E.: Nn-anarx structure based dynamic output feedback linearization for control of nonlinear mimo systems. In: The 15th Mediterranean Conference on Control and Automation, Athens, Greece (June 2007)
11. Billings, S.A., Fadzil, M.B.: The practical identification of systems with nonlinearities. In: Proc. of 7th IFAC/IFORS Symp. Identification Syst. Parameter Estimation, pp. 155–160 (1985)
12. Hagan, M.T., Nenhaj, M.B.: Training feedforward networks with the marquardt algorithm. IEEE Transactions on Neural Networks 1(6), 989–993 (1994)
13. Declercq, F., De Keyser, R.: Comparative study of neural predictors in model based predictive control. In: Proceedings of The International Workshop on Neural Networks for Identification, Control, Robotics, and Signal/Image Processing, Venice, Italy, pp. 20–28 (August 1996)

Incremental Semi-automatic Correction of Misclassified Spatial Objects

Markus Prossegger[1] and Abdelhamid Bouchachia[2]

[1] Carinthia University of Applied Sciences,
School of Network Engineering and Communication, Klagenfurt, Austria
m.prossegger@cuas.at
[2] Alpen Adria University, Department of Informatics, Klagenfurt, Austria
hamid@isys.uni-klu.ac.at

Abstract. This paper proposes a decision tree based approach for semi-automatic correction of misclassified spatial objects in the Austrian digital cadastre map. Departing from representative areas, proven to be free of classification errors, an incremental decision tree is constructed. This tree is used later to identify and correct misclassified spatial objects. The approach is semiautomatic due to the interaction with the user in case of inaccurate assignments. During the learning process, whenever new (training) spatial data becomes available, the decision tree is then incrementally adapted without the need to generate a new tree from scratch. The approach has been evaluated on a large and representative area from the Austrian digital cadastre map showing a substantial benefit.

Keywords: Incremental Decision Tree, Spatial Objects, Semiautomatic Classification.

1 Introduction

Over the past years geoinformation systems have been developed in order to primarily facilitate the visualization of geodata and to enable tagging and enriching this latter with meta-information. Existing free/commercial geoinformation systems are powerful in providing various spatial operations, but lack the ability to (self-) correct the inaccurate and inconsistent data unless a human expert is involved to manually do that on behalf of the system. Very often, the time needed for a manual validation and correction of the spatial objects (in a particular area) is very high. This requires a constant presence of the expert, especially in situations where data arrives over time.

Recently, several systems have emerged lying focus on high quality and error-free data. An instance of such systems is the simulation and optimization engine of fiber optic communication networks [1]. Spatial landuse objects, represented as polygons, are used to generate a cost raster indicating the specific costs for the underground work of a network construction. Misclassified spatial objects could lead to invalid simulation results regarding the cable route and/or the construction costs.

A. Bouchachia (Ed.): ICAIS 2011, LNAI 6943, pp. 16–25, 2011.

As it will be discussed in Sec. 3 there are a number of different criteria known, describing the quality of geodata: completeness, positional accuracy, temporal accuracy, thematic accuracy, logical consistency, external quality, and service quality. In the present research work we focus on the validation and semiautomatic correction of the landuse classification of spatial data. In a previous work, we have developed a semi-incremental approach for the identification of topological errors [10]. This method is, however, not fully incremental, since the identification procedure is triggered from scratch upon arrival of new data. It relies on the decision tree algorithm ID3 proposed in [11]. Whenever a misclassification is detected, the expert/user corrects it manually and then the whole decision tree is reconstructed. The present paper deals with the enhancement of [10] by replacing the ID3 algorithm by a real incremental decision tree algorithm, namely ID5R described in [14]. As shown in Sec. 4 the identification of misclassified or unknown spatial objects is done automatically using the decision tree. The correction of wrong assignments of data objects to the classes is done by the user who adjusts those assignments.

The following sections give a general idea of incremental decision trees (Sec. 2), describe the notion of quality from the perspective of spatial data (Sec. 3) and after the detailed description of our approach in Sec. 4, the results of our initial experiments are given in Sec. 5.

2 Decision Trees

A decision tree (DT) is a decision support representation used in various domains like classification, regression, search, etc. In this paper, we will focus on the process induction of decision trees for classification purposes. Given a dataset of objects with their class labels, the tree will allow to distribute the data on leaf nodes, where each leaf is labeled. The intermediate nodes are generated based on the values of attributes. Such attributes are incrementally selected based on their discriminatory power. During classification, the input is compared against the attribute values of the tree starting from the root node of the tree. The path on which the values of input attributes satisfies those of the tree leads to the predicted class label.

There exist various algorithms and split criteria to induce decision trees from a collection of data objects. For a comprehensive presentation of decision trees we refer to [12].

In this work we focus on an incremental tree induction algorithm called ID5R [14], that is guaranteed to build the same decision tree like the well known ID3 algorithm proposed in [11] but without the need to rebuilding the whole tree from scratch, if a new instance becomes available. In other terms, ID5R is dedicated to online classification of data. Specifically, a branch between a given node in the decision tree and its successor is characterized by an information gain. The most discriminative attribute splits the data X into a set of subsets $X^1, ..., X^l$ according to the l values $v_1, ..., v_l$ of that attribute. The discrimination is quantified by entropy as the impurity measure:

$$Ent(X) = -\sum_{i=1}^{H} p_i log(p_i) \ . \tag{1}$$

where X is a set of samples consisting of H classes and p_i is the fraction of samples of class i in X. To find the information gain on partitioning X into C subsets is defined as:

$$Gain(X, X_1, \cdots, X_C) = Ent(X) - \sum_{j=1}^{C} \frac{|X_j|}{|X|} Ent(X_j) \ . \tag{2}$$

The change of the information gain at a decision node leads to a reorder of the nodes in the branch followed by the transposition of the tree if needed (see Alg. 5).

3   Spatial Data Quality

There are a number of quality criteria defined to measure the degree of agreement between the real world data and the modeled data. Next to the ISO standard 19113 [16], which covers completeness, logical consistency, positional accuracy, temporal accuracy and thematic accuracy, there are more precise definitions for external quality [15] and service quality criteria like soundness, dependability, usefulness and usability [6][7]. The most frequently applied criteria describing the spatial data quality are the logical consistency, the positional accuracy [5] as well as the correct classification of the spatial objects. While the quality criteria like completeness, temporal accuracy and the set of service quality criteria can only be improved by acquiring new spatial data or adding new sources, the logical inconsistencies as well as incorrect spatial classifications can be located and further improved using the available spatial data. In [13], [2] and [9] some approaches are presented on how to validate spatial data using manually defined topological and spatial integrity constraints.

In contrast to the manual defined integrity constraints, the idea of a self-learning decision tree approach to automatically find errors within spatial data seems promising [10]. To investigate such an idea, we apply an incremental decision tree algorithm. This approach will enable semi-automatic correction of spatial objects misclassification. Further details follow in the next section.

4   Details of the Approach

The process that we follow in designing our semiautomatic correction of spatial object misclassification consists of the following steps:

– Generating training instances using error free spatial data
– Constructing and evolving the decision tree
– Semi-automatically validating new spatial data objects and incrementally updating the tree if necessary

In the following we introduce details of these three steps.

A. *Generating Training Instances*

The approach requires the availability of spatial data, covering a large area and containing a representative number of spatial objects. This initial data set has to be free of any misclassified objects since it is used to generate an initial decision tree, covering all different landuse classes found in the data. In our study, we use the Austrian digital cadastre map and all the classes specified therein (for example: roadways, grassland, water areas, building area, buildings ...). Based on this data, we gather the pairwise topological relationship between the spatial objects (see examples in Fig. 1) using the relations defined in the RCC-theory [3]. According to this theory, any pair of spatial objects has a defined relationship that is independent of the coordinate system and measurement scale and does not change under transformation.

Based on the eight RCC-relationships shown in Fig. 2, the initial decision tree is constructed in order to validate new spatial data with respect to the object's landuse classification. If the class of a spatial object cannot be found in the decision tree or the class does not correspond to the resulting leaf of the tree, the spatial object is presented to the user. After the manual reclassification or validation of the assigned class, the data is used as an additional training instance to adjust the decision tree incrementally.

In Alg. 1 all spatial objects (ie. polygons) of the area, except the polygons describing the border (see gray polygons in Fig. 3) are used to generate the set of training instances used in the construction of the initial decision tree. Although there is no need for any training instances to allow the validation process running Alg. 6, it is highly recommended to do so. The algorithm is incremental and updates the decision tree during the validation process, but if

---

Algorithm 1. Generate training instances

1: Import all polygons P of the area
2: **for all** polygons $p_i \in P$ **do**
3:    **if** p_i is a polygon located at the border of the area **then**
4:       Ignore p_i
5:    **else**
6:       Set all initial relation counters to Zero
7:       **for all** polygons $p_j \in P$ **do**
8:          Compute the pairwise RCC-relation
            between p_i and p_j, where $i! = j$
9:          Increase the corresponding relation counter by 1
10:      **end for**
11:      Save the instance using the relation-counter pairs and assign the class $landuse(p_i)$
12:   **end if**
13: **end for**

---

there was no error-free training data available, every instance has to be validated manually until the decision tree covers a large number of cases.

For the sake of illustrating how instances are generated in the form of tuples to induce the decision tree, let us consider an instance of the class *building*. The class is a description expressed in terms of the neighbor relationship. That is, the relationship indicates actually an attribute, while the numerical value following the relationship indicates the value of that attribute as shown below:

$$\langle building{:}NTPP(building,building){=}2,EC(building,street){=}1,...\rangle$$

In the given example the *building* is a non-tangential proper part (NTPP) of two other *buildings* and is external connected (EC) with a spatial object of the class *street*. The instance will look like: $<(2,1,...)$, Building$>$, where the first part indicates the attributes' values and the second part indicates the class label.

To ensure the usability of the decision tree, the spatial data used to generate the training instances has to match the data source to be validated. In our case the data originates from the Austrian digital cadastre map (DKM), containing information about the landuse of the spatial objects. Each object is of exact one defined landuse and have to be a valid polygon. Valid in this case means, that the edges of the polygon does not cross each other and that the polygon is closed (ie. first edge vertex equals last edge vertex).

Having gathered the training instances, the process of decision tree generation can be triggered.

B. *Initial Decision Tree Generation*

Based on the training instances the initial decision tree is generated using Alg. 2 which is a slightly adapted version to the ID5R decision tree algorithm described in [14]. Each instance of the data is used to enhance and adapt the tree if needed.

Algorithm 2. Decision tree generation

1: Gather the training instances I from the error free spatial data using Alg. 1
2: **if** all instances I belong to the same class (i.e., landuse) **then**
3:     Generate single node tree and add all attribute-value pairs of each instance in I as an unexpanded set
4: **else**
5:     **for all** instances $i \in I$ **do**
6:         Update the tree running Alg. 4 using i as parameter
7:     **end for**
8: **end if**

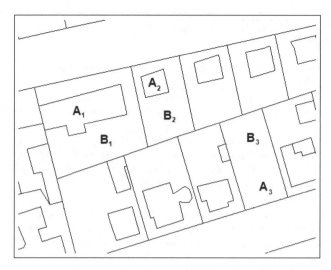

Fig. 1. Examples of pairwise RCC-relationships: $TPP(A_1, B_1)$, $NTPP(A_2, B_2)$, $EQ(A_3, B_3)$ and their inverse equivalents $TPP^{-1}(B_1, A_1)$, $NTPP^{-1}(B_2, A_2)$ and $EQ(B_3, A_3)$

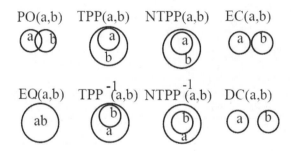

Fig. 2. Region Connection Calculus (RCC-8) relations [3]

Algorithm 3. Classification of an instance

Require: instance i
1: Find node n in tree, satisfying the tested attribute-value pairs of instance i
2: **if** n is a leaf node AND $class(n) == landuse(i)$ **then**
3:    **return** leaf node n
   {Tree satisfies the given instance i}
4: **else if** n is a leaf node AND $class(n)! = landuse(i)$ **then**
5:    **return** expected class $landuse(n)$
   {Tree satisfies the given instance i but shows
   different class: $landuse(i)! = landuse(n)$}
6: **else**
7:    **return** decision node n
   {n is a decision node}
8: **end if**

Algorithm 4. Tree update

Require: instance i
1: **repeat**
2:      Find node n in tree, satisfying the tested attribute-value pairs of instance i
        running Alg. 3
3:      **if** no satisfying leaf or decision node was found **then**
4:          **return** failed to update because of different class
5:      **end if**
6:      Update the classes counts at the tested attributes
7:      Update the classes counts at the non-tested attributes
8:      **if** n is a leaf node AND $landuse(i) = landuse(n)$ **then**
9:          Add non-tested attribute-value pairs of i as
            unexpanded set to n
10:     **else if** n is a leaf node AND $landuse(i)! = landuse(n)$ **then**
11:         Expand the non-tested attribute of n showing the highest information gain,
            creating one or more subtrees depending on the number of corresponding
            values
            {Instance i will not be added in the current iteration}
12:     **else**
13:         Select one arbitrary non-tested attribute of
            decision node n and create a successing
            leaf node n_s
14:         Assign $landuse(i)$ as class to leaf node n_s
15:         Add non-tested attribute-value pairs of i as
            unexpanded set to n_s
16:     **end if**
17: **until** instance i was added
18: Transpose the tree following the predecessors of n respectively n_s running Alg. 5
19: **return** update succeeded

Algorithm 5. Transpose tree

Require: leaf node n
        {Traverse the tree bottom-up starting with n}
        {See Eq. 2 for information gain}
1: **while** there is a predecessor n_p of n **do**
2:      **if** $information\_gain(n) > information\_gain(n_p)$ **then**
3:          Swap the places of n_p and n
4:          Reorder all other subtrees of n_p if there are any
5:      **end if**
6:      Select n_p as n during the next iteration {Do one step bottom-up}
7: **end while**

C. *Semi-automatic validation*

Once the initial decision tree is generated using the training instances it can be used to validate new arriving spatial data over time (Alg. 6). Following the decision nodes in the tree, the attribute-value combinations of the new instance

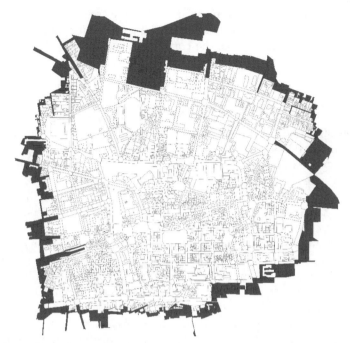

Fig. 3. Spatial data of urban area, bounded by border polygons (gray)

Algorithm 6. Semi-automatic validation

Require: new arriving instance i to be validated
 1: Update the tree running Alg. 4
 2: **if** update failed **then**
 3:     Ask user to validate or change the corresponding class $landuse(i)$
 4:     **if** class was changed **then**
 5:         Assign changed class to instance i
 6:         Update the tree running Alg. 4 again
         {This is the standard case}
 7:     **else if** class assignment of i remained the same **then**
 8:         Do not update the tree using i
         {This is the exceptional case}
 9:     **end if**
10: **end if**

---

are used to predict the supposed class (ie. landuse) of the spatial object. There are three possible findings:

- *Unsatisfying tree* - the tree does not satisfy the attribute-value pairs of the new instance. The tree has to be extended following Alg. 4.
- *Same landuse class* - the new arriving instance is labeled with the same landuse as it was found in the corresponding leaf of the decision tree. Nothing has to be done, the tree remains the same.

- *Different landuse class* - the resulting leaf of the tree shows a landuse class, different from the expected landuse of the new instance. Following Alg. 6, the user is required to select the correct landuse class of the given spatial object.

5   Experimental Results

Having described the various processing stages in detail, we turn now to the evaluation. In particular, we are interested in observing how (the size of) the decision tree evolves during the initial generation (Alg. 1) and how the validation stage (Alg. 6) runs after the arrival of new spatial data.

For quantification purposes, we use the following criteria: the duration, the number of decision nodes, and the depth level of the tree. We are concerned with one large and representative area from the Austrian digital cadastre map, covering urban and suburban surface. The selected area contains more than 4,000 spatial objects (polygons) each classified into one of 16 different classes (for example: roadways, grassland, water areas, building area, buildings ...). All included spatial objects are proven to be free of misclassification and therefore can be used to generate the training instances using Alg. 1. Due to the high number of spatial objects, the number of generated training instances is high as well.

Running each of the in Sec. 4 described steps on a standard Notebook (Dual Core 2.5GHz, 3GB Ram) the generation of the training instances needs about 10 minutes time which is more or less reasonable due to the number of spatial objects to be tested. The next step, the generation of the initial decision tree is the most time consuming process and takes more than 100 minutes. Since this step can be seen as an offline process, the time plays a minor role. The initial decision tree based on the given 4,000 spatial objects, contains nearly 25,000 decision nodes and shows a depth of 80 levels from the root to the leaf nodes. Using the generated tree in the last step, the semi-automatic validation of new arriving spatial data, the time needed to validate 100 new instances is less than one minute.

To investigate the performance of the proposed approach, we have used only 100 instances to generate the initial decision tree followed by 100 instances that are sequentially presented to the classifier. For these 100 instances, 58 interactions with the user have been required in order to validate the assigned landuse class. If we use 1,000 instances to induce the initial decision tree, then no interaction is required for the same 100 instances.

6   Conclusion

In this paper, an incremental self-learning approach based on decision trees has been proposed to deal with online update and semi-automatic correction of spatial objects misclassification. Using the ID5R algorithm, the decision tree can be incrementally adjusted without the need to its reconstruction from scratch over time. The approach is semi-automatic in the way that each instance, not falling in one of the leaf nodes of the tree, has to be validated manually by the user. Moreover given a spatial data, proven to be free of any misclassification, an initial decision tree can be constructed without the need to any interaction with the user. The experiments show that the approach is effective and efficient.

As a future investigation, we intend to explore ways to reduce the time needed for the generation of the initial decision tree and to evaluate the classification performance using various erroneous areas of the Austrian digital cadastre map.

References

1. Bachhiesl, P., Prossegger, M., Stoegner, H., Werner, J., Paulus, G.: Cost optimal implementation of fiber optic networks in the access net domain. In: International Conference on Computing, Communications and Control Technologies, pp. 334–349 (2004)
2. Clodoveu, K., Borges, K., Davis, A., Laender, H.: Integrity constraints in spatial databases. In: Database Integrity: Challenges and Solutions. Ideas Group, USA (2002)
3. David, A., Cui, Z., Cohn, A.: A spatial logic based on regions and connection. In: Proc. KR 1992, pp. 165–176 (1992)
4. Ellson, J., Gansner, E., Koutsofios, L., North, S.C., Woodhul, G.: Graphviz Open Source Graph Drawing Tools. LNCS, vol. 2265, pp. 594–597 (2002)
5. Jakobsson, A., Vauglin, F.: Status of data quality in european national mapping agencies. In: Proceedings of the 20th International Cartographic Conference, Beijing, China, vol. 4, pp. 2875–2883 (2001)
6. Kahn, B., Strong, D., Wang, R.: Information quality benchmarks: Product and service performance. Commun. ACM 45, 184–192 (2002)
7. Leo Pipino, L., Lee, Y.W., Wang, R.Y.: Data quality assessment. Commun. ACM 45(4), 211–218 (2002)
8. Mostafavi, M., Edwards, G., Jeansoulin, R.: An ontology-based method for quality assessment of spatial data bases. In: Proceedings of the Third International Symposium on Spatial Data Quality, vol. 28, pp. 49–66 (2004)
9. Mostafavi, M., Edwards, G., Jeansoulin, R.: An ontology-based method for quality assessment of spatial data bases. In: Proceedings of the Third International Symposium on Spatial Data Quality, vol. 28, pp. 49–66 (2004)
10. Prossegger, M., Bouchachia, A.: Incremental identification of topological errors within spatial data. In: Proceedings of the 17th International Conference on Geoinformatics, pp. 1–6 (2009)
11. Quinlan, J.: Expert systems in the microelectronic age. In: Discovering rules by Induction From Large Collections of Examples. Edinburgh University Press, Edinburgh (1979)
12. Safavian, S., Landgrebe, D.: A survey of decision tree classifier methodology. IEEE Transactions on Systems, Man and Cybernetics 21(3), 660–674 (1991)
13. Ubeda, T., Egenhofer, M.: Topological error correcting in gis. In: In the Proceedings of International Symposium on Spatial Databases (1997)
14. Utgoff, P.: Incremental induction of decision trees. Machine Learning 4, 161–186 (1989)
15. Wang, R., Strong, D.M.: Beyond accuracy: What data quality means to data consumers. Journal of Management Information Systems 12, 5–34 (1996)
16. I. 211, 19113 Geographic Information - Quality Principles, International Organization for Standardization, ISO (2002)

On-Line Human Recognition from Video Surveillance Using Incremental SVM on Texture and Color Features

Yanyun Lu, Anthony Fleury, Jacques Booneart, and Stéphane Lecœuche

Univ Lille Nord de France, F-59000 Lille, France
EMDouai, IA, F-59500 Douai, France
{firstname.lastname}@mines-douai.fr

Abstract. The goal of this paper is to contribute to the realization of a system able to recognize people in video surveillance images. The context of this study is to classify a new frame including a person into a set of already known people, using an incremental classifier. To reach this goal, we first present the feature extraction and selection that have been made on appearance based on features (from color and texture), and then we introduce the incremental classifier used to differentiate people from a set of 20 persons. This incremental classifier is then updated at each new frame with the new knowledge that has been presented. With this technique, we achieved 92% of correct classification on the used database. These results are then compared to the 99% of correct classification in the case of a non-incremental technique and these results are explained. Some future works will try to rise the performances of incremental learning the one of non-incremental ones.

1 Introduction

Nowadays, video surveillance is more and more considered as a solution for safety and is now widely-used in town or in public transports, and more generally in public areas. Human recognition in video sequences is a key ability for video surveillance [15]. However, it is difficult to have a complete knowledge about a person in order to recognize him in video sequences. In a realistic environment, human beings are time-varying objects due to the different possible positions, poses and expressions ; but also due to environmental conditions such as illumination variation or camera motion. Even a very huge static database of people images can not express the whole set of possibilities [14]. That is the reason why on-line learning could be a way to improve the knowledge that we already acquired on a person in order to consider new conditions (environmental, position of the person, etc.).

However, on-line multi-category classification remains a difficult and challenging problem. One of the challenge is to find the features that will correctly represent the class (that defines one person) with only a first sequence of data. After this first stage, we would like to correctly classify new frames from another sequence using the previous knowledge, in and train again the classifier considering this new information. In a first stage, a decision system able to decide whether a data will be used to create a new class or will be classified as an existing one could be design. Then the second stage should be this work, which classifies the considered frame as belonging to one of the class and then adapt the classifier with this new data.

A. Bouchachia (Ed.): ICAIS 2011, LNAI 6943, pp. 26–39, 2011.
© Springer-Verlag Berlin Heidelberg 2011

In this work, we used Support Vector Machines (SVM) as classifier. This classifier, introduced by Vapnik [17], since a long time, used in a very large number of application and gave very good generalization results [4]. The main idea of SVM is initially to construct an hyperplane that separates two classes (linearly) minimizing the risk, by taking the largest margin between the data and the boundary. It has been then extended to non-linear cases (using a Kernel function) and to multi-category problems [3,12]. It turned SVM to a very powerful classifier that can be adapted to a large number of problems.

However, these techniques rely on the fact that we describe correctly, during the training stage, all the classes that are being recognized. As in our case, when all the data describing the classes are not known when learning, an on-line version of SVM has been designed [6], that tries to adapt the boundary with the new data that is considered. In [1], Awad and Motai used an adaptation of the Least-Square SVM (LS-SVM) to achieve a unique, fast and simple multi-category classification of behavioral motions.

The paper is organized as follow: first, we present, in Section 2, the problem that is aimed to be solved and we introduce the used database. Section 3 presents the initial features extraction and three different kinds of feature selection method which performances are compared in our system (feature selection is an important part in order to achieve good results in classification, that is why we present different methods to compare the effects of the selections on the results). Then, section 4, presents the incremental multi-category SVM method that has been implemented in this article. Section 5 discusses the results comparing them to ones with classical SVM. Finally section 6 concludes the paper and outlines our future works on this topic.

2 Human Recognition in Video Frames

Our aim is to contribute to the design of a video surveillance system that is able to recognize the persons that are seen by a camera. In this work, we will consequently present and apply an on-line multi-class SVM algorithm to set-up a surveillance system, which recognizes a person. The goal is to use a first sequence of image to learn to recognize the person (creating the class), and then evaluate the results of this recognition on other sequences. As the algorithm is incremental, each decision that is taken from a frame in a new sequence will be used to update the SVM with this new information. Incremental techniques are adapted to this kind of work because we never have a complete information when starting to learn to recognize a person from such a system (with different illumination, positions etc.), as a consequence we will learn step by step, when a new information comes in the system. The system that we present begins by a preprocessing stage, that is feature extraction (after receiving a frame). As a consequence, part of this paper is dedicated to the methods of feature selection implemented. Then, we used SVM as classifier for an incremental recursive multi-category classification and compared it to non-incremental version of SVM. This system is described by Fig. 1. The main contribution of this paper is the analysis, on a large database, of the important features for human recognition and the investigation on incremental techniques for using the defined features.

Before collecting a real on-board dataset in our system, CASIA Gait Database [5] was used. It is a video database of 20 persons, walking at normal pace. Each person

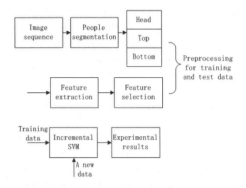

Fig. 1. The framework of proposed human recognition system

Fig. 2. Three persons in different actions in CASIA gait database [5]

walks with different orientations regarding the video camera. Each image contains one unique person and the 20 persons did not changed their clothes between trials. Six trials are presented for each of the twenty subjects: walking from right to left and from left to right, walking in front of the video camera (coming and leaving, two times in each direction), walking in a direction that is at 45° of the camera from the left and from the right. Fig. 2 shows the six different actions that are repeated twice for each of the 20 persons. The whole number of images from the 20 classes is 19135, the distribution of the samples in the different classes is described in Table 1. This table shows us that the 20 classes (considering the average and standard deviation value of the cardinality) are almost represented with the same number of samples for each one.

Table 1. The distribution of 20 classes within the 19135 images in CASIA gait database

Number of classes	20
Number of frame	19135
Average Cardinality	956.75
Std Cardinality	83.5243

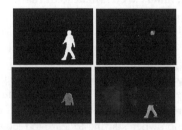

Fig. 3. The silhouette picture and the three parts of the body that have been considered

In CASIA Gait Database, background subtraction has been performed and the silhouette pictures are extracted from the sequences. From this silhouette, we segmented the body in three different parts: the head, the top part (the chest) and the bottom part (the legs), which are shown in Fig. 3. Each part is processed separately and the features are computed for these three parts independently. We have, with this, three different analyses that are more accurate than considering a unique part composed of the whole body (separating the top and the bottom of the body makes us analyze two colors instead of one average color). These three parts have been chosen because they are generally the three ones in which we have different clothes or colors. They are generally used to describe the appearance of a person. Such segmentation of the body have been already introduced by Gasser et al. [8], in order to also recognize people using a video camera. However, this previous work used only one feature (that is an average value on the three parts) and uses non-incremental algorithms. The work that will be presented in the remaining of this paper justifies the use of these three parts by deeply analyzing the feature selection part and testing it with incremental and non-incremental algorithms for classification.

3   Feature Selection and Comparison of the Methods

3.1   Extraction the Initial Feature Sets

Classification of objects, or in our case human beings, needs some variables to define what or who has to be recognized. These features need to correctly represent what we want to classify and correctly differentiate the classes. The first stage of our work consists in extracting robust features from each frame of a person in video sequences, to define this person using the information contained in these images. Most of the known and used features to define human beings are based on face, gait, body sharp and appearance [18,11,19]. In [16], appearance-based method has been successfully used in tracking and recognition. Since the appearance of a person is made up of clothes and visible parts, color features are easy to obtain and describe. Color features are based on the general characteristics of the pixels and invariant to translation, rotation and not sensitive to scale if a correct normalization is used. We combine color and texture features in our research.

Color features are based on the RGB (Red, Green Blue) plans of the image whereas texture features are based on grey levels of the image. Color features of each frame captured by camera are varying depending on several factors, such as illumination conditions, surface reflectance or resolution response of the camera. As a consequence, normalization is necessary. In this paper, the grey-world normalization (GN) is used. It assumes that changes in the illuminating spectrum can be modeled by three constant factors applied to R, G, B, in order to obtain invariance and more robustness to illumination intensity variations [7].

As explained before, we considered three different parts for the body. For each part, we computed the different features that we defined. These features are the mean and standard deviation values for each color component and the energy in four beams of the histogram of the image. This leads to the extraction of 18 color-based features for each part of the body.

Some texture-based features have been previously defined by Haralick [10]. Thirteen features have been given, considering as an input a grey scale image. We still consider the segmentation of the body in three parts and we consider this area of the image that we convert in grey levels. We obtain a one-dimension matrix that represents regions, with values between 0 (black) and 255 (white). From the Spatial Grey Level Dependence Matrix, 13 features are computed. This whole set of features is listed in Table 2.

Based on color and texture features, we obtain a total of 93 features for the 19135 images: 54 color features merging the information of the three parts of the body and of

Table 2. The initial features based on color and texture

Type of Feature	Description
Color	Mean Value for R', for G' and for B'
	Standard Deviation for R', for G' and for B'
	Histogram with 4 beams for R', for G' and for B'
Texture	Energy
	Correlation
	Inertia
	Entropy
	Inverse Difference Moment
	Sum Average
	Sum Variance
	Sum Entropy
	Difference Average
	Difference Variance
	Difference Entropy
	Information Measure of Correlation 1
	Information Measure of Correlation 2

Table 3. The results of three methods of feature selection

FeatureSet	FeatureNumber	Description
CASIA-Wholeset	93	Initial color and texture features
CASIA-PCA	26	linear combinations of original features
CASIA-CFS	40	5-color-head 13-color-top 14-color-bottom 1-texture-head 14-texture-top 3-texture-bottom
CASIA-Wrapper	16	4-color-head 4-color-top 4-color-bottom 1-texture-head 2-texture-top 1-texture-bottom

the three color spaces, and 39 texture features for each body. The features are named firstly with the position (h for head, t for top and b for bottom), and their meaning (mean for average value, std for standard deviation, hist_beam1 or hist_beam2 for the histograms) and then with the color if it applies (r for red, g for green and b for blue). We obtain for instance for the mean value of the top in the red plan the name t_mean_r.

3.2 Feature Selection

To represent our classes, we can think that having a very high dimensional dataset will lead to high discrimination power and to efficiency in classification. However, high dimensional data are difficult to interpret and their processing by a classifier may raise the problem of curse of dimensionality. In order to avoid useless dimensions in the training data, and as a consequence, reduce the computing time and increase the performances, many algorithms are designed to reduce dimensionality to its minimum, still keeping the performances of the original dataset in supervised or unsupervised learning.

In our work, we focus on supervised learning, where the class labels are known. Three methods (PCA, Wrapper and Correlation-based feature selection) are compared, in order to choose the best features for human recognition. In a first place all the dimensions are normalized to remove scale effects between them (because variation can be hugely different between dimensions).

PCA. Feature selection based on PCA aims at reducing the number of dimension without losing the main information by projecting the data on a new orthogonal basis. In our work, when the sum of the variance is equal to 95% of the initial variance of the data, we stop and consider our subspace as optimal to answer to our problem.

As a result, 26 features are extracted, which are the linear combination of the 93 initial features. When computing, the 26 new data for each of the 19135 images are saved, and a new dataset (CASIA-PCA) is constituted.

Correlation-Based Feature Selection. Correlation-based feature selection (CFS) is a simple filter algorithm which ranks feature subsets according to the correlation based on the heuristic of "merit", which is described by M. A. Hall [9] as the following expression:

$$M_s = \frac{k \cdot \overline{r_{cf}}}{\sqrt{k + k \cdot (k-1) \cdot \overline{r_{ff}}}}$$

where k is the number of features selected in the current subset, $\overline{r_{cf}}$ is the mean feature-class correlation, for each element $f \in S$ of our current subset, and $\overline{r_{ff}}$ is the mean feature-feature correlation for each pairwise of elements. From this heuristic, the search method will begin with the empty set and add some features, once at a time, in order to find efficiently the one that possesses the best value. Best first method is applied to search the set with the best merit value.

For our initial set of features, the algorithm gave us a subset of 40 features, the most representative features with the less possible redundancy. The final subset (CASIA-CFS) contains features from all the body including: 5 features that are from the color of the head, 4 from the texture of the top, 3 features from the texture of the bottom, 14 from the color of the bottom. The texture features are less present in the final subset and the most important part of the subset is given by the bottom part of the body.

Wrapper. Wrapper methods were first described by John et al.[13]. It uses, as CFS, a search algorithm to go through the whole combination of features but to compute the merit of a subset, it uses the results of the classification of the dataset with the targeted algorithm. The huge disadvantage of wrapper method is that it has, to compute the rank of a subset, to evaluate the results (given by global error rate) of the classification of the dataset. As a consequence, the execution time before obtaining the desired results can be huge. However, the advantage of this method is that it should give the best results as the classification algorithm is specified before and used to compute the merit.

Over the 93 features, 16 features have been selected by this method. Average and standard deviation values are well represented and for texture entropy is present in the three part of the body. The selected features are presented in Table 3.

3.3   Discussion on the Results of Feature Selection

As described in the above subsections, four sets of features were considered for the classification stage: CASIA-Wholeset (initial set of 93 features), CASIA-PCA, CASIA-CFS and CASIA-Wrapper. The results of feature selection are summarized in following Table 3.

For PCA method, we get 26 features instead of 93 features in 99.6% relevance (the average of ROC Area). However, the disadvantage of this first method is that it highly relies on the data and we can consider, with our initial problem, that another dataset would have given different results for the linear combinations of features.

In CASIA-CFS, most of selected features are color-based. And comparing CASIA-CFS and CASIA-Wrapper feature sets, 11 features are in both sets: h_mean_r, h_std_r, h_mean_b, t_mean_r, t_std_r, t_mean_b, t_std_b, b_mean_r, b_std_r, b_std_g, b_mean_b. In addition, when we carefully look at the values of the covariance matrix (that gives us the importance of each feature in the linear combination creating the new vectors), we can notice that the ones that are selected by the other methods are the ones that have the higher coefficients. It is obvious that color-based features are more useful in people classification in our system. Entropy features of texture-based are usually selected and give the most useful information to human classification in all feature sets.

4   Incremental SVM

SVM is an algorithm based on structure risk minimization principle, by learning from the data and adding a margin between the data and the boundary. In multi-class classification, training data is prone to be large. As all the classifier, when learning, SVM needs to have a good representation of the classes. For human recognition, it is very difficult to give such a database (with the different illuminations, orientation, etc.). One approach to overcome this constraint is to train using an incremental learning technique, whereby only a subset of the data is used at any one time. Multi-category SVM with incremental learning can be depicted as follow: adapt the decision function when a new data is added while retaining the Karush-Kuhn-Tucker (KKT) conditions on all the previous training data.

4.1   Multi-category SVM with Incremental Learning

This work is based on the incremental algorithm presented in [2]. Let's consider a training dataset D of L pairs $(x_i, y_i), i = [1, \cdots, L], x_i \in R^d, y_i \in [1, \cdots, K], K \geq 2$. To solve non-linear problems, the original data x_i is mapped to higher dimensional space by $\Phi(x)$ function. SVM hyper planes are given by: $w_i^T \Phi(x) + b_i = 0$. So the class of a point x is determined by finding i such that $f_i(x) = w_i^T \Phi(x_i) + b_i$ is maximized. In multi-category classification, the margin between class i and j is $2/||w_i - w_j||$. In order to get the largest margin of class i and j, minimization of $||w_i - w_j||$ to all $i, j = 1, ..., L$ is computed. Also, as described in [3], the regularization term $\frac{1}{2} \sum_{i=1}^{L} ||w_i||^2$ is added to the objective function. In addition, a loss function $\sum_{i=1}^{L} \sum_{j=i+1}^{L} \sum_{x_k \in C_{ij}} \lambda_k^{ij}$ is used to find the decision rule with the minimal number of errors in inseparable case, where the slack variable λ_k^{ij} measure the degree of misclassification of the hyper-plan ij of the kth training vector . So, the proposed quadratic function as the following:

$$\min \frac{1}{2} \sum_{i=1}^{L} \sum_{j=i+1}^{L} ||w_i - w_j||^2 + \frac{1}{2} \sum_{i=1}^{L} ||w_i||^2 + C \sum_{i=1}^{L} \sum_{j=i+1}^{L} \sum_{x_k \in C_{ij}} \lambda_k^{ij} \qquad (1)$$

where $C \geq 0$ trades off the term that controls the number of outliers. A larger C is corresponding to assigning a higher penalty to errors.

The constraint conditions are $y_k^{ij} \left[(w_i - w_j)^T \Phi(x_k) + (b_i - b_j) \right] - 1 + \lambda_k^{ij} \geq 0; \lambda_k^{ij} \geq 0;$ $\forall x_k \in C_{ij}$, where $C_{ij} = C_i \cup C_j$, $y_k^{ij} = 1$ if $x_k \in C_i$ and $y_k^{ij} = -1$ if $x_k \in C_j$. The goal is to get the minimum of the objective function, which is a quadratic programming task. We solve it by Lagrange multiplier method. The Lagrange function L_p is defined by:

$$L_p = \frac{1}{2}\sum_{i=1}^{L}\sum_{j=i+1}^{L}\|w_i - w_j\|^2 + \frac{1}{2}\sum_{i=1}^{L}\|w_i\|^2 + C\sum_{i=1}^{L}\sum_{j=i+1}^{L}\sum_{x_k \in C_{ij}}\lambda_k^{ij} - \sum_{i=1}^{L}\sum_{j=i+1}^{L}\sum_{x_k \in C_{ij}}\beta_k^{ij}\lambda_k^{ij}$$

$$-\sum_{i=1}^{L}\sum_{j=i+1}^{L}\sum_{x_k \in C_{ij}}\alpha_k^{ij}(y_k^{ij}[(w_i - w_j)^T\Phi(x_k) + (b_i - b_j)] - 1 + \lambda_k^{ij}) \quad (2)$$

where Lagrange coefficients are $\alpha_k^{ij} \geq 0, \beta_k^{ij} \geq 0, i \neq j$.

The Lagrange L_p has to be minimized w_i, b_i, λ_k^{ij} and maximized α_k^{ij} and β_k^{ij}. Then in the saddle points the solution satisfies for all $i = 1,...,L$: $\frac{\partial L_p}{\partial w_i}$, $\frac{\partial L_p}{\partial b_i}$ and $\frac{\partial L_p}{\partial \lambda_k^{ij}}$ are equal to zero, respectively. In consequence, we get:

$$w_i = \frac{1}{L+1}\sum_{j=1, j \neq i}^{L}(\sum_{x_k \in C_i}\alpha_k^{ij}\Phi(x_k) - \sum_{x_k \in C_j}\alpha_k^{ij}\Phi(x_k)) \quad (3)$$

and $\alpha_k^{ij} + \beta_k^{ij} = C$ then $0 \leq \alpha_k^{ij} \leq C, i = 1,...,L$, $j = i+1,...,L$, this means that all the weights α_k^{ij} are bounded by C.

Based on the KKT conditions, at the saddle points: $\alpha_k^{ij}((w_i - w_j)^T\Phi(x_k) + (b_i - b_j) - 1) = 0$ and $\alpha_k^{ij}\beta_k^{ij} = 0$ for all $i = 1,...,L$, $j = i+1,...,L$. Then by replacing w_i as Equation 3, the problem of minimization of L_p can be solved by minimizing the following objective function:

$$W = \frac{1}{2(L+1)}(\sum_{i=1}^{L}\sum_{j=1+1}^{L}\|\sum_{x_k \in C_i}(2\alpha_k^{ij} + \sum_{\substack{m=1 \\ m \neq i,j}}^{L}\alpha_k^{im})\Phi(x_k) - \sum_{x_k \in C_j}(2\alpha_k^{ij} + \sum_{\substack{m=1 \\ m \neq i,j}}^{L}\alpha_k^{mj})\Phi(x_k) - \sum_{\substack{m=1 \\ m \neq i,j}}^{L}\sum_{x_k \in C_m}(\alpha_k^{im} - \alpha_k^{mj})$$

$$\Phi(x_k)\|^2 + \sum_{i=1}^{k}\|\sum_{\substack{m=1 \\ m \neq i}}^{L}\sum_{x_k \in C_i}\alpha_k^{im}\Phi(x_k) - \sum_{x_i \in C_m}\alpha_k^{im}\Phi(x_k)\|^2) - \sum_{i=1}^{L}\sum_{j=i+1}^{L}\sum_{x_k \in C_{i,j}}\alpha_k^{ij} + \sum_{i=1}^{L}b_i\sum_{\substack{m=1 \\ m \neq i}}^{L}(\sum_{x_k \in C_i}\alpha_k^{im} - \sum_{x_k \in C_m}\alpha_k^{im}) \quad (4)$$

The KKT conditions on the point $x_n \in C_{ij}$ divide data D into three categories according to the value of g_n^{ij} for all $i = 1,...,L$, $j = i+1,...,L$:

$$g_n^{ij} = \frac{\partial W}{\partial \alpha_n^{ij}}\begin{cases} > 0; & \alpha_n^{ij} = 0 \\ = 0; & 0 < \alpha_n^{ij} < C \\ < 0; & \alpha_n^{ij} = C \end{cases} \quad (5)$$

The set S of support vectors sv_n^{ij} which are strictly on the margin ($g_n^{ij} = 0$), and let s^{ij} be the number of support vectors which are on the margin. The set E of error vectors ev_n^{ij} which are incorrectly positioned compared to the margin ($g_n^{ij} < 0$), and the set I of ignored vectors iv_n^{ij} ($g_n^{ij} > 0$).

The main idea of incremental learning SVM is that train an SVM with the partitions and reserve only the support vectors at each training step and add them to the training set for the next step. The key is to preserve the KKT conditions on all training vectors while adiabatically adding a new vector. When a new sample is added, the coefficients g are changed corresponding to the new data to meet the KKT conditions, while ensuring that the exising sample in D continue to satisfy the KKT conditions at each step. In particular, these conditions can be expressed as differential form:

$$\Delta g_n^{ij} = y_n^{ij} \Big(A^{ij,pq} \Delta \alpha_c^{pq} K_{cn} + \sum_{\substack{x_k \in C_i}} (2\Delta \alpha_k^{ij} + \sum_{\substack{m=1 \\ m \neq i,j}}^{L} \Delta \alpha_k^{im}) K_{kn} - \sum_{\substack{x_k \in C_j}} (2\Delta \alpha_k^{ij} + \sum_{\substack{m=1 \\ m \neq i,j}}^{L} \Delta \alpha_k^{mj}) K_{kn}$$

$$- \sum_{\substack{m=1 \\ m \neq i,j}}^{L} \sum_{x_k \in C_m} (\Delta \alpha_k^{im} - \Delta \alpha_k^{mj}) K_{kn} + (\Delta b_i - \Delta b_j) \Big) \tag{6}$$

$$B^i \Delta \alpha_c^{pq} + \sum_{\substack{m=1 \\ m \neq i}}^{L} \Big(\sum_{x_k \in C_i} \Delta \alpha_k^{im} - \sum_{x_k \in C_j} \Delta \alpha_k^{im} \Big) = 0 \tag{7}$$

where $i = 1, ..., L, j = i+1, ..., L$, α_c^{pq} is the coefficient being incremental, initially zero and K is kernel function, $\Phi(x_i)^T \Phi(x_j) = K(x_i, x_j)$ and $K_{kn} = K(x_k, x_n)$. Coefficients $A^{ij,pq}, B^i$ are defined by:

$$A^{ij,pq} = \begin{cases} 2 & \text{if } (i,j) = (p,q) \text{ and } x_c \in C_i \\ -2 & \text{if } (i,j) = (p,q) \text{ and } x_c \in C_j \\ 1 & \text{if } i = p, j \neq q \text{ and } x_c \in C_i \\ & \text{or } i \neq p, j = q \text{ and } x_c \notin C_{ij} \\ -1 & \text{if } i = p, j \neq q \text{ and } x_c \notin C_{ij} \\ & \text{or } i \neq p, j = q \text{ and } x_c \in C_j \\ 0 & \text{otherwise} \end{cases} \tag{8}$$

$$B^i = \begin{cases} 1 & \text{if } x_c \in C_i \\ -1 & \text{if } x_c \notin C_i \end{cases} \tag{9}$$

where $p = 1, ..., L, q = i+1, ..., L$.

For all support vectors sv_n^{ij}, $n = 1, ..., S^{ij}$, $i = 1, ..., L, j = i+1, ..., L$, $g_n^{ij}(sv_n^{ij}) = 0$, then $\Delta g_n^{ij}(sv_n^{ij}) = 0$. We set $b = [b_1, ..., b_L]$ and $\alpha = [\alpha_1^{12}, \alpha_2^{12}, ... \alpha_i^{ij}, \alpha_j^{ij}, ..., \alpha_{L-1}^{(L-1)L}, \alpha_L^{(L-1)L}]$, α_i^{ij} expresses the weights of support vectors sv_n^{ij} that belong to the class C_i. Equations 6 and 7 can be transformed as a matrix equation, where we know that $\Delta b, \Delta \alpha$ change with $\Delta \alpha_c^{pq}$ in matrix parameter R, as described in detail in [2].

$$\begin{bmatrix} \Delta b \\ \Delta \alpha \end{bmatrix} = -RH^{pq} \Delta \alpha_c^{pq} \tag{10}$$

The new sample x_c is added, training set $D^{L+1} = D^L \cup x_c$ initializes $\alpha_c = 0$. If $g_c^{pq} > 0$, x_c is not a margin or error vector, and we terminate. Else we apply the largest possible incremental α_c^{pq}. When $g_c^{pq} = 0$, x_c is considered as a support vector and added to the set S; when $\alpha_c^{pq} = 0$, x_c is a error vector and added to the set E. Otherwise $\Delta \alpha_c^{pq}$ is too small to cause the data move across S, E and I, the largest possible increment $\Delta \alpha_c^{pq}$ is determine by the bookkeeping procedure [6]. The incremental procedure algorithm is described by Algorithm 1 [14,6].

Algorithm 1. Incremental Procedure [14,6]

```
1  x_c → C_p, p ∈ [1,...,L];
2  Set n > 0;
3  for q = 1,...,L,q ≠ p do
4       α_c^{pq} ← 0;
5       z = [b,a];
6       Compute H^{pq};
7       while (g_c^{pq} < 0 and α_c^{pq} < C) do
8            α_c^{pq} = α_c^{pq} + n;
9            z = z − R · H^{pq} · n;
10           g_k^{ij} = g_k^{ij} + Δg_k^{ij}, i = 1,...,L, j = i+1,...,L, x_k ∈ C_{ij};
11           if α_n^{ij} are close to zero then
12                Corresponding support vectors move inside the margin (sv_n^{ij} → dv_n^{ij});
13                Update R,z and H^{pq};
14           end
15      end
16      if α_c^{pq} = C then x_c is added to C_p as an error vector;
17      else x_c is considered as a support vector;
18      Update R;
19 end
```

4.2 The Results of Incremental SVM

In this implementation, an RBF kernel has been used for both algorithms. The value of the hyper-parameter of the kernel has been optimized before running the tests using the train dataset. Both algorithms (incremental and non-incremental) use the same kernel parameter (and also the same value for C).

In our system, the incremental SVM work flow is shown in Fig.4. For the following results, 100 images of each class (10% of the whole dataset, about one sequence) are used for training and the remaining are used for testing. Table 4 describes the performances of the incremental SVM classifier. The results vary a lot with the feature sets and the mean of recognition rate of all classes is 81.82%. The best set is given by

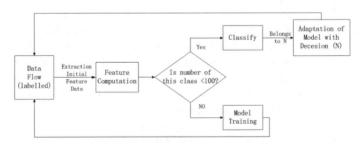

Fig. 4. Incremental learning work flow

CASIA-Wrapper with a 92.93% global recognition rate. Some classes are badly recognized in the other three databases, with recognition rates below 70% for C10, C16, C19 and C20 (showed in bold typesetting in the table). However, encouraging results of 20 classes (only C1 has low results) are obtained by considering the Wrapper dataset with more than 90%. We do not have, in this protocol, overfitting problems (especially with Wrapper dataset) because even if the data that has been used for feature selection could be part of the test datasets, the algorithm is different (incremental one) from the one that has been used before.

5   Comparison with Classical SVM

We performed a comparison experiment using classic SVM based on the same feature datasets in the same experimental conditions, to check if the lower results are caused by inner properties of the class.

In our comparative experiments, the SVM classifier was tested with a stratified cross-validation using 66% for training and 34% for testing (randomly chosen). Table 5 reports the comparative results of classification recognition rate of non-incremental learning according to four sets feature database. For all feature sets, the results are almost identical and the mean of recognition rate of all classes achieves 98.43%. The two tests protocols are different, however, it would have been difficult to achieve two interesting tests with the same protocol. These results on a non-incremental algorithm are used as a reference that one could achieve with an incremental one. As we have no formal comparison of the two techniques, these first results give some clues on the remaining work to improve our incremental procedure.

Some classes, which showed lower recognition rate in incremental SVM, achieve good performances in classical SVM. That is to say, lower results of incremental learning are not due to inner properties of the class.

In classical SVM, during the training process, we have the whole set and then we learn the models. This learning phase is done minimizing the error (with the slack variables). However, even in that case, we have some errors that are made by the classifier, but these vectors are ignored. When performing incremental learning, we update the margins with the result of the classification and as a consequence, if a frame is incorrectly classified, it will be considered as part of a wrong class. When retraining, this frame possibly could become a support vector of this wrong class. Without the whole picture at the beginning, such frame, if it is presented just after the initialization process, could migrate to the Support Vector Set instead of the Error Set (because of the lack of knowledge from the class). And this support vector will create update of the decision function and include a slow movement of the separation between the considered classes. The wrong result by this false support vector will then have an impact on the remaining classification. When presenting a new frame close to the one with error for instance, if again incorrectly classified because of this first error, the inaccuracy will be increased. That is one of the possibility to explain these low results for only few classes (always the same). [2] proved that at the end of the process, the support vectors are the same (and so are the boundaries). However, before this step, we already have classified a huge number of data. This explaination is confirmed by the last column of the table 4,

Table 4. Recognition results of SVM with incremental learning based on four proposed database. The last column gives the results with a different repartition between training and testing (90%/10%)

	Wholeset	PCA	CFS	Wrapper	Wholeset90
C1	88.39	74.82	76.06	**60.61**	98.31
C2	85.77	93.95	89.51	98.98	91.29
C3	74.42	78.14	68.77	91.57	95.90
C4	78.96	76.64	79.42	89.9	95.26
C5	87.47	81.56	88.57	97.92	96.46
C6	87.36	86.04	76.55	92.74	97.23
C7	93.32	89.86	96.3	98.28	95.85
C8	95.81	98.2	97.77	99.17	97.18
C9	80.3	94.8	82.28	98.25	98.30
C10	**37.07**	**48.59**	**36.84**	98.51	93.42
C11	94.06	97.41	94.15	95.2	98.90
C12	99.29	98.47	98.36	96.36	99.99
C13	82.58	78.65	87.7	82.25	96.16
C14	84.49	83.73	82.17	95.33	96.53
C15	90.82	91.26	88.39	93.21	93.13
C16	**56.18**	**58.25**	**60.1**	92.93	97.07
C17	82.9	88.48	86.09	95.2	96.55
C18	96.16	94.26	96.21	92.75	97.29
C19	**15.84**	**16.02**	**18.38**	95.9	95.82
C20	**59.36**	**82.66**	**69.91**	95.4	95.14
Global	78.88	80.93	79.12	92.93	96.29

Table 5. Recognition results of SVM without incremental learning based on four proposed database

	Wholeset	PCA	CFS	Wrapper
C1	99.49	99.12	99.7	99.81
C2	99.48	99.52	99.47	99.68
C3	99.97	99.18	100	100
C4	98.45	94.88	99.11	95.26
C5	99.6	97.05	99.46	99.82
C6	97.4	97.24	96.45	100
C7	100	99.65	100	98.87
C8	99.96	99.18	100	100
C9	99.53	100	100	99.81
C10	100	100	100	100
C11	98.91	98.06	99.65	95.38
C12	99.73	98.7	99.8	100
C13	99.38	98.79	99.47	97.91
C14	99.29	95.76	98.52	100
C15	98.99	97.66	99.55	90.88
C16	92.4	91.88	93.47	89.53
C17	99.96	99.73	99.73	99.9
C18	96.33	92.8	94.94	99.82
C19	100	100	99.49	99.82
C20	100	100	100	99.64
Global	98.96	97.97	98.95	97.91

in which we inverted the size of training and testing dataset for the whole set of features. These second results are close to the one of classical SVM without any class badly recognized. One idea to overcome this problem is to investigate on the support and error vectors assignation (tracing them over the time) in order to find a possibility to avoid such behaviour. We could think of finding a criterion that gives us the opportunity to reject a decision for future update of the classifier.

6   Conclusion and Future Work

In this paper, we presented a human recognition surveillance system based on adaptive multi-category SVM classifier. The classification is done from the body appearance extracted in the image sequences. The first originality introduced in the article is to segment each body into three parts (Head, Top, and Bottom), since three divided analyses are more accurate than the whole body. Considering these three parts of each silhouette, we characterized them by finding the most appropriated features. To do so, after extracting a whole feature set of 93 features based on color and texture of each part, we compared three different feature selection methods to reduce the feature space and obtain the optimal feature set. Then, four sets of database are obtained. The most satisfied result is based on Wrapper feature selection, which consists of 16 features of each person.

To apply our work to human recognition in video surveillance, we have to overcome the problem that the classes are not completely known at the beginning of the process. For this, we implemented an incremental learning algorithm. Using classical SVM for this task would require too much samples for each person to classify and a huge database that would be difficult to map onto memory. Moreover, this incremental procedure makes the classification method evolve to be able to learn a sequence of images and test on other sequences that could be different in terms of exposition or orientation of the person. Incremental SVM is more suitable for the practical situation of surveillance system. In our work, incremental SVM is tested in the situation based on four sets feature database respectively and is compared to classical SVM. The results of the classical SVM are very good in all feature database. The recognition rates of the incremental algorithm are lower, however, the performance for the database extracted with wrapper feature selection is satisfying with 92.93% global accuracy rate.

Our future work will first consist in improving the current results by considering some criterions on the new data that is presented to decide to use it for the adaptation or only to test it. With this first stage, we hope to remove the undesired modifications of the boundaries that is created from one class to another and that creates low results for some of the classes. The second part of our future work is to try to create new classes from data that are collected. For the moment, we only can classify data that are from known person. Novelty detection and class creation will be part of the design of a system that suits for video surveillance applications requirements.

Acknowledgment. Portions of the research in this paper use the CASIA Gait Database collected by Institute of Automation, Chinese Academy of Sciences.

References

1. Awad, M., Motai, Y.: Dynamic classification for video stream using support vector machine. Applied Soft Computing 8(4), 1314–1325 (2008)
2. Boukharouba, K., Bako, L., Lecoeuche, S.: Incremental and Decremental Multi-category Classification by Support Vector Machines. In: 2009 International Conference on Machine Learning and Applications, pp. 294–300. IEEE, Los Alamitos (2009)
3. Bredensteiner, E., Bennett, K.: Multicategory classification by support vector machines. Computational Optimization and Applications 12(1), 53–79 (1999)
4. Burges, C.: A tutorial on support vector machines for pattern recognition. Data Mining and Knowledge Discovery 2(2), 121–167 (1998)
5. CASIA Gait Database (2001): Downloadable on the internet at , http://www.sinobiometrics.com
6. Cauwenberghs, G., Poggio, T.: Incremental and decremental support vector machine learning. In: Advances in Neural Information Processing Systems, vol. 13, pp. 409–415 (2000)
7. Finlayson, G., Schiele, B., Crowley, J.: Comprehensive colour image normalization. In: Burkhardt, H.-J., Neumann, B. (eds.) ECCV 1998. LNCS, vol. 1406, pp. 475–490. Springer, Heidelberg (1998)
8. Gasser, G., Bird, N., Masoud, O., Papanikolopoulos, N.: Human activities monitoring at bus stops. In: Proceedings of the IEEE Inernational Conference on Robotics and Automation, New Orleans, LA, vol. 1, pp. 90–95 (April 2004)
9. Hall, M.: Correlation-based feature selection for machine learning. Ph.D. thesis, University of Waikato, New-Zealand (1999)

10. Haralick, R., Shanmugam, K., Dinstein, I.: Textural features for image classification. IEEE Transactions on Systems, Man and Cybernetics 3(6), 610–621 (1973)
11. Hörster, E., Lux, J., Lienhart, R.: Recognizing persons in images by learning from videos. In: Proceedings of SPIE, vol. 6506, pp. 65060D.1–65060D.9 (2007)
12. Hsu, C., Lin, C.: A comparison of methods for multiclass support vector machines. IEEE Transactions on Neural Networks 13(2), 415–425 (2002)
13. John, G., Kohavi, R., Pfleger, K.: Irrelevant features and the subset selection problem. In: Proceedings of The Eleventh International Conference on Machine Learning, vol. 129, pp. 121–129 (1994)
14. Ma, J., Theiler, J., Perkins, S.: Accurate on-line support vector regression. Neural Computation 15(11), 2683–2703 (2003)
15. Truong Cong, D., Khoudour, L., Achard, C., Meurie, C., Lezoray, O.: People re-identification by spectral classification of silhouettes. Signal Processing 90(8), 2362–2374 (2010)
16. Truong Cong, D., Khoudour, L., Achard, C., Douadi, L.: People Detection and Re-Identification in Complex Environments. IEICE Transactions on Information and Systems 93(7), 1761–1772 (2010)
17. Vapnik, V.: The Nature of Statistical Learning Theory. Springer, Heidelberg (2000)
18. Yoon, K., Harwood, D., Davis, L.: Appearance-based person recognition using color/path-length profile. Journal of Visual Communication and Image Representation 17(3), 605–622 (2006)
19. Zhou, X., Bhanu, B.: Integrating face and gait for human recognition at a distance in video. IEEE Transactions on Systems, Man, and Cybernetics, Part B: Cybernetics 37(5), 1119–1137 (2007)

An Improved Adaptive PID Controller Based on Online LSSVR with Multi RBF Kernel Tuning

Kemal Ucak and Gulay Oke

Department of Control Engineering
Istanbul Technical University
Maslak,TR-34469, Istanbul, Turkey
{kemal.ucak,gulay.oke}@itu.edu.tr

Abstract. In this paper, the effects of using multi RBF kernel for an online LSSVR on modeling and control performance are investigated. The Jacobian information of the system is estimated via online LSSVR model. Kernel parameter determines how the measured input is mapped to the feature space and a better plant model can be achieved by discarding redundant features. Therefore, introducing flexibility in kernel function helps to determine the optimal kernel. In order to interfuse more flexibility to the kernel, linear combinations of RBF kernels have been utilized. The purpose of this paper is to improve the modeling performance of the LSSVR and also control performance obtained by adaptive PID by tuning bandwidths of the RBF kernels. The proposed method has been evaluated by simulations carried out on a continuously stirred tank reactor (CSTR), and the results show that there is an improvement both in modeling and control performances.

Keywords: Adaptive PID, Kernel Polarization, Multi Kernel, Online LSSVR.

1 Introduction

PID Controllers have been the most popular controller structure owing to their simplicity and robustness, in spite of further developments in control engineering. The strength of the PID control lies in the simplicity, lucid meaning and clear effect [1]. The PID's long life force comes from its clear meaning and effectiveness in practice [1]. In adaptive control, tuning of the PID parameters rapidly and optimally is significant to get a good tracking performance in nonlinear systems [2]. Parameters of the model based PID controller can be tuned employing Support Vector Machine (SVM) or Neural Network model of the system.

Support Vector Machine theory has recently been utilized for tuning controller parameters [3,4,5,6], instead of Neural Network approach since it ensures global minima and it has powerful generalization ability. Since parameters of the controller are tuned according to the model of the plant, the control performance of PID based on Support Vector Regression (SVR) is directly related to the performance of the model.

The main design component in SVM is the kernel which is a nonlinear mapping function from the input to the feature space [7]. The main function of the kernel is to convert a linearly non separable classification problem in low dimension to a separable

A. Bouchachia (Ed.): ICAIS 2011, LNAI 6943, pp. 40–51, 2011.

one in high dimension and hence plays a crucial role in the modeling and control performance [2]. Kernel functions are generally parametric [2] and the numerical values of these parameters have significant effect on both modeling and control performance. Depending on the initial values of kernel parameters some features significant for the model may be discarded or redundant or irrelevant features may also be mapped to the feature space and, better performance may be achieved by discarding some features [8]. Owing to such factors, the selection of optimal kernel parameters is crucial in terms of the solution of the SVR problem. In order to seek optimal kernel parameters for regression, particle swarm optimization, pattern search and grid-diamond search have been utilized in [9],[10] and [11]. The common aim in all these approaches is to compute the kernel parameters offline. In [2], gradient descent optimization method has been utilized to tune the bandwidth of the single RBF kernel during online operation. The purpose of this paper is to improve the proposed method given in [2] introducing more flexibility to the kernel function using multi RBF.

In this paper, taking into consideration that more flexibility in kernel provides better SVM model, it's been our aim to estimate optimal values for parameters of multi RBF kernels and controller parameters using gradient information. In section 2, a brief overview of LSSVR and Online LSSVR are given. Tuning of multi RBF kernel parameters using online LSSVR is presented in Section 3. Adaptive PID controller based on online LSSVR is detailed in section 4. Simulation results, performance analysis of the online multi RBF kernel and adaptive PID, are given in section 5. The paper ends with a brief conclusion in Section 6.

2   Online Least Square Support Vector Regression

Given a training data set:

$$(y_1, x_1).....(y_k, x_k) \, , \; x \in R^n, y \in R \quad k = 1, 2, ,,, N \, . \tag{1}$$

where N is the size of training data and n is the dimension of the input matrix, the optimization problem for LSSVR is defined as follows to maximize the geometric margin and minimize the training error:

$$\min_{(w,b,e)} \frac{1}{2} w^T w + \frac{1}{2} C \sum_{k=1}^{N} e_k^2 \tag{2}$$

subject to

$$y_k - w^T \varphi(x_k) - b - e_k = 0 \, , \; k = 1, 2, ..., N \tag{3}$$

The minimization problem presented in equation (2, 3) is called the primal objective function [12]. By utilizing the primal objective function and its constraints, Lagrangian function can be derived as follows:

$$L(w,b,e,a) = \frac{1}{2} w^T w + \frac{1}{2} C \sum_{k=1}^{N} e_k^2 - \sum_{k=1}^{N} \alpha_k (w^T \varphi(x_k) + b + e_k - y_k) \tag{4}$$

In (4), L is the Lagrangian and, α_k are Lagrange multipliers [13-15]. For optimality primal variables have to vanish at the saddle point:

$$\frac{\partial L}{\partial b} = \sum_{k=1}^{N} \alpha_k = 0 \tag{5}$$

$$\frac{\partial L}{\partial w} = \underline{w} - \sum_{k=1}^{N} \alpha_k \varphi(x_k) = 0 \longrightarrow \underline{w} = \sum_{k=1}^{N} \alpha_k \varphi(x_k) \tag{6}$$

$$\frac{\partial L}{\partial e_k} = C \sum_{k=1}^{N} e_k - \sum_{k=1}^{N} \alpha_k = 0 \longrightarrow \alpha_k = Ce_k \tag{7}$$

$$\frac{\partial L}{\partial \alpha_k} = 0 \longrightarrow y_k = w^T \varphi(x_k) + b + e_k \quad k = 1, 2, ..., N \tag{8}$$

The solution of the problem is as follows via (5-8):

$$\begin{bmatrix} 0 & \underline{1} \\ \underline{1}^T & \Omega_{km} + \frac{I}{C} \end{bmatrix} \begin{bmatrix} b \\ \underline{a}^T \end{bmatrix} = \begin{bmatrix} 0 \\ y^T \end{bmatrix} \tag{9}$$

with

$$\underline{y} = [y_1, y_2, ..., y_N] \;\; , \;\; \underline{a} = [a_1, a_2, ..., a_N] \;\; , \;\; \underline{1} = [1, 1, .., 1], \Omega_{km} = K(x_k, x_m) \;\;, \;\; k, m = 1, 2, ..., N$$

Further information about LSSVR is available in [13], [14] and [15].

The dynamics of a non-linear system, can be represented by the Nonlinear AutoRegressive with eXogenous inputs (NARX) model ,

$$y(n+1) = f(u(n), .., u(n - n_u), y(n-1), .., y(n - n_y)) \tag{10}$$

where $u(n)$ is the control input applied to the plant at time n, $y(n+1)$ is the output of the plant , and n_u and n_y stand for the number of past control inputs and the number of past plant outputs involved in the model respectively [8].

The state vector of the system at time index n is represented as follows:

$$\underline{x}(n) = [u(n), .., u(n - n_u), y(n-1), .., y(n - n_y)] \tag{11}$$

The output of the model can be written as:

$$\hat{y}(n+1) = \sum_{i=n-L}^{n-1} a_i(n) K(\underline{x}(n), \underline{x}(i)) + b(n) \tag{12}$$

using equations (8),(10) and (11).

A training data set $(X(n), Y(n))$ can be established using inputs $\underline{X}(n) = [\underline{x}(n-1), ..., \underline{x}(n - L)]$, the corresponding outputs of the system $\underline{Y}(n) = [y(n), .., y(n - L + 1)]$, and L, the length of the sliding window. $\alpha(n)$ and $b(n)$ are obtained as follows assuming $\underline{U}(n) = [\underline{\Omega}(n) + \frac{I}{C}]^{-1}$ and using (9):

$$\underline{\alpha}^T(n) = \underline{U}(n)[\underline{Y}(n) - \underline{1}^T b(n)] \tag{13}$$

$$b(n) = \frac{\underline{1}U(n)\underline{Y}(n)}{\underline{1}U(n)\underline{1}^T} \tag{14}$$

At time index n, we have:

$$X(n) = [\underline{x}(n-1),....\underline{x}(n-L)] \; , \; \underline{Y}(n) = [y(n),..,y(n-L+1)] \tag{15}$$

At time index $n+1$, $\underline{X}(n+1)$ can be expressed as:

$$\underline{X}(n+1) = [\underline{x}(n),\underline{x}(n-1),....\underline{x}(n-L+1)] \; , \; \underline{Y}(n+1) = [y(n+1), y(n),..,(n-L+2)] \tag{16}$$

New data pair $(\underline{x}(n), y(n+1))$ is added to the training data set and, old data pair $(\underline{x}(n-L), y(n-L+1))$ is discarded from the training data set at time index $n+1$.

References [2],[3] and [16] can be referred for detailed information on the online identification procedure of nonlinear systems via online least square support vector regression.

3   Tuning of Multi-RBF Kernel

In this work, an online tuning procedure for the bandwidths and scaling coefficients of a multi RBF kernel has been proposed to improve modeling and control performance. The multi RBF kernel is given as follows:

$$Ker(\underline{x}_c(n), x_{svi}(n)) = \sum_{j=1}^{m} \frac{k_j \exp(-\dfrac{d_{c,svi}(n)}{2\sigma_j^{\;2}(n)})}{\displaystyle\sum_{z=1}^{m} k_z} \tag{17}$$

where $\sigma_j(n)$ is the bandwidth of the kernel function, $\underline{x}_c(n)$ is the current state vector of the plant and $d_{c,svi}(n)$ is the Euclidean distance between current data and the ith support vector.

$$d_{c,svi}(n) = (\underline{x}_c(n) - x_{svi}(n))^T (\underline{x}_c(n) - x_{svi}(n)) \tag{18}$$

In order to reveal the behavior of the multi RBF kernel function with fixed bandwidth, the behavior of the multi RBF kernel has been analyzed by synchronizing it with a single kernel. Assume that the multi kernel is the linear combination of 2 RBF kernels, the new kernel is as follows:

$$Ker(\underline{x}_c(n), x_{svi}(n)) = \frac{k_1(n)}{k_1(n)+k_2(n)} K_1(n) + \frac{k_2(n)}{k_1(n)+k_2(n)} K_2(n) \tag{19}$$

where

$$K_j(n) = K(\underline{x}_c(n), x_{svi}(n), \sigma_j) = \exp(-\frac{d_{c,svi}(n)}{2\sigma_j^{\;2}(n)}) \tag{20}$$

The following equation is written to examine whether this multi kernel can be represented using a single kernel or not.

$$\exp(-\frac{d_{c,svi}(n)}{2\sigma_s^2(n)}) = \frac{k_1(n)}{k_1(n)+k_2(n)}K_1(n) + \frac{k_2(n)}{k_1(n)+k_2(n)}K_2(n) \tag{21}$$

$$\sigma_s^2(n) = -\frac{d_{c,svi}(n)}{2\ln(\frac{k_1(n)}{k_1(n)+k_2(n)}K_1(n) + \frac{k_2(n)}{k_1(n)+k_2(n)}K_2(n))} \tag{22}$$

As can be seen from equation (22), multi kernel with fixed bandwidths equals to a single kernel with varying bandwidth depending on scaling coefficients and Euclidean distance between features. That is, multi RBF kernel with fixed bandwidths behaves like a single kernel with time varying bandwidth. In this paper, it is proposed to tune multi kernel to improve modeling performance of the system using the flexibility of multi kernel. The regression function with multi RBF kernel can be rewritten as in (23)

$$\hat{y}(n) = \sum_{i=n-L}^{n-1} \alpha_i(n)Ker((\underline{x}_c(n), x_{svi}(n))) + b(n) \tag{23}$$

Partial derivatives of LSSVR model with respect to weights and bandwidths of the kernels are obtained as follows:

$$\frac{\partial \hat{y}}{\partial k_j(n)} = \sum_{i=n-L}^{n-1} \alpha_i(n)[\sum_{z=1}^{m} \frac{k_z(n)(K_j(n) - K_z(n))}{[\sum_{z=1}^{m} k_z(n)]^2}] \tag{24}$$

$$\frac{\partial \hat{y}(n)}{\partial \sigma_j(n)} = \sum_{i=n-L}^{n-1} \alpha_i(n)\frac{k_j}{\sum_{z=1}^{m} k_m}K_j\frac{d_{c,svi}^2(n)}{\sigma_j^3(n)} \tag{25}$$

The objective function to be minimized to improve model performance is selected as:

$$J_m(n) = \frac{1}{2}[y(n) - \hat{y}(n)]^2 = \frac{1}{2}[\hat{e}_m(n)^2] \tag{26}$$

where $\hat{e}_m$ is model error. Since $\hat{y}(n)$ is a function of the multi kernel functions, kernel bandwidths and scaling coefficients can be tuned by applying gradient descent method to minimize the objective function given in (26) as follows [18]:

$$\Delta\sigma_j(n) = -\eta(n)\frac{\partial J_m(n)}{\partial \hat{e}_m(n)}\frac{\partial \hat{e}_m(n)}{\partial \hat{y}(n)}\frac{\partial \hat{y}(n)}{\partial \sigma_j(n)} = \eta(n)\hat{e}_m(n)\frac{\partial \hat{y}(n)}{\partial \sigma_j(n)} \tag{27}$$

$$\Delta k_j(n) = -\eta(n)\frac{\partial J_m(n)}{\partial \hat{e}_m(n)}\frac{\partial \hat{e}_m(n)}{\partial \hat{y}(n)}\frac{\partial \hat{y}(n)}{\partial k_j(n)} = \eta(n)\hat{e}_m(n)\frac{\partial \hat{y}(n)}{\partial k_j(n)} \tag{28}$$

where $\eta(n)$ is the learning rate ($0 < \eta(n) < 1$), which can be obtained utilizing any line search algorithm. Thus, the kernel parameters can be tuned using (27, 28) as follows:

$$\sigma_j(n+1) = \sigma_j(n) + \Delta\sigma_j(n)$$
$$k_j(n+1) = k_j(n) + \Delta k_j(n) \tag{29}$$

4   Adaptive PID Controller with Multi RBF Kernel

An adaptive PID controller has been utilized to control a third order continuously stirred tank reactor (CSTR). Online LSSVR has been employed to model the dynamics of the plant. The system Jacobian information has been approximated from the model and this information is used to tune the PID controller coefficients.

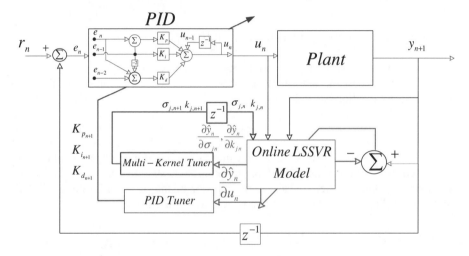

Fig. 1. Adaptive PID controller and kernel tuner

In fig. 1, the adaptive PID controller and the proposed multi-kernel tuner are illustrated, where $\hat{y}(n)$ is the output of the model, $y(n)$ is the output of the system, $\sigma_j(n)$ is the bandwidth of the kernels, $r(n)$ is the reference trajectory for plant, and $e(n), \hat{e}(n)$ are the tracking and model error respectively at time index n.

$$e(n) = r(n) - y(n) \quad, \quad \hat{e}(n) = y(n) - \hat{y}(n) \tag{30}$$

The adaptive PID controller consists of 4 parts: PID controller, online LSSVR, PID and kernel parameter tuners. The classical incremental PID controller produces a control signal as follows [3,6,17]:

$$u(n) = u(n-1) + K_p(n)(e(n) - e(n-1)) + K_i(n)(e(n))$$
$$+ K_d(n)(e(n) - 2e(n-1) + e(n-2)) \tag{31}$$

where K_p, K_i and K_d are the controller parameters to be tuned. At the beginning of the control, the controller and kernel parameters are not optimal [6], and hence, they need to be tuned using optimization techniques [6,18]. The tracking error results from non optimal controller parameters. That is, tracking error is the function of controller parameters.

$$e(n) = f(K_i(n), K_d(n), K_p(n)) \tag{32}$$

The model error is the function of model parameters.

$$\hat{e}(n) = f([\sigma_1(n), ...\sigma_m(n)], [k_1(n), ...k_m(n)], C, \alpha(n), b(n)) \tag{33}$$

Since the Lagrange multipliers and bias of the regression model are obtained using LSSVR, and C is taken as a fixed value, the modeling error can be rewritten as follows:

$$\hat{e}(n) = f([\sigma_1(n), ...\sigma_m(n)], [k_1(n), ...k_m(n)]) \tag{34}$$

In order to make the controller and kernel parameters converge to their optimal values, gradient descent algorithm has been employed. The inputs of the PID controller can be defined as follows:

$$xc(1) = e(n) - e(n-1), \; xc(2) = e(n), \; xc(3) = e(n) - 2e(n-1) + e(n-2) \tag{35}$$

Since the controller parameters are tuned using model based method, gradient descent is utilized to minimize not only the tracking but also the modeling error by approximating the one step ahead future behavior of the plant with online LSSVR. That is, the following objective function is tried to be minimized:

$$J(n) = \frac{[r(n) - y(n)]^2}{2} + J_m(n) = \frac{1}{2}[e^2(n) + \hat{e}_m^2(n)] \tag{36}$$

The PID parameters are tuned as follows:

$$\Delta K_p(n) = -\eta(n)\frac{\partial J(n)}{\partial K_p(n)}, \; \Delta K_i(n) = -\eta(n)\frac{\partial J(n)}{\partial K_i(n)}, \; \Delta K_d(n) = -\eta(n)\frac{\partial J(n)}{\partial K_d(n)} \tag{37}$$

where $\eta(n)$ is the learning rate, determined using line search algorithm. Golden section has been used to compute $\eta(n)$. In this paper, multi kernel adaptation proposed in (27)-(29) has been used to improve the modeling performance and consequently the control performance. In the calculation of the control parameter updates above, Jacobian information, relating the input and output of the controlled system has been provided by the online LSSVR. Thus, parameters are tuned as follows:

$$\frac{\partial \hat{y}(n)}{\partial u(n)} = -\sum_{i=n-L}^{n-1} \alpha_i(n) \frac{\sum_{z=1}^{m} [\frac{k_z(n)K_z(\underline{x}_c(n), x_{svi}(n))}{\sigma_z^2(n)} (u(n) - x_{svi}(1, n-i))]}{\sum_{z=1}^{m} k_z(n)} \qquad (38)$$

$$\Delta K_p(n) = -\eta(n)e(n)\frac{\partial y(n)}{\partial u(n)} xc(1) \ , \ K_p(n+1) = K_p(n) + \Delta K_p(n)$$

$$\Delta K_i(n) = -\eta(n)e(n)\frac{\partial y(n)}{\partial u(n)} xc(2) \ , \ K_i(n+1) = K_i(n) + \Delta K_i(n) \qquad (39)$$

$$\Delta K_d(n) = -\eta(n)e(n)\frac{\partial y(n)}{\partial u(n)} xc(3) \ , \ K_d(n+1) = K_d(n) + \Delta K_d(n)$$

As depicted by the simulation results given in section 5 these update rules improve the controller and modeling performance and the parameters are expected to converge to their optimal values in the long run.

5   Simulation Results

The performance of the proposed kernel parameter adaptation method in modeling and control has been evaluated on a third order continuously stirred tank reactor (CSTR). The dynamics of CSTR is given by the following set of differential equations:

$$\dot{x}_1(t) = 1 - x_1(t) - Da_1 x_1(t) + Da_2 x_2^2(t)$$
$$\dot{x}_2(t) = -x_2(t) + Da_1 x_1(t) - Da_2 x_2^2(t) - Da_3 d_2 x_2^2(t) + u(t) \qquad (40)$$
$$\dot{x}_3(t) = -x_3(t) + Da_3 d_2 x_2^2(t)$$

where $Da_1 = 3$, $Da_2 = 0.5$, $Da_3 = 1$, $d_2 = 1$, $u(t)$ is the control signal and $x_3(t)$ is the output of the process [6,19,20]. The magnitude of the control signal has been restricted between 0 and 1. The Jacobian information obtained as the output of the online LSSVR block in fig.1 is used to tune adaptive PID controller parameters. The initial values of all controller parameters are set to zero. In order to compare the adaptive single and adaptive multi kernel performance, initial values of the kernel bandwidth parameter are set to 1.

Fig. 2 illustrates that PID controllers, obtained using both adaptive single kernel and adaptive multi kernel methods attain good tracking performance, furthermore the control signal produced by controller with multi RBF kernel is more moderate than the other one. As can be seen from fig.2, introducing flexibility using multi RBF accelerates the response of the system. The adaptations of controller parameters are depicted in fig. 3 for both cases and the variation of kernel bandwidth is illustrated in fig. 4 and 5. The kernel parameters converge to their optimal values to obtain better plant model depending on the alternation of reference signal.

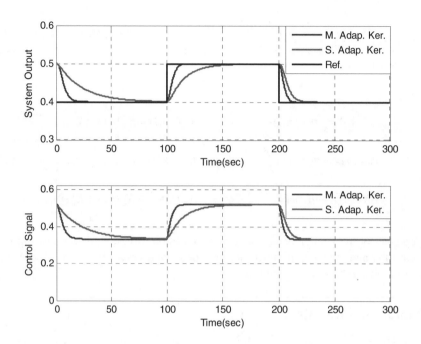

Fig. 2. System outputs for adaptive single(S.) kernel and adaptive multi(M.) kernel

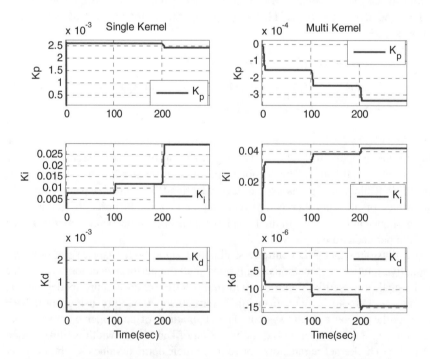

Fig. 3. Controller parameters for single and multi kernel case

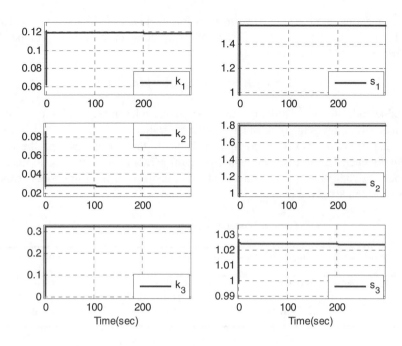

Fig. 4. Kernel parameters for adaptive multi kernel

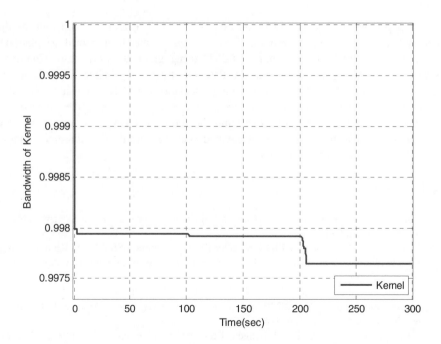

Fig. 5. Bandwidth of the adaptive single kernel

The modeling and tracking performances for single and multi adaptive bandwidth kernels are compared in Table 1. The following equation is used to compare the performance of the controllers:

$$J_{comp} = \sum_{n=1}^{N} (r(n) - y(n))^2 + (u(n) - u(n-1))^2 \tag{41}$$

The table indicates that utilizing multi kernel provides more flexibility in kernel machine and improves the performance of the controller.

As can be seen from third column of Table 1, the performance of the overall system obtained for the case with adaptive multi kernel bandwidth is better than that obtained with adaptive single kernel bandwidth, in terms of tracking-model error and performance index given in (41).

Table 1. Model and Control Performance

Error(MAE)	Single Adaptive Kernel	Multi Adaptive Kernel	Improvement (%)
Tracking Error	0.0160	0.0058	63.6374
Modeling Error	5.4017e-004	3.1902e-004	40.9401
J_{comp}	2.7436	1.1964	56.3928

6 Conclusions

In this paper, taking into consideration that flexibility in kernel function reduces the modeling and control error resulting from kernels, it has been aimed to tune the parameters of a multi kernel online LSSVR using gradient information. Controller parameters are also tuned using gradient descent. Employing online identification to model the system reduces the time consuming calculations of SVR. The results show that the proposed tuning method improves the performance of the controller in terms of tracking and modeling error. By combining the powerful features of fuzzy logic and support vector machines, more sophisticated and successful modeling and control techniques can be employed in future works.

References

1. Choi, Y., Chung, W.K.: PID Trajectory Tracking Control for Mechanical Systems. LNCIS. Springer, Berlin (2004)
2. Ucak, K., Oke, G.: Adaptive PID Controller Based on Online LSSVR with Kernel Tuning. In: International Symposium on Innovations in Intelligent Systems and Applications, Istanbul, Turkey (2011)
3. Wanfeng, S., Shengdun, Z., Yajing, S.: Adaptive PID Controller Based on Online LSSVM Identification. In: IEEE/ASME International Conference on Advanced Intelligent Mechatronics, vol. 1-3, pp. 694–698 (2008)
4. Zhao, J., Li, P., Wang, X.S.: Intelligent PID Controller Design with Adaptive Criterion Adjustment via Least Squares Support Vector Machine. In: 21st Chinese Control and Decision Conference (2009)

5. Takao, K., Yamamoto, T., Hinamoto, T.: A design of PID controllers with a switching structure by a support vector machine. In: International Joint Conference on Neural Network, Vancouver, BC, Canada (2006)
6. Iplikci, S.: A comparative study on a novel model-based PID tuning and control mechanism for nonlinear systems. International Journal of Robust and Nonlinear Control 20, 1483–1501 (2010)
7. Campbell, W.M., Sturim, D.E., Reynolds, D.A.: Support vector machines using GMM supervectors for speaker verification. IEEE Signal Processing Letters 13(5) (2006)
8. Iplikci, S.: Controlling the Experimental Three-Tank System via Support Vector Machines. In: Kolehmainen, M., Toivanen, P., Beliczynski, B. (eds.) Adaptive and Natural Computing Algorithms. LNCS, vol. 5495, pp. 391–400. Springer, Heidelberg (2009)
9. Guo, Y.C.: An Integrated PSO for Parameter Determination and feature selection of SVR and its application in STLF. In: International Conference on Machine Learning and Cybernetics, Baoding, PR China, pp. 359–364 (2009)
10. Momma, M., Bennett, K.P.: A pattern search method for model selection of support vector regression. In: International Conference on Data Mining, Arlington, VA, pp. 261–274 (2002)
11. Hou, L.K., Yang, Q.X.: Study on parameters selection of LSSVR based on Grid-Diamond search method. In: International Conference on Machine Learning and Cybernetics, Baoding, PR China, vol. 1-6, pp. 1219–1224 (2009)
12. Farag, A., Mohamed, R.M.: Regression using support vector machines: basic foundations, Technical Report (2004)
13. Suykens, J.A.K.: Nonlinear modeling and support vector machines. In: IEEE Instrumentation and Measurement Technology Conference Budapest, Hungary (2001)
14. Gunn, S.: Support Vector Machines for Classification and Regression, ISIS Technical Report (1998)
15. Smola, A.J., Scholkopf, B.: A tutorial on support vector regression. Statistics and Computing 14, 199–222 (2004)
16. Zhu, Y.F., Mao, Z.Y.: Online Optimal Modeling of LS-SVM based on Time Window. In: IEEE International Conference on Industrial Technology, Hammamet, Tunisia, vol. 1-3, pp. 1325–1330 (2004)
17. Bobal, V., Böhm, J., Fessl, J., Macháček, L.: Digital-Self Tuning Controllers, Advanced Textbooks in Control and Signal Processing. Springer, London (2005)
18. Luenberger, D.G., Ye, Y.: Linear and Nonlinear Programming, 3rd edn. Springer Science + Business Media, LLC (2008)
19. Wu, W., Chou, Y.S.: Adaptive feedforward and feedback control of non-linear time-varying uncertain systems. International Journal of Control 72, 1127–1138 (1999)
20. Ungar, L.H.: A bioreactor benchmark for adaptive-network based process control. In: Neural Network for Control. MIT Press, Cambridge (1990)

An Extended Sliding Mode Learning Algorithm for Type-2 Fuzzy Neural Networks

Kostadin Shiev[1], Nikola Shakev[1], Andon V. Topalov[1],
Sevil Ahmed[1], and Okyay Kaynak[2]

[1] Control Systems Department, TU – Sofia campus Plovdiv, 25 Tsanko Dustabanov Str.,
4000 Plovdiv, Bulgaria
[2] Department of Electrical and Electronic Engineering, Bogazici University, Istanbul, Turkey
{k.shiev,sevil.ahmed}@gmail.com,
{topalov,shakev}@tu-plovdiv.bg, okyay.kaynak@boun.edu.tr

Abstract. Type-2 fuzzy logic systems are an area of growing interest over the last years. The ability to model uncertainties in a better way than type-1 fuzzy logic systems increases their applicability. A new stable on-line learning algorithm for type-2 fuzzy neural networks is proposed in this paper. It can be considered as an extended version of the recently developed on-line learning approaches for type-2 fuzzy neural networks based on the Variable Structure System theory concepts. Simulation results from the identification of a nonlinear system with uncertainties have demonstrated the better performance of the proposed extended algorithm in comparison with the previously reported in the literature sliding mode learning algorithms for both type-1 and type-2 fuzzy neural structures.

Keywords: type-2 fuzzy logic systems, artificial neural networks, variable structure systems, sliding mode control.

1 Introduction

Uncertainties and imprecisions exist as an undivided part in both dynamic modeling and control problems and in most cases are difficult to handle. They are due to the lack of an accurate model and/or the presence of different external disturbances, measurement and sensor errors. All of these factors could reflect poor performance of the real-time applications. Type-1 fuzzy logic systems (T1FLSs) are not able to model effectively existing uncertainties because their membership functions (MFs) are totally crisp. When it is difficult to determine the place of the membership functions precisely, type-2 fuzzy logic systems (T2FLSs) have an advantage as they can handle better with modeling of such uncertainties owing to the fuzziness of their MFs. Membership functions of the type-1 fuzzy sets (T1-FSs) are two-dimensional, whereas those of the type-2 fuzzy sets (T2-FSs) are three-dimensional. The new third-dimension of the T2-FSs provides additional degrees of freedom that makes it possible to directly model uncertainties [1].

A. Bouchachia (Ed.): ICAIS 2011, LNAI 6943, pp. 52–63, 2011.

T2FLSs are particularly suitable for modeling and control of nonlinear systems with unknown time-varying dynamics. They can also allow more flexibility to avoid problems associated to the uncertainties pertaining to the choice of the system's fuzzy rules and fuzzy membership functions. Based on this T2FLSs have recently been considered as a preferable alternative to T1FLSs in such cases and many successful applications have been reported in various areas where uncertainties occur, such as in decision making [2], signal processing [3], [4], traffic forecasting [5], mobile robot control [6], pattern recognition [7], [8], and intelligent control [9], [10].

It is well know that fuzzy systems are often combined with artificial neural networks (ANNs) due to the good performance they together result in. Fuzzy neural networks (FNNs) combine the advantages of both techniques. Like the fuzzy systems and neural networks, FNNs are proven to be universal approximators too [11]. Fuzzy reasoning is capable of handling uncertain and imprecise information while neural networks are capable of learning from samples. On the other hand, stability of the learning algorithms and rapid convergence of the error towards zero are the main issues, which should be solved when applying such intelligent structures in on-line dynamic modeling and control schemes. Two general approaches that help solving these problems have been reported in the literature. The first one relies on direct implementation of the Lyapunov's stability theory to obtain robust training algorithms for continuous-time neural and neuro-fuzzy structures [12]. Another way to get the solution of the stability problems is to utilize the variable structure systems (VSS) theory in constructing the parameter adaptation mechanism of the FNNs [13-15]. Such intelligent systems exhibit robustness and invariance properties. An additional and important benefit is that VSS-based learning algorithms can ensure faster convergence than the traditional learning techniques in on-line tuning of ANNs and FNNs [16]. Several sliding mode control-based learning algorithms for different computational intelligence structures have been recently reported in the literature. A sliding mode algorithm for parametric adaptation of type-1 fuzzy neural networks (T1FNNs) has been proposed in [14]. It has been followed by a modification that has been successfully applied to type-2 fuzzy neural networks (T2FNNs), [17].

This paper presents a new extended sliding mode learning algorithm for T2FNNs. The tunable parameters of the T2FNNs are more than those of T1FNNs), hence the problem of ensuring the stability and convergence during an on-line adaptation procedure is more difficult. Current investigation has been inspired by the sliding mode control-based training method for interval type-2 fuzzy neural networks that has been reported in [17]. The algorithm, proposed in [17], has been further extended to allow adaptation of the relation between the two components - the lower and the upper membership functions - of T2-FSs. This gives a possibility to manage non-uniform uncertainties in T2-FLSs. Several comparative simulations have been made to confirm the consistency of the newly proposed extended on-line sliding mode learning algorithm. Therefore, it has significant influence on the T2FNNs' performance and adaptation characteristics.

The paper is organized as follows. Section 2 presents a short overview of T2FLSs. The extended on-line sliding mode learning algorithm for T2FNNs with Gaussian membership functions is introduced in Section 3. Simulation results for the proposed approach are shown in Section 4. Finally, concluding remarks are given in Section 5.

2 Overview of the Type-2 Fuzzy Logic Systems

Type-2 fuzzy logic systems have been first introduced by Zadeh in 1970s. However, the rapid implementation of the T2FLSs in engineering applications has been delayed by existing problems related to the characterization of type-2 fuzzy sets, performing operations with T2-FSs, inferencing with T2-FSs and obtaining the defuzzified value from the output of a type-2 inference engine [18].

The membership functions of T2-FSs are three dimensional and include a footprint of uncertainty (FOU), which is a new third dimension of T2-FSs that additionally helps handling uncertainties [1]. If their secondary membership functions are set to 1 over the whole interval formed by FOU, then the fuzzy sets are called interval type-2 fuzzy sets (IT2-FSs). This assumption corresponds to the case of uniform uncertainties and it is preferred by many researchers due to its simplicity.

The architecture of the IT2-FLS is similar to that of the fuzzy logic controllers (FLCs) with T1-FLSs which contain fuzzifier, rule base, fuzzy inference engine, type-reducer, and defuzzifier. IT2-FLSs can provide more robustness than the T1-FLSs when handling uncertainties and disturbances [6], [9]. T2-FLSs are based on fuzzy *if-then* rules which are similar to those of the conventional FLCs.

An interval type-2 Takagi-Sugeno-Kang fuzzy logic system is considered in this investigation, where antecedents are type-2 fuzzy sets and consequents are crisp numbers (IT2 TSK FLS A2-C0). The rth rule has the following form:

$$R_r: \textit{if } x_1 \textit{ is } \tilde{A}_{1j} \textit{ and } x_2 \textit{ is } \tilde{A}_{2j} \textit{ and } \ldots \textit{ and } x_i \textit{ is } \tilde{A}_{ij} \textit{ then } f_r = \sum_{i=1}^{I} a_{ri} x_i + b_r, \qquad (1)$$

where x_i, $(i = 1 \ldots I)$ represents the sequence of the input variables; f_r, $(r = 1 \ldots N)$ is the TSK-type output function; $\tilde{A}_{ij}$ is a jth type-2 membership function for i^{th} input variable; a_{ri} and b_r are the parameters of the consequent part for r^{th} rule.

The firing strength of rth rule is calculated using lower $\underline{\mu}(x)$ and upper $\bar{\mu}(x)$ membership functions. The Gaussian type-2 fuzzy sets can be associated with system uncertainties in two ways – by their mean or by the standard deviation (Fig. 1).

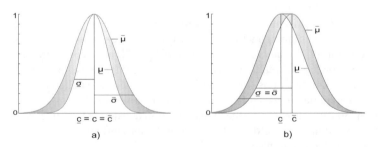

Fig. 1. Type-2 Gaussian fuzzy sets with a) uncertain standard deviation and b) uncertain mean

Membership functions with uncertain standard deviation have been used for the antecedent part of the fuzzy *if-then* rules in this investigation. The lower and upper membership functions with uncertain deviation (Fig.1a) are represented as follows:

$$\overline{\mu}_{ij}(x_i) = \exp\left(-\frac{1}{2}\frac{(x_i - c_{ij})^2}{\overline{\sigma}_{ij}^2}\right) \quad ; \quad \underline{\mu}_{ij}(x_i) = \exp\left(-\frac{1}{2}\frac{(x_i - c_{ij})^2}{\underline{\sigma}_{ij}^2}\right) \tag{2}$$

2.1 Type-2 Fuzzy Neural Networks

The structure of the type-2 fuzzy neural network, used in this investigation, is shown on Fig. 2. The network implements TSK fuzzy *if-then* rules introduced by (1). Each layer of the T2FNN structure carries out a particular part of the T2FLSs strategy.

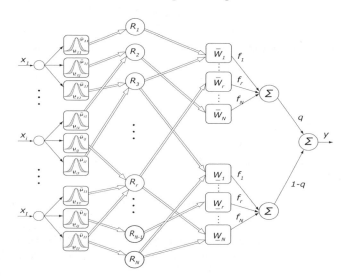

Fig. 2. Structure of type-2 TSK fuzzy neural network

The first layer depicts the inputs of the structure. The number of the neurons in the input layer depends on the dimension of the sequence of input variables. The next layer of the network performs the fuzzification operation over the inputs by IT2 Gaussian fuzzy sets with uncertain standard deviation (Fig. 1a). Each membership function of the antecedent part of (1) is represented by an upper $\overline{\mu}(x_i)$ and a lower $\underline{\mu}(x_i)$ membership function. The degrees of fulfillment for both membership functions (upper and lower) for i^{th} input signal are determined according (2) respectively. Next layer consists of all rules R_N from the TSK rule base (1). The outputs of the neurons here are sequences of the membership degrees of the activated in the previous layer type-2 fuzzy membership functions. They are passed through the fourth layer if the corresponding fuzzy rule is activated. The "prod" T-norm operator is applied in the fourth layer to calculate the strength of each rule R_r. Neurons in this layer are represented as follows:

$$\begin{aligned}
\underline{w}_r &= \underline{\mu}_{\tilde{A}1}(x_1) * \underline{\mu}_{\tilde{A}2}(x_2) * \ldots * \underline{\mu}_{\tilde{A}I}(x_I) \\
\overline{w}_r &= \overline{\mu}_{\tilde{A}1}(x_1) * \overline{\mu}_{\tilde{A}2}(x_2) * \ldots * \overline{\mu}_{\tilde{A}I}(x_I)
\end{aligned} \tag{3}$$

The output weights in the fourth layer are determined as TSK linear functions

$$f_r = \sum_{i=1}^{I} a_{ri} x_i + b_r .$$ (4)

Therefore, the last two layers of the fuzzy neural network perform type reduction and defuzzification operations. The evaluation of the output y of the T2FNN is done in accordance with the type-2 fuzzy inference engine proposed in [19].

$$y = q \sum_{r=1}^{N} f_r \tilde{\underline{w}}_r + (1-q) \sum_{r=1}^{N} f_r \tilde{\overline{w}}_r$$ (5)

where N is the number of fuzzy rules and the normalized values $\tilde{\underline{w}}_r$ and $\tilde{\overline{w}}_r$ are used.

$$\tilde{\underline{w}}_r = \frac{\underline{w}_r}{\sum_{r=1}^{N} \underline{w}_r}, \quad \tilde{\overline{w}}_r = \frac{\overline{w}_r}{\sum_{r=1}^{N} \overline{w}_r}$$ (6)

The parameter q is introduced in (5) to consider the case of non-uniform uncertainties and to allow adjustment of the influence of the lower and the upper membership function of IT2-FLSs on the output determination procedure.

It is convenient to define the following vectors

$$F = [f_1\ f_2\ ...f_r\ ...\ f_N];\ \tilde{\underline{W}} = [\tilde{\underline{w}}_1\ \tilde{\underline{w}}_2\ ...\tilde{\underline{w}}_r\ ...\ \tilde{\underline{w}}_N];\ \tilde{\overline{W}} = [\tilde{\overline{w}}_1\ \tilde{\overline{w}}_2\ ...\tilde{\overline{w}}_r\ ...\ \tilde{\overline{w}}_N]$$ (7)

The extended on-line learning algorithm, proposed in the next section, includes adaptation of: (i) the parameters of IT2 Gaussian functions, (ii) the parameters in the consequent parts of the fuzzy rules and (iii) the parameter q. Note that in the current investigation the TSK linear function is considered as consisting of the parameter b_r only for simplicity.

3   The Extended Sliding Mode On-Line Learning Algorithm

Let us define the learning error of the considered T2FNN as the difference between the network's current output $y(t)$ and its desired value $y_d(t)$:

$$e(t) = y(t) - y_d(t)$$ (8)

The scalar signal $y_d(t)$ represents the time-varying desired output of the neural network. It will be assumed that the rate of change $\dot{y}_d(t)$ is bounded by a predefined positive constant B_{y_dot} (this limitation is valid for all real signal sources due to the physical restrictions).

$$|\dot{y}_d| \le B_{y\_dot}$$ (9)

Using the principles of the sliding mode control theory [20] the zero value of the learning error coordinate $e(t)$ can be defined as a time varying sliding surface, i.e.

$$S(e(t)) = e(t) = y(t) - y_d(t) = 0$$ (10)

When the system is in sliding mode on the sliding surface S that guarantees that the IT2 TSK FLS A2-C0 output $y(t)$ coincides with the desired output signal $y_d(t)$ for all time $t > t_h$ where t_h is the hitting time of $e(t) = 0$.

Definition: A sliding motion will have place on a sliding manifold $S(e(t)) = e(t) = 0$, after time t_h if the condition $S(t)\dot{S}(t) = e(t)\dot{e}(t) < 0$ is true for all t in some nontrivial semi open subinterval of time of the form $[t, t_h) \subset (-\infty, t_h)$.

The learning algorithm for the adaptive parameters $\overline{c}_{ij}, \underline{c}_{ij}, \overline{\sigma}_{ij}, \underline{\sigma}_{ij}, b_r, q$ should be derived in such a way that the sliding mode condition of the above definition will be enforced.

Theorem 1. If the learning algorithm for the parameters of the upper $\overline{\mu}(x_i)$ and the lower $\underline{\mu}(x_i)$ membership functions with a Gaussian distribution is chosen as:

$$\underline{\dot{c}}_{ij} = \overline{\dot{c}}_{ij} = \dot{x}_i \tag{11}$$

$$\underline{\dot{\sigma}}_{ij} = -\frac{\underline{\sigma}_{ij}^3}{(x_i - c_{ij})^2}\alpha sign(e); \quad \overline{\dot{\sigma}}_{ij} = -\frac{\overline{\sigma}_{ij}^3}{(x_i - c_{ij})^2}\alpha sign(e) \tag{12}$$

and the adaptation of the output weights of the fourth and the fifth layer of the neuro-fuzzy network is chosen as follows:

$$\dot{f}_r = -\frac{\left(q\underline{\tilde{w}}_r + (1-q)\overline{\tilde{w}}_r\right)}{\left(q\underline{\tilde{W}} + (1-q)\overline{\tilde{W}}\right)\left(q\underline{\tilde{W}} + (1-q)\overline{\tilde{W}}\right)^T}\alpha sign(e) \tag{13}$$

$$\dot{q} = -\frac{1}{F\left(\underline{\tilde{W}} - \overline{\tilde{W}}\right)^T}\alpha sign(e) \tag{14}$$

where α is a sufficiently large positive number satisfying the inequality:

$$\alpha > \frac{B_{y\_dot}}{2} \tag{15}$$

then, given an arbitrary initial condition $e(0)$, the learning error $e(t)$ will converge to zero during a finite time t_h.

Proof: From (2), (3), and (6) it is possible to obtain the time derivatives:

$$\underline{\dot{\tilde{w}}}_r = -\underline{\tilde{w}}_r \underline{K}_r + \underline{\tilde{w}}_r \sum_{r=1}^{N} \underline{\tilde{w}}_r \underline{K}_r; \quad \overline{\dot{\tilde{w}}}_r = -\overline{\tilde{w}}_r \overline{K}_r + \overline{\tilde{w}}_r \sum_{r=1}^{N} \overline{\tilde{w}}_r \overline{K}_r \tag{16}$$

where the following substitutions are used

$$\underline{A}_{ij} = \frac{x_i - c_{ij}}{\underline{\sigma}_{ij}}; \quad \overline{A}_{ij} = \frac{x_i - c_{ij}}{\overline{\sigma}_{ij}} \tag{17}$$

$$\underline{K}_r = 2\sum_{i=1}^{I} \underline{A}_{ij}\underline{\dot{A}}_{ij} ; \quad \overline{K}_r = 2\sum_{i=1}^{I} \overline{A}_{ij}\overline{\dot{A}}_{ij} \tag{18}$$

Also it is obvious that applying the proposed adaptation laws (11), (12) the value of $\underline{K}_r$ and $\overline{K}_r$ can be calculated in this way

$$\overline{K}_r = \underline{K}_r = \sum_{i=1}^{I} \overline{A}_{ij}\overline{\dot{A}}_{ij} = \sum_{i=1}^{I} \underline{A}_{ij}\underline{\dot{A}}_{ij} = I\alpha sign(e) \tag{19}$$

Consider the following Lyapunov function candidate:

$$V = \frac{1}{2}e^2 . \tag{20}$$

In order to satisfy the stability condition the time derivative $\dot{V}$ has to be negative.

$$\dot{V} = e\dot{e} = e(\dot{y} - \dot{y}_d) \tag{21}$$

Differentiating (5) it is possible to obtain:

$$\dot{y} = \dot{q}\sum_{r=1}^{N} f_r\underline{\tilde{w}}_r + q\sum_{r=1}^{N}\left(\dot{f}_r\underline{\tilde{w}}_r + f_r\underline{\dot{\tilde{w}}}_r\right) - \dot{q}\sum_{r=1}^{N} f_r\overline{\tilde{w}}_r + (1-q)\sum_{r=1}^{N}\left(\dot{f}_r\overline{\tilde{w}}_r + f_r\overline{\dot{\tilde{w}}}_r\right) \tag{22}$$

Substituting (16), (18), (19) consecutively in (22) results in

$$\begin{aligned}
\dot{y} &= \dot{q}\sum_{r=1}^{N} f_r\underline{\tilde{w}}_r + q\sum_{r=1}^{N}\left(\dot{f}_r\underline{\tilde{w}}_r + f_r\left(-\underline{\tilde{w}}_r\underline{K}_r + \underline{\tilde{w}}_r\sum_{r=1}^{N}\underline{\tilde{w}}_r\underline{K}_r\right)\right) - \\
&\quad -\dot{q}\sum_{r=1}^{N} f_r\overline{\tilde{w}}_r + (1-q)\sum_{r=1}^{N}\left(\dot{f}_r\overline{\tilde{w}}_r + f_r\left(-\overline{\tilde{w}}_r\overline{K}_r + \overline{\tilde{w}}_r\sum_{r=1}^{N}\overline{\tilde{w}}_r\overline{K}_r\right)\right) = \\
&= \dot{q}\sum_{r=1}^{N} f_r\underline{\tilde{w}}_r + q\sum_{r=1}^{N}\left(\dot{f}_r\underline{\tilde{w}}_r - 2I\alpha sign(e)f_r\left(\underline{\tilde{w}}_r - \underline{\tilde{w}}_r\sum_{r=1}^{N}\underline{\tilde{w}}_r\right)\right) - \\
&\quad -\dot{q}\sum_{r=1}^{N} f_r\overline{\tilde{w}}_r + (1-q)\sum_{r=1}^{N}\left(\dot{f}_r\overline{\tilde{w}}_r - 2I\alpha sign(e)f_r\left(\overline{\tilde{w}}_r - \overline{\tilde{w}}_r\sum_{r=1}^{N}\overline{\tilde{w}}_r\right)\right)
\end{aligned} \tag{23}$$

Note that the sums of normalized activations are constant.

$$\sum_{r=1}^{N}\underline{\tilde{w}}_r = 1; \quad \sum_{r=1}^{N}\overline{\tilde{w}}_r = 1 \tag{24}$$

Applying (13), (14) and (24) we obtain

$$\dot{y} = -\frac{1}{F\left(\underline{\tilde{W}} - \overline{\tilde{W}}\right)^T}\alpha sign(e)\sum_{r=1}^{N} f_r\left(\underline{\tilde{w}}_r - \overline{\tilde{w}}_r\right) + \sum_{r=1}^{N}\dot{f}_r\left(q\underline{\tilde{w}}_r + (1-q)\overline{\tilde{w}}_r\right) \tag{25}$$

$$\dot{y} = -2\alpha sign(e) \tag{26}$$

Finally (26) can be substituted in (21)

$$\dot{V} = e\dot{e} = e(-2\alpha sign(e) - \dot{y}_d)$$ (27)

$$\dot{V} < -2\alpha|e| + B_{y\_dot}|e| < 0$$ (28)

The inequality (28) means that the controlled trajectories of the learning error $e(t)$ converge to zero in a stable manner.

4   Simulation Studies and Results

The performance of the proposed extended sliding mode on-line learning algorithm has been evaluated in simulations by applying it to a type-2 fuzzy neural identifier of a SISO second order nonlinear system which is described by the following expression [21]:

$$\dot{\chi}_1 = \chi_2$$
$$\dot{\chi}_2 = f(\chi,t) + g(\chi,t)u + \eta(\chi,t)$$ (29)
$$y = \chi_1$$

where $f(\chi,t) = f_0(\chi,t) + \Delta f(\chi,t)$ and $g(\chi,t) = g_0(\chi,t) + \Delta g(\chi,t)$ are smooth nonlinear functions, and $\eta(\chi,t)$ is a bounded uncertainty. Both nonlinear functions consist of nominal (known) parts $f_0(\chi,t) = \chi_1^2 - 1.5\chi_2$ and $g_0(\chi,t) = 2$, and fault terms $\Delta f(\chi,t) = 0.3\sin(t)\chi_1^2 + \cos(t)\chi_2$, $\Delta g(\chi,t) = \cos(\chi_1)$ arising at a certain moment of the operation of the system. The external disturbance term is presented by $\eta(\chi,t) = 0.2\sin(\chi_2) + \chi_1\sin(2t)$ with a known upper bound $\eta_0(\chi,t) = 0.2 + |\chi_1|$.

The type-2 fuzzy neural identifier with the proposed extended sliding mode learning algorithm has been compared in two consecutive experiments with two other identifiers that also use sliding mode on-line learning algorithms (type-1 fuzzy neural identifier and type-2 fuzzy neural identifier with a learning algorithm without adaptation of the parameter q). The performance of the three identifiers has been tested on the nonlinear system described by (29). A sinusoidal input signal with decreasing amplitude and frequency has been applied to the simulated system during both experiments.

Experiment 1. The first experiment starts initially with the nominal case, i.e. $\Delta f(\chi,t) = 0$ and $\Delta g(\chi,t) = 0$, and then at a certain time (t=10 sec) the fault operating regime is introduced.

The errors during the identification procedure are shown on Fig. 4. During the first 10 sec (when $\Delta f(\chi,t) = 0$ and $\Delta g(\chi,t) = 0$) the identification error provided by the type-1 fuzzy neural identifier is the smallest one. The results prove that T1FNNs handle very well in the nominal case. However subsequently, when the system is characterized by the presence of uncertainties (after t=10 sec), type-2 fuzzy neural identifiers perform more accurately. Fig. 4 shows also that the proposed learning algorithm with adaptation of the parameter q leads to better results compared to the learning algorithm with fixed value of the parameter q (introduced in [17]). The change of the parameter q during the experiment with the proposed extended sliding mode on-line learning algorithm is presented on Fig. 5.

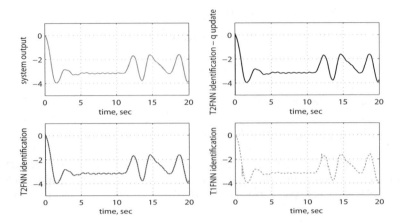

Fig. 3. Exp.1: Identification performance under uncertainty and faults included in t=10 sec

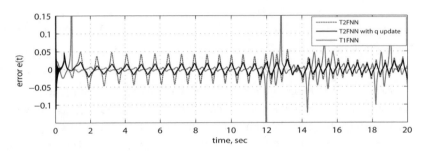

Fig. 4. Exp.1: Identification errors with three different types of FNN with sliding mode learning

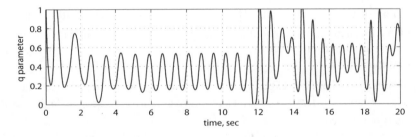

Fig. 5. Exp.1: Variation of the parameter q during the identification procedure with T2FNN using the proposed extended sliding mode on-line learning algorithm

Experiment 2. The second experiment is performed with uncertainties and faults included during the whole simulation time. In this case the type-1 fuzzy neural identifier is not able to handle with system uncertainties and the error is bigger compared to the results during the Experiment 1. The reason for this difference is that in the first experiment the T1FNN is trained during the first 10 sec of the simulation (when $\Delta f(\chi,t)=0$ and $\Delta g(\chi,t)=0$).

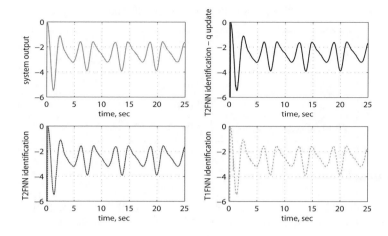

Fig. 6. Exp.2: System identification performance under uncertainty and faults

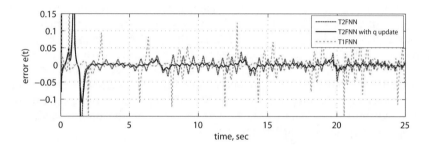

Fig. 7. Exp.2: Errors for the three different types of FNN with sliding mode learning

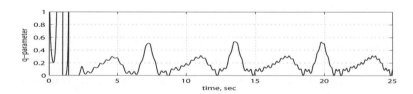

Fig. 8. Exp.2: Variation of the parameter q during the identification procedure with T2FNN using the proposed extended sliding mode on-line learning algorithm

As it can be seen the introduced extended sliding mode learning algorithm decreases significantly the identification error values.

The root mean square error (RMSE) values during the experiments corroborate the better performance of the proposed extended sliding model learning algorithm for interval type-2 FNNs.

Table 1. RMSE during the identification

Type of FNN	RMSE Experiment 1	RMSE Experiment 2
T1 FNN	0.0263	0.0275
T2 FNN	0.0207	0.0199
T2 FNN with q update	0.0103	0.0127

5 Conclusions

A novel extended sliding mode on-line learning algorithm for type-2 fuzzy neural networks is presented. Adaptive elements are situated in the second, the fourth and the fifth layer of the proposed fuzzy neural structure. The second and fourth layers consist of the parameters of TSK fuzzy rules. The antecedents are represented by the center and the standard deviations of each activated type-2 Gaussian membership function with uncertain deviation. The adaptive parameters in the fourth layer are the coefficients of the TSK linear function. The last adaptive element in the fuzzy neural structure is the modeling parameter q. The adaptation of this parameter is the main contribution of this investigation, due to its importance in determination of the output of the T2FNN. The performed simulations have shown better performance of the T2FNN using the proposed sliding mode on-line learning algorithm with adaptation of the parameter q. It is compared with two other sliding mode learning algorithms for T1FNN and for T2FNN with constant parameter q in identification procedure of a SISO nonlinear system with uncertainties and fault.

Acknowledgement. This work was supported in part by the TU Sofia Research Fund Project 112pd009-19 and in part by the Ministry of Education, Youth and Science of Bulgaria Research Fund Project BY-TH-108/2005.

References

1. Mendel, J.M., John, R.: Type-2 fuzzy sets made simple. IEEE Trans. on Fuzzy Syst. 10(2), 117–127 (2002)
2. Garibaldi, J.M., Ozen, T.: Uncertain fuzzy reasoning: A case study in modelling expert decision making. IEEE Trans. Fuzzy Syst. 15(1), 16–30 (2007)
3. Karnik, N.N., Mendel, J.M., Liang, Q.: Type-2 fuzzy logic systems. IEEE Trans. Fuzzy Syst. 7(6), 643–658 (1999)
4. Mendel, J.M.: Uncertainty, fuzzy logic, and signal processing. Signal Process. 80(6), 913–933 (2000)
5. Li, L., Lin, W.-H., Liu, H.: Type-2 fuzzy logic approach for short-term traffic forecasting. Proc. Inst. Elect. Eng. Intell. Transp. Syst. 153(1), 33–40 (2006)
6. Hagras, H.A.: A hierarchical type-2 fuzzy logic control architecture for autonomous mobile robots. IEEE Trans. Fuzzy Syst. 12(4), 524–539 (2004)
7. Mitchell, H.B.: Pattern recognition using type-II fuzzy sets. Inf. Sci. 170, 409–418 (2005)

8. Wu, H., Mendel, J.M.: Classification of battlefield ground vehicles using acoustic features and fuzzy logic rule-based classifiers. IEEE Trans. Fuzzy Syst. 15(1), 56–72 (2007)

9. Castillo, O., Melin, P., Montiel, O., Rodriguez-Diaz, A., Sepulveda, R.: Handling uncertainty in controllers using type-2 fuzzy logic. J. Intell. Syst. 14(3), 237–262 (2005)

10. Sepulveda, R., Castillo, O., Melin, P., Rodriguez-Diaz, A., Montiel, O.: Experimental study of intelligent controllers under uncertainty using type-1 and type-2 fuzzy logic. Inf. Sci. 177(10), 2023–2048 (2007)

11. Lin, C.T., George Lee, C.S.: Neural Fuzzy Systems, Englewood Cliffs, NJ (1996)

12. Suykens, J.A.K., Vandewalle, J., De Moor, B.: Lur'e systems with multilayer perceptron and recurrent neural networks: absolute stability and dissipativity. IEEE Trans. on Automatic Control 44, 770–774 (1999)

13. Yu, S., Yu, X., Man, Z.: A fuzzy neural network approximator with fast terminal sliding mode and its applications. Fuzzy Sets and Systems 148, 469–486 (2004)

14. Topalov, A.V., Kaynak, O., Shakev, N., Hong, S.K.: Sliding Mode Algorithm for On-line Learning in Fuzzy Rule-based Neural Networks. In: 17th IFAC World Congress, Seoul, Korea, pp. 12793–12798 (2008)

15. Shakev, N., Topalov, A.V., Kaynak, O.: A Neuro-Fuzzy Adaptive Sliding Mode Controller: Application to Second-Order Chaotic System. In: IS 2008 – IEEE International Conference on Intelligent Systems, Varna, Bulgaria, p. 9.14–9.19 (2008)

16. Cascella, G., Cupertino, F., Topalov, A., Kaynak, O., Giordano, V.: Adaptive control of electric drives using sliding-mode learning neural networks. In: IEEE International Symposium on Industrial Electronics, vol. 1, pp. 125–130 (2005)

17. Kayacan, E., Cigdem, O., Kaynak, O.: A Novel Training Method Based on Variable Structure Systems Approach for Interval Type-2 Fuzzy Neural Networks. In: IEEE Symposium Series on Computational Intelligence, SSCI, Paris, France, pp. 142–149 (2011)

18. Mendel, J.M.: Uncertain Rule-Based Fuzzy Logic Systems. Prentice Hall, Los Angeles (2001)

19. Biglarbegian, M., Melek, W., Mendel, J.M.: On the stability of interval type-2 tsk fuzzy logic control systems. IEEE Transactions on Systems, Man, and Cybernetics, Part B: Cybernetics 40(3), 798–818 (2010)

20. Utkin, V.I.: Sliding Modes in Control and Optimization. Springer, Heidelberg (1992)

21. Debbache, G., Golea, N.: Neural Network Based Adaptive Sliding Mode Control of Uncertain Nonlinear Systems. Submitted to Int. Journal of Applied Mathematics& Computer Science (2011)

Time Stamping in the Presence of Latency and Drift

Gary R. Marrs, Ray J. Hickey, and Michaela M. Black

School of Computing and Engineering, University of Ulster, Coleraine,
County Londonderry, N. Ireland
marrs-g@email.ulster.ac.uk,
{mm.black,rj.hickey}@ulster.ac.uk

Abstract. Online classification learners operating under concept drift can be subject to latency in example arrival at the training base. The impact of such latency on the definition of a time stamp is discussed against the background of the Online Learning Life Cycle (OLLC). Data stream latency is modeled in Example Life-cycle Integrated Simulation Environment (ELISE). Two new algorithms are presented: CDTC versions 1 and 2, in which a specific time stamp protocol is used representing the time of classification. Comparison of these algorithms against previous time stamp learning algorithms CD3 and CD5 is made. A time stamp definition and algorithmic solution is presented for handling latency in data streams and improving classification recovery in such affected domains.

Keywords: Online Learning, Classification, Concept Drift, Latency, Time Stamp.

1 Introduction

In online learning the issues of noise and concept drift upon a learner are clearly documented; an introduction to existing work and other underlying issues may be found in [1-7]. Furthermore the potential for lack of representative of examples in a data stream is discussed in [8]. It is also the case that, whether explicitly or implicitly defined, online classification involves the inducement and subsequent updating of a classifier from a data stream of time-stamped training examples. Current approaches, as in those referenced above, involving a variety of machine learning algorithms either individually or in ensembles, deploy various approaches to handling concept drift and maintaining a set of valid training examples.

Previously in [9] and [10], an online learner life cycle model was introduced and the various latency scenarios were explored in order to determine distinct latency signatures in classification for normal distribution and negative exponential models of example arrival at an online learner. It was noted that a training example is supposed to be representative of an underlying true rule operating at a particular time, i.e. a temporal event. Since an example may only become available *after* that time, this leads to a time discrepancy or *latency*.

A. Bouchachia (Ed.): ICAIS 2011, LNAI 6943, pp. 64–75, 2011.

2 The Online Learning Life-Cycle, Latency and Time Stamping

In online classification learning, the learning algorithm receives new training examples on a periodic basis and adopts a learning update regime to maintain currency of the classifier. These new examples are time-stamped and placed in a training base. The time-stamps will influence the learner.

In [10] an overview of the Online Learning Life Cycle (OLLC) was given. The OLLC was designed to provide a generalized framework for visualising online learning through the five identified key stages and the boundaries of a domain; identifying additional non-stationary learning specific issues such as trackability and selection filtering, and, latency in example procurement.

In [9] the signature impact of various latency models and scenarios were analysed and the issue of what this meant to the definition and use of a time stamp raised.

While a more thorough explanation of the online learning life cycle can be found in [10], it can be briefly summarised into stages as in Table 1.

Table 1. OLLC Stages

Stage	Description
Initial example collection	Initial supervised example collection takes place using external sources and is placed into the training base.
Initial classifier induction	Upon receiving data from the training base, the learning algorithm is applied and generates the first classifier.
Classification	A new case, <description>, arrives at time t_c for classification, This is given its predicted class, *pclass*, by the current classifier and stored as (t_c, <description>, *pclass*).
Verification and return to the example base	At time, $t_v > t_c$, the true class, *vclass*, may be obtained. Verification latency is $t_1{}^{lat}$. After further delay, $t_2{}^{lat}$, this may be fed back, at ((t_{tb})), to the example training base as *(<description>, vclass)*.
Learning update regime	The learner is applied periodically to examples returned to the training example base since the last episode of learning.

Latency, for the purposes of the OLLC, refers to the time taken from the instantiation of a potential example, e.g. a loan applicant beginning his application, and a prediction / classification is made, e.g. a predicted class to grant loan or reject; through the subsequent period when the verified class is given / discovered; and ending when the final form of example arrives at the online learner training base. As stated in [9], latency only becomes an issue should drift occur.

Depending upon the domain, latency can be either constant (fixed) or random [9]. For example, a system, which predicts rise or fall of share price from the close of one day to the close of the next, has fixed verification latency with no administrative delay. However, in domains attempting to handle fraud, verification and administrative delays are likely to be random. As a result, random latency will cause examples to become available out of their original chronological ordering.

The issue as to what the time stamp of a new training example should be has received little attention in the literature. When a classifier makes a classification at time t, it is attempting to replicate that which would be made by an oracle (possibly a human expert), were such available [9]. This oracle is indexed by time and can change its rules over time, i.e. concept drift. It is the role of the learning regime to try to capture and maintain the oracle's rules over time.

From the OLLC three distinct time stamps can be observed; time of classification (t_c), time of verification (t_v), and time at training base (t_{tb})

The time of classification relates to the earliest identifiable time in an example's life cycle from the viewpoint of an online learner. Once online and in a closed domain, the classifier is likely to first discover the data instances that will subsequently feedback to it as examples. It is the likeliest record of the chronological order of examples and the associated time of drift states.

The time of verification represents the moment whereby an example discovers its verified class: as distinct from the true class definition. Examples can gain their verified classifications through either disclosure of the true class over time in a domain or the assignment of a verified class to date, e.g. a panel of experts.

Finally, there is the arrival time at the training base, i.e. when the example including its verified class finally arrives at the online learner training base ready for the next learning update cycle to occur. This time stamp preserves the final ordering of examples as the result of the summative latencies gained over their life cycle in feeding back to the base.

3   Online Learners

For experimentation the following four online learners were used. CD3 and CD5 [11] being established Time Stamp Attribute Relevance (TSAR) approach [11] learners in the literature and CDTC, Concept Drift Time of Classification, versions one and two being new learners. While base learners may be interchangeable, CD5 and both CDTC algorithms use a weka implementation of Quinlan's C4.5 algorithm, J48 [12].

CD3 uses the decision tree algorithm, ID3 [13], along with post pruning as a base learner. In each learning episode CD3 receives a batch of training examples that have become available since the last episode. These are time-stamped as *new* and added to examples retained from previous episodes, time-stamped as *current*. CD3 assesses the relevance of the time-stamp attribute to classification however it is using a time stamp allocated at the time of the training base; the time-stamp attribute relevance (TSAR) principle [11]. Following induction, rules are extracted from the tree and those which specify the time-stamp value as *current* are deemed to be out of date and purged, along with all examples covered by the rule. Finally, the new examples have their time-stamp changed to *current*. By this means, CD3 aims to dynamically maintain a base of training examples considered to be valid, that is, they reflect the current oracle. It is an important feature of CD3 that it does not remove training examples simply on the basis of age, the argument being that, under concept drift, typically not all rules are subject to drift and so examples covered by un-drifted rules retain their relevance to the learner.

A further development of the batch-based discrete time stamping of CD3, CD5 is designed to use a continuous time stamp applied to each example as it arrives at the training base. Once again this represents the time at training base time stamp definition.

CDTC version one, table 2, is a new algorithm that relies upon a meta data protocol at the point of classification of examples to ensure that accurate time stamps from the moment of classification, t_c, are available to use instead of applying the time of arrival at the training base. It learns every batch call from all examples obtained to the current time.

Table 2. CDTC version one pseudo code

```
Batch Contents Data Structure
(tc , <Description> , vClass)
Learner
while online
 if batch received
    if initial batch
        Call Base_Learner on Training _Base
        Deploy Base_Learner_Classifier
    else if not initial batch
        Append batch contents into Training _Base Table
        Call Base_Learner on Training _Base
        Deploy Classifier
 end while
Classification
while online
  if example_received(<Description>)
    Append Current_TimeStamp(tc, <Description>)
    Classify(tc, <Description>)
    Return(tc, <Description>, Predicted Class) to Domain
 end while
```

In version 2, table 3, additional mechanisms are added that check for accessible rules being present in the classifier, under the current time and only if the most informative attribute is the time stamp, prior to classifying a particular example and to determine whether to begin the example purging procedure. If accessible rules are present, the learner purges examples, from the training base, by checking the existing examples in the training base that were used in creating the previous classifier. The algorithm compares the original time stamp classification of the example against what it would classify as, as the current time, in the new classifier. Examples that classify correctly with their original time stamp but not the current time, or, examples that do not classify correctly at all are purged from the learning base; thus avoiding the version one problem of the training base hanging onto irrelevant examples and an unnecessarily severe impact on computation time during a learning phase.

Classification also uses the accessible rules check and, when accessible rules are not available with the current time stamp, uses the rules immediately prior to the most recent time represented in the classifier rules.

While batches are received, the learner uses a learning curve test on the most recent n, set to 100 in the experiments, examples not used in a classifier to determine whether any change in classification rate beyond the *Range*, in this case 5%, either direction has occurred. If so a learning cycle engages learning on all current and new examples in the training base, purging only takes place after a learning cycle has proceeded. This helps avoid unnecessary learning and purging; ensuring that all relevant examples are still kept for necessary learning updates.

Table 3. CDTC version two pseudo code

```
   Learner
while online
   if batch received
     if initial batch
       Set batch examples' Status to "New"
        Call Base_Learner on Training _Base
       Deploy Base_Learner_Classifier
       Select n "New" examples
       Set Previous_Rate to classification rate of the n examples
       Update all examples Example_Status in Training_Base to Current
     else if not initial batch
       Set batch examples' Status to "New"
       retrieve most recent n examples by TimeStamp where Status is New
       Evaluate current classifier on n
       if new average classification rate outside Previous_Rate +/- Range(%)
         Previous_Rate assign new rate
         Call Base_Learner on Training _Base
         Deploy Classifier
         if Classifier has accessible rules
           Get all Current Examples
           if classifies correctly with original time stamp but not current time
             Delete Current examples with matching (<Description>,vClass)
           else if doesn't classify correctly with original time stamp or current time
             Delete Current examples with matching (<Description>,vClass)
           Update all examples' Status in Training_Base to Current
   end while
   Classification
while online
   if example_received(<Description>)
     Append Current_TimeStamp(t_c, <Description>)
     if Classifier has accessible rules
      Classify(t_c, <Description>)
     else
      use less than most Recent_Time in tree to classify(Recent_Time,<Description>)
     return(t_c, <Description>, Predicted Class) to Domain
   end while
```

In addition, the learning curve test also aids in avoiding time stamp relevance reaction and purging response to a non-domain representative imbalance in the class value distribution; a side-effect of TSAR methodology observed when using C4.5 as a base learner in early experimentation.

No maximum training base size is used; doing so risks the learner never being able to achieve a sufficient number of examples to learn the quantity and complexity of rules active in each concept universe in the domain.

4 Experimental Methodology

To investigate the impact of latency on learning under concept drift, a series of experiments was performed using a variety of latency and drift scenarios. In these, latency was modeled as both fixed and random and was assumed to be independent of description attribute values of the examples and of class. No filtering was applied.

Training and test examples were generated using AutoUniv [14]. AutoUniv creates an artificial universe (U), a complete probabilistic model of the joint distribution of the description attribute and the class, comprising four components: attribute definitions; attribute factorization (into independent factors); attribute factor distributions; and, a rule set. Noise is modelled as the degree of uncertainty in the class distributions of each rule. Retaining attribute and class definitions and altering some of the other components of the universe obtain drifted models. Drift can be in rules only (concept drift) or in attribute distributions only (population drift) or both.

For the experiments, three universes were generated all with the same attributes and classes using 8 relevant attributes, 2 noise attributes, a range of 2-5 attribute values, a range of 2-5 rules and 4 class values. The second universe was obtained by applying concept drift to the first; the third was obtained by applying concept drift to the second. Details are given in tables 4(a) and 4(b). All universes have similar Bayes rates.

Table 4. (a) Universe drift variations, (b) Cross-classification rates (XCR) between universes.

Universe	Rules	Average Rule Length	Noise %	Bayes Rate %
1	60	4.2	21.4	78.6
2	88	4.3	19.5	80.5
3	82	4.3	22.1	77.9

Old	New	XCR (%)
Universe 1	Universe 2	32.1
Universe 2	Universe 3	26.8
Universe 1	Universe 3	33.6

The cross-classification rate (XCR), [11], provides a simple measure of the extent of drift, i.e. that which would be obtained if the universe rules operating before a drift point were applied to classify examples after drift had occurred. From table 4(b) it is seen that XCR is very low, in relation to the corresponding Bayes rate in all cases. If an online learner correctly induces rules for universe 1 but fails to detect the drift to universe 2 and then to universe 3, the classification rate will drop first to about 32% and then rise to about 34%.

Examples were then given a life cycle using ELISE. ELISE was developed to load training and test examples from AutoUniv into a database and to generate initial time point and additional latency values to include with each domain training example as specified in the OLLC [8].

Elise allows for the selection of either constant or random latency types. Random latency offers a further breakdown into latency models generated according to a normal distribution or negative exponential: a normal distribution representing latency scenarios where examples may return early or late but will more likely be closer to an expected time and share a common dependency with each other, and, negative exponential for the scenario where examples will most likely return soon after classification but still allow for very late example return; also have little to no dependency between examples to determine latency. When selecting a normal distribution the user has control over a number of preset variance levels. Overall, random latency is determined from an inputted average latency value.

In addition to the latency periods, the user can specify a regime for examples arriving to be classified. These arrivals can be fixed or random and modeled as above.

The user inputs the drift points, i.e. the time points at which the first example of each new drifted universe is experienced. They also enter the time point at the end of each test batch and the total number of test examples that make up a batch. In all, 21 experiments were scripted to run in ELISE. For each of the drift scenarios in table 5, each latency scenario in table 6 was conducted for both a medium and high latency value, as presented in table 7. The first experiment in each drift scenario, i.e. zero latency experiment, was performed to determine learner baseline performance under each drift scenario prior to the addition of latency. Ten iterations of each of these experiments were performed using different sets of data taken from each drifted universe and the average performance calculated.

Data was supplied as described in table 8. The combined total of examples, 10000, used for learning never changes in the experiments. The effect of increasing the number of drifts reduces the overall time for recovery and therefore represents an increasingly drift-active domain. These experiments only consider the impact of latency on domains susceptible to revolutionary drift, i.e. a sudden and immediate change in the rules, which gives a clearer interpretation of the impact of latency.

Table 5. Drift scenarios

Drifts	Drift points
0	0
1	4501
2	3001, 6001

Table 6. Latency scenarios

Latency Type	Latency Model
Zero	n/a
Constant	n/a
Random	Normal Distribution
Random	Negative Exponential

Table 7. Standard deviations for random latency

Average Latency	Normal Distribution Standard Deviation	Negative Exponential Standard Deviation
500	96	500
2000	516	2000

Table 8. Example data artificial universe(U) breakdown for each drift scenario

Category	Training Examples	Domain Examples	Test Examples
No drift	U1 (1000)	U1(9000)	U1(10000)
One drift	U1 (1000)	U1(4500), U2(4500)	U1(10000), U2(10000)
Two drift	U1 (1000)	U1(3000), U2(3000), U3(3000)	U1(10000), U2(10000), U3(10000)

Finally, learning and testing cycles were performed in the ELISE simulation every 500 time points.

5 Analysis of Results

The initial experiments involving no drift performed as expected. With the learners commencing at time point zero, having already conducted an initial learning run of 1000 training examples, quickly achieving a high classification accuracy bordering on the Bayes rate for the universe. Under latency, the only difference was in the return of examples after the last true time point of 9001, indicating that the examples were returning later than their true time, i.e. lagging as the result of latency.

The two drift experiments performed similarly to the one drift experiments, just with more pronounced impacts. As such, understanding the two drift scenario with high latency values provides comprehension of the one drift and medium latency versions.

As can be seen below, figure 1, in the two drift baseline experiments, i.e. zero latency, CDTC version 1 and CD5 perform identically in a zero latency environment since time of classification and time at training base become identical; both showing a marked improvement in recovery performance over CD3 and the batch time stamp approach. Interestingly, CDTC version 2 has a marked improvement over all others in recovery. Like, CD3 it deploys a purging mechanism that allows for removal of no longer relevant and noise examples. By evaluating the examples according to the continuous time stamp and purging it is capable of improving over version one. This is in fact maintaining a training base using time of classification relevance rather than using a sliding fixed window.

By examining time point 6501, the significance of the time of classification for defining a time stamp is clearly represented with a difference of 14.088% between the classification rates of CD3 and CDTC version 2. It is also notable that the lowest accuracy in each of the latency and drift scenarios is comparable to the cross-classification rate (XCR). However, the pattern of recovery is entirely different under latency conditions.

For constant latency, figure 2, a low classification plateau occurs for the duration of the example latency, i.e. the nature of constant latency presents as being an overall constant lag behind the current domain.

In the high latency scenario the example latency was for 2000 time points and this matches the duration of the lag prior to recovery. It must be observed that the constant latency prevents concept universe two full recovery prior to the second drift. However, once again in the recovery phase it is CDTC version 2 that recovers first, managing to achieve a stabilizing performance before the end of the real domain time stream at 9001.0.

An interesting observation is that CDTC and CD5, although using different definitions of time stamp, perform identically. This can be attributed to the fact that constant latency does not alter the chronological ordering of examples prior to arrival at the training base. It strongly suggests that the time stamp definition is interchangeable between time of arrival at the training base and that time when it was first classified in the case of constant latency.

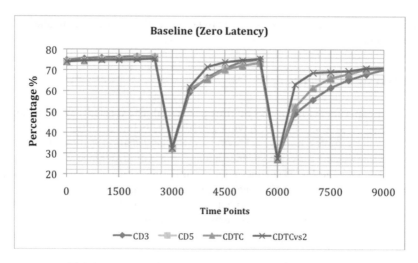

Fig. 1. Test result for two drift with zero latency experiment

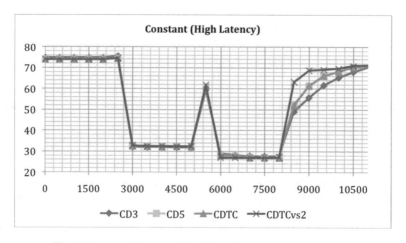

Fig. 2. Test result for two drift with constant latency experiment

It is the case that the definition for the time stamp becomes of critical importance when handling random latency domains, figure 3. Both for normal and negative exponential latency, it can clearly be demonstrated that learners using time stamps derived from time of arrival at the training base, either as discrete batch based or as continuous example-based, have a distinct disadvantage in recovery from drift.

With normal distribution latency, the impact is obvious by the first drift. Both versions of CDTC using the time of classification time stamp achieve a much earlier recovery commencement and achieve a higher classification rate performance prior to the second drift point. Between CDTC version 2 and CD5 at time point 5501 there is a difference in performance of 9.823% and at time point 8501 the difference is an extremely substantial 27.6%.

Negative exponential latency provides the most interesting results. While initially beginning its recovery quicker than under constant latency, the overall rate of recovery is much slower than the other latency models with a failure to achieve anywhere near the Bayes rate.

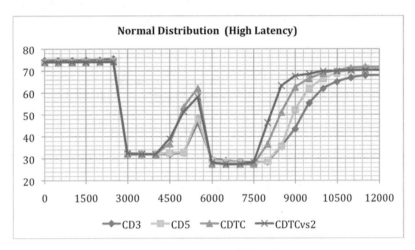

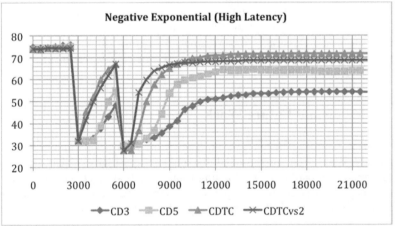

Fig. 3. Test results for two drift with random latency experiment

In this instance it is seen that CD3 is beginning to struggle significantly by the second drift: failing to achieve a near Bayes rate classification by the last example's true domain time point of 9001. The reduction in time between each drift sees a compounding realisation in the classification rate crash and recovery, with the second drift point occurring prior to full recovery.

CD5 does perform considerably better than CD3 however the cost of a time at training base time stamp is apparent. Both versions of CDTC handle the negative exponential latency with a performance in recovery that is near the baseline performance when latency was zero.

Upon further consideration, the cause of the negative exponential latency's severe impact upon learners using time at training base is clear. At the first drift point the learner is still receiving late examples from universe one delaying its recovery. By the second drift point, the learner is still receiving examples from both universe 1 and universe 2 in addition to the new universe. See table 9 where the compositions of the first two batches after the second drift point are displayed.

Table 9. Batch composition for two drift, high negative exponential latency

	Average Percentage %		
Batch Times (t)	**Universe 1**	**Universe 2**	**Universe 3**
6001 - 6501	16	72	12
6501 - 7001	12.7	55.7	31.6

The contamination caused from the mixing of the universes presents itself to the learner as a new compounded pseudo-universe. However, when using time at the training base, the examples relation to the drift point is already blurred by random latency and loss of accuracy in deducing the drift point or relating examples to the drift point. As a result, the learner is more prone to lose the relevance of the time stamp and try to learn the pseudo-universe.

Negative exponential latency in this experiment gives a mixture of examples that are not only contaminated but that also have a majority representation from a previous universe. As a result, it is not possible for a time at training base time stamp to achieve a successful classifier. Those learners using time of classification are able to distinguish the old universe examples, as they are able to relate examples more accurately to a drift point.

6   Conclusion and Future Work

Time stamp definitions in the presence of latency are highly important; used explicitly or implicitly. It has been demonstrated that a learner must have a clear representation of an example's chronological positioning when operating in a temporal environment when latency is an issue; these experiments were repeated on alternative domains (including binary class value) and real protein data with similar results. It is clear that a protocol for online example collection and a time stamp definition close to the example's instantiation, time of classification, should be used.

Two new algorithms have been presented that use a time of classification protocol to solve the latency issue. Due to the constraints of the real world on example storage and performance, CDTC version 2 provides the best all round solution to handling the various latency scenarios. It may also be viewed as a TSAR wrapper algorithm for other learner approaches, used alongside a relevant example collection protocol, as a replacement for the C4.5 base learner.

There is an additional extension of latency that is also being explored and will be presented in future work, latency de-synchronisation. In this scenario, average random latencies of different class values may have different dependencies that result in different durations for progression through a domain to the training base. It is hoped that through additional use of meta-data analysis, our new third version of CDTC will be able to re-synchronise the examples through latency analysis from the time of classification to arrival, and, use intelligent batch processing to secure an accurate comprehension of the data stream.

References

1. Kolter, J.Z., Maloof, M.A.: Dynamic Weighted Majority: An ensemble method for drifting concepts. Journal of Machine Learning Research 8, 2755–2790 (2007)
2. Minku, L.L., White, A.P., Yao, X.: The Impact of Diversity on On-line Ensemble Learning in the Presence of Concept Drift. IEEE Transactions on Knowledge and Data Engineering, 730–742 (2009)
3. Gao, J., Fan, W. and Han, J.: On appropriate assumptions to mine data streams: Analysis and practice. In: Proc. ICDM 2007, pp. 143–152 (2007)
4. Gama, J.: Knowledge Discovery from Data Streams. Chapman & Hall/CRC, Boca Raton (2010)
5. Lughofer, E., Angelov, P.: Handling Drifts and Shifts in On-line Data Streams with Evolving Fuzzy Systems. Applied Soft Computing 11, 2057–2068 (2011)
6. Angelov, P., Lughofer, E., Zhou, X.: Evolving Fuzzy Classifiers with Different Architectures. Fuzzy Sets and Systems 159, 3160–3182 (2008)
7. Klinkenberg, R.: Learning Drifting Concepts: example selection vs. example weighting. Intelligent Data Analysis 8(3), 281–300 (2004)
8. Wang, H., Yin, J., Pei, J., Yu, P., Yu, J.: Suppressing model over-fitting in mining concept-drifting data streams. In: Proc. KDD 2006, Philadelphia, pp. 736–741 (2006)
9. Marrs, G.R., Hickey, R.J., Black, M.M.: The Impact of Latency on Online Classification Learning with Concept Drift. In: Bi, Y., Williams, M.-A. (eds.) KSEM 2010. LNCS (LNAI), vol. 6291, pp. 459–469. Springer, Heidelberg (2010)
10. Marrs, G.R., Hickey, R.J., Black, M.M.: Modeling the Example Life-Cycle in an Online Classification Learner. In: Online Proc. of 1st International Workshop on Handling Concept Drift in Adaptive Information Systems: Importance, Challenges and Solutions, HaCDAIS, ECML/PKDD, pp. 57–64 (2010)
11. Black, M., Hickey, R.J.: Maintaining the performance of a learned classifier under concept drift. Intelligent Data Analysis 3, 453–474 (1999)
12. Quinlan, J.R.: C4.5: Programs for Machine Learning. Morgan Kaufmann, San Francisco (1993)
13. Quinlan, J.R.: Induction of decision trees. Machine Learning 1, 81–106 (1986)
14. Hickey, R.J.: AutoUniv.,
    http://archive.ics.uci.edu/ml/datasets/AutoUniv

Artificial Recurrence for Classification of Streaming Data with Concept Shift

Piotr Sobolewski and Michał Woźniak

Department of Systems and Computer Networks, Faculty of Electronics, Wroclaw University
of Technology, Wybrzeże Wyspiańskiego 27, 50-370 Wroclaw, Poland
{piotr.sobolewski,michal.wozniak}@pwr.wroc.pl

Abstract. The article presents a method for improving classification of
streaming data influenced by concept shift. For this purpose the algorithms
designed for recurring concept drift environments are adapted. To minimize
classification error after concept shift, an artificial recurrence is implemented
serving as a better starting point for classification. Three popular algorithms are
tested on three different scenarios and their performance is compared with and
without the application of an artificial recurrence.

Keywords: concept shift, recurring concept drift, artificial recurrence, non-
stationary data streams.

1 Introduction

In real cases, so-called *concept drift* occurs frequently [10, 13]. The potential for
considering new training data [14] is an important feature of machine learning
methods used in security applications (spam filters or IDS/IPS) [15] or decision
support systems for marketing departments, which need to follow the changing client
behavior [9]. Unfortunately, the occurrence of this phenomena dramatically decreases
classification accuracy. Concept drift could be caused by changes in the probabilities
of classes or/and conditional probability distributions of classes [11]. The most
popular taxonomy of the *concept drift* was formulated in [12]:

- Gradual drift (gradual changes, evolutionary changes, concept drift) – if the
  changes are mild in nature.
- Sudden drift (substitution, abrupt changes, concept substitution, concept
  shift) – if the changes are abrupt.
- Recurring context (recurring trends) – if the context changes either
  periodically or changes in an unordered fashion.

In this work we focus on methods which deal with recurring concept drift, which was
introduced by Widmer et al. [7]. System proposed by authors can extract models from
the data repository and train classifiers, which serve as a tool for classification if
corresponding concept recurs in the future. A possibility of using already trained
classifiers when facing a concept shift greatly increases adaptability of classification
systems.

A. Bouchachia (Ed.): ICAIS 2011, LNAI 6943, pp. 76–87, 2011.

In general, most of the approaches, which deal with concept shift can be described by following procedure:

```
1. Check if a batch of samples indicates concept shift,
2. If not, use a trained classifier,
3. If yes, use an outdated classifier and train a new classifier
   when data with class labels are available.
```

If the classification of data stream is influenced by recurring concept drift then point 3 of mentioned procedure could be improved in the following way:

```
3. If yes, check if the concept is known (e.g. it has occurred
   in the past),
   a. If yes, use a classifier trained on historical concept,
   b. If not, use an outdated classifier and train a new
      classifier if data with class labels are available.
```

When recurrence is not detected (3b), the classification system does not have an accurate tool to perform the classification and it has to wait for a new well-grounded classifier in a new model, what requires a certain amount of samples with revealed class labels. During this time system is forced to classify incoming samples with a not prepared classifier, which will result in the diminished accuracy and an overall decrease of performance. The scale of the decrease depends on the impact of concept drift, namely the impetuosity of changes. Most of the algorithms, which deal with concept drift, try to minimize the time of a new classifier training. Efficient solutions to this problem are based on almost unlimited availability of data with labels, but usually the access to true labels of data is very costly and in some applications even impossible [5].

The main aim of the method presented in this paper is to minimize the drop in performance of the classification system after a shift in concept which results in a new, unknown concept. The demonstrated method makes use of strengths of algorithms designed for recurring concept drift environments in data streams with non-recurring concept shifts. We exploit this advantage in scenario, which does not consider concept recurrence, but we assume a maximal concept shift strength. Thanks to this assumption we can predict some future scenarios, i.e. possible concepts, which could be treated as a starting point for a new classification model. Let us notice that in many real cases, e.g. stores, which seasonally have to adjust their marketing strategy to the trends in fashion do not have to consider supplying the warehouses with car parts, so these items are outside the area of an allowed concept shift. Therefore, the main objective of the work is to propose a method of data streams classification, which could exploit fast adaptability of methods dedicated to recurrent data drift.

2 Related Works

In the area of recurring concept drift there are several popular algorithms which are further evaluated in this paper. The method described in [1] considers the use of two layers learning scheme – the first level (a base classifier) performs the classification of unlabeled data, the second one (a referee) remembers if the classification was correct or not, learning the areas of feature space, where level one classifier performs either correctly or incorrectly. Drift detection is based on an assumption, that if the distribution of the examples is stationary, then the error-rate of the learning algorithm will decrease when the number of examples increases. Referees act as detectors of recurring drift, checking if the model fits the occurred situation. In [2] authors represent each batch of samples in a form of a conceptual vector, created on the basis of feature means and variances (if data are numeric) or on the basis of numbers of samples with the same values of certain features in a batch (if the data are nominal). The difference between two batches is measured by calculating the Euclidean distance between their conceptual vectors. The batches are then clustered according to the distance and each cluster represents a different concept. On each cluster a separate classifier is trained, which is then used for the classification of the concept represented by the corresponding cluster. Recurrence in data stream is detected on the basis of the sample features in a data chunk and their distance to clusters. In [3], a classifier ensemble is used. Each elementary classifier in the ensemble is trained on a different concept extracted from the recorded samples with known labels. During the testing phase, weights are given to all classifiers proportionally to their performance on training data. As a result, most accurate classifiers are selected as active and their decisions are evaluated according to given weights. Data labels are available only for some portions of samples in data stream only and can be used for training elementary classifiers and updating the ensemble with new weights. If during training an ensemble does not reach a certain performance threshold, a new classifier is trained on the batch of samples and added to the global set.

3   Artificial Recurrence Approach

Concept recurrence carries an opportunity to choose a better starting point for classification after concept shifts, however such an opportunity disappears when the recurrence is not present. Our solution to this problem is to create an artificial recurrence, namely to generate a repository of artificial data on the basis of real data. It would represent concepts which could occur after a concept shift. New set of classifiers are trained on artificial data and they are used in the same manner as classifiers trained on real historical records. The consecutive process is the same as in the case of a recurring concept drift, except the fact that models are generated artificially. An advantage of generating artificial data points is that there is no limit of training data samples for classifiers, so there is no threat of under-training. After concept shift, the classifiers trained on the artificially generated samples serve as temporary classifiers for streaming data, until the classifiers which are trained on real data surpass their performance. A chosen "artificial" classifier may also serve as a starting point for the new classifier training process. Classifiers trained on artificial data are not updated, and are kept separate from real classifiers, so both models can function independently. Artificial repository of concepts is rebuilt or updated on the basis of information carried by labeled samples, depending if concept shift is detected or not. A general overview of the solution is described in the pseudo-code below:

```
 1:  Parameters: C: current data distribution (concept),
          PCᵢ: the i-th previous data distribution,
          ACᵢ: the i-th artificial data distribution,
          nPC: number of previous data distributions,
          nAC: number of artificial data distributions,
          D_C: set of data belonging to distribution C,
          Φ_C: classifier trained on dataset D_C,
          B: batch of samples drawn from data stream.
 2:  while new B do
 3:     for i=0 to nAC do
 4:         generate D_{ACi} based on D_C,
 5:         train Φ_{ACi}.
 6:     end for
 7:     if B belongs to C then
 8:         classify B with Φ_C,
 9:         add B to D_C,
10:         update Φ_C.
11:     else
12:         set recurrence_check = 0.
13:         for i=0 to nPC do
14:             if B belongs to PCᵢ then
15:                 classify B with Φ_{PCi},
16:                 add B to D_{PCi},
17:                 update Φ_{PCi},
18:                 set C = PCᵢ,
19:                 set recurrence_check = 1.
20:             end if
21:         end for
22:         if recurrence_check = 0 then
23:             for i=0 to nAC do
24:                 if B belong to ACᵢ then
25:                     classify B with Φ_{ACi},
26:                     create new D_C = B,
27:                     create new C based on D_C,
28:                     train new Φ_C,
29:                     increment nPC,
30:                     set D_{nPC} = D_C,
31:                     set P_{CnPC} = C.
32:                 end if
33:             end for
34:         end if
35:     end while
```

Fig. 1. Pseudo-code of an artificial recurrence approach

Artificial recurrence method is a continuation of work presented in [19].

4 Experiments

4.1 Scenarios

Artificial recurrence is evaluated on three scenarios with three popular algorithms, described in the section 2. For the remainder of this paper, the algorithm described in [1] will be called "*MetaLearn*", in [2] a "*ConVec*" and the algorithm described in [3] – "*EnsC*". Their performance is compared with and without the implementation of artificial recurrence mechanism. The experiments were carried out on the same datasets as used by authors of mentioned methods, i.e.

- "SEA Concepts" dataset [6] for evaluation of *MetaLearn*,
- "Nursery" dataset [20] for evaluation of *EnsC*,
- "Simple Gaussian" for evaluation of *ConVec*,

An exception is *ConVec*, where originally datasets *Usenet1* and *Usenet2* were used, however as these datasets have too many features to implement artificial recurrence in its current state, a custom scenario has been designed instead. Let us describe the set-up of experiments shortly.

Simple Gaussian. "Simple Gaussian" is an artificially generated scenario to test ConVec algorithm. Data is divided into two classes with the same prior probability and described by two features with Gaussian distributions with equal variances $(\mathrm{var}(X1) = \mathrm{var}(X2) = 1)$ and different means (initially $\mu1 = (2,2)$ and $\mu2 = (7,2)$), what is shown in Fig. 2. Shift in concept is simulated by changing the means of sample features belonging to each class. The shift in means is limited by a fixed distance and a static central point, allowing them to drift anywhere along the circular path, as shown in Fig. 3.

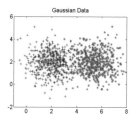

Fig. 2. Initial state of data distribution in "Simple Gaussian" scenario – points represent data samples on the feature space distributed between two classes (red and blue)

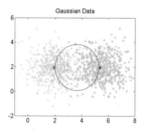

Fig. 3. Allowed concept shift in means of classes, represented by a circular path (green). Means of two classes (red and blue) are marked on the opposite sides of the circle. Artificial recurrence generates datasets with class means distributed uniformly along the circular path, simulating possible drifts in concept.

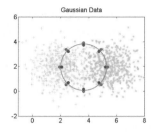

Fig. 4. Artificial class means generated by artificial recurrence method. Basing on the means, eight artificial concepts are generated

Artificial class means are equally distributed around the circle, as shown in Fig. 4. After concept shifts, a classifier trained on data belonging to the closest artificial concept to unlabeled batch of samples is used to perform classification until a real classifier trained on incoming data achieves better performance. Eight artificial concepts have been chosen arbitrally, basing on the assumption about possible shift area for this problem and 4 real concept shifts are simulated, with the following class means:

Table 1. Class means in different concepts in "Simple Gaussian" scenario

Concept	μ_1	μ_2
Concept 1	(2,2)	(7,2)
Concept 2	(4.5,4.5)	(4.5,-0.5)
Concept 3	(7,2)	(2,2)
Concept 4	(4.5,-0.5)	(4.5,4.5)

Concept pairs 1 with 3 and 2 with 4 are mirror distributions, perpendicular to each other. Concept shift occurs every 1000 samples, artificial concepts are generated with 500 samples for each class, a batch consists of 50 samples and after classifying each batch, the true class labels become available for the system.

SEA Concepts. "SEA Concepts" was introduced in [6] and used for the evaluation of *MetaLearn*. Samples are described by three features with random numeric values which range from [0;10] and are distributed between two classes. Class distribution is made according to the following formula:

$$\text{Class}(X_i) = \begin{cases} 1, \text{if } f_1 + f_2 \le \theta \\ 2, \text{if } f_1 + f_2 > \theta \end{cases}, \tag{1}$$

where:

Class(X_i) - class of *i*-th sample,
f_1, f_2 – first two features of sample *i*.

In [6], four θ values were chosen for different concepts: 8, 9, 7 and 9.5. In [1], authors added four additional concepts by repeating the same θ values to create the concept recurrence, also increasing the size of the dataset to 120000 samples. To show an advantage of an artificial recurrence in non-recurring environment, we used the same experiment set-up as in [6], namely the four concepts occurring in intervals between 15000 samples, so the test data stream consists of 60000 samples. We added 10% of class noise by generating an incorrect, opposite class for each concept. Artificial recurrence is implemented by distributing artificially generated samples to classes with 10 different values of θ, resulting in 10 artificial concepts created every time data labels are available, specifically every 500 samples in the test scenario. Values of artificial θ are created on the basis of estimated value of θ for the current distribution, according to the equation:

$$a\theta_i = e\theta - 5 + i, i \in \{1,2, \ldots, 10\}, i \neq 5 , \tag{2}$$

where:

$a\theta_i$– θ of i-th artificial concept,
$e\theta$ – estimated θ of the current concept.

The value of $e\theta$ is estimated by calculating a mean of an average of $f_1 + f_2$ for both classes from all samples in the current concept according to:

$$e\theta = \frac{\frac{\sum_{i=1}^{n_1}\left(f_{1,1}^i + f_{2,1}^i\right)}{n_1} + \frac{\sum_{i=1}^{n_2}\left(f_{1,2}^i + f_{2,2}^i\right)}{n_2}}{2} \tag{3}$$

where:

$f_{f,c}^i$– feature f of the i-th sample from class c,
n_c – number of samples in class c.

Classifiers based on artificial concepts also have their own referees and take part in the recurrence tracking process together with the referees of classifiers trained on the real data.

Nursery. "Nursery" is a dataset used for evaluation of *EnsC* algorithm [3]. Each sample belongs to one of four classes (after removing points from the "recommended" class) and it is described by 8 nominal features. Concept shift is simulated in the same way, as presented by the authors of an algorithm in [3], namely a new concept is created by changing a value of a feature to another value present for this feature in the dataset in a consistent way, without changing the class label. The values change for each class by rotating clockwise or anti-clockwise over all samples. Concept shift is limited to a change in only one feature at once. Artificial recurrence is implemented by generating data samples, which simulate every possible concept within the allowed shift area, by rotating each feature one value clockwise or anti-clockwise without changing other features and class labels, which results in 16 artificial concepts updated every time a new set of data with labels is available (samples have 8 features, each with 2 possible directions of rotation). Classifiers which are trained on artificially generated data are considered as regular classifiers trained on real data and are added to the ensemble in the same manner. New artificial data is generated after each new data chunk with labelled samples, replacing data generated on the basis of previous data chunk. Classifiers trained on artificial data are also replaced by new ones, so their number remains constant. In data stream, labelled data chunks are available every 2000 samples and consist of 400 labelled records. Testing and evaluation of classification accuracy is performed only on unlabelled data. Concept shifts occur every 2000 samples and with each concept one feature is rotated for all the following data. Every new concept rotates the next feature, interchangeably clockwise and anti-clockwise, until all 8 features have been rotated. As a result, 8 different concepts are present in data stream and the experiment is performed on 16000 samples in total.

4.2   Results

To ensure the reliability of the comparative study, during the experiments the same classifiers, as chosen by the authors of considered systems were applied, namely for *EnsC* decision trees trained by ID3 algorithm, for *MetaLearn* Naïve Bayes for both the level 0 classifiers and the referees and for *ConVec*, CCP Framework with Leader-Follower clustering algorithm described in [8] and a Naïve Bayes classifier. Also, the same algorithm parameters were used, as proposed in mentioned above papers [1-3].

The results shown in Tab. 2 present an overall accuracy of tested algorithms with and without the implementation of an artificial recurrence in the domain of the average error-rates and average errors on batches of 50 samples. The cumulative error-rates of the analysed solutions are depicted in Fig. 5-7.

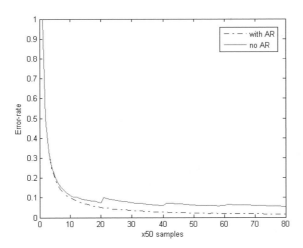

Fig. 5. Error-rates of *ConVec* algorithm, with and without artificial recurrence. The blue dotted line represents the error-rate of an algorithm with artificial recurrence and the green solid line shows the error-rate without artificial recurrence.

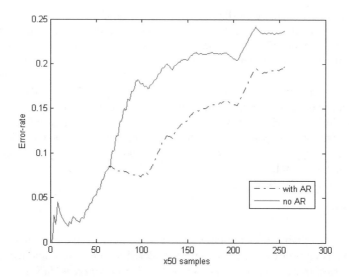

Fig. 6. Error-rates of *EnsC* algorithm, with and without artificial recurrence. The blue dotted line represents the error-rate of an algorithm with artificial recurrence and the green solid line shows the error-rate without artificial recurrence.

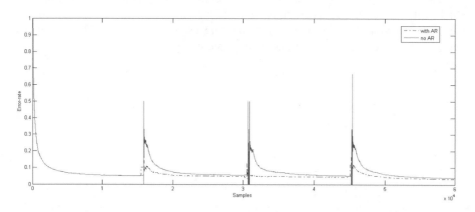

Fig. 7. Error-rates of *MetaLearn* algorithm, with and without artificial recurrence. The blue dotted line represents the error-rate of an algorithm with artificial recurrence and the green solid line shows the error-rate without artificial recurrence.

Table 2. Average error-rates and errors on batches of 50 samples with and without artificial recurrence for each test scenario

Experiment	Average error-rates			Average error on 50 samples	
	MetaLearn	*ConVec*	*EnsC*	*ConVec*	*EnsC*
With A.R.	6,05%	5,42%	11,18%	0,47%	19,68%
Without A.R.	9,61%	9,85%	15,87%	4,1%	23,68%

Implementation of artificial recurrence in the existing algorithms has significantly increased the performance of classification systems. For the first experiment with *ConVec* algorithm (Fig. 5) we can observe a noticeable increase of error when concept shifts in the scenario without artificial recurrence. It is caused by the need to create new clusters and training new classifiers, what requires a temporary use of the old, erroneous classifiers to classify a new, unknown concept. This trend disappears when artificial recurrence is implemented. Error rate smoothly decreases, as new labeled data is available to update the classifiers and tune the artificial data. After each shift in concept, the closest artificial cluster is chosen by the distance estimator and then the classifier trained on this cluster is used to perform classification. As artificial data covers all the allowed concept drift area, classifiers trained on the artificial concepts are well prepared for the classification of the new concept data. Artificial recurrence decreases an average error overall almost twice and an average error on a batch of 50 samples by almost 85%. Such an impressive decrease of the error of classification is caused by the fact that the artificially generated clusters of data consist of more samples, than the real clusters. As a consequence, classifiers trained on the artificially generated datasets are better prepared for classification, than classifiers trained on real clusters which is directly reflected in an average error on a batch of samples.

EnsC algorithm has been tested with the same parameters, as originally proposed by the authors in [3], specifically *PermittedError* is set to 0.05 and *AcceptanceFactor* is 0.4. The results are shown in Fig. 6.

The difference in the cumulative error-rates becomes noticeable from the moment of the first concept shift in data stream, as before it the system performs the classification with only one single classifier which is trained on the first available data chunk with labels. An average error of mentioned algorithm without artificial recurrence is about 40% higher than with artificial recurrence and the difference in error on a batch of 50 samples is about 25%. The misclassification-rate grows, because only 20% of data are available with labels, what does not fully represent the whole dataset. As random data samples are labeled, some classes within concepts may not appear within the labeled data chunks at all, precluding the classifiers from learning them. Also, combining classifiers trained on the real and artificial data has produced better results, than considering separate ensembles.

The results of the last experiment, with *MetaLearn* algorithm are depicted in Fig. 7. Error-rates are reset with each shift in concept, as in [1]. Without artificial recurrence, misclassification-rate increases significantly with each new detected concept, because a new classifier needs to be trained from scratch, with every shift in concept. After implementing artificial recurrence, this severe drop in performance has been radically decreased, as the system became equipped with a tool which allows a prior preparation for every possible new concept. The classifiers trained on artificial data together with their referees properly predict new distributions, allowing the system to maintain a better level of performance, overall. Difference between mean error-rates is around 50%, what is mainly caused by an accurate estimation of $e\theta$ and as a consequence, a proper selection of $a\theta$ for generating artificial distributions. Drift detection mechanism derived directly from [1] performed acceptably both with and without artificial recurrence, allowing the system to switch to a new mode at the right time.

5 Conclusions

The main purpose of implementing artificial recurrence into recurring concept drift classification algorithms was to minimize an increase of the error-rate after concept shift and in consequence improve the overall performance of the systems. The method has been evaluated with three popular algorithms, in the different scenarios with data characterized by various types of features (nominal and numeric) and distributions. The results of the experiments have shown that after implementing artificial recurrence, the performance of recurring concept drift algorithms increased by at least 25% in each of the tested scenarios. Such an increase in the overall accuracy was possible mainly by minimizing a drop in the performance caused by the concept shift.

Although the results of our approach seem promising, artificial recurrence still requires deeper study and improvement. We have to notice the limitation of the proposed method. After concept shifts, a set of new models (classifiers) has to be generated. Its number increases significantly, according to the number of features used by the classification models. Also, as the accuracy of the method depends on how densely artificial models cover the area of potential shifts, the problem may be compared to the task of establishing a grid size in the grid search algorithm, where quality of solution depends on the size of grid, while on the other hand the smaller grid size causes increase of computational costs [16].

This drawback together with the heuristic method of creating artificial concepts will be taken into consideration in the future research with an aim to create an analytical method for generating artificial concepts and to replace the two step process of generating artificial data and training classifiers with one step classifier creation by parameter tuning. It may lower the need for computing power and make the method more universal. Also, as there are no algorithms dedicated specifically for the artificial recurrence approach, it may also be an interesting field for scientific exploration.

Acknowledgement. This work is supported in part by The Ministry of Science and Higher Education under the grant which is realizing in the period 2010-2013.

References

1. Gama, J., Kosina, P.: Tracking Recurring Concepts with Meta-learners. In: Lopes, L.S., Lau, N., Mariano, P., Rocha, L.M. (eds.) EPIA 2009. LNCS, vol. 5816, pp. 423–434. Springer, Heidelberg (2009)
2. Katakis, I., Tsoumakas, G., Vlahavas, I.P.: An Ensemble of Classifiers for coping with Recurring Contexts in Data Streams. In: ECAI, pp. 763–764 (2008)
3. Ramamurthy, S., Bhatnagar, R.: Tracking recurrent concept drift in streaming data using ensemble classifiers. In: ICMLA, pp. 404–409 (2007)
4. Gama, J., Castillo, G.: Learning with Local Drift Detection. In: Li, X., Zaïane, O.R., Li, Z.-h. (eds.) ADMA 2006. LNCS (LNAI), vol. 4093, pp. 42–55. Springer, Heidelberg (2006)
5. Seewald, A.K., Fürnkranz, J.: An Evaluation of Grading Classifiers. In: Hoffmann, F., Adams, N., Fisher, D., Guimarães, G., Hand, D.J. (eds.) IDA 2001. LNCS, vol. 2189, pp. 115–124. Springer, Heidelberg (2001)

6. Street, W.N., Kim, Y.: A streaming ensemble algorithm (SEA) for large-scale classification. In: KDD, pp. 377–382 (2001)
7. Widmer, G., Kubat, M.: Learning in the Presence of Concept Drift and Hidden Contexts. Machine Learning, 69–101 (1996)
8. Duda, R.O., Hart, P.E., Stork, D.G.: Pattern Classification. John Wiley & Sons, New York (2000)
9. Black, M.M., Hickey, R.J.: Classification of Customer Call Data in the Presence of Concept Drift and Noise. In: Bustard, D.W., Liu, W., Sterritt, R. (eds.) Soft-Ware 2002. LNCS, vol. 2311, pp. 74–87. Springer, Heidelberg (2002)
10. Gaber, M.M., Zaslavsky, A.B., Krishnaswamy, S.: Mining data streams: a review. SIGMOD Record, 18–26 (2005)
11. Kelly, M.G., Hand, D.J., Adams, N.M.: The Impact of Changing Populations on Classifier Performance. In: KDD, pp. 367–371 (1999)
12. Narasimhamurthy, A.M., Kuncheva, L.I.: A framework for generating data to simulate changing environments. In: Artificial Intelligence and Applications, pp. 415–420 (2007)
13. Tsymbal, A.: The problem of concept drift: Definitions and related work. Technical Report. Department of Computer Science, Trinity College: Dublin, Ireland (2004)
14. Zhu, X., Wu, X., Yang, Y.: Effective classification of noisy data streams with attribute-oriented dynamic classifier selection. Knowl. Inf. Syst., 339–363 (2006)
15. Patcha, A., Park, J.: An overview of anomaly detection techniques: Existing solutions and latest technological trends. Computer Networks, 3448–3470 (2007)
16. Kuffner, J.J.: Efficient Optimal Search of Euclidean-Cost Grids and Lattices. In: Proceedings of the IEEE/RSJ Int. Conf. on Intelligent Robots and Systems (IROS 2004), vol. 2, pp. 1946–1951 (2004)
17. Lughofer, E., Angelov, P.: Handling Drifts and Shifts in On-line Data Streams with Evolving Fuzzy Systems. Applied Soft Computing 11(2), 2057–2068 (2011)
18. Kurlej, B., Wozniak, M.: Active Learning Approach to Concept Drift Problem. Logic Journal of IGPL (2011); doi:10.1093/jigpal/jzr011
19. Sobolewski, P.: Concept selecting classifiers as a solution to recurring concept drift in streaming data. Modelling and Simulation of Systems (2011)
20. Asuncion, A., Newman, D.J.: UCI ML Repository. University of California, School of Information and Computer Science, Irvine, CA (2007),
    http://www.ics.uci.edu/~mlearn/MLRepository.html

New Drift Detection Method for Data Streams

Parinaz Sobhani and Hamid Beigy

[1] Department of Computer Engineering, Sharif University of Technology, Tehran, Iran
psobhani@ce.sharif.ir, beigy@ce.sharif.ir
[2] Department of Computer Engineering, Sharif University of Technology, Tehran, Iran

Abstract. Correctly detecting the position where a concept begins to drift is important in mining data streams. In this paper, we propose a new method for detecting concept drift. The proposed method, which can detect different types of drift, is based on processing data chunk by chunk and measuring differences between two consecutive batches, as drift indicator. In order to evaluate the proposed method we measure its performance on a set of artificial datasets with different levels of severity and speed of drift. The experimental results show that the proposed method is capable to detect drifts and can approximately find concept drift locations.

Keywords: Concept drift, stream mining, drift detection, evolving data.

1 Introduction

Traditional techniques of data mining assume that data have stationary distributions. This assumption for recent challenges where tremendous amount of data are generated at unprecedented rates with evolving patterns, is not true anymore. Examples of such applications include text streams, surveillance video streams, credit card fraud detection, market basket analysis, information filtering, computer security, etc. An appropriate method for such problems should adapt to drifting concepts without need to store all data.

In machine learning methods to handle concept drift can be categorized as: approaches that adapt to current concept without explicit drift detections and approaches that detect changes when they come then adapt the learner to cope with new concept.

In this paper, we use the second approach, drift detection, as a way to respond and handle concept drift in evolving data. In order to detect a change, two different approaches can be fallowed: One is monitoring the evolution of performance indicators such as accuracy, precision and recall and the other one is monitoring distributions on two different time-windows [11]. We proposed a new method to measure and detect changes in data by processing data chunk by chunk and measuring differences between two consecutive batches. Differences are calculated by finding nearest neighbor in previous batch of data for each instance in current batch and comparing their corresponding labels.

The experimental results illustrate efficacy of using this detection method to find concept drift locations with much less false detections.

A. Bouchachia (Ed.): ICAIS 2011, LNAI 6943, pp. 88–97, 2011.

The rest of paper is organized as fallows. Next Section presents the related works in drifts detection and then the proposed method is presented in Section 3. In Section 4, we examine our method with artificial datasets and Section 5 concludes the paper.

2 Related Work

Detecting concept drift is important for dealing with data streams. Lots of methods for drift detection have been proposed in the literature. Most of these approaches are statistical methods that mostly depend on modeling the probability distributions of data and monitoring the likelihood of new instances [1], [8]. An example of statistical methods is the multivariate Wald-Wolfowitz test which is based on differences between data points as measured by a metric [14]. These approaches usually need all past data without considering space limits and are with high computational complexity [2].

Recent approaches concentrate more on measurements related to the running accuracy of the classifier [3], [4], [6], [9], [13]. According to probably approximately correct learning (PAC learning) model if the distribution of examples is stationary, as the number of examples increases the error rate decreases [12]. So a significant increase in the error of the algorithm during training, while using more examples, indicates a concept drift.

Among these approaches drift detection method (DDM) and early drift detection (EDDM) are more popular. DDM proposed in [3] works using two thresholds, t_1 and t_2. If the average error rate e, which is assumed to have binomial distribution, goes above t_1 a warning is alarmed and if e exceeds t_2, it is assumed that a concept drift has happened. After detection of the drift, the model induced by the learning method resets and a new model is learnt using the instances stored since the warning level triggered. To improve detection of gradual changes, EDDM is presented in [4]. It relies on the idea that the distance between two occurrences of classification errors increases as a stable concept is being learnt. So, a significant decrease in distance indicates a concept drift.

Klinkenberg and Joachims suggested accuracy, recall and precision of learner as drift indicators in [9]. In this approach, these indicators are monitored constantly and compared to a confidence interval of standard sample errors for a moving average value. The average is calculated using values of each indicator in the last M batches. The biggest problem of these approaches is parameters that are needed to be tuned for each particular application.

DDM, EDDM and most other existing performance-based methods proposed in the literature process data one by one, Chu suggested a drift detection method based on the framework of statistical decision theory [13]. In this framework, two tests are done to detect concept drifts, a significant test for abrupt changes and a hypothesis test for gradual changes. Significant test assesses how well no-change hypothesis explains ensemble accuracy on recent block of data (θ) and hypothesis test is performed by likelihood ratio test on probability density function θ under the no-change hypothesis and that under the change hypothesis.

3 Proposed Drift Detection Method

In this section, we propose a new method to detect changes in data streams by processing data chunk by chunk and measuring differences between two consecutive batches. Differences are calculated by finding nearest neighbor in previous batch of data for each instance in current batch and comparing their corresponding labels. The proposed drift detection algorithm is more effective for problems with well separated and balanced classes.

Let examples arrive in bundles. Assume that a new set of training data D_t is available at time instant t, previous training data D_{t-1} is also accessible. In order to measure differences between D_t and D_{t-1}, we first calculate the distance between each instance of D_t to instances in D_{t-1} . Different distance functions can be used. We used heterogeneous Euclidean/overlap metric (HEOM) [5]. HEOM is calculated according (1). In HEOM, for numeric features and categorical features the Euclidean distance and the overlap distance are used respectively, as given in (2).

$$d_{heom}(x_1, x_2) = \sqrt{\sum_{a=1}^{m} heom_a^2 \quad (x_1, x_2)} , \tag{1}$$

$$heom_a(x_1, x_2) = \begin{cases} 0 & if\ a\ is\ categorical\ and\ x_{1a} = x_{2a} \\ 1 & if\ a\ is\ categorical\ and\ x_{1a} \neq x_{2a} \\ \frac{x_{1a} - x_{2a}}{range_a} & if\ a\ is\ numeric \end{cases} , \tag{2}$$

where x_1 and x_2 are two instances with m features and for a numeric feature a the distance is normalized by the width of the range of values of the corresponding feature on the training set $range_a$.

Using distance map, the index and corresponding value of the nearest neighbor in D_{t-1} for each data in D_t is calculated. In order to detect the drift, we suggest using the fallowing relation.

$$\text{Degree of drift} = \frac{\sum_{i=1}^{n} \theta\,(i) * disagree(i)}{\sum_{i=1}^{n} \theta\,(i)} , \tag{3}$$

where n is the number of instances in D_t , $\theta\,(i)$ is a distance-based relevance coefficient and *disagree(i)* is calculated as given in (4). In our method, we consider $\theta\,(i)$ as the inverse HEOM distance between i-th instance of D_t and its nearest neighbor in D_{t-1} .

$$disagree(i) = \begin{cases} 1 & if\ label\ of\ nearest\ neighbor\ to\ x_i\ doesn't\ match\ it \\ 0 & if\ label\ of\ nearest\ neighbor\ to\ x_i\ match\ it \end{cases} \tag{4}$$

Significant increase in values of degree of drift (DoF) indicates the concept drift with high probability. In order to find peaks in the sequence of DoFs, we fallow the approach used in [10]. At time t, the average and the standard deviation of all DoFs, up to that time (except those which indicate concept drift), are computed and if current indicator value is away more than s standard deviation from the average, the system alarms concept drift, where s is a parameter of the algorithm.

4 Experiments and Results

In this section we evaluate the performance of the proposed concept drift detection method. Specifically, we would like to identify concept drift locations by finding peaks in sequences of drift measurements. Because in real datasets it's not known when a drift has occurred, evaluating accuracy of our approach to detect drifts by using only pure real world dataset is impossible.

In order to test our method in presence of different types of drifts we used artificial datasets described in [7]. In [7], drifts are categorized according to severity and speed criteria. Severity describes the extent of changes offered by a new concept and speed is inverse of the time taken for a new concept to replace the old one [7].

Criteria for evaluating the performance of drift detection methods include: probability of true detection, probability of false alarms and delay in detection [11]. Using these criteria we compared our algorithm's ability with the one proposed in [13]. In [13] Chu used two tests based on the framework of statistical decision theory to detect drifts. This proposed method has two thresholds, one for hypothesis test of gradual changes and the other one for significant test of abrupt changes.

To evaluate efficiency of our proposed method to distinguish concept drifts, we applied it to a set of artificial datasets where the location, speed and severity of concept drifts are known. The artificial data sets were used here [7] include circle, sine moving vertically, sine moving horizontally and line problems [7]. Nine instances of each problem which contains nine different drifts with varied level of severity and speed are available. Each dataset contains 2000 instances and each instance corresponds to one time step. In each dataset, first 1000 instances were produced according to first concept and after that concept change starts to happen. For more information about datasets, refer to [7].

Table 2 shows the results of experiments on all datasets. These results were obtained using $s = 4$ for our method and $t_1 = 10$ and $t_2 = 0.1$ for Chu's method and each batch of data assumed to have 100 instances. The first column of this table shows dataset's name, the second column specifies severity and speed of drift, third and forth columns indicate number of time steps between beginning of drift and detection of drift and whether drift was detected or not, in our and Chu's method respectively. Finally, the numbers in the two last columns give the number of incorrectly detected concept drifts for each method.

Table 2 shows that the proposed detection method is capable to detect drifts. In almost all datasets, drifts were detected at approximately right position. As the speed and severity of drift increase, the number of false detections and delay to detect change decrease, in other words, drifts can be better detected. This is due to the fact that when a drift has high severity and high speed, it causes big changes very suddenly so differences between batch of old concept and batch of new concept are more noticeable. Comparing to Chu's method, our distance-based method can detect drifts with much fewer false detections. As shown in table 2, especially as the speed of drift decreases, our distance-based method dominates Chu's method. The * in table 2 indicates the cases the proposed algorithm outperforms Chu's method.

The minimum delay time is equal to batch size. This is due to processing data chunk by chunk and before the next batch becomes available we cannot compare it to previous one and hence detect the drift. So the larger the batch size is the longer delay we would have to detect drifts. The number of false detections of the proposed algorithm with respect to batch size is given in Figure 1. In this figure, we applied the algorithm to nine instances of line problem and numbers of false detections with different batch sizes were averaged on these sets. As figure 1 shows, when batch size increases the number of false detections decreases.

Figure 2 through 4 gives an example of concept drift detection by peak identification on line data set. Solid line shows drift indicator which is one when drift is detected and zero otherwise. Dash line shows degrees of dominance of the new concept (DODONC) given by the fallowing rule [7].

$$
f = \begin{cases} 0 & t < t_0 \\ \dfrac{t - N}{drift\_time} & t_0 \le t \le drift\ time + t_0 \\ 1 & t > t_0 \end{cases}, \qquad (5)
$$

where, N is the number of time steps before the drift started to occur which is 1000 in these datasets and drifting time depending on speed, varied among 1, 250 and 500 time steps.

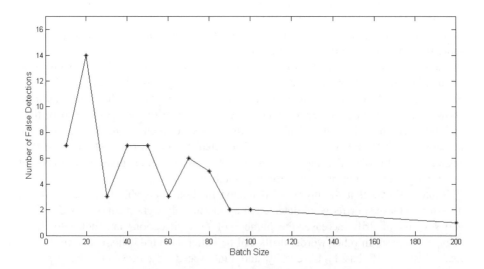

Fig. 1. The number of false detections of the proposed algorithm with respect to batch size

Table 1. Results of the experiments on artificial datasets, the * indicates the cases that the proposed algorithm outperforms Chu's method

Dataset	Properties	Delay of drift detection of our method	Delay of drift detection of Chu's method	Number of false detections of our method	Number of false detections of Chu's method
Line*	Low severity, High speed	100	100	0	1
Line	Low severity, Medium speed	200	200	1	0
Line*	Low severity, Low speed	200	300	1	1
Line	Medium severity, High speed	100	100	0	0
Line	Medium severity, Medium speed	200	200	0	0
Line	Medium severity, Low speed	200	200	0	0
Line	High severity, High speed	100	100	0	0
Line	High severity, Medium speed	100	100	0	0
Line	High severity, Low speed	200	200	0	0
Circle	Low severity, High speed	100	100	0	0
Circle	Low severity, Medium speed	200	200	0	0
Circle*	Low severity, Low speed	300	No drift	0	0
Circle*	Medium severity, High speed	100	100	0	2
Circle*	Medium severity, Medium speed	200	200	1	2
Circle*	Medium severity, Low speed	200	200	1	3
Circle*	High severity, High speed	100	100	2	3
Circle*	High severity, Medium speed	200	200	0	4
Circle*	High severity, Low speed	300	300	0	4
SineV	Low severity, High speed	100	100	0	0
SineV	Low severity, Medium speed	No drift	300	0	1
SineV*	Low severity, Low speed	400	400	0	2
SineV	Medium severity, High speed	100	100	2	1
SineV	Medium severity, Medium speed	100	200	2	0
SineV*	Medium severity, Low speed	200	200	0	1
SineV*	High severity, High speed	100	100	0	1
SineV	High severity, Medium speed	200	100	0	1
SineV*	High severity, Low speed	300	300	0	1
SineH*	Low severity, High speed	100	100	0	1
SineH	Low severity, Medium speed	No drift	No drift	0	0
SineH*	Low severity, Low speed	300	No drift	0	0
SineH*	Medium severity, High speed	100	100	0	2
SineH*	Medium severity, Medium speed	200	100	0	1
SineH*	Medium severity, Low speed	200	200	0	1
SineH*	High severity, High speed	100	100	0	1
SineH	High severity, Medium speed	200	100	0	0
SineH*	High severity, Low speed	200	200	0	1

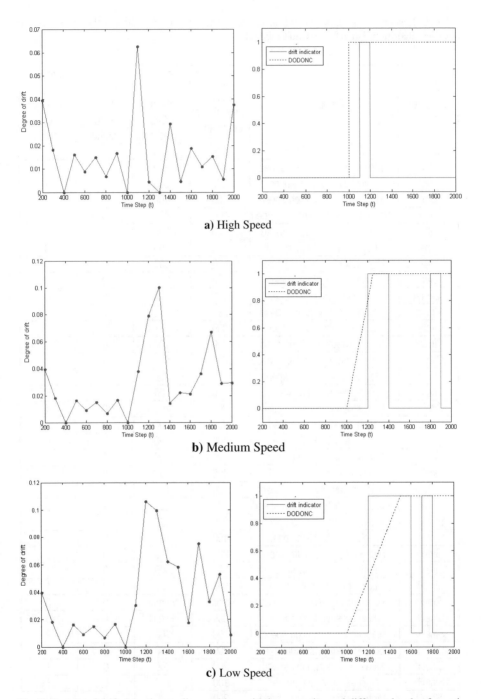

a) High Speed

b) Medium Speed

c) Low Speed

Fig. 2. Results of drift detection on line problem with low severity and different levels of speed

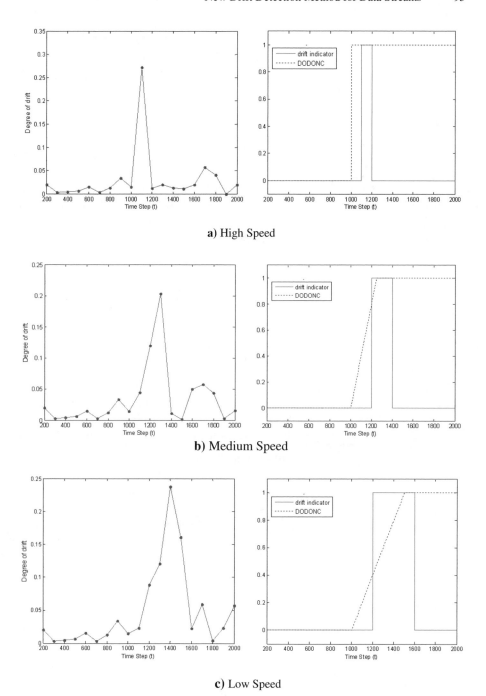

a) High Speed

b) Medium Speed

c) Low Speed

Fig. 3. Results of drift detection on line problem with medium severity and different levels of speed

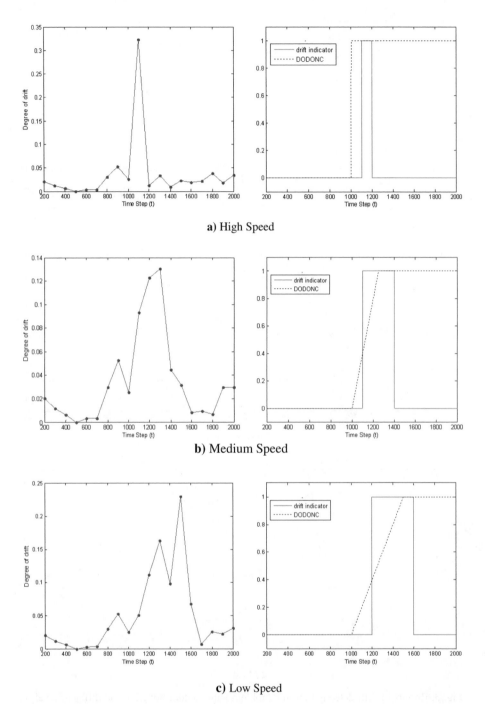

a) High Speed

b) Medium Speed

c) Low Speed

Fig. 4. Results of drift detection on line problem with high severity and different levels of speed

5 Conclusions

This paper introduced a new method for detecting concept drifts based on processing data chunk by chunk and measuring differences between two consecutive batches. Differences are calculated by finding nearest neighbor in previous batch of data for each instance in current batch and comparing their corresponding labels. The benefit of this approach, compared to the other methods, is that it can detect different types of drifts with varied speed and severity especially gradual concept drifts. In all experiments we have carried out, the proposed approach can find the drift location with very few exceptions. Artificial datasets that used here include four problems and nine instances of each problem with different levels of severity and speed of drift.

In future works, we intend to use this detection method for classification of data streams.

References

[1] Markou, M., Singh, S.: Novelty detection: A review, Part I: Statistical approaches. Signal Processing 83(12), 2481–2521 (2003)

[2] Kuncheva, L.I.: Classifier ensembles for detecting concept change in streaming data: Overview and perspectives. In: Proc. of the Second Workshop SUEMA, Patras, Greece, pp. 5–9 (2008)

[3] Gama, J., Medas, P., Castillo, G., Rodrigues, P.: Learning with drift detection. In: Bazzan, A.L.C., Labidi, S. (eds.) SBIA 2004. LNCS (LNAI), vol. 3171, pp. 286–295. Springer, Heidelberg (2004)

[4] Baena-Garcia, M., Del Campo-Avila, J., Fidalgo, R., Bifet, A.: Early drift detection method. In: Proc. of the 4th ECML PKDD International Workshop on Knowledge Discovery from Data Streams, Berlin, Germany, pp. 77–86 (2006)

[5] Wilson, D.R., Martinez, T.R.: Improved heterogeneous distance functions. Journal of Artificial Intelligence Research 6(1), 1–34 (1997)

[6] Nishida, K., Yamauchi, K.: Detecting concept drift using statistical testing. In: Corruble, V., Takeda, M., Suzuki, E. (eds.) DS 2007. LNCS (LNAI), vol. 4755, pp. 264–269. Springer, Heidelberg (2007)

[7] Minku, F.L., White, A., Yao, X.: The impact of diversity on on-line ensemble learning in the presence of concept drift. In: IEEE TKDE, vol. 22, pp. 730–742 (2010)

[8] Salganicoff, M.: Density-adaptive learning and forgetting. In: Proc. of the 10th Int. Conf. on Machine Learning, pp. 276–283 (1993)

[9] Klinkenberg, R., Joachims, T.: Detecting concept drift with support vector machines. In: Proc. of the 17th Int. Conf. on Machine Learning, pp. 487–494 (2000)

[10] Dries, A., Ruckert, U.: Adaptive concept drift detection. In: SDM, pp. 233–244. SIAM, Philadelphia (2009)

[11] Gama, J.: Knowledge discovery from data streams. Data Mining and Knowledge Discovery Series. USA (2010)

[12] Mitchell, T.M.: Machine Learning. McGraw-Hill, New York (1997)

[13] Chu, F., Zaniolo, C.: Fast and light boosting for adaptive mining of data streams. In: Dai, H., Srikant, R., Zhang, C. (eds.) PAKDD 2004. LNCS (LNAI), vol. 3056, pp. 282–292. Springer, Heidelberg (2004)

[14] Friedman, J.H., Rafsky, L.C.: Multivariate generalizations of the Wald-Wolfowitz and Smirnov two-sample tests. Annals of Statistics 7(4), 697–717 (1979)

Learning Curve in Concept Drift While Using Active Learning Paradigm

Bartosz Kurlej and Michał Woźniak

Department of Systems and Computer Networks, Faculty of Electronics
Wroclaw University of Technology
Wybrzeze Wyspianskiego 27, 50-370 Wrocław, Poland
{bartosz.kurlej,michal.wozniak}@pwr.wroc.pl

Abstract. Classification of evolving data stream requires adaptation during exploitation of algorithms to follow the changes in data. One of the approaches to provide the classifier the ability to adapt changes is usage of sliding window - learning on the basis of the newest data samples. Active learning is the paradigm in which algorithm decides on its own which data will be used as training samples; labels of only these samples need to be obtained and delivered as the learning material. This paper will investigate the error of classic sliding window algorithm and its active version, as well as its learning curve after sudden drift occurs. Two novel performance measures will be introduces and some of their features will be highlighted.

Keywords: machine learning, pattern recognition, concept drift, adaptation, active learning, sliding window, nearest neighbour, algorithm convergence.

1 Introduction and Related Works

Pattern recognition is one of the basic tasks met by humans. We face it since birth, we learn how to recognize parents look and sound, we taste food and distinguish flavours. We are recognizing different animals and are able to generalize and assign them to the spices apart from they unique features. Some of the concepts we are using are quite stable during the time (e.g. "cat") others change (e.g. "old man"). Nowadays we try to teach computers to perform this task.

These days amount of data provided every day to people, institutions or governments forces us to develop new methods or retrieving information from them. In order to achieve it we have developed machine learning algorithms that allow us to teach our computers to recognize offered incoming patterns. Today we have at our disposal many methods which provide effective solutions for problems with unchanged models. On the other hand, in a real situation. evolving data streams, so-called concept drift occurs frequently [13]. We need to deal with conditions that have different description in different time slots. The main areas of usage covers: security (spam filtering[4] and intrusion detecting system[9]), economics (market analysis[3], fraud detection[6]), robotics (DARPA Challenge[12], navigation system[10] or soccer robot player [8]) to enumerate only few.

A. Bouchachia (Ed.): ICAIS 2011, LNAI 6943, pp. 98–106, 2011.

The first attempts to formalize and handle this phenomenon started in the last century. The term *concept drift* was introduced in 1986 by Schlimmer and Granger along with STAGGER algorithm [11]. Other early algorithms are IB3[1] published in 1991 and FLORA[14] in 1996. From these papers the widely accepted taxonomy that divides the drifts to: sudden(abrupt), gradual, incremental and recurring context was proposed[13]. Three main sources of concept drift were defined as (1) changes of class prior probabilities, (2) change of one or several classes probability distribution (3) and changes of posterior distributions of class membership [7]. This work we considers an sudden concept drift caused by change of the classes probability distribution.

Despite the fact that *concept drift* has been investigated for some time, there is a lack of measures that allow to rate algorithms. Widely used mean classification error during classifier exploitation suffers from the fact of reliance on the drift frequency rate and in case of low, prefers the classifier that has worse convergence properties, but is slightly better between drifts. This paper aims to propose two additional measures of quality and show that results can be interpreted in different ways.

This paper is arranged as follows. In section 2 we provide formal description of problem. We develop and derive additional performance measures. Section 3 delivers description of active learning method, an alternative to reference sliding window algorithm. Description and scenario of experiments are enclosed in section 4. Section 5 contains evaluation of results that present performance of algorithm and mentions differences between measures. Finally, section 6 consist of final remarks and suggests further examination of the issue.

2   Problem Formalization

2.1   Classic Classification Problem

The aim of classic classification problem is to assign the object x described as a vector of features to one of predefined categories (classes) $i \in \mathbf{M} = \{1, ..., M\}$ on the basis of its features values [5]. In standard approach of supervised learning we provide training data in form of data samples with class label assigned to them. We aim to obtain the classifier, function that maps feature space X to class labels set $\mathbf{M}$.

$$\Psi : X \mapsto \mathbf{M} \tag{1}$$

Performance of these associations is measured by the loss function $L(i, j)$ that describes the loss incurred if object from class j is classified as class i. The right decision usually do not cause the loss so $L(i, i) = 0$. Common method of describing loss function is the loss matrix $\mathbf{L}_{i,j} = L(i, j)$. In this paper we consider only 0-1 loss function[5].

$$L(i, j) = \begin{cases} 0 & i = j \\ 1 & i \neq j \end{cases} \quad i, j \in \mathbf{M} \tag{2}$$

As the optimal classifier Ψ^* we assume the one for witch expected loss during exploitation time

$$\Psi^* = \mathrm{argmin}_{\Psi(\mathbf{x})}\mathbf{E}[L(\Psi(\mathbf{x}), class(\mathbf{x}))] \tag{3}$$

where $class(\mathbf{x})$ is the correct class of given $\mathbf{x}$ object.

2.2 Concept Drift

In many practical applications the model presented above cannot be applied because of dynamic nature of described phenomenon - it is time dependency. Our objective is to construct the model that will keep its quality by reflecting the changes in described form and be consistent with current data distribution. The feature space evolves, to reflect this in our model we have to make them time dependent. So now our objects are described as

$$\mathbf{x}(t) \in X(t)$$

our classifier changes also in the time, we denote it by Ψ_t. Our goal is to minimalize expected loss function of Ψ_{t-1} classifier on $X(t)$ object space.

2.3 Efficiency Measures

Traditional measure used in evaluation of classification efficiency is mean error (or mean loss if we use 0-1 loss function) of classification estimated in time of classifier exploitation . In each step error is equal to error of classifier obtained in previous step on current data:

$$error_\Psi(t) = \mathbf{E}[L(\Psi_{t-1}(\mathbf{x}), class(\mathbf{x}))] \tag{4}$$

Because conditions change in the time and in every time slot the classifier may obtain different performance, we use mean error (in time domain) as the measure. This indicator is described by following pattern:

$$error_\Psi = \mathbf{E}[error_\Psi(t)] \tag{5}$$

However in concept drift problem this measure does not describe time dependency of error after concept drift occurs. That is why we propose to introduce two additional measures Samples to Recovery (StR) as the number of samples that needs to be presented before the classifier reaches stable level of performance. To describe these measures we have to define *stable level* of - $error^*$ firstly. In this work we assume that *stable level* of error is the mean error $error_\Psi$ however in future this assumption should be investigated. StR needs additional parameter $\alpha > 1$ to indicate how close to *stable level* we want them to operate.

$$\mathtt{StR}_\alpha = min(t_0 : t_n^* < t, t_0 < t_{n+1}^* \text{ and } error(t) < \alpha * error^* \text{ for } t > t_0) \tag{6}$$

Additionally we propose to introduce measure that reflects the amount of information supplied to the classifier. We provide information by adding labels to presented samples therefore we called the additional measure Labels to Recovery (LtR).

$$\text{LtR}_\alpha = \sum_{t_n^*}^{t_n^*+\text{StR}_\alpha} l(x(t)) \text{ where } l(x(t)) = \begin{cases} 0 & \text{if } x(t) \text{ is not labelled} \\ 1 & \text{if } x(t) \text{ is labelled} \end{cases} \qquad (7)$$

3 Proposed Algorithms

We use classic sliding window method applied to Nearest Neighbour algorithm as the reference classifier. It uses the *windowSize* elements as reference set, when the new sample comes in it replaces the oldest one in the reference set. Active learning paradigm leads us to make some modification. Let's d_e and d_d be responsible for guarding the discriminant and exploration of new area of feature space. If incoming sample is close enough to discriminant line (distance to two respective samples in reference set from different classes is lower than d_d^*) or is not investigated part of feature space (distance to nearest sample in reference set is higher than d_e^*) then we propose to use it as a training sample and add it to our reference set (and remove from it the oldest sample - the one which was presented before anyone else in reference set).

4 Experiments

To investigate learning curve and present efficiency measures difference, we conducted the following experiments.

4.1 Scenario

At the beginning the classifier was trained with *windowSize* samples randomly chosen from the training dataset. The experiment was divided into 1000 "test and learn" steps. In each step the performance on the whole test set was evaluated and then one sample from training set was presented as the opportunity to adapt. Classic sliding window algorithm used all presented samples as training material, while active approach made the decision about usage on the basis of the sample features only. The above mentioned procedure was repeated 10 times for each dataset.

4.2 Datasets

The normalized iris and wine datasets from UCI[2] and the banana set were used as the benchmark databases. Number of classes, features and objects for each dataset is presented in Tab.1 (i.e. each feature was normalized). In order to simulate abrupt concept drift each dataset was rotated 90 degrees every 200 samples. The rotation was performed in the planes defined by randomly paired features, in every iteration of the experiment.

Table 1. Datasets description

dataset	# of features	# of classes	# of elements in classes
iris	4	3	50 50 50
wine	13	3	59 71 48
banana set	2	2	200 200

4.3 Classifiers

We used reference sliding window and Nearest Neighbour algorithm with the following parameters:

- k (number of neighbours) = 1 or 3
- $d_e^* = 0.2$
- $d_d^* = 1$.

4.4 Results

The mean error time line based on iteration in every step(learning curve) with global mean error(horizontal lines) are presented in Fig.1:

The closer look in time domain on single drift (iris dataset, *windowSize*=40) is presented on Fig.2.

The StR and StL measures for different α are presented in the Tab.2,3 and 4 (we use mean error over iteration as entry data for measuring StR and StL with $\alpha = 1$)

Table 2. Quality measures values for iris dataset

windowSize	active			classic		
	$error^*$	StR	LtR	$error^*$	StR	LtR
40	0.067	131.2	85.3	0.076	163.3	163.3
50	0.061	107.3	68.6	0.070	145.8	145.8
60	0.056	74.5	49.3	0.066	124.7	124.7
70	0.055	76.3	49.9	0.063	114.3	114.3
80	0.053	66.0	44.1	0.060	111.0	111.0
90	0.051	68.1	45.6	0.058	88.8	88.8
100	0.051	69.6	46.5	0.056	85.5	85.5

5   Evaluation of Results (conclusions)

In evidence of presented results it is clear that the measures used in experiment judge the classifiers differently. It is also believed that each of them has its own purpose:

- mean error is the most common quality measure used in machine learning
- StR is a measure that reflects convergence of classificator in the domain of samples, what usualy can be treated as time

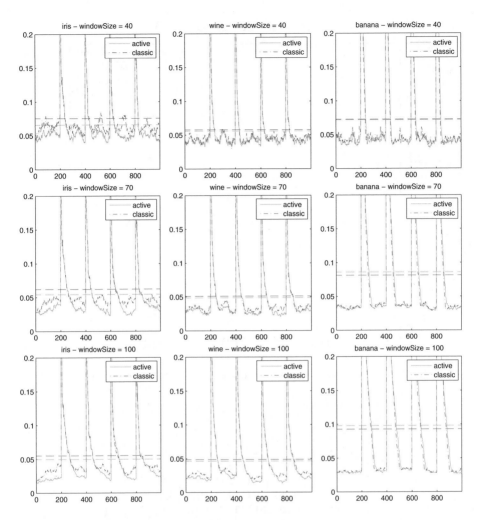

Fig. 1. Mean error of classification for datasets in each step, and global mean error

Table 3. Quality measures values for wine dataset

windowSize	active			classic		
	$error^*$	StR	LtR	$error^*$	StR	LtR
40	0.056	161.8	97.9	0.058	169.3	169.3
50	0.053	133.7	72.4	0.055	158.5	158.5
60	0.051	102.2	49.0	0.053	143.0	143.0
70	0.049	98.8	46.7	0.051	119.2	119.2
80	0.048	89.1	40.8	0.050	102.1	102.1
90	0.047	86.2	38.8	0.050	90.3	90.3
100	0.047	87.6	39.8	0.049	92.3	92.3

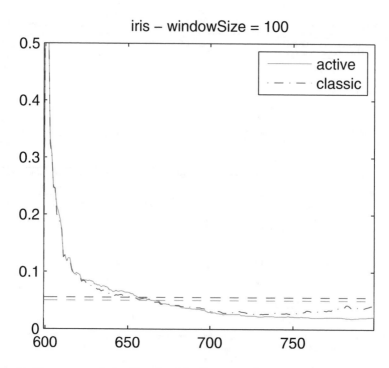

Fig. 2. Mean error of classification iris dataset - after second drift steps 599-799

Table 4. Quality measures values for banana dataset

	active			classic		
windowSize	$error^*$	StR	LtR	$error^*$	StR	LtR
40	0.074	72.8	59.3	0.073	115.4	115.4
50	0.077	61.6	52.7	0.075	73.6	73.6
60	0.081	55.5	49.6	0.078	59.1	59.1
70	0.086	61.5	54.9	0.082	56.8	56.8
80	0.090	67.6	60.9	0.085	63.1	63.1
90	0.094	73.9	66.8	0.089	68.7	68.7
100	0.098	78.7	71.0	0.093	73.8	73.8

– LtR is a measure appropriate for dealing with datastreams where aqusition of data is costless, because in this case labelling cost is the main part of overall learning costs

It can be observed that mean error is sensitive to overall classification performance, and slightly better result after reaching stable level of performance could have more influence on this measure than fast convergence of algorithm after drift has occurred (example on Fig.2). StR measure is the general purpose measure that can rate adaptive algorithms but it has to be parametrised therefore it needs widely accepted parameters standardization. It is also sensitive to different mean error level. LtR measure is appropriate only in a situation where data are available on demand, and drift does not depend of number of samples taken from data stream.

6   Final Remarks and Future Works

The properties of algorithms that deal with concept drift problem, could be pretty well presented on learning curve figures, but we are seeing the need of measures that will allow us to rate those algorithms. In our opinion today we do not have the proper tool to compare algorithms on statistics basis because our measures are sensitive to phenomena that are not concept drift related. Our future investigation will be aimed at improving presented measures and developing new ones, that will be devoid of influence phenomena which are not concept drift related.

Acknowledgement. This work is supported in part by The Ministry of Science and Higher Education under the grant which is realizing in the period 2010-2013.

References

1. Aha, D.W., Kibler, D., Albert, M.K.: Instance-based learning algorithms. Machine Learning 6, 37–66 (1991)
2. Asuncion, A., Newman, D.J.: UCI ML Repository. University of California, School of Information and Computer Science, Irvine, CA (2007),
   http://www.ics.uci.edu/~mlearn/MLRepository.html
3. Black, M.M., Hickey, R.J.: Classification of customer call data in the presence of concept drift and noise. In: Bustard, D.W., Liu, W., Sterritt, R. (eds.) Soft-Ware 2002. LNCS, vol. 2311, p. 74–87. Springer, Heidelberg (2002)
4. Delany, S., Cunningham, P., Tsymbal, A.: A comparison of ensemble and case-base main- tenance techniques for handling concept drift in spam filtering. In: Proc. of the 19th Int. Conf. on Artificial Intelligence. AAAI Press, Menlo Park (2006)
5. Duda, R.O., Hart, P.E., Stork, D.G.: Pattern Classification, 2nd edn. John Wiley & Sons, NY (2001)
6. Hilas, C.: Designing an expert system for fraud detection in private telecommuni- cations networks. Expert Syst. 36(9), 11559–11569 (2009)
7. Kelly, M., Hand, D., Adams, N.: The impact of changing populations on classifier performance. In: Proc. of the 5th ACM SIGKDD Int. Conf. on Knowledge discovery and data mining. ACM, New York (1999); Kurlej, B., Woźniak, M.: Active Learning Approach to Concept Drift Problem. Logic Journal of IGPL, Oxford Journals; doi: 10.1093/jigpal/JZR011 (in-press)
8. Lattner, A., Miene, A., Visser, U., Herzog, O.: Sequential pattern mining for situa- tion and behavior prediction in simulated robotic soccer. In: Bredenfeld, A., Jacoff, A., Noda, I., Takahashi, Y. (eds.) RoboCup 2005. LNCS (LNAI), vol. 4020, pp. 118–129. Springer, Heidelberg (2006)
9. Patcha, A., Park, J.: An overview of anomaly detection techniques: Existing solu- tions and latest technological trends. Comput. Netw. 51(12), 3448–3470 (2007)
10. Procopio, M., Mulligan, J., Grudic, G.: Learning terrain segmentation with classi- fier ensembles for autonomous robot navigation in unstructured environments. J. Field Robot. 26(2), 145–175 (2009)

11. Schlimmer, J., Granger, R.: Incremental learning from noisy data. Machine Learning 1(3), 317–354 (1986)
12. Thrun, S., et al.: Winning the DARPA Grand Challenge. Journal of Field Robotics 23(9), 661–692 (2006)
13. Tsymbal, A.: The problem of concept drift: definitions and related work, Technical Report TCD-CS-2004-15, Department of Computer Science, Trinity College Dublin (2004)
14. Widmer, G., Kubat, M.: Learning in the presence of concept drift and hidden contexts. Machine Learning 23(1), 69–101 (1996)

Utility-Based Self-adaption with Environment Specific Quality Models

Camilo Fitzgerald, Benjamin Klöpper*, and Shinichi Honiden

National Institute of Informatics, 2-1-2 Hitotsubashi, Chiyoda-ku, Tokyo, Japan

Abstract. In order to adjust to changing environments and internal states, self-adaptive systems are enabled to autonomously adjust their behaviour. The motive is to achieve better performance while minimising human effort in setting up and maintaining these systems. Ensuring correct functionality across a system's lifetime has been largely addressed. Optimisation of their performance, however, has received little attention. This paper presents an approach that applies goal modelling and decision making theory to calculate the quality of a system's performance in terms of a given configuration's utility with respect to its current environment. Thereby functionally valid configurations can be evaluated within the self-adaptive loop. The approach increased human players' performances in experiments based on a computer game. These results suggests that utility modelling is a promising approach for optimising the quality of behaviour in self-adaptive system.

Keywords: Self-adaptive Systems, Utility Theory, Goal Modelling, Decision Analysis.

1 Introduction

The principle motive for the new paradigm of self-adapting or self-managing software is the minimisation of human effort in setting up and maintaining software systems. To limit human participation in configuration and maintenance these systems are able to modify their behaviour in response to changing operational environments if their goals are currently not accomplished, or if better functionality and performance can be achieved [7]. If self-adaption is implemented through architectural reconfiguration then a good behaviour is equivalent to a good configuration of the system's components [16]. A self-adaptive software system must have the ability to answer the following two questions at runtime with minimal or no human interaction:

1. What is a good system configuration?
2. How to transform the current configuration into a good configuration?

While the second question is well researched, there is a lack of methodologies to enable software systems to evaluate their own performance and that of alternative configurations autonomously. In [6] we introduced a planning approach able

---

* Benjamin Klöpper is a visiting researcher and scholarship holder of the (DAAD).

A. Bouchachia (Ed.): ICAIS 2011, LNAI 6943, pp. 107–118, 2011.

to identify an optimal configuration for a specified system of physical computation nodes given utility information on alternative components. A similar approach is introduced in [21]. Both approaches do not fully define a methodology to model behavior quality, but instead rely on human entry of this information. Hence, regarding the previously defined two questions, systems based on these approaches are not entirely autonomous and self-adaptive.

2   Related Work

2.1   Self-adaptive Systems

When self-adaptation is implemented by architectural reconfiguration planning is often used to find a reconfiguration strategy for transforming the current configuration into a preferable one. Satzger et al. [18] introduced an automated planning approach for organic computing systems, but rely on users or administrators to specify goal state conditions which must be met in the final configuration. Nafz et al. [14], meanwhile, introduce the Organic Design Pattern (ODP) which can be used to identify configuration states. The ODP describes a number of constraints on functional valid configurations. Given the specific layout of a distributed computational system including nodes, communication channels and available resources a genetic algorithm [19] can be used to determine feasible configurations. The resulting validity of configurations, however, is described in terms of functional properties and qualitative aspects are not considered.

In an extension of their three layer architecture for self-managing systems [20] Kramer et al. [21] consider Quality Of Service (QoS) attributes. In this approach, the user specifies information about the technical QoS aspects of particular components, such as battery life or monetary costs. The user is not required to provide full and accurate information and the assembly process falls back onto arbitrary choices when it is not. In this way the approach avoids extensive and detailed design-time analysis which would need to be repeated every time a new component becomes available. To require the user to specify his preference regarding QoS attributes for the complete software system presents some drawbacks. First, the user requires an extensive technical understanding of the system. Second, accepting an incomplete definition of the constraints increases the risk of undesirable system behaviour. These two drawbacks conflict with the aims of self-adaptive systems - minimizing human effort in setting up and maintaining software systems.

2.2   Goal-Oriented Requirements Engineering

Goal-oriented requirements engineering (GORE) is an incremental approach to elicit, analyse and specify requirements of a software system to be [1]. A goal is defined as 'an objective the system under consideration should achieve' [9], and the goal's formulation describes the intended properties of the system that should be ensured. Thus, the term goal in requirements engineering has the character of a functional constraint. GORE approaches are rooted on *goal models* - structured hierarchical graphs in which goals are elicited by asking why and how questions. Not every goal has to be satisfied absolutely. To capture partial goal satisfaction methods for quantitative reasoning Letier et al. [10] added objective functions and quality variables to the goal model. Quality variables measure the extent to which goals are satisfied, while objective functions describe goal-related quantities to be maximized or minimized. Propagation rules are defined that propagate lower level objective functions up the goal hierarchy. Throughout the whole process, objective terms and their calculation remains on a technical level. This makes the comparison of objectives from different domains and different semantics difficult. The intention, however, is not to provide an integrated objective function, but to decide several objective functions used by the developer to analyse alternative system designs.

GORE has already been applied to self-adaptive systems. Moradini et al. [12] use GORE to develop self-adaptive systems based on the Belief-Desire-Intention engine JADEX [17]. KAOS goal modelling [8] is used by Nakagawa et al. to facilitate the extraction of multiple self-adaptive control loops [15]. KAOS is also applied by Cheng et al. [3] to develop the requirements of dynamically adaptive systems - a subclass of self-adaptive systems that switch between behavioural configurations in different environmental settings. These approaches, however, are limited to modelling functional objectives and runtime decision making is either not directly considered [3], or expressed in binary logic rule systems [12,15]. In the latter case fine-grained low-level rules must be defined precisely, which is extremely difficult given the complexities of real self-adaptive systems.

2.3 Multiple Attribute Utility Theory

Multiple attribute utility theory is an approach for eliciting a preference function or ranking for a multi-criteria decision problem [5]. A decision maker first defines a set of attributes relevant to the decision problem and assigns values to them for each alternative decision option. They then define monotonic utility functions for each attribute that convert their values into a common scale between the interval [0,1]. The results of these conversions are then aggregated into a final score describing the desirability of the option. Several methods exist for deriving the aggregation and utility functions [13].

The selection of the most suitable method for deriving a utility function depends largely on the nature of the attributes. Direct rating, for instance, is suitable for attributes without a commonly agreed scale of measurement. Direct assessment and piecewise linear functions, meanwhile, are most suitable if the attributes posses intuitive numerical scales of measurement [22].

The starting point for defining an aggregation function, meanwhile, is often a value tree where for each junction in the tree an aggregation operator is defined [5]. The simplest and most popular aggregation operator is weighted averaging [2], where weights are defined throughout the tree structure and propagated upwards. Another approach, non-additive measures, is based on a Choquet integral [11], which avoids the independence assumption of the weighted average method and considers interactions between attributes.

3   Utility Based Self-adaption

3.1   Quality in the Self-adaptive Control Loop

Self-adaptive systems often implement four actions in a *control loop* [16][4]: Sense, analyse, decide, and act. Figure 1 shows a self-adaptive loop that considers the quality of alternative configurations in the decision stage. One of the main questions regarding this *quality aware* self-adaptive loop is how available configurations can be evaluated or ranked to select an appropriate new configuration for the reconfiguration process. In this paper, we suggest the definition of an environmentally dependent utility function for this task.

Fig. 1. Self-Adaptive Control Loop

3.2   Defining the Utility Based Adaption Problem

In [6] a class of self-adaptive systems were introduced which the utility based adaption problem applies to. Essentially the system model encompasses a set of *tasks* that carry out system activities, and a set of *components* for each task that implement it. Each component offers a specific *performance level* when implementing a task and consumes certain number of *resources*. The possible configurations of a system are defined by the assignment components to tasks, with the constraint that the total number of resources consumed does not exceed the total available. A solution to the utility based adaption problem should provide a systematic method for calculating the utility of a given configuration in a specific environment, defined by a set of *environmental influences*. A planning approach can then be used to optimise the self-adaptive system's performance given a set of possible valid configurations.

We introduce some additional concepts to fully define the problem. A *quality variable*, from goal modelling literature [10], is a measurable physical attribute of a self-adaptive system measured in terms of a *quality level*. The distinction between tasks and quality variables allows us to reason about a configuration's effects on a self-adaptive system's behaviour, as opposed to the internal performance of its software. Finally, *effect functions* reflect the physics of a system by transforming performance levels into a decision relevant quality level.

3.3   The Self-adaptive Guardian Game

For our research we developed a demonstrator used in this paper as a running example, and later to validate our work. In the *Self-Adaptive Guardian*, a human or automated player controls a self-adaptive space ship with the goal of maximising their score during a given time period. 10 points can be earned by shooting UFOs with the ship's laser or picking up a human and returning it to the base. 20 points, meanwhile, are lost by allowing a UFO to abduct a human and drag it off the screen, or by loosing a ship.

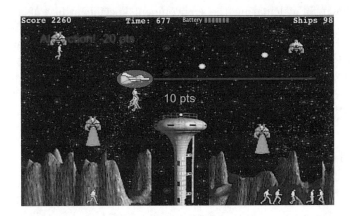

Fig. 2. Self-Adaptive Guardian: Gameplay

The gameplay environment can be altered via a set of environmental influence variables. These are the human spawn rate, the initial and maximum number of humans in play, the rate at which UFOs attempt to abduct humans, and the UFO bullet speed, fire rate and spawn rate.

The space ship implements a component-task model, Figure 3, and feasible adaptive configurations can be described by a number of constraints. In the

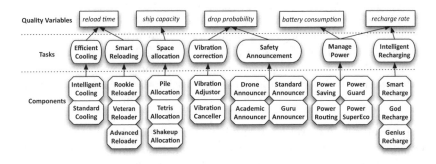

Fig. 3. Self-Adaptive Guardian: Component/Task Model

current version one constraint is implemented - the availability of a memory resource that can be used to install software components. Each component offers a trade-off between the resources it consumes and the performance it offers for implementing a specific task. Task performance levels modify the ship's usability by altering one or more quality variables in accordance with a set of effect functions.

4   Environment Specific Quality Modelling

Our approach for calculating the environment specific utility of a configuration applies goal-oriented design and multi-attribute utility theory, discussed in Sections 2.2 and 2.3. The designer first constructs a goal model defining the objectives of the self-adaptive system. They then choose a set of likely scenarios, and assign weights and utility functions to the goal model for each one. Finally, decision analysis is used to calculate how well alternative configurations satisfy the goal model for each scenario. That which provides the most satisfaction is selected as the configuration for the scenario in question.

4.1   Goal Model Design

A designer follows goal oriented analysis to construct a goal model - high level goals are identified and refined until measurable quality variables can be assigned to leaf nodes, or *requirements*. Two constraints are enforced on this model in our approach. There must be only one top level goal, who's level of satisfaction is used to calculate the overall utility of a configuration, and the satisfaction of all requirements must be measurable in terms of a single quality variable. The quality variables are ideally measured by the self-adaptive system, but can be composed from a set of task performance levels and corresponding effect functions. A goal model for the Self-Adaptive Guardian can be seen in Figure 4, where the quality variables for the requirements are shown in brackets.

4.2   Scenario Modelling

The designer identifies a set of scenarios spread across the range of typical environmental situations - assigning weights and utility functions to the goal model for each scenario by treating it as a multi-attribute utility problem. Figure 5 shows such an assignment for a partial section of the self-adaptive guardian goal model in a scenario where there are many humans and a low number of UFOs.

In the example utility functions are defined using *direct assessment*, in which the designer specifies an equation that fits the shape of utility function. For the maximise fire rate goal the reload time quality variable has been transformed into a goal satisfaction level by fitting it to a chi-square distribution function.

Weighted averaging was used to define the aggregation function that propagates satisfaction levels up the goal model. Relative weights are assigned to each set of child nodes adding up to 1. Preference has been given to the maximise rescues goal over its siblings as the scenario represented contains a high number of humans. The satisfaction of a parent goal is calculated by summing the products of each child's satisfaction level and their weight.

The time spent assigning weights and utility functions can be reduced. A technical designer can construct the goal model and assign a set of weights and utility functions that generalise the quality aspects in all situations. Then for each specific scenario the designer re-assigns weights for only the higher-level goals. This technique, although less precise, allows for situation specific utility models to be constructed in far less time. Further, users of the system can generate new scenario specific models without knowledge of underlying framework.

Modelling in this way allows a designer to calculate the scenario specific utility of a given configuration. The quality variables associated with the configuration are transformed into goal satisfaction levels by the utility functions and propagated up the goal model using the aggregation functions. The satisfaction level of the top goal is taken to be the configuration's utility for the modelled scenario.

4.3   Integration into the Self-adaptive Control Loop

Using our approach the utility of a specific configuration in a given scenario can be determined. Two questions remain if this functionality is to be integrated into the self-adaptive control loop. First, how to identify an optimal configuration, and second, how to map a set of environmental influences to a scenario.

Given a set of available components and constraints specifying a functionally correct configuration, the identification of an optimal configuration can be formulated as a discrete optimisation problem. In the limited application example of the self-adaptive guardian a random search strategy is acceptable. For more complex systems, however, a more sophisticated exploration of the search space may be necessary and could be accomplished using meta-heuristics, such as genetic algorithms or tabu-search.

There are two options for mapping an environmental situation to a scenario. If the set of possible situations is discrete and small enough then a designer can map

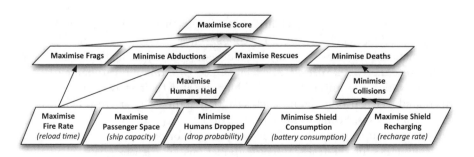

Fig. 4. Self-Adaptive Guardian: Goal Model

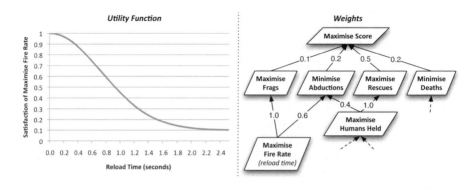

Fig. 5. Self-Adaptive Guardian: Scenario Specific Weights and Utility Functions

them directly. A continuous set of situations, however, will need to be grouped into sets, each mapped to a scenario. In essence, this resembles a clustering or classification problem. A system designer, for instance, could provide a training set on which a decision tree can be generated to perform this mapping.

5 Adaptation Experiments

We have validated our approach for calculating scenario specific configuration utility in the Self-Adaptive Guardian game. A first set of experiments was conducted using humans to play the game, and then a second with an autopilot we developed to behave in a similar fashion to that observed in humans. The questions we wished to answer were:

1. Can a designer create adaptive configurations that enable players of the game to get scores preferable that of a static configuration.
2. Under what circumstances are adaptive configurations preferable static ones?
3. How do the benefits of adaptive configurations vary for different types of runtime behaviour?

A game in the Self-Adaptive Guardian environment consisted of four environmental situations, each lasting 50 seconds. These were *normal*, in which the environmental influences are roughly balanced, *frenzy*, in which the UFO spawn and fire rate increases, *roswell*, in which the UFO abduction rate increases, and *rabbit*, in which the initial number of humans and their spawn rate increases. We created a scenario model for each situation and derived corresponding *adaptive configurations*. Scenario models were designed by creating a general model that we believed to generalise all situations, and for each scenario changing the relative weights for the frags, rescues, abductions and deaths goals.

As a baseline for the human experiments we picked the configuration that resulted from the normal scenario, as we believed this to be the optimal *static configuration* for playing the game. In the autopilot experiments, meanwhile, we were able get the autopilot to play non-stop and therefore obtain an additional static configuration baseline using brute force. 3000 random configurations were used to play the game. Those that achieved the top ten scores were then used to play 50 games each, and that which achieved the best average score selected as the baseline. This 'best possible' static configuration would in fact be difficult to estimate where brute force simulation is not possible, either due to a high level of system complexity or difficulties in accurate measurement of the top-level goal.

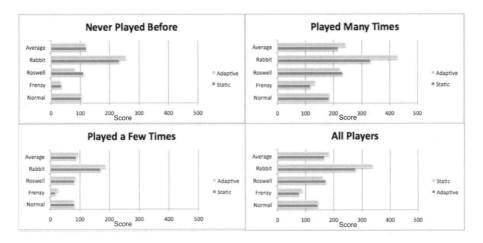

Fig. 6. Human Player Scores using Alternative Configuration Selection Strategies

In the human experiments, Figure 6, participants were asked to play the game once with the static configuration and once with the adaptive ones. The configuration they played with first was randomly selected to avoid bias in a player learning as they played the game. A questionnaire asking how many times they had played before was given to participants before they played. A total of 86 such experiments were conducted. In the autopilot experiments, Figure 7, the game was played using the adaptive configurations and the two static configurations 170 times each. In both sets of results the average scores in each situation for the different configurations are shown. The first three graphs in the human results subdivide the players into the number of times they had played before, and the last is the average of these results.

The significance of the human results, in which less games were played, was confirmed with a Chi-square homogeneity test for each situation. Player scores were grouped into a (0.2,0.4,0.6,0.8) quantile. The null hypothesis that the scores from the static and adaptive configurations are from identical probability distributions was rejected with 70% , 99,9%, and 99.9% probabilities for the frenzy, rabbit and roswell situations. In the normal situation where the configuration was identical the hypothesis was accepted with a probability of 99.9%.

In the human experiments greater improvements in score were observed for players with more experience playing the game. We suspect that this is due to

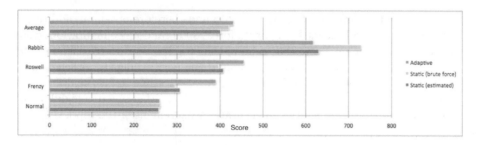

Fig. 7. Autopilot Scores using Alternative Configuration Selection Strategies

the fact that as a player gains experience their behaviour matches more closely that imaged by the scenario model designer, who was also an experienced player. This suggests that a designer needs a good knowledge of the system's run-time behaviour for our approach to be advantageous, and that moderate variations in this behaviour could lead to poor performance.

The average score decreased in the roswell situation for human players and in the rabbit situation for the autopilot. This further demonstrates the difficulties a designer has in estimating the weights and utility functions in accordance with system behaviour, as slight variations may cause the model for specific scenarios to be inaccurate. If, and only if, a specific scenario were found to perform poorly the designer could update the adaptive models.

In both human and autopilot games played using the adaptive approach, however, a significant increase in the average score over the baselines can be observed, showing promise for its usage in adaptive problems.

Further, the results of the autopilot experiment indicate that our self-adaptive approach may be more robust than simply identifying a best static configuration using the brute force method. It appears as though the brute force method has selected a configuration that works very well in the rabbit situation. This is likely due to the fact that a higher score is achievable in this situation than in the others, thereby maximising the average score achieved by the configuration across all scenarios. In a real environment the proportion of time spent in alternate situations may differ. If this were the case and less time was spent in the rabbit situation the adaptive system would not suffer the effects, while the average score of the brute force method would decline drastically.

6   Discussion

The approach described in this paper allows a designer to select a good, or even optimal, configuration from a large set of functionally feasible configurations in a changing environment. This problem has lacked attention in previous literature, which has been mainly concerned with functionally valid configurations [14,15,12]. Using this approach, therefore, adaptive configurations can be chosen that qualitatively optimise the behaviour of a software system, as opposed to simply guaranteeing that it will function. The improvements in score for adaptive configurations over the static baselines in the experiments on the self-adaptive guardian show promise for application of utility based self-adaption to optimise the performance of adaptive systems.

We have designed the approach with the flexibility and plugability of the component model in mind. Candidate components can easily be added or removed from self-adaptive system without altering the underlying models - the utility of a set of possible configurations is simply recalculated. This addresses a criticism of self-adaptive systems expressed in [21], which states that the static upfront design required in current approaches requires entire underlying models to be heavily transformed if architectural changes later take place.

Principle areas for further work concern both extended evaluation of the modelling process and the development of a complete utility-based self-adaptation loop. The results from the roswell situation with human players indicate that the average weighting assumption is not perfectly suited. In this situation both frags and rescues interact when determining the number of abductions. Thus, it would be interesting to redesign the scenario models with an aggregation function that omits the independence assumption. Further, experiments with different model designers would help to determine the effects of their domain knowledge on adaptive performance. Regarding the completion of the self-adaptive loop, the mapping of environmental situations to the most appropriate scenario model is an open research question. An investigation into how best to define scenarios that offer a good coverage of the possible situations that a self-adaptive system might encounter during its life-time would also be of interest. Finally, the purely reactive decision making that responds to current changes in the environment could be replaced with a more sophisticated look-ahead method, considering the costs of reconfiguration and resulting risks of performance loss.

Acknowledgment. The *Self-adaptive Guardian* is based on the open source engine JGame and the example game *Guardian* developed by Boris van Schooten. JGame can be downloaded under `http://www.13thmonkey.org/~boris/jgame/`.

References

1. Anwer, S., Ikram, N.: Goal oriented requirement engineering: A critical study of techniques. In: 13th Asia Pacific Software Engineering Conference (2006)
2. Belton, V., Stewart, T.J.: Multi-Criteria Decision Analysis - An Integrated Appraoch. Kluwer Academic Publishers, Dordrecht (2002)
3. Cheng, B.H.C., Sawyer, P., Bencomo, N., Whittle, J.: A goal-based modeling approach to develop requirements of an adaptive system with environmental uncertainity. In: ACM/IEEE 12th International Conference on Model Driven Engineering Languages and Systems (2009)
4. Dobson, S., Denazis, S., Fernández, A., Gaïti, D., Gelenbe, E., Massacci, F., Nixon, P., Saffre, F., Schmidt, N., Zambonelli, F.: A survey of autonomic communications. ACM Trans. Auton. Adapt. Syst. 1, 223–259 (2006)
5. Giove, S., Brancia, A., Satterstrom, F., Linkov, I.: Decision Support Systems and Environment: Role of MCDA. In: Decision Support Systems for Risk-Based Management of Contaminated Sites, pp. 1–21. Springer, Heidelberg (2009)

6. Klöpper, B., Meyer, J., Tichy, M., Honiden, S.: Planning with utilities and state trajectory constraints for self-healing in automotive systems. In: 4th IEEE International Conference on Self-Adaptive and Self-Organizing Systems (2010)
7. Laddaga, R.: Self adaptive software problems and projects. In: Second International IEEE Workshop on Software Evolvability, pp. 3–10 (2006)
8. van Lamsweerde, A.: Requirements engineering in the year 00: A research perspective. In: 22nd International Conference on Software Enginerring, pp. 5–19 (2000)
9. van Lamsweerde, A.: Goal-oriented requirements engineering: A guided tour. In: 5th IEEE International Symposium on Requirements Engineering, p. 249 (2001)
10. Letier, E., van Lamsweerde, A.: Reasoning about partial goal satisfaction for requirements and design engineering. In: 12th ACM SIGSOFT International Symposium on Foundations of Software Engineering, pp. 53–62 (2004)
11. Marichal, J.: Dependence between criteria and multiple criteria decision aid. In: 2nd International Workshop on Preference and Decisions (1998)
12. Moradini, M., Penserini, L., Perini, A.: Towards goal-oriented development of self-adaptive systems. In: SEAMS 2008, pp. 9–16 (2008)
13. Mustajoki, J., Hämäläinen, R.P.: Web-hipre: Global decision support by value tree and ahp analysis. INFOR 38, 208–220 (2000)
14. Nafz, F., Ortmeier, F., Seebach, H., Steghöfer, J.-P., Reif, W.: A universal self-organization mechanism for role-based organic computing systems. In: González Nieto, J., Reif, W., Wang, G., Indulska, J. (eds.) ATC 2009. LNCS, vol. 5586, pp. 17–31. Springer, Heidelberg (2009)
15. Nakagawa, H., Ohsuga, A., Honiden, S.: gocc: A configuration compiler for self-adaptive systems using gloal-oriented requirement descriptions. In: 6th International Symposium on Software Engineering for Adaptive and Self-Managing Systems (2011)
16. Oreizy, P., Gorlick, M.M., Taylor, R.N., Heimbigner, D., Johnson, G., Medvidovic, N., Quilici, A., Rosenblum, D.S., Wolf, A.L., Wolf, E.L.: An Architecture-Based Approach to Self-Adaptive Software. IEEE Intelligent Systems 14, 54–62 (1999)
17. Pokahr, A., Braubach, L., Lamersdorf, W.: Jadex: A bdi reasoning engine. Multi-Agent Programming 15(2), 149–174 (2005)
18. Satzger, B., Pietzowski, A., Trumler, W., Ungerer, T.: Using automated planning for trusted self-organising organic computing systems. In: Rong, C., Jaatun, M.G., Sandnes, F.E., Yang, L.T., Ma, J. (eds.) ATC 2008. LNCS, vol. 5060, pp. 60–72. Springer, Heidelberg (2008)
19. Siefert, F., Nafz, F., Seebach, H., Reif, W.: A genetic algorithm for self-optimization in safety-critical resource-flow systems. In: IEEE Symposium Series in Computational Intelligence 2011 (2010)
20. Sykes, D., Heaven, W., Magee, J., Kramer, J.: From goals to components: a combined approach to self-management. In: 2008 International Workshop on Software Engineering For Adaptive and Self-Managing Systems, pp. 1–8 (2008)
21. Sykes, D., Heaven, W., Magee, J., Kramer, J.: Exploiting non-functional preferences in architectural adaptation for self-managed systems. In: 2010 ACM Symposium on Applied Computing, pp. 431–438 (2010)
22. Von Winterfeldt, D., Edwards, W.: Decision Analysis and Behavioral Research. Cambrigde University Press, Cambridge (1986)

Self-adaptive Service Monitoring

Kassidy Clark, Martijn Warnier, and Frances M.T. Brazier

Faculty of Technology, Policy and Management
Delft University of Technology, The Netherlands
{K.P.Clark,M.E.Warnier,F.M.Brazier}@tudelft.nl

Abstract. Online marketplaces are emerging in which services are provided and consumed. Parties make online agreements regarding the terms and conditions of service provisioning. For certain kinds of services, it may be necessary to know whether it is being provisioned according to the agreement. To this end, the service may be monitored. For instance, a web application service may be monitored to guarantee that the response time of the application is within acceptable limits. The decision of whether or not to monitor a service is correlated to the perceived level of risk that a violation will occur. If there is a low level of perceived risk, monitoring may not be required, and vice versa. The perceived level of risk associated with a service transaction can change over time. However, traditional monitoring techniques are not able to react to this change. This paper proposes a self-adaptive service monitor that adapts to changes in the perceived level of risk. This monitor combines a traditional service monitor with a self-monitoring protocol, referred to as *passive monitoring*. This monitor is implemented in the AgentScape Middleware.

1 Introduction

Online marketplaces are emerging in which services are provided and consumed. In these marketplaces, parties can advertise, negotiate and purchase services. These services include access to hardware, such as storage or compute power and access to software, such as databases or other applications. Examples of such marketplaces include the Grid services market [2], the Web services market [4] and the Cloud services market [3].

Parties negotiate the terms and conditions of their services, including the price, Quality of Service and other service obligations. These terms and conditions are embodied in an agreement. This agreement also specifies what actions should be taken if any party violates the agreement. To know if, when and by whom an agreement is violated, services can be monitored. Relevant service metrics (e.g. response time) are measured at periodic intervals to offer assurance that a service is being provided as promised. These measurements are performed either by each party individually or by a separate monitoring service.

In some cases, a Trusted Third Party (TTP) is used as a separate monitoring service. The TTP offers additional assurance that measurements are performed impartially. Dependence on a separate monitoring service, such as a TTP, can

A. Bouchachia (Ed.): ICAIS 2011, LNAI 6943, pp. 119–130, 2011.
© Springer-Verlag Berlin Heidelberg 2011

be problematic. For instance, it may not always be preferable to give external parties access to local resources and (sensitive) data. However, monitoring services require this access to perform measurements. Moreover, monitoring services generate additional overhead costs (e.g. CPU, messages, and so forth). Furthermore, centralized monitoring services form an obstacle to the scalability of the marketplace. Reducing dependence on a separate monitoring service allows the system to scale better.

It might also be the case that parties do not feel that monitoring is always necessary. For instance, if the parties' past experience with one another has given them a high level of trust in each other, the perceived risk that there will be a violation is very low. In this case, monitoring just produces unnecessary overhead costs. Parties should be able to adjust the monitor. This makes it possible to reduce monitoring overhead when the perceived level of risk is low, and vice versa.

Monitoring systems and services in distributed environments is an area of ongoing research. Monitoring is used for Grid and Cloud environments to monitor a wide spectrum of metrics, from low-level hardware health to high-level service compliance [15]. Two of the most well known monitoring systems are Nagios [11] and Ganglia [9]. Both of these systems offer a wide range of configurable monitoring options, including the ability to modify the interval between measurements. However, these systems were not designed to adjust the level of monitoring dynamically or autonomously.

Some monitoring services are able to dynamically adapt their monitoring policy at run-time based on environmental limits or changes in priorities. For instance, the monitor proposed in [6] collects system notifications from distributed nodes and can dynamically adjust the frequency of the notifications, based on CPU load. The higher the load (e.g. more users in the system), the lower the frequency of notifications. Another example of a dynamic monitor is the adaptive system monitor described in [10]. This monitor attempts to reduce monitoring overhead by pre-selecting and focusing on key metrics. Only when an anomaly is detected in one of these key metrics, does the monitor adapt by increasing the number of related metrics that are continuously monitored. Effectively, this monitor is able to 'zoom in and out' of areas when problems are detected.

This paper proposes an alternative self-adaptive monitoring technique that reacts to changes in the perceived level of risk by dynamically adjusting the level of monitoring. This monitor combines a traditional monitoring service with a self-monitoring protocol, referred to as *passive monitoring* [7]. In addition to switching between these two modes, the self-adaptive monitor is able to decrease the frequency of measurements to decrease overhead, or increase the frequency to offer higher assurance.

The self-adaptive monitor proposed in this paper differs from the approaches discussed above in two major ways. First, in addition to reacting to changes in system overhead, the motivation to modify the monitoring policy is to dynamically adapt to the level of perceived risk as it changes during service provisioning. Secondly, rather than only adjusting the measurement interval, the monitor is able to switch between two major modes of monitoring: active and passive. In the passive mode, dependence on a separate monitoring service decreases. An effect of this reduced dependence is that the system is able to scale.

This paper is organized in the following way. Section 2 explains both traditional monitoring and the self-monitoring protocol, referred to as *passive monitoring*. Section 3 describes the proposed self-adaptive monitor in more detail. Section 4 presents the adaptation model used to determine when and how to adjust the monitor. This includes a more detailed explanation of the monitoring architecture. Section 5 evaluates an implementation of the self-adaptive monitor in the AgentScape Middleware. Finally, Section 6 concludes the paper.

2 Monitoring Techniques

Monitoring can be performed either by each individual party or by a separate monitoring service. Most traditional monitoring services periodically test various metrics to determine if the system is operating as expected [9,11]. This mode of monitoring is referred to in the remainder of this paper as *active monitoring*. Using this technique, an impartial monitoring service (e.g. TTP) takes measurements on behalf of the parties. If a violation is detected, the monitoring service can take action. Such action could be to cancel the service or penalize the offending party. The chosen action depends on the policy agreed upon by the parties during service negotiation.

An alternative to active monitoring is a *passive monitoring* [7]. When using passive monitoring, each party performs their own measurements. Therefore, this monitoring technique does not require or depend on a separate monitoring service. Essentially, passive monitoring uses cryptographic primitives to build a secure, non-repudiable audit log. Each party to the agreement must commit to add an entry to the audit log. For instance, all parties must be satisfied with the current level of service before an entry can be added. However, if one party is not satisfied, no entry is added. Therefore, this protocol is also referred to as a *mutual commit* monitoring protocol. This section contains a general overview of the protocol. The full protocol, including conflict mediation is detailed in [7].

Each party is responsible for local service measurements and no external monitoring service is used, such as a Trusted Third Party (TTP). Service provisioning is divided into discrete intervals. For provisioning to continue for the next interval, all parties of the agreement must agree that they are thus far satisfied with the service and have not detected any violations. Once all parties agree, a token (e.g. password) is exchanged. The token is cryptographically encrypted and signed to ensure that, once sent and received, no party can deny sending or receiving the token. These tokens are aggregated using other cryptographic primitives to form an audit log of compliance.

If no violations are detected, no intervention is needed. Tokens are exchanged directly between the parties, so no external monitoring services are required. This reduces the costs normally associated with interaction with a separate monitoring service. However, if a party detects a violation, conflict mediation must be performed. There are several possible ways to perform conflict mediation. In the simplest case, the service is immediately canceled. Another option is that the parties work together to examine the audit log to determine which party is responsible for the violation. Optionally, the examination of the audit log can also be performed by a TTP.

The conflict mediation process requires the audit log from each party, along with the last two messages from the interval in dispute. Using the non-repudiation properties of the messages, the last point can be established at which the parties were satisfied with the service. For example, if the service spans 10 intervals and the violation was detected in the last interval, any penalties are limited to the last interval. One possible result of conflict mediation can be to switch to active monitoring and continue the service. This is possible with self-adaptive monitoring.

3   Self-adaptive Monitoring

Monitoring offers assurance that violations are detected. Some service transactions require more assurance than others. The level of assurance required is a reflection of the perceived level of risk associated with the service. For instance, the importance of detecting a violation in a mission critical service is different from that of detecting a violation in a non-mission critical service. These violations ultimately have different levels of impact (e.g. financial, operational and so forth). Different services have different perceived levels of risk and therefore have different monitoring requirements. To this end, monitoring can be expressed in the 'amount' or 'level' of monitoring. In general, a high level of monitoring equates to frequent measurements of all relevant metrics. In contrast, a low level of monitoring equates to less frequent measurements of a subset of the metrics.

Furthermore, levels of trust and perceived risk between parties are not constant and can change during the course of their interactions. In this context, trust is defined as a combination of several metrics used in electronic markets [16,8,5]. These include personal metrics, such as transaction history, transaction cost and the ability to verify results. These also include community metrics, such as the popularity, activity and position of a party in the community. These metrics are dynamic in that they change over time. For instance, a successful transaction 10 years ago has less impact on the trust level than a successful transaction yesterday.

Reputation is also an important factor in determining trust levels. This is often the case when determining initial trust levels. For instance, reputation is used when a consumer chooses a service provider [13]. If the provider is well-known (e.g. Amazon Web Services), this increases the initial trust the consumer has and lowers the perceived risk of doing business. Once service provisioning has begun, a consumer dynamically adjusts the level of perceived risk based on the number of successful transactions and the size of transactions (e.g. 1 dollar versus 1000 dollars).

The first time two parties do business together, there is often a low level of trust and thus a high level of perceived risk. This has the effect that both parties may need a high level of assurance from monitoring and accept the extra costs it generates. As these parties interact with one another, they build a relationship based on their experience. If these experiences are bad, in that the parties fail to meet their agreement obligations, the level of trust remains low and perceived risk remains high. However, if these experiences are good, in that parties honor their obligations, the level of trust increases. As the level of trust increases, perceived risk and the need for monitoring decreases.

When using a separate monitoring service, such as [11,9], a single, static monitoring policy is used for the entire session that cannot reflect the dynamic changes in the levels of trust and perceived risk. However, changes in the level of perceived risk between parties can be immediately and directly reflected in the self-adaptive monitor. This is accomplished by dynamically switching between active and passive modes, as well as increasing or decreasing the measurement interval. In effect, these changes increase the level of assurance when needed, or reduce overhead and dependence on the TTP when possible.

4 Adaptation Model

The choice of which monitoring level to use for a particular transaction is based on a risk function. This function takes the current *risk level* and a *monitoring policy* and chooses an appropriate monitoring level. The monitoring level is expressed with the mode (e.g. active, passive) and the interval (e.g. time between measurements). Each party to an agreement executes this function before a transaction to determine which level of perceived risk applies, and therefore which level of monitoring is required. In the case that the levels of monitoring required by two or more parties differs, the highest level is used. This guarantees that all parties have at least the minimum level of assurance required.

This model is independent of the particular method used to compute a party's perceived risk level. An example of how the perceived risk level can be computed is illustrated below.

4.1 Risk Level

The first input to the adaptive monitoring function is the current perceived risk level. The perceived risk level is determined using both knowledge from the environment and local knowledge. Environmental knowledge can be a reputation authority, such as that proposed in [16], that offers additional information about a particular party, including their activity and popularity in the environment.

Local knowledge includes the price (or cost) of the current transaction and the history (if any) of transactions with the given party. These two variables are combined to form a matrix, similar to the trust matrix presented in [8]. The *transaction cost* of the current transaction and the *transaction history* correspond to a level of perceived risk. Essentially, the higher the cost of a transaction, the higher the perceived risk level. Conversely, the better the transaction history, the lower the perceived risk level.

Transaction cost is an artificial value that reflects the negative impact that would occur if a certain transaction were to fail (e.g. the other party violates the agreement). This value is derived by first mapping levels of transaction cost to ranges of actual price. For instance, for a particular party any transaction below 100 euro corresponds to a cost of 1. Whereas transactions between 100 and 200 euro correspond to a cost of 2 and so on. This mapping is specific to each individual party.

Transaction history is a value that reflects the level of satisfaction with a given party, based on past interactions with that party. The higher the number of successful interactions in the past, the higher the transaction history. This value also takes into consideration the effect of *information decay*, as discussed in [16]. In this context, this means that the recent transactions influence transaction history more than transactions that occurred long ago. Therefore, a weighting scheme is used to give more weight to the outcome of the most recent transaction and less weight to a transaction, the older it is.

4.2   Monitoring Policy

Each party maintains their own policy that specifies which monitoring mode and interval correspond to which level of perceived risk. For instance, for a particular party, an risk level of 1 may correspond to a low level of monitoring, such as passive mode with an interval of 90 seconds. Whereas an risk level of 10 may correspond to a high level of monitoring, such as active mode with an interval of 5 seconds. Each party's policy therefore specifies this mapping between the level of perceived risk and the level of monitoring.

Additionally, the policy specifies the particular weights that an agent attaches to each element of knowledge. Weights can be used to indicate how important an element of knowledge is based on its age or type. For instance, the 10 most recent transactions are more important than the rest. Weights are also used to indicate the importance of local knowledge (e.g. transaction history, transaction cost) and additional environmental knowledge (e.g. central reputation authority). The policy also contains a threshold to indicate how much the perceived risk level is able to change before the monitor is adapted. In effect, this number allows the monitor to react immediately to any change in perceived risk (e.g. paranoid) or assume that slight changes in the perceived risk level are anomalies and therefore react only if perceived risk consistently increases or decreases (e.g. optimistic). Finally, the policy contains additional information, including an optional name that describes the policy (e.g. optimistic, paranoid and so forth).

Two example policies are illustrated in Figure 1. The *Paranoid* policy has a low reaction threshold and thus quickly adapts the monitor to any changes in the risk level. This policy also gives a larger weight to the most recent 10 transactions. Furthermore, this policy is more sensitive to transaction cost than history. In contrast, the *Optimistic* policy has a higher reaction threshold and thus allows more variation in the perceived risk level before adapting the

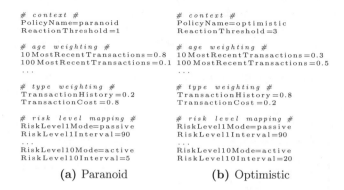

```
# context #                          # context #
PolicyName=paranoid                  PolicyName=optimistic
ReactionThreshold=1                  ReactionThreshold=3

# age weighting #                    # age weighting #
10MostRecentTransactions=0.8         10MostRecentTransactions=0.3
100MostRecentTransactions=0.1        100MostRecentTransactions=0.5
...                                  ...

# type weighting #                   # type weighting #
TransactionHistory=0.2               TransactionHistory=0.8
TransactionCost=0.8                  TransactionCost=0.2

# risk level mapping #               # risk level mapping #
RiskLevel1Mode=passive               RiskLevel1Mode=passive
RiskLevel1Interval=90                RiskLevel1Interval=90
...                                  ...
RiskLevel10Mode=active               RiskLevel10Mode=active
RiskLevel10Interval=5                RiskLevel10Interval=20
```

(a) Paranoid   (b) Optimistic

Fig. 1. Examples of (a) paranoid and (b) optimistic monitor policies

monitor. This policy balances the weight of the most recent transactions with older transactions. Furthermore, this policy considers the history of transactions more important than the cost of a particular transaction.

The policy allows each party to customize their monitoring needs, based on their individual perception of risk. The policy may also change over time. For instance, a party may choose a very paranoid policy when joining an online marketplace for the first time. After gaining experience in this marketplace, the party may choose to modify the policy to reflect the lessons learned (e.g. raise the threshold). In this regard, the self-adaptive monitor can also be manually adjusted, if necessary.

4.3   Monitoring Architecture

There are three main parties to a service agreement: the service provider, the service consumer and the service monitor. Each of these parties requires certain data depending on the monitoring mode: active or passive. Furthermore, communication patterns between parties differ depending on the current mode.

For active mode, shown in Figure 2a, the consumer and provider require only their unique Risk Level calculation and Monitoring Policy. The parties require no further monitoring data. The Service Monitor is responsible for performing measurements and checking for agreement violations. Therefore, this service must have access to the Agreement Terms, the Measurement Logic (e.g. which variables must be tested) and the Results of the measurements. All monitoring communication is initiated by the Service Monitor directly to each party individually.

In contrast, passive mode shifts the monitoring responsibility to the consumer and provider. In this mode, shown in Figure 2b, the Service Monitor requires no knowledge of the Agreement Terms or Measurement Logic. Furthermore, the Results (e.g. audit log) are no longer stored at the Service Monitor, but rather at each of the parties to the agreement. Additionally, the Agreement Terms,

Measurement Logic and Results are stored at each individual party, rather than at the Service Monitor. All monitoring communication goes directly between the Consumer and Provider. Only in the case of mediation do the parties optionally communicate with the Service Monitor to send the required audit logs.

The only extra data required are the Cryptographic Keys. These are used by each party to enable the mutual commit protocol and encrypt the audit log. The Service Monitor also maintains a set of keys to enable mediation in the case that a violation is detected.

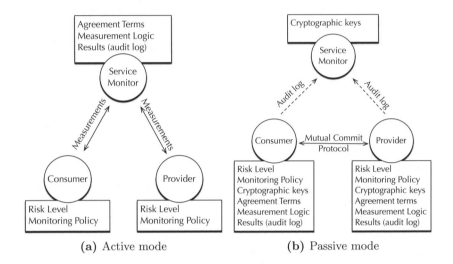

(a) Active mode   **(b)** Passive mode

Fig. 2. Data and communication of (a) active and (b) passive monitoring

5   Experimental Evaluation

The feasibility of the self-adaptive monitor is illustrated with an implementation. Several experiments are performed to compare the overhead of the active and passive modes. First, parties use a static active or a static passive monitor. Finally, parties use the self-adaptive monitor. Overhead is measured as the average CPU usage of monitoring activity.

The self-adaptive monitor is implemented in the AgentScape distributed middleware [12]. In this environment, Consumers, Producers and Monitors (TTP) are represented by self-contained, mobile software agents. This implementation performs asymmetric cryptography using the Rivest-Shamir-Adleman (RSA) [14] algorithm and the Boneh-Lynn-Shacham (BLS) [1] algorithm[1].

---

[1] The BLS implementation uses existing code provided by Dalia Khader and the Java Pairing Based Cryptography Library (jPBC) provided by Angelo de Caro (http://gas.dia.unisa.it/projects/jpbc/). Source code is available upon request.

Experiments run on two machines connected across gigabit ethernet. The first machine has a 2.0GHz dual core CPU and 1GB of RAM. The second machine has a 2.0GHz dual core CPU and 2GB of RAM. Both machines run the Linux operating system and AgentScape middleware. Two AgentScape Locations are used, one on each machine: *Location C* and *Location P*. Consumer agents are loaded into Location C and Producer agents into Location P.

5.1   Experimental Setup

Three experiments are performed in total: *Baseline A, Baseline P* and *Self-Adaptive*. The first two experiments compare the baseline CPU usage of each monitoring mode (active and passive) separately. The third experiment shows the changes in CPU usage as the monitor dynamically switches between intervals and modes. An overview of these experiments is shown in Table 1.

Table 1. Overview of experiments

Experiment	Monitor	# of Agents	Interval
Baseline A	Active	2	10
Baseline P	Passive	2	60
Self-Adaptive	Active & Passive	2	10,20,60,90

In *Baseline A*, a single consumer and a single provider negotiate an agreement that uses an active monitor with an interval of 10 seconds. In *Baseline P*, a single consumer and a single provider negotiate an agreement that uses a passive monitor with an interval of 60 seconds. No conflict mediation is performed during these experiments. Each baseline experiment is repeated 10 times and the CPU load results are averaged.

In *Self-Adaptive*, one consumer and one provider negotiate an agreement that begins with an active monitor with an interval of 10 seconds. Both parties use the same monitoring policy. This policy specifies that after 5 minutes without violations, the Risk Level decreases. This decrease is reflected in the monitoring level by increasing the interval to 20 seconds. After another 5 minutes without violations, the Risk Level decreases further. This decrease is reflected in the monitoring level by changing the mode to passive with an interval of 60 seconds. After another 5 minutes without violation, the Risk Level decreases further still. This decrease is reflected in the monitoring level by increasing the interval to 90 seconds. When a violation is detected, mediation is requested. The result of mediation is to increase the Risk Level. This increase is reflected in the monitoring level by returning to active mode with an interval of 10 seconds. The self-adaptive experiment is repeated 10 times and the CPU load results are averaged.

5.2   Experimental Results

The *Baseline* experiments, shown in Figure 3, demonstrate the contrast in CPU usage generated by the two different monitors. The active monitor has a consistent CPU usage baseline reflecting the 10 second monitoring interval. Usage peaks are relatively low, but occur often. This steady surge reflects the measurement request, execution, response and evaluation. The passive monitor also has a consistent CPU usage baseline reflecting the 60 second monitoring interval. Usage peaks are relatively high, when compared to the active monitor, but occur less frequently. This steady surge reflects the computationally intense cryptography that is used in the mutual commit monitoring protocol.

The *Self-Adaptive* experiment, shown in Figure 4, gives an overview of the self-adaptive monitoring process. In the active modes, the CPU usage has a consistent pattern reflecting the 10 and 20 second monitoring interval, respectively. In the passive modes, the CPU also has a consistent CPU usage that reflects the 60 and 90 second monitoring interval, respectively. A noticeable CPU usage surge occurs when conflict mediation is requested. This surge reflects the additional cryptography required to verify the messages and aggregate signatures used in the audit logs.

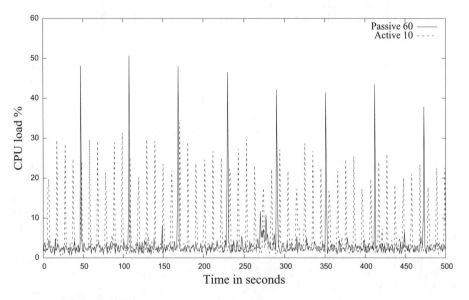

Fig. 3. CPU usage of active and passive monitor with two agents

5.3   Discussion of Results

In this implementation, it is difficult to compare the monitoring modes, due to the different results that they produce. The passive mode produces a cryptographically secured audit log, whereas the active mode produces an audit log

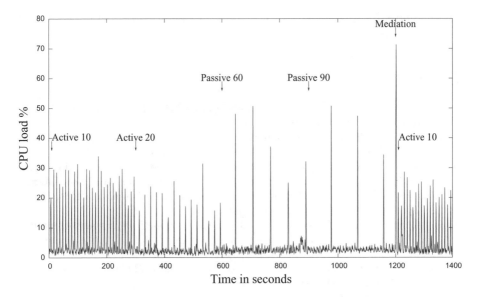

Fig. 4. CPU usage of self-adaptive monitor with two agents

without any cryptographic security. The cryptography used in passive monitoring increases the computational overhead[2] as can be seen in Figures 3 and 4. In these figures, it can be seen that the peaks in CPU load associated with the passive monitor are higher than those associated with the active monitor. To reduce the impact of this cryptographic overhead, a larger interval is used for the passive mode, in this implementation.

Figure 4 also shows the relatively high computation required for conflict mediation. This is also due to cryptography required to verify the data stored in the audit log. When mediation occurs often, it may present a significant load to system resources. Therefore, the frequency of conflict mediation may influence the choice of monitoring mode. This consideration can be included in the monitoring policy.

6   Conclusion

This paper proposes a self-adaptive monitor that reacts to changes in the level of perceived risk by adjusting the level of monitoring. This monitor can automatically switch between two modes, active and passive, and automatically adjust the polling interval for both. This paper demonstrates how the perceived level of risk can be calculated and how different monitoring policies can be applied.

Future work will examine the scalability of the self-adaptive monitor in a larger, distributed environment. Other trust mechanisms, such as reputation authorities, will also be incorporated to quantify the level of trust between parties.

---

[2] In particular, the BLS implementation is chosen only for its functionality. This code is not optimized for production level systems.

Acknowledgements. This work is a result of support provided by the NLnet Foundation (http://www.nlnet.nl).

References

1. Boneh, D., Lynn, B., Shacham, H.: Short signatures from the Weil pairing. Journal of Cryptology 17(4), 297–319 (2004)
2. Buyya, R., Vazhkudai, S.: Compute power market: Towards a market-oriented grid. In: ccgrid, p. 574. IEEE Computer Society, Los Alamitos (2001)
3. Buyya, R., Yeo, C., Venugopal, S.: Market-oriented cloud computing: Vision, hype, and reality for delivering it services as computing utilities. In: 10th IEEE International Conference on High Performance Computing and Communications, HPCC 2008, pp. 5–13. IEEE, Los Alamitos (2008)
4. Cheng, S., Chang, C., Zhang, L., Kim, T.: Towards competitive web service market. In: 11th IEEE International Workshop on Future Trends of Distributed Computing Systems, FTDCS 2007, pp. 213–219. IEEE, Los Alamitos (2007)
5. Hsu, C.: Dominant factors for online trust. In: International Conference on Cyberworlds 2008, pp. 165–172 (September 2008)
6. Keung, H., Dyson, J., Jarvis, S., Nudd, G.: Self-adaptive and self-optimising resource monitoring for dynamic grid environments. In: Galindo, F., Takizawa, M., Traunmüller, R. (eds.) DEXA 2004. LNCS, vol. 3180, pp. 689–693. Springer, Heidelberg (2004)
7. Khader, D., Padget, J., Warnier, M.: Reactive Monitoring of Service Level Agreements. In: Book chapter in CoreGRID Springer Series, pp. 13–23. Springer, Heidelberg (2010)
8. Manchala, D.: E-commerce trust metrics and models. IEEE Internet Computing 4(2), 36–44 (2000)
9. Massie, M., Chun, B., Culler, D.: The ganglia distributed monitoring system: design, implementation, and experience. Parallel Computing 30(7), 817–840 (2004)
10. Munawar, M., Ward, P.: Adaptive monitoring in enterprise software systems. Tackling Computer Systems Problems with Machine Learning, SysML (2006)
11. NagiosEnterprises: Nagios - the industry standard in it infrastructure monitoring (May 2011), http://nagios.org/
12. Overeinder, B.J., Brazier, F.M.T.: Scalable Middleware Environment for Agent-Based Internet Applications. In: Dongarra, J., Madsen, K., Waśniewski, J. (eds.) PARA 2004. LNCS, vol. 3732, pp. 675–679. Springer, Heidelberg (2006)
13. Resnick, P., Kuwabara, K., Zeckhauser, R., Friedman, E.: Reputation systems. Communications of the ACM 43(12), 45–48 (2000)
14. Rivest, R., Shamir, A., Adleman, L.: A method for obtaining digital signatures and public-key cryptosystems. Communications of the ACM 21(2), 120–126 (1978)
15. Sahai, A., Machiraju, V., Sayal, M., van Moorsel, A., Casati, F., Jin, L.: Automated SLA Monitoring for Web Services. In: Feridun, M., Kropf, P.G., Babin, G. (eds.) DSOM 2002. LNCS, vol. 2506, pp. 28–41. Springer, Heidelberg (2002)
16. Tajeddine, A., Kayssi, A., Chehab, A., Artail, H.: A comprehensive reputation-based trust model for distributed systems. In: Workshop of the 1st International Conference on Security and Privacy for Emerging Areas in Communication Networks, pp. 116–125 (September 2005)

Automatic Task Resolution and Adaptation in Pervasive Environments

Imen Ben Lahmar[1], Djamel Belaïd[1], Hamid Mukhtar[2], and Sami Chaudhary[1]

[1] Institut Telecom; Telecom SudParis, CNRS UMR SAMOVAR, Evry, France
{imen.ben_lahmar,djamel.belaid,sami.chaudhary}@it-sudparis.eu
[2] National University of Sciences and Technology, Islamabad, Pakistan
hamid.mukhtar@seecs.edu.pk

Abstract. Using a component-based approach, a user task can be defined as an assembly of abstract components (i.e. services), requiring services from and providing services to each other. To achieve the task's execution, it has to be resolved in concrete components, which involves automatic matching and selection of components across various devices. For this goal, we propose in this article a task resolution approach that allows for each service of a user task, the best selection of the device and component used for its execution. The task resolution approach considers in addition to the functional aspects of the task, the user preferences, devices capabilities, services requirements and components preferences.

Moreover, applications in pervasive environments are challenged by the dynamism of their execution environments. Towards this challenge, we use a monitoring mechanism to detect the changes of environments and we propose an adaptation approach that is based on the reselection of a subset of devices and components.

Keywords: Component-based task, resolution, monitoring, adaptation, pervasive environments.

1 Introduction

The recent research work related to automatic service composition in pervasive environments has gained much maturity. Emphasis has been on the automatic selection of services for users, without their intrusion, in the pervasive environment. In most cases, such an approach considers an abstract user task on the user device, which leads to automatic selection of services across various devices in the environment.

Using Service-Oriented Architecture (SOA), it is possible to describe a user task as an assembly of services (i.e. abstract components) without any information on how these services are implemented. The implementation of these services can be found by looking up concrete and deployed components in devices of the environment. A service is matched with a component if their interfaces match. A user task is said to be resolved if for all of its services, we find matching components implementing these services.

A. Bouchachia (Ed.): ICAIS 2011, LNAI 6943, pp. 131–144, 2011.

The complexities involved in resolving such applications have been addressed by many previous approaches. Most of existing approaches consider in addition to the functional aspects of services, some non-functional ones like quality of service (QoS), user preferences to achieve the task resolution [4] [6] [13] [12].

In [10], we have proposed an approach for devices selection that evaluates devices by considering the user preferences and devices capabilities. Given the evaluation results, services are assigned to devices starting from high to low device value. Thus, the evaluation function may result in the selection of more than one device, where each device may ensure a particular service in the user task.

However, services may also express their requirements towards the devices capabilities, which constraints the devices selection. Indeed, this selection approach does not guarantee that the selected devices may satisfy the services requirements since the devices ranking is done independently of services requirements. Thus, it is possible that a device with a lower device value may satisfy a requirement for a specific service better compared to a device with a higher value.

To achieve the task resolution, we require matching them with concrete components provided by the selected devices. Current task resolution approaches assign services arbitrarily to components provided by the environment [4] [10]. However, many components that implement the service functionality, may be found in the same selected device. Therefore, there is a need to a mechanism allowing the selection of the component that best matches the service's description.

Furthermore, users' tasks in pervasive environments are challenged by the dynamism of their execution environment due to, e.g., users and devices mobility, which make them subjects to unforeseen failures. Thus, there is a need to adapt the tasks to meet the detected changes.

The motivation for this article is two-folds: 1) selection of the best device and component for each service of the user task and 2) adaptation of a user task due to the changes of the execution environment.

The remainder of this paper is organized as follows. Section 2 defines the problems addressed in this paper, while Section 3 provides an overview of existing related work. Section 4 describes the non-functional requirements that are considered for our task resolution approach. In Section 5, we present the principle of the task resolution that is illustrated by an example scenario in section 6. In Section 7, we describe the principle of the task adaptation. Finally, Section 8 concludes the article with an overview of our future work.

2   Problem Description

We consider a video player task that provides the functionality of displaying video to the user. The task can be composed of three services (i.e. abstract components) namely, controlling, decoding and displaying video.

The resolution of services into respective concrete components is required for the realization of the task. We assume that a number of devices exist in the pervasive environment with different characteristics, ranging from small hand-held devices with limited capabilities, to powerful multimedia computers with abundant resources. These devices host one or more concrete components, which correspond to the services of the video player task.

For each service in the task, we may find one or more matching components across different devices; however, while these components offer similar functional interfaces, they may differ from each other in terms of the capabilities of the devices. Hence, a video player component on a smart phone is not considered the same as one on a flat screen. Therefore, there is a need of a mechanism for a dynamic selection of a particular device over the other, when they host the same components.

Moreover, it is possible that the selected device provides several components that implement the same service. For example, a laptop device provides a VLC player and Real player components that implements the same video display service. Thus, there is a need to carry out dynamically the selection of convenient components for the task resolution.

Furthermore, the task's execution is challenged by the dynamism of the execution environment due to the mobility of devices and users. This means that devices as well as components may appear and disappear in ad hoc manner, which may prevent the task to be well executed. Thus, there is a crucial need to select other components or devices to ensure a continuous execution.

3   Related Work

The task resolution and adaptation issues have been extensively studied in different contexts, notably in the area of software components that has become an accepted standard for building complex applications. In this section, we detail some of the existing related approaches as well as their limitations.

The Aura project defines an architecture that realizes user tasks in a transparent way [13]. The user tasks defined in Aura are composed of abstract services to be found in the environment. Gaia [12] is a distributed middleware infrastructure that enables the dynamic deployment and execution of software applications. In this middleware, an application is resolved in available resources of a specific active space. This resolution can be either assisted by the user or automatic. Gaia supports the dynamic reconfiguration of applications. For instance, it allows changing the composition of an application dynamically upon a user's request (e.g., the user may specify a new device providing a component that should replace a component currently used).

Both of the previous platforms introduce advanced middleware to ease the development of pervasive applications composed out of networked resources. However, they are too restrictive regarding the networked resources that may be integrated since resources have to host the specific middleware to be known by pervasive applications.

[6] provides a Dynamic Service Composition in Pervasive Computing mechanism to support context awareness for tasks composition at runtime. This mechanism implements a process for resolving an abstract specification to a concrete service composition. The proposed service composition mechanism

models services as directed attributed graphs. The hierarchical service composition mechanism based on a device overlay formed through the latch protocol. The basic principle of latching is that a device with lower resource availability latches itself to another device with higher resource availability. Thus, devices are structured as a tree that implies the device level.

While their approach is quite general, it has two limitations. First, the latch protocol compares the devices capabilities without considering the services requirements. Thus, a device with a low level may respond better to the services requirements than the device with a higher level. Second, the selection of components is done in arbitrarily way that they do not consider the selection of the best component among different alternatives.

The PCOM system [2] allows specification of distributed applications made up of components. Each component explicitly specifies its dependencies in a contract, which defines the functionality offered by the component and its requirements with respect to local resources and other components. The resulting application architecture is a tree formed by components and their dependencies. PCOM supports a component reselection whenever this later is no longer able to provide its functionality. With respect to the application model defined by PCOM, this means that a problem in a component is escalated to the next, i.e. higher, level of the tree. The escalation continues until a component resolves the conflict by reselecting components.

Thus, the replacement of a sub-tree starts from the predecessor of the component and may include its successors if it is necessary. However in our work, we ensure the reselection only of the concerned components. Moreover, they do not provide any mechanism that allows the selection of suitable component if there are others components providing the same service.

In [5], Ibrahim et al. propose a spontaneous Service Integration Middleware for pervasive Environment (MySIM) that allows the service composition based on semantic description of services. MySIM is split into four components: the Translator, the Generator, the Evaluator, and the Builder. The request descriptions are translated to a system comprehensible language in order to be used by the middleware. Once translated, the request specification is sent to the Generator that provides the needed functionalities by composing the available services. It tries to generate one or several composition plans with the same or different technology services available in the environment based on syntactic and semantic. The last step is to evaluate these plans to choose the best one based on QoS of services.

The major drawback of this approach is that the evaluator module does not consider the services requirements while composing services. Moreover, the adaptation of services composition consists on the revaluation of the composition plans for the whole task, while in our work, we are able to reselect only the concerned services.

The COCOA framework [4] supports the dynamic composition of abstract user tasks. User tasks are modeled as service conversations (or workflows), which are dynamically matched with the available networked service instances using a conversation based matching algorithm. Their solution builds on semantic Web services (OWL-S) to enable semantic matching of interfaces. Several service QoS properties are considered for service selection (e.g. performance, latency, etc).

In their approach, they claim to consider user preferences, but their treatment of user preferences is only nominal. Moreover, the COCOA framework permits the arbitrary selection of the resulting service composition as they all conform to the target user task.

In view of all these identified problems in the above cited works, we now propose our own approach that overcomes these problems.

4 Selection Constraints

Resolving a task corresponds to the selection of concrete components that best match with its services across various devices provided by the execution environment. In order to select the most promising components for the preferred devices for the user, we require considering some non-functional constraints like devices capabilities, user preferences, services requirements and components preferences. This ensures the resolution of user task on the distributed components. In the following, we describe each of these non-functional constraints.

Device Capabilities (DC). Considering the problem of having various devices capabilities that host a number of components providing the same functionality, it becomes practically impossible to choose one particular component on a specific device without considering the mentioned factors.

We addressed this problem by proposing an extension for CC/PP [7] device description model, which classifies a device capabilities into hardware, software and network categories [9]. All of the capabilities are either boolean or literal type, which can represent the device ability for a specific device capability. We use this extension to model the devices capabilities and we denote by 1 that the device is able to provide a specific capability and 0 if it could not.

Service Requirements (SR). Services in the user task may also describe their requirements for devices capabilities. These requirements may be specified by the application and they tailor the selection of devices to task resolution. In [10], we have proposed to model the services requirements by boolean or literal type, implying the ability of a device to respond to that requirement. If any of the required capability's value is false, the service cannot be executed on that device. Hence, this later is eliminated as the service requirements are not satisfied there. Thus, by introducing service requirements, we can reduce the solution space largely by decreasing the number of candidate devices.

User Preferences (UP). In [10], we have proposed a preference model that considers user preference as a real number ranging between (-1.0 , 1.0) values. Using 1.0 value represents a very important capability, thus, a device should provide that capability else it will be eliminated. The -1.0 value represents users dislike to avoid using a device with such a capability, whereas, the 0.0 value represents a do not care condition, i.e., the availability or unavailability of such a capability is not important for the user. Based on the user preferences, the user task will be executed on a set of devices for which maximum of their preferences are satisfied.

Components Preferences (CP). Components may express their preferences for the device capabilities in order to be executed properly. Compared to services requirements, we consider that the components preferences are concrete ones. For example, if the service requires some inputs, the component referring to that service may specify the input type like keyboard or touch screen, etc. Thus, there is a need to consider these preferences when selecting components. We propose to model components preferences using values that range between (0.0 , 1.0). The 1.0 value represents a very important capability that a device should provide. If a component does not have any preference, we assume that it does not care, and its value is 0.

5   Task Resolution

In [10], we presented an algorithm to select devices for the overall task by considering only the devices capabilities and user preferences. If the selected device has more than one component implementing the service, the algorithm does not provide any selection method for a component.

In this article, we propose an improvement for the previous algorithm to ensure the selection of the best device for each service of the task by considering the devices capabilities, user preferences and services requirements. Moreover, we propose a selection method of the best component by considering the devices capabilities and components preferences.

5.1   Device Selection

To select the devices used for the user task's resolution, we evaluate them as following:

$$CalculateDV = \sum \omega_i + Match(R_u, R_d) + \frac{I_s}{I_t} + \frac{D_s}{D_t} \qquad (1)$$

Given a capability c_i of a device and the user preference or dislike value v_i for the c_i, a weighted capability ω_i is calculated as:

$$\omega_i = \begin{cases} v_i & if \ c_i = 1 \ , \ -1 \leq v_i \leq 1 \\ -v_i & if \ c_i = 0 \ , \ -1 \leq v_i \leq 1 \end{cases}$$

The Match method returns a value representing the matching degree between the preferred screen resolution R_u and the effective screen resolution R_d of the device. The I_s/I_t ratio is used to calculate the number of preferred capabilities (i.e. I_s) satisfied among the total number of preferred capabilities (i.e. I_t). We consider also the number of disliked capabilities by subtracting the ratio D_s/D_t from the device value. The D_s denotes the number of disliked capabilities present on a device, while D_t denotes the total number of dislikes specified by the user.

We denote by CalculateDV(DC, UP) a value of a device calculated using the formula 1 for all of its capabilities. However, the CalculateDV(SR, DC, UP) represents a value of a device for a specific service that is calculated using the formula 1 by considering only the device capabilities(DC) and the user preferences (UP) related to the service requirements (SR).

Algorithm 1. DeviceSelection(Task, DevicesList)

1: ServicesList contains set of services in Task;
2: DevicesList contains list of devices;
3: **for** each service s in ServicesList **do**
4:     DevicesValues is used to store devices value for s
5:     **for** each device d in DevicesList **do**
6:         **if** fit(s, d) and fit(colocation(s), d) **then**
7:             **for** each service s' in $\{s, colocation(s)\}$ **do**
8:                 **if** $Requirement(s') \neq \oslash$ **then**
9:                     DV = DV + CalculateDV(SR, DC, UP)
10:                **else**
11:                    DV = DV + CalculateDV(DC, UP)
12:                **end if**
13:            **end for**
14:            store DV in DevicesValues
15:        **end if**
16:    **end for**
17:    sort DeviceValues
18:    select the device with the highest value for s and colocation(s)
19: **end for**

Algorithm 1 shows the main feature of the device selection process. A user task consists of a list of services to resolve in a set of components provided by devices of the execution environment. We consider the fitness constraint to indicate that a service is executable on a device using a fit() method (line 6) that returns true if the service is executable on the device, or false otherwise.

Moreover, two or more services may specify their colocation dependence on each other, which means that they must be executed on the same device. For this goal, the algorithm checks the fitness of the colocation services (i.e. colocation() method in line 6) to determine if they fit in the same device as the task's service.

To calculate the devices values for the service and its colocation, the algorithm uses the formula 1. If the service specifies some requirements (Requirement method in line 8), the device value is calculated using CalculateDV(SR, DC, UP) (line 9). Otherwise, the device value is calculated using CalculateDV(DC, UP) (line 11).

After that, it sums the device values calculated for the execution of the service and its colocations. The device with the highest value will be selected to fit a service and its colocations in.

5.2   Component Selection

Some selected devices may provide more than one component implementing the same service. Thus, there is a need to select a component that best matches the service's description. For this, we propose the Algorithm 2 that allows the selection of the convenient component for each service of the user task.

The Algorithm 2 evaluates components by considering their preferences towards the devices capabilities in order to select a component with a highest value. A component value is calculated as following:

$$CalculateCV = \sum \omega_i + \frac{I_s}{I_t} \qquad (2)$$

The ω is a weighted capability of a device that depends on the component's preferences. The I_s/I_t corresponds to the number of preferred capabilities (i.e. I_s) satisfied among the total number of preferred capabilities (i.e. I_t) of the component.

Algorithm 2. ComponentSelection(s, d)

1: ComponentsList contains list of components that match s and deployed on d;
2: ComponentsValues contains components values;
3: **for** each c in ComponentsList **do**
4:     CV=calculateCV(CP,DC)
5:     store CV in ComponentsValues
6: **end for**
7: sort ComponentsValues
8: select the component with the highest value for s

The Algorithm 2 uses the formula 2 to calculate components' values (line 4) by considering their preferences (CP) towards the device capabilities (DC). Then, the components values are sorted in order to select the component with the highest value. To achieve the task resolution, this algorithm will be executed in each selected device to select the convenient component for each service.

6   Example Scenario

Referring back to the video player task in the Section 2, we consider that the task is represented by an assembly of three services: a VideoDecoder, a VideoDisplay and a Controller services. The Controller service sends a command to the VideoDecoder service to decode a stored video into appropriate format. Once the video is decoded, it is passed to the VideoDisplay service to play it. Assume that the VideoDisplay service depends on the VideoDecoder one, thus they should be executed in the same device.

Table 1. Device capabilities and user preferences

Capabilities	SP	FS	User
Resource.Software.VideoPlayer=VLC	1	0	0.1
Resource.Hardware.Output.VideoCapable.Screen.Width	320	1920	1920
Resource.Hardware.Output.VideoCapable.Screen.Height	240	1200	1200
Resource.Hardware.Output.SoundCapable.InternalSpeaker	1	1	0.2
Resource.Hardware.Output.SoundCapable.ExternalSpeaker	1	1	1.0
Resource.Hardware.Input.Keyboard	1	0	0.1
Resource.Hardware.Input.TouchScreen	1	0	0.3
Resource.Hardware.Memory.MainMemory	1	1	0.0
Resource.Hardware.Memory.Disk	1	0	0.0

For the task execution, the services should be resolved in concrete components available in the execution environment. Consider that this later consists of a Smartphone (SP) and Flat-screen (FS) devices. Table 1 shows some capabilities of the two devices and their corresponding user preferences.

Table 2. Requirements of the Video player services

Service	Service Requirements
Controller	Resource.Hardware.Input
VideoDisplay	Resource.Hardware.Output.VideoCapable
	Resource.Hardware.Output.SoundCapable

Moreover, services may express their requirements towards the devices capabilities. For example in table 2, the VideoDisplay service requires an output VideoCapable and SoundCapable capabilities to achieve its execution, whereas, the Controller service requires an input capability to command the Video Player task.

We have evaluated FS and SP devices using the previous approach [10]. The SP device has a higher value (2.88) than the FS device (2.1). Thus, the SP device will be selected to resolve the video player task since it provides the requested components. However, it is not the best device regarding the user preference related to the screen size.

Table 3 shows the devices values calculated for each service and their colocation following the Algorithm 1. For this purpose, we have considered only the capabilities related to the services requirements and their user preferences. Compared to results of the previous algorithm, the Controller service will be executed in SP device, while the VideoDisplay and VideoDecoder services will be executed in FS device, which best satisfies the user preference (i.e. bigger screen size).

Table 3. Devices values for Controller and VideoDisplay services

Service	SP	FS	Selected device
Controller	1.4	-0,4	SP
VideoDisplay & VideoDecoder	5.2	5.3	FS

To achieve the service resolution, the Algorithm 2 is used to select the convenient component for each service of the video player task. In Table 4, we list the preferences of components provided by FS device. The VideoDisplay2 component requires a main memory to cache the video, whereas the VideoDisplay1 component is less interested in Disk memory than the Main one. These preferences is used by the Algorithm 2 for the selection of the suitable component.

Table 4. Preferences of video display components in FS device

Preference	VideoDisplay1	VideoDisplay2
FS.Hardware.Memory.MainMemory	0.8	1.0
FS.Hardware.Memory.Disk	0.2	0.0

Table 5 present the values of VideoDisplay components provided by FS device. The VideoDisplay2 component has a higher value than the VideoDisplay1 component. Thus, it will be selected for the execution of the VideoDisplay service. As it can be seen, our approach presents the advantage of selecting the best device and component for each service of the task.

Table 5. Selection of component for VideoDisplay Service

VideoDisplay1	VideoDisplay2	Selected Component
1.1	2.0	VideoDisplay2

7   Task Adaptation

Applications in pervasive environments are challenged by the dynamicity of their execution environments. In such situations, applications are subject to unforeseen changes due to users and devices mobility. Thus, there is a need to capture these changes and then adapt the user's task given the new situation.

7.1   Monitoring of the Execution Environment

A generalized notion of context has been proposed in [1] as *any information that can be used to characterize the situation of an entity (person, location, object, etc.).* We consider the adaptation context as any event that may trigger the adaptation of a user task in pervasive environments. These events may include the disappearance of a used device or the undeployment of a selected component. They may also involve the appearance of a new device or the deployment of a new component that may be interesting for task's execution. Moreover, the changes of user preferences or devices capabilities may affect the devices values thus triggering the adaptation of the user task.

To capture these adaptation events, there is a need to monitor the execution environment. Monitoring process consists in notifying the interested components in the changes of the environment.

For this purpose, we have considered that the environment is modeled as a set of components providing some properties through which they can be monitored. Similarly, a user can be modeled as a component exposing some properties referring to its preferences.

To monitor the changes of the properties of a component, we have used the monitoring framework in [3] that allows components to subscribe to the changes of local or remote components in order to be notified of their changes. Using this mechanism, it is possible to detect the changes of the user preferences and the devices capabilities components.

For the appearance and disappearance of devices, we propose to use a device discovery registry, which contains a list of all available devices in the environment. This registry receives notifications about the arrival and departures of devices by using for example the Universal Plug and Play (UPnP) technology.

Since the selection component Algorithm is executed in each selected device, we consider that this later provides a local components registry to list its provided components. Thus, it is possible to be aware of the deployment of new components or the undeployment of existing ones.

7.2   Adaptation Actions

The problem of adapting component-based applications has been extensively studied in different contexts. In the literature, we distinguish two main adaptive techniques: parametric or compositional adapatations [8]. Parameterization techniques aim at adjusting internal or global parameters in order to respond to changes in the environment. Compositional adaptation consists on replacing components implementation or the restructuring of the application without modifying its functional behaviour.

In this article, we propose a dynamic compositional adaptation approach that consists in resolving only the concerned services of a task since there may be cases in which all services or the devices are not affected by the context's changes. The adaptation corresponds to the reselection of some devices or components or to the both for a continuous execution of the task in the new context. It is achieved by the following adaptation actions.

Disappearance of a used device. One important event triggering the adaptation of a user task is the disappearance of a used device, which implies the disappearance of components used for the task execution. Towards this issue, we propose the selection of the subsequent device in the device list provided by Algorithm 1 to resolve the concerned services. For example, in the video player application, the FS device is used for the execution of the VideoDisplay and VideoDecoder service. If this device disappears, then the subsequent device, i.e. SP device, will be used to resolve the services.

Disappearance of a used component. In case of the disappearance of a used component from a selected device, we can keep the device if it has other components matching with the service. Thus, the subsequent component in a component list provided by the Algorithm 2, is selected. For example, if the VideoDisplay2 component of the FS device disappears, the VideoDisplay1 component will be used to fit the service with the FS device. However, if the device does not provide an alternative for the disappeared component, we require selecting the subsequent device in the device list provided by the Algorithm 1, to assign the service to one of its components.

Appearance of a new device. Another important event triggering the adaptation of a user task is the appearance of a new device whose capabilities may be interesting for the execution of a user task. Thus, there is a need to calculate its value for each service of the task to determine whether it has a higher value than the value of the used device. If it is, the new device will replace the already selected device to match the services with its provided components. Otherwise, there is no need to adapt the task. For example, during the execution of the video player task, a new laptop device appears. To determine the device usefulness, there is a need to calculate its value for each service of the user task. If it represents an interesting device for a specific service, it will be selected.

Appearance of a new component in a selected device. During the execution of a user task, a new component may be deployed on a selected device. This new component can be interesting for service execution. Thus, if it matches with a service of the task, we require calculating its value to decide whether it provides a highest value than the used component or not. For instance, assume that the FS device provides a new videoDisplay component. This later may trigger the adaptation of the task if it has a higher value than the value of the used VideoDisplay2 component.

Changes of a device capabilities or user preferences. For each service, we consider the changes of the user preferences and the device capabilities that are related to its requirements and that may induce the changes of the devices values. Thus, if the device is already in use and its value changes from higher to lower, then the subsequent device in the device list provided by Algorithm 1 is selected to resolve that service. However, if a device value becomes higher than the value of the used device, the service will be assigned to one of its matched component.

As it can be seen, our adaptation approach allows the reselection of partial devices and components to fulfill a continuous execution of tasks.

8   Conclusion

In this article, we propose algorithms that ensure for each service of a user task the selection of the best device and component for its execution. This is done by considering in addition to the functional behaviour of a task, some non-functional ones like user preferences, devices capabilities, services requirements and components preferences.

Moreover, we have handled some monitoring mechanisms to detect the events that may affect the services execution due to the dynamicity of pervasive environment. These events may range from the appearance and disappearance of devices/components to the changes of device capabilities or user preferences. To overcome these changes, we have proposed an adaptation approach that is based on the partial reselection of devices and components.

We have also implemented, as a proof of concept, a java prototype of task resolution and adaptation services. We have used SCA (Service Component Architecture) [11] to describe components since it provides the ability to write applications abstractly and then resolve them to the concrete components.

Further, we are looking forward to integrate these services with the monitoring framework of [3] before providing any evaluation results.

References

1. Abowd, G.D., Dey, A.K., Brown, P.J., Davies, N., Smith, M., Steggles, P.: Towards a better understanding of context and context-awareness. In: Gellersen, H.-W. (ed.) HUC 1999. LNCS, vol. 1707, pp. 304–307. Springer, Heidelberg (1999)
2. Becker, C., Handte, M., Schiele, G., Rothermel, K.: Pcom - a component system for pervasive computing. In: The Second Conference on Pervasive Computing and Communications, PerCom 2004, Orlando, FL, USA, pp. 67–76 (2004)
3. Belaïd, D., Ben Lahmar, I., Mukhtar, H.: A Framework for Monitoring and Reconfiguration of Components Using Dynamic Transformation. International Journal on Advances in Software 3(3), 371–384 (2010)
4. Ben Mokhtar, S., Georgantas, N., Issarny, V.: Cocoa: Conversation-based service composition in pervasive computing environments with qos support. Journal of System and Software 80(12), 1941–1955 (2007)
5. Ibrahim, N., Le Mouel, F., Frénot, S.: Mysim: a spontaneous service integration middleware for pervasive environments. In: The International Conference on Pervasive Services, ICPS 2009, London, United Kingdom, pp. 1–10 (2009)
6. Kalasapur, S., Kumar, M., Shirazi, B.A.: Dynamic service composition in pervasive computing. IEEE Transactions on Parallel and Distributed Systems 18, 907–918 (2007)
7. Kiss, C.: Composite Capability/Preference Profiles (CC/PP): Structure and Vocabularies 2.0. W3C Working Draft (April 30, 2007),
   http://www.w3.org/TR/2007/WD-CCPP-struct-vocab2-20070430/
8. McKinley, P.K., Sadjadi, S.M., Kasten, E.P., Cheng, B.H.C.: Composing adaptive software. Journal of IEEE Computer 37, 56–64 (2004)
9. Mukhtar, H., Belaïd, D., Bernard, G.: A model for resource specification in mobile services. In: The 3rd International Workshop on Services Integration in Pervasive Environments, SIPE 2008, Sorrento, Italy, pp. 37–42 (2008)

10. Mukhtar, H., Belaïd, D., Bernard, G.: User preferences-based automatic device selection for multimedia user tasks in pervasive environments. In: The 5th International Conference on Networking and Services, ICNS 2009, Valencia, Spain, pp. 43–48 (2009)
11. Open SOA Collaboration. Service component architecture (sca): Sca assembly model v1.00 specifications (2007), http://www.osoa.org/
12. Román, M., Campbell, R.H.: A middleware-based application framework for active space applications. In: Endler, M., Schmidt, D.C. (eds.) Middleware 2003. LNCS, vol. 2672, pp. 433–454. Springer, Heidelberg (2003)
13. Sousa, J.P., Garlan, D.: Aura: An architectural framework for user mobility in ubiquitous computing environments. In: The 3rd Working IEEE/IFIP Conference on Software Architecture, Montral, Canada, pp. 29–43 (2002)

Subsumption Architecture for Enabling Strategic Coordination of Robot Swarms in a Gaming Scenario

Anna Hristoskova, Enric Junqué de Fortuny, and Filip De Turck

Department of Information Technology, Ghent University - IBBT,
Gaston Crommenlaan 8 bus 201, 9050 Ghent, Belgium
{anna.hristoskova,filip.deturck}@intec.ugent.be,
enric.junquedefortuny@ugent.be

Abstract. The field of swarm robotics breaks away from traditional research by maximizing the performance of a group - swarm - of limited robots instead of optimizing the intelligence of a single robot. Similar to current-generation strategy video games, the player controls groups of units - squads - instead of the individual participants. These individuals are rather unintelligent robots, capable of little more than navigating and using their weapons. However, clever control of the squads of autonomous robots by the game players can make for intense, strategic matches.

The gaming framework presented in this article provides players with strategic coordination of robot squads. The developed swarm intelligence techniques break up complex squad commands into several commands for each robot using robot formations and path finding while avoiding obstacles. These algorithms are validated through a 'Capture the Flag' gaming scenario where a complex squad command is split up into several robot commands in a matter of milliseconds.

Keywords: Swarm robotics, Subsumption, Robot behaviours, Strategic control, Robot formations, Path finding.

1 Introduction

The increasing amount of robotics researchers and technology developers results in new innovations and opportunities attracting attention outside the factory. Korea is taking the lead in promoting the use of robots for service applications, such as elderly care. The United States employs robots to assist soldiers on the battlefield. Robots are manufacturing solar panels for European companies. Projects where robots collaborate to successfully complete tasks are becoming increasingly common. An indicator of this rise in interest is the growing number of challenges, leagues and participants of the RoboCup initiative [1,2]. It promotes robotics research by providing appealing scenarios such as robot soccer.

The idea of 'robot gaming' is not a new one. In the past, however, the application of this concept has been rather limited. Current robot games involve

A. Bouchachia (Ed.): ICAIS 2011, LNAI 6943, pp. 145–156, 2011.

individual robots fighting each other in a last-robot-standing competition. Others are actually robot building and programming competitions, rather than true games. In swarm robotics, the challenge is to solve problems by using numerous simple robots by maximizing the performance of the collective behaviour of the swarm. These robots run on limited hardware supporting basic behaviour limiting their AI. Few swarm robotic systems use small finite state machine as the core controlling mechanism of the individual robots. This is due to the fact that most of them are inspired by the behaviour of insects having limited intelligence.

This article presents a framework enabling game players with strategic control over robot squads. The player has access to a gaming interface managing the health and power of his robots and the coordination of the squads. A swarm intelligence component is distributed between the central framework and the individual robots supporting dynamic real-time autonomous robot movement, robot formations, path finding, sensor reading, event detection and obstacle avoidance. Novelty is the implemenation of a subsumption architecture supporting the swarm intelligence. It decomposes a complex squad behaviour into many basic robot behaviours which are organized into layers and activated based on priority. Validation of the proposed framework for a 'Capture the Flag' scenario shows that the swarm intelligence is able to split a single strategic squad command into several robot commands in 570 ms.

The remainder of the paper is structured as follows. Section 2 presents the current research in the field of swarm robotics. Section 3 elaborates on the developed framework with special attention on the swarm intelligence in Section 4. The swarm behaviour is evaluated for a gaming scenario in Section 5. Finally, the main conclusions and future improvements are drawn in Section 6.

2   Related Work

Platforms requiring the simultaneous achievement of complex tasks focus on techniques related to multi-robot coordination and task allocation. RoboSwarm [3] supports global behaviour through centralized robot orchestration consisting of task planning and allocation using bidding mechanisms between robots. The distributed approach of I-Swarm [4] is based on collective behaviours observable in honeybees. Instead of high-level robot-to-robot communication a network of weak robot-to-robot interactions (collisions) leads to specific spatial constellations that promote a collective decision. Another insect-inspired (ants) project is Swarm-bots where teams of robots overcome challenges such as object movement, path formation and hole avoidance by autonomously attaching to each other and moving around in coordination [5,6,7]. Though these s-bots do not talk among themselves, they receive low-level signals - such as individual push and pull forces - allowing coordinated group movement. The process of self-assembling is governed by the attraction and the repulsion among s-bots, and between s-bots and other objects. The successor to the Swarm-bots project, Swarmanoid, supports self-assembly through the training of artificial neural networks in order to transport an object [8]. The project focuses on the creation of three kinds of robots; eye-bots, hand-bots, and foot-bots. While the foot-bots move back and forth between a source and a target location, the eye-bots are deployed in stationary positions against the ceiling, with the goal of guiding the foot-bots [9].

In [10] the construction of a world model plays essential role for determining the positions of robot players on a soccer field, merging observations from vision, messages from teammates, and odometry information from motion. The position estimates are used by different behaviours to decide the robot's actions. These behaviours include skills (low-level robot abilities such as kicking the ball), tactics (behaviour of a single robot), and plays (coordination of the team) [11].

The framework in this article is based on the announce/listen metaphor, found in current routing protocols. A robot subscribes to and publishes messages on a specific topic/channel. Novelty is the implementation of a subsumption architecture decomposing a complicated swarm behaviour into many simple behaviours for each individual robot. It is based on the sliding autonomy [12] technique which enables humans to interact and take over control of a given subtask, while the rest of the system operates autonomously. Interventions include robots requesting help when a failure occurs or a user requesting robot assistance with some task. Studies show that sliding autonomy provides an increase in efficiency of 30-50% over teleoperation together with an increase in reliability of up to 13% over autonomous operation depending on the user's ability [13].

3   Framework Design and Implementation

The proposed framework should be able to adapt dynamically to changing number of robots, players and most importantly messages as communication is a key concept required for the intelligent coordination of robot swarms. Therefore a Publisher-Subscriber pattern extended with an Event Channel is developed, as presented in Figure 1. Eventing allows for a scalable architecture processing and forwarding events generated by the Game Client, robots, Game Logic and

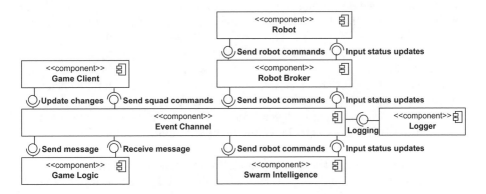

Fig. 1. Architecture of the publish-subscribe gaming framework showing the communication of the components through the Event Channel

Swarm Intelligence (all discussed in the following paragraphs). This results in a dynamic real-time control of the robot squads.

The Event Channel is responsible for the communication between the different components. As performance is a key issue ActiveMQ [14] is adopted which is designed for high performance clustering, client-server, and peer-based communication. It is an open sourced implementation of JMS 1.1 as part of J2EE 1.4 and supports a variety of cross language clients and protocols such as Java, C, C++, C#, Ruby, Perl, Python, PHP.

The Game Client connects the player to the game capturing and transmitting player actions (e.g. robot, squad and game configuration, chat sessions, strategic squad commands, status updates, monitoring messages, music) and visualizing the battlefield. This is supported by a PAC-pattern as a hierarchical structure of agents, each consisting of a triad of Presentation, Abstraction and Control. The agents are responsible for the players' actions communicating with each other through the Control. The Abstraction retrieves and processes the actions and the Presentation formats the visual and audio presentation of the battlefield.

The Game Logic sets up a game by connecting players with each other and with their robots. It manages the battlefield map, player and robot data, game settings and status, and player-squad communication through the realization of the player commands by the Swarm Intelligence. Several Game Logic modules can be connected to each other handling an increasing load of players and robots.

The Swarm Intelligence contains the AI of the framework, safe from the Robot Intelligence on the robots. It is presented in detail in Section 4.

The Robot has a layered design in Figure 2 keeping hardware dependencies local. The upper layer contains the Robot Intelligence, sensors and actuators. The Robot Intelligence acts as the "brain" of the robot interpreting orders from the Swarm Intelligence, gathering information from its sensors and deciding which sequence of actions has to be performed to execute the orders (detailed description provided in Section 4.4). The sensors and actuators control the robot's hardware. The Data Model prevents illegal robot operations by following the rules defined by the players at the start of the game. It controls the robot's vital parameters such as health, firepower, and provides the Robot Intelligence with a high-level abstraction of the robot's sensors, actuators and its communication interface. This Communication layer sends and receives messages and commands from and to other robots and the Game Logic through the Robot Broker.

The Logger monitors the game actions through the use of the open source program log4j [15]. It enables detection of conflicts and determines their source.

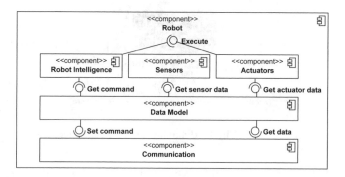

Fig. 2. The Layered Pattern of the Robot

4   Detailed View on the Robot and Swarm Intelligence

While designing the Swarm Intelligence two main resource-related obstacles arise when working with limited devices such as robots. On one hand it is undesirable to have a huge amount of state information on each robot due to limited memory and communication overhead. Furthermore, not all robots posses enough computational resources required to perform advanced swarm behaviours. Therefore the designed architecture employs the **sliding autonomy** principle that is split into two distinct parts working together: reflexive behaviours or simple commands reside on the robot itself (**Robot Intelligence**), whereas complex swarm coordination computations are 'outsourced' to the server (**Server-side Swarm Intelligence**). The outcome is an architecture where the amount of intelligence residing on the robots is adaptable to their hardware capabilities. Before discussing them in detail, we will first focus on a description of the subsumption principle and path finding in combination with robot formations.

4.1   Subsumption and Behavioural Layers

The core of the Robot and Swarm Intelligence is built using the **subsumption architecture** in Figure 3. Subsumption is a way of decomposing a complicated intelligent behaviour into many simple behavioural modules which in turn are organized into layers. An Arbitrator activates one and only one behaviour having the highest priority when a choice between several behaviours is presented.

The cooperating parts on the server (**Swarm Intelligence**) and on the robot (**Robot Intelligence**) consist of different behavioural layers, stacked on top of each other. A user can easily add a behaviour by implementing the provided interface and adding it to the Arbitrator who will then include the behaviour in the arbitration procedure. The following main behavioural layers are defined:

– *Squad behaviours* have the lowest priority and are usually sequences of commands, performed by a squad of robots as a group. They are always initiated by a player command and processed at the server.

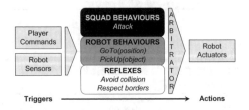

Fig. 3. Behavioural layers

- *Robot behaviours* consist of basic individual robot commands such as GoTo(x,y), PickUp(object) and are a resultant of squad behaviours.
- *Reflexes* have the highest priority. Examples include last-minute collision avoiding and staying within map boundaries.

4.2   Formations

A critical part in any robotics application is path finding. In the presented architecture, the A^*-algorithm[1] is adopted for swarm navigation on the battlefield. Swarm navigation coordinates a group of robots to get into and maintain a formation with a certain shape [16,17]. The Swarm Intelligence guides the robots into composing several formations depending on the situation at hand. The following are provided (Robot$_i$ with diameter d, number of robots n):

- Line (horizontal):

$$\text{Destination D} = (D_x, D_y)$$
$$\text{Robot}_{i,x} = D_x + d(i - \frac{n-1}{2})$$
$$\text{Robot}_{i,y} = D_y$$

- Circle for defending objects:

$$\text{Destination D} = (D_x, D_y)$$
$$\text{Radius R} = nd$$
$$\text{Robot}_{i,x} = D_x + R\cos\left(\frac{i\,360°}{n}\right)$$
$$\text{Robot}_{i,y} = D_y + R\sin\left(\frac{i\,360°}{n}\right)$$

- Half Circle for attacking enemy robots/squads:

$$\text{Destination D} = (D_x, D_y)$$
$$\text{Radius R} = nd$$
$$\text{Robot}_{i,x} = D_x + R\cos\left(\frac{i\,270°}{n}\right)$$
$$\text{Robot}_{i,y} = D_y + R\sin\left(\frac{i\,270°}{n}\right)$$

- (Inverse) Wedge: combination of two diagonal line formations.

---

[1] Source: http://www.gamegardens.com/

4.3   Server-Side Swarm Intelligence

During game flow a player orders a robot squad to execute a certain high-level command (e.g. "Attack!", "Defend the base!") through the Game Client. These commands are posted on the Event Channel and processed by the Swarm Intelligence on the server before being passed on to the respective squads. A *Squad Arbitrator*, which acts as a squad leader decision intelligence, activates the correct *Squad Behaviour*. This behaviour breaks down the high-level commands into *Robot Behaviours*, smaller *(Sequence)Commands*, for each individual squad member. The following main *Squad Behaviours* are defined:

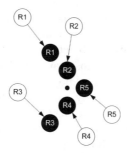

Fig. 4. Gathering robots in a wedge formation at a central point (black dot). Before gathering (white) and after gathering (black).

- *Gather:* The gather mechanism is presented in Figure 4. When a squad is initially created or is dispersed, the robots need to gather in their respective positions in a chosen formation. This is achieved by sending all robots to a central formation point. When no central point has been given, a centroid is calculated. Hereafter each robot is assigned a point in the final formation (based on minimal distance) and a path is calculated using the A^*-algorithm:
  1. $D(x, y)$ = central point.
  2. Calculate the best path $\mathcal{P}$ to $D(x, y)$ using A^*.
  3. Convert $\mathcal{P}$ into n turn-points $P_i(x_i, y_i)$.
  4. Create sequence of commands using the points from Step 3.

$$\text{SequenceCommand} = \{\text{GoTo}(x_1, y_1), \text{GoTo}(x_2, y_2), ..., \text{GoTo}(x_n, y_n)\}$$

  5. Send *SequenceCommand* to the robots.
- *GoTo(x,y):* moves a group of robots from their respective locations to the given coordinates. First the robots in the squad are gathered in formation. Following the path $\mathcal{P}$ is calculated for the squad as a whole since moving in a straight line could lead to collisions. The player can also define the given path using click and drag or just individual commands.
- *Defend(object):* consists of:
  1. Get object's coordinates as $P(x, y)$.
  2. GoTo(x, y) using circle or half-circle (moving object) formation.

- *Attack(object):* similarly to *Defend(object)* it consists of:
  1. Get object's coordinates as $P(x, y)$.
  2. GoTo(x, y) using half-circle formation.

  A problem that might occur is that targets will often be moving. This is solved by recalculating the path which is fairly efficient given that only the action-radius of the target object has to be taken into account. On receiving a movement of the target:
  1. Do a partial A^* on the battlefield map given the old data and the current position of the attacker.
  2. Update the old data entry on the map to the recent version.
  3. Send the new command to the robots.
- *Shoot(object):* is automatically done when an enemy robot is in range. The attacker 'shoots' at a preconfigured shooting rate with preconfigured damage. This damage is deducted from the enemy robot's health.
- *Avoiding Collisions:* For static objects on the battlefield map A^* is used to avoid collisions. Furthermore, close range collision prevention is covered in the robot (*Reflex Behaviour*). It is however important to realize the dangers of moving objects such as enemy robots. These are not accounted for in path-finding algorithms due to exponentially high complexity. A mitigation strategy of the *Squad Behaviour* is to check for inbound collisions in a specific range for each squad. Once a possible inbound collision has been found, the squad's path is adjusted (Figure 5).

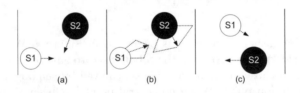

(a)   (b)   (c)

Fig. 5. Avoid collisions for dynamic objects Squad1 and Squad2; (a) a collision situation occurs, (b) mitigation vectors are calculated and commands are adjusted, (c) avoidance commands are performed, previous path is resumed

4.4 Robot Intelligence

The robot is where all behaviours resulting from the *Squad Behaviours* of the server-side Swarm Intelligence eventually end up. It also adopts the subsumption architecture consisting of *SequenceCommands*, *Commands* and *Reflexes*. *Reflexes* are instantly activated and always get control when required. The following in Table 1 are defined:

- *Avoiding collisions:* Although the server-side Swarm Intelligence calculates a big part of path-finding and collision avoidance some collisions could still occur. Therefore a basic collision behaviour for the individual robot is necessary in order to prevent any unwanted collisions or even possible damage.
- *Respecting borders:* Robots should not move beyond the gaming area or ignore physical map boundaries, such as water, while executing commands.

Table 1. Avoiding collisions and Respecting borders behaviours

Name	Avoid collision		Respect border
Trigger	Collision detected by the touch sensors (front and rear)	Object with $d(R, O) <$ d_{crit} detected by the sonar (viewing angle α)	Border-line detected by the infrared sensor (front)
Behaviour	Turn the robot 90° away from the point of contact.	Turn the robot 90° and move forward for a length of $d_{crit}\tan(\alpha)$.	Turn the robot 90° away from the border.

Commands (Table 2) received from the server-side Swarm Intelligence are performed on exactly one robot. They can be interrupted by *Reflexes* or overridden by new commands. There is always at most one command present in the robot. If a complex behaviour using multiple commands is required (e.g. Attack(object)), a *SequenceCommand* is used.

Table 2. Defined basic *Command behaviours*

Name	Command behaviour
Beep	Produces a short beep, useful for shooting at enemies and testing.
Rotate(α)	Rotates the robot over α-degrees.
GoTo(x,y)	Rotates the robot and moves it in a straight line to the given point.
Shoot(enemy)	Shoots at an enemy robot at a preconfigured shooting rate and damage.

5   Validation of the Swarm Intelligence

The implemented swarm gaming[2] framework is executed using Lego Mindstorms NXT [18], a robotics toolkit for building different robots. Building instructions for 4 main models (Shooterbot, Colour Sorter, Alpha Rex, Robogator) ranging in complexity are supplied. All measurements are performed on a DELL Latitude E5400 notebook with 2.40 GHz Intel Core 2 Duo, and 4 GB RAM.

During normal game flow the game and robots (health power based on budget, squad division, robot type: scout, tank, infantry, amphibian) are configured. Several scenarios, such as 'Capture the Flag' and 'Death Match', are executed depending on the players' preferences. Measurements of the Swarm Intelligence are performed on squad A of 3 robots capturing the flag of an enemy team B. Figure 6 displays the robot positions and path taken in wedge formation by the bottom Team A. Player A selects squad Team A and indicates flag B. Recognized as an enemy flag by the Swarm Intelligence, this results in an GoTo(flag B) squad command. The *Squad Behaviour* breaks the command up into several (in this case 10 GoTo and a PickUp(flag B)) robot commands, *Sequence Command*, for the 3 robots. The robots are gathered in wedge formation and a path is calculated for the squad. The water and border obstacles are avoided both during squad

---

[2] http://ciri.be/blog/?p=234

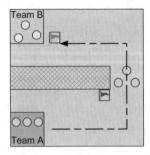

Fig. 6. 'Capture the Flag' battlefield including a water obstacle between the two teams

path calculation and individual robot navigation. Results in Table 3 show the performance of the different architectural components between the assignment of the strategic order by the player and sending the separate commands to the robots. As expected the main bottleneck is the Swarm Intelligence where the path finding for each robot in the squad is calculated. While the average execution time ($\bar{x}$) out of 20 measurements is 570 ms, the standard deviation (σ) is quite large (109 ms) due to the large variation displayed by the arbitration procedure of the subsumption loop checking the different behavioural priorities.

Table 3. Swarm Intelligence performance for a player command sent to a squad

ms	Player → SI	Swarm Intelligence	SI → Robot Squad
$\bar{x}$	9	570	7
σ	3	109	6
Min	6	365	2
Max	15	756	24

Scalability of the Swarm and Robot Intelligence subsumption functionality is measured for a squad of 3 robots moving in line formation. A *Squad* GoTo(x,y) command is sent at different intervals ranging from 100 to 5000 ms. The average out of 10 measurements is presented for each interval in Table 4. In order to optimize the path finding algorithm the Swarm Intelligence waits for 300 ms before processing the player commands. This results in longer execution time for short intervals (100 and 250 ms) as more information is computed. Due to the possible recalculations of the Swarm Intelligence and consistency reasons, the Robot Intelligence considers only the last received command for execution by the robot as mentioned in Section 4.4 keeping the processing time stable.

Table 4. Scalability of the Swarm and Robot Intelligence subsumption framework

Interval(ms)	100	250	500	750	1000	1500	2000	2500	5000
Swarm Intelligence(ms)	1059	740	362	270	375	173	182	314	190
Robot Intelligence(ms)	629	696	603	657	500	627	597	587	551

The average Round Trip Time (RTT) in Table 5 for the physical NXT robots is measured when sending 100 messages between PC to NXT while an overloading thread constantly calculates the product of 2 random 10x10 matrices to simulate other calculations on the robot. Results show delays of up to 2 seconds.

Table 5. Round Trip Time from PC to NXT and back in ms

(ms)	Number of bytes sent			
# overloading threads	140	200	240	300
5	1007	1014	1293	1388
10	1034	1162	1516	1640
15	1176	1324	1732	1898
20	1326	1607	2042	2240

6 Conclusion

This article presents a swarm-intelligent framework achieving meaningful behaviour at swarm-level, instead of the individual robot-level. Keeping in mind the physical robot squads, the designed framework decomposes strategic player commands into individual robot actions using a layered subsumption architecture. Validation through a 'Capture the Flag' scenario shows that a squad command is split up into several robot commands in a matter of 570 ms.

In the future the robots will be enriched with semantics enabling dynamic discovery of their capabilities. This will result on one hand in run-time planning and assignment of tasks depending on the available robot functionality and on the other in automatic distributed interactions between the robots and their environment enabling seamless communication with devices such as sensors, computers, and cameras.

Acknowledgments. A. Hristoskova would like to thank the Special Research Fund of Ghent University (BOF) for financial support through her PhD grant.

References

1. RoboCup, http://www.robocup.org/
2. Gabel, T., Riedmiller, M.: On Progress in RoboCup: The Simulation League Showcase. In: Ruiz-del-Solar, J. (ed.) RoboCup 2010. LNCS, vol. 6556, pp. 36–47. Springer, Heidelberg (2010)
3. Mokarizadeh, S., Grosso, A., Matskin, M., Kungas, P., Haseeb, A.: Applying Semantic Web Service Composition for Action Planning in Multi-robot Systems. In: Fourth International Conference on Internet and Web Applications and Services (ICIW 2009), pp. 370–376. IEEE Press, Italy (2009)
4. Schmickl, T., Thenius, R., Moeslinger, C., Radspieler, G., Kernbach, S., Szymanski, M., Crailsheim, K.: Get in touch: cooperative decision making based on robot-to-robot collisions. In: Autonomous Agents and Multi-Agent Systems, vol. 18(1), pp. 133–155. Springer, Heidelberg (2009)

5. Groß, R., Bonani, M., Mondada, F., Dorigo, M.: Autonomous self-assembly in swarm-bots. In: IEEE Transactions on Robotics, vol. 22(6), pp. 1115–1130. IEEE Press, Los Alamitos (2006)
6. Trianni, V., Nolfi, S., Dorigo, M.: Cooperative hole avoidance in a swarm-bot. In: Robotics and Autonomous Systems, vol. 54(2), pp. 97–103. Elsevier, Amsterdam (2006)
7. Nouyan, S., Dorigo, M.: Chain based path formation in swarms of robots. In: Dorigo, M., Gambardella, L.M., Birattari, M., Martinoli, A., Poli, R., Stützle, T. (eds.) ANTS 2006. LNCS, vol. 4150, pp. 120–131. Springer, Heidelberg (2006)
8. Groß, R., Dorigo, M.: Towards group transport by swarms of robots. International Journal of Bio-Inspired Computation 1(1-2), 1–13 (2009)
9. Ducatelle, F., Di Caro, G.A., Gambardella, L.M.: Cooperative self-organization in a heterogeneous swarm robotic system. In: 12th Annual Conference on Genetic and Evolutionary Computation Conference (GECCO), pp. 87–94 (2010)
10. Coltin, B., Liemhetcharat, S., Meriçli, C., Tay, J., Veloso, M.: Multi-Humanoid World Modeling in Standard Platform Robot Soccer. In: 10th IEEE-RAS International Conference on Humanoid Robots, USA (2010)
11. Browning, B., Bruce, J., Bowling, M., Veloso, M.: STP: Skills, tactics, and plays for multi-robot control in adversarial environments. IEEE Journal of Control and Systems Engineering 219, 33–52 (2005)
12. Dias, M., Kannan, B., Browning, B., Jones, E., Argall, B., Dias, M., Zinck, M., Veloso, M., Stentz, A.: Sliding autonomy for peer-to-peer human-robot teams. In: 10th Intelligent Conference on Intelligent Autonomous Systems (IAS 2008), Germany, pp. 332–341 (2008)
13. Turgut, A.E., Çelikkanat, H., Gökçe, F., Şahin, E.: Self-organized flocking in mobile robot swarms. In: Swarm Intelligence, vol. 2(2), pp. 97–120. Springer, Heidelberg (2008)
14. ActiveMQ, http://activemq.apache.org/
15. Apache log4j, http://logging.apache.org/log4j/
16. Rampinelli, V.T.L., Brandao, A.S., Martins, F.N., Sarcinelli-Filho, M., Carelli, R.: A multi-layer control scheme for multi-robot formations with obstacle avoidance. In: International Conference on Advanced Robotics (ICAR 2009), pp. 1–6. IEEE Press, Germany (2009)
17. Gamage, G.W., Mann, G., Gosine, R.G.: Formation control of multiple nonholonomic mobile robots via dynamic feedback linearization. In: International Conference on Advanced Robotics (ICAR 2009), pp. 1–6. IEEE Press, Germany (2009)
18. Lego Mindstorms NXT, http://mindstorms.lego.com/

Runtime Generation of Robot Control Code from Ontology File

Yuri Gavshin and Jevgeni Shumik

Tallinn University of Technology, Centre for Biorobotics,
Akadeemia tee 15a-111, 12618 Tallinn, Estonia
{yury,jevgeni}@biorobotics.ttu.ee
http://www.biorobotics.ttu.ee

Abstract. This paper provides an initial implementation of the novel module to transform OWL-S ontology into executable robot control code. We explore the idea of formalizing robot behavior descriptions using Semantic Web knowledge representation. The paper describes the methodology and implementation details of the robot control code generator to translate ontology file descriptions to a compilable Java code, as well as the robot control framework to execute the code at run-time.

We validate our approach with the experiment, conducted on Sctios G5 robot. The task "follow the red object" is translated into a working Java code from OWL-S ontology file. The generated Java code is compiled and executed at run-time. As a result, the robot is following the person with a red folder in his hands.

1 Introduction

Robots are entering our lives by moving from industrial environments and research laboratories closer to humans. Initially, robots were physical machines inside factories and worked in isolation. Now the robots are helping us every day – some household robots, like autonomous vacuum cleaners and lawnmowers became mainstream products. It is possible to buy them in a big electronics store or make an order over the Internet.

These robots, however, are fairly simple and lack the ability to be taught externally by user or by means of the Internet. Currently robots are programmed with a control code, which was developed, optimized and tweaked by software developers and engineers. Such straight-forward approach in teaching robot behaviors is fairly sufficient for simple single-purpose robots, like lawnmowers and vacuum cleaners.

However, the latest statistical report in [1] shows that a multi-purpose robot-assistant is the vision for the future. New software capabilities are needed in order to develop more complex work patterns and interactions between working robots and to provide adaptive and learning features. As the power of on-board computers for autonomous robots is growing, it became possible to install complex software architectures on robots and have them connected to the Internet.

A. Bouchachia (Ed.): ICAIS 2011, LNAI 6943, pp. 157–167, 2011.

A natural learning possibility is needed to teach robots new tasks and behaviors. People should be able to teach robots similar to the way parents teach children. The way children learn in schools – by reading books – is also very attractive.

However, it means that a human should be able to teach robots using abstract means and descriptions. The Internet may become a perfect learning territory for robots and robotic services if the information on the Web would be fittingly formalized.

The Semantic Web technology provides a good opportunity to store information in the Internet in a well-structured machine-readable form. World is partially at Web 2.0 now and is moving towards 3.0, where usage of Semantic Web will grow. It is strategically important now to connect the robot software development with the Internet and Semantic Web technologies. Semantic Web is understandable for machines, humans may understand semantic web through visualization and analysis graphical user interfaces, like web pages.

Many projects contribute to creation of ontology files describing objects in Semantic Web formats, for example [2], [3], [4]. Semantic Web is also being used in composition with robots. The term Semantic Robot Space is being introduced by [5], where sensor information is mapped to high-level Semantic Web representation to provide high-level reasoning and state identification and to decide which actions to perform on physical robot.

The Semantic Agent Programming Language (S-APL) that integrates the semantic description of the domain resources with the semantic prescription of the agents behavior is introduced in [6]. It uses pre-programmed Reusable Atomic Actions in Java language, deployed on a robot. Which atomic action to execute is decided by their semantic reasoning engine.

Another example is the reasoning engine Gandalf, which is used to derive sequences of robot actions from Semantic Web structured knowledge [7]. In [8] the web services are deployed on each robot engine and executed by Web Service Modeling Execution Environment (WSMX). A similar approach can be found in [9] and [10] where knowledge represented by ontology files is used to automatically compose robot action plans. The plans are composed of a sequence of calls to predefined web services deployed on a robot.

The initiatives described above operate on an upper level of knowledge representation and reasoning. Lower-level robot control code consists of predefined program in C/C++ or Java programming language, used directly or thorough web-services. In other words, existing approaches use Semantic Web directly or generating some sort of rules in simpler form to change robot behavior.

In contrast to the aforementioned approaches, we generate new control code from Semantic Web descriptions and change the code at run-time. Behaviors are described in OWL-S format [11] in such a way, that Java code can be generated from them using the developed *OntologyParser* component.

To test our approach, we set up a simple experiment with a real Scitos G5 robot. The task is to follow a red object; control code is sent to robot in OWL-S format, robot parses it, generates Java code and executes it. The task consists of data read operations (distance and bearing of the object), data manipulation operations and command execution operation to rotate or move the robot.

Data manipulation operations can be described by a simple set of instructions – rotate to keep object directly in front, then stay close, but not too close. Such instructions are translated into lower-level ones – hold the value of object bearing near 0, then hold the value of distance between 1 and 3 meters. As a result, the robot successfully follows the red object in hands of the person conducting the experiment.

Next section explains in detail our approach to generate Java code from the ontology file. Section 3 describes the robot control framework, used to compile and execute the generated code at run-time. In section 4 the experimental setup with implementation details are presented. Section 5 describes and discusses results of the experiment. The last section contains conclusions and directions for future work.

2 Code Generation from Ontology

2.1 Semantic Web Description Specifications

The Semantic Web is a web of data that machines can understand. It contains various technologies and specifications to represent data. A very important technology is a Resource Definition Framework(RDF), which offers a base vocabulary to describe objects in the Internet. It is based upon the idea of making statements about objects in the form of triplets – subject-predicate-object expressions – a very flexible way to describe object properties. Another advantage is the possibility to refer to one object description inside another object description, which gives an excellent opportunity to reuse already defined objects.

However, there is not enough vocabulary in RDF to describe complex properties. To overcome this problem the RDF extensions like Web Ontology Language (OWL), RDF Schema (RDFS), Friend Of A Friend (FOAF), etc. were made. Vocabularies stated above can describe various objects, but can not describe behaviors or actions.

The OWL-S (Web Ontology Language for web Services) specification is an extension of the OWL vocabulary and offers an opportunity to describe program workflow. Although it is initially meant for web services, it can also describe robot control code.

2.2 The OntologyParser

In our approach we use the OWL-S specification to describe robot behavior. The robot control code can be described in form of triplets using the OWL-S, then a valid Java code can be generated from triplets. The *OntologyParser* software component was written to take an OWL-S structured ontology file as an input, parse it and output the generated code. To make ontology parsing easier, the Jena framework [12], written in Java, has been used. Jena creates the in-memory model from ontology file and then the *OntologyParser* uses Jena API methods to query for the resources and properties in the model.

The *OntologyParser* architecture is similar to a Servant software design pattern – it has a number of "parse" methods each handling its own property or resource. When the desired resource or property is found in the model, *OntologyParser* calls the corresponding method and the block of code is generated as a result. The generated block of code is then appended to a resulting program string; it is also possible to output a list of separate generated program strings from a single ontology file. Such architecture is very simple and intuitive because each method knows which resource or property it parses and which resources and properties will go next and what to do with them. The methods may call each other several times until they reach the end of the ontology file ladder and then return in the LIFO order. The generated code can then be sent to the framework that controls the robot.

2.3   OntologyParser Methods

Every method name of OntologyParser starts from the word "parse" and continues with the name of the resource it parses. Methods have two input parameters:

- *Resource* – the Jena Resource object instance.
- *StringBuilder* – the global string program object, that is passed to all "parse" methods, each appending its own pieces of code.

The following OWL-S specification resources and properties are parsed and transformed into Java code: ControlConstructList, parseComposedOf, IfThenElse, Else, HasDataFrom, HasOutput, ParameterType, Perform, Process, RepeatWhile, Sequence, TheVar, ValueData.

Below are described the additional properties and resources defined under the *xmlns* : *pahpam* namespace to serve OntologyParser specific needs:

- pahpam:AtomicProcessCode – an extension of process:AtomicProcess to describe atomic processes that contain hard-coded Java code fragments.
- pahpam:code – is used in pahpam:AtomicProcessCode and contains a hard-coded Java code.
- pahpam:programKnowledgeBase, pahpam:Entries, pahpam:hasEntry, pahpam:Entry, pahpam:entryKey, pahpam:entryValue – these resources and properties are used to describe a map of constants that are used inside the generated programs.
- pahpam:isScopedSequence – tells the OntologyParser that the following block of code should be surrounded by brackets. It was made to avoid duplicate variable declarations. The variables in Java with the same names declared in the different scoped blocks do not conflict with each other.
- pahpam:inputParamList – describes a list of input parameters of a function.
- pahpam:BaseAction – shows the OntologyParser that this action should be executed by the PAHPAM framework after its code has been generated.

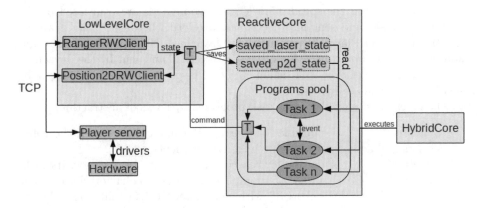

Fig. 1. The PAHPAM framework architecture

3   PAHPAM Framework

To show that generated robot control code is valid, it needs to be compiled and executed on a robot. For that purpose, the robot control framework called Programmable Architecture for Hierarchical Perception, Actuation and Modeling (PAHPAM) was written. To simplify the development, the Javaclient library [13] is used to communicate with the Player server [14], which offers high level interfaces to interact with sensors and actuators of the robot. The PAHPAM is a multi-threaded multi-layered architecture. It consists of several layers called cores; each one contains a set of core-specific tasks. Task is an atomic synchronous or asynchronous control program that may communicate with other tasks using events. If some task A needs another task B to operate, it sends a request to launch the task B. If there is no task B available yet, then task A waits for it. Task B may also become available, if a control code with the name B is sent to the PAHPAM framework at run-time. Control code is in a form of Java String and it can be read from a Java source file, a database or generated from OWL-S ontology file by the *OntologyParser*. The Javassist library [15] is used to compile Java classes from plain strings and load them to Java Virtual Machine at run-time. Fig. 1 depicts the PAHPAM architecture in a simplified form.

Robot's hardware is accessed through the Player server. *RangerRWClient* and *Position2DRWClient* use the Javaclient library to communicate with the Player server over TCP channel. They are located in a *LowLevelCore* and deal with the laser sensor data and 2D position commands respectively. The states are translated by the translation tasks (squares marked with "T") and sent into the *ReactiveCore* through the *ServerCoresMediator*, which is not shown here to simplify the drawing. The states are saved globally in the *ReactiveCore* by the "save state" tasks to provide an access to them for another tasks (Task 1, Task2, ... , TaskN) located in the program pool. These tasks are executed by the *HybridCore* and they may initiate the robot commands, for example "move forward with the speed 0.5m/s". The commands are translated by the "translate" tasks and sent into the *LowLevelCore* where they may again be translated to the Player format used by Javaclient. The command that was addressed to the *Position2DRWClient*, is accepted and sent by the Javaclient to the Player server over TCP channel. The Player server moves the robot by sending commands to its actuators.

The cores are designed to split task programs by levels of abstraction:

- *LowLevelCore* – responsible for sensing. It communicates with the robot sensors and actuators through reader/writer clients.
- *ReactiveCore* – responsible for reactive actions with low latency. Its tasks use *LowLevelCore*'s tasks to accomplish the desired behavior. For example a low level task "MoveBFLR" with parameters [0.5, 0] that tells robot to move forward with the speed of 0.5m/s, may be initiated.
- *HybridCore* – responsible for higher-level functionality, this core can be located on a separate machine. It contains the *OntologyParser* functionality as a separate task contained in programs pool. After parser has generated the robot control program it sends the code to lower level cores – *ReactiveCore* and *LowLevelCore*.

4   Experimental Setup

Purpose of the conducted experiment is to test the approach of generating working Java code from OWL-S ontology file. The robot controlled by PAHPAM framework pursuits a red object. It means that pursuing robot needs to find the red object in the world and hold him in sight. The red object need to be in the center of the pursuing robot's sight and not so far from it, otherwise it will loose the target. For example if the red object is to the right of the pursuing robot then it should turn right. If it is to the left, then turn left. If the red object is very close, then move back. If it is too far away then it must be pursued by moving forward. These two behaviors: "hold the red object in center of the sight" and "hold the distance" can be more abstractly described as "hold value within boundaries"; the task of the pursuing robot has both behaviors.

A "hold value within boundaries" resource has been defined and two different conditions have been applied to it:

- Hold the red object in the sight center:
    - if the red object's position is 2 pixels to the left of sight center, then turn left with speed 0.4rad/s
    - if the red robot's position is 2 pixels to the right of sight center, then turn right with speed 0.4rad/s
- Hold the distance:
    - if the obstacle is less than 1 meter away, then move back with speed 0.5 m/s
    - if the obstacle is more than 3 meters away, then move forward with speed 0.5 m/s

The prepared ontology file, containing the task description, is given to the *OntologyParser* and the Java code is generated from it. Then the Java code is sent to the *ReactiveCore* program pool and executed. The experiment is conducted using the real Scitos G5 differential-drive robot at the Centre for Biorobotics in Tallinn University of Technology. The Player server runs on the robot and provides the interfaces to the robot's sensors and actuators over the TCP/IP network. The PAHPAM framework communicates with the Player server over TCP sockets, reading data from sensors and writing commands to actuators.

The red folder is used as a trackable object, a person holds it in hands, moves around and the robot should follow him. Scitos G5 has two cameras positioned on eyes level. In the experiment only one camera is used to track the red object and the *cmvision* driver provides the *blobfinder* interface to track the red object within camera's field of view.

4.1   PAHPAM Framework

The execution of the framework begins with creation and launch of the sensor reader/writer clients. The Player server is running on local machine (127.0.0.1), reader/writer clients read the data with 200ms intervals and send it to framework cores. The sensor handler programs in the *ReactiveCore*'s programs pool take the data and register it as states in the core to be used by the task programs. The tasks have access to the most recently received robot states.

The following sensor handlers were made for the experiment:

- *r_state_process__p2dmain* – saves current speed states of the *position2d* interface.
- *r_state_process__rangerlaser* – saves laser rangefinder states of the *ranger* interface.
- *r_state_process__blobfinder* – saves a list of identified objects provided by the *blobfinder* interface.

Letter "r" means that the sensor handler is in ReactiveCore program pool.

Also, the following predefined task programs are used in the experiment:

- *r_task_process__attributesextractor* – reads *blobfinder* state, extracts its attributes (color, size, coordinates,etc) and sends the *r_event_process__blobfinderattributesextracted* event about it .
- *r_task_process__redcolordetector* – reacts to event produced by the attributes extractor. If the event contains the red color attribute then it sends the *r_event_process__redcolordetectedevent* event about it.
- *r_task_process__laserfrontminimumextractor* – reads the laser ranger state, extracts the distance to the closest obstacle and stores it to a new state *r_state_process__laserfrontminimum* .

Task programs use events to communicate with each other. They produce all the necessary information for the main program *r_task_process__followredobject*. This task program is not predefined and is not in the program pool at startup.

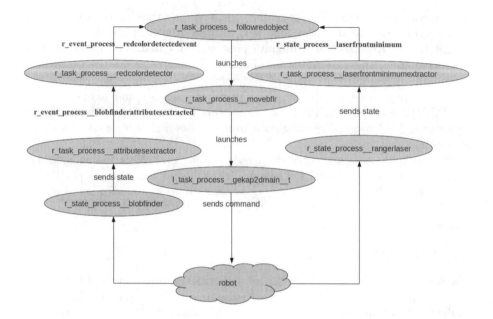

Fig. 2. Robot tasks hierarchy for the experiment

It is generated by the *OntologyParser* from the ontology file and sent to program pool at run-time. After that, it is executed and it executes other task programs, described above, that produce necessary data for it. It is also possible to change the ontology, regenerate the task, update robot control code and update robot behavior at run-time by executing the new version of the task. All the task programs run in parallel in their own threads, Fig. 2 depicts the robot tasks hierarchy in the experiment.

5   Results and Discussion

5.1   Results

The PAHPAM framework with the predefined task programs is launched to establish connection to the robot. After connection is established and framework is successfully launched, the ontology file with the main task description is given to the *OntologyParser*. The resulting java code is 56 rows long.

The three time measurements were done during the code generation and compilation process from the ontology file written for the experiment. The way from the ontology file to a compiled Java class consists of three phases, that are shown below with the time measurements made on a laptop with Intel Core Duo CPU T2500 @ 2.00GHz processor and 1 GB of RAM:

- Reading the 1300 rows ontology file into an in-memory Jena model using Jena API: 460 – 510ms.

Fig. 3. Robot following a person with a red folder. Robot is moving towards the person, if distance is more than 3 metres (left). Robot stops, when the distance is less than 3 metres (right).

- Generating 56 rows of Java control code from the in-memory Jena model by the *OntologyParser*:   26 – 34ms.
- Compilation of the generated code into the Java class by the Javassist library: 6 – 8ms.

The ontology file reading into an in-memory model takes most of the time. The *OntologyParser* operates fast because it works with the model located in the memory. The generated code is sent to the *ReactiveCore* program pool at runtime.

As a result, the robot exhibits the desired behavior "follow the red object":

- If the object moves to the right, then it rotates clockwise.
- If the object moves to the left, then it rotates counter-clockwise.
- If the object is directly in front and the distance is less than 1 metre, then it moves forward.
- If the object is directly in front and the distance is more than 3 metres, then it moves backward.

The video of Scitos G5 robot following a person with the red folder is available at: http://www.youtube.com/watch?v=Nz6B7unluTc.

5.2   Discussion

The *OntologyParser* managed to successfully transform the prepared ontology file into working Java code, but the component is still in the early development stage. The biggest advantage of the approach is its ability to create virtually any type of executable code, which allows to describe the whole behavioral logic of a robot from top to the ground.

The biggest problem in its current state is the inability to transform object hierarchies into Java code. Some projects already analyzed and solved the problem of mapping OWL object model into Java class model, for example in [16].

However, the existing approaches generate static class models of the whole hierarchy. Alternatively, more suitable approach for us would be to transform the object hierarchies into procedural Java code, so that only task- and context-specific data is used. This would enable using the relevant data from ontology in lower-level and less powerful components of robot control architecture.

Another problem of the current implementation is usage of hard-coded pieces of Java code in conditional statements, like *while* and *if*. We plan to address this issue by using the SWRL rule language to make ontology independent of the output language.

6   Conclusions

The goals of this paper were:

- Show that working Java control code can be generated from OWL-S descriptions:
  - Describe robot control code with OWL-S specification.
  - Show that the description blocks (AtomicProcesses, Sequences of actions, If-Then-Else constructs, etc.) can be reused.
- Implement compilation, class loading and execution of the generated code at run-time.

Based on the result of the experiment it can be concluded that it is possible to describe robot control code in a Semantic Web OWL-S format. The ontology file that describes "follow the red robot" behavior was written using constructs AtomicProcess, Perform, If-then-Else, Repeat-While. Many defined blocks were reused during the development of ontology description file. The AtomicProcess and Perform constructs as well as the If-Then-Else block were reused most frequently. The complete control code description file is in total 1300 rows, which may seem a big overhead to describe 56 rows of generated code. However, the description file contains a lot of initial descriptions that can be reused in future descriptions. The secondary goal that was achieved is to send generated code to robot at run-time and execute it. The behavior code "follow the red robot" is generated and executed on robot. The resulting behavior can be observed on the Scitos G5 robot in the actual lab.

6.1   Future Work

In the nearest future the *OntologyParser* should be enhanced. For example, now all the variable names must be described in description files. It is desirable that unique variable names are generated at the parse time. Predefined utility functions can also be described using OWL-S in the future. The support for rule languages like SWRL should be added to avoid hard-coded Java code in condition blocks. Additionally, to successfully teach real robots, the OWL-S control code descriptions need to be consolidated with the Semantic Web ontologies located in the Internet.

The far perspective is to find a way to automatically create control code description files.

References

1. Litzenberger, G.: Service robots – getting successfully established, the robot companion still a vision? (September 2010),
   http://www.worldrobotics.org/downloads/PR_2010-09-14_service_EN.pdf
2. Ashburner, M., Ball, C., Blake, J., Botstein, D., Butler, H., Cherry, J., Davis, A., Dolinski, K., Dwight, S., Eppig, J., Harris, M., Hill, D., Issel-Tarver, L., Kasarskis, A., Lewis, S., Matese, J., Richardson, J., Ringwald, M., Rubin, G., Sherlock, G.: Gene ontology: Tool for the unification of biology. Nature Genetics 25(1), 25–29 (2000), http://www.geneontology.org/
3. Raskin, R., Pan, M.: Knowledge representation in the semantic web for earth and environmental terminology (sweet). Computers and Geosciences 31(9), 1119–1125 (2005), http://sweet.jpl.nasa.gov/ontology/
4. Co-ode project, http://www.co-ode.org/
5. Jang, M., Sohn, J.C., Cho, Y.: Building semantic robot space based on the semantic web. In: RO-MAN 2007, pp. 499–504 (2007)
6. Katasonov, A., Terziyan, V.: Semantic agent programming language (S-APL): A middleware platform for the semantic web. In: ICSC 2008, pp. 504–511 (2008)
7. Vain, J., Tammet, T., Kuusik, A., Reilent, E.: Software architecture for swarm mobile robots. In: BEC 2008, pp. 231–234 (2008)
8. Vasiliu, L., Sakpota, B., Kim, H.G.: A semantic web services driven application on humanoid robots. In: WCCIA 2006, pp. 236–241 (2006)
9. Ha, Y.G., Sohn, J.C., Cho, Y.J.: Service-oriented integration of networked robots with ubiquitous sensors and devices using the semantic web services technology. In: IROS 2005, pp. 3947–3952 (August 2005)
10. Mokarizadeh, S., Grosso, A., Matskin, M., Kungas, P., Haseeb, A.: Applying semantic web service composition for action planning in multi-robot systems. In: ICIW 2009, pp. 370–376 (2009)
11. OWL-S: Semantic markup for web services,
    http://www.w3.org/Submission/OWL-S/
12. Jena - a semantic web framework for java, http://jena.sourceforge.net/
13. Javaclient project, http://java-player.sourceforge.net/
14. Gerkey, B., Vaughan, R., Howard, A.: The player/stage project: Tools for multi-robot and distributed sensor systems. In: ICAR 2003, pp. 317–323 (2003)
15. Chiba, S., Nishizawa, M.: An easy-to-use toolkit for efficient java bytecode translators. In: Pfenning, F., Macko, M. (eds.) GPCE 2003. LNCS, vol. 2830, pp. 364–376. Springer, Heidelberg (2003)
16. Gobin, B.A., Subramanian, R.K.: Mapping knowledge model onto java codes. In: World Academy of Science, Engineering and Technology, vol. 61, pp. 140–145 (2010)

Mobile Robot Self-diagnosis with a Bank of Adaptive Particle Filters

Michał Zając

Institute of Control and Computation Engineering, University of Zielona Góra,
ul. Podgórna 50, 65-254 Zielona Góra, Poland
M.Zajac@weit.uz.zgora.pl

Abstract. The diagnosis of mobile robot faults is one of the most serious problems which have to be overcome if one considers applications of mobile robotics in real life, outside laboratories. It would be desirable to perform the diagnosing routine in parallel with the standard activity of the robot, e.g., navigation, but without generating additional computational overhead. Recently the particle filter has become a very popular tool for state estimation of mobile robots. This is because it makes it easier to solve, e.g., the simultaneous localization and mapping problem. One of the biggest drawbacks of the method is its high computational burden closely related to the number of particles used. Therefore, it is often necessary to work out a compromise between the computational time and the quality of results. This work proposes a fault diagnosis system for a mobile robot which is based on a bank of adaptive particle filters. The idea behind is to reduce the total number of particles used in state estimation through activating and deactivating individual filters when needed, as well as by adapting the number of particles in each filter.

1 Introduction

1.1 Fault Diagnosis of Mobile Robots

As mobile robots step outside from the laboratory playgrounds and start being applied in various types of tasks and a wide range of domains, an acute need for uninterrupted, faultless and safe operation of such systems becomes obvious. The problem is especially important for systems which operate in critical conditions with a high risk of fault occurrence [8,2]. In the last years, since its introduction in [5], a new tool for solving state estimation problems, namely the particle filter, has proven to be a very powerful method for nonlinear systems [12]. Its attractive properties, such as the ability of estimating states of highly nonlinear systems which may be disturbed by process noise described by virtually any probability distribution, make it a powerful tool to use in fault detection and isolation (FDI) applications.

1.2 Related Research

Generally, we can distinguish three groups of research subjects which are related to the work reported in this paper. The first group contains research on particle filter-based FDI methods directly aimed at obtaining real-time diagnosis of

A. Bouchachia (Ed.): ICAIS 2011, LNAI 6943, pp. 168–179, 2011.

mobile robots. In [3] a Rao-Blackwellized particle filter-based solution of real-time fault diagnosis, where the one step look-ahead seems to provide superior performance in applications when compared with the standard Kalman filter based approach. In turn, an algorithm closely related to the Rao-Blackwellized particle filter for non-linear system diagnosis, called the Gaussian particle filter, is presented in [6]. In this method each particle samples a discrete mode and approximates the continuous variables by a multivariate Gaussian distribution at each time step by means of an unscented Kalman filter. Although the presented simulation results are promising, the paper lacks results of tests on a real system. A number of interesting particle based FDI techniques for mobile robots, which complement the Gaussian particle filter, such as a variable-resolution particle filter, a risk-sensitive particle and a one-step look-ahead particle filter are introduced in [19]. The ideas seem to work well in simulations, but extensive real-life tests are not provided. Another method is the Gaussian process proposals particle filter as given in [15]. A number of real robot tests performed show that the developed system was able to track the state of the robot more reliably through collision events than an optimized version of the standard particle filter with uninformed proposals, but the systems deals only with binary failure variables.

The second group includes some general FDI research, unrelated to the mobile robotics directly, but employing particle filter state estimation methods which can be particularly interesting from the point of view of mobile robot diagnosis. In [10] the FDI task is formulated in the multiple model environment where the particle filter is combined with the likelihood ratio test. This approach is further developed in [7] and [11] to account for abrupt and incipient faults in the detection and isolation phases. However, the approach is only investigated on a simulation benchmark problem and no results have been reported regarding a real system. A set of further nonstandard applications of particle methods to change detection, system identification and control in nonlinear non-Gaussian state-space can be found in the survey paper [1].

The third group incorporates research aimed at improving the efficiency of particle filters and therefore boosting the performance of mobile robots. One of the most serious challenges when designing a particle filter-based solution is the problem of sample size adaptation. This problem arises even further, when one considers a real-time (or quasi real-time) system, such as a mobile robot. One of the most common approaches to the problem are the methods based on maintaining the filter quality by the measure of the effective sample size (ESS) as outlined in, e.g., [16]. Few other sample size adaptation methods which could also address the considered problem, such as Shannon differential entropy-based or neural network-based adaptation schemes, are given in the comprehensive survey [17].

The results presented in this paper are inspired by the aforementioned works, especially in [11,19], and constitute a continuation and extension of the research presented in [20]. The contribution of this paper is threefold. First, it provides a practical implementation of a particle filter-based FDI system with likelihood ratio-test, similar in its idea to the one presented and benchmarked in [11]. The second contribution is the filter activation scheme, which was inspired by the variable resolution particle filter as presented in [19]. It activates the computationally demanding fault isolation process with a bank of adaptive particle filters in the case of a fault occurrence. In this method, in the case of fault, the current (nominal) model is switched to a specific (adaptive) model which is computationally more demanding due to the increased dimensionality of the search space. The third contribution is the proposed sample size adaptation heuristics, which can be an alternative to the methods presented, e.g., in [16].

2   Robot Motion Model

We assume that the mobile robot used in the following research is a unit with an (approximately) differential drive system with pneumatic wheels and position encoders on each axle. Additionally, the robot is equipped with a laser range finder system which facilitates local localization of the robot on a known map of the environment. The purpose of the FDI system is to detect a robot wheel damage (flat tire) which may occur during the robot motion.

In general, the dynamics of a mobile robot can be expressed in terms of a discrete time nonlinear state space model [18]:

$$
\begin{aligned}
\mathbf{x}_t &= \mathbf{f}(\mathbf{x}_{t-1}, \mathbf{u}_{t-1}, \mathbf{\Psi}, \mathbf{w}_{t-1}), \\
\mathbf{y}_t &= \mathbf{h}(\mathbf{x}_t, \mathbf{\Psi}, \mathbf{z}_t),
\end{aligned}
\tag{1}
$$

where $\mathbf{x}_{t-1}$ and $\mathbf{x}_t$ represent the state vector at subsequent time instants $t-1$ and t with a known initial probability density function $p(\mathbf{x}_0)$, $\mathbf{u}_{t-1}$ is the control vector, $\mathbf{f}(\cdot)$ and $\mathbf{h}(\cdot)$ are respectively nonlinear transition and measurement functions, parametrized by an m-element parameter vector $\mathbf{\Psi} = [\psi_1, \psi_2, \ldots, \psi_m]^T$ of the model and $\mathbf{w}_{t-1}$ and $\mathbf{z}_t$ represent respectively the process and measurement noise signals with known probability density functions.

2.1   Velocity Motion Model

The motion of a mobile robot can be described by the velocity motion model, see, e.g., [18] for details. In this model the vector of controls consists of two velocities: angular ω_t and linear v_t, and at time $t-1$ is of the form $\mathbf{u}_{t-1} = [v_{t-1}, \omega_{t-1}]^T$. It is then assumed that $\mathbf{u}_{t-1}$ is constant between $t-1$ and t.

The state vector at time $t-1$ is of the form $\mathbf{x}_{t-1} = [x_{t-1}, y_{t-1}, \theta_{t-1}]^T$, and its subsequent elements denote Cartesian coordinates of the center of gravity of the robot on a plane (x_{t-1} and y_{t-1}) and the heading angle θ_{t-1} relative to the origin of the global coordinate system. State transition of the robot from $\mathbf{x}_{t-1}$ to $\mathbf{x}_t = [x_t, y_t, \theta_t]^T$ can be described as follows:

$$
\begin{aligned}
x_t &= x_{t-1} - \frac{v_{t-1}}{\omega_{t-1}} \sin(\theta_{t-1}) + \frac{v_{t-1}}{\omega_{t-1}} \sin(\theta_{t-1} + \omega_{t-1}\Delta t), \\
y_t &= y_{t-1} + \frac{v_{t-1}}{\omega_{t-1}} \cos(\theta_{t-1}) - \frac{v_{t-1}}{\omega_{t-1}} \cos(\theta_{t-1} + \omega_{t-1}\Delta t), \\
\theta_t &= \theta_{t-1} + \omega_{t-1}\Delta t,
\end{aligned}
\tag{2}
$$

where Δt denotes a fixed time increment between $t-1$ and t. Such a model is quite general since it does not account for physical parameters of a robot (e.g., dimensions, sensor parameters, etc.).

2.2   Process and Measurement Noise Modeling

The state equations (2) do not account for the process noise. It is therefore assumed that the process noise $\mathbf{w}_{t-1} = [w^v_{t-1}, w^\omega_{t-1}]$ is incorporated additively to the vector of controls, which yields the modified controls $\hat{\mathbf{u}}_{t-1} = [\hat{v}_{t-1}, \hat{\omega}_{t-1}]^T$ in the following manner:

$$\hat{v}_{t-1} = v_{t-1} + w^v_{t-1}, \qquad \hat{\omega}_{t-1} = \omega_{t-1} + w^\omega_{t-1}. \tag{3}$$

For simplicity, we assume that the measurement procedure provides direct measurements of the system state vector elements (i.e., one can measure the pose $[x_t, y_t, \theta_t]^T$ of the robot, e.g., by means of vision system or GPS). Then, assuming additive measurement noise $\mathbf{z}_t = [z^x_t, z^y_t, z^\theta_t]$, it is possible to model the perturbed vector of measurements as

$$\mathbf{y}_t = \mathbf{x}_t + \mathbf{z}_t. \tag{4}$$

Basically, the probability density functions of the process and the measurement noise can assume various forms, but for our purposes zero-mean Gaussian noise with known covariance matrices (denoted respectively by $\mathbf{P}$ and $\mathbf{Q}$) was chosen. The matrices can be determined in an off-line calibration procedure as outlined, e.g., in [13].

2.3   Model Parameters

To illustrate the functioning of the proposed FDI system, a "flat tire scenario" was chosen, as an example of a fault which may occur in the case of a wheeled mobile robot platform. This choice can be justified by a simple implementation both on a real robot and in simulation. It invokes no loss of generality and does not exclude the applicability of the presented approach to other types of faults.

In order to achieve the capability of modeling the defects of physical components of the robot, it is necessary to augment the motion model (2) by a set of parameters which reflect the actual system elements. In the case of flat tires diagnosis and the differential drive robot, these parameters are as follows:

- R_r and R_l – the nominal wheel radii of the right and left wheel,
- r_r and r_l – the actual wheel radii of the right and left wheel, respectively.

Additionally, we have to take account of the dependencies between the indications of the right (e_r) and left (e_l) wheel encoders and the controls after time Δt. They are as follows:

$$e_r = K\Delta t \frac{2v_t + \omega_t a}{2R_r}, \qquad e_l = K\Delta t \frac{2v_t - \omega_t a}{2R_l}, \tag{5}$$

where a is the wheel base of the robot and K is the encoder gain. The resulting values can be applied to determine the real control vector $\mathbf{u}_t^R = [v_t^R, \omega_t^R]^T$, which takes into account the current parameter values:

$$v_t^R = \frac{r_l e_l + r_r e_r}{2K \Delta t}, \qquad \omega_t^R = \frac{r_r e_r - r_l e_l}{aK \Delta t}. \tag{6}$$

For the actual parameter values equal to the nominal ones, the control vector $\mathbf{u}_t^R$ becomes the vector $\mathbf{u}_t$. In the case where the actual value of a parameter is different from its nominal one, by means of applying the control vector $\mathbf{u}_t^R$ as the input to the motion model (2), it is possible to obtain the model response as for the system in a faulty state.

3   Fault Detection and Isolation System

The proposed FDI system is composed of a bank of adaptive particle filters. A detailed description of the employed particle filter algorithm can be found in [11] and the general scheme of the proposed solution is presented in Figure 1. The particle filter bank consists of the nominal filter with constant parameters and adaptive filters. In the nominal filter $f^{[0]}$ the state vector is of the form $\mathbf{x}_t^{[0]} = [x_t, y_t, \theta_t]^T$, and an m-element vector of constant (nominal) parameters is $\mathbf{\Psi}^{[0]} = [\psi_1, \psi_2, \ldots, \psi_m]^T$. In the case of considered system, the subsequent elements of the vector Ψ denote wheel parameters such as wheel radii, wheel base or encoder gain. In the adaptive filter $f^{[k]}$, where $k = 1, \ldots, n$, the state vector is augmented with one (we assume that a fault is interpreted as a change in the value of a system parameter) additional element ψ_j, where $j \in 1, \ldots, m$, which is at the same time the j-th element of the parameter vector $\mathbf{\Psi}^{[k]}$ and is of the form $\mathbf{x_t}^{[k]} = [x_t, y_t, \theta_t, \psi_j]^T$.

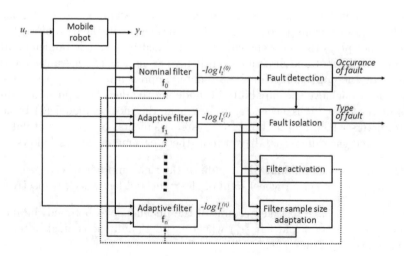

Fig. 1. The proposed FDI system scheme

For the robot in nominal state, each of the filters is able to estimate the state of the system. Hence, in order to reduce the use of computational resources, a filter activation block is introduced. The main task of the block is to activate or deactivate filters, according to the current needs. In practice, a result is that only one filter is active most of the time, which in turn reduces the computational demands of the system. Additionally, the sample size in each filter is set as a result of an adaptive procedure described in the sequel, which decreases the computational burden even further.

The key element of the FDI system is the decision function computed for the k-th particle filter as proposed in [7,10,11]:

$$
\begin{aligned}
d_t^{[k]} &= -\frac{1}{M} \sum_{j=t-M+1}^{t} \ln(p(\mathbf{y}_j|\mathbf{y}_1,\ldots,\mathbf{y}_{j-1}, \mathbf{\Psi}^{[k]})) \\
&\approx -\frac{1}{M} \sum_{j=t-M+1}^{t} \ln(\frac{1}{N_j} \sum_{i=1}^{N_j^{[k]}} \ell_j^{[k]}(i)),
\end{aligned}
\tag{7}
$$

where $\ell_j^{[k]}(i)$ is the likelihood function of the i-th predicted particle $\mathbf{x}_j^{[k]}(i)$ at time j for the k-th particle filter, M is the sliding window width and $N_j^{[k]}$ is the sample size (number of particles) of the k-th particle filter at the time instant j. In the case of additive zero-mean Gaussian measurement noise with covariance matrix $\mathbf{Q}$, the likelihood $l_j^{[k]}(i)$ can be expressed as:

$$
\ell_j^{[k]}(i) = \frac{\exp\left(-\frac{1}{2}(\mathbf{r}_j^{[k]}(i))^T \mathbf{Q}^{-1} \mathbf{r}_j^{[k]}(i)\right)}{\sqrt{(2\pi)^m [\det(\mathbf{Q})]}},
\tag{8}
$$

where $\mathbf{r}_j^{[k]}(i) = \mathbf{y}_j - \mathbf{h}(\mathbf{x}_j^{[k]}(i), \mathbf{\Psi}^{[k]}, \mathbf{0})$ and $\mathbf{h}(\cdot)$ is the nonlinear measurement function as defined in (1).

3.1 Fault Detection and Fault Isolation

The detection of a fault is based on the evaluation of the decision function value for the nominal filter $f^{[0]}$. Here, if the value of the function increases to satisfy the condition $d_t^{[0]} > h$, where h denotes an arbitrarily chosen detection threshold, then a fault occurrence is signaled and subsequently the fault isolation process is being started.

The isolation of a fault is a result of choosing a filter $f^{[k]}$, for which the value of the decision function first drops below the detection threshold to satisfy condition $d_t^{[k]} < h$, and at that time instant has its minimum value with respect to other (nominal and adaptive) filters.

3.2 Filter Activation

The filter activation process is similar and closely related to the fault isolation. At any given time t each of the filters $f^{[0]}, \ldots, f^{[n]}$ can be in state $S^{[f]}$ ($f \in$

$\{0, \ldots, n\}$), where for an active filter $S^{[f]} = 1$ and for a deactivated filter $S^{[f]} = 0$. The decision on which filter is to be active at a given time step is made based on the following set of simple heuristic rules:

- IF at time t the value of the decision function for the nominal filter $f^{[0]}$ satisfies the condition $d_t^{[0]} < h$, THEN $S^{[0]} = 1$, and the other filters are not active $(S^{[1]}, \ldots, S^{[f]} = 0)$.
- IF at time t the value of the decision function for each filter $f^{[0]}, \ldots, f^{[n]}$ satisfies the condition $d_t^{[0]} > h, \ldots, d_t^{[n]} > h$, THEN all filters are active $(S^{[0]}, \ldots, S^{[n]} = 1)$.
- IF at time t the value of the decision function for the filter $f^{[k]}$ satisfies the condition $d_t^{[k]} < h$ and $d_t^{[k]} = \min\{d_t^{[0]}, \ldots, d_t^{[n]}\}$, THEN $S^{[k]} = 1$, and the other filters are not active $(S^{[f]} = 0$, where $f \neq k$ and $f = 0, \ldots, n)$.

The third condition is equivalent to the fault isolation condition, hence, in the case of having a fault stably isolated, only one filter will be active.

As can be easily seen, an inactive filter $f^{[k]}$ after transition from the state $S^{[k]} = 0$ to the state $S^{[k]} = 1$ has outdated information about the actual system state. Hence, such a filter has to be initialized with the current value of the state estimate from the active filter $f^{[j]}$. Unfortunately, in the case of faults which are characterized by step changes in one of the system parameter value, such a procedure may be insufficient. That is why a buffer of length $b > 1$ was introduced into the structure of the system. It stores the recent b controls, measurements and system state estimates (mean values), which allow for the initialization of any filter at the activation time t through b-fold iteration of the particle filter algorithm with the values from the buffer from time $t - b$ to t. Such a procedure vastly reduces the time of parameter adaptation and improves correct system state estimation.

3.3   Sample Size Adaptation

Adaptation of the sample size $N_t^{[k]}$ for a filter $f^{[k]}$ which is active at time t is performed with respect to the current value of the efficient sample size (ESS). The ESS describes the number of particles N_t^{ESS} sampled from the filtering probability distribution function p sufficient to achieve the same estimate quality as N_t samples form the sampling probability distribution function π [16]. It is given by the following formula:

$$N_t^{ESS} = N_t \frac{1}{1 + d(\pi, p)}, \tag{9}$$

where $d(\pi, p)$ is the χ^2 distance between π and p. Usually, the distance $d(\pi, p)$ is usually being empirically estimated by the coefficient of variation cv^2 of the sample weights according to [16]:

$$d(\pi, p) \approx cv^2 = \frac{N_t \sum_{i=1}^{N_t} (q_t(i))^2}{(\sum_{i=1}^{N_t} q_t(i))^2} - 1, \tag{10}$$

where $q_t(i)$ denotes the weight of the i-th particle in a filter. The sample adaptation of the k-th filter is performed in accordance with the following rules:

- IF $N_t^{\text{ESS}[k]} \geq T^{\text{ESS}} N_t^{[k]}$, THEN $N_t^{[k]} = N_{t-1}^{[k]} Z_s$, where $Z_s \in (0,1)$ is the sample size drop parameter and $T^{\text{ESS}} \in (0,1)$ is an arbitrary chosen threshold.
- IF $N_t^{\text{ESS}[k]} < T^{\text{ESS}} N_t^{[k]}$, THEN $N_t^{[k]} = N_{t-1}^{[k]} Z_w$, where $Z_w > 1$ is the sample size rise parameter.
- IF $N_t^{[k]} > N_{\max}$, THEN $N_t^{[k]} = N_{\max}$, where $N_{\max}$ is the maximum sample size parameter.
- IF $N_t^{[k]} < N_{\min}$, THEN $N_t^{[k]} = N_{\min}$, where $N_{\min}$ is the minimum sample size parameter.

The above adaptation procedure maintains the sample size of each filter so as to achieve the quality of filtering fixed by the threshold parameter T^{ESS}. Then the new number of particles is generated in the resampling step of the particle filter.

3.4 Adaptation of the Parameters of Particle Filters

As a result of unpredictability and the lack of a parameter evolution model, in the proposed scheme the parameters $\mathbf{\Psi}^{[j]}$ included as elements of the state vector in filters $f^{[k]}$ evolve as additive Gaussian noise with arbitrarily chosen variances. To bound the search space, constraints were set for each of the adaptive filters $f^{[k]}$ on their adaptive parameters in the form of a range $\Xi^{[k]} = (a^{[k]}, b^{[k]})$. This reduces the need for searching inadequate areas of the search space (e.g., the wheel diameter cannot be negative or much greater than its nominal value). In the case of a range violation by an adaptive parameter of any particle, its value is modified by the *modulo* operator (due to its simple and efficient implementation), to fall into the plausible range.

4 Experimental Results

To verify the proposed FDI system, a number of simulation experiments in MATLAB and tests on a real robot were performed. The considered task of the mobile robot is following a randomly generated planar trajectory, which consists of T waypoints in the form of Cartesian coordinates which the robots should visit during its task. The controls at the consecutive time steps can be calculated based on the current poses and the next waypoint coordinates. It is assumed that the task is perturbed by a fault occurrence, which results from a wheel failure. The right wheel failure is simulated by a step change in the right wheel radius parameter R_{r}. It is assumed that the considered system is Gaussian with additive process noise given by the covariance matrix $\mathbf{Q}$ and the additive measurement noise with the covariance matrix $\mathbf{R}$. The likelihood function $\ell_j^{[k]}(i)$ from (7) is thus given by a multidimensional normal distribution. The values of parameters used in simulations and real robot tests (in curly brackets) are as follows: time increment $\Delta t = 0.2$ [s], robot wheel base $a = 0.3$ [m]

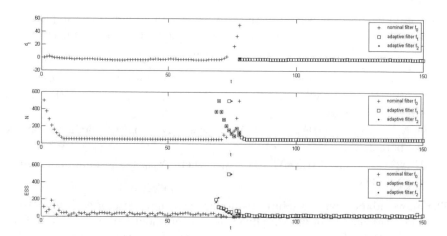

Fig. 2. Flat tire detection in simulation: the decision function values (d_t), the sample size (N) for each filter (the fault occurred at $t = 70$) and the value of the ESS estimates for each filter

$\{0.4 \text{ [m]}\}$, nominal right wheel radius $R_r = 0.1$ [m] $\{0.11 \text{ [m]}\}$, nominal left wheel radius $R_l = 0.1$ [m] $\{0.11 \text{ [m]}\}$, encoder gain $K = 800$ $\{34000\}$, number of simulation steps $t_{\max} = 150$ $\{700\}$, step of fault occurrence $t_{\text{fault}} = 70$ $\{468\}$, sliding window width $M = 10$ $\{10\}$, buffer length $b = 5$ $\{5\}$, maximum number of particles in each filter $N_{\max} = 1000$ $\{3000\}$, minimum number of particles in each filter $N_{\min} = 10$ $\{50\}$, initial number of particles in each filter $N_0 = 500$ $\{3000\}$, detection threshold $h = 30$ $\{30\}$, number of adaptive filters $n = 2$ $\{2\}$, range of parameter adaptation $\Xi^{[1]} = (0.05, 0.11)$ $\{(0.05, 0.15)\}$, range of parameter adaptation $\Xi^{[2]} = (0.05, 0.11)$ $\{(0.05, 0.15)\}$, variance of adaptation $V^{[1]} = 0.001$ $\{0.001\}$, variance of adaptation $V^{[2]} = 0.001$ $\{0.001\}$, initial state $\mathbf{x}_0 = [0, 0, 0]^T$ $\{[0, 0, 0]^T\}$, covariance matrix of the initial state $\mathbf{P}_0 = \text{diag}([0.0001, 0.0001, 0.0001)$ $\{\text{diag}([0.0001, 0.0001, 0.000001)\}$, covariance matrix of process $\mathbf{Q} = \text{diag}([0.01, 0.005])$ $\{\text{diag}([0.01, 0.05])\}$ and covariance matrix of measurements $\mathbf{R} = \text{diag}([0.01, 0.01, 0.001])$ $\{\text{diag}([0.1, 0.1, 0.01])\}$.

4.1   Flat Tire Simulation

The damage of the right wheel is modeled by a change in the value of the parameter R_r from 0.1 to 0.07. Figure 2 presents the simulation results.

The plots present the decision function values, the current number of particles involved into the FDI process at each time step and the value of ESS estimates for the active filters. Fault detection occurred at the time instant $t = 72$, and the fault isolation at time $t = 78$. It can be observed that the detection latency is relatively small and the sample size is low and stable before and after the detection point. The number of particles is increased only at the time of detection, when all the filters are active.

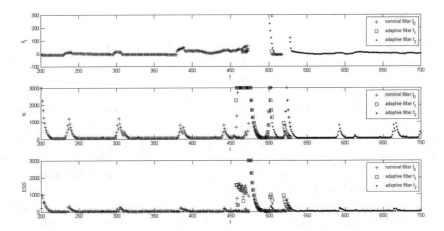

Fig. 3. Flat tire detection on the real robot: the decision function values (d_t), the sample size (N) for each filter (the fault occurred at $t = 468$) and the value of the ESS estimates for each filter

4.2   Real Robot Tests

Figure 3 presents the results for FDI of a real mobile robot. The tests were performed on a mobile robot Pioneer 3-AT, which is a 4-wheel skid-steering type vehicle. However sophisticated models of such a robot exist (see e.g., [9]), it is also possible to approximate its kinematics with a differential drive kinematic model as e.g., in [4], and it is known that particle filters perform better in conjunction with simple models [18]. Thus, the latter approach was adopted with the motion model introduced in the Section 2. The robot is equipped with four pneumatic wheels, which allow for simulation of a flat tire by deflating the wheels on one side of the robot, while temporary interrupting the operation of the robot. The plots present the decision function values, the number of particles involved into the FDI process and current ESS estimate values. Fault detection occurred at the time instant $t = 468$, and the fault isolation process stabilized at the time moment $t = 525$, which means 7 seconds of the detection latency.

A stable low sample size can be observed before and after the time of detection. The number of particles increases only at the time of fault detection, when all the filters are activated. As expected, when compared with the simulation results, one can observe larger deviations of the process, which is reflected by rougher plots and a larger total number of particles involved in the estimation process. As can be observed, some disadvantage of the system is its inertia which results from the time which is necessary to adapt the parameter values in the case of a fault occurrence. This results in a delay between the fault detection and isolation. Despite the aforementioned drawback, the achieved reaction times (few seconds for the fault isolation) seem acceptable.

5   Conclusions

In this paper an FDI system based on a bank of particle filters was proposed. The performed tests show that the FDI scheme with the sample size and filter activation mechanisms can considerably reduce the computational cost of the fault diagnosis process, while providing satisfactory estimates of adaptive parameters. As a consequence, it was possible to estimate the system state even in a fault state, which in turn can be further used for designing a fault-tolerant control system. At the same time it was possible to limit the total number of particles involved in the state estimation process, which was beneficial in terms of the computational burden when compared with a system with a constant sample size or without the filter activation procedure.

The goal of future research is to elaborate and implement methods of automatic identification and calibration of the system, as is presented, e.g., in [13,14]. Furthermore, it is necessary to perform thorough analysis of the system taking into account detection times, detection latencies, false alarms, undetected faults, false detections, etc., as well as a comparison with other FDI systems.

To achieve quasi real-time performance of the fault isolation process in the case of a real robot, an implementation of the computationally-intensive fault isolation part of the system in a massive computational environment such as a computer cluster or modern multi-core GPU is considered. The particle filter can be in a natural way parallelized, which offers an opportunity of implementing intensive parts of the computations in a multiprocessor framework, such as MPI. This idea is currently being extensively examined, and the results of these investigations will be published in the near future.

Acknowledgment. The author is a scholar within Sub-measure 8.2.2 Regional Innovation Strategies, Measure 8.2 Transfer of knowledge, Priority VIII Regional human resources for the economy Human Capital Operational Programme co-financed by the European Social Fund and the Polish state budget.

References

1. Andrieu, C., Doucet, A., Singh, S.S., Tadić, V.: Particle methods for change detection, system identification, and control. In: IEEE Proc. (2004)
2. Chen, J., Patton, R.: Robust model-based fault diagnosis for dynamic systems. Kluwer, Boston (1999)
3. de Freitas, N., Dearden, R., Hutter, F., Morales-Menendez, R., Mutch, J., Poole, D.: Diagnosis by a waiter and a mars explorer. In: IEEE Proc. (2004)

4. Goel, P., Dedeoglu, G., Roumeliotis, S., Sukhatme, G.: Fault detection and identification in a mobile robot using multiple model estimation and neural network. In: Proc. IEEE Int. Conf. Robotics and Automation (2000)
5. Gordon, N., Salmond, D., Smith, A.: Novel approach to nonlinear/non-gaussian bayesian state estimation. In: IEEE Proc.–F, vol. 35, pp. 107–113 (1993)
6. Hutter, F., Dearden, R.: The gaussian particle filter for diagnosis of non-linear systems. In: Proc. 14th Int. Conf. Principles of Diagnosis, Washington D.C., USA (2003)
7. Kadirkamanathan, V., Li, P., Jaward, M.H., Fabri, S.G.: Particle filtering-based fault detection in non-linear stochastic systems. Int. J. Sys. Sci. 33, 259–265 (2002)
8. Korbicz, J., Kościelny, J., Kowalczuk, Z., Cholewa, W.: Fault Diagnosis: Models, Artificial Intelligence, Applications. Springer, Heidelberg (2004)
9. Kozłowski, K., Pazderski, D.: Modeling and control of a 4-wheel skid-steering mobile robot. Int. J. Appl. Math. Comput. Sci. 14(4) (2004)
10. Li, P., Kadirkamanathan, V.: Particle filtering based likelihood ratio approach to fault diagnosis in nonlinear stochastic systems. IEEE Trans. Syst., Man, and Cybern., C, Appl. Rev. 31, 337–343 (2001)
11. Li, P., Kadirkamanathan, V.: Fault detection and isolation in non-linear stochastic systems–a combined adaptive monte carlo filtering and likelihood ratio approach. Int. J. Contr. 77, 1101–1114 (2004)
12. Liu, M., Zang, S., Zhou, D.: Fast leak detection and location of gas pipelines based on an adaptive particle filter. Int. J. Appl. Math. Comput. Sci. 15(4), 541–550 (2005)
13. Martinelli, A.: The odometry error of a mobile robot with a synchronous drive system. IEEE Trans. Rob. Aut. 18, 399–405 (2002)
14. Martinelli, A., Tomatis, N., Siegwart, R.: Simultaneous localization and odometry self calibration for mobile robot. Auton. Rob. 22, 75–85 (2007)
15. Plagemann, C., Stachniss, C., Burgard, W.: Efficient failure dtection for mobile robots using mixed abstraction particle filters, vol. 22, pp. 93–107 (2006)
16. Straka, O., Šimandl, M.: Particle filter adaptation based on efficient sample size. In: Proc. 14th IFAC Symp. System Identification, pp. 991–996 (2006)
17. Straka, O., Šimandl, M.: A survey of sample size adaptation techniques for particle filters. In: Proc. 15th IFAC Symp. System Identification, vol. 15 (2009)
18. Thrun, S., Burgard, W., Fox, D.: Probabilistic Robotics. MIT Press, Cambridge (2005)
19. Verma, V., Gordon, G., Simmons, R., Thrun, S.: Particle filters for rover fault diagnosis. IEEE Rob. Aut. Mag. 11(1), 56–66 (2004)
20. Zając, M., Uciński, D.: Adaptive particle filter in fault detection and isolation of mobile robots. Pr. Nauk. Polit. Warsz., Elektronika 175, 635–644 (2010)

Emergence of Safe Behaviours
with an Intrinsic Reward

Yuri Gavshin and Maarja Kruusmaa

Tallinn University of Technology, Centre for Biorobotics,
Akadeemia tee 15a-111, 12618 Tallinn, Estonia
{yury,maarja}@biorobotics.ttu.ee
http://www.biorobotics.ttu.ee

Abstract. This paper explores the idea that robots can learn safe behaviors without prior knowledge about its environment nor the task at
hand, using intrinsic motivation to reverse actions. Our general idea is
that if the robot learns to reverse its actions, all the behaviors that
emerge from this principle are intrinsically safe. We validate this idea
with experiments to benchmark the performance of obstacle avoidance
behavior. We compare our algorithm based on an abstract intrinsic reward with a Q-learning algorithm for obstacle avoidance based on external reward signal. Finally, we demonstrate that safety of learning can be
increased further by first training the robot in the simulator using the
intrinsic reward and then running the test with the real robot in the real
environment.

The experimental results show that the performance of the proposed
algorithm is on average only 5-10% lower than of the Q-Learning algorithm. A physical robot, using the knowledge obtained in simulation, in
real world performs 10% worse than in simulation. However, its performance reaches the same success rate with the physically trained robot
after a short learning period. We interpret this as the evidence confirm-
ing the hypothesis that our learning algorithm can be used to teach safe
behaviors to a robot.

1 Introduction

This paper is concerned with applying an intrinsic reward signal to robot learning. In our case, the intrinsic motivation of the robot is to learn to reverse
actions. The rationale for such a motivational system is to teach the robot to
behave safely. We surmise that a robot governed by such an intrinsic motivation will behave inherently safely as it will avoid actions that cause irreversible
damage.

Intrinsic motivation is a concept derived from psychology and in its original
meaning refers to an activity done for one's inherent satisfaction rather than
to achieve some specific external goal [1]. In computer science and robotics intrinsic motivation has been studied in developmental robotics and reinforcement
learning. Some models are derived seeking an analogy with neural processes

A. Bouchachia (Ed.): ICAIS 2011, LNAI 6943, pp. 180–191, 2011.

in the brain [2]. Schmidhuber's research ([3],[4]) introduces a system with autonomous and active exploratory behavior motivated by "artificial curiosity". Barto et al. [5] and Stout et al. [6] use advanced RL techniques in their research of robot learning motivated by the concepts of "novelty" and "surprise". These approaches are tested in a grid-world abstract agent simulation.

Kaplan and Oudeyer showed that a robot can develop visual competences from scratch driven only by internal motivations independent of any particular task: predictability, familiarity and stability [7]. They generalized their approach further and derived a mechanism of Intelligent Adaptive Curiosity, an intrinsic motivation system which pushes a robot towards situations in which it maximizes its learning progress [8]. Experiments by Kaplan and Oudeyer are made with real robots using real sensor data.

In this paper we derive an intrinsic motivation system that forces the robot to learn to reverse actions and gives the preference to reversible ones. In the opposite to [8] where the motivational system encourages robot curiosity, our system is driven towards stability and safety.

The drive to suppress irreversible actions is thus a kind of an adaptive homeostatic predictive motivation according to the classification given in the recent overview paper of computational approaches to intrinsic motivation [9]. Homeostatic systems force the robot to maintain some of their properties (e.g. the energy level). Another example of a homeostatic system is the motivation to maintain a comfortable level of social interaction [10]. In our case the homeostatic system of the robot forces it to build a connected state space where all other states can always be reached and returned back to.

Our motivation to build a learning system that learns action reversibility is to build safe autonomous learning robots. We assume that reversible actions are intrinsically safe because the robot is always able to deal with the consequences. The abstract intrinsic motivation also makes the goal of the robot independent of the environment it works in or the task it fulfills (as an external goal). Instead of specifying routines such as avoiding obstacles, falls, traps, risky regions or routes or staying near to some known landmark, it is rather told not to do things it cannot undo. It explains "why" a robot should behave that way and if a new problematic action/situation occurs, a robot avoiding irreversible actions will avoid these new dangers after some learning period.

Papers of Kruusmaa and Gavshin have provided an initial evidence that the principle "Don't do things you can't undo" generates a concrete safe behavior of obstacle avoidance ([11],[12]). This behavior emerges from the intrinsic goal of the robot to avoid irreversible actions as after bumping to an object/wall or wheels slippage, a simple robot cannot reverse to the previous state with the same sensor readings. In this paper we have developed their ideas further, conducted experiments on simulated Khepera II and Scitos G5 robots as well as on the real SCITOS G5 robot. With these experiments we aim at investigating:

- How well does our approach compare to some classical benchmark obstacle avoidance algorithm?

- Does it increase the safety of robot learning if we first train the robot in a simulator to avoid irreversible actions and then run the trained robot in a real environment?

In the following section we present our ideas in a more formal way. In section 3 we describe the experimental setup, the algorithms used, explain the differences between the physical and simulated robots used in experiments, their test environments and specific implementation details. In section 4 we present the results and discuss them together with general applicability of the approach. Section 5 contains conclusions and possible directions of future work.

2   Theoretical Framework

This section briefly describes the general theoretical framework used to ground the reversibility based algorithm and to test the robots.

2.1   Definitions

A robot's world is a labelled transition system $(S, \Lambda, \rightarrow)$, where S is a set of experienced states, Λ is a set of labels (a label contains an action or a sequence of actions), and $\rightarrow$ is a set of labelled transitions between the states. When the result of an action a in state s is not wholly determined by the robot, multiple transitions from s are labelled with the same action a and it is the world that determines which transition actually happens.

A reversibility for world W is a quintuple of three states and two actions: $(s_{init}, a_{forward}, s_{interim}, a_{reverse}, s_{final})$. Generally speaking, a composite action $a_{forward}a_{reverse}$ produces a transition from s_{init} to s_{final} through $s_{interim}$ in W.

Also, the action sequence $a_{forward}a_{reverse}$ is expected to work for any states x and y with $d_{orig}(x, s_{init}) \leq \varepsilon_{orig}$ and $d_{dest}(y, s_{interim}) \leq \varepsilon_{dest}$, where d_{orig}, d_{dest} are metrics on states and ε_{orig}, ε_{dest} are their thresholds.

The reversibility $(s_{init}, a_{forward}, s_{interim}, a_{reverse}, s_{final})$ holds in W if there exists a transition path from s_{init} to s_{final} through $s_{interim}$ consisting of two transitions labelled accordingly $a_{forward}$ and $a_{reverse}$, and $d_{rev}(s_{init}, s_{final}) \leq \varepsilon_{rev}$, where d_{rev} is a prametric ($d_{rev}(x, y) \geq 0$ and $d_{rev}(x, x) = 0$) on states and ε_{rev} is a threshold; fails otherwise.

An action $a_{forward}$ in an arbitrary state s is expected to be reversible (by action $a_{reverse}$), if the reversibility $(s_{init}, a_{forward}, s_{interim}, a_{reverse}, s_{final})$ holds and $d_{orig}(s, s_{init}) \leq \varepsilon_{orig}$. A reversibility model of the robot is a set of reversibilities that are expected to hold.

2.2   Explanations

A reversibility model can be given to the robot in advance, transferred from another robot, extracted by a human from the knowledge about the world or learned by the robot. Using this model a robot can predict whether the action from the state is reversible by iterating through its experience and using obtained reversibilities to ground the predictions.

The actions used are symbolic actions and it is irrelevant whether they are atomic or complex actions. These actions can also be interpreted as discrete choices if used by a high level symbolic decision maker. The only requirement is that every action must have a reverse action, i.e. the action that undoes (reverses) it.

States are also discrete but with metrics d_{orig} and d_{dest} defined on the set of the states. These metrics are used to search for the reversibilities to ground the predictions. Metric d_{orig} together with its threshold value ε_{orig} are used to filter reversibilities by calculating the distance between its initial state and the current state. The smaller the distance, the higher is the probability that the actual outcome of making the same action from the current state will generate a similar reversibility. In other words, d_{orig} and ε_{orig} are used to identify a "region" or a "cluster" of states.

A prametric d_{rev} is used to calculate how strongly the reversibility holds. A prametric is used instead of a metric to make it possible to reward transitions from "worse" states to "better" ones (in case of goal-oriented learning); if d_{rev} is a metric, then the calculated number would measure stability.

The intrinsic reward for making an action is counter-proportional to the value of d_{rev}. When applied to our learning algorithm it forces the robot to give higher weight to the actions that are reversible. The intrinsic reward can be generated, when a sequence of an action with its reverse-action is observed. In this case, the reversibility $(s_{init}, a_{forward}, s_{interim}, a_{reverse}, s_{final})$ is observed and the value of $d_{rev}(s_{init}, s_{final})$ is calculated. The intrinsic reward can then be calculated, for example, using the following expression:

$$r = \varepsilon_{rev} - d_{rev}(s_{init}, s_{final}) \,.$$

3   Experimental Setup

The purpose of the experiment is to validate the reversibility-based approach to safe learning proposed in this paper. The experiment consists of:

- Tests 1 and 2: two test runs of the same length with simulated Khepera II and Scitos G5 (5200 steps each).
- Test 3: the physical test run (1000 steps long) on Scitos G5 pre-loaded with simulation data (first 4000 steps from Test 2).

Each test run is divided into two phases: data collection (phase 1) and simulation (phase 2).

During the first phase the robot (physical or simulated) makes pseudo-random moves and the input data (sensors data, actions made and outcomes of the actions) are collected and saved into log files. The predictions are made during the second phase using the data collected in the first phase. The performance is measured by sampling algorithms' predictions of whether the next action will succeed, followed by calculation of the success rate of those predictions.

3.1   The Robots

Comparative experiments are conducted on two common research robot plat-forms, Khepera II by K-Team and Scitos G5 by MetraLabs. For this paper both robots are tested in the simulator and Scitos G5 robot is tested physically.

Both Khepera II and Scitos G5 are differential drive robots but with different size and slightly different geometry. Khepera II has a circular shape and the rotation axis is exactly at the center of the circle. Therefore it can rotate freely in very close proximity (1-2 mm) to the obstacle without touching it. Scitos G5 also has a circular shape but with an additional compartment at the back side for the passive third wheel, which considerably changes the way it can rotate its own body: a 360° turn can be completed without touching the obstacle only if the distance to the obstacle is larger than approximately $200mm$ (the size of the passive wheel compartment). The laser range finder is used in the test reported in this paper.

3.2   The Environments

Both Khepera II and Scitos G5 robots are simulated by Gazebo simulator (version 0.8-pre3, OGRE version 1.4.9, ODE version 0.10.1) through Player (modified version 2.1.0) interface [13].

The physical environment for Scitos G5 is a rectangular box of size $970mm$ by $1500mm$ (see Fig. 1). Absolute size for simulated Scitos G5 and its environment matches closely the real one and the laser rangefinder is located in the correct position and pose in respect to the robot's body. However, only 22 of 541 laser rays were simulated to optimize performance, since only 8 rays were used in the experiments.

Khepera II infra-red sensors are simulated by 8 short laser rays distributed evenly around the robot with the maximum measurable distance of $100mm$. The environment for Khepera II simulated environment is a right-angled triangle with side lengths $196mm$, $125mm$ and $233mm$.

3.3   Robot Movements

In the experiments the state vector is $s = (d_0, d_1, d_2, d_3)$, where d_i are sensor values for front, back, left and right sensors, accordingly. The robot is given a set of actions with corresponding reverse actions: movements forward-backward and turning left-right are pair-wise reverse-actions to each other. A discrete set of actions is used in the experiments: F – make a step forward, B – make a step backward, L – rotate counter-clockwise, R – rotate clockwise, where $F = -B$, $B = -F$, $L = -R$, $R = -L$.

Actions are defined in terms of commands to move forward/backward or rotate. An action $a = [m_{trans}, m_{rot}]$ consists of a pair of target movement deltas – m_{trans} is in metres and , m_{rot} is in degrees. For simulated Khepera II the values were set as follows:

$F = [+0.016, 0]$ – make a step forward,
$B = [-0.016, 0]$ – make a step backward,

Fig. 1. Environments for the experiments. Simulated Khepera II is on the left. Simulated Scitos G5 is in the center. Real Scitos G5 is on the right.

---

1. Record current state $s_i = (d_0, ..., d_3)$.
2. Execute a random action as a_i.
3. Record the state $s_{i+1} = (d_0, ..., d_3)$.
4. Execute the reverse action for a_i as a_{i+1} .
5. Record the resulting state as s_{i+2}.
6. Execute a random action as a_{i+2}.
7. Add 3 to i and repeat (goto 1).

Fig. 2. Movement algorithm (Phase 1)

$L = [0, +30]$ – rotate counter-clockwise,
$R = [0, -30]$ – rotate clockwise.
For both simulated and real Scitos G5 the values were set as follows:

$F = [+0.15, 0]$ – make a step forward,
$B = [-0.15, 0]$ – make a step backward,
$L = [0, +42]$ – rotate counter-clockwise,
$R = [0, -42]$ – rotate clockwise.

The robot moves using the algorithm described in Fig. 2 – robot makes a random move followed by its reverse action, then makes another random action, but without a reverse action, and then repeats the pattern. The purpose of the first two actions is to generate at least one pair of actions to generate intrinsic reward signal.The purpose of the next (random) action without a matching reverse action is to make the robot to explore the environment.

3.4 Software Design

The code consists of the following units:

- an independent agent that generates the sequence of actions to move the robot during the first phase.
- Q-Learning and reversibility based algorithms running in parallel
- a "switch" to route data between the agent and the algorithms, or to simulate the test run in the second phase.

1. Read current state $s_i = (d_0, ..., d_3)$ and the next action a_i from log.
2. Choose a number of reversibilities from the set of experienced ones with $a_{forward} = a_i$, based on $d_{orig}(s_i, s_{init})$ of experienced reversibility.
3. If no reversibilities are selected, make no prediction.
4. Calculate the expected irreversibility value (intrinsic reward) v_{rev} using $d_{rev}(s_{init}, s_{final})$ of experienced reversibilities.
5. If $v_{rev} > \varepsilon_{rev}$, then predict negative outcome, positive otherwise.
6. If $i < 2$, add 1 to i and repeat.
7. Read the last action as a_{i-1} and the previous action a_{i-2} from log.
8. If a_{i-1} is not a reverse-action of a_{i-2}, add 1 to i and repeat.
9. Add the new obtained reversibility as $(s_{i-2}, a_{i-2}, s_{i-1}, a_{i-1}, s_i)$ to the set of experienced reversibilities.
10. Add 1 to i and repeat (goto 1).

Fig. 3. Prediction data collection algorithm (Phase 2)

In the first phase real-world or simulated data is gathered from the test run and saved into a log file. The file contains sensor readings data, actions made and the outcomes of the actions. The second phase is a virtual run using collected data to calculate predictions and can be executed without a robot or a simulator. The log file from the first phase is loaded into memory, parsed as sensor readings and actions and then this history is fed to the algorithms, getting predictions of actions' successfulness simultaneously.

3.5   Reversibility Based Algorithm

The aim of the reversibility based algorithm is to predict if a certain action from a certain state is reversible or not. This is done by generating the intrinsic reward signal based on the distance between the initial and final state representations. The algorithm is described in Fig. 3. It takes a sequence of states and actions as an input: $s_0, a_0, s_1, a_1, s_2, a_2, s_3, ...$.

At every $i > 1$, if $a_{i-1} = -a_{i-2}$ then the reversibility $(s_{i-2}, a_{i-2}, s_{i-1}, a_{i-1}, s_i)$ is added to robot's experience, which is a vector of reversibilities.

To predict the outcome of making action a_t from state s_t, an intrinsic reward is calculated as an expected irreversibility value v_{rev} using a set of reversibilities, selected from the experience vector. In the experiments we select reversibilities with the same forward action and $d_{orig}(s_{init}, s_t) < \varepsilon_{orig}$, where s_{init} is the initial state of the reversibility under consideration.

The value of v_{rev} is a weighted average of $d_{rev}(s_{i-2}, s_i)$ values of selected reversibilities. Reversibilities are sorted by $d_{orig}(s_{init}, s_t)$ in an ascending order and their weights are $1/i^3$ (1, 1/8, 1/27, 1/256, etc), i.e. reversibilities with a "closer" initial state have considerably stronger influence.

In the experiments we use the Euclidean metric to calculate d_{orig} and d_{rev} ; the values ε_{orig} and ε_{rev} are finite and selected manually. The metric d_{dest} was not used in the experiments, i.e. $\varepsilon_{dest} = +\infty$.

3.6   Reinforcement Learning Algorithm

Reinforcement learning is a commonly used learning method to learn obstacle avoidance by trial and error ([14],[15],[16]). Therefore we have chosen a Q-Learning algorithm to compare the performance of the reversibility based learning to a standard method.

The main difference between reinforcement learning algorithms and the reversibility based algorithm is that a reinforcement learning algorithm receives an external reward signal indicating the success of an action. Reversibility based algorithm, on the other hand, uses only sensor data to determine the success of an action (which may also be interpreted as an intrinsic reward rising from the similarity of the initial and final states).

In the Q-Learning algorithm the expected reward of a state-action pair is updated using the following expression:

$$Q(s_t, a_t) \leftarrow Q(s_t, a_t) + \alpha_t(s_t, a_t)[r_t + \gamma Q(s_{t+1}, a_t) - Q(s_t, a_t)] .$$

Our experiment consists of random movements, therefore the long-term reward is irrelevant and only short-term reward should be used, for this reason we take $\gamma = 0$.

The prediction value is calculated as $sign(Q(s_t, a_t))$, i.e. negative Q means a negative prediction, positive Q means a positive prediction. Initially, Q values are set to 0 and if $Q = 0$, then no grounded prediction can be made.

3.7   Other Implementation Details

Real Scitos G5's default configuration file was altered to set rotational PID controller's Kp value to 0.2. Sensor values for Scitos G5 are in metres, therefore they are multiplied by 1000 to be of similar scale to the ones of Khepera II. This doesn't affect the reversibility based algorithm, but makes saving and loading the log files simpler.

During the experiments $\alpha_t(s_t, a_t)$ for Q-Learning update expression was set to 0.01. Threshold values ε_{orig}, ε_{rev} and the tile size for Reinforcement learning state identification were constant: $\varepsilon_{orig} = 11000$, $\varepsilon_{rev} = 10000$, $RLtilesize = 168$.

4   Results and Discussion

4.1   Results

During the tests 1 and 2 both learning methods are predicting collisions of simulated robots with simulated obstacles (walls). Fig. 4 and 5 represent the test results for simulated Khepera II and Scitos G5 environments respectively. In the test 3, shown in Fig. 6, the reversibility model from simulated test run is used to predict collisions of the real Scitos G5 robot with walls during the physical test run.

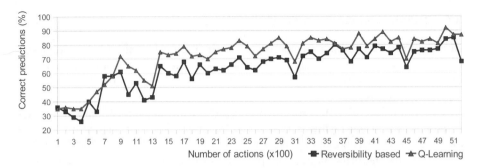

Fig. 4. Results of Test1 – simulated Khepera II

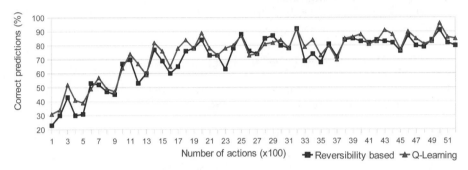

Fig. 5. Results of Test2 – simulated Scitos G5

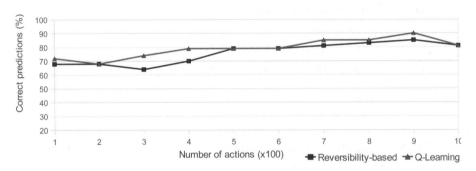

Fig. 6. Results of Test 3 – real Scitos G5 using simulated experience

The rate of correct prediction is calculated by sampling how many predictions out of a 100 were correct. If no prediction is made, then it counts as incorrect prediction. Downward spikes in prediction rate graphs are caused by novelty of the states, since no grounded prediction can be made for such unvisited states.

The rates of correct prediction of both algorithms in simulated environments start at 20–40% and gradually reach the level of 70–90% after 3900 steps. The robot with preloaded experience, obtained in simulation, performs quite well from the beginning. The rates of correct prediction in the real environment start at 70–75% and reach the level of 80–90% after 900 additional steps.

4.2   Q-Learning vs. Reversibility-Based Learning

On both simulated robots and the real Scitos G5 robot Q-Learning converges to a 5-10% higher prediction success rate than the reversibility-based learning. The Q-Learning algorithm is explicitly designed to avoid obstacles – at every collision the robot gets a negative reward signal proportional to the size of unfinished movement. The robot motivated to be able to reverse its actions has no concept of an obstacle or collision. The reversibility-based algorithm does not use the external reward signal and merely tries to predict whether the action will be reversible or not, based on its internal representations of similarities between the states. Also, the method of measuring the rate of correct predictions works in advantage of the Q-Learning algorithm, which predicts future rewards based on the experienced rewards, while the reversibility based algorithm predicts future rewards based on sensor data alone.

4.3   Real-Life Tests with Preloaded Simulator Data

The aim of the test 3 is to train the robot in the simulator to behave safely and then test the performance of the real robot in the real environment. The physical test run with the reversibility model built during the simulation test run shows success rate 65-70% from the very beginning of the test run. During the test in the real environment the performance improves further reaching to the success rate of the simulated run (ca 80%). This is because when put to the real environment, the robot still first encounters states it has not been trained for in the simulator. However, it adapts to the changes fairly fast and reaches the performance of the simulated robot of the test 2. This shows that a reversibility model can be learned in simulation to increase the safety of robot learning and then be corrected further on a physical robot.

4.4   Generality of the Approach

In general, we interpret the results as positive, since, indeed, a concrete robot behavior of obstacle avoidance is observed to emerge from the abstract principle "Don't do things you can't undo". However, there are problems with this straight-forward plain-sensor approach: it is influenced by many factors like sensor precision, sensor noise, actions' precision, etc. Although, this problem belongs more to the realm of the state identification: Q-Learning algorithm suffers from the same problems.

It is difficult to distinguish sensors by their importance for the particular action. Different kinds of sensors can also be a problem, since Euclidean distance takes all numbers equally into account. Thus, a sensor returning current time stamp or a sensor returning distance in millimetres and others in metres will be a problem in this case and will render both algorithms almost useless without additional tuning. Another problem is to choose threshold values ε_{orig}, ε_{dest} and ε_{rev}. We chose those values manually using statistical information of the data from a particular test run.

We therefore conclude that for the present approach it is not possible to run the same code absolutely interchangeably on different platforms. Despite that the goal to learn to reverse actions is purely abstract and the reward signal is intrinsic, it is still based on the real underlying sensor values, which makes the algorithm implementation somewhat dependent on the physical embodiment.

5   Conclusions

The aim of these experiments was to validate the concept of learning using an intrinsic reward signal based on the reversibility of robot's actions. We argued that by learning to reverse its actions the robot develops understanding of its own motion in the surrounding environment. We argued that in contrast with learning algorithms designed for a special purpose (e.g. obstacle avoidance) the reversibility based algorithm has an abstract intrinsic goal of being able to reverse actions. At the same time we aimed at showing that this abstract goal can lead to concrete safe behaviors, such as obstacle avoidance, when irreversible actions are suppressed. Our aim was to investigate further if this general idea works on different robots and how it performed with respect to a benchmark Q-learning algorithm. Furthermore, we aimed at showing that if such a robot is trained in simulations and then ran in real life, the performance of the robot is safer.

In general, we interpret the results as positive, since, indeed, a concrete robot behavior of obstacle avoidance is observed on two different robots to emerge from the abstract principle "Don't do things you can't undo". We encountered some problems with this straight-forward plain-sensor approach: it is influenced by many factors like sensor precision, sensor noise, actions' precision, etc. However, such state-identification problems are inherent for any state-based approach.

The experimental data analysis leads to the following conclusions:

1. The Q-learning algorithm based on an external reward signal is 5-10% more successful than the reversibility based algorithm using an intrinsic reward signal.
2. The real robot running with simulator pre-loaded data is ca 10% less successful than the robot trained in real environment. After additional learning steps it is able to quickly adjust its performance and measures up to the results achieved with the robot trained in real life. This suggests that the algorithms can mostly be learned in a simulator to increase safety of the robot and its environment.

5.1   Future Work

In the future we will continue testing the same principle in more complicated scenarios. We are trying to use environment-model-aware state identification, planning and internal simulation to further increase the complexity of generated behaviors. Another possible direction is to use the principle of reversibility to make other learning algorithms learn faster or safer, or both. Our ultimate goal is a multi-purpose personal robot-assistant with intrinsically safe autonomous decisions.

References

1. Ryan, R.M., Deci, E.L.: Intrinsic and extrinsic motivations: classic definitions and new directions. Contemporary Educational Psychology 25(1), 54–67 (2000)
2. Prescott, T.J., Montes Gonzalez, F.M., Gurney, K., Humphries, M.D., Redgrav, P.: A robot model of the basal ganglia: Behavior and intrinsic processing. Neural Networks 19(1), 31–61 (2006)
3. Schmidhuber, J.: Exploring the predictable. In: Ghosh, A., Tsutsui, S. (eds.) Advances in Evolutionary Computing, pp. 579–612. Springer, Heidelberg (2003)
4. Schmidhuber, J.: Self-Motivated Development Through Rewards for Predictor Errors / Improvements. In: 2005 AAAI Spring Symposium on Developmental Robotics, pp. 1994–1996 (2005)
5. Barto, A.G., Singh, S., Chentanez, N.: Intrinsically Motivated Learning of Hierarchical Collections of Skills. In: ICDL 2004, pp. 112–119 (2004)
6. Stout, A., Konidaris, G.D., Barto, A.G.: Intrinsically Motivated Reinforcement Learning-A Promising Framework For Developmental Robot Learning. In: The AAAI Spring Symposium on Developmental Robotics (2005)
7. Kaplan, F., Oudeyer, P.Y.: Motivational principles for visual know-how development. In: 3rd International Workshop on Epigenetic Robotics, pp. 73–80 (2003)
8. Oudeyer, P.Y., Kaplan, F.: Intrinsic Motivation Systems for Autonomous Mental Development. IEEE Trans. Evol. Comput. 11, 265–286 (2007)
9. Oudeyer, P.Y., Kaplan, F.: What is intrinsic motivation? A topology of computational approaches. In: Front. Neurorobotics, vol. 1 (2007)
10. Breazeal, C.: Designing Sociable Robots. Bradford Books/MIT Press, Cambridge (2002)
11. Kruusmaa, M., Gavshin, Y., Eppendahl, A.: Don't Do Things You Can't Undo: Reversibility Models for Generating Safe Behaviours. In: ICRA 2007, pp. 1134–1139 (2007)
12. Gavshin, Y., Kruusmaa, M.: Comparative experiments on the emergence of safe behaviours. In: TAROS 2008, pp. 65–70 (2008)
13. Gerkey, B., Vaughan, R., Howard, A.: The player/stage project: Tools for multi-robot and distributed sensor systems. In: ICAR 2003, pp. 317–323 (2003)
14. Lin, M., Zhu, J., Sun, Z.: Learning Obstacle Avoidance Behavior Using Multi-agent Learning with Fuzzy States. In: Bussler, C.J., Fensel, D. (eds.) AIMSA 2004. LNCS (LNAI), vol. 3192, pp. 389–398. Springer, Heidelberg (2004)
15. Gutnisky, D.A., Zanutto, B.S.: Learning Obstacle Avoidance with an Operant Behavior Model. Artificial Life 10(1), 65–81 (2004)
16. Macek, K., Petrovic, I., Peric, N.: A Reinforcement Learning Approach to Obstacle Avoidance of Mobile Robot. In: IEEE AMC 2002, pp. 462–466 (2002)

A Trajectory Tracking Application of Redundant Planar Robot Arm via Support Vector Machines

Emre Sariyildiz, Kemal Ucak, Gulay Oke, and Hakan Temeltas

Department of Control Engineering, Istanbul Technical University,
34469 Istanbul, Turkey
{esariyildiz,kemal.ucak,gulay.oke,hakan.temeltas}@itu.edu.tr

Abstract. In this paper we present a kinematic based trajectory tracking application of redundant planar robot arm by using support vector machine method (SVM). The main advantages of using the proposed method are that, it does not suffer from singularity that is the main problem of redundancy in robot kinematics and better results for the kinematic model of redundant robot arm can be obtained by using less training data. Training data are obtained by using the forward differential kinematic model of the robot arm. We also implement the trajectory tracking application by using Artificial Neural Networks (ANN). Two methods are compared with respect to their generalization performances, and training performance. Simulation results are given.

Keywords: Artificial Neural Networks, Redundancy, Robot Arm, Singularity, Support Vector Machine, Trajectory Tracking.

1 Introduction

The control of redundant robot manipulators has a wide research area in robotics. The redundant robot manipulators offer the potential to overcome many difficulties by increased manipulation ability and versatility [1, 2]. Thus, they are usually used in many robotic applications such as obstacle avoidance, singularity avoidance, complex manipulation etc. [3, 4, and 5]. However the redundant robot manipulators have many advantages, they require quite complex control structures and suffer from singularity problem.

A fundamental research task of redundant robot manipulation is to find out the appropriate way to control the system of redundant robot manipulator in the work space at any stage of the trajectory tracking. The equations of the kinematic problem of redundant robot manipulator are highly complex and nonlinear. Thus, obtaining an analytic solution for the kinematic problem of redundant robot arm is generally very hard even impossible task. Therefore, iterative solution methods are frequently used in redundant robot kinematics. Differential kinematic is one of the most important solution methods to cope with the redundancy problem [6, 7]. The main advantage of the differential kinematic is that it can be easily implemented any kind of mechanism.

A. Bouchachia (Ed.): ICAIS 2011, LNAI 6943, pp. 192–202, 2011.

Also, accurate and efficient kinematic based trajectory tracking applications can be easily implemented by using this method. Jacobian is used as a velocity mapping operator which transforms the joint velocities into the Cartesian linear and angular velocities of the end effector. A highly complex and nonlinear inverse kinematic problem of redundant robot manipulators can be numerically solved by just inversing the Jacobian matrix operator. However, differential kinematic based solutions can be easily implemented any kind of mechanisms, it has some disadvantages. The first one is that differential kinematic based solutions are locally linearized approximation of the inverse kinematic problems [8]. Thus, we can only obtain the approximate solutions of the inverse kinematic problem by using this method. Although the solution results of this method are not real, the approximation results are generally quite sufficient. The second disadvantage of this method is that it has heavy computational loads and big computational time because of numerical iterative approach. To obtain the inverse kinematic solution, we need to calculate the inverse of the Jacobian matrix. Taking inverse of a matrix is generally hard task and the singularity is one of the main problems of this calculation. There are many researches and applications of singularity problem of robot manipulators. There are, in general, four main techniques to cope with the singularity problem of robot manipulators. These are avoiding singular configuration method, robust inverse method, a normal form approach method and extended Jacobian method [9-12]. However given techniques have some disadvantages which include computational load and errors. And the last disadvantage of the differential kinematic method is that, it requires numerical integration which suffers from numerical errors, to obtain the joint positions from the joint velocities [13].

In recent years, Artificial Neural Network (ANN) based solution methods of kinematic problem of robot manipulators have been demonstrated [14-16]. There are two important advantages of ANN based inverse kinematic solution methods. The first one is that these methods do not suffer from the complex and highly nonlinear inverse kinematic equations and they can be easily implemented any kind of mechanism. And the second one is that ANN based inverse kinematic solution methods do not suffer from singularity problem. ANN based models can be obtained locally and it uses back propagation algorithm. SVM is also another Intelligent System Identification method which ensures global minimal solution. The strengths of SVM based modeling are that it doesn't get stuck at local minima and it has powerful generalization abilities with very few training data. Therefore, in recent years, Support Vector Machine theory has been used in many Identification problems, instead of Artificial Neural Network approach.

In this paper we present a new Artificial Intelligent based inverse kinematic solution method for the planar redundant robot manipulator. This solution method uses Support Vector Machine method. Satisfactory trajectory tracking result is obtained by using the proposed method and the simulation results of redundant planar robot arm are given in section 4. This paper is also include, the mathematical model of the system in section 2, a brief overview of Support Vector Regression in section 3. Conclusion and future works are drawn in the final section.

2   Differential Kinematics

It is very hard or even impossible to find the analytical solutions of the inverse kinematic problem of the redundant robot manipulators except the limited special structures or very easy mechanisms. Therefore, differential kinematic based solution of the inverse kinematic problem of redundant robot manipulators is widely used [15]. In the differential kinematic based solutions, a velocity mapping which transforms the Cartesian linear and angular velocities of the end effector of robot manipulators to the joint velocities, is used as the following,

$$\dot{\mathbf{q}} = J^g(\mathbf{q}) \mathbf{V_{tip}} \tag{1}$$

where $\mathbf{q} = \begin{bmatrix} q_1 & q_2 & \cdots & q_n \end{bmatrix}$ and $\dot{\mathbf{q}} = \begin{bmatrix} \dot{q}_1 & \dot{q}_2 & \cdots & \dot{q}_n \end{bmatrix}$ indicate joint angles and joint velocities respectively, $J^g(\mathbf{q})$ indicates generalized inverse of the Jacobian matrix and $\mathbf{V_{tip}}$ indicates the linear and angular velocities of the robot manipulator's end effector. Jacobian can be obtained by using analytical or geometric approaches which can be found in many basic robotic books [16-17]. The joint angles can be found by integrating the joint velocities given by

$$\mathbf{q} = \int_0^t \dot{\mathbf{q}} dt = \int_0^t J^g(\mathbf{q}) \mathbf{V_{tip}} dt \tag{2}$$

3   Support Vector Regression

3.1   Linear Regression

Given a training data set:

$$(y_1, \underline{x}_1)\dots(y_k, \underline{x}_k), \quad x \in R^n, y \in R \quad k = 1, 2, ,,, k. \tag{3}$$

where k is the size of training data and n is the dimension of the input matrix can be approximated by a linear function, with the following form,

$$f(\underline{x}) = \langle \underline{w}, \underline{x} \rangle + b \tag{4}$$

where $\langle ., . \rangle$ denotes the inner product. The optimum regression function is determined by the minimum of equation (5).

$$\Phi(\underline{w}) = \frac{1}{2} \|\underline{w}\|^2 \tag{5}$$

$\mathcal{E}$ - Tolerance Loss Function, shown in Figure 1, sets the constraints of the primal form. The primal form of the optimization problem for $\mathcal{E}$ -SVR is defined as follows to maximize the geometric margin and minimize the training error:

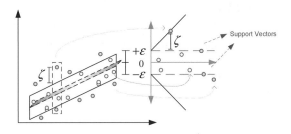

Fig. 1. ε - Tolerance Loss Function

$$\min_{(w,b,\xi_i,\xi_i^*)} \frac{1}{2}\|w\|^2 + C\sum_{i=1}^{l}(\xi_i + \xi_i^*)$$

subject to

$$y_i - \langle w, x_i \rangle - b \leq \varepsilon + \xi_i$$
$$\langle w, x_i \rangle + b - y_i \leq \varepsilon + \xi_i^* \qquad (6)$$
$$\xi_i, \xi_i^* \geq 0$$

The term $\|w\|$ is the Euclidean norm of weights, which symbolizes the model complexity, and the second term of the objective function is the empirical risk of weight vector. By means of the C parameter, predetermined parameter, the trade-off between model complexity and empirical loss function can be determined.

ξ_i, ξ_i^* are slack variables representing the upper and lower constraints on the output of the system [19]. The model complexity and the training error are minimized through $\frac{1}{2}\|w\|^2$ and $C\sum_{i=1}^{l}(\xi_i + \xi_i^*)$ respectively. The minimization problem presented in equation (4) is called the primal objective function [19,20 and 22]. The key idea in SVMs is to construct a Lagrange function from the primal objective function and the corresponding constraints, by introducing a dual set of variables [20].

By utilizing the primal objective function and its constraints, Lagrangian function can be derived as follows:

$$L = \frac{1}{2}\|w\|^2 + C\sum_{i=1}^{l}(\xi_i + \xi_i^*) - \sum_{i=1}^{l}\alpha_i(\varepsilon + \xi_i - y_i + \langle w, x_i \rangle + b)$$
$$-\sum_{i=1}^{l}\alpha_i^*(\varepsilon + \xi_i^* + y_i - \langle w, x_i \rangle - b) - \sum_{i=1}^{l}(\eta_i\xi_i + \eta_i^*\xi_i^*) \qquad (7)$$

In (7), L is the Lagrangian and $\eta_i, \eta_i^*, \alpha_i, \alpha_i^*$ are Lagrange multipliers [20]. Hence the dual variables in (7) have to satisfy positivity constraints, i.e. $\alpha_i^*, \eta_i^* \geq 0$.

Due to the fact that the Lagrangian function has a saddle point with respect to the primal and dual variables at the solution, the partial derivatives of L with respect to primal variables (w, b, ξ_i, ξ_i^*) have to vanish for optimality[20]:

$$\frac{\partial L}{\partial b} = \sum_{i=1}^{l} (\alpha_i^* - \alpha_i) = 0 \tag{8}$$

$$\frac{\partial L}{\partial w} = \underline{w} - \sum_{i=1}^{l} (\alpha_i - \alpha_i^*)\underline{x}_i = 0 \tag{9}$$

$$\underline{w} = \sum_{i=1}^{l} (\alpha_i - \alpha_i^*)\underline{x}_i$$

$$\frac{\partial L}{\partial \xi_i^{(*)}} = C - \partial_i^{(*)} - \eta_i^{(*)} = 0 \tag{10}$$

(Note: $\partial_i^{(*)}$ refers to α_i and α_i^*).

It is transformed to dual form, by utilizing equation (9) above. Dual form of the regression problem is defined as follows:

$$\min_{\alpha_i, \alpha_i^*} \frac{1}{2} \sum_{i=1}^{l} \sum_{j=1}^{l} (\alpha_i - \alpha_i^*)(\alpha_j - \alpha_j^*)\langle \underline{x}_i, \underline{x}_j \rangle - \sum_{i=1}^{l} [\alpha_i(y_i - \varepsilon) - \alpha_i^*(y_i + \varepsilon)] \tag{11}$$

subject to

$$0 \le \alpha_i \le C \quad i = 1, 2, 3, , , , , , , , , l$$
$$0 \le \alpha_i^* \le C \quad i = 1, 2, 3, , , , , , , , , l \tag{12}$$
$$\sum_{i=1}^{l} (\alpha_i - \alpha_i^*) = 0$$

As can be seen from the dual form of the optimization problem, the objective function is convex. That's, the problem has single local minima which is also global solution of the problem. This dual problem can be solved by finding Lagrange multipliers utilizing a quadratic programming technique (in our implementation, the "quadprog" command from Matlab optimization toolbox was used). The support vectors are the training data related to nonzero Lagrange multipliers [19,20 and 21]. The solution of the regression problem can be approximated by the support vectors and the related Lagrange multipliers.

3.2 Non-linear Regression

Occasionally, the training data may be nonlinearly distributed and cannot be separated with a linear regression surface. In this case, the training data is mapped onto a high dimensional feature space by means of a kernel function as depicted in Figure 2. This allows us to use linear regression techniques to solve non-linear regression problems. In this paper, Gaussian function has been employed as the kernel function:

$$K\left(\mathbf{x},\mathbf{y}\right)=\exp\left(-\frac{\|\mathbf{x}\text{-}\mathbf{y}\|^2}{2\sigma^2}\right)$$

(13)

where σ is the bandwidth of the Gaussian radial basis kernel function.

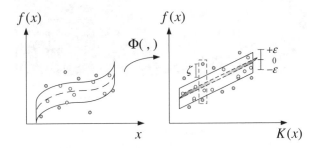

Fig. 2. Transition of data not represented by a linear regression surface to the feature space using kernel

All linear regression formulas can be transformed to non-linear regression equations using $K(\underline{x}_i,\underline{x}_j)$ instead of $\langle\underline{x}_i,\underline{x}_j\rangle$ shaped inner product. Thus, the non-linear regression or approximation function, the optimal desired weights vector of the regression hyperplane and an optimal bias of the regression hyperplane can be expressed in terms of support vectors as given in (14)-(16) [19,22] :

$$f(\underline{x})=\sum_{i\in SV}\lambda_iK\langle\underline{x}_i,\underline{x}\rangle+b\ ,\ \lambda_i=\alpha_i-\alpha_i^*$$

(14)

$$\langle\underline{w},\underline{x}\rangle=\sum_{i\in SV}\lambda_iK\langle\underline{x}_i,\underline{x}\rangle$$

(15)

$$b=\frac{1}{l}\sum_{i=1}^{l}(y_i-\sum_{i\in SV}\lambda_iK\langle\underline{x}_i,\underline{x}\rangle)$$

(16)

4 Simulation Results

Three link planar robot arm which can be seen in figure 3 is utilized in the simulation studies. The simulation study of the trajectory tracking application is performed by using Matlab and the animation application is performed by using virtual reality toolbox (VRML) of Matlab.

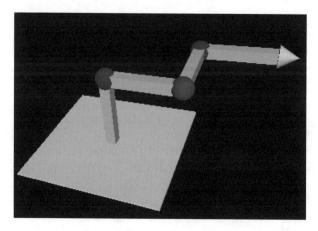

Fig. 3. Three Link Planar Robot Arm

So as to reveal all dynamics of the manipulator, a random signal has been applied to the manipulator. 300 data are selected randomly for training process. The inputs and outputs of the SVM and ANN models are as in fig. 4.

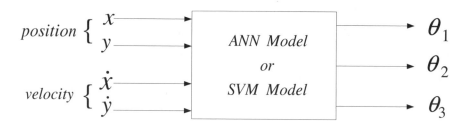

Fig. 4. ANN and SVM Model

As all training data is arranged according to model in fig. 4, training process is converted to finding the solution of the regression problem. Same training data has been utilized both in ANN and SVM. The models of the system, as in fig. 4, have been trained in the series-parallel (SP) mode. Three separate SVR MISO structures have been combined to model the MIMO model of the manipulator. C is set to 10000 in order to keep the number of the support vector as low as possible. ε and σ have been selected 0.001 and 0.1 respectively. In order to compare ANN and SVM model one hidden layer with 50 neuron has been employed in ANN. The results of the ANN and SVM models are depicted in fig. 5,6,7 for all links.

Figure 5 illustrates the simulation result of ANN Model and SVM model with 23 support vectors. SVM model in fig. 6 and 7 has 40 and 61 support vectors respectively. As can be seen from figures, in spite of using same training data, SVM models the dynamics of the manipulator better than ANN owing to finding global solution of the regression problem. The following equation is used to evaluate the improvement in performance:

$$\text{Impr} = 100 \sum_{n=1}^{N} \frac{\left| x_{ANN}(n) \right| - \left| x_{SVM}(n) \right|}{\left| x_{ANN}(n) \right|} \tag{17}$$

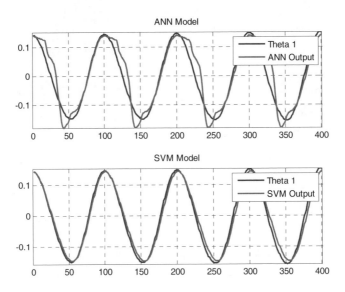

Fig. 5. Outputs of the SVM and ANN Models for theta 1 (θ_1)

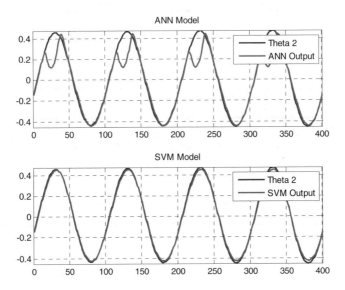

Fig. 6. Outputs of the SVM and ANN Models for theta 2 (θ_2)

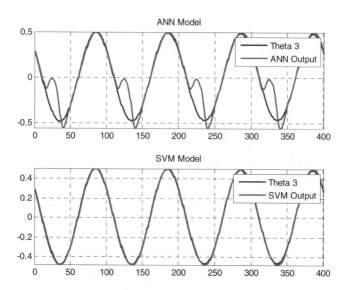

Fig. 7. Outputs of the SVM and ANN Models for theta 3 (θ_3)

Table 1. Training and Validation Performances

Error(MAE)	ANN 1	SVR 1	Improvement (%)
Training Error	4.0676e-005	2.8491e-007	99.2996
Validation Error	0.0012	2.0744e-004	82.3523

Table 2. Training and Validation Performances

Error(MAE)	ANN 2	SVR 2	Improvement (%)
Training Error	9.0317e-006	3.4958e-007	96.1294
Validation Error	0.0112	2.2100e-004	98.0286

Table 3. Training and Validation Performances

Error(MAE)	ANN 3	SVR 3	Improvement (%)
Training Error	6.2502e-006	5.5473e-007	91.1246
Validation Error	0.0161	1.5761e-004	99.0229

As can be seen from fig. 5-7, ANN model of manipulator can not learn some dynamics although same training data has been utilized. The tables indicate that SVR has better generalization performance and models the dynamics of manipulator better than ANN although both ANN and SVM model have few training error.

5 Conclusion

A kinematic based trajectory tracking application of a redundant planar robot arm is presented by using Support Vector Machine method. The main advantages of the SVM based modeling are that it doesn't get stuck at local minima and it has powerful generalization abilities with very few training data. The proposed method and ANN based solution method are compared with respect to their training and generalization performances. As it can be seen from tables in simulation section, model based on SVR has better generalization performance than ANN based model since SVM ensures global minima.

In the future works, dynamic modeling of redundant robot manipulator will be studied by using SVM method combined with the powerful features of fuzzy logic.

References

1. Chang, P.H.: A Closed-Form Solution for Inverse Kinematics of Robot Manipulators with Redundancy. IEEE Journal of Robotics and Automation RA-3(5) (October 1987)
2. Yoshikawa, T.: Analysis and Control of Robot Manipulators with Redundancy. In: Robotics Research–The First International Symposium, pp. 735–747. MIT Press, Cambridge (1984)
3. Uchiyama, M.: Study in Dynamic Control of Artificial Arm-Part I. Trans. JSME 45(391), 314–322 (1979)
4. Ping, G., Wei, B., Li, X., Luo, X.: Real-Time Obstacle Avoidance for Redundant Robot. In: IEEE International Conference on Mechatronics and Automation, pp. 223–228 (August 2009)
5. Lin, C.C.: Motion Planning of Redundant Robots. Journal of Robotic Systems 14(12), 839–850 (1997)
6. Wolovich, W.A., Elliott, H.: A Computational Technique for Inverse Kinematics. In: Proceedings of 23rd Conference on Decision and Control (December 1984)
7. Caccavale, F., Chiacchio, P., Chiaverini, S., Siciliano, B.: Experiments of Kinematic Control on a Redundant Robot Manipulator. Laboratory Robotics and Automation 8, 25–36 (1996)
8. Siciliano, B., Khatib, O.: Handbook of Robotics. Springer, Heidelberg (2008)
9. Hu, Z., Fu, Z., Fang, H.: Study of singularity robust inverse of Jacobian matrix for manipulator. In: International Conference on Machine Learning and Cybernetics, Beijing, pp. 406–410 (2002)
10. Nakamura, Y., Hanafusa, H.: Inverse kinematic solutions with singularity robustness for robot manipulator control. Journal of Dynamic Systems, Measurement and Control 108, 163–171 (1986)
11. Wampler, C.W.: Manipulator inverse kinematic solutions based on vector formulations and damped least-squares methods. IEEE Transactions on Systems, Man and Cybernetics 16, 93–101 (1986)
12. Balestrino, A., De Maria, G., Sciavicco, L.: Robust control of robotic manipulators. In: International Proceedings of the 9th IFAC World Congress, Budapest, vol. 6, pp. 80–85 (1984)

13. Lin, S., Huang, C.W.: Numerical Integration of Multibody Mechanical Systems Using Baumgarte's Constraint Stabilization Method. Journal of the Chinese Institute of Engineers 25(2), 243–252 (2002)
14. Hasan, A.T., Ismail, N., Hamouda, A.M.S., Aris, I., Marhaban, M.H., Al-Assadi, H.M.A.A.: Artificial Neural Network-Based Kinematics Jacobian Solution for Serial Manipulator Passing through Singular Configurations. In: Advances in Engineering Software 41, 359–367 (2010)
15. Karilk, B., Aydin, S.: An improved approach to the solution of inverse kinematics problems for robot manipulators. J. Eng. Appl. Artif. Int. 13, 159–164 (2000)
16. Ogawa, T., Matsuura, H., Kanada, H.: A Solution of inverse kinematics of robot arm using network inversion. In: Proceedings of the 2005 International Conference on Computational Intelligence for Modelling (2005)
17. Spong, M.W., Hutchinson, S., Vidyasagar, M.: Robot Modeling and Control. Wiley, Chichester (2005)
18. Craig, J.J.: Introduction to robotics: Mechanics and Control, 3rd edn. Prentice-Hall, Englewood Cliffs (2006)
19. Gunn, S.: Support Vector Machines for Classification and Regression, ISIS Technical Report (1998)
20. Smola, A.J., Scholkopf, B.: A Tutorial on Support Vector Regression. Statistics and Computing 14, 199–222 (2004)
21. Vapnik, V.: The Nature of Statistical Learning Theory. Springer, New York (1995)
22. Suykens, J.A.K.: Nonlinear Modeling and Support Vector Machines. In: IEEE Instrumentation and Measurement Technology Conference Budapest, Hungary, vol. 1, pp. 287–294 (2001)

Intelligent Crossroads for Vehicle Platoons Reconfiguration

Baudouin Dafflon[1], Franck Gechter[1], Jean-Michel Contet[1],
Abdeljalil Abbas-Turki[1], and Pablo Gruer[1]

Laboratoire Systèmes et Transports
Université de Technologie de Belfort-Montbéliard
{firstname.lastname}@utbm.fr
http://set.utbm.fr

Abstract. Nowadays, urban environments suffer from recurrent traffic jam with associated side effects. One reason of this is the social implicit priority given to personal cars, which are preferred to public transportation systems the main drawback of which is the time and path rigidity. Recently, some alternative transportation systems have been developed based on size adaptable trains of vehicles called platoon. These approaches still suffer from rigid path planning. The paper presents one possible solution to overcome this drawback. The proposal is based on the use of existing crossroads as hubs able to reconfigure vehicles train while crossing. Thanks to this solution, each train component could have its specific path in the public transportation grid. This paper presents also a comparative study of exposed algorithms relatively to a classical traffic light schedule.

Keywords: active crossroad, platoon, vehicles train, train dynamical reconfiguration.

1 Introduction

Nowadays, urban environments suffer from recurrent traffic jam. Consequently, undesirable side effects occur such as greenhouse effect gas (COx NOx,...) and particle emission, noise pollution, transportation time increase... One of the reasons that lead to this situation is the priority choice of a personal car instead of public transportation devices. Moreover, statistical studies established that a high percentage of urban moving cars are occupied by the driver only. However, widely developed, public transportation systems seem to stay unattractive. Many reasons can explain this fact: regular transportation system is rigid (timetable, table, itinerary,...). They are uncomfortable, several transportation systems are required to reach one specific destination,...

To convince people, some research is devoted to create a new transportation service aimed at offering some properties generally associated to personal car. Indeed, these new systems must possess a set of properties such as **adaptability** to the user demand, **autonomy** to be able to act independently to schedule or predetermined path, **reconfigurability** to accommodate a variable number

A. Bouchachia (Ed.): ICAIS 2011, LNAI 6943, pp. 203–214, 2011.

of people to transport. One possible solution, demonstrated in the CRISTAL project[1], is the use of small mobility units that can both be used by a regular driver as a standard electrical vehicle in car sharing and be structured as vehicles immaterial train (i.e. with no material link between vehicles) driven by a professional. To perform This way, each mobility unit is autonomous and proposed service both separately or integrated within a platoon (cf. figure 1).

Fig. 1. Example of vehicle platoon system (CATS European Project)

The key element of such an approach is the platoon function, i.e. the function that makes vehicles able to follow each other without a material link. This function can be considered as the control of the vehicle's inter-distance. This control problem is addressed through two sub problems: longitudinal control and lateral control. The longitudinal control consists in regulating braking and acceleration in order to fix the inter-vehicle distance to a predefined regular distance. By the same, lateral control consists in computing a wheel direction according to the platoon trajectory.

In literature, platoon control can be encountered as global or local approaches. **Global** approaches are composed of a decision-making vehicle, generally integrated in the first vehicle of the train, which computes some reference informations (trajectory points, steering and speed instruction, ...) and send them to each follower vehicle. For example, [1,2] uses a global positioning system to compute trajectory points and communicate them to the follower vehicles. Another approach [3] consists in broadcasts driving information (steering and speed) to each follower vehicle, as what was made in *Chauffeur* European project. Literature exposes that this approach yield good trajectory matching. However, global positioning sensors or other technologies require road adaptation. Besides, a safe, reliable vehicle-to-vehicle communication network is required. Global control approaches yield adequate results, subject to strong constraints on sensors (high cost), road adaptation and communication reliability between vehicles.

Local approaches are based only on vehicle's perception capabilities. Vehicles are equipped with low cost sensors, which compute measurements such as inter-vehicle distance vectors. Each vehicle computes the acceleration and wheel

---

[1] http://projet-cristal.net/

direction commands with its own perceptions. In literature, local control strategies proposed within local approaches general use PID controllers [4,5,6] or other regulation-loop based algorithm [7,8,9]. Other proposed approaches are based on a physics-inspired, inter-vehicular interaction link from which vehicle's control references can be computed, as in [10] or in [11]. The main interest of local approach is the technical simplicity, require neither expensive road infrastructure, nor reliable inter-vehicle communication and use cheaper and more reliable sensors than the global approaches. However, these approaches suffer from the anticipation error problem. Some recent researches tend to cover this problem. [12] is a local approach which minimizes the anticipation error by taking into account local curve properties with performance levels close to those obtained by global control.

Even with reliable and efficient embedded platoon functionalities, vehicle virtual train transportation systems still have several drawbacks. Among these, the most handicapping is the fixed-line constraints since people who use the platoon are obliged to follow the pre-determined path, even if this was set on the fly. A solution to overcome this problem is to allow a vehicle platoon to merge, split and reconfigure at specific points in order to make users can build their own path using small mobility units that are able to move autonomously hanging on existing vehicles trains. Existing crossroads can be good candidates for these reconfiguration points. The goal of this paper is to present a solution for the reconfiguration of vehicles virtual train on crossroads. This solution is based on a merge of vehicle behaviors and crossroads intelligent priority assignment. In the presented solution, the reconfiguration procedure is totally autonomous. This contrasts with classical methods where each driver has to take the control of its own vehicle on crossroads, following standard circulation rules, making a new train coupling after the crossroad.

The paper is structured as follows: Section 2 presents a state of the art of active crossroads systems. Then, sections 3 and 4 give a detail explanation of the crossroad model and a presentation of the associated experimental results. The paper concludes with an overview of future works (Section 5).

2   Active Crossroads: State of the Art

Since the vehicle virtual train transportation systems are neither vehicles nor trains, then one of the most important challenges that the concept has to face is the intersection. On the one hand, the traditional traffic lights do not take into consideration long and slow virtual trains of vehicles that cross the intersection. Indeed, the traffic light can change the color without considering whether all the vehicles that belong to the same platoon are released [15]. A similar problem can occur in an intersection with a stop sign. On the other hand, in cities, tramway's signalization considers the previously known number of rail cars. The green time is accordingly fixed to few seconds [16]. However, the core of the proposed system is that the number of virtually attached vehicles is variable. Thus, the initially computed green time may not match the length of the virtual train. Hence, the traffic signalization at intersections deserves a particular attention.

One way to overcome this matter is to use the Traffic-Responsive Strategy based on the vehicle-interval method [17]. A critical interval (CI) is created, during which any detected vehicle leads to a green prolongation that allows a vehicle to cross the intersection. If no vehicle is detected during CI, the strategy proceeds to the next stage. However, this strategy requires some adaptations. Indeed, this strategy is applicable to two-stage intersections and designed for ordinary vehicles [18]. More precisely, a crossroad of virtual trains needs more than two stages, the minimum and the maximum-green durations are not required, the length of the critical interval needs to be accurately estimated and the usual location of the inductive loop detectors (40m upstream of the stop line) is not adapted to our application. Moreover, only the virtual locomotive needs to be informed about whether or not it has the right of way. So, the prolongation of the green light is useless.

From the point of view of the traffic efficiency, the work presented in [19] proposes an interesting approach for building the solution to our system. The authors assume an intersection and vehicles that can wirelessly communicate together. The authors use the well-known Littles formula, for optimizing the traffic. As a result, the stage that releases the greatest number of vehicles is selected. Nevertheless, the use of wireless communication raises the problems of the rates of successful messages and of the communication delay [20]. Hence, an innovative traffic signalization at intersections is required for the vehicle virtual train transportation systems. We will call this signalization: Active Signalization.

3   Crossroads and Vehicle Models

3.1   Global Overview

In this paper, crossroads are considered to be reconfiguration hubs for incoming platoons (i.e. vehicle trains). Each platoon is composed of several mobility units, which can be autonomous (in train configuration) or human drivable (in single configuration). In a standard traffic light crossroad, this re-configuration requires to turn each vehicle from autonomous mode to driven mode in order to complete merge and split maneuvers. The goal of the approach presented in this paper is to bring to crossroads intelligent routing abilities in order to keep each vehicle in autonomous mode. In this section, vehicle and crossroad models are detailed.

3.2   Vehicle Specification

Required functionalities

The vehicles used are supposed to have got autonomous abilities. To that way, they are equipped by sensors aimed at perceiving surrounded environment. They also are able to decide, which is the best command to apply in a specific situation. In particular, vehicles have platoon functionality, i.e. they can follow the trajectory of a front perceived object/vehicle. This functionality is used in our case for the train crossroads entrance and exit. Moreover, they also have the

Fig. 2. SeTCAR: one of Système et Transports Laboratory vehicles

capability to perceive the crossroads signals aimed at stopping the vehicle when necessary and giving it drive authorization.

Figure 2 represents such a platoon able vehicles. This, called SeTCAR, has been transformed in our laboratory based on standard electrical cars (GEM cars). It was upgraded by integrating direction, speed and breaking control using a Dspace Microautobox[2]. Moreover, SeTCAR is equipped by several sensors such as Laser Range Finders, Lidar, mono-camera, stereo-camera, RTK GPS, Gyroscope, magnetic field detector, ...

Vehicle behavior

Vehicle behavior can be split into three phases:

– **Crossroad entrance:** Vehicles arrive within a platoon, each vehicle following its predecessor except for head vehicle, which is human driven. When an incoming train is near the crossroad (i.e. when it arrives into crossroad perception range), each vehicle turns into autonomous mode. In this mode, vehicles follow incoming predetermined trajectory thanks to specific sensors/beacons[3]. Moreover, vehicles turning signal lights are also autonomously controlled depending on the goal path of each vehicle.

– **Crossroad control:** When in crossroad, each vehicle follows trajectories enlightened by the crossroad decision process. Decisions are made depending on crossroad configuration and vehicle constraints (see next section for more details. The enlightenment process consists in activating the specific vehicle perceivable beacons which virtually draw authorized trajectories over the road. Each vehicle follows one trajectory in order to reach its destination point. If no beacon is detected vehicle stays at its place waiting for beacon activation.

– **Crossroad exit:** After passing the crossroad, vehicles turn from autonomous mode to regular platoon mode. The driver in the head vehicle takes control of the train.

---

[2] http://www.dspace.de/en/pub/home/products/hw/micautob.cfm
[3] In our case a Laser Range Finder and reflective beacons placed on the road.

3.3 Crossroads Model

Crossroad decision process is based on a perception rule-based decision loop. This section describes first the perception abilities of the crossroad, and then exposes two proposals for the decision process.

Perception

Crossroad is able to perceive pending cars and exiting cars. Each incoming road has got a pending car detector. This runs as a simple switch the result of which is equal to 1 when a car is waiting and 0 when there is no car. Moreover, each pending detector is able to count the number of car, which leaves the incoming road to enter the hub area. In simulation, this detector has been made thanks to boxcollider as shown in figure 3 left. In real crossroads, regular magnetic loop can be used.

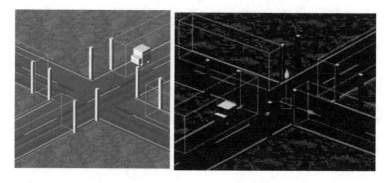

Fig. 3. Pending car detector (left) and output car detector (right) in Vivus Simulator

By the same, each output road is equipped by an output car detector, the goal of which is to count the number of vehicle exiting the hub. Combining this information with the number of vehicles in the hub counted by pending detectors, it is possible to determine if vehicles are still in the hub. These detectors have been also made with boxcollider in simulation (cf. figure 3 right) and can be made with magnetic loop in real road configuration.

Behavior: Regular traffic light. This behavior has been developed in order to obtain a reference in adaptive decision process evaluation. The solution used is based on the simplest possible control system. It uses a timer with a fixed passing time (T_p) whatever the chosen lane (i.e. there is no priority of one lane over the other). Each phase of the signal lasts for a specific duration before the next phase occurs; this pattern repeats itself regardless of traffic. When one light turns to red, traffic lights of the perpendicular lanes stay red for a fixed time called full red time (T_{fr}). This is made to avoid collision between cars that have passed the crossroad on orange and those that start early when light turns green. Older traffic light systems still use this synchronization model.

Behavior: Priority to first incoming vehicle. This first adaptive decision process is based on simple rules:

1. The first vehicle to enter in the perception range of the crossroad has the priority.
2. If more than one vehicle enter the perception at the same time priority is given to right.
3. If four vehicles enter at the same time (i.e. this corresponds to a situation which can not be solved by the two previous rules), priority is given randomly.
4. When all vehicles of one turn left the hub, decision process returns in step 1 until crossroad is empty.

Behavior: Configuration Analysis based decision process The previous hub adaptive behavior can improve the release time of the crossroad. However, there is still one drawback that should be overcome. Indeed, previous behavior processes only one vehicle at each loop. When the processed vehicle leaves the crossroad, hub takes into account next one. In order to optimize the release time, it has been decided to maximize the number of cars entering the hub. The main difficulty is not to introduce more road's conflicts. To that way, all the possible input configuration has been listed taking into account both the presence of the vehicle and the goal of them using turning light perception. Each configuration corresponds to a string of characters. The particularity of this encoding is that it is relative. it does not describe the routes according to the departure and arrival, but in relation to action that will realize the car (go right, go left ...). Table 1 shows the list of usable characters.

Table 1. Usable characters for description of crossroad input configuration

R	L	F	X
Vehicle goes to **Right** direction	Vehicle goes to **Left** direction	Vehicle goes **Forward**	There is no vehicle in the lane

For each configuration, we are now able to generate the corresponding code starting from bottom right and turning counterclockwise. Then the rank of each computed. It corresponds to the number of vehicle that is able to pass the hub at the same time. Table 2 shows all the possible configurations.

The other possible combinations can be deduced from these by rotation. This corresponds to circular permutation of the code. Once the code of the configuration is determined, the crossroad chooses the one which allows to get pass the maximum of vehicles.

4   Experimental Results

4.1   Simulation Description

Vivus Simulator

Many simulators aimed at studying vehicles dynamics are existing. Among the most popular, we can cite Callas and Prosper and widely used in automotive

Table 2. Possible input configurations with their associated code

Rank	4	3	3	2	2	2
Coding	R R R R	R R R X	R F X R	R R X X	R X R X	F X F X
Example						
Rank	2	2	2	1	1	1
Coding	F X R X	F X X R	R L X X	R X X X	F X X X	L X X X
Example						

industry. Most of them are focusing on mechanical simulation of the vehicle with a special focus on tyre/road contact. The main drawback of these is the requirement of real vehicle to build a dynamical model and the difficulty to integrate virtual sensors and onboard artificial intelligence abilities.

In this context, System and Transportation Laboratory decided to develop a simulation/prototyping tool, named Virtual Intelligent Vehicle Urban Simulator (VIVUS), aimed at simulating vehicles and sensors, taking into account their physical properties and prototyping artificial intelligence algorithms such as platoon solutions [12] or obstacle avoidance devices [13].

VIVUS was initially based on Java 3D for the 3D graphical part and on PhysX for sensors and vehicle dynamic behaviors [14]. The main problem of this solution is the communication between 3D and Physical part, since they are in different programming languages (Java for the 3D part and C++ for the physical one). Thus, it has been decided to use a simulation environment which can integrate both parts. VIVUS is now based on Unity3D[4]. Unity3D is an integrated authoring tool for creating interactive content such as architectural visualizations or real-time 3D animations. This engine allows to create real-time 3D environment with a real physic interaction between the elements situated in the 3D environment.

In VIVUS, simulating a vehicle consists in physical behaviors, sensors/perception and control board simulations.

Physics 3D model is based on the Physx engine, integrated into Unity3D. This engine is one of the best considering the accuracy and the realistic behavior obtained. In order to obtain simulation results as near as possible from the reality, a complete physical model of vehicles has been made. Models designed for Physx are based on composition of Physx elementary objects. The simulated vehicle is then considered as a rectangular chassis with four engine/wheel components. This choice can be considered to be realist, the chassis being made as a rectangular un-deformable shape. As for the engine/wheel components, vehicle

---

[4] http://unity3d.com/

platform owns 4 wheel drive each of them being directly linked to one electrical engine.

Each simulated vehicles are equipped by sensors. VIVUS allows to simulate different sensors:

- *image sensor* produces a bitmap
- *video sensor* produces a sequence of bitmaps
- *geometric sensor* produces information of collisions on a predefined set of rays or between object
- *location sensor* produces the vehicle position and orientation
- *state sensor* produces the state of the vehicle or one of its components (communications, engine, etc.) or the state of the simulated environment's components like weather report.

Algorithm	Traffic light	First in priority	Configuration Analysis
Release Time	102.70	67.34	60.09
Mean vehicle waiting time	59.75	38.97	33.91

Fig. 4. Small trains reconfiguration and associated results

Algorithm	Traffic light	First in priority	Configuration Analysis
Release Time	264.70	210.34	156.47
Mean vehicle waiting time	151.91	105.56	98.25

Fig. 5. Big train reconfiguration and associated results

Algorithm	Traffic light	First in priority	Configuration Analysis
Release Time	145.2703	132.62	98.94
Mean vehicle waiting time	85.88	73.21	51.89

Fig. 6. Example of mixed train and associated results

This simulator has been successfully used as a prototyping tool for sensor design/positioning and a development tested for artificial intelligence algorithms.

Experimental configurations and results
In order to compare the presented approaches, three typical configurations have been chosen:

1. a sequence with one car at each lane with a R L F F configuration cf. figure 4.
2. a sequence with four 3-car trains. The configuration is then FRR, RLL, FFL, and LFL cf. figure 5.
3. a sequence with a mixing between small and big train with the following configuration FRLR, FF, L, FL cf. figure 6.

Associated tables of figures 4, 5 and 6, gives the results obtained these three sequences. Release time, expressed in simulation cycle time, is the time required to process all the incoming vehicles. Mean waiting time is also expressed in simulation cycle time.

Results obtained show that both proposals drastically improve hub release time and mean waiting time as compared to regular traffic lights. The main benefits for the configuration analysis based decision process is linked to the waiting time since several vehicles can enter the hub at the same time provided they are not in conflict.

5   Conclusion

This paper presented two algorithms aimed at allowing platoon's reconfiguration while optimizing hub release time. These algorithms suppose several constraints on vehicle and crossroad perception abilities. Vehicles must be able to be part of a platoon and to detect specific active beacons placed on road. As for crossroad, it must perceive the presence and the expected direction of the first waiting vehicle for each incoming lane (the number of waiting vehicles is not perceived). It must also perceive if one vehicle exits the hub. This perception can be easily made thanks to magnetic loop detectors. Results obtained show that algorithms fulfilled their function (i.e. platoon reconfiguration) and gives better results than a standard traffic light solution.

From now on, we focus on composition of several crossroads into the grid. The goal of this is both to develop global path planning algorithms aimed at computing the best path in the grid for each mobility unit and to study the behavioral interaction between crossroads in order to improve time travel. We also are trying to adapt this developed solution to other crossroads configurations and to traffic circles.

References

1. Martinet, P., Thuilot, B., Bom, J.: Autonomous Navigation and Platooning using a Sensory Memory. In: International IEEE Conference on Intelligent Robots and Systems, IROS 2006, Beijing, China (October 2006)
2. Woo, M.J., Choi, J.W.: A relative navigation system for vehicle platooning In: SICE 2001, Proceedings of the 40th SICE Annual Conference. International Session Papers (IEEE Cat. No.01TH8603), pp. 28–31 (2001)
3. Fritz, H.: Longitudinal and lateral control of heavy duty trucks for automated vehicle following in mixed traffic: Experimental results from the CHAUFFEUR project. In: Proceedings IEEE Conference on Control Applications, vol. 2, pp. 1348–1352 (1999)
4. Ioannou, P., Xu, Z.: Throttle and brake control systems for automatic vehicle following. IVHS Journal 1(4), 345 (1994)
5. Moskwa, J.J., Hedrick, J.K.: Nonlinear algorithms for automotive engine control. IEEE Control Systems Magazine 10(3), 88–93 (1990)
6. Daviet, P., Parent, M.: Longitudinal and lateral servoing of vehicles in a platoon. In: Proceedings of IEEE Intelligent Vehicles Symposium, pp. 41–46 (1996)
7. Sheikholeslam, S., Desoer, C.A.: Longitudinal control of a platoon of vehicles with no communication of lead vehicle information: A system level study. IEEE Transactions on Vehicular Technology 42, 546–554 (1993)
8. Hyeongcheol, L., Tomizuka, M.: Adaptive vehicle traction force control for intelligent vehicle highway systems (IVHSs). IEEE Transactions on Industrial Electronics 50(1), 37–47 (2003)
9. Kehtarnavaz, N., Griswold, N.C., Lee, J.S.: Visual control of an autonomous vehicle (BART)The vehicle-following problem. IEEE Transactions on Vehicular Technology 40(3), 40, 654–662 (1991)
10. Gehrig, S.K., Stein, F.J.: Elastic bands to enhance vehicle following. In: Proceedings of IEEE Conference on Intelligent Transportation Systems, ITSC, pp. 597–602 (2001)
11. Yi, S.-Y., Chong, K.-T.: Impedance control for a vehicle platoon system. Mechatronics (UK) 15(5), 627–638 (2005)
12. Contet, J.-M., Gechter, F., Gruer, P., Koukam, A.: Reactive Multi-agent approach to local platoon control: stability analysis and experimentations. International Journal of Intelligent Systems Technologies and Application (2010)

13. Gechter, F., Contet, J.-M., Gruer, P., Koukam, A.: Car driving assistance using organization measurement of reactive multi-agent system. Procedia CS 1(1), 317–325 (2010)
14. Lamotte, O., Galland, S., Contet, J.-M., Gechter, F.: Submicroscopic and Physics Simulation of Autonomous and Intelligent Vehicles in Virtual Reality. In: The Second International Conference on Advances in System Simulation (SIMUL 2010), Nice, France, August 22-27 (2010)
15. Miller, A.J.: A computer control system for traffic networks. In: Proc. 2nd Int. Symp. Traffic Theory, pp. 200–220 (1963)
16. Ma, W., Yang, X.: A passive transit signal priority approach for bus rapid transit system. In: IEEE Intelligent Transportation Systems Conference, Seattle, WA, USA, vol. (413) (2007)
17. Papageorgiou, M., Diakaki, C., Dinopoulou, V., Kotsialos, A., Wang, Y.: Review of Road Traffic Control Strategies. Proceedings of the IEEE 91(12), 2043–(2067)
18. Vincent, R.A., Young, C.P.: Self-optimizing traffic signal control using microprocessor: The TRRL MOVA strategy for isolated intersections. Traffic Eng. Control 27, 385–387 (1986)
19. Pitu, B.M., Ning, Z.: Queuing Models for Analysis of Traffic adaptive Signal Control. Transaction on Intelligent Transportation System 8(1), 50–59 (2008)
20. Griinewald, M., Rust, C., Witkowski, U.: Using mini robots for prototyping intersection management of vehicles. In: Proceedings of the 3rd International Symposium on Autonomous Minirobots for Research and Edutainment, pp. 288–294 (2006)

Genetic Algorithm Based Structure Identification for Feedback Control of Nonlinear MIMO Systems

Kristina Vassiljeva[1], Juri Belikov[2], and Eduard Petlenkov[1]

[1] Department of Computer Control, Tallinn University of Technology,
Ehitajate tee 5, 19086, Tallinn, Estonia
{kristina.vassiljeva,eduard.petlenkov}@dcc.ttu.ee
[2] Institute of Cybernetics, Tallinn University of Technology,
Akadeemia tee 21, 12618, Tallinn, Estonia
jbelikov@cc.ioc.ee

Abstract. Choice of the architecture of the neural network makes it possible to find its optimal structure for the control of nonlinear multi-input multi-output (MIMO) systems using the linearization feedback.Genetic algorithm is proposed as the optimization method for finding the appropriate structure. The controller is based on the parameters of the obtained neural network. The error based criterion is applied as evaluation function for model identification procedure.

Keywords: genetic algorithms, neural networks, nonlinear control, MIMO systems.

1 Introduction

This paper examines the system identification problem from the standpoint of control system design. Model selection is one of the central problems in control theory. The performance of the model based control algorithms considerably depends on the model accuracy of the controlled process. However, the model is not usually well-defined, because of existing uncertainties and non-modeled dynamics, among other causes. Thus, the key steps are to identify structure and the parameters of the system based on the available data, which requires a good understanding of the system.

The structure identification itself can be divided in two types: identification of the input variables of the model and the input-output relations. In most conventional black-box modeling approaches the input variables are given, thus only the input-output relation has to be found. Unfortunately, in real life we often have little or not enough data to properly identify which of the available input variables of the dynamic model (order of the system) should be taken into account during modeling procedure, see [1] and [2]. Some authors address using of fuzzy and neural networks systems have been used for modeling and designing control systems by exploiting their learning and function approximation capabilities, see [3].

In the approach presented in this paper it is assumed that a little or no knowledge about the structure of the controlled system is given a priori. Therefore theoretically there are an infinite number of input variables of the dynamic system for the known

A. Bouchachia (Ed.): ICAIS 2011, LNAI 6943, pp. 215–226, 2011.

outputs exist, which has to be restricted to a certain number. So, the first step for modeling is to find the order of the MIMO system using some of the regression analysis techniques, see [4]. A nonlinear system usually can be nonlinear in many ways, thus "classical" methods to find the regressors have had apparently limited success. Recently, neural networks (NN) have attracted much interest in system modeling and control communities because of their ability to approximate any nonlinear mappings. So, knowing the order of the system, and consequently, finding the optimal structure of neural network, we can design a controller for our nonlinear MIMO system. Previously the specific NN structure has been considered for dynamic feedback control using state-space controller in [5] and [6]. The major goal was devoted to the minimal NN-based state-space representation of the system and implementation of the state-space based algorithm for control of nonlinear MIMO systems. In these articles most of the attention was paid to the feedback linearization. One of the possible implementations of this algorithm is to use a class of models with NN-ANARX (Neural Network based Additive NARX) structure, see [7] and [8]. It's main advantage that it can always be linearized by appropriate feedback, and observable state-space equations can be directly written down from NN-ANARX form without any additional computations. This gives possibility to combine a classical state feedback linearization with approach based on using neural networks. The contribution of this paper is devoted to genetic algorithm based structure identification for feedback control of nonlinear MIMO systems.

Hence, for the best model identification a set of neural networks must be trained. Correct choice of the NN-model improves the control quality of the nonlinear processes. The main problem to obtain a good model using neural networks is to find its optimal structure. Besides, quality of the model very much depends on the choice for the initial values of the parameters. These two problems can be solved simultaneously using genetic algorithm. That leads to point, that structure of the neural network could be defined by the genetic algorithm (GA), which finds optimal NN parameters and dependencies between the inputs of dynamic model and outputs of the controlled system. Typically success of the model is evaluated using a performance criterion, thus on the basis of the obtained model controller can be designed and its efficiency checked during the simulation. The result of the control simulation can be used as an evaluation function for further calculation of the fitness function of a "chromosome" in current population. Thus, as a result of the GA, we obtain a neural network of a specific structure, which contains both types of structural identification described above.

Many systems have been developed in recent years that evolve both neural topologies and weights. These methods contain a variety of ideas about how Topology and Weight Evolving Artificial Networks (TWEANNs) should be implemented: Parallel Distributed Genetic Programming (PDGP) systems, Cellular Encoding (CE) method, GeNeralised Acquisition of Recurrent Links (GNARL), NeuroEvolution of Augmenting Topologies (NEAT). Most neuroevolution systems deal with reinforcement learning tasks, see [9] and [10].

At the same time, our approach involves the use of classical supervised training of neural networks. At the first stage the general structure of the neural network model is determined. Then search of better initial values takes place. This conditioned by the property of NN, where neural networks even with the same structure and the same learning mechanism will have different parameters depending on the results of the initialization process. The power of GA's derives from their ability to exploit efficiently this vast amount if accumulating knowledge by means of relatively simple selection mechanisms, see [11].

The rest of the paper is organized as follows. Section 2 identifies the problem of encoding and the evaluation function of a genetic algorithm. Description of the GA is given in Section 3. Numerical example demonstrating practical applicability of the proposed state controller is presented in Section 4. Conclusions are drawn in the last section.

2   GA Encodings and Optimization Problems

Usually most genetic algorithms have only two main components that are problem dependent: the problem of encoding and the evaluation function. According to [12] and [13] the first step is encoding the neural network into binary strings called chromosomes that is determined by the structure of the neural network.

2.1   Architecture of the Neural Network

Consider a discrete-time MIMO nonlinear autoregressive network with exogenous inputs (NARX), described by the input-output difference equation

$$y(k) = f(y(k-1), \ldots, y(k-n), u(k-1), \ldots, u(k-n)), \tag{1}$$

where $u(k)$ and $y(k)$ are inputs and outputs of the system, $f(\cdot)$ is an analytical function.

This model can be easily obtained by using classical fully connected neural network and covers a wide class of nonlinear systems. However, classical representation of that model does not assure using the minimal/optimal number of parameters in the NN. Thus, for a more flexible structure, which allows excluding all redundant interconnections and parameters of the neural network, it is necessary to modify its architecture, as shown below. Above all, each sub-layer should be divided into groups of neurons, each of which is responsible for the interconnection of inputs to each specific output. Thus, connections between inputs and hidden sub-layer can be eliminated if both subsystems do not depend on the same regressors.

2.2   Illustrative Example

Assume that black-box model has two inputs and two outputs. Examine in more detail the obtained structure of the model, which maximal order of a subsystem was found using some regression analysis as three.

Thus, architecture of the fully connected NN-NARX model is defined as follows: the maximal order of the subsystem, number of system inputs and outputs, determine the number of inputs of neural network. As number of outputs is two, each sub-layer should be divided into two groups L_{11} and L_{12} as it is shown in Fig. 1. Consider that solid and dashed lines are showing a presence of the connection between layers/neurons.

This structure is flexible and allows us to describe nonlinear MIMO system with any interconnections between inputs and outputs of the dynamic model using NN-NARX

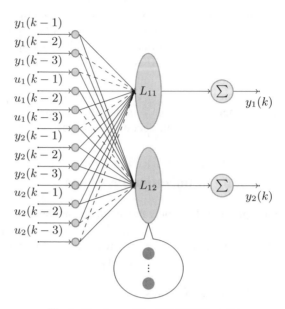

Fig. 1. Structure of the NN-NARX model

architecture. It makes this architecture available to use in the genetic algorithms for finding the optimal structure of the NN in black-box model identification.

First, determine the length of the chromosome, which describes the neural network in Fig. 1. Parameters that determine its length are:

$$l = o \cdot (n + m) \cdot m, \tag{2}$$

where l is a length of the gene, o is a maximal order among subsystems of the controlled MIMO system, n and m are numbers of inputs and outputs of the system, respectively.

In our case $l = 3 \cdot (2 + 2) \cdot 2 = 24$. Hence, for a fully connected NN-NARX the gene would be as follows

$$gene = [1\,1\,1\,1\,1\,1\,1\,1\,1\,1\,1\,1 \quad 1\,1\,1\,1\,1\,1\,1\,1\,1\,1\,1\,1],$$

where the first bit of the chromosome shows the connection between input $y_1(k-1)$ of the first sub-layer L_{11} and output $y_1(k)$, the second bit - connection between input $y_1(k-1)$ of the first sub-layer L_{12} and output $y_2(k)$, third bit - connection between input $y_1(k-2)$ of the first sub-layer L_{11} and output $y_1(k)$, etc.

If any connection between an input and any output does not exist, it can be represented as 0 in the chromosome encoding. Let existing connections are presented by the solid lines and the absent connections by the dashed lines. Thus, the structure demonstrated in Fig. 1 can be described using the following gene

$$gene = [1\,1\,0\,1\,0\,1\,1\,1\,1\,0\,0\,1 \quad 1\,1\,1\,1\,1\,1\,1\,1\,1\,0\,0\,1].$$

In order to minimize the number of parameters used, in case when all inputs of one sub-layer are interconnected with all outputs of the neural network, there is no need to divide this sub-layer into groups of neurons. In our case this would reduce the number of neurons on the first sub-layer in 2 times (in this work we assume that groups of neurons on the hidden sub-layers have the same size). Therefore, if NN-NARX model is fully connected, we obtain the classical representation of that structure.

2.3   Evaluation Function

In this paper we consider the set-point tracking problem. The primary aim of our work is to find a suitable controller for the nonlinear MIMO process, so fit of the model should be evaluated using one of the control criteria. The most common structure is feedback (Fig. 2), as this structure can monitor variations in the process and successfully compensate for the unwanted executions in a manner consistent with the performance objectives. In this work a criterion based on the shape of the complete closed-loop response or so-called error-based criterion was chosen.

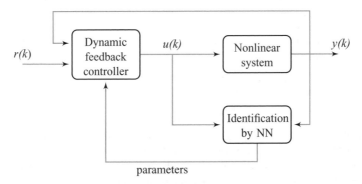

Fig. 2. Structure of the control system

Further, the quality criterion is calculated on the basis of obtained MSE of the control.

$$quality = e^{-k \cdot MSE} \tag{3}$$

where k is proportional coefficient. The use of (3) is justified by the fact that, when calculating a fit function, the poor control performance (large MSE) could outweigh and distort the overall picture. In this case, even a small decrease for small values of MSE will have an effect in the case of forming the new offspring. In addition scaling of the population fitness helps to avoid premature convergence.

3   Genetic Algorithm Description

In this work the canonical genetic algorithm is used, see [12]. First, the number of chromosomes is specified. This number remains constant for all future generations. Each gene corresponds to a specific NN-NARX structure with unspecified weights values. These weights are determined during the neural network training phase. Next, a controller based on the parameters of neural network is automatically designed, see [5] and

[6]. Onward all genes are estimated with the aid of properly selected evaluation function. In our case the performance is checked using MSE based criterion. On the next step fit function is calculated.

Hereinafter, speaking about evaluation and fitness function, we mean distinguish functions. Evaluation function, providing a measure of performance, is independent of evaluation of any other chromosomes. However, fitness is defined by: $f_i/\bar{f}$, where f_i is the evaluation associated with $gene_i$ and $\bar{f}$ is average evaluation of all chromosomes in the population. In other words, the fitness is always defined with respect to other members of the current population.

Intermediate generation filled by the chromosomes of the current generation using stochastic sampling with replacement. Crossover with a single recombination point is applied to randomly paired strings. After recombination, a mutation operator is used and according to the elitism operator the best chromosomes of the current generation is copied to the next generation. Elitism is the last step of our search. After evaluation, each gene is ordered according to its fitness value. Thus, the new population is established and a new generation begins. The algorithm terminates whenever a controller designed on neural network parameters with structure obtained with the aid of gene has an error less than an a priori defined threshold or a pre-specified number of generations has been reached. Thus, the whole algorithm can be represented by schema depicted in Fig. 3.

3.1   Practical Implementation

Proposed algorithm has been formalized using the programming language of MATLAB environment. Further, a separate application package was written with the number of functions. Efficiency of the algorithm was tested on a number of academic examples, the results of which lead to the conclusion about the viability of this technique. This makes sense to its further improvement and development.

Since we consider the identification process as a part of the control task it is logical to use the subclass of NARX models called ANARX. Neural network based additive NARX structures allow directly use technique based on dynamic feedback linearization [14]. Another not the least of the factors is that observable state-space equations can be obtained without any additional computations [5].

Thus, technique for obtaining a custom structure of NN-NARX models can be applied to its subclass NN-ANARX models. In that case the classical equation (see [15])

$$y(k) = \sum_{i=1}^{max(n_p)} C_i \phi_i(W_i \cdot z(k-i)), \tag{4}$$

where $\phi_i(\cdot)$ is an activation function of neurons of the corresponding sub-layer, $W_i \in \mathbb{R}^{l_i \times (m+m)}$ and $C_i \in \mathbb{R}^{m \times l_i}$ are matrices of synaptic weights of inputs and outputs of i-th sub-layer, $z(k) = [y_1(k), \ldots, y_m(k), u_1(k), \ldots, u_m(k)]^T$, l is a number of sub-layers of the neural network and m is a number of the system outputs; converts to the next form

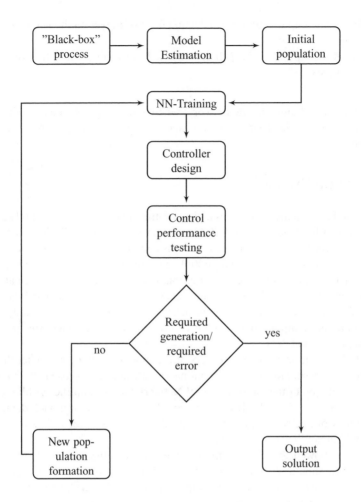

Fig. 3. Reduced model finding algorithm

$$
y_{i'} = \sum_{i=1}^{max(n_p)} \sum_{j=1}^{q_i} \sum_{s \in R_{ij}} c_{ijs} \cdot
$$

$$
\cdot \phi_{ijs}\left(w_{ijs} \cdot \left[\left\{ \delta^{i-1} y_{d_{yij}} \right\}_{d_{yij} \in D_{yij}}, \left\{ \delta^{i-1} u_{d_{uij}} \right\}_{d_{uij} \in D_{uij}} \right]^T \right), \quad (5)
$$

if $s = i'$ and $s \in R_{ij}$, then corresponding terms are taken, otherwise they are excluded. Where

$max(n_p)$ - maximal order among all subsystems;
qi - maximal number of the decomposed sub-layers on the i-th layer;
s - number of the output of the NN, with which current sub-layer is connected;
R_{ij} - set of all connections between i-th hidden layer and output of the j-th subsystem;

d_{yij} - index of the output y on the j-th decomposed sub-layer on the i-th layer;
D_{yi} - set of indexes d_{yij};
d_{uij} - index of the input u on the j-th decomposed sub-layer on the i-th layer;
D_{uij} - set of indexes d_{uij};
δ - time shift.

In other words we obtain a neural network, where each output depends on the specific number of time instances. Using such representation we can easily eliminate all redundant connections.

4   Numerical Example

The model to be estimated is given as a discrete-time black-box MIMO model. Estimation process can be done using MATLAB System Identification Toolbox with NARX type black-box models. The input vector $u(k)$ is composed of 2 variables and the output vector $y(k)$ contains 2 variables with 600 data samples. First, for model identification and in order to obtain a state-space representation, it is necessary to estimate the regressors of the given MIMO system. Thus, each output of the model can be taken as a function of regressors which are transformations of past inputs and past outputs. Typical regressors are simply delayed input or output variables, which are functions of measured input-output data.

First of all, to define regressors, orders of the model has to be set. After the choice of model order, we should choose the nonlinearity estimator to be used. To obtain state-space representation of the model a Neural Network based Simplified Additive NARX (NN-SANARX) (see [5] and [6]) structure could be employed for model identification. As neural network activation functions were chosen as sigmoid, so it was decided to use sigmoid net nonlinear estimators.

Estimation showed that the maximum order of the subsystems is 3, therefore the neural network should be trained with three sub-layers on the hidden layer. On the other hand, the given system has two outputs; it means that each sub-layer should be divided into two groups of neurons.

According to the proposed algorithm, see Fig. 3 the next step is a creation of an initial population. First of all, the length of the chromosome should be defined using (2)

$$length = 3 \cdot (2 + 2) \cdot 2 = 24.$$

As for the calculation of the control signals $u_i(k)$ (see [5]) we need to know

1. the influence of the control signal on the previous time step to both outputs, so restriction should be imposed on the values of 5-8 bits of the genes: $gene_i(5 : 8) = 1$;
2. second state of the model, it means that we need to have it explicitly or be able to calculate it using subsequent states. That leads us to the point, that obtained chromosome should be tested for the presence of that interconnections.

On the basis of the obtained genes neural network of specific structure was generated. Levenberg-Marquardt (LM) algorithm was used to perform the training. At this stage the number of training epochs was taken small. In the future, if structure will be appropriate, we can train our network additionally to obtain a more precise control. The linear activation function was chosen on the first sub-layer with 2 neurons, with respect to NN-SANARX structure, and the hyperbolic tangent sigmoid activation function on the other hidden sub-layers with 4 nodes for each group of neurons.

On the next step neural network parameters were used to design a controller, based on the state-space feedback algorithm, see [5]. Closed loop control system was simulated with piece-constant and sinusoidal reference signals and quality criterion was calculated.

Genetic algorithm described in Section 3 with different initial population size, crossover rate and mutation probability was applied to find the optimal structure of the neural network. Distinctive feature of the applying GA to the neural networks is that the same gene could correspond to different NNs. Namely, neural networks have the same structure, but due to the different initial parameters their final weights are different. On this basis two approaches were used: in the first case several NNs were trained for one chromosome and the best of them was chosen for the representation of the gene. This was substantiated by the fact on the chance of good structure, but inappropriate initial values obtained chromosome was not lost. In the second case only one NN for the gene was trained. Further experiments showed that total time needed for optimal NN search was almost the same. The only difference was that in the second approach first took place structural identification and only then for the best structure the most optimal neural network was chosen. In the first case structural and parametrical identification took place for the same time what naturally increased time of formation of a new generation.

If obtained structure and designed with its aid controller gave unstable behavior of the system, then MSE equate to 50 which automatically made fit function equal to 0. Another significant remark should be done. Several experiments were conducted there in initial population were added a few genes which described a fully connected neural network. All results have shown that for this kind black-box model the classical structure that was used earlier is not an optimal one.

Most of the experiments came to the same structure, described by the next gene

$$gene = [1\ 1\ 1\ 1\ 1\ 1\ 1\ 1 \quad 0\ 1\ 0\ 1\ 1\ 1\ 1\ 1 \quad 0\ 0\ 1\ 0\ 0\ 0\ 1\ 1].$$

On this basis, the custom architecture of the NN-SANARX structure could be as depicted in Fig. 4.

Some experiments with population more than 150 individuals had two groups of genes one of them is mentioned above and another was

$$gene = [1\ 1\ 1\ 1\ 1\ 1\ 1\ 1 \quad 0\ 0\ 1\ 0\ 1\ 1\ 1\ 1 \quad 0\ 1\ 1\ 1\ 0\ 1\ 1\ 1].$$

Closed loop control system was simulated with piece-constant and sinusoidal reference signals. The results of this simulation are depicted in Fig. 5. It can be seen that controls $u_1(k)$ and $u_2(k)$ are capable of simultaneous tracking of the desired reference signals $v_1(k)$ and $v_2(k)$, respectively.

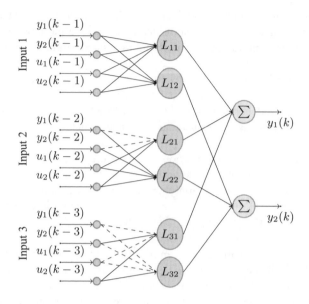

Fig. 4. Structure of the NN-SANARX model

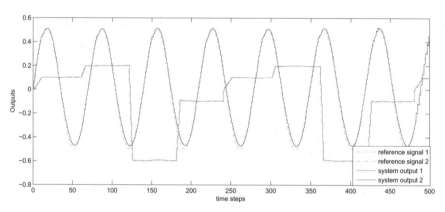

Fig. 5. Control of nonlinear MIMO system

5   Conclusions

The main contribution of this paper is in proposed novel representation of the NARX structure, which leads to the possibility of using such a structure for the formation of any genes. Consequently, this allows to solve the problem of finding the optimal structure of the neural network from the control point of view. Namely, for the NN based state-space representation of a wide class of nonlinear MIMO systems as well as its application to the state control based on feedback linearization. Parameters identified by training of NN-SANARX can directly be rewritten to the state-space representation for further use in control algorithm. The possibility of obtaining optimal structure which is not necessarily fully connected enables to reduce the number of the parameters used in NN. This is a significant factor especially in adaptive control, when improvement of the neural network parameter occurs in online mode. Summarizing the above said a set of test models generated by genes are in the range from the minimal state-space order to the maximal possible order (max_ord) of system. That order could be found by maximal order of one of the subsystem multiplied by the number of subsystems

$$max\_ord = max\_ord\_subsys \cdot subsys\_num. \tag{6}$$

Usually, since we use a black-box model, we do not know the minimal order of the system and data received from the regression analysis is not necessarily the right one. Having in mind that direct value of the minimal order (min_ord) of the system is absent, so for our practical needs, we choose the best model from the GA point of view being in the interval

$$min\_ord \leq NN\_order \leq max\_ord. \tag{7}$$

In other words, from these models we select the best from the perspective of control.

Acknowledgments. This work was partially supported by the Governmental funding project no. SF0140113As08, the Estonian Science Foundation Grant no. 8738 and European Social Funds Doctoral Studies and Internationalisation Programme DoRa.

References

1. Bastian, A., Gasós, J.: A type i structure identification approach using feedforward neural networks. In: IEEE World Congress on Computational Intelligence: ICNN, Orlando, FL, USA, June 27 - July 02, pp. 3256–3260 (1994)
2. Helmicki, A.J., Jacobson, C.A., Nett, C.N.: Fundamentals of control-oriented system identification and their application for identification in h_∞. In: American Control Conference, Boston, MA, USA, pp. 89–99 (June 1991)
3. González-Olvera, M.A., Tang, Y.: Black-box identification of a class of nonlinear systems by a recurrent neurofuzzy network. IEEE Transactions on Neural Networks 21(4), 672–679 (2010)
4. Feil, B., Abonyi, J., Szeifert, F.: Determining the model order of nonlinear input-output systems by fuzzy clustering. In: Benitez, J.M., Cordon, O., Hoffmann, F., Roy, R. (eds.) Advances in Soft Computing, Engineering Design and Manufacturing, pp. 89–98. Springer, Heidelberg (2003)
5. Vassiljeva, K., Petlenkov, E., Belikov, J.: State-space control of nonlinear systems identified by anarx and neural network based sanarx models. In: WCCI 2010 IEEE World Congress on Computational Intelligence: IJCNN, Barcelona, Spain, pp. 3816–3823 (July 2010)
6. Vassiljeva, K., Petlenkov, E., Belikov, J.: Neural network based minimal state-space representation of nonlinear mimo systems for feedback control. In: 2010 the 11th International Conference on Control Automation, Robotics and Vision, Singapore, December 7-10, pp. 2191–2196 (2010)
7. Petlenkov, E., Nõmm, S., Kotta, Ü.: Nn-based anarx structure for identification and model-based control. In: The 9th International Conference on Control Automation Robotics and Vision, Singapore, pp. 2284–2288 (December 2006)

8. Petlenkov, E.: Nn-anarx structure based dynamic output feedback linearization for control of nonlinear mimo systems. In: The 15th Mediterranean Conference on Control and Automation, Athens, Greece, pp. 1–6 (June 2007)
9. Stanley, K., Miikkulainen, R.: Efficient reinforcement learning through evolving neural network topologies. In: Genetic and Evolutionary Computation Conference, San Francisco, CA, USA, pp. 569–577 (2002)
10. Stanley, K., Miikkulainen, R.: Evolving neural networks through augmenting topologies. Evolutionary Computation 10(2), 99–127 (2002)
11. Grefenstette, J.J.: Optimization of control parameters for genetic algorithms. IEEE Transactions on Systems, Man and Cybernetics 16(1), 122–128 (1986)
12. Whitley, D.: Genetic algorithms and neural networks. In: Winter, G., Periaux, J., Galan, M., Cuesta, P. (eds.) Genetic Algorithms in Engineering and Computer Science, pp. 191–201. John Wiley, New York (1995)
13. Son, J.S., Lee, D.M., Kim, I.S., Choi, S.K.: A study on genetic algorithm to select architecture of a optimal neural network in the hot rolling process. Journal of Materials Processing Technology 153-154, 643–648 (2004)
14. Pothin, R., Kotta, Ü., Moog, C.: Output feedback linearization of nonlinear discrete-time systems. In: Proc. of the IFAC Conf. on Control System Design, Bratislava, pp. 174–179 (2000)
15. Kotta, Ü., Nõmm, S., Chowdhury, F.: On a new type of neural network-based input-output model: The anarma structure. In: The 5th IFAC Symposium on Nonlinear Control Systems NOLCOS, St. Petersbourg, Russia, pp. 1535–1538 (July 2001)

Regenerative Abilities in Modular Robots Using Virtual Embryogenesis

Ronald Thenius, Markus Dauschan, Thomas Schmickl, and Karl Crailsheim

Artificial Life Laboratory of the Department of Zoology, Karl-Franzens University
Graz, Universitätsplatz 2, A-8010 Graz, Austria
ronald.thenius@uni-graz.at

Abstract. One task in the field of modular robotics is to develop robotic organisms as fault-tolerant as possible. Even in case of damage of the robotic organism, the robotic units have to be able to autonomously repair the organism. We have adapted a technique called Virtual Embryogenesis (VE) to the problem of self organised assembly of a robotic organism, and tested the ability of the VE to regenerate damage of the organism. It showes, that due to randomly appearing events during the evolutionary process, that shapes the VE-process, the developed robotic organism has regenerative abilities.

1 Introduction

The field of modular robotics has been intensely researched in the last years [12,22,16]. In this field methods to organise autonomous robotic units to cooperatively solve a given task are investigated. These tasks can reach from swarms of robots that aggregate to overcome a gap, to pre-assembled robotic organisms, that has to exchange a damaged subunit autonomously.

These robotic units (figure 1(a)) can operate autonomously in the environment (swarm mode) or mechanically connect to each other and build a robotic organism (figure 1(b)), that is able to solve tasks that cannot be solved by a single autonomous robotic unit. Examples for this are the avoidance of hazardous areas (e.g., crossing holes), passing barriers (e.g., climbing walls), building sensor networks, or sharing energy for a power intensive task of a single unit inside the robotic organism. These artificial systems have to be able to autonomously adapt to a given problem in an unknown environment (e.g., rescue missions in a collapsed building, during space exploration missions).

One of the major questions in this field is how to react to damages during organism mode. Investigations regarding this topic were already done by ([18,17]). Many of these approaches include global communication, a global positioning system, and a high ability of the robots to communicate. If these abilities are limited by hardware constraints, or disadvantageous environmental conditions (e.g., noise jamming the communication channels), these approaches might fail. Our approach to organise the multi-robotic organism formation is based on observations made during the growth processes of biological lifeforms [28]. The

A. Bouchachia (Ed.): ICAIS 2011, LNAI 6943, pp. 227–237, 2011.

(a) SYMBRION robotic modules   (b) Simulation of robotic organism

Fig. 1. Hardware and concepts in the field of modular robotics. Left subfigure: Two autonomous robotic modules developed by the Institute for Process Control and Robotics of the university Karlsruhe during the SYMBRION project [22]. Each module is equipped with a 2D-omnidirectional drive, and 4 genderless docking-ports. This allows to assemble the robots to a huge variety of robotic organisms. Each module also can be equipped with a high-torque hinge (round structure on the right robot), that enables a robotic organism to move in 3D. Right subfigure: Simulation of assembled moving robotic organism (6-legged walker), consisting of several robotic modules.

scientific field investigating the processes of embryogenetic development and evolutionary adaptation of lifeforms is called Evolutionary Developmental Biology (EvoDevo). For details see [2,26,13].

Based on the findings by the field of EvoDevo, we developed the Virtual Embryogenesis (VE) [24], which allows us to evolve processes, that manage to assemble units of mobile agents using artificial evolutionary processes (see also [4]).

The questions we want to investigate in this paper, are:

- Are robotic structures developed by the VE-process able to compensate damage during the growth process?
- Are such regenerative abilities evolvable through VE?

2   Materials and Methods

2.1   Methodological Background

The modelling of embryogenetic growth processes is not new, first models about the processes organising an embryo were already made by Turing [25]. The first empiric measurements to this topic were done by Wolpert [28], what triggered the development of a big number of models about the developmental processes[3,6,10]. In the following decades the processes organizing the growth of embryos were intensely investigated [11,29]. In the last years, along with the development of adequate computational power more and more complex models of EvoDevo processes emerged [15,14].

The second topic this paper focuses on is modular robotics. In the last years research in this field has intensified. The research aim for both, evolvable robotic structures [22,16] and the organization of predefined body shapes [21,18]. Also highly relevant for this field is the control of assembled modular robots [20,7].

Fig. 2. Screenshot of the Netlogo 4.1.2 simulation of the VE-process, adapted for the purpose of modular robotics. Blue boxes indicate docked robotic modules that form the robotic organism. Brown boxes indicate autonomous mobile robotic modules which are performing random walk. Green areas indicate docking signals which attract mobile autonomous robotic modules. As soon as a mobile module reaches the module emitting the docking-signal, it docks there and becomes part of the robotic organism.

2.2   The VE-Process

The VE process [24,23] is a model of processes observable in biological embryos. In nature the function of a cell in an embryo is determined by its position within the growing body. The localisation of a cell is based on selforganised processes, which include the interaction of diffusing substances, called morphogenes (for more details see [2,13,9]). These substances are emitted and detected by the cells of the embryo. The reaction of a cell (e.g., growth, specialisation, duplication) to a given concentration is determined by the genome of the cell.

All experiments shown in this paper are based on simulation experiments performed using the simulation environment Netlogo 4.1.2 [27]. The models presented in [24] were adapted to the problem of organising assembly processes in modular robotics. The cells of an embryo are represented by virtual individual robotic modules (see figure 2). For technical details (e.g, genetic encoding, simulated physics) see citeTheniusEtAlMathMod09. Following changes were applied to the former model:

– Besides robotic units (corresponding to the cells of the growing embryo), that are part of the robotic organism, a second class of agents was introduced: mobile robotic units, driving around in the environment, performing random walk.
– Cells (i.e, robots) are no more able to duplicate. Instead of a duplication, all cells in the robotic organism are able to send out a "docking-signal" on one of the free docking ports. Mobile robotic units are able to detect a docking signal over a distance of 5 spatial units, one of which is equivalent to one

edge length of one robot. Autonomous robots approach this docking signal, and dock to the robotic organism. As soon as docked, the genome of the robotic organism is transferred to the robotic unit. This way the autonomous robotic unit becomes part of the robotic organism. The diffusion of morphogenes is handled as described in [24].

- To simulate the damaging of the robotic organism a given part of the robotic organism disassembles into mobile robotic units.
- A simple artificial evolution was applied, to shape the genome of the virtual embryo to develop a given bodyshape. For details, see section 2.3
- The first robotic unit, that "founds" the robotic organism ("root cell"), emits a base-gradient, on which other morphogen gradients can build on. This feature is not evolved, but hand-coded into the robot, and can be seen as a technical analogon to the "bicoid"-gradient in biological lifeforms [5].

2.3   Experimental Setup

To investigate the regenerative abilities of an evolved robotic organism, we have used a genome that had evolved using a given pattern for 300 generations, each including 200 individual genomes. During evolution, each individual genome has been tested regarding its ability to develop a defined body shape within 100 time steps. The fitness f of an individual genome β has been calculated according to

$$f_\beta = \frac{|\Omega \cup \Psi| - |\Omega \cap \Psi|}{|\Psi|} \tag{1}$$

whereby Ω is the set of all cells of the final embryo and Ψ is a predefined spatial pattern (see figure 3). Using this method, a robotic organism (respectively its genome) is rewarded for each robotic unit inside the target pattern, and punished for each robotic unit outside the target pattern. Please note, that other fitness functions (e.g., testing for features of the embryo) where also successfully tested (data not shown). To test the regenerative abilities of the VE a simple fitness-function in combination with a simple pattern was chosen.

In a second step, we used the evolved genomes to test the tolerance of the resulting robotic organism against damage and the regenerative ability by allowing the organism to grow for 100 time steps. After this we removed a part of the organism and observed the reaction for 200 time steps. The number of robots, which were removed from the robotic organism was added as mobile robotic units to the experiment. Please note that the tested genome had evolved to build a defined shape of the robotic organism, but not to regenerate damage take during the growth process, or after the end of the growth process. This experiment has been done to investigate how the VE-process reacts to damage during growth.

Fig. 3. Target pattern that defines fitness of a growing robotic organism during an evolutionary process. Yellow areas increase fitness of an embryo by 0.1 point per robotic unit in this field, red areas by 1 point, and black areas decrease it by 1 point.

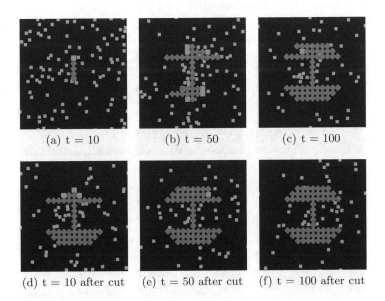

(a) t = 10	(b) t = 50	(c) t = 100
(d) t = 10 after cut	(e) t = 50 after cut	(f) t = 100 after cut

Fig. 4. Screenshots of first experiments: The robotic organism was allowed to grow for 100 timesteps. Then the 2 upper rows of the organism were cut away. Robotic units removed from the organism were added as autonomous robotic units to the experiment. Within the next 100 timesteps, the robotic organism started to regenerate. Please note, that a exemplary run is depicted and that the results can slightly vary in repeated runs, as mentioned below. Blue boxes indicate docked robotic modules (organism), brown boxes indicate autonomous mobile robotic modules, green areas indicate docking signals. For more details, please see section 2.2.

3   Results

3.1   Damaging the Embryo

The experiments described in section 2.3 have shown that embryos which never
evolved for regeneration, have the regenerative abilities. This was surprising,
due to the fact, that during evolution no damage was applied to the growing
organisms. As depicted in figure 4, the top 2 rows of the robotic organism were
removed after 100 timesteps. The organism started to regrow from the central
axis, and finished regeneration after almost 100 timesteps.

Further experiments have shown, that the degree of the regenerative ability
was not faultless and could lead to small differences in the resulting reconstructed
shape (figure 5). Depending on the degree of damage, the regenerated shape
could slightly differ from the shape of the organism before the damage. Figure
5(d) depicts the regeneration process of an organism, that was cut in the half.
After the damage was applied, growth processes rebuilding the lost parts of the
organism could lead to a deformation of the resulting shape.

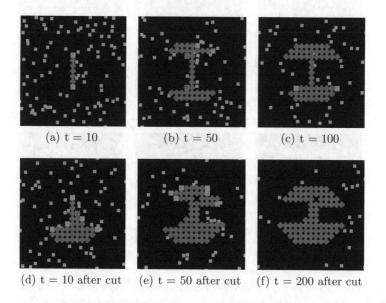

(a) t = 10   (b) t = 50   (c) t = 100

(d) t = 10 after cut   (e) t = 50 after cut   (f) t = 200 after cut

Fig. 5. Screenshots of second experiment: After the robotic organism was allowed to
grow for 100 timesteps, the 5 upper rows of the organism were cut away. Within the
next 200 timesteps, the robotic organism started to regenerate. Due to unbalanced
growth processes during the regenerative phase, the regenerated organism differs from
the undamaged organism. Blue boxes indicate docked robotic modules (organism),
brown boxes indicate autonomous mobile robotic modules, green areas indicate docking
signals. For more details, pleas see section 2.2.

3.2   Analysing the Regenerative Abilities

We started to analyse the regenerative abilities in more detail. To investigate the dependencies between damage and regeneration, we performed a set of experiments with different degrees of damage applied to the organism. In these experiments we allowed the robotic organism to grow for 100 time steps and then removed a fraction of robotic modules, beginning from the top. We increased the fraction in each experiment and repeated each experiment several times. After damaging the organism, we observed it for 200 time steps, and measured its fitness according to equation 1. It showed, that the organism was able to regenerate until about half of the organism was removed (figure 6). The reason for this massive loss of regenerative ability was found in the fact, that in the given experimental set-up the removal of more than 50 percent of the robotic organism removed the "root" robot from the organism. After this "root"-robot was removed, the evolved selforganised process inside the robotic organism broke down, and heavy deformations occurred during the following growth process.

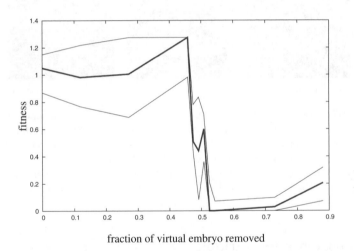

Fig. 6. Result of analysis. Please note the distribution of results in case no part of the robotic organism is removed. It is based on the random behaviour of the mobile robotic units, and results in the ability of the the evolved embryo to compensate damages. Please note, that the depicted figure is the result of several experiments with one individual genome. Several tests with other genomes where performed and led to comparable results (data not shown). N = 10; bold line indicates the median; fine lines indicate quartile 1 and quartile 3.

3.3   Finding the Reason for the Integral Regenerative Abilities

Another question to answer, which was brought up the results mentioned above, was: How can the regenerative abilities develop during evolution, without any modification of the fitness function or damaging process happening while the genomes evolve? Repeated tests of the same genome showed that the results varied, due to irregularities in the building (see figure 4(c)) process based on the random arrival of an autonomous robotic unit at the docking position (see figure 6). To compensate these irregularities, the VE-System evolved the ability to repair itself within given constraints. This ability evolved independently form the kind of damage, be it damage based on noise in the environment or manually added damage. To test this hypothesis, we repeated the evolutionary runs, but instead of autonomous moving agents, that had to find a docking-signal, we automatically placed a robot wherever a docking signal was emitted. This way, the probability for a robot to arrive at an open docking port was 100 percent in the time step the port opened. For an exemplary result see figure 7(a). We again tested the ability of the robotic organism to regenerate damage. It showed that the regenerative ability had not evolved in this experiment (see figure 7).

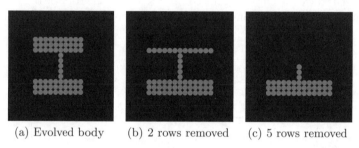

(a) Evolved body   (b) 2 rows removed   (c) 5 rows removed

Fig. 7. Screenshots of results of an experiment without mobile autonomous robots. Subfigure a): Evolved organism-shape after 300 Generations. Subfigure b,c): after 100 timesteps of regular growth, 2 respectively 5 top rows of robotic modules were removed and the organism was allowed to proceed growing for another 200 timesteps. No regenerative activity was observable. Please note, that the depicted figure is the result of experiments with one individual genome. Several tests with other genomes where performed and led to comparable results (data not shown).

4   Discussion and Outlook

With the work at hand we show that the VE process is able to evolve modular robotic structures, that are able to repair themselves within described limits (section 3.1). Even more interesting is the fact, that these abilities can evolve in an artificial evolutionary process, without any implementation of destructive events in the evolutionary process. The reason for the evolution of regenerative abilities can be found in the randomised arrival times of autonomous robotic units at open docking ports during the growth process (section 3.2). Genomes, that had a high tolerance against randomly occurring lacks of mobile robotic units during the growth-process have performed better in building robotic organisms, than genomes that were dependant on a constant flow of building material (= autonomous robotic units). This hypothesis is also supported by the fact, that the ability to regenerate does not evolve, as soon as we use a setup with a constant presence of autonomous robotic units an an docking port if available (section 3.3).

In a real-world robotic scenario, robots that lose contact to the robotic organism, can switch back to a default-program (comparable to our random walker program presented here) and this way become the building material for the regeneration process of the robotic organism. Individual robotic units can detect the loss of contact e.g., by a drop of the primary gradient, emitted by the "root" robot.

Advantages of the presented system compared to autoregenerative robotic systems [18,17] are the ability to work without global positioning systems or global communication. The VE is based on simple neighbour-to-neighbour communication. Even in the organism-mode, the communication between robotic units is limited to the communication of a set of morphogen values (e.g., 16 for the work at hand). Due to the low computational power needed to calculate the described process it is possible to evolve the genome for a needed body structure even on-board the individual robot. As shown in this paper, the resulting body-plans and building processes are highly robust and fault-tolerant, with a minimum of communication requirements.

In the future we plan to investigate how to increase the ability of a robotic organism to regenerate. Also, we plan to use more sophisticated models of the robotic hardware to simulate the process of organism assembly more precisely. We further plan to test the VE-process on real robotic hardware (see figure 1(a)). Compared to other on-board evolving systems (e.g., [1]) the VE has limited computational requirements, which will enable us to run the process also on "smaller" swarm-robotic modules. One question we also want to focus on is: How do the results of our simulation experiments compare to results fund in wound-healing processes in nature?

The VE process has shown to be highly usable for the development of assembly instructions, that are stable against disturbances from the environment, or mechanical malfunctions of subunits. We plan to combine the VE-process with other related bio-inspired controllers (e.g., AHHS [19]) to enable the evolved robotic organisms to perform complex tasks, whereby the mapping of controller structures to morphological structures [8] by the genome will be of major interest.

Acknowledgements. This work was supported by: EU-IST-FET project SYMBRION, no. 216342; EU-ICT project REPLICATOR, no. 216240; The Austrian Federal Ministry of Science and Research (BM.W_F); The European Commission (EC).

References

1. Bongard, J., Zykov, V., Lipson, H.: Resilient machines through continuous self-modeling. Science 314(5802), 1118–1121 (2006)
2. Carroll, S.B.: Endless forms: the evolution of gene regulation and morphological diversity. Cell 101(6), 577–580 (2000),
   http://view.ncbi.nlm.nih.gov/pubmed/10892643

3. Crick, F.: Diffusion in embryogenesis. Nature 225(5231), 420–422 (1970), http://dx.doi.org/10.1038/225420a0

4. Dauschan, M., Thenius, R., Schmickl, T., Crailsheim, K.: Using virtual embryogenesis multi-robot organisms. In: Bouchachia, A. (ed.) ICAIS 2011. LNCS (LNAI), vol. 6943, pp. 227–237. Springer, Heidelberg (2011)

5. Ephrussi, A., Johnston, D.S.: Seeing is believing - the bicoid morphogen gradient matures. Cell 116(2), 143–152 (2004)

6. Gierer, A., Meinhardt, H.: A theory of biological pattern formation. Biological Cybernetics 12(1), 30–39 (1972), http://dx.doi.org/10.1007/BF00289234

7. Hamann, H., Stradner, J., Schmickl, T., Crailsheim, K.: Artificial hormone reaction networks: Towards higher evolvability in evolutionary multi-modular robotics. In: Fellermann, H., Dörr, M., Hanczyc, M.M., Laursen, L.L., Maurer, S., Merkle, D., Monnard, P.A., Støy, K., Rasmussen, S. (eds.) Proc. of the ALife XII Conference, pp. 773–780. MIT Press, Cambridge (2010)

8. Hoffmann, M., Marques, H.G., Arieta, A.H., Sumioka, H., Lungarella, M., Pfeifer, R.: Body Schema in Robotics: A Review. IEEE Transactions on Autonomous Mental Development 2(4), 304–324 (2010)

9. Jaeger, J., Surkova, S., Blagov, M., Janssens, H., Kosman, D., Kozlov, K.N., Manu, Myasnikova, E., Vanario-Alonso, C.E., Samsonova, M., Sharp, D.H., Reinitz, J.: Dynamic control of positional information in the early Drosophila embryo. Nature 430, 368–371 (2004), http://dx.doi.org/10.1038/nature02678

10. Meinhardt, H., Gierer, A.: Applications of a theory of biological pattern formation based on lateral inhibition. Journal of Cell Science 15(2), 321–346 (1974), http://view.ncbi.nlm.nih.gov/pubmed/4859215

11. Meinhardt, H., Gierer, A.: Pattern formation by local self-activation and lateral inhibition. Bioessays 22, 753–760 (2000)

12. Mondada, F., Pettinaro, G.C., Guignard, A., Kwee, I., Floreano, D., Deneubourg, J.L., Nolfi, S., Gambardella, L.M., Dorigo, M.: SWARM-BOT: a New Distributed Robotic Concept. Autonomous Robots, special Issue on Swarm Robotics 17(2-3), 193–221 (2004)

13. Müller, G.B.: Evo-devo: Extending the evolutionary synthesis. Nature Reviews Genetics 8, 943–949 (2007)

14. Müller, G.B., Newman, S.A.: The innovation triad: an evodevo agenda. Journal of Experimental Zoology Part B: Molecular and Developmental Evolution 304(6), 487–503 (2005), http://dx.doi.org/10.1002/jez.b.21081

15. Newman, S.A., Müller, G.B.: Origination and innovation in the vertebrate limb skeleton: an epigenetic perspective. Journal of Experimental Zoology Part B: Molecular and Developmental Evolution 304(6), 593–609 (2005), http://dx.doi.org/10.1002/jez.b.21066

16. REPLICATOR: Project website (2011), http://www.replicators.eu

17. Rubenstein, M., Sai, Y., Choung, C.M., Shen, W.M.: Regenerative patterning in swarm robots: mutual benefits of research in robotics and stem cell biology. The International Journal of Developmental Biology 53, 869–881 (2009)

18. Rubenstein, M., Shen, W.M.: Automatic scalable size selection for the shape of a distributed robotic collective. In: IROS (October 2010)

19. Schmickl, T., Hamann, H., Crailsheim, K.: Modelling a hormone-inspired controller for individual- and multi-modular robotic systems. Mathematical and Computer Modelling of Dynamical Systems 17(3), 221–242 (2011)

20. Shen, W.M., Krivokon, M., Chiu, H., Everist, J., Rubenstein, M., Venkatesh, J.: Multimode locomotion via SuperBot reconfigurable robots. Autonomous Robots 20(2), 165–177 (2006)

21. Støy, K.: How to construct dense objects with self-reconfigurable robots. In: Christensen, H. (ed.) European Robotics Symposium 2006, Springer Tracts in Advanced Robotics 22, vol. 22, pp. 27–37. Springer, Heidelberg (2006)
22. SYMBRION: Project website (2011), http://www.symbrion.eu
23. Thenius, R., Bodi, M., Schmickl, T., Crailsheim, K.: Growth of structured artificial neural networks by virtual embryogenesis. In: Kampis, G., Karsai, I., Szathmáry, E. (eds.) ECAL 2009, Part II. LNCS, vol. 5778, pp. 118–125. Springer, Heidelberg (2009)
24. Thenius, R., Schmickl, T., Crailsheim, K.: Novel concept of modelling embryology for structuring an artificial neural network. In: Troch, I., Breitenecker, F. (eds.) Proceedings of the MATHMOD (2009)
25. Turing, A.M.: The chemical basis of morphogenesis. Philosophical Transactions of the Royal Society of London. Series B, Biological Sciences B237(641), 37–72 (1952)
26. Weatherbee, S.D., Carroll, S.B.: Selector genes and limb identity in arthropods and vertebrates. Cell 97(3), 283–286 (1999)
27. Wilensky, U.: Netlogo. Center for Connected Learning and Computer-Based Modeling, Northwestern University. Evanston, IL (1999), http://ccl.northwestern.edu/netlogo/
28. Wolpert, L.: Positional information and the spatial pattern of cellular differentiation. Journal of Theoretical Biology 25(1), 1–47 (1969)
29. Wolpert, L.: One hundred years of positional information. Trends Genet. 12(9), 359–364 (1996), http://view.ncbi.nlm.nih.gov/pubmed/8855666

Using Virtual Embryogenesis in Multi-robot Organisms

Markus Dauschan, Ronald Thenius, Thomas Schmickl, and Karl Crailsheim

Artificial Life Laboratory of the Department of Zoology,
Karl-Franzens University Graz, Universitätsplatz 2, A-8010 Graz, Austria
markus.dauschan@uni-graz.at

Abstract. We introduce a novel method to apply a pluripotent process of virtual embryogenesis (VE) on modular robotics. The VE software is able to perform simulations on recent computer hardware and can be used to control robotic hardware. Each robot controlled by our VE-software mimics a cell within a virtual embryogenesis process and is able to signal other robots to dock, thus initiating or advancing the build process of a multi-robot organism. In addition to that, our system can also be used to perform primitive locomotion e.g. wall avoidance behaviour in single robots.

1 Introduction

Building homogeneous or heterogeneous artificial organisms using autonomous robots has been intensely investigated within recent years [2,1,6,16]. Both docked within an organism and as a swarm, the robot collective is more than the pure sum of its parts. The possibility to dock robots together to a multifunctional organism unlocks a new series of options to solve technical problems [15]. Such problems could be autonomous locating and retrieval of buried humans after an earthquake which involves the independent identification of obstacles and their overcoming. With this task in mind, one can see the advantages of both configuration modes - swarm and organism. Running a search is easier using the mechanics of a swarm, thus increasing the searchable space by the number of individuals searching. On the other hand the overcoming of obstacles or even the retrieval of a body may be much easier using a solid organism. The design of such an organism should be closely reflecting the situation this organism is applied to. Several strategies have been investigated to deal with this emerging difficulties [6,19,20].

Our approach to this problem is a process of virtual embryogenesis (VE) which results in the shape of a multi-robot organism using evolutionary computation. Evolution has been solving these very problems for a long time and provides us with a wealth of inspiring examples for the design and shaping of organisms.

Modelling embryogenesis processes has a long tradition in both Biology and Computer Science. One of the first models was proposed by Alan Turing [29], one of the grounding fathers of modern Computer Science. The modelling method

A. Bouchachia (Ed.): ICAIS 2011, LNAI 6943, pp. 238–247, 2011.

used in our work [28] is based on Evolutionary Developmental Biology (EvoDevo) [3,31,17,4] and is constructed to mimic the most basic processes found in real-life embryogenesis. The model is implemented as a two-dimensional multi agent simulation in which each cell represents an agent that acts upon its respective individual status and reacts on the input from surrounding agents respectively cells. Based on these inputs each cell chooses in each time step one or several actions from a catalogue of activities. These activities are encoded within a genome provided for each individual embryo consisting of several cells. Our VE is natively designed to allow individual cells to connect to each other thus forming an Artificial Neuronal Network (ANN) [28,25]. In the work at hand we focused only on the morphological aspects of the system and the creation of ANNs is disregarded. Cell emitted substances, so called morphogens, form the embryo by triggering genome based behaviours in cells and thus allow specialization of cells which may lead to the development of different tissues within the developing embryo. These actions include: proliferation (duplication), change of sensitivity to a certain morphogen and the emittance of morphogens. Morphogens spread throughout our virtual embryo via a simplified diffusion process [5,9,35,33]. The resulting morphogen gradients act inter alia as positional cues for the cells. A primary morphogen gradient [23,7], emitted by the first cell, which lies in the center of the virtual grid, is provided in each simulation to support this. Proliferation may occur in three different ways: lateral, vertical and omnidirectional. Each cell may duplicate once per time step at most. The direction chosen from the three possibilities is the direction holding the minimal number of cells. This effect is introduced to emphasize the weight of the surrounding cells to the duplicating cell. However, duplication may also be prevented in a certain direction, if the border of the simulation environment is reached. For the experiments done this environment is usually set to a grid of 40 times 40 spatial units, each able to host one cell.

2   Materials and Methods

2.1   Implementation

The first implementation of our VE has been done in NetLogo [32] to provide a solid base for rapid prototyping and immediate visualization of results. An extensive overview of the possibilities using this implementation of our VE process is given in [26,28]. To open way for fast computation and to consider certain hardware requirements of the robots a C++ implementation has been developed including all core features of the original NetLogo version. Following an object oriented approach [21] the program consists of several classes working secluded from each other on their respective tasks. To represent cells within the virtual two-dimensional world, class 'CellController' has been created. This class is designed to represent a cell within the VE simulation but also to be able to correspond to a robot within a multi-robot organism. To distinguish between these two different situations, the class includes a boolean variable that indicates whether it is executed in robot-mode. We do not use the inheritance concept of

C++ [24] as one of our aims is to show that the exact same system, meaning the exact same class that runs on recent computer hardware, is also able to be executed on robotic hardware. We show three consecutive steps, already using robotic hardware:

1. A decoupled 'CellController' class is executed on the robot and provided with three different genomes which are supposed to trigger different docking signals to other robots.
2. A modified decoupled 'CellController' class is executed on the robot and is receiving proximity sensor values from the robot as morphogen levels. This may result in the production of special 'proteins' that are able to address the movement actuators. Provided with the correct genome this setup is supposed to show a primitive (genome-based) collision avoidance behaviour by the robot.
3. The whole VE is cross-compiled and executed on the robot.

All genomes used in these experiments are hand coded to show proof of concept.

2.2 Evolution Controller

To find a genome resulting in an embryo that matches an assumed ideal shape, evolutionary computation is applied. Two additional classes are added to the program - class 'Generation' and class 'Evolution'. 'Generation' is in charge of the calculation and administration of all individuals belonging to one generation. As output several created genomes are handed over to 'Evolution' that collects all genomes and also picks a start-genome for the upcoming generation. The very first start-genome may be read in or created randomly.

A template schema, currently consisting of 460 cells, is used for internal representation of the maximum fitness within the evolution process. Fitness points are assigned to each individual according to the number of cells lying within or outside the borders of this template schema. For *ingoal* cells which lie within the template pattern one point is awarded whereas for outliers *outgoal* two points are subtracted. The fitness for each embryo is then calculated using

$$fitness = (ingoal - 2 * outgoal)/maxFitness \qquad (1)$$

whereby *maxFitness* holds the maximal achievable fitness value. The resulting individual fitness is a value between 0 and 1 with 1 representing a perfect mapping of the template pattern by the embryo. A value of 0 is awarded if the fitness would be negative or more than 90% of the grid is beset with cells which corresponds to uncontrolled growth (cancer). One example for an evolutionary run using our VE software is depicted in figure 1.

2.3 Optimizations

To increase the performance of the calculation of a single individual, several optimizations are applied on different stages of the program. At first every index

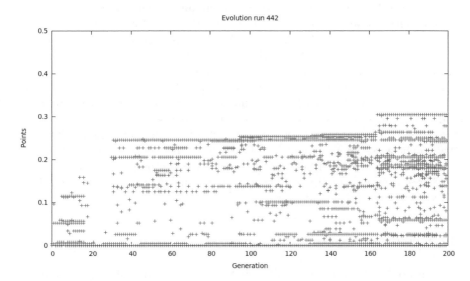

Fig. 1. Example of an evolutionary run using the VE evolution engine. Crosses indicate individual fitness points. As time (and generations) pass, more and more individuals manage to achieve higher fitness values and therefore create a closer mapping of the resulting individual to the template pattern given to the system.

of a lattice point in the two-dimensional grid is reduced to a single index using the following method described by D. E. Knuth [14]:

$$z = x + gridsize * y \tag{2}$$

respectively:

$$x = z \text{ modulo } gridsize \tag{3}$$

and

$$y = int((z - x)/gridsize) \tag{4}$$

with z corresponding to the one dimensional index and x, y to the respective axes of the two-dimensional index.

To reduce the overhead of the object oriented implementation of the program the -O3 compiler option is used. Among many other optimizations this option compiles all methods that are not bigger than a certain threshold (amount of lines) as 'inline' functions, which improves performance drastically. Apart from that, loop vectorization is applied to take advantage of vector registers in modern Intel CPUs. A direct comparison between the GNU compiler [8] and the Intel compiler [10] did not result in a difference in runtime of the program.

2.4   Robotic Hardware

We use robotic hardware from the Symbrion [2] and Replicator [1] EU projects, in particular the robots designed by the Karlsruhe Institute for Technology. These are cubical robots with docking elements, proximity, light and docking sensors on four sides and are described extensively in [12] and [13]. Due to their cubical form and their ability to dock to other robots in each direction in 2D, they perfectly correspond to our 2D VE where each cell may have a maximum of four neighbours. On the bottom of the machines are two actuators to provide mobility [13]. The main controller for the robot is a *Blackfin* (ADSP-BF537E from ANALOG DEVICES) board that includes a fixed point digital signal processor and runs an uCLinux [30] operating system. All relevant sensor and actuator information is handled by a high level API (Application Programming Interface) that can be accessed via a C++ interface. Due to the fact that the robots are still in development we could only make use of three prototypes. Those prototypes have been running a preliminary version of the final operating system which was not yet able to physically dock robots.

3   Results

For our applications, VE on multi-robot organisms and evolutionary computation using the C++ version of VE, first results could be obtained.

3.1   Virtual Embryogenesis

The C++ implementation of VE is able to produce forms similar to a given template schema using evolutionary computation. Results can be compared with

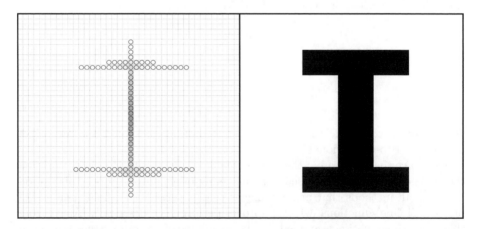

Fig. 2. Plot of a resulting embryo showing the gradient of morphogen 0 in green (left figure). This shape was produced by assigning fitness points according to the similarity to the template schema depicted in the figure on the right side. For each *ingoal* cell one point is awarded whereas two points are subtracted for each cell that overshoots the template pattern (*outgoal*). Resulting negative fitness values for the embryo are set to be zero.

those obtained by using the NetLogo implementation as the two versions use the same set of most basic rule sets (see section 1, [28]). Differences within the results of the two implementations build up as the NetLogo version has a more complex way to manage the individual reproduction process and choice of start genome for each generation. One of the resulting forms and its corresponding ideal template schema shown are depicted in figure 2.

Fig. 3. First results using the 'CellController' class to indicate docking signals using LEDs. Each side of the robot has three color-adjustable LEDs, which are lit according to the provided genome. Green LEDs indicate a docking signal, red LEDs none. A robot which signals to dock with one side, but refuses docking on the other is depicted above.

3.2   Results Using Robotic Hardware

Using the most recent prototype of the robot designed by the Karlsruhe team [12] [13], we show that both - VE core application and the decoupled 'CellController' class - are able to be compiled using the GNU cross-compiler [8] adapted for the *Blackfin* platform and can be executed on the robot.

The decoupled 'CellController' class has been tested on the robot and has taken full command of the machine. This implementation is based on a high level interface provided by the middleware. Green LEDs acting as docking signals are switched on and off according to the provided genome (figure 3) using the calculations that have been made by the main routine of 'CellController'. Simple tests have been performed using three different genomes - one that results in

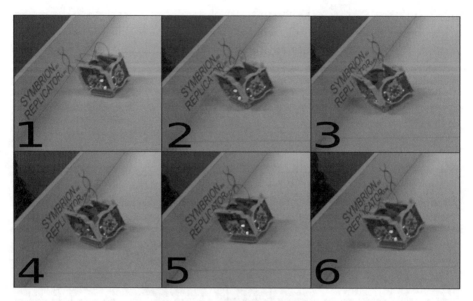

Fig. 4. First results using the 'CellController' class to steer a robot and obtain collision avoidance behaviour. The following is depicted: The robot is moving forward as there is no obstacle within its sensor range (1). Then a wall is coming in range (2), so the proximity sensor value, that is induced as a morphogen is building up to a certain threshold encoded in the genome and the robot reacts by stopping its movement. This is also indicated by switching the color of the front LEDs to red (3). The high level of the morphogen also triggers a second gene on the genome which is responsible for a turn movement (4). During the turn, the morphogen level decreases again, because the robot is turning away from the wall. With a lower level of morphogen, the gene responsible for the turn is not triggered anymore, but the gene for foward movement is triggered once again (5). With its morphogen level stabilized, the robot continues with forward motion throughout the arena.

lateral proliferation respectively docking signals to other robots, the other two resulting in vertical and omnidirectional docking signals. All three tests have lead to the correct distribution of red and green LEDs on all sides of the robot (picture 3).

Using a slightly modified version of class 'CellController' it is possible to steer the robot and observe basic collision avoidance. In this case the sensor values for obstacle-proximity are induced into the 'CellController' as morphogens and behaviour according to the level of this morphogen is encoded inside the genome. Providing a hand-coded genome has then resulted in a collision avoidance behaviour of the robot which is depicted in figure 4.

4   Outlook

The first step on the way to build multi-robot organisms using VE has been achieved by showing that our software runs on current robotic hardware and is able to switch on docking signals. This feature will be used to initiate the building of a robotic organism. First simulation studies regarding this process are presented in [27]. We show that, depending on the genome provided, different forms of multi-robot organisms can develop as projected in our simulations. Hereafter we plan to use VE for automated docking of robots according to the docking signals - first manually, then autonomously.

We have also shown that our decoupled 'CellController' class is able to steer a robot and demonstrates basic collision avoidance behaviour corresponding to a provided genome. As a next step we will adapt the VE process to autonomously react to docking signals. One advantage of our VE is that it can run on a single robot which opens the opportunity of each single robot being aware not only of its neighbours, but of the complete organism shape. We plan to investigate the application of on-board evolution on the robots. One final application will be to solve a given problem as an organism.

5 Discussion

In the work at hand we show that our bio-inspired VE process performs well in both design and construction of multi-robot organisms. Previous investigations in swarm robotics use global information to a large extend [19,20]. This information consists of the exact position of each robot at each time. Also many bio-inspired works on shape development processes depend on the existence of a global positioning system, that often encodes positional information in the genome [34,18,22,11]. In contrast to that, our self-organised approach does not necessarily require a single robot to be aware of its position at each time. Positional cues in our organisms are available using morphogen gradients [23,7] that are based on pure neighbour communication between robots. During construction of the organism every robot is equally suited to extend the organism by docking to it. These features of VE provide a high fault tolerance for building virtual and robotic organisms.

Acknowledgements. This work was supported by: EU-IST-FET project SYM-BRION, no. 216342; EU-ICT project REPLICATOR, no. 216240.

The writing of this article was supported by the Austrian Federal Ministry of Science and Research (BM.W_ F).

References

1. REPLICATOR: Robotic Evolutionary Self-Programming and Self-Assembling Organisms, 7th Framework Programme Project No FP7-ICT-2007.2.1. European Communities (2008-2012)
2. SYMBRION: Symbiotic Evolutionary Robot Organisms, 7th Framework Programme Project No FP7-ICT-2007.8.2. European Communities (2008-2012)
3. Carroll, S.B.: Endless forms: the evolution of gene regulation and morphological diversity. Cell 101(6), 577–580 (2000),
   http://view.ncbi.nlm.nih.gov/pubmed/10892643

4. Carroll, S.B.: Endless Forms Most Beautiful: The New Science of Evo Devo. W. W. Norton (April 2006)
5. Crick, F.: Diffusion in embryogenesis. Nature 225(5231), 420–422 (1970), http://dx.doi.org/10.1038/225420a0
6. Dorigo, M., Tuci, E., Groß, R., Trianni, V., Labella, T.H., Nouyan, S., Ampatzis, C., Deneubourg, J.L., Baldassarre, G., Nolfi, S., Mondada, F., Floreano, D., Gambardella, L.M.: The SWARM-BOTS project, pp. 31–44 (2005), http://www.springerlink.com/content/e4klufrqeqe6nvc2
7. Ephrussi, A., Johnston, D.S.: Seeing is believing - the bicoid morphogen gradient matures. Cell 116(2), 143–152 (2004)
8. GNU Project: GCC, the GNU compiler collection, version 4.4.3, http://www.gnu.org/software/gcc/gcc.html
9. Gurdon, J.B., Bourillot, P.Y.: Morphogen gradient interpretation. Nature 413(6858), 797–803 (2001), http://dx.doi.org/10.1038/35101500
10. Intel Corporation: Intel c++ compiler, version 12.0.2, http://software.intel.com/en-us/articles/intel-compilers/
11. Jin, Y., Schramm, L., Sendhoff, B.: A gene regulatory model for the development of primitive nervous systems. In: INNS-NNN Symposia on Modeling the Brain and Nervous Systems. Springer, Heidelberg (2008)
12. Kernbach, S., Schmickl, T., Hamann, H., Stradner, J., Schwarzer, C., Schlachter, F., Winfield, A., Matthias, R.: Adaptive action selection mechanisms for evolutionary multimodular robotics. In: Proc. of the 12th International Conference on the Synthesis and Simulation of Living Systems (AlifeXII). MIT Press, Denmark (2010)
13. Kernbach, S., Scholz, O., Harada, K., Popesku, S., Liedke, J., Raja, H., Liu, W., Caparrelli, F., Jemai, J., Havlik, J., Meister, E., Levi, P.: Multi-robot organisms: State of the art. In: ICRA 2010, Workshop on Modular Robots: State of the Art, Anchorage (2010)
14. Knuth, D.E.: The art of computer programming, sorting and searching, 2nd edn. Addison Wesley Longman Publishing Co., Inc., USA (1998)
15. Kornienko, S., Kornienko, O., Nagarathinam, A., Levi, P.: From real robot swarm to evolutionary multi-robot organism. In: 2007 IEEE Congress on Evolutionary Computation, pp. 1483–1490 (2007)
16. Levi, P., Kernbach, S. (eds.): Symbiotic Multi-Robot Organisms: Reliability, Adaptability, Evolution. Springer, Heidelberg (2010)
17. Müller, G.B.: Evo-devo: Extending the evolutionary synthesis. Nature Reviews Genetics 8, 943–949 (2007)
18. Roggen, D., Federici, D., Floreano, D.: Evolutionary morphogenesis for multicellular systems. Genetic Programming and Evolvable Machines 8, 61–96 (2007)
19. Rubenstein, M., Shen, W.M.: Scalable self-assembly and self-repair in a collective of robots. In: Proceedings of the IEEE/RSJ International Conference on Intelligent Robots and Systems (IROS), St. Louis, Missouri, USA (October 2009)
20. Rubenstein, M., Shen, W.M.: Automatic scalable size selection for the shape of a distributed robotic collective. In: IROS (October 2010)
21. Rumbaugh, J., Blaha, M., Premerlani, W., Eddy, F., Lorenson, W.: Object-Oriented Modeling and Design, 1st edn. Prentice-Hall, Englewood Cliffs (1991)
22. Schramm, L., Jin, Y., Sendhoff, B.: Evolutionary synthesis and analysis of a gene regulatory network for dynamically stable growth and regeneration. BioSystems (2010) (submitted)

23. Shvartsman, S.Y., Coppey, M., Berezhkovskii, A.M.: Dynamics of maternal morphogen gradients in drosophila. Current Opinion in Genetics & Development 18(4), 342–347 (2008)
24. Stroustrup, B.: The C++ Programming Language, 3rd edn. Addison-Wesley Longman Publishing Co., Inc., USA (2000)
25. Thenius, R., Bodi, M., Schmickl, T., Crailsheim, K.: Growth of structured artificial neural networks by virtual embryogenesis. In: Kampis, G., Karsai, I., Szathmáry, E. (eds.) ECAL 2009, Part II. LNCS, vol. 5778, pp. 118–125. Springer, Heidelberg (2008)
26. Thenius, R., Bodi, M., Schmickl, T., Crailsheim, K.: Using virtual embryogenesis for structuring controllers. In: Hart, E., McEwan, C., Timmis, J., Hone, A. (eds.) ICARIS 2010. LNCS, vol. 6209, pp. 312–313. Springer, Heidelberg (2010)
27. Thenius, R., Dauschan, M., Schmickl, T., Crailsheim, K.: Regenerative abilities in modular robots using virtual embryogenesis. In: Bouchachia, A. (ed.) ICAIS 2011. LNCS (LNAI), vol. 6943, pp. 238–247. Springer, Heidelberg (2011)
28. Thenius, R., Schmickl, T., Crailsheim, K.: Novel concept of modelling embryology for structuring an artificial neural network. In: Troch, I., Breitenecker, F. (eds.) Proc. of the MATHMOD (2009)
29. Turing, A.M.: The chemical basis of morphogenesis. Philosophical Transactions of the Royal Society of London. Series B, Biological Sciences 237(641), 37–72 (1952)
30. Ungerer, G., Dionne, J., Durant, M.: uClinux: Embedded Linux/Microcontroller Project (September 2008), http://www.uclinux.org
31. Weatherbee, S.D., Carroll, S.B.: Selector genes and limb identity in arthropods and vertebrates. Cell 97(3), 283–286 (1999)
32. Wilensky, U.: Netlogo. Center for Connected Learning and Computer-Based Modeling, Northwestern University Evanston, IL (1999), http://ccl.northwestern.edu/netlogo/
33. Wolpert, L.: Positional information and the spatial pattern of cellular differentiation. Journal of Theoretical Biology 25(1), 1–47 (1969)
34. Wolpert, L.: Positional information revisited. Development 107, 3–12 (1989)
35. Wolpert, L.: One hundred years of positional information. Trends Genet 12(9), 359–364 (1996), http://view.ncbi.nlm.nih.gov/pubmed/8855666

Adaptive Bearings Vibration Modelling for Diagnosis

Ryszard A. Makowski[1] and Radoslaw Zimroz[2]

[1] Wroclaw University of Technology, Wybrzeze Wyspianskiego 27
Signal Theory Section
[2] Wroclaw University of Technology, Wybrzeze Wyspianskiego 27
Diagnostic and Vibroacoustics Science Laboratory
50 370 Wroclaw, Poland
{ryszard.makowski,radoslaw.zimroz}@pwr.wroc.pl

Abstract. An adaptive algorithm for vibration signal modeling is proposed in the paper. The aim of the signal processing is to detect the impact signals (shocks) related to damages in rolling element bearings (REB). Damage in the REB may result in cyclic impulsive disturbance in the signal, however they are usually completely masked by the noise. Moreover, impulses may have amplitudes that vary in time due to changes transmission path, load and properties of the noise. Thus, the solution should be an adaptive one. The proposed approach is based on the normalized exact least-square time-variant lattice filter (adaptive Schur filter). It is characterized by an extremely fast start-up performance, an excellent convergence behavior, and a fast parameter tracking capability and make this approach interesting. The method is well-adapted for analysis of the non-stationary time-series, so it seems to be very promising for diagnostics of machines working in time varying load/speed conditions.

Keywords: Adaptive stochastic modeling, linear prediction, adaptive Schur filter, rolling element bearings, damage detection, vibration time series.

1 Introduction

Identification of quasi-periodic (or cyclic) impulsive signal components in a raw vibration signal generated by Rolling Element Bearings (REB) is one of the most exploited issue in the subject focused on condition monitoring. It is important for many types of machines where REB are commonly used i.e. rotating and reciprocating machines including gearboxes, fans, engines, compressors, etc [1]-[17]. Typical damages in the REB give cyclic disturbance in the signal [1],[5], however, they are usually completely masked by the noise [6]-[13]. Moreover impulses may have amplitudes that vary in time due to changes of transmission path, time varying load and time varying properties of noise [14],[15].

Thus, there is a need to use an adaptive method, i.e. an adaptive system that can be tuned according to changing environment [16]-[18] for a signal with

A. Bouchachia (Ed.): ICAIS 2011, LNAI 6943, pp. 248–259, 2011.

varying time-frequency structure. By changing environment we understand here several factors that affect vibration signal captured from the bearing' housing. Basic reason for non-stationarity of the signal is short, transient disturbance associated with the damage. Additionally, properties of the signal depend on variation of the rotational speed and external load related to the material stream transported on the belt (amount of material being transported). Finally, the time varying mixture consists also of time varying response from other parts of the drive unit (gearbox) and other sources including Gaussian and non-Gaussian noise.

In order to meet the expectation (i.e. to extract the information about damage) a novel approach for stochastic modeling, namely the algorithm that is based on the adaptive optimal orthogonal parameterization, i.e. the adaptive Schur filter is proposed [19]. Based on the linear prediction theory which uses the innovative filters, we propose an advanced structure of adaptive filter that is known in signal processing community as the adaptive Schur filter. However, it should be highlighted, that it was difficult to find any example of application of the Schur filter for vibration signals.

The idea of the stochastic modeling of the signal will be presented first, and than several features aimed to enhance the detection efficiency will be proposed. The results of applying the adaptive Schur filter to synthetic and real time series (vibrations) will be shown. The filter calculates an optimal orthogonal signal representation using second-order statistics of the signal, resulting in a set of time-varying Schur coefficients. Some simple procedures (derivatives of reflection coefficients (RCs), sum of them etc.) of further processing designed to improve the damage detection are proposed. It will be shown that the method is well-adapted for analysis of the non-stationary time-series [20], and it seems to be very promising for condition monitoring of machines working in time varying load/speed conditions. It should be noted that damage detection in bearings is an important topic in the literature. It is possible to find many examples of using the existing techniques (wavelets, adaptive LMS filter, optimal Wiener filter, etc), (see [23]). However, most of the known techniques referred to laboratory test data and stationary load/speed conditions. Any information about applying the Schur filter in bearings diagnostics were found.

2 Theoretical Background

The basic theory concerning the linear prediction, first for stationary case and next for non-stationary case, which use adaptive approach will be briefly described in this section. It is necessary to understand the idea of used signal processing method.

2.1 Stochastic Modeling of Signal in Stationary Case

Modeling of the signal used here origins from classical linear prediction problem [17],[21]. It is well known that for stationary autoregressive process with discrete time of rank P, the next value $x(t)$ of signal at any time t may be estimated using previous P samples

$$\hat{x}(t) = \sum_{n=1}^{P} a_n x(t - n); \quad t = P, \dots \tag{1}$$

where $\{a_n : n = 1, \dots, P\}$ are coefficients which depend on signal, forming a prediction filter. Prediction described by (1) is named as forward prediction; by analogy backward one also exists. Estimation error, called also the prediction error, is defined as

$$e_P(t) = x(t) - \hat{x}(t) \tag{2}$$

Values of coefficients of the filter are calculated using minimization of mean square error, i.e.:

$$\varepsilon = \min_{a_1, \dots, a_P} E\{e_P^2(t)\} \tag{3}$$

where E is an expected value operator. This kind of filter is also called mean-square filter. Quality of modeling the signal (i.e. value of prediction error) is a function of: length P of filter, values of coefficients and signal itself.

The prediction filtering scheme is presented on Fig. 1. The input is a signal history of rank P, and the output is the estimator of signal sample for given time t.

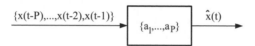

Fig. 1. Scheme of prediction filtering of signal

By substitution $\{\alpha_n = -a_n : n = 1, \dots, P\}$ and $\alpha_0 = 1$ it is possible to obtain the complementary filter called innovative or whitening filter. The idea of the innovative filtering is presented on Fig. 2.

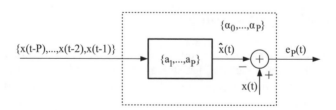

Fig. 2. Scheme of innovative filtering of signal

The output from the innovative filter is the prediction error called also the innovative signal, which tends to be white noise if rank of the filter increases.

Filters presented above are suitable for stationary signals. However they are not able to react in case of rapid impulsive changes in the signal. Obviously, vibration signals, especially when damage occurs in the machine, are non-stationary. Hence, to process a non-stationary signal it is necessary to have an adaptive filter that will change filter coefficients according to changes of the signal statistics.

2.2 Stochastic Modeling of Signal via Adaptive Schur Filter

An adaptive Schur filter calculates recursively the solution for the signal prediction following from the orthogonal projection theorem (the least-square approach) [22] at every time step. Obviously, in the case considered here, due to non-stationary nature of time-series, the solution is time-dependent. The ladder-form realization of the Schur filter is presented in Fig. 3.

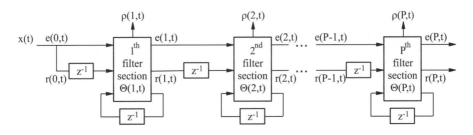

Fig. 3. The ladder-form realization of the adaptive Schur filter

The filter consists of P equal sections. Each section $\Theta(n,t)$ is entirely described by the reflection coefficient $\rho(n,t)$ and it is updated, in time and in order, by a set of double-recursive, as follows:

$$\rho(n+1,t) = \rho(n+1,t-1)\sqrt{1-e^2(n,t)}\sqrt{1-r^2(n,t-1)}+e(n,t)r(n,t+1) \quad (4)$$

$$e(n+1,t) = \frac{e(n,t)-\rho(n+1,t)r(n,t-1)}{\sqrt{1-\rho^2(n+1,t)}\sqrt{1-r^2(n,t-1)}} \quad (5)$$

$$r(n+1,t) = \frac{r(n,t-1)-\rho(n+1,t)e(n,t)}{\sqrt{1-\rho^2(n+1,t)}\sqrt{1-e^2(n,t-1)}} \quad (6)$$

where $e(n+1,t)$ and $r(n+1,t)$ denote the forward prediction error and backward prediction error on the $(n+1)^{th}$ section at time t respectively.

The number of filter sections P is a function of the analyzed signal type. The estimation quality depends on the decreasing rapidity of covariance function $C(k)$ where k denotes a time-lag. If the rapidity is high, estimation quality decreases slowly with increase of P and as a result it is necessary to use higher filter order. If the rapidity is low, estimation quality decreases quickly and lower filter order is needed.

In previous applications [6],[7],[10] of adaptive filters (LMS) based on linear prediction two output signals were considered: denoised signal (predicted deterministic contribution) or prediction error. In mechanical applications for REB damage detection, the signal of interest is the prediction error. In case of adaptive normalized Schur algorithm, the obtained results are the prediction errors and reflection coefficients (RCs). When for given signal and for given time instant, a local disturbance of signal statistics appears, updating procedure will modify set of prediction errors and set of reflection coefficients. If signal doesn't contain impulsive disturbances, prediction errors and reflection coefficients become constant (excluding changes connected with estimation errors of statistics). Authors propose here several approaches for stochastic modeling of the signal to detect fault. They will be discussed in next sections.

2.3   Filter Initiation

As it was said, the reflection coefficients, forward and backward prediction errors in each section and time instant are calculated recursively. Simultaneously, to ensure the stability of the filter and its good numerical properties, the analyzed signal should be normalized, hence:

– The first sample $x_s(0)$ is normalized according to the formula

$$x(0) = \frac{x_s(0)}{\sqrt{c_0}} \tag{7}$$

where

$$c_0 = x_s^2(0) + \delta \tag{8}$$

where δ is small positive constant to avoid division by 0
– Initiation of forward/backward prediction errors for $t = 0$

$$e(0,0) = r(0,0) = x(0) \tag{9}$$

and

$$r(n,-1) = 0; \quad n = 0, ..., P - 1 \tag{10}$$

– Initiation of reflection coefficients

$$\rho(n,-1) = 0; \quad n = 0, ..., P - 1 \tag{11}$$

– The next signal samples, are normalized according to the formula

$$x(t) = \frac{x_s(t)}{\sqrt{c_t}} \tag{12}$$

where

$$c_t = \lambda c_{t-1} + x_s^2(t) \tag{13}$$

c_t represents estimator of variance of signal assuming that its mean equals zero. In turn, $\lambda \in (0, 1)$ is a forgetting factor. The role of this factor is to minimize the weight of previous values in comparison with the new signal samples.

After initiation only two a priori parameters are required: filter order P and the forgetting factor λ. As it was mentioned, filter order depends on signals properties. In practice $P = 8$ or $P = 10$ was established. The forgetting factor may be adaptive in some cases however here the value of $\lambda = 0.998$ is assumed.

It should be clearly stressed that in fact, setting value of parameters for this filter is not critical. Parameter λ should be set to assure that the adaptation time $(T_s = 1/(1 - \lambda)$ - in samples) equals expected distance between impulses. Filter order P should provide satisfactory model of the signal. However, if P is too big, prediction errors and reflection coefficients of higher index will converge to constant values. Future effort will be focused on automatic, blind selection of the parameters that means fully adaptive (self-organizing) system with unsupervised training phase.

3   Performance Analysis Using Simulations

To test the performance of the proposed approach a synthetic signal was used. It simulates a noisy observation from real machine, i.e. it is a mixture of impulsive signal and narrow-band deterministic signal (several sine waves), Fig. 4.

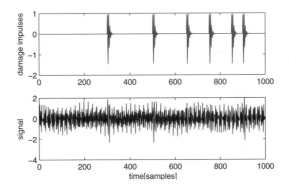

Fig. 4. Synthetic signal used for testing of modeling efficiency: local impulsive shocks (informative) - top and noisy observation -bottom

Fig. 5 and 6 shows results of signal analysis. They show variation of prediction errors and reflection coefficients, respectively. It can be clearly seen, that prediction error of the 8th section provides valuable result. A much better situation (significant changes for several sections) can be found on Fig. 6. Occurrence of impulses in noisy observation affects the values of RCs at each section. It may be concluded that results are very promising and in the next section the performance of the filter will be tested for industrial data.

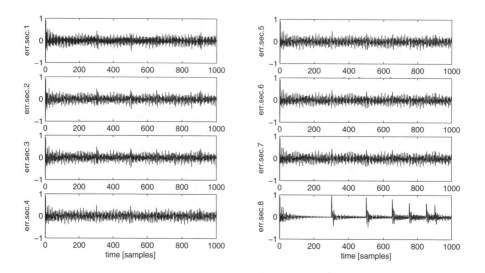

Fig. 5. Prediction errors for sections: 1-4(left) and 5-8 (right)

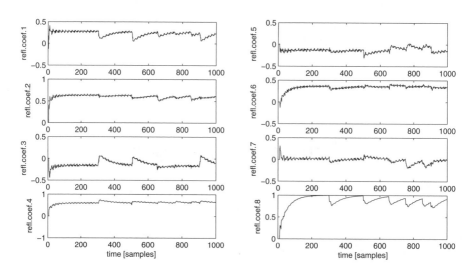

Fig. 6. Reflection coefficients for section: 1-4 (left) and 5-8 (right)

4   Application to Industrial Data

In this section the results of application of Schur filter to real data, i.e. vibration time series acquired from the machine working in the mining company, will be presented. A scheme and photographs of the machine during experiments are presented on Fig. 7.

Several acquisition sessions have been performed. For each signal has been acquired with following parameters: sampling frequency Fs=19200Hz, duration

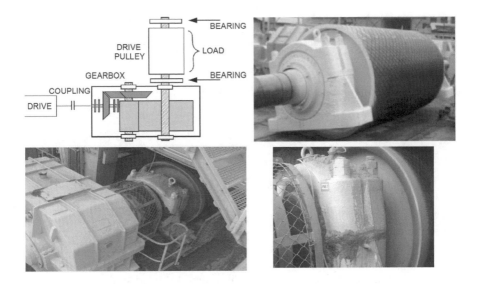

Fig. 7. Scheme and photographs of diagnosed object

T=5s. Location of accelerometer is shown on the Fig. 7 (right bottom corner); sensor has been mounted horizontally using the screw. The parameters have been established by experts from company providing the monitoring system. Characteristic damage frequencies (calculated based on shaft rotational speed and geometry of the bearings) are: 12.35Hz, 16.1Hz and 8.9Hz (inner ring, outer ring and rolling element, respectively).

The task defined here (from diagnostics point of view) is to detect the local disturbance signal with one of cycles corresponding to the fault frequency. Unfortunately, the signal of interest (impulsive, cyclic contribution related to the damaged bearings) is completely masked by high energy source related to the gearbox located nearby (see Fig. 7 (left bottom) and Fig. 8 (top)). In the paper the task is limited to the signal of interest extraction. Further identification of fault type is a classical one and it is based on the envelope analysis (the Hilbert transform to get the envelope signal and spectral analysis to identify periodicity of the envelope). More information can be found in other papers concerning the diagnostics of these machine (for example [14]).

The idea of results description is as follow. Raw (not processed) vibration time series are difficult to interpret due to strong noise contribution. It is expected to get an enhanced signal after processig. Several cyclic spikes (impacts) related to the damage should be clearly visible. At this stage there is no objective, mathematical criterion to compare results. They are assesed based on visual inspection. For comparison, two cases will be analysed: vibration time series from damaged and undamaged REB.

Apart from using prediction errors and reflection coefficients, two new features has been defined, i.e. derivatives of reflection coefficients [20]:

$$d(n,t) = \rho(n,t) - \rho(n, t - \tau); \quad \tau = 1 \qquad (14)$$

and sum of absolute values of derivatives of RC, F_{SAVDRC}

$$F_{SAVDRC}(t) = \sum_{n=1}^{P} |d(n,t)| \qquad (15)$$

4.1   Vibration Time Series from Damaged REB

Fig. 8 presents raw time series and results of processing for damaged REB. As it was mentioned, for raw time series any regular, cyclic impact are not seen. Unfortunately, prediction error signals and reflection coefficients at any section did not provide satisfactory results. When applying the new features, defined in previous section, very good results were obtained, both for sum of derivatives of RCs and sum of absolute values of derivatives of RCs. These results are presented on Fig. 8 (middle and bottom subplot). Expected impulses in the all two forms of signal are marked by ellipses.

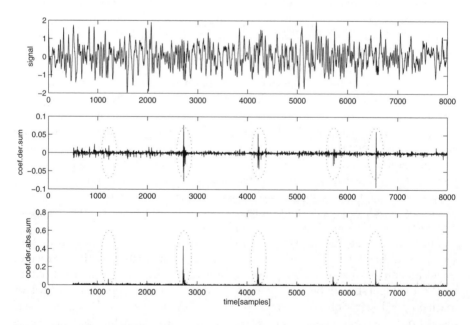

Fig. 8. Raw vibration time series (top) and results of modeling: sum of derivatives of RCs (middle) and sum of absolute values of derivatives of RCs (bottom) - "bad condition" case

4.2   Vibration Time Series from REB in Good Condition

By analogy, the same approach has been applied to the data from undamaged machine. In this case it is not expected to see any impulses - no damage in the REB has been noticed. Fig 9 shows: raw vibration time series, sum of derivatives of RCs and sum of absolute values of derivatives of RCs, respectively. No artefacts have been found; in case of good condition there are no cyclic disturbances in reflection coefficients as it was found for data from damaged bearings (note difference in the Y axis scale).

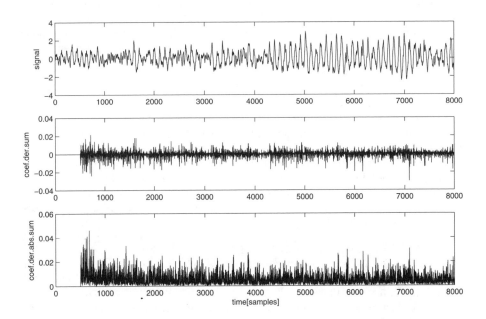

Fig. 9. Raw vibration time series (top) and results of modeling: sum of derivatives of RCs (middle) and sum of absolute values of derivatives of RCs (bottom) - "good condition" case

5   Conclusion

A novel technique of vibration signals analysis based on the adaptive Schur filter is presented in the paper. It has been investigated in the context of REB damage detection. Proposed approach can be interpreted as a preprocessor i.e. classical adaptive filter with prediction error as output signal or tool for stochastic modeling of non-stationary signal with several features based on reflection coefficients variation. Several innovative approaches for damage detection in bearings, such as using the reflection coefficients, derivative of RCs and sum of absolute value of derivative of RCs were defined. All these features provided good results, however, the last one is probably the best, especially for industrial data. Further efforts will focus on defining the criterion in order to compare results. It needs to be noticed that, without signal pre-processing, detection of impulses (that indicate local damage) is not possible at all. Results presented in this paper have been obtained based on synthetic as well as real signals captured from industrial machines working in surface lignite mines.

References

1. McFadden, P.D., Smith, J.D.: Vibration monitoring of rolling element bearings by the high-frequency resonance technique-a review. Tribology International 17, 3–10 (1984)
2. McFadden, P.D., Smith, J.D.: Model for the vibration produced by a single point defect in a rolling element bearing. Journal of Sound and Vibration 96, 69–82 (1984)
3. Antoni, J., Randall, R.B.: A stochastic model for simulation and diagnostics of rolling element bearings with localized faults. Journal of Vibration and Acoustics, Transactions of the ASME 125, 28–289 (2003)
4. Antoni, J., Bonnardot, F., Raad, A., Badaoui, M.: Cyclostationary Modelling of Rotating Machine Vibration Signals. Mechanical Systems and Signal Processing 18, 1285–1314 (2004)
5. Zimroz, R., Bartelmus, W.: Gearbox condition estimation using cyclo-stationary properties of vibration signal. Key Engineering Materials 413-414, 471–478 (2009)
6. Ho, D., Randall, R.B.: Optimisation of bearing diagnostic techniques using simulated and actual bearing fault signals. Mechanical Systems and Signal Processing 14, 763–788 (2000)
7. Antoni, J., Randall, R.B.: Differential diagnosis of gear and bearing faults. ASME Journal of Vibration and Acoustics 124/2, 165–171 (2002)
8. Boustany, R., Antoni, J.: Blind extraction of a cyclostationary signal using reduced-rank cyclic regression - A unifying approach. Mechanical Systems and Signal Processing 22, 520–541 (2008)
9. Lee, S., White, P.: The enhancement of impulsive noise and vibration signals for fault detection in rotating and reciprocating machinery. Journal of Sound and Vibration 21(3), 485–505 (1998)
10. Barszcz, T.: Decomposition of vibration signals into deterministic and nondeterministic components and its capabilities of fault detection and identification. Int. J. Appl. Math. Comput. Sci. 19(2), 327–335 (2009)
11. Boustany, R., Antoni, J.: A subspace method for the blind extraction of a cyclostationary source: Application to rolling element bearing diagnostics. Mechanical Systems and Signal Processing 19(2), 1245–1259 (2005)
12. Barszcz, T., Randall, R.B.: Application of spectral kurtosis for detection of a tooth crack in the planetary gear of a wind turbine. Mechanical Systems and Signal Processing 23(2), 1352–1365 (2009)
13. Barszcz, T., Zimroz, R., Jablonski, A., Bartelmus, W.: Bearings fault detection in gas compressor with high impulsive noise level. In: The Seventh International Conference CM 2010/MFPT 2010, Stratford-upon-Avon, p. 13. Coxmoor Publishing Company, England (2010)
14. Zimroz, R.: Some remarks on local damage diagnosis in presence of multi-faults and non-stationary operation. In: The Sixth International Conference CM 2009/MFPT 2009, pp. 33–44. The BINDT, US Society for MFPR, Dublin, Ireland (2009)

15. Bartelmus, W., Zimroz, R.: Vibration condition monitoring of planetary gearbox under varying external load. Mechanical Systems and Signal Processing 23, 246–257 (2009)
16. Gelman, L., Zimroz, R., Birkel, J., Leigh-Firbank, H., Simms, D., Waterland, B., Whitehurst, G.: Adaptive vibration condition monitoring technology for local tooth damage in gearboxes. Insight: non-destructive testing and condition monitoring 47(8), 461–464 (2005)
17. Lin, J., Zuo, M.: Gearbox fault diagnosis using adaptive wavelet filter. Mechanical Systems and Signal Processing 17(6), 1259–1269 (2003)
18. Brie, D., Tomczak, M., Oehlmann, H., Richard, A.: Gear Crack Detection By Adaptive Amplitude And Phase Demodulation. Mechanical Systems and Signal Processing 11(1), 149–167 (1997)
19. Zarzycki, J.: Multidimentional Nonlinear Schur Parametrization of Non-Gausian Stochastic Signals, Part One: Statement of the problem. Multidimensional Systems and Signal Processing 15(3), 217–241 (2004)
20. Lopatka, M., Adam, O., Laplanche, C., Zarzycki, J., Motsch, J.-F.: Effective Analysis of Non-Stationary Short-Time Signals Based on The Adaptive Schur Filter. In: IEEE/SP 13th Workshop on Statistical Signal Processing, pp. 251–256 (2005)
21. Rabiner, L., Juang, B.-H.: Fundamentals of Speech Recognition. Prentice Hall, Englewood Cliffs (1993)
22. Lee, D.T.L., Morf, M., Friedlander, B.: Recursive least squares ladder estimation algorithms. IEEE Trans. Circuit and Systems 28(6), 627–641 (1981)
23. Randall, R.B., Antoni, J.: Rolling element bearing diagnostics-A tutorial. Mechanical Systems and Signal Processing 25(2), 485–520 (2011)

Hybrid Learning System for Adaptive Complex Event Processing

Jean-René Coffi[1,2], Christophe Marsala[2], and Nicolas Museux[1]

[1] Thales Research and Technology,
1, Avenue Augustin Fresnel 91767 Palaiseau, France
[2] LIP6/UPMC,
4, Place Jussieu 75005 Paris, France

Abstract. In today's security systems, the use of complex rule bases for information aggregation is more and more frequent. This does not however eliminate the possibility of wrong detections that could occur when the rule base is incomplete or inadequate. In this paper, a machine learning method is proposed to adapt complex rule bases to environmental changes and to enable them to correct design errors. In our study, complex rules have several levels of structural complexity, that leads us to propose an approach to adapt the rule base by means of an Association Rule mining algorithm coupled with Inductive logic programming for rule induction.

1 Introduction

A major concern in the field of Critical Infrastructures Protection is anticipation and reactivity to threats aimed at the vital infrastructures of a nation. The building blocks to protect efficiently those elements are linked to the concept of *Situation Understanding* ([9], [20]). A *situation* is recognized based on various activities detected on the environment - for example the activation of a fire alarm based on smoke or heat detection - in some cases the situation is confirmed and an appropriate reaction is initiated by the operator, in others it is rejected (a fire did not occur) and we have a *false positive*. It can also happen that a situation is not recognized when it should have been, we have then a *false negative*.

To obtain a global view of a situation based on detected activities we use Complex Event Processing (CEP, [19], [11]), which is a paradigm for representing systems that react automatically based on events occurrence. It uses a set of reactive rules which takes basic events as input, verifies their inter-relationships and parameters in order to generate new events or launch actions (fig 1). It is used in many application domains, in particular for multi-sensor surveillance ([26], [25]). Due to the low occurrence of attacks, the initial detection model cannot be built via machine learning but must be defined by a domain expert. This particular bias can lead to incomplete and subjective models and furthermore to detection errors. First because its relative to the expert's knowledge, then because the environment is evolving due to new threats appearing or new *modus operandis* from the actors.

A. Bouchachia (Ed.): ICAIS 2011, LNAI 6943, pp. 260–271, 2011.

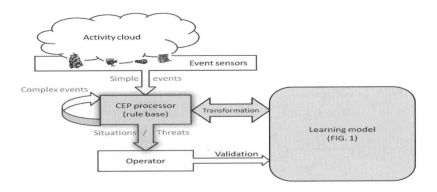

Fig. 1. Complex Event Processing cycle

We propose here to associate the initial model with a technique to correct the detection errors. Knowledge revision in rule based system is a difficult task, even more so when the domain knowledge, initial data and new facts to take into account are represented in a complex structure. As the environment evolves overtime we aim to adapt our set of beliefs while maintaining consistency with the old information available. There are many ways to extract new knowledge using additional data, the majority those methods works very well in the propositional setting but are hard to extend to higher level logics mostly because of the complexity involved. A new paradigm based on the human immune system was proposed in [7]; although some complexity issues were tackled, the interpretation of the result is still problematic especially in the security field. We propose here a method combining Relational Association Rules Mining (R-ARM) with Inductive Logic Programming (ILP, [6]) in order to extract first order hypotheses structured data. The learning process is composed of several steps described in figure 2.

This paper introduces first the problem of adaptation in a complex, reactive context. This is followed by a presentation of the learning process, which is finally evaluated by comparison with previous algorithms.

2   A Reactive-Rules Based Detection System

2.1   Theory of Event Processing

While many CEP languages exist, such as SAMOS ([13]), COMPOSE ([14]) or SNOOP ([8]), very little as been done about conceiving and reasoning on a system ([12]). That's why we propose a generic representation of a rule, where any types of correlation can be written:

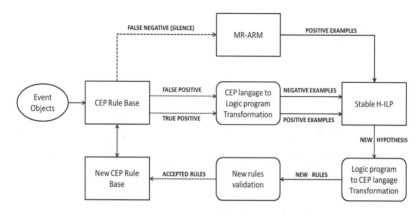

– dotted arrows: decision making steps - full arrows: data flow
– rounded squares: intermediary steps - squares: data processing steps

Fig. 2. Modification process of a complex decision system

TYPE Rule content (*the type of situation detected*)
DECLARE EventClass virtual events list(*input event classes'*);
ON Event Pattern (*relationships between events*)
SUCH-THAT Constraints satisfied (*contextual constraints on detections*)
DO generate NewEvent (*arglist*)
    throw Command (*parameters*) (*event generation and/or command launching*)

The set of events is provided under the form of an ontology since the set is organised as a hierarchy and each event has its own structure. In first-order logic, an event class can be represented as an unary predicate: $A(x)$, meaning that instance x is of type A.

In CEP each class of event is defined by a vector of attributes common to every events belonging to that class. Because of that, behind the predicate $A(x)$ we included an object structure defining the properties of that predicate. For example, every event of type *sound* could be described by its class (*sound*), its own unique identification, its date, but also its *intensity, spectrum*, etc. The hierarchical structure of event class is a lattice, and, in terms of logic, can be though as direct implications (figure 3).

To construct CEP rule, the events' classes are connected by operators to form the patterns we expect to be detected. Most operators are specializations of logical conjunctions and disjunctions, and they can be of any arity. An operator o can also be represented by a predicate of the same arity ($o(x, y)$, means their is a relationship o between x and y). They are also related to each other in a hierarchical manner (for example the *causality* operator is a specialization of the *sequence* operator which itself is a specialization of the *conjunction*). Moreover, the existence of a relationship can be verified by testing the events' attributes, for example a *sequence* is verified by comparing the *dates* of two events (figure 4).

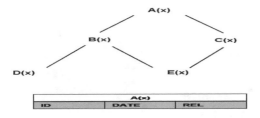

– Event Logic: $D(x) \to B(x)$, $B(x) \to A(x)$, $C(x) \to A(x)$, $E(x) \to B(x) \wedge C(x)$

Fig. 3. Events Hierarchy and Structure

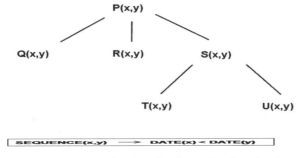

Relationship Logic: $T(x,y) \to S(x,y)$, $U(x,y) \to S(x,y)$, $Q(x,y) \to P(x,y)$,
$R(x,y) \to P(x,y)$, $S(x,y) \to P(x,y)$

Fig. 4. Relationships Hierarchy and Structure

A rule is written by combination of those two elements. They can be used in many types of applications, however we focus in this paper on its use for multi-sensor surveillance, with the aim to correct design errors and adapt the system to environmental changes.

2.2 Illustrative Application

In the field of security - more precisely infrastructure protection - very few data is readily available. We decided to simulate real-life scenarios in a multi-agent environment ([2]) to construct a learning database. Although the conditions of a detection (rule-base) are pre-determined, the behaviour of the system has been made partially random by introducing probabilities on agents' behaviours and sensors detection rates (in a case of faulty sensors). The basic event are fed into a rule engine, Esper ([1]), and the outputs are recorded after evaluation (figure 5).

To have an objective evaluation of the output, the rule engine implements two sets of rules: the first is used as a *reference* and only gives correct outputs, the second is a set of degraded rules (*dummy*) which outputs are compared to the reference to be marked as positive or negative example. The goal of the learning

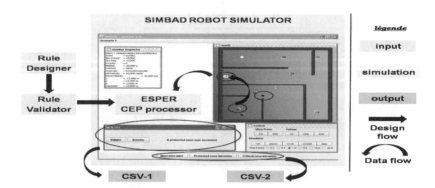

Fig. 5. The simulation Environment

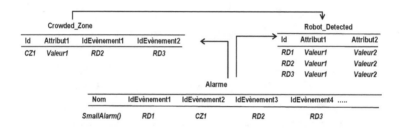

Fig. 6. Relational tables for a false negative

process is to make the *dummy* as close to the *reference* as possible in terms of detection rates.

To avoid information loss, the data is recorded in a structured model. The false negative is described by the IDs of all the recorded events. Each complex event is described by the IDs of events that led to its creation, plus its own descriptive attributes. Finally a simple event is described by its own attributes (see figure 6).

The logic program corresponding to figure 6 has to be built from scratch by a pattern mining algorithm. In case a false positive occurs, the trace of the rules that triggered the alarm is collected. Each alarm is described by the patterns leading to its detection and each pattern to the events composing it. If the event is *complex*, it's linked to its own pattern, if its *simple* its described by the values of its attributes (figure 7).

The corresponding logic program for figure 7 would be:

```
not(SmallAlarm()) :=
CrowdedZone(CZ1), RobotDetected(RD1), cause(CZ1, RD1)
CrowdedZone(CZ1) :=
RobotDetected(RD2), RobotDetected(RD3), conjunction(RD2, RD3)
```

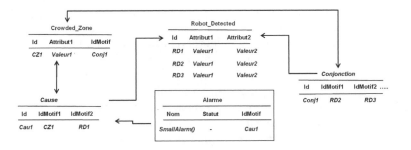

Fig. 7. Relational table for a false positive

This initial system will be updated overtime by exploiting the detection errors of the situation $S1$. When a false negative is detected, the current rules are *generalized* or a new rule is added. On the other hand, when a false positive is detected, the current rules are *specialized* or a rule is deleted.

3   The Learning Algorithm

Our learning model consists of two phases: in case a *false negative* is detected, a positive example e^+ is constructed and the model generalized to include it; when we have a *false positive*, the corresponding negative example e^- is recorded and the model is specialized to exlude it.

3.1   Finding of New Hypotheses with Induction

The representation of our problem under the form of a logic program allows us to address two main difficulties compared to classical machine learning paradigms. First of all, its has a much larger knowledge representation capability (as opposed to propositional logic). Moreover we can use domain knowledge in the learning process. Those two points are vital given the structured nature of our reactive system. Represented in logic programs are the background theory B (our initial CEP rule base or the previously inferred rule base); a set of positive examples E^+ (the examples obtained through the rule-mining phase and the examples that were correctly labeled by our initial system); a set of negative examples E^- (obtained after a false positive occurred); a set of well-formed hypothesis H. The goal in ILP is to find an hypothesis $h \in H$ such that:

- $B \wedge h \models E^+$ (*posterior sufficiency*), h allows us to explain E^+,
- $B \wedge h \not\models E^-$ (*posterior satisfiability*), B and h are consistent with E^-.

The problem can therefore be seen as searching H for the best hypothesis h, search algorithms include inductive and deductive inference rules for generalization and specialization. A deductive inference rule maps a hypothesis h to a more specific hypothesis h' that exclude a negative example. An inductive inference rule maps a hypothesis h to a more general hypothesis h' that matches a positive example. The application of those inference rules guides the exploration of our search space H. However the efficiency of the algorithm also depends on the search strategy applied and the hypothesis evaluation method. The search space H in our case is limited by our events' and relations hierarchies. The search strategy is also conditioned by those. If an error can be corrected by specialization or generalization of a predicate then the rules of *Inverted Resolution* are used ([15]), otherwise the rules of θ-*subsumption* may be applied ([21]). Some special cases are possible, especially concerning negative predicates. For hypothesis evaluation, state of the art learning models mainly use bayesian information based techniques ([17]).

3.2   Constructing Positive Examples from False Negatives

Traditionally in ILP, the finding of a new rule that covers a missed detection is done through *abduction* ([23]). This particular method doesn't suit completely our setting. The most important drawback being that the concept of hierarchies between predicate is not taken into account.

For example, during the abduction phase the fact that an event might be a specialization of another one might be important, just like the hierarchies between relations can lead to better generalization.

Frequent Itemset Generation: What we propose is to compare this manner of creating new rules from false negative with the use of a simple method of association rule mining. Agrawal extends the applications of *a-priori* to structured concepts ([24], [4]). Furthermore much work has been done on mining temporal ([18]) and spatial relationships between concepts ([5]). We propose a modified version of *a-priori*, that test the presence of any kind of relationships between the frequent concepts by exploring the relationships hierarchy.

During the construction of our frequent itemsets three additional operations are mandatory:

- the collecting of events' classes from events' IDs,
- the marking of the same event class appearing twice or more in a single transaction,
- the elimination of redundant IDs.

Those operations can be done during the generation of the candidates items in the *a-priori* algorithm ([3]). They require the modification of the function generating the candidates items in a way that when an ID, id, is found we first check if it doesn't appear as an antecedent to another event ($id \notin id'.relations$) then we recover $id.class$ and if it is not already in the transaction we set:

```
1: for all c ∈ eventclasses do
2:     count_class = 0
3:     for all items do
4:         if id.class = c then
5:             count_class + +
```

6:          $candidates = candidates \cap c(count\_class)$
7:        **end if**
8:      **end for**
9: **end for**

Relationships Mining: In order to talk about multi-relational association rules, the notion of a frequent query and query subsumption need to be defined. Instead of the frequent itemsets of the single relation case, in the multi-relational case there are frequent queries.

Example queries in the CEP context (A and B are event classes):

1. $Disjunction(A, B) \rightarrow A(x) \vee B(y)$
2. $Conjunction(A, B) \rightarrow A(x) \wedge B(y)$
3. $Sequence(A, B) \rightarrow A(x) \wedge B(y) \wedge Date(x) \leq Date(y)$

Example hierarchy of predicates in the CEP context (queries subsumption):

1. $Conjunction(A, B) \rightarrow Disjunction(A, B)$
2. $Sequence(A, B) \rightarrow Conjunction(A, B)$

Discovery of rules is accomplished by a systematic search in the space of database queries. To tackle the problem of a very large, potentially infinite, search space of queries, two basic strategies are used: first, the search is systematic and orders queries based on subsumption; second, support and confidence thresholds are used to guide the search and sort out uninteresting rules. A important observation is that support is non-increasing when moving from a more general to a more specific query in the search graph, therefore if the support is not sufficient for a particular query, its children will be pruned from the search tree. The algorithm for mining relationships between items takes the frequent itemsets computed by *a-priori* and the queries graph as input. We use a search algorithm that starts with the topmost query and explores the refinement graph from top to bottom to extract frequent association rules R.

4   Experimental Results

In this section we will call *scenarios* the model of a situation, that is the set of rules used to detect a threat, and *observation* a particular instance (detected threat) of a scenario which, in real life, is marked as positive or negative by the operator.

The first set of scenarios are located in a train station. Our test CEP system contains nine rules used to detect three types of threats: a terrorist attack on a electric box, a chemical contamination and an act of vandalism.

The second environment is an administrative building in which we want to detect an attack on an official with six CEP rules[1]. Each type of threat we want

---

[1] The scenarios are taken from the french Competitiveness Pole System@tic through the project SIC: Securisation des Infrastructures Critiques 2008-2010.

to detect correspond to an independent dataset. After the simulation we have 165 *terrorist attacks*, 293 *chemical attacks*, 317 *acts of vandalism* and 159 *attacks on official*.

The original database is split in two parts - while conserving the proportions of detection errors - one is used for model construction (roughly two third of the database), and the other for model evaluation.

Two ILP tools were experiment with: FOIL ([22]) and INTHELEX ([10]). The former is use to learn *Horn clauses* definitions, it goes from to most general clause specializes it successively by adding more litterals that cover the positive examples will keeping the negative examples out. Unlike FOIL, INTHELEX is a fully incremental method that uses an abductive phase. This means we can use the *dummy* as a knowledge base and slowly improve it, and also construct new rule from the false negatives; whereas our implementation of FOIL builds a rule base from scratch and ignores the false negative, although there are extensions that include abduction ([16]).

In our experiments we compare three mesures: the good classification rate (the higher, the better), the false positve and false negative rates (the lower, the better).

The goal of our experiment is first to test existing ILP tools and determine if they are appropriate for this domain of application. In that aim we compare the expert's rule base with one built via Machine Learning. A cross-validation is performed on the two models: we draw ten times a third of the dataset for testing, the remaining two third are used for model building.

The results in figure 8 show us that a system designed from experts' knowledge is roughtly equivalent to a model built from scratch with FOIL. The induced model seems however more stable than the declared one.

For the second experiment we used our Multiple-Relations Association Rules Mining (MR-ARM) algorithm on the false negatives of each datasets. The rules extracted are frequent correlations within a set of frequent events for a given threat, the minimal support required for both frequent events and frequent correlations is 2/3 of the data. This method is compared with the incremental INTHELEX algorithm which uses abduction on false negatives.

DATA SET (Number of Observations)	Initial Rule Base			FOIL-Inducted Rule Base		
	GCR (SD)	FP (SD)	FN (SD)	GCR	FP	FN
Terrorist Attack (165)	41,2 %(±14,6)	36,8%(±15,1)	22,4%(±8,6)	49,8%(±7,1)	29,9%(±6,4)	20,1%(±7,7)
Chemical Attack (293)	64,3%(±12,9)	20,3%(±8,1)	15,4%(±7)	61,2%(±11,9)	20,2%(±5,5)	17,9%(±7,8)
Vandalism (317)	50,7%(±17,5)	30,2%(±14,6)	19,1%(±11,8)	48,1%(±8,3)	25,2%(±4,7)	26,4%(±9,3)
Attack on Official (159)	36,9%(±20,2)	35%(±16,5)	28%(±18,4)	39,1%(±13,7)	31,6%(±11,2)	29,1%(±15,3)

Fig. 8. Classification rates (± SD) of Initial Rule base and FOIL

The results on the test set - shown in figure 9 - confirm that the false negative rate dropped considerably. However, the overall detection rate is barely superior to the classical learning algorithm. This is mainly due to the inclusion of new false positives by over generalization, but also to the fact that our test set introduces new aspects of the model that are not included in the learning set.

DATA SET (Number of Observations)	INTHELEX-Improved Rule Base			MRARM-INTHELEX Rule Base		
	GCR	FP	FN	GCR	FP	FN
Terrorist Attack (165)	82,1%	8,1%	9,8%	84,4%	10,9%	4,7%
Chemical Attack (293)	90%	4,3%	5,7%	91,5%	4,6%	3,9%
Vandalism (317)	87,2%	4,9%	7,8%	90,7%	5,3%	4%
Attack on Official (159)	79,6%	8,4%	12%	83,3%	10,7%	6%

Fig. 9. Classification rates Abductive INTHELEX vs MARM-INTHELEX

Finally our MRARM-INTHELEX algorithm is performed again while incrementing the number of examples used for learning (figure 10). At each iteration ten random examples are added to the learning set.

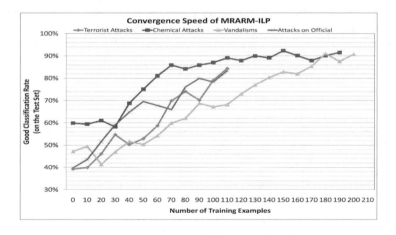

Fig. 10. Convergence speed of MARM-ILP

For a low number of rules such as the detection of chemical attacks, a peak is quickly reached as opposed to complicated rule sets, which need a high number of examples (vandalisms).

5 Conclusions

We presented here the problem of adaptation of a complex reactive rule based system to detection errors. The learning process was briefly introduced and experimental results on simulated scenarios shown.

If incremental ILP methods are seen to be efficient in this type of context and the effect of MR-ARM on the detection of false negatives is clear, questions remain to be answered about the inductive phase of the process.

First in our hypotheses testing phase, we can take into account the balancing between false positives and false negatives minimisation by using the concepts of *precision* (α) and *recall* (β) and their combination measure: F_i-*score*. When i is greater than 1 more importance is given to the false negative rate, and when i is lower than 1 more importance is given to the false positive rate. We will also study inference rules for the generalization and specialization of negative predicates. Finally in later experiments we will study the generality of our learning algorithm by making random sampling for the test set.

References

1. Esper-complex event processing (2008), http://esper.codehaus.org/
2. Simbad 3d robot simulator (2008), http://simbad.sourceforge.net/
3. Agrawal, R., Srikant, R.: Fast algorithms for mining association rules in large databases. In: VLDB 1994: Proceedings of the 20th International Conference on VLDB, pp. 487–499. Morgan Kaufmann Publishers Inc., San Francisco (1994)
4. Allen, J.F.: An interval-based representation of temporal knowledge. In: IJCAI 1981: Proceedings of the 7th International Joint Conference on Artificial Intelligence, pp. 221–226. Morgan Kaufmann Publishers Inc., San Francisco (1981)
5. Ashwin, R.K., King, R.D., Srinivasan, A., Dehaspe, L.: Warmr: A data mining tool for chemical data (2001)
6. Biba, M., Maria, T., Basile, A., Ferilli, S., Esposito, F.: Improving scalability in ilp incremental systems (2006)
7. De Castro, L.N., Timmis, J.I.: Artificial immune systems as a novel soft computing paradigm. Soft Computing - A Fusion of Foundations, Methodologies and Applications 7, 526–544 (2003)
8. Chakravarthy, S., Krishnaprasad, V., Anwar, E., Kim, S.K.: Composite events for active databases: Semantics, contexts and detection. In: VLDB 1994: Proceedings of the 20th International Conference on Very Large Data Bases, pp. 606–617. Morgan Kaufmann Publishers Inc., San Francisco (1994)
9. Dousson, C., Gaborit, P., Ghallab, M.: Situation recognition: Representation and algorithms (1993)
10. Esposito, F., Semeraro, G., Fanizzi, N., Ferilli, S.: Multistrategy theory revision: Induction and abduction in inthelex. Machine Learning, 133–156 (2000)
11. Etzion, O., Niblett, P.: Event Processing in Action. Manning (2010)
12. Fenkam, P., Jazayeri, M., Reif, G.: On methodologies for constructing correct event-based applications. In: International Workshop on Distributed Event-Based Systems (DEBS), pp. 38–43 (2004)
13. Gatziu, S., Dittrich, K.R.: Samos: an active object–oriented database system. In: IEEE Bulletin of the TC on Data Engineering (1992)

14. Gehani, N.H., Jagadish, H.V., Shmueli, O.: Event specification in an active object-oriented database. SIGMOD Rec. 21(2), 81–90 (1992)
15. Kavurucu, Y., Senkul, P., Toroslu, I.H.: Ilp-based concept discovery in multi-relational data mining. Expert Systems with Applications 26, 11418–11428 (2009)
16. Lamma, E., Mello, P., Milano, M., Riguzzil, F.: Introducing abduction into (extensional) inductive logic programming systems. In: Lenzerini, M. (ed.) AI*IA 1997. LNCS, vol. 1321, pp. 183–194. Springer, Heidelberg (1997)
17. Landwehr, N., Kersting, K., Raedt, L.D.: Integrating nave bayes and foil. Journal of Machine Learning Research 8, 481–507 (2007)
18. Lee, E., Chan, K.: Discovering Association Patterns in Large Spatio-temporal Databases. In: Sixth IEEE International Conference on Data Mining - Workshops (ICDMW 2006), pp. 349–354 (2006)
19. Luckham, D.: The Power of Events. Addison-Wesley, Reading (2002)
20. Museux, N., Vanbockryck, J.: Event based sensors fusion for public place surveillance. In: Proceedings of 10th International Conference on Information Fusion, pp. 1–8 (July 2007)
21. Plotkin, G.: A note on inductive generalisation. Machine Intelligence 5, 153–163 (1970)
22. Quinlan, J.R., Cameron-jones, R.M.: Induction of logic programs: Foil and related systems. New Generation Computing 13, 287–312 (1995)
23. Ray, O.: Nonmonotonic abductive inductive learning. Journal of Applied Logic (2008)
24. Srikant, R., Agrawal, R.: Mining sequential patterns: Generalizations and performance improvements. In: Apers, P.M.G., Bouzeghoub, M., Gardarin, G. (eds.) EDBT 1996. LNCS, vol. 1057, pp. 1–17. Springer, Heidelberg (1996)
25. Tian, Y.L., Hampapur, A., Brown, L., Feris, R., Lu, M., Senior, A., Shu, C.F., Zhai, Y.: Event detection, query, and retrieval for video surveillance. In: Information Science Reference. ch. 15 (2009)
26. Zhai, Y., Tian, Y.L., Hampapur, A.: Composite spatio-temporal event detection in multi-camera surveillance networks. In: Workshop on Multi-camera and Multi-modal Sensor Fusion Algorithms and Applications (October 2008)

A New Space Defined by Ant Colony Algorithm
to Partition Data

Hamid Parvin and Behrouz Minaei-Bidgoli

School of Computer Engineering, Iran University of Science and Technology
(IUST), Tehran, Iran
{parvin,b_minaei}@iust.ac.ir

Abstract. To reach a robust partition, ensemble-based learning is always a very promising option. There is straightforward way to generate a set of primary partitions that are different from each other, and then to aggregate the partitions via a consensus function to generate the final partition. Another alternative in the ensemble learning is to turn to fusion of different data from originally different sources. In this paper we introduce a new ensemble learning based on the Ant Colony clustering algorithm. Experimental results on some real-world datasets are presented to demonstrate the effectiveness of the proposed method in generating the final partition.

Keywords: Ant Colony, Data Fusion, Clustering.

1 Introduction

Choosing a single clustering algorithm and appropriate parameters for a given dataset requires both clustering expertise and insights about dataset itself. Instead of running the risk of picking an inappropriate clustering algorithm, we can leverage the different options available by applying all of them to dataset and then combining their clustering results. This is the basic idea behind cluster ensembles (Strehl and Ghosh, 2002).

There are many types of consensus functions that solve this problem heuristically. Most of them require the number of clusters to be specified as a priori, but in practice the number of clusters is usually unknown. In this paper, we propose a new consensus function for cluster ensembles based on swarm intelligence (Kennedy and Russell, 2001) that addresses this problem. In particular, given a set of partitions, we apply ant clustering to the co-association matrix computed from the ensemble to produce the final partition, and automatically determine the number of clusters.

The first ant colony clustering model was introduced by Deneubourg et al. (1991). His model possesses the swarm intelligence of real ants, and was inserted into a robot for the object collecting task. Lumer and Faieta (1994) improved upon Deneubourg's model by adding the Euclidean distance formula to the similarity density function and giving ants three kinds of abilities: speed, shortterm memory, and behavior exchange.

It is inspired by how ants organize their food in their nests. Ant clustering typically involves two key operations: picking up an object from a cluster and dropping it off

A. Bouchachia (Ed.): ICAIS 2011, LNAI 6943, pp. 272–284, 2011.

into another cluster (Tsang and Kwong, 2006). At each step, some ants perform pick-up and drop-off based on some notions of similarity between an object and the clusters. Azimi et al. define a similarity measure based on the co-association matrix (Azimi et al., 2009). Their clustering process is completely decentralized and self-organized, allowing the clustering structure to emerge automatically from the data. As a result, we can accurately determine the number of clusters in the data. The experimental results show that the proposed consensus function is very effective in predicting the number of clusters and also achieves reliable clustering performance. In addition, by introducing some simple heuristics, we can detect the marginal and outlier samples in the data to improve our final clustering.

```
initializing parameter;
for each ant a
          place random a in a position not occupied by other ants;
end;
for each object o
          place random o in a position not occupied by other objects;
end;
for t=1:t_max
          for each ant a
                    g=select a random number uniformly from range [0,1];
                    r=position(a)
                    if(loaded(a) and (is_empty(r)))
                              if(g<p_drop)
                                        o=drop(a);
                                        put(r,o);
                                        save(o,r,q);
                              end;
                    end;
                    elseif(not (loaded(a) or (is_empty(r))))
                              if(g<p_pic)
                                        o=remove(r);
                                        pick_up(a,o);
                                        search_and_jump(a,o);
                              end;
                    end;
                    else
                              wander(a,v,N_dir);
                    end;
          end;
end;
```

Fig. 1. Pseudo code of original ant colony clustering algorithm

Liu et al. propose a method for incrementally constructing a knowledge model for a dynamically changing database, using an ant colony clustering. They use information-theoretic metrics to overcome some inherent problems of ant-based clustering. Entropy governs the pick-up and drop behaviors, while movement is guided by pheromones. They show that dynamic clustering can provide significant benefits over static clustering for a realistic problem scenario (Liu et al., 2006).

The rest of the paper is organized as follows. Section 2 deals with ant colony clustering. The proposed new space is presented in Section 3. In Section 4, experimental results of the clustering algorithm over original feature space versus mapped feature space are compared. The paper is concluded in Section 5.

2 Ant Colony Clustering

General form of ant colony clustering algorithm is presented here. The algorithm includes a population of ants. Each ant is operating as an autonomous agent that reorganizes data patterns during exploration to reach an optimal clustering. Pseudo code of ant colony clustering algorithm is depicted in Fig. 1.

At the first step each object represented by a multi-dimensional vector in the original feature space is randomly scattered in a two-dimensional space. In each step each ant randomly searches the space. They use its short-term memory to jump into a location that is potentially near to an object. They can pick up or drop an object using a probability density obtained by equation 1.

$$f(o_i) = \max\left\{0, \frac{1}{s^2} \sum_{o_j \in Neigh_{sxs}(r)} \left[1 - \frac{d(o_i, o_j)}{\alpha(1 + \dfrac{v-1}{v_{max}})}\right]\right\} \tag{1}$$

$Neigh_{sxs}(r)$ is the observable local area (or the set of observable rooms) for an ant located at room r. $Neigh_{sxs}(r)$ must be adjacent to the location r. It is worthy to mention that each room including $Neigh_{sxs}(r)$ and r is a two-dimensional vector. The function $d(o_i, o_j)$ is the distance between two objects o_i and o_j in the original feature space. It is calculated by equation 2. Threshold α is a parameter that scales the distance between each pair of objects and speed parameter v control the volume of feature space that an ant explores in each epoch of algorithm.

$$d(o_i, o_j) = \sqrt{\sum_{k=1}^{m} (o_{ik} - o_{jk})^2} \tag{2}$$

where m is the number of original features and where o_{ik} is k-th feature of object o_i. Probability that an unloaded ant takes an object that is in the room occupied by the ant, obtained from the equation 3.

$$P_{pick}(o_i) = (\frac{k_1}{k_1 + f(o_i)})^2 \tag{3}$$

k_1 is a fixed threshold to control the probability of picking an object. The probability that a loaded ant lays down its object is obtained by equation 4.

$$P_{drop}(o_i) = \begin{cases} 2f(o_i) & if \ f(o_i) < k_2 \\ 1 & if \ f(o_i) \geq k_2 \end{cases} \tag{4}$$

k_2 is a fixed threshold to control the probability of dropping an object. Similarity measure, speed parameter, local density and short-term memory are described in following.

2.1 Perception Area

Number of data objects observed by an ant in a two-dimensional area s. It is considered as one of the effective factors controlling the overall similarity measure and consequently the accuracy and the computational time of the algorithm. If s is large, it will cause the rapid formation of clusters and therefore generally fewer developed clusters. If s is small, it will cause the slower formation of clusters and therefore the number of clusters will be larger. It is worthy to mention that selecting this parameter is a very important factor. While selecting a large value can cause premature convergence of the algorithm, selecting a small value also causes late convergence of the algorithm.

2.2 Similarity Scaling Factor

Scaling parameter value α is defined in the interval (0, 1]. If α is large, then the similarities between objects will increase, so it is easier for the ants to lay down their objects and more difficult for them to lift the objects. So if α is large, fewer clusters are formed and it will be highly likely that well-ordered clusters will not form. If α is small, the similarities between objects will reduce, so it is easier for the ants to pick up objects and more difficult for them to remove their objects. So many clusters are created that can be well-shaped. On this basis, the appropriate setting of parameter α is very important and should not be data independent.

2.3 Speed Parameter

Speed parameter v can uniformly be selected form range $[1, v_{max}]$. Rate of removing an object or picking an object up can be affected by the speed parameter. If v is large, few rough clusters can irregularly be formed on a large scale view. If v is small, then many dense clusters can precisely be formed on a small scale view. The speed parameter is a critical factor for the speed of convergence. An appropriate setting of speed parameter v may cause faster convergence.

2.4 Short Term Memory

Each ant can remember the original real features and the virtual defined two-dimensional features of the last q objects it drops. Whenever ant takes an object it will search its short term memory to find out which object in the short term memory is similar to the current object. If an object in memory is similar enough to satisfy a threshold, it will jump to the position of the object, hoping the current object will be dropped near the location of the similar object, else if there is no object in memory similar, it will not jump and will hold the object and will wander. This prevents the objects originally belonging to a same cluster to be spitted in different clusters.

2.5 Drawbacks of Original Ant Colony Clustering Algorithm

The original ant colony clustering algorithm presented above suffers two major drawbacks. First many clusters are produced in the virtual two-dimensional space and it is hard and very time-consuming to merge them and this work is inappropriate.

The second drawback arises where the density detector is the sole measure based on that the clusters are formed in the local similar objects. But it fails to detect their dissimilarity properly. So a cluster without a significant between-object variance may not break into some smaller clusters. It may result in forming the wrong big clusters including some real smaller clusters provided the boundary objects of the smaller clusters are similar. It is because the probability of dropping or picking up an object is dependent only to density. So provided that the boundary objects of the smaller clusters are similar, they placed near to each other and the other objects also place near to them gradually. Finally those small clusters form a big cluster, and there is no mechanism to break it into smaller clusters. So there are some changes on the original algorithm to handle the mention drawbacks.

2.6 Entropy Measure of Local Area

Combining the information entropy and the mean similarity as a new metric to existing models in order to detect rough areas of spatial clusters, dense clusters and troubled borders of the clusters that are wrongly merged is employed.

Shannon entropy information has been widely used in many areas to measure the uncertainty of a specified event or the impurity of an arbitrary collection of samples. Consider a discrete random variable X, with N possible values $\{x_1, x_2, ..., x_N\}$ with probabilities $\{p(x_1), p(x_2), ..., p(x_N)\}$. Entropy of discrete random variable X is obtained using equation 5.

$$H(X) = -\sum_{i=1}^{N} p(x_i) \log p(x_i)$$

(5)

Similarity degree between each pair of objects can be expressed as a probability that the two belong to the same cluster. Based on Shannon information entropy, each ant can compute the impurity of the objects observed in a local area L to determine if the object o_i in the center of the local area L has a high entropy value with group of object o_j in the local area L. Each ant can compute the local area entropy using equation 6.

$$E(L \mid o_i) = -\sum_{o_j \in Neigh_{s \times s}(r)} p_{i,j} \times \frac{\log_2(p_{i,j})}{\log_2 |Neigh_{s \times s}(r)|}$$

(6)

where the probability $p_{i,j}$ indicates that we have a decisive opinion about central object o_i considering a local area object o_j in its local area L. The probability $p_{i,j}$ is obtained according to equation 7.

$$p_{i,j} = \frac{2 \times |D(o_i, o_j)|}{n}$$

(7)

where n ($n=|Neigh_{sxs}(r)|$) is the number of neighbors. Distance function $D(o_i,o_j)$ between each pair of objects is measured according to equation 8.

$$D(o_i,o_j) = \frac{d(o_i,o_j)}{norm(o_i)} - 0.5$$

(8)

where $d(o_i,o_j)$ is Euclidian distance defined by equation 2, and $norm(o_i)$ is defined as maximum distance of object o_i with its neighbors. It is calculated according to equation 9.

$$norm(o_i) = \max_{o_j \in Neigh_{sxs}(r)} d(o_i,o_j)$$

(9)

Now the function $H(L/o_i)$ is defined as equation 10.

$$H(L|o_i) = 1 - E(L|o_i)$$

(10)

Three examples of local area objects on a 3×3 (=9) neighborhood depicted in the Fig. 2. Different classes with different colors are displayed.

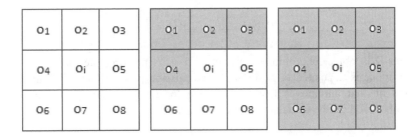

Fig. 2. Three examples of local area objects

When the data objects in the local area L and central object of the local area L exactly belong to a same cluster, i.e. their distances are almost uniform and low values, such as the shape or the form depicted by the left rectangle of Fig. 2, uncertainty is low and $H(L/o_i)$ is far from one and near to 0. When the data objects in the local area L and central object of the local area L belong to some completely different separate clusters, i.e. their distances are almost uniform and high values, such as the shape or the form depicted by the right rectangle of Fig. 2, uncertainty is again low and $H(L/o_i)$ is far from one and near to 0. But in the cases of the form depicted by the middle rectangle of Fig. 2 where some data objects in the local area L and central object of the local area L exactly belong to a same cluster and some others does not, i.e. the distances are not uniform, the uncertainty is high and $H(L/o_i)$ is far from 0 and close to 1. So the function $H(L/o_i)$ can provide ants with a metric that its high value indicates the current position is a boundary area and its low value indicates the current position is not a boundary area.

In ant-based clustering, two types of pheromone are employed: (a) cluster pheromone and (b) object pheromone. Cluster pheromone guides the loaded ants to valid clusters for a possible successful dropping. Object pheromone guides the unloaded ants to loose object for a possible successful picking-up.

Each loaded ant deposits some cluster pheromone on the current position and positions of its neighbors after a successful dropping of an object to guide other ants for a place to unload their objects. The cluster pheromone intensity deposited in location j, by m ants in the colony at time t is calculated by the equation 11.

$$rc_j(t) = \sum_{a=1}^{m} \left[\mu^{(t-t_a^1)} \times C \times E(L \mid o_j) \right] \qquad (11)$$

where C is cluster pheromone constant, t_a^1 is the time step at that a-th cluster pheromone is deposited at position j, and μ is evaporation coefficient. On other hand, an unloaded ant deposits some object pheromone after a successful picking-up of an object to guide other agents for a place to take the objects. The object pheromone intensity deposited in location j, by m ants in the colony at time t is calculated by the equation 12.

$$ro_j(t) = \sum_{a=1}^{m} \left[\mu^{(t-t_a^2)} \times O \times H(L \mid o_j) \right] \qquad (12)$$

where O is object pheromone constant, and t_a^2 is the time step at that a-th object pheromone is deposited at position j. Transmission probabilities of an unloaded ant based on that ant moves from the current location i to next location j from its neighborhood can be calculated according to equation 13.

$$P_j(t) = \begin{cases} 1/w & if \sum_{j=1}^{w} ro_j(t) = 0 \forall j \in N_{dir} \\ \dfrac{ro_j(t)}{\sum_{j=1}^{n} ro_j(t)} & otherwise \end{cases} \qquad (13)$$

where N_{dir} is the set of possible w actions (possible w directions to move) from current position i. Transmission probabilities of a loaded ant based on that ant moves from the current location i to next location j from its neighborhood can be calculated according to equation 14.

$$P_j(t) = \begin{cases} 1/w & if \sum_{j=1}^{w} rc_j(t) = 0 \forall j \in N_{dir} \\ \dfrac{rc_j(t)}{\sum_{j=1}^{n} rc_j(t)} & otherwise \end{cases} \qquad (14)$$

```
Input:
    QD, itr, q, AntNum, Data, O, C, k₁, k₂, vₘₐₓ, period, thr, st, distributions of v, α and μ
initializing parameter using distributions of v, α and μ;
for each ant a
            place random a in a position not occupied by other ants in a plane QD*QD;
end;
for each object o
            place random o in a position not occupied by other objects in the plane QD*QD;
end;
success(1:ant)=0;
failure(1:ant)=0;
for t=1: itr
            for each ant a
                    g=select a random number uniformly from range [0,1];
                    r=position(a)
                    if(loaded(a) and (is_empty(r)))
                            if(g<p_drop)
                                    o=drop(a);
                                    put(r,o);
                                    save(o,r,q);
                            end;
                    elseif(not (loaded(a) or (is_empty(r))))
                            if(g<p_pic)
                                    o=remove(r);
                                    pick_up(a,o);
                                    search_and_jump(a,o);
                                    success(a)=success(a)+1;
                            else
                                    failure(a)=failure(a)+1;
                            end;
                    end;
                    else
                            wander(a,v,N_dir); // considering the defined pheromone
                    end;
            end;
            if( t mod period==0)
                    for each ant a
                            if(success(a)/(failure(a)+success(a))>thr)
                                    α(a)=α(a)+st;
                            else
                                    α(a)=α(a)-st;
                            end;
                    end;
            end;
end;
```

Fig. 3. Pseudo code of modified ant colony clustering algorithm

2.7 Modified Ant Colony Clustering

Combining the information entropy and the mean similarity as a new metric to existing models in order to detect rough areas of spatial clusters, dense clusters and troubled borders of the clusters that are wrongly merged is employed. When the data objects in the local area L and central object of the local area L exactly belong to a same cluster, i.e. their distances are almost uniform and low values, such as the shape or the form depicted by the left rectangle of Fig. 3, uncertainty is low and $H(L/o_i)$ is far from one and near to 0. When the data objects in the local area L and central object of the local area L belong to some completely different separate clusters, i.e. their distances are almost uniform and high values, such as the shape or the form depicted by the right rectangle of Fig. 3, uncertainty is again low and $H(L/o_i)$ is far from one and near to 0. But in the cases of the form depicted by the middle rectangle of Fig. 3 where some data objects in the local area L and central object of the local area L exactly belong to a same cluster and some others does not, i.e. the distances are not uniform, the uncertainty is high and $H(L/o_i)$ is far from 0 and close to 1. So the function $H(L/o_i)$ can provide ants with a metric that its high value indicates the current position is a boundary area and its low value indicates the current position is not a boundary area.

After all the above mentioned modification, the pseudo code of ant colony clustering algorithm is presented in the Fig. 3. For showing an exemplary running of the modified ant colony algorithm, take a look at Fig. 4. In the Fig. 4 the final result of modified ant colony clustering algorithm over Iris dataset is presented.

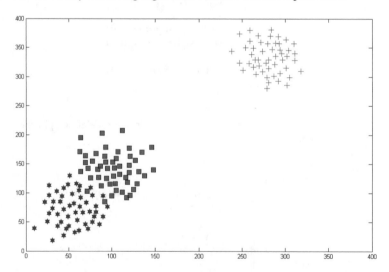

Fig. 4. Final result of modified ant colony clustering algorithm over Iris dataset

It is worthy to mention that the quantization degree parameter (QD), queue size parameter (q), ant number parameter ($AntNum$), object pheromone parameter (O), cluster pheromone parameter (C), $k1$ parameter, $k2$ parameter, maximum speed parameter (v_{max}), period parameter, update parameter (thr) evaporation parameter μ

and step of update for α parameter (*st*) are respectively set to 400, 5000000, 20, 240, 1, 1, 0.1, 0.3, 150, 2000, 0.9, 0.95 and 0.01 for reaching the result of Fig. 4. Parameter α for each ant is extracted from uniform distribution of range [0.1, 1]. Parameter v for each ant is extracted from uniform distribution of range [1, v_{max}].

Consider that the result shown in the Fig. 4 is a well separated running of algorithm. So it is a successful running of algorithm. The algorithm may also converge to a set of overlapping clusters in an unsuccessful running.

3 Proposed New Space Defined by Ant Colony Algorithm

The main idea behind proposed method is using ensemble learning in the field of ant colony clustering. Due to the huge sensitiveness of modified ant colony clustering algorithm to initialization of its parameters, one can use an ensemble approach to overcome the problem of well-tuning of its parameters. The main contribution of the paper is illustrated in the Fig. 5.

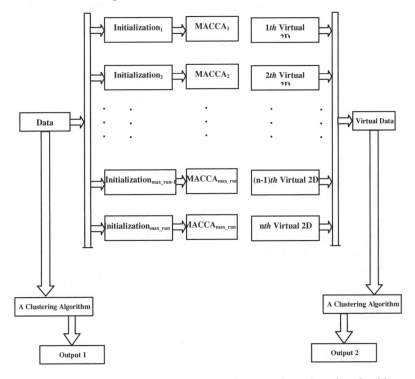

Fig. 5. Proposed framework to cluster a dataset using ant colony clustering algorithm

As it is depicted in Fig. 5 a dataset is feed to as many as *max_run* different modified ant colony clustering algorithms with different initializations. Then we obtain *max_run* virtual 2-dimensions, one per each run modified ant colony clustering algorithm. Then by considering all these virtual 2-dimensions as new space with

2*max_run dimensions, we reach a new data space. We can employ a clustering algorithm on the new defined data space.

4 Experimental Study

This section evaluates the result of applying proposed algorithm on some real datasets available at USI repository (Newman et al. 1998). The main metric based on which a partition is evaluated is discussed in the first subsection of this section. The details of the used datasets are given in the subsequent section. Then the settings of experimentations are given. Finally the experimental results are presented.

4.1 Evaluation Metric

After producing the output partition, the most important question is "how good a partition is?". The evaluation of a partition is very important as it is mentioned. Here the normalized mutual information between the output partition and real labels of the dataset is considered as the main evaluation metric of the final partition (Strehl and Ghosh, 2002; Alizadeh et al., 2011). The normalized mutual information between two partitions, P^a and P^b, is calculated as:

$$NMI(P^a, P^b) = \frac{-2 \sum_{i=1}^{k_a} \sum_{j=1}^{k_b} n_{ij}^{ab} \log\left(\frac{n_{ij}^{ab} \cdot n}{n_i^a \cdot n_j^b}\right)}{\sum_{i=1}^{k_a} n_i^a \log\left(\frac{n_i^a}{n}\right) + \sum_{j=1}^{k_b} n_j^b \log\left(\frac{n_j^b}{n}\right)}$$

(23)

where n is the total number of samples and n_{ij}^{ab} denotes the number of shared patterns between clusters $C_i^a \in P^a$ and $C_j^b \in P^b$; n_i^a is the number of patterns in the cluster i of partition a; also n_j^b are the number of patterns in the cluster j of partition b.

Another alternative to evaluate a partition is the accuracy metric, provided that the number of clusters and their true assignments are known. To compute the final performance of a clustering algorithm in terms of accuracy, one can first re-label the obtained clusters in such a way that have maximal matching with the ground truth labels and then counting the percentage of the true classified samples. So the error rate can be determined after solving the correspondence problem between the labels of derived and known clusters. The Hungarian algorithm is employed to solve the minimal weight bipartite matching problem. It has been shown that it can efficiently solve this label correspondence problem (Munkres, 1957).

4.2 Datasets

The proposed method is examined over 6 different standard datasets. Brief information about the used datasets is available in Table 1. More information is available in (Newman et al. 1998).

Table 1. Details of used dataset

Dataset Name	# of dataitems	# of features	# of classes
Image-Segmentation	210	19	7
Zoo	101	17	7
Thyroid	215	5	3
Soybean	683	35	4
Iris	150	4	3
Wine	178	13	3

4.3 Experimental Settings

The quantization degree parameter (QD), queue size parameter (q), ant number parameter ($AntNum$), object pheromone parameter (O), cluster pheromone parameter (C), $k1$ parameter, $k2$ parameter, maximum speed parameter (v_{max}), period parameter, update parameter (thr) evaporation parameter μ and step of update for α parameter (st) are respectively set to 400, 5000000, 20, 240, 1, 1, 0.1, 0.3, 150, 2000, 0.9, 0.95 and 0.01 in all experimentations as before. Parameter α for each ant is extracted from uniform distribution of range [0.1, 1]. Parameter v for each ant is extracted from uniform distribution of range [1, v_{max}]. Fuzzy k-means (c-means) is employed as base clustering algorithm to perform final clustering over original dataset and new defined dataset. Parameter max_run is set to 30 in all experimentations. So the new defined space has 60 virtual features. Number of real cluster in each dataset is given to fuzzy k-means clustering algorithm in all experimentations.

Table 2. Experimental results in terms of accuracy

Dataset Name	Fuzzy k-means output 1		Fuzzy k-means output 2	
	Accuracy	Normaliz ed Mutual Information	Accuracy	Normaliz ed Mutual Information
Image-Segmentation	52.27	38.83	54.39	40.28
Zoo	80.08	79.09	81.12	81.24
Thyroid	83.73	50.23	87.94	59.76
Soybean	90.10	69.50	94.34	80.30
Iris	90.11	65.67	93.13	75.22
Wine	74.71	33.12	76.47	35.96

As it is inferred from the Table 2, the new defined feature space is better clustered by a base clustering algorithm rather than the original space.

4.4 Experimental Results

Table 2 shows the performance of the fuzzy clustering in both original and defined spaces in terms of accuracy and normalized mutual information. All experiments are reported over means of 10 independent runs of algorithm. It means that experimentations are done by 10 different independent runs and the final results are averaged and reported in the Table 2.

5 Conclusion and Future Works

In this paper a new clustering ensemble framework is proposed which is based on a ant colony clustering algorithm and ensemble concept. In the proposed framework we use a set of modified ant colony clustering algorithms and produce a intermediate space considering their outputs totally as a defined virtual space. After producing the virtual space we employ a base clustering algorithm to obtain final partition. The experiments show that the proposed framework outperforms in comparison with the clustering over original data space. It is concluded that new defined the feature space is better clustered by a base clustering algorithm rather than the original space.

References

1. Alizadeh, H., Minaei-Bidgoli, B., Parvin, H., Mohsen, M.: An Asymmetric Criterion for Cluster Validation. SCI, vol. 363. Springer, Heidelberg (2011)
2. Newman, C.B.D.J., Hettich, S., Merz, C.: UCI repository of machine learning databases (1998), http://www.ics.uci.edu/~mlearn/MLSummary.html
3. Strehl, A., Ghosh, J.: Cluster ensembles - a knowledge reuse framework for combining multiple partitions. Journal of Machine Learning Research 3, 583–617 (2002)
4. Kennedy, J., Russell, S.: Swarm Intelligence. Morgan Kaufmann, San Francisco (2001)
5. Azimi, J., Cull, P., Fern, X.: Clustering ensembles using ants algorithm. In: Mira, J., Ferrández, J.M., Álvarez, J.R., de la Paz, F., Toledo, F.J. (eds.) IWINAC 2009. LNCS, vol. 5601, pp. 295–304. Springer, Heidelberg (2009)
6. Tsang, C.H., Kwong, S.: Ant Colony Clustering and Feature Extraction for Anomaly Intrusion Detection. SCI, vol. 34, pp. 101–123 (2006)
7. Liu, B., Pan, J., McKay, R.I.: Incremental clustering based on swarm intelligence. In: Wang, T.-D., Li, X., Chen, S.-H., Wang, X., Abbass, H.A., Iba, H., Chen, G.-L., Yao, X. (eds.) SEAL 2006. LNCS, vol. 4247, pp. 189–196. Springer, Heidelberg (2006)
8. Deneubourg, J.L., Goss, S., Franks, N., Sendova-Franks, A., Detrain, C., Chretien, L.: The dynamics of collective sorting robot-like ants and ant-like robots. In: International Conference on Simulation of Adaptive Behavior: from animals to animates, pp. 356–363. MIT Press, Cambridge (1991)
9. Lumer, E.D., Faieta, B.: Diversity and adaptation in populations of clustering ants. In: International conference on simulation of adaptive behavior: from animals to animates, pp. 501–508. MIT Press, Cambridge (1994)
10. Munkres, J.: Algorithms for the Assignment and Transportation Problems. Journal of the Society for Industrial and Applied Mathematics 5(1), 32–38 (1957)

Extracting and Exploiting Topics of Interests from Social Tagging Systems

Felice Ferrara and Carlo Tasso

University of Udine, Via delle Scienze 206, 33100 Udine, Italy
`{felice.ferrara,carlo.tasso}@uniud.it`

Abstract. Users of social tagging systems spontaneously annotate resources providing, in this way, useful information about their interests. A collaborative filtering recommender system can use this feedback in order to identify people and resources more strictly related to a specific topic of interest. Such a collaborative filtering approach can compute similarities among tags in order to select resources associated to tags relevant for a specific interest of the user. Several research works try to infer these similarities by evaluating co-occurrences of tags over the entire set of annotated resources discarding, in this way, information about the personal classification provided by users.

This paper, on the other hand, proposes an approach aimed at observing only the set of annotations of a single user in order to identify his topic of interests and to produce personalized recommendations. More specifically, following the idea that each user may have several distinct interests and people may share just some of these interests, our approach adaptively filters and combines the feedback of users according to a specific topic of interest of a user.

Keywords: Recommender systems, collaborative filtering, social tagging, adaptive, personalization.

1 Introduction

The social Web is constituted by services aimed at promoting socialization and communication among users which are allowed to create, share, and organize information. In particular, social tagging systems deal with sharing and organizing resources: each user can both share her resources with the other peers and assign some labels (named tags) to resources in order to simplify future retrieval.

The collection of resources tagged by a user is called *personomy*. A personomy is a personal classification of resources which are interesting to the specific user and it can be explored by other users by means of tags. However, the classification generated by a user usually is not very precise since users freely choose tags without following rules to avoid ambiguities and, for this reason, the tags applied by a user cannot have a clear semantic. On the other hand, the union of all personomies (referred as *folksonomy*) can be analyzed in order to infer semantic relations taking into account how the community of Web 2.0 users combines tags.

A. Bouchachia (Ed.): ICAIS 2011, LNAI 6943, pp. 285–296, 2011.

This analysis can extract semantic relations among tags which emerge from the collaborative social work of users. Such 'social semantic' relations among tags can potentially be used in order to enhance the access to information by empowering, for example, information filtering systems such as Collaborative Filtering (CF) recommender systems.

CF recommender systems implement the word-of-mouth mechanism: they simulate the behavior of humans which usually share their opinions with friends when they need to take a decision. In a user-based CF recommender system [1], the simulation of this social process is exploited in two steps. The first step is usually referred as 'neighbor selection' and it is the phase when the system identifies the set of people which share an interest with the target user (referred in this paper as 'active user'). In the second step, the system generates the list of recommendations by combining feedback (i.e. information about what is relevant for a user) provided by the best (most similar) neighbors: resources more relevant to the community of the best neighbors are suggested to the active user. The rationale of this model is that users with a common interest are interested in the same resources and could be interested in the same information also in the future. In order to accomplish this mechanism, a CF system models the opinions of each user by a vector which contains her ratings (rating vector). In this way, the similarity between two users depends on the similarity between the two rating vectors associated to them.

However, this basic model does not take into account the fact that each user may be interested in more than one Topic of Interest (ToI). This can reduce the accuracy of both the first and the second steps exploited by a user-based CF system. In fact, by computing just one similarity value for each pair of users, the system ignores that the active user could be similar to a set of users for a certain specific topic, but she could share another ToI with a completely different neighborhood. This issue has been recognized also in [2], where the authors proposed the BIPO (Best Item Per Overlapping) framework aimed at finding for each resource a locally adaptive neighborhood. Following the 2-step workflow described above it is straightforward to recognize a further criticality, since the system considers all the feedback provided by the neighborhood, without taking into account that such feedback could partly refer to different ToIs. This means that the system could suggest resources which are interesting to the community of neighbors but which are completely not related to the ToIs of the active user.

In this work we describe an approach aimed to overcome these limitations in social tagging systems by using social semantic relations among tags.

More specifically, we face the first criticality by analyzing the personomy of the active user: tags applied by the active user are grouped according to the strategy used by the active user to combine tags. Given a user, this first analysis produces a set of clusters of tags where each cluster contains tags which have been frequently used together to annotate resources. Different clusters of tags are considered to correspond to different ToIs of the active user. Given the list of the ToIs of the active users, we select the resources associated to a specific ToI (associated to the tags belonging to the same cluster associated to that ToI) in order to detect a set of neighbors (users) interested in that specific ToI. This is accomplished by selecting the users which have tagged the specific resources associated to the considered ToI.

To tackle the second criticality we take into account the tags utilized by neighbors. More specifically, given a neighbor, the collection of her tagged resources is filtered discarding the resources which have not been labeled by tags relevant to the specific ToI. In order to compute the relevance of the tags exploited by a neighbor, we consider the set of resources that the neighbor shares with the active user for the specific ToI: tags applied on shared resources are more 'trustworthy' than others for finding new items related to that specific ToI.

The choice of extracting relations among tags by analyzing the set of annotations of the specific user (instead of evaluating the co-occurrences over the entire collection of annotations) is aimed at filtering the user feedback according to the personal classification provided by the active user in order to better fit his specific informative needs.

The paper is organized as follow: in Section 2 related works are discussed, the construction of the user profile is the object of Section 3, Section 4 deepens the discussion on the mechanism used to compute recommendations for a specific topic of interest, the ongoing evaluation activities are illustrated in Section 5 and, finally, conclusions and future works conclude the paper in Section 6.

2   Related Work

The growing usage of Web 2.0 applications and the social dimension introduced by these tools are appealing features for researchers interested in systems devoted to personalize the access to Web information.

In fact, the collaborative work of Web 2.0 users in social tagging systems have been analyzed to extract social semantic relations since semantic information generated by the social work of users can be used to infer similarities among tags, resources and users [3]. These relations are inferred by evaluating co-occurrences among tags and the majority of the work in the literature takes into account co-occurrences over the entire folksonomy, i.e., by collapsing the annotations produced by all the users.

The resulting 3-dimensional relation involving tags, users and resources cannot be trivially managed to infer social semantic relations since it merges relations among objects of the same type as well among objects of different types. A common approach to overcome such limitation is to project projecting the 3-dimensional relationship among users, items and tags into two 2-dimensional relationships by hiding information about one dimension. Following this approach, the social semantic relations can be described by three matrices:

1. The *Tag-Resource* (*TR*) matrix which describes the two-way relation between tags and resources. Each row of the matrix, associated to a tag, is a vector, which counts how many times a tag has been applied on each resource.

2. The *User-Tag* (*UT*) matrix which describes the two-way relation between users and tags. Each row of the matrix, associated to a user, is a vector, which counts how many times a user applied each tag.
3. The *User-Resource* (*UR*) matrix which describes the two-way relation between users and resources. Each row of the matrix, associated to a user, is a unary vector which allows to describe if a user tagged or not a resource.

As we described in [4], several approaches aimed at inferring similarities among users, tags, and resources by using these matrices have been proposed and integrated in recommender systems.

For example, by computing the cosine similarity between the rows of TR matrix associated to the tag t_i and t_j the similarity between the two tags, $sim(t_i, t_j)$, is quantified according to the number of times the two tags co-occur on the same resources. On the other hand, the similarity between the users u_i and u_j, $sim(u_i, u_j)$, can be estimated by computing the cosine similarity between the rows of the UT matrix associated to the two specific users.

These two measures of similarity have been used in SocialRanking [5], a user based CF recommender system which, given a tag t_k, assigns a score $R(p)$ to each resource p for the user u as

$$ R(p, t_k) = \sum_{u_i} \left(\sum_{t_x} sim(t_x, t_k) \right) \cdot (sim(u, u_i) + 1) $$

where t_x is a tag that the user u_i assigned to the resource p. In this case, given a user u and a tag t_k, the relevance of a resource p is higher if

- p has been tagged by people which used many tags applied by u;
- p has been labeled by tags which have been often used (by the entire community of users) to classify the same resources tagged with the tag t_k.

We also proposed a user based CF recommender framework [6] which groups 'similar' tags utilized by the active user for modeling his interests. In this CF framework, the similarity among two tags depends on the number of times the two tags co-occur on the same resources in the folksonomy and the relevance of a new resource is computed by evaluating also the relevance of the tags assigned to it. However, both these approaches uses tag relations introduced by all users without taking into account how the active user specifically combines tags. In fact, a folksonomy merges the annotations provided by the entire community without taking into account specific personal interests and tagging strategies of different users. On the other hand, a personomy embodies information strictly related to the personal interests of a user. This means that the analysis of a personomy can reveal relations among tags which are meaningful just for that user.

Authors of [7] proposed a framework to catch semantic relations built by each user. This CF framework is based on a community detection algorithm for clustering tags that the active user applied frequently together: each user is modeled by sets of tags and the similarity among users is computed by evaluating the similarity among the sets of tags they used. However, users that share an interest could label the same concept using different set of tags, and this limits the possibility to identify similarities among users.

In this work we also group tags utilized by the active user by taking into account the semantic relations built by her. However, differently from the approach described in [7], we recognize that some tags are used to refer also to other different interests. This means that some tags utilized by the active user are more relevant than others for describing a specific ToI. We also face the limitation of neighbor selection by adaptively choosing a set of neighbors interested in the specific ToI. To reach this aim we take into account the set of resources tagged within a specific ToI since we recognize that different users may use different tags to refer to the same concept. Finally, we also filter feedback from neighbors by using tags (not necessarily the tags applied by the active user) that the neighbor applied on resources relevant for the specific ToI.

3   Identifying the Topic of Interests

The set of ToIs $\{ToI_{au}^1, \ldots, ToI_{au}^t\}$ identified within the personomy of the active user, constitutes her interest profile. The ToI_{au}^k is defined as

$$ToI_{au}^k = \left(T_{au}^k, R_{au}^k\right)$$

where

$$T_{au}^k = \left\{(t_1, w_{t_1}^k), \ldots, (t_n, w_{t_n}^k)\right\}$$

is the set of weighted tags used by the active user au to annotate his resources in the topic k and

$$R_{au}^k = \left\{(r_1, w_{r_1}^k), \ldots, (r_m, w_{r_m}^k)\right\}$$

is the set of resources tagged by the user au with the tags in T_{au}^k.

More specifically, T_{au}^k is defined on a set of semantically related tags

$$tag(T_{au}^k) = \{t_1, \ldots, t_n\}$$

applied by the active user, where two tags are considered to be in a semantic relation if the active user has applied them together to classify one or more resources. The weight associated to each tag represents the relevance of the tag with respect to that ToI and it is used to compute the relevance of each resource $res(R_{au}^k) = \{r_1, \ldots, r_m\}$ tagged by the active user within that ToI.

In order to identify the semantic relations defined by the active user we analyze her personomy throwing out information about the tagged resources. In particular, given the personomy of the active user we build an undirected weighted graph P where: each node represents a tag; an edge connects two tags if they have been used together to label one or more resources; an edge connecting two tags is weighted by the number of times two tags have been used together.

Figure 1 shows the graph P for one of the user of the BibSonomy social tagging system [8], where we do not show the weights associated to edges to make the graph readable.

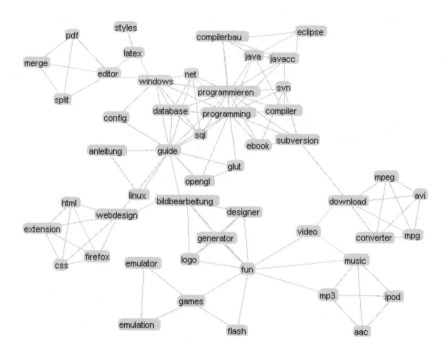

Fig. 1. An example of the graph P for a user of the BibSonomy system

Given the graph representation of a personomy, we apply a graph clustering technique for grouping tags with a shared semantic. In particular, we follow the idea proposed in [9] where a node (representing a tag in our model) may be in more than one cluster identifying, in this way, overlapping clusters of tags. This clustering technique identifies clusters of tags by identifying subgraphs from the starting graph P, where each subgraph G maximizes the following fitness property

$$f_G = \frac{K_{in}}{(K_{in} + K_{out})^\alpha}$$

where K_{in} is the sum of the weights of the edges which connect two tags belonging to G, K_{out} is the sum of the weights which connect tags in G with the rest of the graph, and α is a parameter which controls the size of clusters. In other words, the fitness of a subgraph increases when we add to the subgraph a tag that the user has exploited frequently in co-occurrence with tags in the subgraph and rarely with the other. The algorithm builds, for a given node, a cluster of tags by adding, at each step, the node which maximizes the following fitness function $f_G^a = f_{G+a} - f_{G-a}$, where $G+a$ $(G-a)$ is the subgraph obtained by adding (removing) the node a to the subgraph G. The process which adds tags to the cluster stops when there are not tags with a positive fitness value.

Using this method, our approach defines the cluster for the most used tag. Then, the approach identifies the cluster for the most used tag which has not been yet included in a cluster. The clustering algorithm ends when each tag is at least in one cluster. At the end, each subgraph detected by the clustering phase contains the set of tags associated to a certain ToI for the active user.

However, given a subgraph G^k, some of the tags in G^k are less relevant than others since they possibly are used also for referring to other different ToIs. Therefore, we associate a weight w_t^k to each tag t in the subgraph G^k by computing the betweeness centrality [10] of t in the specific subgraph identifying, in this way T_{au}^k. Applying this strategy on the example showed above for the most used tag 'programming' with $\alpha = 1.0$ we obtain the weighted set of tags: (programming, 1.0), (programmieren, 0.77), (guide 0.54), (java, 0.45), (javacc, 0.40), (compilerbau,0.36), (windows,0.31), (database, 0.27), (net,0.27), (sql, 0.27), (glut,0.22), (opengl,0.22), (eclipse,0.22), (compiler, 0.18), (svn, 0.18), (subversion 0.18), (ebook, 0.18), (anleitung, 0.09), (linux,0.09).

The set T_{au}^k is used to infer the set R_{au}^k such that $res(R_{au}^k)$ is composed by the resources that the active user labeled by tags in $tag(T_{au}^k)$ and the weight w_r^k for the resource r is equal to the maximum weight of tags in $tag(T_{au}^k)$ which the active user associated to r.

4   Recommending Resources for a ToI

This section focuses on the recommendation process by describing how the approach filters and ranks resources for a specific $ToI_{au}^k = (T_{au}^k, R_{au}^k)$. We will show how the set of weighted resources R_{au}^k can be used to select adaptively the neighbors (Section 4.1) and then how feedback from neighbors are filtered and combined (Section 4.2).

4.1   Adaptive Neighbor Selection

Given the $ToI_{au}^k = (T_{au}^k, R_{au}^k)$ of the active user, the set of weighted resources R_{au}^k is used to filter the set of neighbors for the ToI. In particular, the approach identifies people interested in the specific ToI by taking into account only the users who tagged the resources in $res(R_{au}^k)$. We assume that people interested in ToI_{au}^k share with the active user relevant resources within the specific ToI. For this reason, let $R_{shared}(u, R_{au}^k)$ be the set of resources that the user u share with the active user in $res(R_{au}^k)$, we compute how much the specific interest of the active user is matched by the neighbor u by computing the following

$$InterestMatch(u, ToI_{au}^k) = \frac{\sum_{r_i \in R_{shared}(u, R_{au}^k)} w_{r_i}^k}{\sum_{r_i \in res(R_{au}^k)} w_{r_i}^k}$$

The logic behind this formula is that higher is the number and the relevance of the resources in R_{au}^k that the neighbor u tagged, higher is the interest of u in the specific ToI. By using the InterestMatch function, we can filter the set N_{au}^k of neighbors interested in ToI_{au}^k.

4.2   Filtering and Combining Feedback for the ToI

The neighbor selection phase takes in account only resources in the ToI of the active user. In order to produce recommendations we need to identify new resources labeled by neighbors which are related to the specific ToI. Therefore, to do this, we consider the tags that the neighbor u applied on the set of shared resources $R_{shared}(u, R_{au}^k)$: the resources labeled by u with these tags are considered relevant for the specific ToI. e follow the idea that, some tags in the personomy of the neighbor u are more trustworthy than others for finding relevant resources for the ToI. In fact also the neighbor may have several ToIs and, for this reason, we are interested in discovering which tags utilized by u better account for the ToI of the active user. We consider more trustworthy the tags which have been used by the neighbor to label many relevant resources within ToI_{au}^k and, specifically, we measure the trustworthiness of a tag t_j in the collection of the neighbor u with respect to ToI_{au}^k as follow:

$$trustworthiness_u(t_j, ToI_{au}^k) = \frac{\sum_{r_i \in R_{shared}(u, R_{au}^k)} w_{r_i}^k \cdot \phi(u, t_j, r_i)}{\sum_{r_i \in R_{shared}(u, R_{au}^k)} w_{r_i}^k}$$

where $\phi(u, t_j, r_i) = 1$ if the user u applied the tag t_j on the resource r_i, 0 otherwise. Following the principle that trustworthy tags are associated to relevant resources of the neighbor u, we assign an higher relevance to resource labeled by more trustworthy tags. Specifically, we compute $rel_u(r_j, ToI_{au}^k)$, which is the relevance of the resource r_j in the personomy of the neighbor u with respect to ToI_{au}^k, as the highest trustworthiness associated to tags that the neighbor u assigned to r_j.

Finally, the relevance of a resource r_j for the active user with respect to ToI_{au}^k is computed summing the relevance of r_j over the collections of the neighbors N_{au}^k as follow:

$$rel(r_j, ToI_{au}^k) = \sum_{u \in N_{au}^k} InterestMatch(u, ToI_{au}^k) \cdot rel_u(r_j, ToI_{au}^k)$$

This allows to produce the ranked list of resources that are recommended to the active user.

5   Evaluation

Two main approaches can be used to evaluate the accuracy of the suggestions produced by a recommender system: a live approach and an off-line approach. In the first case, experimentation involves human participants which explicitly provide information about their interests. The recommender system can, in turn, build user profiles and produce a set of recommendations for each user. Finally, the involved humans can personally judge if the suggested items match their interests. On the other hand, an off-line evaluation uses an historical dataset which contains the rate history (the tagging history) of a certain set of users. In this case, the dataset is divided into two chunks of data where a block of data is used as training set in order to build user profiles and the other block is used as test set, in order to compare the resources rated/tagged by the user to the ones predicted/suggested by the system. Both the live and the off-line approach have some advantages and shortcomings since live experimentations are more precise but are also more expensive while, on the other hand, off-line evaluation is cheaper but cannot be very precise. More specifically, the main limitation of off-line evaluation depends on the high number of unrated resources: the users in the dataset usually evaluated just a small part of the available resources. This means that the system can produce meaningful recommendations which have not been rated/tagged by the active user: therefore an off-line evaluation considers these recommendations as not relevant for the active user (i.e. he did not rate/tag them) and this lowers the estimated precision. Obviously, this prevents an effective evaluation of the recommender system. For this reason, we have planned to evaluate our approach by using both a live and an off-line approach. At the moment we have exploited only some off-line experimentations in order to demonstrate the validity of our technique.

More specifically, in this work, we are interested in evaluating if the idea of filtering feedback for a single topic of interest by using the semantic relations built by the active user and his neighbors can significantly improve the approaches in the literature. For this reason, we have implemented the SocialRanking recommender system [5], which similarly to our approach produces recommendations for a specific tag/topic, and we have used it as a baseline reference for performance measurement.

We used a dump of the BibSonomy system [11] to compare the results provided by the two recommender systems. More specifically, we divided the BibSonomy dataset into two chunks of data: the training set which includes all bookmarks until the first of January 2008; the test set which has the bookmarks from the first of January 2008 to the 31 December 2008. We created the user profile only for the m users who tagged at least 60 resources until the first of January 2008 and who tagged at least 10 resources during the 2008. This is reasonable since collaborative filtering approaches produce effective recommendations only when users rated a significant number of items [1].

For each user, we used our approach to identify his topic of interests. Then, we computed a set of recommendations for the ToI which contained the tag that he used most frequently in the subsequent period (i.e. in the test set).

We used the same tag as input in the SocialRanking case. Both the Social-Ranking mechanism and our approach have been exploited for producing 10 recommendations, using feedback from the top 10 and from top 20 neighbors.

The quality of the computed recommendations produced by the two mechanisms was evaluated by adopting two measures, named respectively *hit-rate*(HR) and *average reciprocal hit-rank* ($ARHR$), which have been used also in [12] to compare two collaborative filtering recommender systems. More specifically, the HR measure is defined as follow

$$hit\text{-}rate = \frac{Number\ of\ hits}{m}$$

where m is the total number of users considered in the evaluation and we count a hit when the system produces at least one correct recommendation (i.e. a recommendation for a resource that the active user has actually tagged in the subsequent period). Given the lists of recommendations for the m users produced by a recommendation mechanism, the hit-rate is a value in $[0, 1]$ which is higher when there is a larger number of users who received at least one recommendation for a resource that they will tag in the test period.

Table 1 shows that our approach has an higher HR both when 10 neighbors and 20 neighbors are used: according to this metric the approach proposed in this paper outperforms SocialRanking.

Table 1. Hit-rate with 10 and 20 neighbors

	HR (10 neighbors)	HR(20 neighbors)
SocialRanking	0.13	0.15
Our Approach	0.34	0.40

The main limitation of the HR measure is given by the fact that hits are evaluated regardless of their position, i.e, a hit that occurs in the first position of the list of recommendations is treated equally to a hit that occurs in the last position. In other words, the capability of the recommender system to better rank resources is not recognized. In order to face this limitation we also used the $ARHR$ measure which is defined as

$$ARHR = \frac{1}{m} \sum_{i=1}^{h} \frac{1}{p_i}$$

where h is the number of hits and p_i is the position of i-th hit. $ARHR$ is still a value in $[0, 1]$ but it represents a measure of how well the recommender mechanism is capable to rank a hit in high-score positions. In Table 2 we show that our approach outperforms SocialRanking also when we use the $ARHR$ metric.

Table 2. ARHR with 10 and 20 neighbors

	ARHR (10 neighbors)	ARHR (20 neighbors)
SocialRanking	0.05	0.07
Our Approach	0.14	0.19

The main advantage of SocialRanking is that it can face the sparsity problem. Such limitation is due to the fact that users in CF filtering systems usually rate only a small part of the total number of items globally considered in the system and this makes harder the task of finding similarities on the basis of shared resources. Our approach can actually increase the sparsity since only a part of the user feedback is used to produce the set of recommendations (i.e., only the part relevant to a specific ToI).

However, Table 1 and Table 2 show that by inferring topic of interests from the set of the user annotated resources we obtain a more adequate description of the user interests since the number of hits increases as well as the position of the hits in the lists of recommendations. This depends on the fact that by computing similarities among tags by using only the similarities inferred from the *Tag-Resource* matrix, SocialRanking cannot account personal tagging strategies, i.e., semantic relations which are not adopted by a significant number of users in the community. Moreover, by taking into account only the number of times two tags co-occur in order to infer their semantics, approaches (such as SocialRanking) ignore that the tagged resources embed the information able to clarify the meaning of tags. For this reason we compute similarities among users by also taking into account the number of shared resources: higher is the number of shared resources, higher is the probability that the users are using two set of (possibly distinct) tags to describe a shared ToI.

6 Conclusions

In this work we propose a novel method to improve the precision of recommendations computed by a user-based CF system for social tagging systems. In order to reach this aim we address two main open issues.

In particular, traditional user-based CF recommender systems do not take into account that each user may have several distinct interests and people may share just some of these interests. In order to face this limitation, our approach adaptively filters and combines the feedback of neighbors according to a specific topic of interest identified for the active user. More specifically, in our approach, a topic of interest of the active user is defined by a set of tags with a shared meaning. In order to identify it we do not use approaches based on the analysis of the entire folksonomy, since they tend to completely discard information about the specific user. On the other hand, we group the tags of the active user according to the personal tagging strategy adopted by the user.

The results show that the proposed approach is reasonable and it outperforms other approaches proposed in literature. At the moment, we are planning a more effective evaluation to validate this claim by exploiting off-line evaluations on new datasets and by exploiting an on-line evaluation.

Moreover, we are interested both in:

- extending the approach following some idea proposed in [9] in order to identify hierarchical organization of user interests;
- adding a more semantic layer by means of content/ontology based analysis.

This step could potentially empower our approach by extracting semantic information able to disambiguate and enrich the description of user interests, merging more strictly the social and the semantic perspectives.

References

1. Schafer, J.B., Frankowski, D., Herlocker, J., Sen, S.: Collaborative filtering recommender systems (chapter 9). In: Brusilovsky, P., Kobsa, A., Nejdl, W. (eds.) Adaptive Web 2007. LNCS, vol. 4321, pp. 291–324. Springer, Heidelberg (2007)
2. Baltrunas, L., Ricci, F.: Locally adaptive neighborhood selection for collaborative filtering recommendations. In: Nejdl, W., Kay, J., Pu, P., Herder, E. (eds.) AH 2008. LNCS, vol. 5149, pp. 22–31. Springer, Heidelberg (2008)
3. Marinho, L., Nanopoulos, A., Schmidt-Thieme, L., Jaschke, R., Hotho, A., Stumme, G., Symeonidis, P.: Social tagging recommender systems. In: Ricci, F., Rokach, L., Shapira, B., Kantor, B. (eds.) Recommender Systems Handbook, pp. 615–644. Springer, Heidelberg (2011)
4. Dattolo, A., Ferrara, F., Tasso, C.: On social semantic relations for recommending tags and resources using folksonomies. In: Human-Computer Systems Interaction. Backgrounds and Applications, vol. 2 (in printing)
5. Zanardi, V., Capra, L.: Social ranking: Finding relevant content in web 2.0. In: Proc. of the 2nd ACM Int. Conf. on Recommender Systems, Lausanne, Switzerland (2008)
6. Dattolo, A., Ferrara, F., Tasso, C.: Supporting personalized user concept spaces and recommendations for a publication sharing system. In: Houben, G.-J., McCalla, G., Pianesi, F., Zancanaro, M. (eds.) UMAP 2009. LNCS, vol. 5535, pp. 325–330. Springer, Heidelberg (2009)
7. Zhou, T., Ma, H., Lyu, M., King, I.: Userrec: A user recommendation framework in social tagging systems. In: Proc. of the 24th AAAI Conf., Atlanta, Geogia, USA, pp. 1486–1491 (2010)
8. Benz, D., Hotho, A., Jaschke, R., Krause, B., Mitzlaff, F., Schmitz, C., Stumme, G.: The social bookmark and publication management system bibsonomy. The VLDB Journal 19, 849–875 (2010)
9. Lancichinetti, A., Fortunato, S., Kertész, J.: Detecting the overlapping and hierarchical community structure in complex networks. New Journal of Physics 11 (2009)
10. Opsahl, T., Agneessens, F., Skvoretz, J.: Node centrality in weighted networks: Generalizing degree and shortest paths. Social Networks 32 (2010)
11. BibSonomy: Bibsonomy dataset, dumps for research purposes, http://www.kde.cs.uni-kassel.de/bibsonomy/dumps
12. Deshpande, M., Karypis, G.: Item-based top-n recommendation algorithms. Transaction on Information Systems 1, 143–177 (2004)

Border Pairs Method – Constructive MLP Learning Classification Algorithm

Bojan Ploj[1], Milan Zorman[2], and Peter Kokol[2,3]

[1] School centre Ptuj, Higher vocational college
Vicava 1
SI-2250 Ptuj, Slovenia
bojan.ploj@scptuj.si
[2] University of Maribor, Faculty of Electrical Engineering and Computer Science
Smetanova 17
SI-2000 Maribor, Slovenia
[3] University of Maribor, Faculty of Health Sciences
Žitna ulica 15
SI-2000 Maribor, Slovenia
{milan.zorman,kokol}@uni-mb.si

Abstract. In this paper we present Border pairs method, a constructive learning algorithm for multilayer perceptron (MLP). During learning with this method a near-minimal network architecture is found. MLP learning is conducted separately by individual layers and neurons. The algorithm is tested in computer simulation with simple learning patterns (XOR and triangles image), with traditional learning patterns (Iris and MNIST) and with noisy learning patterns. During the learning we have less possibilities to get stuck in the local minima, generalization of learning is good. Learning with noisy, multi-dimensional and numerous learning patterns work well. The Border pairs method also supports incremental learning.

Keywords: artificial intelligence, machine learning, multilayer perceptron, constructive neural network, border pairs method (BPM).

1 Introduction

Neural Networks (NN) are one of the best known learning devices, with multi-layer perceptron (MLP), a neural network with one or more hidden layers, being the most popular of them (Fig.1.). This is a feedforward neural network, where connections between the units do not form a directed cycle. Its classical learning algorithm is backpropagation - a supervised learning method - lengthy iterative generalization of the delta rule. Sets of constants (weights) first get random values, which heavily influence the number of required iterations [1]. During the learning process the values gradually change until the learning error is small enough. There is a strong probability that we stay in local minima, so the outcome of learning is uncertain. The optimal size of MLP (number of neurons and layers) is unknown during a learning process, so a

A. Bouchachia (Ed.): ICAIS 2011, LNAI 6943, pp. 297–307, 2011.
© Springer-Verlag Berlin Heidelberg 2011

rule of thumb is often applied. Constructive neural network (CoNN) removes most of the disadvantages [2]. Most CoNN algorithms are still iterative.

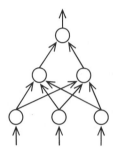

Fig. 1. Structure of MLP with three inputs, two nodes in hidden layer and one output, appropriate for learning with BPM

Border pairs method (BPM) is a constructive method which is presented in details in the following section. BPM is not a classical iterative approach, values of weights and biases are directly determined from the geometry of learning patterns, similar to the 'nearest neighbour classification'.

Specificity of the BPM is:

- Learning of each neuron individually.
- Learning with the selected (small) subset of the learning patterns.

Research work was conducted by the method of 'Tabula rasa', independently of the knowledge of other researches. It was observed how individual neurons behave in successfully learned MLP's. The resulting method was subsequently compared with the most common methods from the field of machine learning.

The most similar methods are called DistAl [3] and 'Geometrical Synthesis of MLP NN' [4]. Some similarities were also found with the method of 'Support Vector Machine' (SVM) [5] and 'NN weight initialization method using decision trees' [6]. DistAl method applies to neurons with spherical threshold in the hidden level. These neurons measure Euclidean distance from the centre of the sphere and ignite when the distance from the centre is less than threshold. This method provides similar results with border pairs method. In the case of 'Geometrical Synthesis of MLP' we have normal neurons with linear threshold (LTU). Since the method of border pairs differs in how a hyper plane separate patterns of different classes is searched. Instead of border pairs polyhedrons are used and all learning patterns, even those not located near the border hyper planes. The similarity to the method of SVM is that it uses solely selected learning patterns. The method of 'initialization of weights using decision trees' is similar to border pairs method by the fact that the initial values of the weights are closely to those learned, but it does not provide the MLP with near-minimum architecture. In the table 1 we represent an overview of advantages and disadvantages of related methods.

Table 1. Properties of different methods

Method	Advantages	Disadvantages
Support Vector Machine	• Fast training • Always search for global minimum	• Complex model and no control over complexity • Lack of result transparency
Geometrical synthesis of MLP	• Fast training • Fragmentation of classification problem	• All patterns are used for training
Initialisation of NN using DT	• Constructive method	• Complex model

2 Description of the Border Pairs Method

Our main goal was to avoid the disadvantages of traditional MLP learning, described in the introduction. The basic idea was to find the appropriate size of hidden layers and learning them individually, independently from the rest. Thus a demanding learning is divided into several simpler subtasks. Therefore, the hidden layers of learned MLP with two continuous inputs, and one discrete output were observed to discover the behaviour of individual neurons. Here are the basic rules:

1. In the first hidden layer:
   - Output values are binary (0 or 1).
   - Similar learning patterns are treated equally (clustering).
   - Neighbouring clusters differ only by one bit.
2. In the following layers MLP logical operations are performed with data from the first layer.

The first layer linearly divides patterns of the different classes. The second one performs the logical AND operation and the third layer performs a logical OR operation. These basic logical operations are trivial for neurons, so their learning does not pose any problems. For non-complex learning patterns the second and the third may be omitted, so in general, we can say that they are optional.

For an incremental learning only incorrectly classified patterns are used. We make additional border pairs and check the existing ones. Seeking of new border pairs is a fast and simple task, performed without difficulties. During the incremental process, additional learning of individual neurons is repeated.

On the Fig. 2 we see a graphical representation of two-dimensional patterns (x and y) labelled with two classes (o and +). The circles represent the learning patterns with the desired value of 1, the crosses with the desired value of 0. Three border lines (a, b and c) are required to separate the circles from the crosses. With these lines we

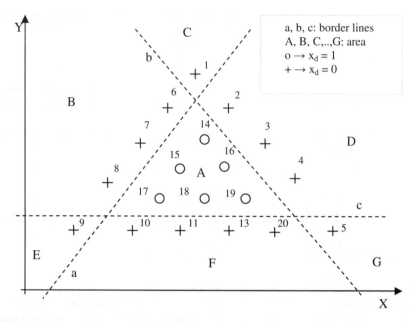

Fig. 2. Graphical diagram of the clustering of two-dimensional learning patterns

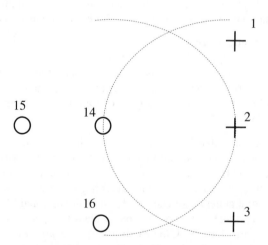

Fig. 3. Border pairs graph. Patterns 2 and 14 don't have any patterns inside the circle intersection so they can be used as a border pair

divided the input space into seven smaller areas (A, B, C, D, E, F and G). Now we start to search for border pairs, which are later used to determine the border lines. Border pairs are heterogeneous pairs (o and +) of learning patterns that lay as close to each other as possible, but on different sides of the border line. For example, between patterns 2 and 14 there is no other object and therefore this is a border pair. Patterns 2 and 15 are not a border pair, because there is a pattern 14 between them.

The exact description of border pair is shown in Fig. 3. Circles have centres in two patterns of different classes (patterns 2 and 14). Both radii are equal to Euclidean distance between the centres. If there is no other pattern found in the intersection then these patterns form a border pair. In a multi-dimensional space a circle is replaced by a multi-dimensional equivalent.

When the border pairs are formed, we can search for border lines (lines a, b and c in Fig. 2). All border pairs must be separated by at least one border line. Each border line must separate as many border pairs as possible and ultimately minimize the number of border lines. After setting border lines, we can check the individual areas.

If an area contains patterns of different classes, then we continue to search for additional border pairs and border lines. In this process we use only samples from the particular area. Learning is finished, when all areas contain patterns of only one class.

Table 2. Area (cluster) codes of learning patterns

Area	Code
A	1 1 1
B	0 1 1
C	0 0 1
D	1 0 1
E	0 1 0
F	1 1 0
G	1 0 0

The positions of the border lines are determined during learning of the neurons in the first hidden layer of MLP. At the beginning we start with one border line and try to match it with as many border pairs as possible. For unmatched border pairs we construct another border line and we try again to match as many previously unmatched border pairs as possible. We repeat this procedure, until all borders pairs are covered. The number of border lines is therefore between one and the number of border pairs.

Each border line corresponds with one neuron in the first hidden layer. All border pairs must be separated at the end of the learning process. The more border pairs are separated by a single neuron (single border line), the better the generalization of learning gets. In the worst case (no generalization) the number of border lines (neurons) is equal to the number of border pairs. Fewer border pairs can also be omitted in the training process when the training data is noisy.

First hidden layer assigns a binary code to each area of the input space (A, B, C, D, E, F and G in Fig.2.), so we get as many bits as there are border lines. The codes of two neighbouring areas differ only by one bit. In our case the first layer can have output codes (vectors), shown in table 2.

Learning the first layer runs according to the following algorithm:

```
Step 1: Search for the border pairs.
 Step 2: Take a new neuron and learn it with the
data of next border pair.
  Step 3: Add new (nearby) border pair and teach
  the same neuron. If learning succeeds, retain
  the added pair and mark it as used, otherwise
  discard it.
  Step 4: Continue with step 3 until the last
  border pair.
  Step 5: Continue with step 2 until all border
  pairs are used.
Step 6: Check all areas of input space
(clusters). If some area contains some patterns
of the opposite class (outliers) then search for
additional border pairs in this area and
continue with step 2.
```

Higher layers compute logical operations with binary vector (see example in Table 2). In our case (Fig. 2.) only one AND operation is needed. In the triangle there are patterns which are on the right side of border lines a, b and c. In general we have many convex areas in the input space, which contain only positive patterns. To each such convex area corresponds an adequate AND term. This function is preformed in the second hidden layer. The output layer performs logical OR operation of convex areas and is mandatory in cases, where we have more, than one triangle (not shown in this case). This is also the reason why BPM's classification error converge to zero on all finite and non-contradictory datasets.

3   Testing of the Border Pairs Method

The testing of BPM was performed using five different datasets, described below: XOR, triangle, Iris, MNIST and simple noisy data.

3.1   XOR

The first test of BPM was performed on well known XOR problem, shown in Fig. 4. Despite only four learning patterns (A, B, C in D) and only two-dimensional input space, many algorithms have problems with it. Our learning patterns form four border pairs: AB, AC, BD and CD.

Now we try to combine the border pairs. Pairs AB and AC could be separated with the same border line, represented with one neuron. The same is true for pairs BD and CD. So we get two border lines (a and b) or two neurons in the first layer. This is done fast and accurately without getting stuck in any local minima. Now we must obtain the final result from the first layers of binary code. This is done with an additional layer of neurons. In this case only logical OR operation with first layers data is needed.

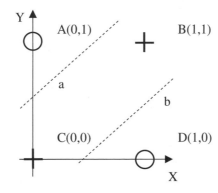

Fig. 4. The Graph of the XOR learning patterns

3.2 Triangle

This dataset is also two-dimensional. We try to find out if given point falls into the triangle. Dataset is similar to one, see in Fig.2. We used 200 learning patterns where approximately a quarter of them were circles (o) and the remaining were crosses (+). The learning process was repeated ten times with both algorithms (BPM and Backpropagation), and then the average and standard deviation of the RMSE error was calculated. The results are shown in Table 3.

Unfortunately, the BPM does not combine the border pairs optimally. Instead of three (optimal number for triangle) it frequently finds four or even more border lines.

3.3 Iris

"Iris" is an established data set for the various tests. Data is four-dimensional, continuous and without missing values. It is classified into three classes, each having

Table 3. Comparison of the results of two-dimensional learning

| | RMSE error | |
Number of a test	BPM	Backpropagation
1	0,036	0,200
2	0,075	0,128
3	0,008	0,417
4	0,016	0,072
5	0,024	0,240
6	0,048	0,051
7	0,048	0,339
8	0,115	0,026
9	0,008	0,155
10	0,016	0,042
Average	0,039	0,167
Standard deviation	0,034	0,133

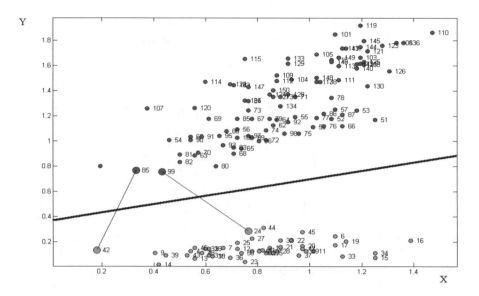

Fig. 5. Patterns from *Iris* dataset. Patterns 1-50 class Setosa, 51-100 class Versicolor and 101-150 class Virginica

50 instances (Fig. 5.). On horizontal axis (X) the sum of first and second input data (sepal length and width in cm) is shown, and on vertical axis (Y) there is the sum of third and fourth data (petal length and width in cm).

To determine whether or not an Iris fits in class "Setosa" (patterns 1-50), we got only two border pairs (42-85 and 24-99), so only one border line was enough (thick line) to separate them. To distinguish between classes Versicolor and Virginica, we needed more border lines, as seen in the table 4. From the data in Table 4 (2+12=14 and 1+4 = 5) it is clear that the class Versicolor lies between the other two classes, as demonstrated in Fig. 5. Trained MLP is able to classify correctly all 150 learning patterns.

Table 4. MLP for Iris dataset

Given class	Number of border pairs	Number of neurons in a hidden layer	RMSE error
Setosa	2	1	2.3e-11
Versicolor	14	5	3.6e-12
Virginica	12	4	2.0e-12

3.4 MNIST

MNIST is an established, proven and comprehensive set of data from the real world, containing handwritten decimal digits. The digits are size-normalized and centred in a fixed-size image.

Table 5. Comparison of learning results for the MNIST database

Digit	Misclassified patterns [%]		
	BPM	SVM	DT
0	2.5	2.0	1.7
1	6.8	7.7	9.6
2	4.2	4.9	4.5
3	5.2	1.5	5.2
4	1.7	1.3	2.6
5	4.8	8.3	6.0
6	0.8	0.3	2.8
7	2.2	3.9	7.1
8	3.4	4.8	5.5
9	4.7	2.9	5.2
Average	3.63	3.76	5.02

In a data set there is a collection of 250 samples from 44 different writers, described with 16 attributes without missing values. All input attributes are integers in the range between 0 and 100. The output attribute is the class code between 0 and 9. We used only 200 samples (20 of them were positive). The rest of the samples (3498) was used for testing. Classification was made with BPM and two other related methods - SVM and DT. The results of comparison are given in Table 5.

3.5 Noisy Data

We wanted to find out how successful the Border pairs method is when learning data contains noise. At the beginning data without noise was used, then the noise is gradually added. The input data is two-dimensional, with continuous values and can

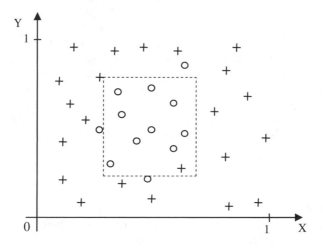

Fig. 6. Learning patterns with noise

Table 6. MSE error with different noise rates and different algorithms

Algorithm		Noise rate (%)				
		0	1	2	5	10
Back-propagation	Average RMSE	0,0692	0,1257	0,1094	0,1333	0,1519
	Std. dev.	0,0290	0,1136	0,0953	0,1146	0,0782
Border pairs	Average RMSE	0,0399	0,0308	0,0497	0,0302	0,1046
	Std. dev.	0,0304	0,0250	0,0491	0,0235	0,0280

be represented as points in the plane. Value 1 at the output of MLP means that a point lays inside a square, and the value 0 means the sample lays outside.

We used 500 randomly distributed patterns: the first 250 patterns took part in the learning process, and the other 250 in evaluation of learning results, both sets having almost equal class distribution. Table 6 contains the obtained results of the averages and standard deviations of the RMSE. The noise rate is given in percentages. Ten percents noise rate means that the P data after adding noise comes in an interval from P-5% to P+5%. The position of the points changes somewhat after adding the noise. The learning was repeated twenty times for each noise rate. Learning with both algorithms was conducted under the same conditions. Noise rate was 0%, 1%, 2%, 5% and 10%.

4   Conclusion

Border pairs method has found near minimal MLP architecture in almost all described cases. For classification of Iris Setosa only two border pairs or only four patterns out of 150 were enough for learning the whole data set correctly.

In the classification of handwritten digits (MNIST) only 200 learning patterns were used for learning. The BPM correctly identified more than 95% from 3498 handwritten digits, which did not participate in learning. Even with a noisy data, some very good results were obtained. RMSE error of the BPM was significantly lower than that of Backpropagation, especially for the noise lower than 10%.

During learning we always managed to avoid the local minima. The initial results of the research give us a good starting point for further work. Possible directions for future research are:

- Noise reduction using border pairs.
- Improvement of algorithm for combining border pairs.

Proper order of adding pairs improves the success of association. For noise reduction is reasonable to use only the patterns which participate in border pairs. We could correct them in the direction of nearby patterns of the same class which do not participate in border pairs.

References

1. Alsmadi, M.S., Omar, K.B., Noah, S.A.: Back Propagation Algorithm: The Best Algorithm Among the Multi-layer Perceptron Algorithm. IJCSNS International Journal of Computer Science and Network Security 9(4) (2009)
2. do Carmo Nicoletti, M.: Constructive Neural Networks: Constructive Neural Network Algorithms for Feedforward Architectures Suitable for Classification Tasks. Springer, Berlin (2009)
3. Yang, J., Parekh, R., Honavar, V.: DistAl: An inter-pattern distance-based constructive learning algorithm. In: Intelligent Data Analysis, vol. 3, pp. 55–73. Elsevier, Amsterdam (1999)
4. Delogu, R., Fanni, A., Montis, A.: Geometrical synthesis of MLP neural networks. Neurocomputing 71, 919–930 (2008)
5. Cortes, C., Vapnik, V.: Support-Vector Networks. Machine Learning 20 (1995)
6. Banerjee, A.: Initializing neural networks using decision trees. In: Computational learning theory and natural learning systems, vol. IV. MIT Press, Cambridge (1997)

Ranking-Based Feature Selection Method for Dynamic Belief Clustering

Sarra Ben Hariz and Zied Elouedi

LARODEC, Institut Supérieur de Gestion de Tunis, 41 Avenue de la Liberté,
2000 Le Bardo, Tunisie
sarra.benhariz@gmail.com zied.elouedi@gmx.fr

Abstract. In this paper, we investigate the problem of dynamic belief clustering. The developed approach tackles the problem of updating
the partition by decreasing the attribute set in an uncertain context.
We propose a based-ranking feature selection method that allows us to
preserve only the most relevant attributes. We deal with uncertainty related to attribute values, which is represented and managed through the
Transferable Belief Model (TBM) concepts. The reported results showed
that, in general, there is a beneficial effect of using the developed selection method to cluster dynamic feature set in comparison with the other
static methods performing a complete reclustering.

1 Introduction

Clustering consists in assignment of a dataset into groups such that the objects in
the same cluster have a high degree of similarity. Known also as cluster analysis
or unsupervised classification, data clustering has been addressed in many fields
like marketing, medicine, banking, finance, security, etc.

Generally, clustering techniques have typically focused on numerical datasets
such as K-means method [13]. However, clustering categorical data is a recent
research problem in data mining. Thus, many efforts have been considered on
clustering data with categorical attributes. Indeed, the K-modes method [10] is
one of the most popular of such techniques since it is inspired from the well-
known K-means method.

The problem of pattern maintenance, consisting in updating the data, is a
fundamental task in data management process. However, most existing clustering
approaches [11] suppose that databases are static. Such approaches are known
as off-line, and the scanning of both old and new information is required for
their updates. The proposal of dynamic techniques of any new information will
be more efficient and this is ensured by taking into account model evolution over
time. The detected changes may concern dataset characteristics (feature set or
data objects) or cluster's partition. In fact, a dynamic dataset is a set of elements
whose parameters change over time. This latter task often concerns large and
high dimensional data. For such datasets, features may affect clusters differently,
some are important while others may bother the clustering procedure. Some
of the previously used features to cluster the dataset may become redundant,

A. Bouchachia (Ed.): ICAIS 2011, LNAI 6943, pp. 308–319, 2011.

irrelevant or may even misguide clustering results. In addition, reducing the number of features may increase problem's comprehensibility.

On the other hand, there are numerous applications, where a dataset already clustered with respect to an initial set of attributes, is altered by the addition of new feature(s). Consequently, a re-clustering is required. Recently, [3,15] propose incremental clustering methods dealing with the increasing of the attribute set, while, works in [1,19] create the clusters by incrementally adding the dataset objects. Furthermore, in [20], authors provided both incremental and decremental procedures to cluster dynamic objects sets. Moreover, preliminary dynamic clustering approaches are proposed in [4,5], handling dynamic clusters' number. However, most of these non-standard methods, except [3,4,5], assume that the datasets are certain and then could not deal with the challenge of uncertainty management.

Another issue in practical applications is uncertainty. Indeed, there is a large amount of data with imperfect characteristics. The necessity of handling both imprecision and uncertainty of the data, in addition to the dynamic problem, leads to the use of several mathematical theories, such as the belief function theory [16]. This was the objective of some of the already exposed dynamic clustering techniques [3,4,5]. Therefore, the idea, here, is to combine clustering methods with this theory for representing and managing this uncertainty. In this work, under a dynamic environment, we will focus on the previously developed belief K-modes method (BKM) [2], using the belief function theory as interpreted in the Transferable Belief model [18] to overcome this limitation since our symbolic datasets have uncertain attribute values. Let us mention that several other works have been developed within this uncertain framework such as in [9]. However, the proposed method exposed a static approach.

This paper focuses on developing a new dynamic clustering approach in an uncertain context and proposes a selection methodology of features which are characterized by uncertain values. The selection methodology is achieved by sorting the features in order to eliminate the most irrelevant one(s) for an afterward up-to-date clustering process. This in fact allows finding better cluster partition quality.

The remainder of this paper is organized as follows. Section 2 recalls the basics of belief K-modes method (BKM) and briefly reviews the standard approach K-modes as well as the belief function theory core concepts. Section 3 describes our new feature selection method based on a ranking principle under uncertainty. Section 4 outlines our developed dynamic clustering methodology. Section 5 presents the outcome of the experiments. Finally, Section 6 sums up the paper with some conclusions.

2   Background on BKM Approach

The K-modes approach [10] was proposed to tackle the problem of clustering large categorical datasets. By using the K-means [13] paradigm, this categorical extension considers a simple matching dissimilarity measure, modes instead of means as cluster representatives. To update modes, during the clustering process, a frequency-based approach is used. Note that the K-modes algorithm preserves the efficiency of the K-means algorithm.

However, for practical applications, there is a large amount of data with imperfect characteristics. So, the necessity of their handling leads to use an appropriate mathematical theory, such as the belief function theory [16]. In this work, we will focus on this tool to represent and manage the uncertainty's parameter. So, we will briefly expose its main concepts, used within BKM framework, under the Transferable Belief Model (TBM). More details can be found in [2,16,17,18].

By considering Θ, a finite non empty set of elementary events to a given problem, also called the frame of discernment and containing hypotheses about one problem domain, the set of all its subsets is referred by the power set of Θ, denoted by 2^Θ. The impact of a piece of evidence on the different subsets of this frame of discernment is represented by the so-called basic belief assignment (bba). Indeed, bba is a function denoted m that assigns a value in [0,1] to every subset A of Θ, and it is defined as follows: $m : 2^\Theta \mapsto [0,1]$ such that $\sum_{A \subseteq \Theta} m(A) = 1$. Each quantity m(A), named basic belief mass (bbm) is considered as the part of belief that supports the event A, and that, due to the lack of information, does not support any strict subsets.

The belief K-modes method (BKM) [2] was developed, based on the K-modes algorithm and uses the belief function theory, more precisely the bba concept, in order to represent and handle this uncertainty.

Contrary to the certain training set which includes only precise information, here, we deal with n objects where each of their S attributes is represented by a bba expressing beliefs on its values. The corresponding bba of an attribute A_j, where $1 \leq j \leq S$, is then given by m_j. Thus, each attribute is represented via one conjunction of all possible values and their corresponding masses. Hence, each attribute value respectively to each instance is denoted by $x_{i,j} = \{(c_j, m_i(c_j)) \mid c_j \in 2^{\Theta_j}\}$. Notice that this training set offers a more generalized framework than the standard one.

BKM first parameter: Cluster mode

The mean operator permits combining bba's respectively to each attribute provided by all objects of one cluster as well as satisfying the commutativity and the idempotency properties [7]. Then, the idea was to apply this operator to this uncertain context, for more details see [2].

Thus, given a cluster $C_l = \{X_1, ..., X_{n_l}\}$ of n_l objects characterized by uncertain attribute values, with $1 \leq l \leq K$, the mode of the cluster C_l can be defined by the following belief mode or representative $Q_l = (q_{l,1}, .., q_{l,j}, .., q_{l,S})$, such that:

$$q_{l,j} = \{(c_j, m_l(c_j)) \mid c_j \in 2^{\Theta_j}\} \tag{1}$$

where $m_l(c_j)$ is the relative bbm of the attribute value c_j within C_l which is defined as follows: $m_l(c_j) = \frac{\sum_{i=1}^{n_l} m_i(c_j)}{|C_l|}$, where $|C_l|$ is the number of objects in

C_l, while $m_l(c_j)$ expresses the part of belief about the value c_j of the attribute A_j corresponding to this cluster mode.

BKM second parameter: Dissimilarity measure
The dissimilarity measure has to take into account the new dataset structure, where one bba is defined for each attribute per object. So, the idea was to adapt the belief distance defined by [6] to this uncertain clustering context. It can be expressed as follows:

$$D(X_i, Q_l) = \sum_{j=1}^{S} d(m_{i,j}, m_{l,j}) \quad (2)$$

where $m_{i,j}$ and $m_{l,j}$ are the relative bba's of the attribute A_j provided by respectively the object X_i and the mode Q_l.

The component **d** takes into account both the bba's distributions provided by the object X_i and the cluster mode Q_l and one similarity matrix D (for more details see [2]). This is a metric defined on the power set non based on the pignistic transformation.

The BKM algorithm has the same skeleton as the standard K-modes method [2]. It can be summarized as follows: After the selection of K initial modes, all other objects must be allocated to the nearest clusters based on the dissimilarity defined by Equation 2. Then, an update of all cluster representatives (Equation 1) and re-testing of the object assignments must be required. We have to reiterate the mode update and the instance reassignment until no object has changed cluster.

3   Ranking-Based Feature Selection under Uncertainty

Feature selection algorithms can be categorized as either filter or wrapper [12] approaches. Filter approaches preselect the features, and then apply the selected feature subset to the clustering algorithm, whereas, the wrapper ones incorporate the clustering algorithm in the selection feature process. We choose, here, to explore the problem differently because we are interested in processing the feature search independently of the clustering algorithm but we have to consider its output clusters arrangement or partition to detect the feature impact during the clustering process.

In the following, the selection features process as well as its preprocessing step namely the ranking one will be detailed under uncertainty. Note that our proposal takes into account the belief structure of our uncertain datasets, whereas, the already developed ranking approaches in the literature deal with certain feature values. Our proposal is a two-stage procedure. Firstly, it sorts the features, locally in each cluster, based on the dissimilarity measures. These distances reflect the feature relevance within each cluster. The result of this first stage is subsequently used in the second one in order to decide which feature(s) must be eliminated to improve the afterward clustering quality. Note that all this study is based on the resulting cluster partition obtained via a complete execution of the BKM algorithm. These two feature selection phases under uncertainty will be detailed in what follows.

3.1 Local Feature Ranking Step

Let us assume that the partition P of K clusters, resulting by applying BKM clustering method, constitutes the starting point of the whole selection approach. The notion of attribute preference has a central role in our study. This is ensured by comparing the scores of all attributes respectively to an appropriate metric. Indeed, we propose the dissimilarity to decide on the features ranking. For each attribute A_j belonging respectively to each cluster C_l, we have to compute this metric between the cluster mode and all instances of this same group as follows:

$$D_{j,l} = \sum_{i=1}^{n_l} d(x_{i,j}, q_{l,j}) \qquad (3)$$

where n_l represents the cluster cardinality. The **d** component is already exposed in Section 2 (see Equation 2) since we treat uncertain attribute values. Furthermore, this distance measures the impact of this attribute A_j, having uncertain values, on the intra-cluster quality/compactness. Thus, the attribute with the highest distance value represents the one who participated least in this cluster formation. Then, it is judged as the most irrelevant one. Finally, the ranking of our S attributes within each cluster, called R_l, is directly built based on these distances sort in an increasing order. By the following pseudo-algorithm, we summarize this first step of the ranking-based feature selection method.

Local feature ranking algorithm(P)

> Data: P
> Result: R_l
> **begin**
> > **for** *Each cluster C_l, $1 \leq l \leq K$* **do**
> > > **for** *Each attribute A_j, $1 \leq j \leq S$* **do**
> > > > Compute $D_{j,l}$ by Equation 3
> > >
> > > Sort these distances in an increasing order
> > > Generate directly R_l, the ranking of S attributes
>
> **end**

3.2 Selecting the Most Irrelevant Features Step

Giving the K arrangements respectively to the K clusters, only the most relevant features must be preserved during the dynamic process after this selection step. The attribute(s) which is/are judged as the most irrelevant one(s), via the general feature ranking, must be eliminated. The sum of the scores will be computed for each attribute by considering all corresponding distance measures already calculated. Thus, a general feature ranking is generated respectively to these scores by their sort in an increasing order. These scores, respectively to S attributes, are computed a follows:

$$D_j = \sum_{l=1}^{K} \mu_l D_{j,l} \qquad (4)$$

Where μ_l reflects the weight of the corresponding cluster during this general feature ranking step. We assume that all μ_l are equal to 1, thus all clusters have the same impact for this step. It is possible that this weight will be fixed by the expert or computed by using the cluster cardinality.

Let us mention that two attributes or more, having the same sum of scores, can be judged as the most irrelevant ones and thus must be eliminated.

Indeed, the selection belief feature process consists in the execution of the already exposed local feature ranking algorithm followed by the current one namely the selecting of the most irrelevant features algorithm to return finally the index/indices of the most irrelevant feature(s) to eliminate. Recall that the considered features set contains uncertain attribute values represented via the belief function theory concepts. To illustrate the developed belief feature selection approach, the following pseudo algorithm is proposed.

Selecting the most irrelevant features algorithm(R_l)

Data: R_l
Result: index/indices
begin

    for *Each attribute A_j, $1 \leq j \leq S$* **do**
        Compute D_j by Equation 4

    Sort these distances in an increasing order
    Generate directly R, the general ranking of S attributes
    Preserve the index/indices of the attribute(s) which is/are judged as the most irrelevant one(s).

end

4   Dynamic Clustering Methodology

4.1   DSBKM Principal

We will present a novel dynamic belief clustering approach called Dynamic S Belief K-modes method (DSBKM) by extending the uncertain K-modes method version (BKM) to non-static environment. Note that S represents the initial attributes number to reduce. It consists in dynamically decreasing the feature set of S attributes and update the clustering result to guarantee a higher quality partition. This is done by considering the dissimilarity/similarity measure concept.

Recall that, like in BKM static framework, within $DSBKM$ context our dataset objects may be characterized by uncertain attribute values represented through the bba's and managed via the belief function concepts.

To this end, we initially run the BKM algorithm to build K clusters, as point of departure of the developed decremental clustering process. Then, the problem to deal with is how to manage this partition and update it without reclustering our reduced dataset again, only described via the most S relevant attributes ?

In our case, we make use of the previously presented feature selection approach to decide which feature(s) to eliminate. DSBKM starts with an initial partition. Then, it performs initialization and updating steps:

- Step 1: The initialization phase aims to detect which cluster(s) must be rearranged. It uses the resulting feature selection method ranking.
- Step 2: The updating phase re-estimates the cluster partition for the dataset of reduced attribute set. In fact, it consists in an iterative update until clusters' stability.

Basically, the key idea of our dynamic algorithm is as follows: having initially K clusters characterized by S attributes, we detect and eliminate, dynamically over time, those attributes that become irrelevant and update consequently the input clusters.

It is possible to reiterate this dynamic process and the selection feature one until an expected clustering quality is reached.

4.2   *DSBKM* Algorithm

The *DSBKM* algorithm's inputs are *BKM* final partition, of K clusters, *noMaxIter* as the maximum number of iterations, the uncertain dataset *UT* as well as the index/indices of the attribute(s) to eliminate. Recall that this latter parameter is the feature selection method output.

For the following algorithm like the selection belief feature one, the dissimilarity measure plays an important role.

This proposed belief dynamic clustering approach can be considered as probabilistic technique when the attribute uncertainty is expressed via the bayesian belief function [16]. Moreover, the standard certain database can be handled via certain bba's [16] within DSBKM framework. Thus, it offers a more generalized approach.

Let us mention that the cluster(s), for which the removed attribute(s) is/are judged as the most irrelevant one(s), remain(s) unchanged.

The revised set R is a temporary group which is created and used during an intermediate step in order to assign to it the revised set objects.

Regarding the time complexity, as shown in the next pseudo-code, the initial step of the dynamic approach has order of $O(K)$, when updating the clusters, $O(K.n_l.S'.noMaxIter)$ is reached. With K is the cluster's number, n_l is the cardinality of the cluster C_l and S' is the attribute's number of the reduced features set.

Our proposal *DSBKM* algorithm is summarized by the following pseudo-algorithm.

DSBKM Algorithm (P, $noMaxIter$, UT, $index(es)$)

Data: P, UT, $noMaxIter$, $index/indices$

Result: P'

begin

> ***Initialization step***
>
> 1. Update the K cluster modes by eliminating the attribute(s) having $index/indices$ number(s).
>
> 2. Preserve only K' clusters among all K clusters, which must be updated. They are the groups for which the eliminated attribute(s) is/are averagely important.
>
> ***Updating step***
>
> 3. **for** *Each cluster C_l, $1 \leq l \leq K'$ with $K' \leq K$* **do**
>
> > Compute its compactness expressed via its intra-cluster similarity measure as follows $D(C_l) = \sum_{i=1}^{n_l} D(X_i, Q_l)$, where $n_l = |C_l|$ represents the cardinality of the cluster C_l with $l \in \{1, .., K\}$ and Q_l is its mode.
>
> 4. Compute the average compactness as threshold for the following.
>
> 5. **for** *Each cluster C_l, $1 \leq l \leq K'$* **do**
>
> > **if** *Compactness $\leq$ Threshold* **then**
> >
> > > The cluster must be revised by checking the instances memberships
> > > - Compute the inter-objects dissimilarities respectively to all instances by using $D(X_{i_1}, X_{i_2}) = \sum_{j=1}^{S} d(m_{i_1,j}, m_{i_2,j})$, where i_1 and $i_2 \in \{1, .., n\}$ and $j \in \{1, .., S\}$.
> > > - Assign to the revised set R the most dissimilar one(s) from other objects.
> >
> > **else**
> > > No detected change for this group
>
> 6. Update all cluster modes.
>
> 7. Assign the revised set objects to appropriate clusters.
>
> 8. Re-update the cluster representatives.
>
> 9. Re-test the dissimilarity of objects against the current modes.
>
> 10. Repeat steps 8 and 9 until no object has changed clusters or the noMaxIter is performed.

end

5 Experimental Study

5.1 Used Data Sets

To evaluate our proposal, we have performed several tests on real databases obtained from the UCI repository [14]. A brief description of these databases is presented in Table 1. Note that no missing attribute values are detected.

Since there are not available real datasets containing uncertainty within the belief function framework, we have modified these databases by introducing uncertainty in the attribute values of their instances in order to obtain uncertain versions. To do this, we use three uncertainty's parameters namely the certain attributes' values of the training instances, the degree of uncertainty p per attribute and the percent of both uncertain objects and uncertain attributes.

The idea is to assign to each attribute, a bba over the set of remaining attributes of this object, based on the set of their possible values, for more details see artificial creation of belief dataset versions process as described in [2]. Details for uncertain versions are omitted, due to lack of space. Let us, just, recall that attribute values are converted to bba's distribution.

Table 1. Description of UCI databases

Databases	#instances	#attributes	#classes
Hayes-Roth	160	5	3
Lenses	24	4	3
Lymphography	148	18	4
Spect heart	267	22	2
Zoo	101	17	7

5.2 Experimental Evaluation Parameters

The selected criteria used to judge the performance of our proposed clustering method are:

1. Clustering quality indices namely the clustering accuracy [10] as external evaluation criterion, besides the widely used validity function namely the Davies-Bouldin (DB) index [8] as internal validation index.

   The first was proposed by Huang [10] as follows $r = \frac{\sum_{l=1}^{K} a_l}{n}$, where n is the number of instances in the dataset, K is the number of clusters, a_l is the number of instances occurring in both cluster l and its corresponding labeled class. If r is equal to 100%, then the cluster partition is judged as excellent, whereas a 'null' or bad cluster arrangement has a clustering accuracy equal to 0%.

   The second is a function of the ratio of the sum of intra-cluster scatter to inter-cluster separation and defined by $DB = \frac{1}{K} \sum_{i=1}^{K} max_{j,j\neq i}\{\frac{S_i+S_j}{d_{ij}}\}$, where S_i and S_j are respectively the average distance of all objects belonging to cluster C_i and C_j to their cluster's centers, and d_{ij} is the distance between clusters centers. S_i and S_j components reflect the intra-cluster variability. By d_{ij} measure, the inter-cluster distance is given. Hence, the ratio is small if the clusters are compact and far from each other. Consequently, Davies-Bouldin index has a small value, going to zero, for a good clustering.

2. Time performance measures namely the running time which represents the time complexity needed to obtain a final stable partition and the iterations number which indicates how many iterations are performed until the partition stability. So, the first criterion is used to find the faster classifier among the dynamic proposed ones and the static method.

5.3   Experimental Results

Two cases must be considered, namely dynamic and static contexts in order to compare them and evaluate our proposals. To this end, we have to proceed by applying the BKM approach initially to build K clusters for each uncertain dataset characterized by all S attributes. We consider then the resulting output partition as ranking-based feature selection input. By running this selection method, the index/indices of the most irrelevant attribute(s) is/are returned. Our proposal, namely $DSBKM$, updates the cluster partition after this reduction of the feature set.

To judge its quality, the proposed approach must be compared to the static version. We have to retain the corresponding experimental evaluation criteria resulting by using DSBKM, as exposed above, and BKM method to cluster dataset characterized by, now, the reduced feature set.

We run the algorithms ten times. The clustering quality indices are measured according to the mean values. According to the obtained results, summarized in Tables 2 and 3, we can observe that the dynamic belief clustering generates better results than those returned by applying the static clustering version. This proves that our dynamic method is resilient to feature set reduction by using the proposed ranking-based selection approach instead of a random feature selection.

Table 2. Clustering quality indices results (BKM versus DSBKM)

Databases	DB index (%)		Clustering accuracy (%)	
	BKM	DSBKM	BKM	DSBKM
Hayes-Roth	7.82	7.05	76.7	78.4
Lenses	4.15	3.26	87.88	90.75
Lymphography	8.56	7.99	84.56	83.99
Spect heart	10.69	8.88	86.25	87.08
Zoo	8.35	8.56	71.8	74.5

Moreover, results in Table 2 confirm that our proposal is well appropriate within such uncertain context and, DSBKM, generally, outperforms BKM and has a better DB measure (the minimum one) and a higher clustering accuracy (the maximum one).

Furthermore, DSBKM provides high accuracy values for all testing data, except Lymphography database, where all values are greater than 74.5% and yields good results in terms of DB index.

Using dynamic clustering mainly aims to improve the classifier performance. In order to appropriately monitor the behavior of DSBKM approach, we also calculate the running time requirement and the iterations number.

Table 3 presents the time performance results for the used datasets. As previously done for the clustering quality indices, here again, we report the mean values of ten times run. We observe that, according to iterations number, reclustering the whole data objects after decreasing the attribute set could not be considered as a good practice comparing to the decremental developed process.

Table 3. Time performance measures (%)(BKM versus DSBKM)

Databases	BKM		DSBKM	
	Running time(s)	Iterations	Running time(s)	Iterations
Hayes-Roth	196	12	183	9
Lenses	71	6	57	5
Lymphography	209	10	187	6
Spect heart	199	9	152	6
Zoo	198	6	187	6

This is due to the highest number of iterations required by the static approach to find the final stable partitions compared to the one required by DSBKM approach. Indeed, it is clear that, for most databases, both running time and iterations number are significantly better using our dynamic framework than the static method. Note that by eliminating the most irrelevant attribute(s), which is/are selected via the proposed ranking-based selection method, the clustering process generates higher quality partitions with reduced time requirements and minimal iterations' numbers.

As expected, these time execution values, slightly higher, can be explained by the fact that each attribute is represented, within DSBKM framework, via one conjunction of all possible values and their corresponding masses instead of one precise category. The same is observed for static version since identical data structures are considered.

6   Conclusion

In this paper, we proposed a new clustering approach which dynamically updates the clusters partition, after reducing the feature set, in order to guarantee a higher quality result. We developed a novel feature selection method under uncertainty to detect and preserve, among all attributes, only the most relevant ones. The uncertainty is considered in attribute values and is represented and managed by the belief function theory as understood by the TBM. We tested our proposed method on real datasets versions soiled by uncertainty, and the obtained experimental results showed its efficiency. As a future work, we plan to investigate and set up a more general clustering method allowing us to handle additional dynamic aspects and uncertainty forms.

References

1. Aranganayagi, S., Thangavel, K.: Incremental Algorithm to Cluster the Categorical Data with Frequency Based Similarity Measure. International Journal of Computational Intelligence 6, 24–32 (2010)
2. Ben Hariz, S., Elouedi, Z., Mellouli, K.: Clustering Approach using Belief Function Theory. In: Twelfth International Conference on Artificial Intelligence: Methodology, Systems, Applications, pp. 162–171 (2006)

3. Ben Hariz, S., Elouedi, Z.: An Incremental Clustering Approach within Belief Function Framework. In: Twelfth IASTED International Conference on Artificial Intelligence and Soft Computing, pp. 98–103 (2008)
4. Ben Hariz, S., Elouedi, Z.: IK-BKM: An Incremental Clustering Approach Based on Intra-Cluster Distance. In: Eighth ACS/IEEE International Conference on Computer Systems and Applications, pp. 1–8 (2010)
5. Ben Hariz, S., Elouedi, Z.: DK-BKM: Decremental K Belief K-modes Method. In: Fourth International Conference on Scalable Uncertainty Management, pp. 84–97 (2010)
6. Bosse, E., Grenier, D., Jousselme, A.L.: A new distance between two bodies of evidence. Information Fusion 2, 91–101 (2001)
7. Catherine Murphy, K.: Combining belief functions when evidence conflicts. Decision Support Systems 29, 1–9 (2000)
8. Davies, D.L., Bouldin, D.W.: Cluster Separation Measure. IEEE Transactions on Pattern Analysis and Machine Intelligence 1(2), 95–104 (1979)
9. Denoeux, T., Masson, M.: EVCLUS: Evidential Clustering of Proximity Data. IEEE Transactions on Systems, Man and Cybernetics 34(1), 95–109 (2004)
10. Huang, Z.: Extensions to the k-means algorithm for clustering large data sets with categorical values. Data Mining Knowledge Discovery 2(2), 283–304 (1998)
11. Jain, A.K., Dubes, R.C.: Algorithms for clustering data. Prentice Hall, Englewood cliffs (1988)
12. John, G.H., Kohavi, R., Pfleger, K.: Irrelevant features and the subset selection problem. In: Eleventh International Conference on Machine Learning, pp. 121–129 (1994)
13. MacQueen, J.: Some methods for classification and analysis of multivariate observations. In: Fifth Berkeley Symposium on Math., Stat. and Prob., pp. 281–296 (1967)
14. Murphy, M., Aha, D.W.: UCI repository (1996), http://www.ics.edu/mlearn
15. Serban, G., Câmpan, A.: Core Based Incremental Clustering, Studia Univ., Babes-Bolyai. Informatica L (1), 89–96 (2005)
16. Shafer, G.: A mathematical theory of evidence, vol. 30. Princeton Univ. Press, Princeton (1976)
17. Smets, P.: The Transferable Belief Model and Other Interpretations of Dempster-Shafer's Model. In: Bonissone, P.P., Henrion, M., Kanal, L.N., Lemmer, J.F. (eds.) Uncertainty in Artificial Intelligence, vol. 6, pp. 375–384. North Holland, Amsteram (1991)
18. Smets, P.: The transferable belief model for quantified belief representation. In: Gabbay, D.M., Smets, P. (eds.) Handbook of Defeasible Reasoning and Uncertainty Management Systems, vol. 1, pp. 267–301 (1998)
19. Su, X., Lan, Y., Wan, R., Qin, Y.: A Fast Incremental Clustering Algorithm. In: International Symposium on Information Processing, pp. 175–178 (2009)
20. Truta, T.M., Campan, A.: K-Anonymization Incremental Maintenance and Optimization techniques. In: Symposium on Applied Computing, pp. 380–387 (2007)

Distributed Constraint Programming with Agents

Carl Christian Rolf and Krzysztof Kuchcinski

Department of Computer Science, Lund University, Sweden
{Carl_Christian.Rolf,Krzysztof.Kuchcinski}@cs.lth.se

Abstract. Many combinatorial optimization problems lend themselves to be modeled as distributed constraint optimization problems (DisCOP). Problems such as job shop scheduling have an intuitive matching between agents and machines. In distributed constraint problems, agents control variables and are connected via constraints. We have equipped these agents with a full constraint solver. This makes it possible to use global constraint and advanced search schemes.

By empowering the agents with their own solver, we overcome the low performance that often haunts distributed constraint satisfaction problems (DisCSP). By using global constraints, we achieve far greater pruning than traditional DisCSP models. Hence, we dramatically reduce communication between agents.

Our experiments show that both global constraints and advanced search schemes are necessary to optimize job shop schedules using DisCSP.

1 Introduction

In this paper, we discuss distributed constraint programming with agents (DCP). We introduce advanced agents with global constraints, and advanced search to solve distributed constraint satisfaction problems (DisCSP), in particular distributed constraint optimization problems (DisCOP). DCP is a special form of constraint programming (CP), where variables belong to specific agents and can only be modified by their respective agents.

We differentiate DCP from DisCSP since DisCSP has traditionally assumed one variable per agent [18]. In contrast, we study the case where agents can control several variables, making it possible to use global constraints. Such constraints are often needed when solving complex CP problems, such as job shop scheduling problems (JSSP).

Using global constraints in DCP requires that each agents has its own constraint solver. Having a full solver in each agent also makes modeling and communication more efficient. As far as we know, no published work on DisCSP has studied global constraints. In earlier work, these constraints were transformed into equivalent primitive or table constraints. This led to inefficient solving and model representation.

There are two main contributions in this paper:

- We empower the individual agents with a full constraint solver; and
- We introduce an advanced search scheme.

A major advantage of each agent having a full solver is that we can create advanced search methods by adding constraints during search. In this paper, we study JSSP and

A. Bouchachia (Ed.): ICAIS 2011, LNAI 6943, pp. 320–331, 2011.

search that adds ordering-constraints before the actual assignments, significantly increasing the performance. We are not aware of any previous research on DisCSP that studies this type of search.

Formally, a constraint satisfaction problem (CSP) can be defined as a 3-tuple $P = (X, D, C)$, where X is a set of variables, D is a set of finite domains where D_i is the domain of x_i, and C is a set of primitive or global constraints containing several of the variables in X. Solving a CSP means finding assignments to X such that the value of $x_i \in D_i$, while all the constraints are satisfied. P is referred to as a constraint store.

Finding a valid assignment to a constraint satisfaction problem is usually accomplished by combining backtracking search with consistency checking that prunes inconsistent values. In every node of the search tree, a variable is assigned one of the values from its domain. Due to time-complexity issues, the consistency methods are rarely complete. Hence, the domains will contain values that are locally consistent, i.e., they will not be part of a solution, but we cannot prove this yet.

DisCSP, as used in [17], can be defined similarly to CSP with the 4-tuple $P = (A, X, D, C)$, where A is a set of agents and X is a set of variables so that $x_i \in a_i$. D is a set of finite domains, and C is a set of sets of *binary* constraints. Each variable x_i has a finite domain d_i, and each set of constraints c_{ij} connects two agents a_i and a_j, where $i \neq j$. Furthermore, each variable is controlled by exactly one agent. Lastly, the constraint network builds a connected graph. In other words, each agent is connected to another agent. Hence, there is at least one path from agent a_i to agent a_j.

Our model of DCP extends the DisCSP definition to a higher level. We retain the properties that a variable is controlled by exactly one agent, and that there is a path from any agent a_i to agent a_j. Now, however, X is a set of sets of variables, C is a set of sets of n-ary constraints, and D is a set of sets of finite domains. Every agent a_i has a set of variables x_i and a set of constraints c_i. In [13], a similar definition is introduced, but not expanded upon. In fact, we are not aware of anyone actually using the main advantage of having many variables per agent. The fact that our agents can have global constraints enables us to use the full power of modeling and pruning in CP.

In DCP, we can perform the consistency and search phase asynchronously [20]. First, we let each agent establish consistency internally, then send its prunings to the agents that are connected via constraints. Figure 1 depicts the structure of the constraint network for a small JSSP. Each agent holds two variables and ensures no overlap

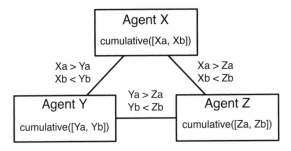

Fig. 1. Model of a distributed JSSP, where each agent holds several variables

between tasks via a cumulative constraint [2]. The constraints between agents are the precedence constraints, stated at the edges. Whenever a variable that is part of a connected constraint changes, the prunings will be propagated to the connected agents. Using our formal model, we, e.g., have $A = \{X, Y, Z\}$, $x_x = \{Xa, Xb\}$, $c_x = \{cumulative([Xa, Xb]), Xa > Ya, Xb < Yb\}$ and $c_{xy} = \{Xa > Ya, Xb < Yb\}$.

The rest of this paper is organized as follows. Section 2 introduces the background and the related work. In Section 3, our model of DCP with global constraints and advanced search is described. Section 4 describes our experiments and results. Finally, Section 5 gathers our conclusions.

2 Background and Related Work

Most work on DisCSP deals with the scenario where each agent holds a single variable and only binary constraints exist between the agents [18]. These problems are typically solved with an asynchronous search, where consistency is enforced between the connected agents [20]. One notable exception is [13]. However, that paper mentions neither global constraints nor advanced search methods.

The model of each agent only controlling one variable and only having binary constraints can technically be used to model any problem. However, even the latest search algorithms need to send a huge amount of messages to other agents [6] to solve such problems. This makes such a limited model less feasible when dealing with large or complex problems. This is especially problematic for optimization problems, since there is a greater need for search than for simple satisfiability problems.

One main difference between our model and previous work, such as [20,6,4,17,13], is that we can communicate entire domains. When a domain has been received, the prunings it carries are evaluated. This is much more efficient than sending one value from a domain at a time and getting a *Good* or *NoGood* message back.

Privacy is often used to motivate distribution of variables. Previous work, such as [21] shows that perfect privacy is possible for DisCSP. However, in the real world, complex encryption and minimal communication are impractical if they decrease performance too much. Our ultimate goal is to use our work for scheduling in autonomous unmanned aerial vehicles [9]. Hence, we focus more on performance than privacy.

A great limitation of previous work is that the problem model is usually translated into a table form [11]. These tables represent all possible assignments by the cartesian product of the domains in the constraint. For many problems, this representation is unfeasibly large [17]. In scheduling, a single cumulative constraint, ensuring no overlap of tasks [2], would have to be translated to binary constraints for every single time point. Even small scheduling problems would need thousands of constraints.

Many complex optimization problems need global constraints to solve in reasonable time. Some papers on DisCSP build advanced structures of agents. Others add a master-like agent that controls the global limits of the problem [12]. However, as far as we know, no one provides global constraints in each agent.

In order for DCP to solve large problems which are relevant to the real world, like JSSP, we need more advanced agents. Theoretically, one variable per agent is sufficient to model any DisCSP. However, just as global constraints can be reduced to binary constraints, the decreased pruning makes such an approach unrealistic for large optimization problems. This paper introduces agents with full constraint solvers, in order to make DCP feasible for industry use.

3   Distributed Solvers

Figure 2 depicts our model of DCP. Each agent holds a separate copy of the JaCoP solver [8], and only controls the variables that are needed for that part of the problem model. For instance, in JSSP, each agent holds the variables representing the tasks on the machine that the agent models. The precedence constraints between tasks assigned to different machines are stored in the connected constraints, since they constrain tasks controlled by different agents. This is how prunings are sent between agents.

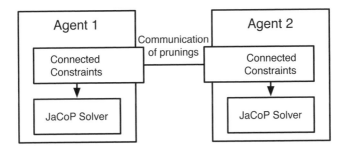

Fig. 2. Our model of DCP, each agent holds a full constraint solver

Figure 3 depicts a simplified view of the distributed constraint evaluation process and the search. All time consuming steps in our solving are parallel. As depicted in Fig. 3, the algorithm evaluates consistency and the agents vote on the next master in parallel. However, in order to guarantee synchronicity, the agents must wait for all prunings to be finished before they can move on to select the next master. Hence, the algorithm moves from synchronous to asynchronous execution of the agents, and back again, with every assignment.

When consistency is evaluated, all prunings are sent directly between the agents that are part of the connected constraint. Hence, the master agent is not controlling communication. It serves only to make an assignment decision and ensure that all agents are synchronized for the next step in the execution. The next step after an assignment may be to backtrack, or locate the next master, or to communicate a solution.

An example of the operations of our model is depicted in Fig. 4, which shows all execution steps. The execution progresses as follows.

1. When the solving is initialized, all agents start to run consistency of their constraints, see Fig. 4(a).
2. If there are changes to a variable that is in a connected constraint, those prunings are sent to the agent holding the other variable of the connected constraint, see Fig. 4(b). In this paper, we only study the case of binary constraints between agents.

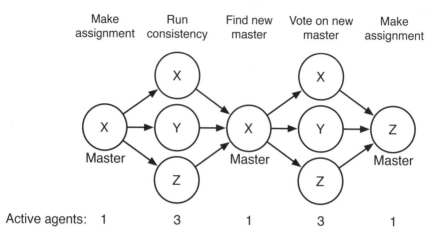

| Make
assignment | Run
consistency | Find new
master | Vote on new
master | Make
assignment |

Active agents: 1   3   1   3   1

Fig. 3. The progress from assignment to next assignment. X, Y, and Z are agents.

Each agent holds a queue of pruning messages, when changes have been received, consistency is again evaluated in the agent. This process continues iteratively until there are no more prunings sent between agents.

3. As soon as the consistency is finished, a negotiation determines which agent will start the search, see Fig. 4(c). This follows the principles of distributed election [5].
4. The agent holding the variable with the highest priority, defined by a user configurable heuristic, gets the master token, see Fig. 4(d)-(e). In this paper, we look at synchronized search. This means that only one agent holds the master token and only this master gets to make the next assignment decision.
5. The master makes an assignment and enforces consistency, see Fig. 4(f).
6. The master sends the prunings to the agents that have connected constraints containing changed variables, see Fig. 4(g).
7. When the agents receive prunings, they automatically run consistency, see Fig. 4(h).
8. When consistency has finished again, we are at the same position as in Fig. 4(c). We renegotiate which agent is to be the new master.

The procedure above continues until all variables have been assigned a value. When a master finds a solution, the cost of the solution can be shared amongst all agents by propagating it to all agents connected to the master. These agents then propagate it further, and so on, until all agents are aware of the solution cost. This is similar to the communication in [3]. Sharing solution costs is necessary in order to use branch and bound search.

If backtracking is necessary, we will undo the assignment leading to the inconsistency. If the current master has run out of possible assignments, it will send a message to the previous master telling it to backtrack. Hence, all agents that have been masters keep track of which agent was master before itself. Furthermore, since agents have several variables, an agent can become master several times in the same search tree branch. Agents therefore also need to keep track of backtracking to themselves.

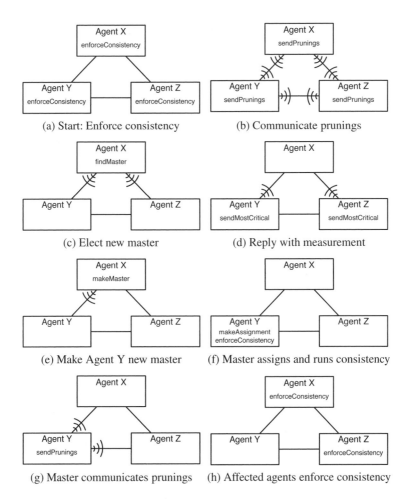

Fig. 4. The operating sequence for consistency and search in our model. The waves along the edges indicate communication.

The pseudo-code for our model is shown in Fig. 5. The `receive` method will be called automatically by the agent whenever a message has been received. Communication between agents are performed by similar syntax to that of [7]. All communication of costs is handled by connected constraints and is therefore controlled by the problem model. This gives great versatility to our model.

The biggest challenge in our distributed model is to detect that all agents are synchronous. For instance, detecting that consistency has reached a fixpoint and it is time to make the next assignment. That detection takes place in the handling of the message `Wait_For_Consistency`. Verifying whether agents are running and consistent can be done as for DisCSP, by using the process of [3].

```
 1  // variables controlled by the agent V
 2  // actors that participate in the problem A
 3
 4  receive(message) {
 5    switch (message.type) {
 6
 7      case Make_Master(oldMaster):
 8        master = true
 9        previousMaster = oldMaster
10        this ! Start_Search
11
12      case Start_Search:
13        v = selectionHeuristic.selectVariable
14        if (v == null)
15          storeSolution
16          this ! Backtrack
17        else
18          k = valueHeuristic.selectValue
19          store.makeAssignment(v, k)
20          this ! Enforce_Consistency
21
22      case Enforce_Consistency:
23        running = true
24        if (store.enforceConsistency)
25          forall (c in connectedConstraints)
26            forall (v in c.remoteVariables)
27              if (v.hasChanged)
28                v.remoteAgent !
29                  Pruning(v.name, v.domain)
30        else
31          consistent = false
32        if (master)
33          this ! Wait_For_Consistency
34        running = false
35
36      case Pruning(varName, domain):
37        v = store.findVariable(varName)
38        v.domain = domain
39        this ! Enforce_Consistency
```

(a)

```
 1  case Wait_For_Consistency:
 2    forall (a in A)
 3      if (a.isRunning)
 4        this ! Wait_For_Consistency
 5        return
 6    forall (a in A)
 7      if (a.inconsistent)
 8        this ! Backtrack
 9        return
10    this ! Select_Next_Master
11
12  case Backtrack:
13    store.forbidLastAssignment
14    store.undoLastAssignment
15    if (store.stillInconsistent)
16      previousMaster ! Backtrack
17    else
18      this ! Start_Search
19
20  case Select_Next_Master:
21    forall (a in A)
22      a ! Find_Best_Variable(this)
23
24  case Find_Best_Variable(theMaster):
25    v = selectionHeuristic.selectVariable
26    k = v.fitness
27    theMaster ! Fitness(k, this)
28
29  case Fitness(fitness, actor):
30    if (fitness > bestFitness)
31      bestFitness = fitness
32      bestActor = actor
33    fitnessReplies += 1
34    if (fitnessReplies == A.size)
35      master = false
36      bestActor ! Make_Master(this)
37  }
38 }
```

(b)

Fig. 5. The pseudo-code for the agents. The receive method is called whenever a message arrives. An exclamation mark indicates communication to an agent.

3.1 Advanced Search in Distributed Constraint Programming

In order to solve complex JSSP, we need the more advanced search that is made possible by our model. The algorithm presented in Fig. 5 is somewhat simplified. For JSSPs, we use a sequence of two search methods. The first orders the tasks on each machine by adding precedence constraints. The second assigns actual start times for each task. This is based on the principles described in [1]. While some problems may solve without the ordering, many require an ordering to solve in reasonable time.

Figure 6 depicts the algorithm for the ordering search. During the ordering, the machine with the least slack in the tasks scheduled on it is selected. Then we pick the task, running on that machine, with the smallest start time. Finally, we impose that the selected task has to execute before the other tasks on that machine, and we remove it from the list used to calculate slack. This procedure is repeated recursively.

This type of advanced search is not possible in all DisCSP solvers. Many DisCSP solvers cannot impose constraints during the search. Even solvers that can impose new constraints, are often limited by mostly supporting table constraints [11]. If only table

```
1  // M is a vector of vectors representing tasks assigned
2  // to a machine. Each task is specified by its starting
3  // task start time t, task duration d
4
5  boolean Jobshop_Search(M)
6    if store.enforceConsistency
7      if M ≠ ∅
8        m ← selectCriticalMachine(M)
9        sort tasks in m in ascending values of t.min()
10       for each i = 1, ..., n
11         for each j = 1, ..., n
12           if (i ≠ j)
13             impose mᵢ.t + mᵢ.d ≤ mⱼ.t
14       M' ← M \ mᵢ
15       if Jobshop_Search(M')
16         return true
17       else
18         return false
19         return false
20     else
21       store solution
22       return true
23   else
24     return false
25
26 vector selectCriticalMachine(M)
27   for each mᵢ ∈ M
28     min ← min(min(mᵢ.t₀), min(mᵢ.t₁), ..., min(mᵢ.tₙ))
29     max ← max(max(mᵢ.t₀ + mᵢ.d₀), max(mᵢ.t₁ + mᵢ.d₁), ...,
30               max(mᵢ.tₙ + mᵢ.dₙ))
31     supply ← max − min
32     demand ← ∑ mᵢ.dᵢ
33     critical ← supply − demand
34   return machine mᵢ with the lowest value of critical
```

Fig. 6. The code for the ordering search

constraints are supported, the memory use of the solver will increase greatly whenever new constraints are imposed for every time unit of the schedule.

4 Experimental Evaluation

For our experiments, we used the JaCoP solver [8]. The agent system is written using actors in Scala [14]. The experiments were run on a Mac Pro with two 3.2 GHz quad-core Intel Xeon processors running Mac OS X 10.6.2 with Java 6 and Scala 2.8.1. These two processors have a common cache and memory bus for each of their four cores. The parallel version of our solver is described in detail in [16]. We used a timeout of 30 minutes for all the experiments. All experiments were run 20 times, giving a standard deviation of less than 5 %.

We ran several standard benchmark scheduling problems described in [19,10]. The characteristics of the problems are listed in Table 1. These are all JSSP, where n jobs with m tasks are to be scheduled on m different machines. We study the case of non-preemptive scheduling.

We created two DisCOP models of each problem: one for our version of DCP with global constraints, and the other representing the traditional case with only primitive

Table 1. Characteristics of the problems for the global constraint model

Problem	Jobs	Tasks	Variables	Constraints	Optimum
LA01	10	5	61	56	666
LA04	10	5	61	56	590
LA05	10	5	61	56	593
MT06	6	6	43	43	55

constraints. When using our model, each agent represents one machine. It contains one global cumulative constraint with n tasks [2], to ensure no overlap of tasks.

In the primitive model, each agent represents one variable. For the problems we studied, the primitive constraints are binary in the sense that they only contain two variables. Our primitive constraint models did not use table constraints. Instead, they used the constraint $start_i + duration_i \leq start_j \vee start_j + duration_j \leq start_i$ for every pair of tasks, to ensure no overlap. This constraint is technically a binary constraints, since the duration is a constant. These primitive constraints can replace cumulative for JSSP since we only have one instance of each resource.

Each problem was started with no prior knowledge of the optimal solution. Hence, the domains of the variables representing the start time tasks were $\{0..1000\}$. When using many resources, translating a single cumulative constraint into table constraint requires primitive constraints in every time point. For many problems, this could result in an excessive number of rows in the table constraint. This is often infeasible due to memory size.

4.1 Experimental Results

The results for finding and proving the the optimal solution are shown in Table 2 and Table 3. Clearly, the primitive representation of the problems rarely found the optimal within the 30 minute timeout. The only exception was MT06, the simplest problem we tested. Still, finding the solution for MT06 took almost 30 times as long as the global model.

Table 2. Execution time in seconds that the global constraint model took to find the optimal solution and the best solution found within the 30 minute timeout

Problem	Time to find optimum	Time to prove optimum	Solution
LA01, Global	3.8	4.0	666
LA04, Global	10.8	12.1	590
LA05, Global	0.7	0.97	593
MT06, Global	3.0	3.0	55

Table 3. Execution time in seconds that the primitive constraint model took to find the optimal solution and the best solution found within the 30 minute timeout

Problem	Time to find optimum	Time to prove optimum	Solution
LA01, Primitive	Timeout	Timeout	936
LA04, Primitive	Timeout	Timeout	976
LA05, Primitive	Timeout	Timeout	720
MT06, Primitive	87.7	Timeout	55

Our model of DCP with global constraints in each agent gives superior performance in our experiments. The traditional model with only one variable per agent never managed to prove the optimality within the timeout. This performance increase comes partly from the fact that we can order variables before we start search. When agents control only one variable, this type of ordering is not possible. In this case, adding the ordering constraints will mostly serve to increase the number of pruning messages that need to be sent.

When we turn off the ordering of tasks, the performance drops significantly for the global model. However, even though we could not prove optimality without ordering, we found better solutions within the timeout than the primitive model for almost all problems. Hence, the benefit of our model is not simply in the use of advanced search, but also in the use of global constraints.

Although our search is synchronous, using asynchronous search would probably not benefit the traditional primitive model much. Our model would probably still be better, because in our experiments we use a simulated distribution, thus minimizing the penalty of sending many messages. The primitive model communicates many more messages to reach the consistency fixpoint. When using a network, the communication would be an order of magnitude more time consuming than on a shared-memory multicore machine.

Using asynchronous search would bring benefits to both the global constraint model and the primitive one. However, the search space of CP is exponential with regard to domain size. Parallel search only gives a polynomial speed-up [15]. Hence the performance advantage of the global constraint model is likely to remain, even though the model with one variable per agent allows for more parallelism.

We also created a third model, where each agent control several variables, but have no global constraints. Just as for the global representation, each agent models one machine. However, the cumulative constraint has been replaced by the same kind of constraints as in the primitive model for every pair of tasks.

The performance of this third model, shown in Table 4, was better than that of the single variable per agent model. However, the performance was usually much lower than of the global constraint representation. For the simplest problem it was slightly faster. But for the most difficult problem, it did not find the optimum within the timeout.

The performance benefit of our model of DCP is not simply because of our advanced search. The ordering of tasks on each machine is possible in the model with several variables per agent but without global constraints. However, the pruning is much weaker when there are no global constraints.

Our results for the model in Table 4, compared to the results in Table 3, illustrate the cost of communication. We get much better performance than the scenario of one variable per agent, despite using the same constraints. Hence, the difference between the performance of these two models comes mostly from the communication of prunings.

The cost of communication depends on the agent framework. However, we ran our experiments on a shared-memory machine. Running on a cluster, with network communication, would increase the performance penalty of communication severely. If anything, our experiments over estimate the competitiveness of traditional DisCSP models.

Table 4. Results for multi-variable agents, *without* global constraints, but *with* ordering

Problem	Time to find optimum	Time to prove optimum	Best Solution
LA01	3.8	6.9	666
LA04	Timeout	Timeout	667
LA05	0.47	9.7	593
MT06	2.5	2.6	55

5 Conclusions

In this paper, we have introduced a completely new model of distributed constraint programming. Unlike any work we are aware of, we equip each agent with a full constraint solver. Our model is the the only one we have seen published that can use global constraints. It also allows advanced search, during which we can order tasks before assigning actual start times of scheduling problems.

By equipping each agent with a full constraint solver, we allow much more efficient modeling of problems. Unlike most work on DisCSP, we do not translate our models into table constraints. This allows us to communicate domains and constraints between agents during the search. Such communication is much more efficient than that of traditional DisCSP. Reducing communication is a major concern in DisCSP solving.

Our main conclusion of this paper is that both global constraints and advanced search are needed in order to solve complex scheduling problems using distributed constraint programming. Traditional work on DisCSP has focused on agents that only control one variable and only have primitive constraints. We conclude that these older models are unlikely to offer good performance for real world use, even when using asynchronous search.

Another conclusion is that using the traditional approach to DisCSP of one variable per agent should be very well motivated. Using one variable per agent may provide better robustness and privacy. However, we show that letting agents control several variables, using global constraints, and using advanced search methods are all important for good performance.

References

1. Baptiste, P., Pape, C.L., Nuijten, W.: Constraint-Based Scheduling. Kluwer Academic Publishers, USA (2001)
2. Caseau, Y., Laburthe, F.: Improving branch and bound for jobshop scheduling with constraint propagation. In: Combinatorics and Computer Science, pp. 129–149 (1995)
3. Chandy, K.M., Lamport, L.: Distributed snapshots: determining global states of distributed systems. ACM Trans. Comput. Syst. 3, 63–75 (1985)
4. Ezzahir, R., Bessiere, C., Belaissaoui, M., Bouyakhf, E.: DisChoco: A platform for distributed constraint programming. In: Proceedings of the IJCAI 2007 Distributed Constraint Reasoning Workshop (DCR 2007), pp. 16–27 (2007)
5. Gallager, R.G., Humblet, P.A., Spira, P.M.: A distributed algorithm for minimum-weight spanning trees. ACM Trans. Program. Lang. Syst. 5, 66–77 (1983)
6. Gershman, A., Meisels, A., Zivan, R.: Asynchronous forward bounding for distributed COPs. Journal of Artificial Intelligence Research 34, 61–88 (2010)
7. Hoare, C.A.R.: Communicating sequential processes. Commun. ACM 21, 666–677 (1978)
8. Kuchcinski, K.: Constraints-driven scheduling and resource assignment. ACM Transactions on Design Automation of Electronic Systems (TODAES) 8(3), 355–383 (2003)
9. Kvarnstrom, J., Doherty, P.: Automated planning for collaborative UAV systems. In: 11th International Conference on Control Automation Robotics Vision, pp. 1078–1085 (2010)
10. Lawrence, S.R.: Resource-constrained project scheduling: An experimental investigation of heuristic scheduling techniques. Graduate School of Industrial Administration, Carnegie-Mellon University, Pittsburgh PA (1984)
11. Léauté, T., Ottens, B., Szymanek, R.: FRODO 2.0: An open-source framework for distributed constraint optimization. In: Proceedings of the IJCAI 2009 Distributed Constraint Reasoning Workshop (DCR 2009), pp. 160–164 (2009)
12. Meisels, A., Kaplansky, E.: Scheduling agents – distributed timetabling problems(DisTTP). In: Burke, E.K., De Causmaecker, P. (eds.) PATAT 2002. LNCS, vol. 2740, pp. 166–177. Springer, Heidelberg (2003)
13. Meisels, A., Zivan, R.: Asynchronous forward-checking for DisCSPs. Constraints 12, 131–150 (2007)
14. Odersky, M., Spoon, L., Venners, B.: Programming in Scala: A Comprehensive Step-by-step Guide, 1st edn. Artima Incorporation, USA (2008)
15. Rao, V. N., Kumar, V.: Superlinear speedup in parallel state-space search. In: Kumar, S., Nori, K.V. (eds.) FSTTCS 1988. LNCS, vol. 338, pp. 161–174. Springer, Heidelberg (1988)
16. Rolf, C.C., Kuchcinski, K.: Load-balancing methods for parallel and distributed constraint solving. In: The 10th IEEE International Conference on Cluster Computing, pp. 304–309 (2008)
17. Rossi, F., van Beek, P., Walsh, T.: Handbook of Constraint Programming (Foundations of Artificial Intelligence). Elsevier Science Inc., New York (2006)
18. Salido, M.: Distributed cSPs: Why it is assumed a variable per agent? In: Miguel, I., Ruml, W. (eds.) SARA 2007. LNCS (LNAI), vol. 4612, pp. 407–408. Springer, Heidelberg (2007)
19. Thompson, G.L.: Industrial scheduling. In: Muth, J.F., Thompson, G.L. (eds.) Collaboration of P.R. Winters. Prentice-Hall, Englewood Cliffs (1963)
20. Yokoo, M., Hirayama, K.: Algorithms for distributed constraint satisfaction: A review. Autonomous Agents and Multi-Agent Systems 3(2), 185–207 (2000)
21. Yokoo, M., Suzuki, K., Hirayama, K.: Secure distributed constraint satisfaction: Reaching agreement without revealing private information. In: Van Hentenryck, P. (ed.) CP 2002. LNCS, vol. 2470, pp. 43–66. Springer, Heidelberg (2002)

A Combinatorial Auction Negotiation Protocol for Time-Restricted Group Decisions

Fabian Lang and Andreas Fink

Helmut Schmidt University Hamburg, Germany

Abstract. This paper focuses on multi-agent contract formation by automated negotiation. Commonly individuals are not willing to share information or cooperate and negotiation protocols may give way to unwanted strategic behavior. Socially beneficial contract agreements require a lot of negotiation time. Furthermore, possible interdependencies of contract items lead to complex contract spaces which restrain contract agreements. Therefore, we propose a novel negotiation protocol applying combinatorial auctions for contract formation which consider interdependencies and yield a rapid decision rights allocation. Additionally, this market-based approach utilizes Vickrey-Clarkes-Groves-mechanisms which may lead to truthful preference uncovering and information sharing through bids. However, combinatorial auctions have a computational drawback: winner determination is $\mathcal{NP}$-hard. In simulation experiments, two approximation algorithms as well as an optimal computation are tested in comparison with an established negotiation protocol. The results show that our protocol yields an effective solution and requires very short run time.

1 Introduction

Multi-agent technology is a growing field in artificial intelligence research and practice. Automated negotiation between digital agents is considered to be one of the most effective tools for multi-agent coordination [6] and represents a multi-agent application discipline by itself [14]. Multi-issue contracts are often characterized by interdependencies, i.e., agents have different utilities for several items in combination than for those items on their own [8]. For instance, processing speed of a data package depends on the fact whether another one has to be processed simultaneously or not using the very same computing instance. When simultaneously computed, both data packages have a lower utility than their sole processing due to scarcer resources. These interdependencies lead to complex contracts which are characterized by non-linearity. This may result in a stagnation of the negotiation process due to individual local optima. However, these local optima often constitute a Pareto-suboptimal outcome, i.e., an agent can improve its outcome without worsening anyone else. Besides, there are some incentives issues as well: Since autonomous agents do not share information about their preferences voluntarily, protocols also have to consider behavioral issues [11]. Moreover, multi-agent coordination on an operational level is typically

A. Bouchachia (Ed.): ICAIS 2011, LNAI 6943, pp. 332–343, 2011.

characterized by a multitude of decisions with restricted decision time. Thus, runtime might be a crucial factor for protocol design. For example, job allocation in Cloud computing, machine coordination in production, or other real-time coordination tasks have very limited available time for decision making.

This research presents and evaluates a combinatorial auction based negotiation protocol with the aim of achieving incentive compatible, beneficial (in terms of welfare), and run-time efficient outcomes. We expect that the proposed protocol is adequate for these objectives and can contribute to the coordination of autonomous agents.

2   Scenario and Objectives

2.1   Formal Scenario

Within a multi-agent setting, the agents $j \in \{\mathbb{N}|0 \leq j < J\}$ negotiate about a common contract $c = \{d_0, \ldots, d_n, \ldots, d_{N-1}\}$. This contract comprises N items which can take binary values, i.e., the decision about an issue or item $n \in \{\mathbb{N}|0 \leq n < N\}$ is $d(n) \in \{0, 1\}$. The utility of an accepted (i.e., value of 1) single item P_j is distributed equally over the interval $\mathcal{U}[-100; 100]$ and their utility is given by the values of the main diagonal of a matrix. To address the problem of non-linearity, the items are mutually interdependent. Thus, a utility mark-up or mark-down for a pair of accepted items p and q is calculated as follows:

$$P_j(p, q) = (P_j(p, p) + P_j(q, q)) * (1 + \omega_{pq}) \quad \text{with } \omega_{pq} \in [-\alpha; \alpha] \qquad (1)$$

Economically speaking, the scenario contains complementary (superadditivity) and substitute (subadditivity) pairs. The utility of a contract c is calculated by

$$U_j(c) = \sum_{p=0}^{N-1} \sum_{q=p}^{N-1} P_j(p, q) * d(p) * d(q) \qquad (2)$$

If the utility of agent j in the final contract c is negative ($U_j(c) < 0$), the agent has an outside option and finishes the negotiation with a utility of zero ($U_j(c) \leftarrow 0$). This restriction is commonly referred to as *individual rationality constraint (IRC)* [2].

2.2   Objectives

Firstly, a negotiation protocol should yield a desirable **social outcome**. Fast decisions shall lead to beneficial contracts. Since transferable cardinal utility values are supposed, we propose the social welfare, which aggregates the utilities of all agent, as performance index. The social welfare is a restrictive criterion constituting a subset of Pareto-efficient outcomes. The social welfare SW of a contract c is calculated by

$$SW(c) = \sum_{j=0}^{J-1} U_j(c) \qquad (3)$$

Secondly, a protocol shall have **short run-time** characteristics to ensure real-time coordination of multi-agent systems. Many computer science applications as well as operational business planing need nearly real-time decision making. Therefore, we assume very constrained decision time for contract formation. Thirdly, a protocol has to warrant **individual rationality and incentive compatibility** to ensure strategy-proofness and prevent malicious behavior worsening the social outcome.

3   Negotiation Protocols

3.1   Combinatorial Auction Protocol (CA-P)

The CA-P is based upon the idea of allocating decision rights to single agents. As the items are interdependent, common (single-item) auctions are not appropriate. The combinatorial auction (CA) is more suited because agents can bid on combinations of goods (here: decision rights).

The concept of the proposed CA-P is novel because the auction does not allocate goods but decision rights. These rights are exercised to form a contract. Usually, this contract affects all agents – not only for the auction's winners. In contrast, in a common auction the goods just affect the winning parties and hence there are no *externalities*. In our case, the utilities of the agents are determined not only by their own decision right bundles but also by the bundles of other agents.

1: **procedure** CA-P   ▷ **Combinatorial Auction Protocol**
2:     $B = \{B_0, \ldots, B_i, \ldots, B_{I-1}\} \leftarrow ReceiveBids()$ ▷ $B_i = \{S_i, p_i, id_i\}$
3:     $w = \{w_0, \ldots, w_n, \ldots, w_{N-1}\} \leftarrow SolveWDP(B)$
4:     **for all** $j \in \{\mathbb{N}|0 \leq j < J\}$ **do**
5:         $VickreyPrice_j \leftarrow ComputeVCG(SolveWDP(B \setminus B_i|id_i = j))$
6:     **end for**
7:     $c = \{d_0, \ldots, d_n, \ldots, d_{N-1}\} \leftarrow Decide(w)$
8: **end procedure**

At first, the agents submit their bids B consisting of a set of contract items S_i, a bid price p_i, and a bidder identification id_i. If their valuation is positive, the bidders will be willing to bid just as much as their valuation. If the valuation is negative, the bidders will be willing to bid as much as their absolute value of their valuation to prevent utility losses (bidder's opportunity costs for losing the auction) so that $p_i = |P_{j|j=id_i}(p, q)|$ $(p, q \in S_i)$. In the next step, the winner determination problem (WDP) is solved and a winner w_n of the decision right is assigned for every item n. Afterwards, this has to be repeated for every agent under the supposition that this agent would not participate in the auction resulting in the Vickrey-prices needed for incentive compatibility (see following subsection). As the auction's revenue can be redistributed from the auctioneer to the agents, the social welfare stays unaffected and payments can be disregarded. Finally, the winners decide about the contract items $(d_n = 1 \vee d_n = 0)$ meaning that the allocated decision rights are exercised. In the end, these decisions form the final contract $c = \{d_0, \ldots, d_n, \ldots, d_{N-1}\}$.

Complexity and Incentive Compatibility. The proposed CA-P has computational drawbacks: as an instance of the *weighted set packing problem*, the occurring *winner determination problem (WDP)* is $\mathcal{NP}$-hard [13]. However, CAs have also some very favorable features: Based on bidding prices, it can reveal cardinal information about utility dimensions of the agents although agents have no incentives to set their private information about their preferences free. Furthermore, CAs can utilize a Vickrey-Clarke-Groves-mechanism (VCG) which is a multi-item generalization of the Vickrey-Auction (Second Price Sealed Bid Auction). In a Vickrey-Auction the winner pays the price which would have occurred without her or his participation (second price). Hence, the bidders cannot improve their outcome with strategic bidding so that truthful bidding is the single dominant strategy (incentive compatibility) [16][10]. The payout function π_j is as follows (b_j is the bidding price of agent j whereas $max(b_{-j})$ is the highest bidding price of the other agents, v_j represents the valuation of agent j):

$$\pi_j = \begin{cases} v_j - max(b_{-j}) & \text{if } b_j > max(b_{-j}) \\ 0 & \text{else} \end{cases} \quad (4)$$

No strategy, be it overbidding $(b_j > v_j)$ or underbidding $(b_j < v_j)$, can improve the bidder's outcome in comparison to the optimal strategy $b_j^* = v_j$. Overbidding can lead to the situation $b_j > max(b_{-j}) > v_j$ causing a loss in the amount of $max(b_{-j}) - v_j$, whereas underbidding is inferior in case of $v_j > max(b_{-j}) > b_j$ preventing a gain in the amount of $v_j - max(b_{-j})$.

To guarantee short computing times, heuristics for the WDP may have to be used. Therefore, two constructive methods with suitable runtime characteristics will be presented later on. However, the usage of heuristics may lead to incentive incompatibility. As Nisan and Ronen [12] show, any approximative allocation algorithm, and hence every reasonable algorithm, theoretically leads to non-truthful bids. However, since valuations and bid prices are privately known, the agents have practically no information about how to alter their bids, so that an improving deviation may be hard to achieve. We argue that non-truthful agents would suffer a loss without information about the preferences about other agents because the dominant strategy may not be discoverable. This opinion is widespread in literature. In this manner, Lehmann et al. [9] state as well that approximate algorithms, e.g. the Greedy algorithm, are essentially truthful if agents do not have sufficient resources or information to analyze the global situation.

Agent Behavior. On the whole, the agents determine two actions: bidding and deciding about won contract items. For the former, we have argued in the previous subsection that agents behave truthfully in practical applications.

For the latter, we applied a heuristic decision rule:

$$d_n = \begin{cases} 1 & P_j(n,n) \geq 0 \\ 0 & P_j(n,n) < 0 \end{cases} \quad \forall n | w_n = j \tag{5}$$

with w_n: winner of item n

Using this decision function the interdependencies are disregarded due to partially unknown information about the other decisions. Since the values of most decision are not available (they are mainly decided by the other agents), the agents just focus on single items. We also have tested an internal optimization problem where agents set up expectations about the decision of the other agents but experiments revealed that this method has a very small positive effect on social welfare but demands more decision time. By limiting the decision time, software agents can be forced to adopt this heuristic decision function for applications with very restrictive time constraints.

Solving the Winner Determination Problem (WDP). A mathematical solver and two constructive heuristics were used to solve the WDP:

1. Mathematical Solver (CPLEX). A mathematical model, proposed by Sandholm et al. [15], was implemented using the CPLEX solver and connected with an interface to the simulation software. The decision right allocation is optimal so that this procedure is incentive compatible. The model was solved by using the following integer program (with x_i: allocation variable):

$$\max_{x_i} \sum_{i=0}^{I-1} p_i * x_i \tag{6}$$

$$s.t. \sum_{i|n \in S_i}^{I-1} x_i \leq 1 \quad \forall n \in \{\mathbb{N}|0 \leq n < N\}, \quad x_i \in \{0,1\}$$

2. Greedy Randomized Adaptive Search Procedure (GRASP). GRASP is an iterative construction heuristic which has been used by several researchers as an approach to solve the WDP effectively (see Buer and Pankratz [1] or Delorme [3]; for GRASP in general see Feo and Resende [4]).

```
 1: procedure GRASP        ▷ Greedy Randomized Adaptive Search Procedure
 2:     for all S do
 3:         B_i^* ← argmax_{p_i}(B_i = {S_i, p_i, id_i})
 4:     end for
 5:     for all τ = {0, 1, ..., T^G − 1} do
 6:         R ← SortByPricePerItem(B^*)
 7:         while R ≠ ∅ do
 8:             if |R| ≤ l then
 9:                 l ← |R|
10:             end if
11:             Clist ← {R[0], ..., R[l − 1]}
12:             InBid ← ChooseRandomly(Clist)
13:             if ItemAlloc_τ ∩ (S ∈ InBid) = ∅ then
14:                 BidAlloc_τ ← BidAlloc_τ ∪ InBid
15:                 ItemAlloc_τ ← ItemAlloc_τ ∪ S ∈ InBid
16:             end if
17:             R ← R \ InBid
18:         end while
19:         BidAlloc^* ← argmax_{Revenue} Revenue(BidAlloc_{τ={0,...,T^G−1}})
20:     end for
21: end procedure
```

Firstly, the algorithm chooses the dominating bids B_i^* by selecting the highest bid price p_i for a given item bundle S_i among the bidders. Afterwards, it orders the bids by a priority rule (here: bid price per item) resulting in a ranking R. Then the algorithm creates a candidate list $Clist$ with the l highest ranked bids in R. An entering bid In is randomly chosen from the l candidates and it is checked if the items of this bid are already allocated. If not, the bid enters the allocation. In is then removed from R. This procedure is repeated until all items are allocated. The GRASP algorithm as a whole is repeated several times ($\tau \in \{0, 1, \ldots, T^G − 1\}$) and the best solution yields the actual allocation (BidAlloc*).

3. Greedy Algorithm (GA). We regard the GA as a special instance of the GRASP algorithm. The results are identical if the candidate list length l is set to one. Since there is no randomness, results are stable and repetition is not necessary. The GA deploys a simple procedure: The bids are sorted by descending bids per item. Starting with the first ranked bid, the bids are designated as winning bids in the descending order unless a bid would lead to an unfeasible allocation. By this means, the GA delivers a feasible approximation in a very short time. A more detailed description of the GA for the solution of CAs is given, among others, by Zurel and Nisan [17].

3.2   Mediated Negotiation Protocol (MN-P)

Mediated negotiation protocols are often mentioned as possible negotiation frameworks. A non-biased mediator manages the negotiation process and determines and monitors the protocol rules. Here, a concept initially proposed by Klein et al. [7] (updated version: [8]) and enhanced by Fink [5] is presented and used as benchmark.

1: **procedure** MN-P $\qquad\qquad\qquad$ ▷ **Mediated Negotiation Protocol**
2: $\quad c_0^* \leftarrow GenerateInitialContract$
3: $\quad$ **for all** $t = \{0, 1, \ldots, T-1\}$ **do**
4: $\quad\quad c_t' \leftarrow Mutate(c_t^*)$
5: $\quad\quad$ **for all** $j \in \{\mathbb{N} | 0 \leq j < J\}$ **do**
6: $\quad\quad\quad Z_j \leftarrow AcceptOrReject(c_t', c_t^*, j)$
7: $\quad\quad$ **end for**
8: $\quad\quad$ **if** $\sum\limits_{j=0}^{J-1} Z_j = J$ **then**
9: $\quad\quad\quad c_{t+1}^* \leftarrow c_t'$
10: $\quad\quad$ **else** $c_{t+1}^* \leftarrow c_t^*$
11: $\quad\quad$ **end if**
12: $\quad$ **end for**
13: $\quad c \leftarrow c_{T-1}^*$
14: **end procedure**

The mediator generates randomly an initial contract which becomes the first contract draft (c_t^*). Afterwards, the mediator mutates one (or more) item(s) of this contract draft resulting in a new contract proposal c_t'. Thereafter, every agent j compares this proposal with the contract draft and decides whether the proposal should be accepted or rejected ($Z_j \in \{1, 0\}$). If all agents accept, the proposal becomes the current contract draft and the iteration starts over. Finally, the accepted contract draft of the last round c_{T-1}^* becomes the final contract c.

Agent Behavior. Klein et al. [8] present two agent types with specific behavior properties. The first one is the avaricious agent (AvA). The AvA acts opportunistically and is myopically interested in its utility maximization. Therefore, the acceptance function is designed accordingly:

$$Z_j = \begin{cases} 1, U_j(c_t') \geq U_j(c_t^*) \\ 0, U_j(c_t') < U_j(c_t^*) \end{cases} \tag{7}$$

The second type is the cooperative agent (CoA). In contrast to the AvA, the CoA acts accommodative and is willing to facilitate its negotiation counterparts by partially supporting contracts with an individual worse outcome. The acceptance function is assumed to be designed like the Metropolis criterion that is used in simulated annealing metaheuristic, i.e., the CoA is willing to accept contracts with a small deterioration but this willingness declines over time using a decreasing parameter TE_t:

$$Z_j = \begin{cases} 1, U_j(c'_t) \geq U_j(c^*_t) \vee e^{-[U_j(c^*_t) - U_j(c'_t)]/TE_t} \geq \mathcal{U}(0,1) \\ 0, U_j(c'_t) < U_j(c^*_t) \vee e^{-[U_j(c^*_t) - U_j(c'_t)]/TE_t} < \mathcal{U}(0,1) \end{cases} \quad (8)$$

A Mechanism Design Extension. Having the two behavior types in mind, we can compare the outcomes of two negotiating agents ($j = 1, 2$) by means of game theory. Given two players, who can act avariciously or cooperatively, the strategy set of the players is represented by $\{strategy_1, strategy_2\}$. As repeatedly shown in literature, the social welfare of the strategy set $\{CoA, CoA\}$ can be near optimal and we suppose this as our point of origin. Unfortunately, being avaricious is individually beneficial when meeting a cooperative agent, so player 1 prefers $\{AvA, CoA\}$ to $\{CoA, CoA\}$. The opposed player can do better by becoming avaricious as well because player 2 prefers $\{AvA, AvA\}$ to $\{AvA, CoA\}$. In the end, no-one would individually deviate from the strategy set $\{AvA, AvA\}$ which constitutes the Nash equilibrium and the social welfare minimum. This game is an instance of the famous prisoner's dilemma [8][5].

To prevent this malicious behavior, adequate mechanisms have to be in place. We propose a mechanism design extension of the protocol based on acceptance quotas (previously presented in [5]). The mechanism aims for agents accepting a certain ratio of contract proposals and hence can overcome local optima. Therefore, we propose that a mediator specifies certain acceptance quotas $p = \{p_1, \ldots, p_\gamma, \ldots, p_\Gamma\}$ (with $p_1 > p_2 > \cdots > p_\Gamma$) for Γ different phases of the negotiation. For instance, we could demand $p_1 = 30.0\%$ accepted proposals for the first 1000 negotiation round and $p_2 = 29.5\%$ for the next thousand and so on. By doing so, the agents are forced to apply a strategy taking these quotas into account. Since the strategy of the presented cooperative type (CoA) is reasonable, we assume that the agents act in this manner. For the application of the Metropolis criterion, a cooling schedule is needed. The agents determine their cooling schedules so that they are can fulfill the acceptance quotas. In each phase γ (e.g. lasting 1,000 rounds), the agents repeatedly (e.g. every 100 rounds) compare their acceptance quotas to the exogenous quotas and increase (if acceptance is below mandatory quota at this point) or decrease (if acceptance is above mandatory quota at this point) their temperature TE_t accordingly.

4   Simulation Results

In the following section the results of our experimental simulations are presented and discussed. For the simulations, 1,000 different preference data sets were created and tested. The additivity variable ω_{pq} is supposed to be normally distributed with $\omega_{pq} \sim \mathcal{N}(\mu = 0.2; \sigma = 0.1)|\omega_{pq} > 0$. The protocols were simulated for three and seven agents considering 25, 50, and 100 contract items. The simulations took between a few milliseconds and several seconds using a common, but state-of-the-art, personal computer. The GRASP algorithm was applied with 100 repetitions. Usually, the algorithm is repeated multiple times of this, but we chose this small quantity to fulfill runtime criteria.

Table 1. Auction Revenue

N	J=3		J=7	
	Greedy	GRASP	Greedy	GRASP
25	96.6%	97.8%	98.0%	99.0%
50	96.6%	97.4%	97.9%	98.5%
100	96.7%	97.2%	97.9%	98.3%

3 agents on the left and 7 agents on the right. CPLEX represents 100%.

Table 1 shows the revenue of the auction which is the objective of the auctioneer. The GRASP algorithm reaches a little more revenue compared to the Greedy algorithm. Both perform about 1-3 percent worse than the optimal solution computed with the CPLEX solver. The heuristics perform relatively better with 7 agents than with 3 agents. The results of the Greedy algorithm are stable over rising item numbers yet the GRASP results decline with rising item numbers.

Table 2. Relative Performances of the Combinatorial Auction

N	CA-P CPLEX		CA-P Greedy		CA-P GRASP	
25	76.6%	57.8%	76.5%	57.9%	76.5%	58.0%
50	76.2%	55.7%	76.0%	55.8%	75.9%	55.8%
100	76.4%	56.4%	76.1%	56.4%	76.2%	56.6%

3 agents on the left and 7 agents on the right. Welfare optimum represents 100%.

At first, we examine the Combinatorial Auction Protocol (CA-P). The auction allocates the decision rights to the agents and they exercise these rights. Table 2 shows the social welfare of the formed contract after the decisions of the agents. The social welfare is represented by the mean of the results in relation to the theoretical welfare optimum. This optimum can be computed by assuming knowledge of an aggregated social welfare function. Because the agents just have private information, this function is unknown to the agents.

Notably, all three winner determination methods yield similar welfares results. The social welfare decreases slightly with rising item and significantly with rising agent quantity. These findings are to be expected because the negotiation is more complex with longer contracts and more participants. Whereas the performance is relatively stable with fewer agents, the deterioration due to more contract items is stronger when more agents participate in the negotiation.

Since all three methods yield similar social welfare results, runtime becomes a major criterion of the evaluation. Table 3 represents the runtimes of the three

Table 3. Relative Runtime of the Combinatorial Auction

N	CA-P CPLEX		CA-P Greedy		CA-P GRASP	
25	188	156	1	1	47	33
50	54	39	1	1	53	43
100	32	25	1	1	60	52

3 agents on the left and 7 agents on the right. Greedy algorithm represents 1.

winner determination methods as a multiple of the fasted heuristic, the Greedy algorithm. Both, the exact method and the GRASP algorithm, need from 25 to 188 times of the runtime of the Greedy algorithm. The optimal solution with CPLEX becomes relatively faster with increasing items and agents quantity whereas the GRASP algorithm even demands more runtime than for small instances. As an interim result, the Greedy algorithm outperforms the other method in terms of runtime but achieves comparable results in terms of social welfare. Therefore, the Greedy algorithm appears to be a dominant method for the problem set presented in this paper.

Table 4. Relative Performances of the Mediated Negotiation

N	CA-P Greedy		MN-P w/ Quotas		MN-P w/o Quotas	
25	76.5%	57.9%	79.3%	66.3%	46.2%	28.0%
50	76.0%	55.8%	76.0%	57.7%	43.2%	20.6%
100	76.1%	56.4%	67.8%	44.9%	41.6%	15.6%

3 agents on the left and 7 agents on the right. Welfare optimum represents 100%.

To validate the protocol externally, we introduced the Mediated Negotiation Protocol (MN-P) with two potential agent types – the avaricious agent (AvA) and the cooperative agent (CoA) – as benchmark. The occurring agent type is depending on the mechanism. Originally agents would behave greedily like the AvA but we have argued that they can be forced to behave like the CoA by means of exogenous acceptance quotas.

The MN-P is scalable and hence can be executed in every desired runtime. To compare the performance with the Greedy algorithm, we limited the runtime of the MN-P to one and a half times (1.5) of the measured Greedy runtime. Table 4 shows a comparative social welfare analysis. The first finding is that the MN-P does not perform very well without quotas. When agents are not forced to accept contracts they presumably cannot overcome local optima and the negotiation gets stuck. The more agents participate the less agreements can be achieved and the less social welfare can be obtained. The latter finding is valid for the MN-P with mandatory quotas as well. With few contract items, the MN-P with quotas performs comparably to the CA-P. However, the decline of social welfare due to more items is greater using the MN-P. This decline of the

MN-P gains speed with more agents. For instance, the MN-P reaches just 44.9 % of the social welfare optimum (CA-P with Greedy 56.4 %) for 100 contract items and 7 agents. In contrast, the CA-P achieves relatively stable results. The CA-P's decline of welfare caused by more items and agents is relatively smaller than the decline of the MN-P. Although the MN-P had 50 % more available runtime, the CA-P performed comparable for small instances and was superior for large instances in the simulation.

5   Conclusion and Outlook

This paper presents a novel approach for coordination of autonomous agents. The approach proposes a market-based coordination method. Automated negotiation is subject to different constraints. On the one hand, a good social welfare performance is desired, but on the other, decision time is limited. For example, data allocation in data centers or job processing in cloud structures requires a fast coordination of agents and contract formation. Furthermore, protocols should prevent unwanted strategies of the agents characterized by a disproportionate gain of an individual at the social welfare's charge. The proposed protocol involves solving the winner determination problem (WDP), which is $\mathcal{NP}$-hard. However, the simulation experiments show that simple heuristics can handle CA very easily – at least with mutual interdependency, as supposed here. We argued as well that the heuristic is realistically truthful and so may prevent strategic actions of the agents. The simulations indicate that the CA-P can achieve good results in very short runtime.

Future work will include the adaptation and evaluation of another methods from the combinatorial auction domain. For instance, a combinatorial clock auction where agents could bid collusive for items as well as item decisions is conceivable. Alternative scenarios like opposed valuations or coalitions are also imaginable and will be analyzed. Since every protocol's performance decreases with a rising number of agents, the analysis of coordination problems with larger numbers of agents is an interesting and open question in multi-agent research.

References

1. Buer, T., Pankratz, G.: GRASP with Hybrid Path Relinking for Bi-Objective Winner Determination in Combinatorial Transportation Auctions. BuR - Business Research 3(2), 192–213 (2010)
2. Conitzer, V., Sandholm, T.: Self-interested Automated Mechanism Design and Implications for Optimal Combinatorial Auctions. In: Proceedings of the 5th ACM Conference on Electronic Commerce, EC 2004 (2004)
3. Delorme, X., Gandibleux, X., Rodriguez, J.: GRASP for Set Packing Problems. European Journal of Operational Research 153(3), 564–580 (2004)
4. Feo, T., Resende, M.G.C.: Greedy Randomized Adaptive Search Procedures. Journal of Global Optimization 6(2), 109–133 (1995)
5. Fink, A.: Supply Chain Coordination by Means of Automated Negotiations Between Autonomous Agents. In: Chaib-draa, B., Müller, J. (eds.) Multiagent based Supply Chain Management. SCI, vol. 28, pp. 351–372. Springer, Heidelberg (2006)

6. Jennings, N.R., Faratin, P., Lomuscio, A.R., Parsons, S., Sierra, C., Wooldridge, M.: Automated Negotiation: Prospects, Methods and Challenges. Group Decision and Negotiation 10(2), 199–215 (2001)

7. Klein, M., Faratin, P., Sayama, H., Bar-Yam, Y.: Negotiating Complex Contracts. Group Decision and Negotiation 12(2), 111–125 (2003)

8. Klein: M., Faratin, P., Sayama, H., Bar-Yam, Y.: Negotiating Complex Contracts, MIT Sloan Working Paper No. 4196-01 (2007), http://ssrn.com/paper=290147

9. Lehmann, D., Callaghan, L., Shoham, Y.: Truth Revelation in Approximately Efficient Combinatorial Auctions. Journal of the ACM 49(5), 577–602 (2002)

10. Milgrom, P.R.: Putting Auction Theory to Work. Cambridge University Press, Cambridge (2004)

11. Nisan, N., Ronen, A.: Algorithmic Mechanism Design. Games and Economic Behavior 35, 166–196 (2001)

12. Nisan, N., Ronen, A.: Computationally Feasible VCG Mechanisms. Journal of Artificial Intelligence Research 29, 19–47 (2007)

13. Pekec, A., Rothkopf, M.H.: Combinatorial Auction Design. Management Science 49(11), 1485–1503 (2003)

14. Sandholm, T.: Distributed Rational Decision Making. In: Weiß, G. (ed.) Multiagent Systems: A Modern Introduction to Distributed Artificial Intelligence, pp. 201–258. MIT Press, Cambridge (1999)

15. Sandholm, T., Suri, S., Gilpin, A., Levine, D.: Winner Determination in Combinatorial Auction Generalizations. In: Proceedings of the First International Joint Conference on Autonomous Agents and Multiagent Systems, AAMAS (2002)

16. Vickrey, W.: Counterspeculation, Auctions, and Competitive Sealed Tenders. The Journal of Finance 16(1), 8–37 (1961)

17. Zurel, E., Nisan, N.: An Efficient Approximate Allocation Algorithm for Combinatorial Auctions. In: Proceedings of the 3rd ACM Conference on Electronic Commerce (EC 2001), pp. 125–136 (2001)

A Multi-agent Approach for Adaptive Virtual Organization Using JADE

Claudiu Ionut Popirlan* and Laura Stefanescu

University of Craiova, Faculty of Mathematics and Computer Science
A.I. Cuza Street, 200585 Craiova, Romania
popirlan@inf.ucv.ro,
laurastef73@yahoo.com
http://inf.ucv.ro/~popirlan

Abstract. By sharing knowledge resources via information technologies, a virtual organization (VO) enables member enterprises to share skills, costs, access to one anothers knowledges. Multi-agent systems (MAS) are capable of adapting themselves to unforeseen changes of their environment in autonomous manner, and differ from more traditional software systems because agents are intended to be independent autonomous, reactive, pro-active and sociable software entities.

In this paper we present a multi-agent approach for handling virtual organization (VO) knowledge management operations. This research proposes to develop a multi-agent system using JADE (Java Agent Development Environment) for knowledge management in a virtual organization, considering agent characteristics, functionalities, communication, cooperation and coordination. Agents have the ability to reorganize themselves in order to bring closer agents capable of cooperating in knowledge problem. We are interested, in this paper, to adaptation in virtual organizations where agents share a same goal.

Keywords: Multi-agent systems, MAS, Virtual Organization, VO, knowledge management, JADE.

1 Introduction

Virtual organization (VO) [2,3] refers to the temporary teaming of enterprises. Today every enterprise uses electronic information processing systems (production and distribution planning, stock and supply management, customer and personnel management) and usually these systems are coupled with a Knowledge-based Systems (KBS) [1] (e.g. databases of customers, suppliers, parts etc.). However knowledge processing alone is not enough. General patterns, structures, regularities go undetected and often such patterns can be exploited to increase turnover. To realize this new generation of business model, the ability to form, operate, and dissolve of virtual enterprise is of most pivotal importance. Agent

---

* The present work was supported by CNCSIS - UEFISCDI through Grant PCE-II-2008-IDEI-450 no. 954/2009.

A. Bouchachia (Ed.): ICAIS 2011, LNAI 6943, pp. 344–355, 2011.

technology [5,6] has been claimed to be a promising tool for knowledge management in a virtual organization. Nowadays there is a clear trend towards using methods and tools that can develop multi-agent systems (MAS) [7,8] capable of reorganization and adapting to changes within their environment.

In this paper we present a multi-agent architecture in context of virtual organization (VO) for knowledge management operations. In this way, we develop a multi-agent system using JADE, considering agent characteristics, functionalities, communication, cooperation and coordination.

The research proposed in this paper are based on three concepts: Multi-Agent Systems, Virtual Organization, and JADE [9,10], which we describe them separately in this section. The rest of this paper is organised as follows. Section 2 discusses the MAS architecture for knowledge management in virtual organization. Section 3 overviews our multi-agent system in terms of its architecture, design and implementation using JADE Platform and describes our experimental domain. Section 4 shows some comparisons of the MAS architecture proposed with other architectures. Finally, the last section presents our conclusions and discusses future works.

1.1 Multi-Agent Systems (MAS)

Software agents originally were discussed in the 70's, and in the mid 90's briefly gained some momentum but then stalled. The "software agent" term has found its way into a number of technologies and has been widely used, for example, in artificial intelligence, databases, operating systems and computer networks literature. Although there is no single definition of an agent [1,5,6] all definitions agree that an agent is essentially a special software component that has autonomy that provides an interoperable interface to an arbitrary system and/or behaves like a human agent, working for some clients in pursuit of its own agenda.

Most discussions on agents focus on their autonomy, intelligence, mobility and interaction [22,23,24,25,26]. Agent-based systems [7,8] claim to be next generation software capable of adapting dynamically to changing business environment and of solving a wide range of knowledge processing application. Although sophisticated software agents can be difficult to build from scratch due to the skills and knowledge needed, the widely available agent construction toolkits may provide a quick and easy start to building software agents without much agent expertise. Significant research and development into multi-agent systems (MAS) has been conducted in recent years [13,14,15], and there are many architectures available today [16,17]. Nevertheless, several issues still need to be faced to make the multi-agent technology widely accepted:

− Secure and efficient execution supports;
− Standardization;
− Appropriate programming languages and coordination models.

1.2 Virtual Organization (VO)

A Virtual Organization (VO) or enterprise can be defined as *a cooperation of legally independent enterprises, institutions or individuals, which provide a service on the basis of a common understanding of business. The cooperating units mainly contribute their core competences and they act to externals as a single corporation. The corporation refuses an institutionalization e.g., by central offices; instead, the cooperation is managed by using feasible information and communication technologies* [2]. Thus we can define VO as:

- A network of people or organizations which are independents;
- Those people and organizations are realizing a common project or common economic activity;
- The communication and information processes are hold through information technologies;
- The organization does not depend on time and space to be made up.

Figure 1 shows the principal's characteristics of the virtual organization concept.

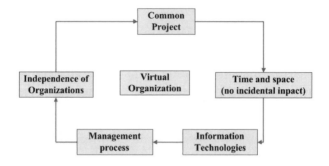

Fig. 1. Principal's characteristics of virtual organization

Recent developments on environments for computer supported collaborative work, distributed knowledge management and *grid architectures* for sharing resources and computational services have lead to an increased interest in what has been termed *virtual organizations*: a set of individuals and institutions that need to coordinate resources and services across institutional boundaries [3,4].

1.3   Java Agent Development Environment (JADE)

JADE is a software platform that provides basic middleware-layer functionalities which are independent of the specific application and which simplify the realization of distributed applications that exploit the software agent abstraction [9]. A significant merit of JADE is that it implements this abstraction over a well-known object-oriented language, Java, providing a simple and friendly API. JADE was implemented [10] to provide programmers with the following ready-to-use and easy-to-customize core functionalities:

- A fully distributed system inhabited by agents;
- Efficient transport of asynchronous messages via a location-transparent API;

- The platform selects the best available means of communication and, when possible, avoids marshalling/unmarshalling java objects;
- A simple, effective, agent life-cycle management;
- Simple APIs and graphical tools are provided to both locally and remotely manage agent life cycles;
- Support for agent mobility: agent migration is made transparent to communicating agents that can continue to interact even during the migration process;
- A subscription mechanism for agents, and even external applications, that wish to subscribe with a platform to be notified of all platform events, including life-cycle-related events and message exchange events;
- A set of graphical tools to support programmers when debugging and monitoring;
- Full compliance with the FIPA specifications [11].

2   A Multi-agent Approach for a Virtual Organization

Our multi-agent approach for virtual organization is motivated by several considerations:

- The nature of the virtual organization is well adapted to the MAS approach, and thus, mapping the VO into a MAS generate adaptive virtual organization;
- The MAS paradigm introduced in the virtual organization environment allows us to benefit from the solutions provided by the research undertakings in the field of software agents: negotiation [18], planning, modelling, etc.
- The co-ordination and resolution of distributed problems are critical for VO management. These problems can be given acceptable solutions within a multi-agent approach. Every phase of virtual organization life cycle requires the completion of several different activities that are well adapted to MAS approach.
- A multi-agent approach provides a good implementation solution for the VO, while taking into account sensitive requirements that must be met satisfactorily:
  - cooperation;
  - co-ordination;
  - execution of distributed business process;
  - preservation of autonomy.

While the MAS is frequently used to develop virtual organization in several domains like that economics, medicine, industry, we think that this approach can suit for knowledge management in virtual organization, with certain adaptation for the basic concepts.

2.1   The MAS Architecture

The system must be able to process distributed knowledge bases from virtual organization. In this respect, the agents visit, one after another, all or a part of the VO's servers to whom they ask for certain information. When an agents gathers all the knowledge requested by user it returns home and shows the results.

Our agent architecture hierarchically organizes component systems for perception, action, and cognition processes, as shown in Figure 2.

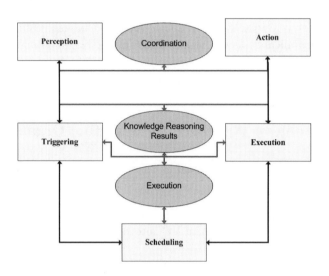

Fig. 2. Principal's characteristics of virtual organization

Perception processes acquire, abstract, and filter sensed data before sending it to other components. Action systems control the execution of external actions on effectors. Perception can influence action directly through reflex arcs or through perception-action coordination processes. The cognition system interprets perceptions, solves problems, makes plans, and guides both perceptual strategies and external action. These processes operate concurrently and asynchronously. They communicate by message passing. It has also other modules for the interaction with the user and distributed knowledge bases:

- The Communication Module: containing all the processes required to handle the messages, namely: reception, filtering, and translation of incoming messages, and formulation and sending of outgoing messages.
- The User Interface: permits the interaction between the master agent and the human agent (user). It is a support interface for the human agent.
- The Planning Module: is the module responsible for managing the cooperation and formulating the offers for achieving sub-goals (parts of the decomposition of the global goal) announced by the master agent; it allows

the agent to compete with other agents for membership in the virtual organization.
- The Execution Module: contains information about the internal resources of the individual organization (knowledge sources, application, users, etc.), which makes possible the performance of local tasks that are assigned to the master agent.

The proposed architecture is agent-based and is designed to support all the processes of VOs life cycle. That is, the proposed architecture is meant to include all the concepts necessary to perform all activities related to the life cycle. We shall adopt a generic, knowledge-based architecture. The enterprise members are represented by autonomous agents, geographically scattered, which are able to cooperate to achieve a common business goal.

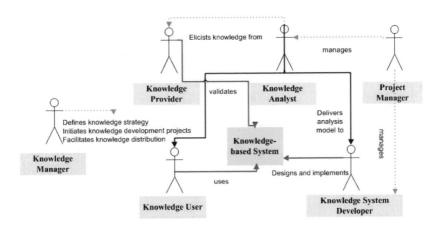

Fig. 3. Relevant agents roles involved in virtual organization construction

The various agents constituting the virtual organization, in order to process distributed knowledge bases, assume the following roles, as shown in Fig. 3.

- Knowledge Manager: is in the top of the hierarchy, and acts as a project manager, but in higher levels. It's like a knowledge strategist, cooperating, defining, and distributing the knowledge to coordinate all the other roles.
- Knowledge Provider: is the owner of human "knowledge". It is typically an expert in the application domain, but could be another person in the organization who does not have the expert status.
- Knowledge Analyst: uses a range of methods and tools that make the analysis of a standard knowledge-intensive task relatively straightforward.
- Knowledge System Developer: is responsible for the design and implementation. The developer must have a basic background of analysis methods. In knowledge system development, the main knowledge problems have been solved by the knowledge analyst. Therefore, this role must have some skills of software designers.

- Knowledge User: makes use, directly or indirectly, of a knowledge system. His interaction with the KBS is important for the project development and validation.
- Project Manager: manages the project, specially the knowledge engineer and the knowledge system developer.

In addition to the agents representing the distributed knowledge base, a Master Agent is introduced in the MAS community. This agent reacts by seizing deal opportunities present in the virtual organization, and proceed thus to establish the corresponding virtual entities.

Structure of the master agent. The Master Agent (MA) is the heart of this multi-agent system architecture, is the representative of the knowledge problem when communicating with other coordination agents. The major responsibilities for the MA include:

- receiving instructions and reporting to other's agents in virtual organization, through an interface;
- assigning data collection to and receiving data from other's agents (data collection agents);
- assigning tasks to, and receiving feedback from other agents;
- communicating with and providing requested data to other MA.

With their domain knowledge, the Master Agents have the ability to monitor, communicate, and collaborate with other agents, react to various requests, as well as assign tasks to other agents.

Communication and Collaboration Mechanism between Agents. In this architecture, the communication and collaboration mechanism between agents is a problem that must be well considered in the design of the agent structure. The communication and collaboration mechanism covers the message transfer between agents, information exchange between agent and distributed knowledge bases, and the agent behaviors in the entire process from request submission, request handle, to result return. These procedures can be summarized as follows:

- Master Agent deploys appropriate agents on its local Knowledge Base, performs the registration on the knowledge bases, and establishes the communication link to the central knowledge base.
- Master Agent submits the information of its sharable Knowledge to the central Knowledge Base through its release agent.
- The retrieval agent of every organization accesses the system periodically. It gets retrieval requests of other enterprises and searches its local Knowledge Base.
- The result agent returns the retrieval result to the system after the local search finishes.

- The Master Agent implies a classification and a sort order to the retrieval result according to its corresponding retrieval request.
- User views the retrieval results on the interface and selects the needed Knowledge. With the information about the Knowledge Base embedded in the retrieval result, the user then contacts the relevant enterprise to obtain the Knowledge.
- The result agent accesses the system periodically. It gets the retrieval results relevant to its retrieval request and stored them locally to wait for the user to view.

3   Developing Multi-Agent Systems with JADE

To illustrate the previous architecture of multi-agent systems for virtual organization, we chose to develop a system that passes two plain-text parameters (an object name and one of its attributes names) on activation and then searches through the knowledge data set to find a result (the attribute value).

One goal of JADE is to simplify development while ensuring standard compliance through a comprehensive set of system services and agents. During the development of the system with JADE, the following types of classes are created and implemented:

- Agent classes to describe various types of agents.
- User Interface classes for customer interaction.
- Agent activity classes for behaviours.
- Database classes to handle the database of the system.
- Communication classes to manage the negotiation between agents.
- Ontology classes to define concepts, predicates and agent actions for the domain.

3.1   Class Diagram

We define the concepts and attributes using UML, as shown in Fig. 4.

3.2   JADE Implementation

An agent lives in a particular environment, and therefore JADE provides one. An agent class is implemented in JADE by extending the provided Agent base class and overriding the default implementation of the methods that are automatically invoked by the platform during the agent lifecycle. Shown below is a sample of the source code included in this application, created in JADE and written in Java:

```
//...
public class MasterAgent extends Agent{

    //...
```

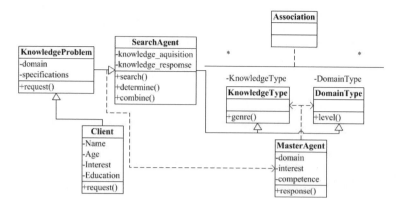

Fig. 4. UML Class Diagram

```
    class Knowledge extends TickerBehaviour{

//...
        ACLMessage msg = new ACLMessage(ACLMessage.INFORM);
        AMSAgentDescription [] agents = null;
        try {
            SearchConstraints c = new SearchConstraints();
            }
        catch (Exception e){
            System.out.println("Exception 1: "+e);
        }
//...
        try {
            msg.setContentObject(kt);
            } catch (IOException ex) {
            Logger.getLogger(KnowledgeType.class.getName()));
            }
        }
    @Override
    protected void setup(){
        Object[] args = new Object[2];
        args = getArguments();
//...
    }
}
```

In JADE, behaviour represents a task that an agent can carry out and is implemented as an object of a class that extends *jade.core.behaviours.Behaviour.* The JADE platform provides a yellow pages service which allows any agent to dynamically discover other agents at a given point in time. The JADE communication paradigm is based on asynchronous message passing. A message in JADE is implemented as an object of the *jade.lang.acl.ACLMessage* object and then calling the *setup()* method of the *Agent* class. Agents must share semantics if the communication is to be effective.

For our example, we start the Master Agent that is designed and implemented in JADE.

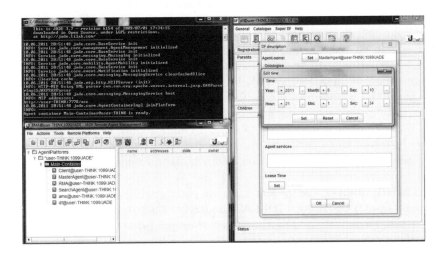

Fig. 5. JADE Remote Monitoring with DF GUI

Figure 5 shows the JADE *Remote Monitoring Agent DF GUI* which controls the life cycles of the implemented multi-agent system (all registered agents).

4   Comparison with Other Architecture

Although our architecture is not the only one that supports adaptation, it is one of a small set of candidate architectures currently in the literature. However, most of these other architectures focus on selected aspects of adaptation, as illustrated by the following examples. CIRCA [19] offer a two-layer architecture in which unpredictable MAS are used to set goals and priorities for a real-time scheduler that guarantees to meet hard deadlines (assuming that is feasible) and to use slack resources effectively. This architecture adapts its real-time schedule to available resources and current priorities, but it does not provide other forms of adaptation, particularly within its use of the AI methods. Several researchers are working on particular forms of adaptation independent of architectural context. Notable examples are: design-to-time scheduling algorithms for maximizing the use of available resources while meeting deadlines on critical tasks [20], flexible adaptation to unanticipated event orderings [21], approximate processing techniques that provide acceptably degraded responses when resources are short [27]. We view these approaches as useful capabilities that we would strive to integrate within our architecture.

5 Conclusions and Future Work

This paper has shown the architecture and JADE development of a multi-agent system which requires communication and collaboration in context of virtual organization. By analysing the system as a set of roles and tasks, a system designer is naturally led to the definition of autonomous agents that co-ordinate their actions to solve the overall system goals. JADE agents embedded with virtual organization have qualities over intelligent reasoning abilities. The MAS development has met the aims and goals expected and has been tested for knowledge processing in virtual organization context.

As a further, we will try to implement agents in order to adopt a control-oriented point of view, for example to request services while they require data files. With the adoption of a blackboard or a tuple space on each data base server, data can be accessed without requiring the presence of peculiar services and in a more natural data-oriented style. We aim to improve the ability of the agents in regard to conflict resolution using negotiation skills by incorporating more advanced negotiation protocols and negotiation rules.

Acknowledgments. The present work was supported by CNCSIS - UEFISCDI through Grant PCE-II-2008-IDEI-450 no. 954/2009 : *Knowledge Management for Virtual Organization. Possibilities of Management Assisting using Knowledge Management Systems.*

References

1. Russell, S., Norvig, P.: Artificial Intelligence: A Modern Approach. Prentice-Hall, Englewood Cliffs (1995)
2. Rocha, A.P., Oliveira, E.: Agents advanced features for negotiation in electronic commerce and virtual organisations formation processes. In: AgentLink, pp. 78–97 (2001)
3. Zheng, Q., Zhang, X.: Automatic Formation and analysis of multi-agent Virtual organization. Journal of the Brazilian Computer Society (JCBS) Special Issue on agents Organizations 11(1), 74–89 (2005)
4. Boella, G., Hulstijn, J., van der Torre, L.: Virtual organizations as normative multiagent systems. In: Proceedings of the 38 Annual Hawaii International Conference on System Sciences (2005)
5. Genesereth, M.R., Ketchpel, S.P.: Software Agents. Communications of the ACM 37(7), 48–53 (1994)
6. Wooldridge, M.J., Jennings, N.R.: Intelligent Agents: Theory and Practice. Knowledge Engineering Review 10(2), 115–152 (1995)
7. Sycara, K.P.: Multiagent Systems. AI Magazine, 79–92 (1998)
8. Wooldridge, M.: Introduction to Multiagent Systems. John Wiley and Sons, UK (2002)
9. Bellifemine, F.L., Caire, G., Greenwood, D.: Developing Multi-Agent Systems with JADE. Wiley, Chichester (2007)
10. JADE, Java Agent Development Environment, website: http://jade.tilab.com
11. FIPA, Foundation for Intelligent Physical Agents, website: http://www.fipa.org

12. Wooldridge, M.J., Jennings, N.R., Kinny, D.: The Gaia Methodology for Agent-Oriented Analysis and Design. Journal of Autonomous Agents and Multi-Agent Systems 3, 285–312 (2000)
13. Kabbaj, A.: Development of Intelligent Systems and Multi-Agents Systems with Amine Platform. In: Schärfe, H., Hitzler, P., Øhrstrøm, P. (eds.) ICCS 2006. LNCS (LNAI), vol. 4068, pp. 286–299. Springer, Heidelberg (2006)
14. Balachandran, B., Enkhsaikhan, M.: Developing Multi-agent E-Commerce Applications with JADE. In: Apolloni, B., Howlett, R.J., Jain, L. (eds.) KES 2007, Part III. LNCS (LNAI), vol. 4694, pp. 941–949. Springer, Heidelberg (2007)
15. Rodrguez, S., Fernndez, V., Julin, V., Corchado, J.M., Ossowski, S., Botti, V.: A THOMAS Based Multi-Agent System for Recommendations and Guidance in Malls. Journal of Physical Agents 3(2), 21–26 (2009)
16. Hagras, H., Callaghan, V., Colley, M.: Intelligent Embedded Agents. Journal of Information Sciences, 289–292 (2005)
17. Bouchachia, A., Prossegger, M.: A Bi-Clustering Agent-based Approach for Map Segmentation. In: Proceedings of the IEEE Symposium on Intelligent Agents, IA 2009, Part of the IEEE Symposium Series on Computational Intelligence, pp. 99–105 (2009)
18. An, B., Lesser, V., Sim, K.M.: Strategic Agents for Multi-resource Negotiation. Autonomous Agents and Multi-Agent Systems 23(1), 114–153 (2011)
19. Musliner, D.J., Durfee, E.H., Shin, K.G.: CIRCA: A cooperative intelligent real-time control architecture. IEEE Transactions on Systems, Man, and Cybernetics 23, 1561–1574 (1993)
20. Garvey, A.J., Lesser, V.R.: Design-to-time real-time scheduling. IEEE Transactions on Systems, Man and Cybernetics 23(6), 1491–1502 (1993)
21. Agre, P.E., Chapman, D.: Pengi: An implementation of a theory of activity. In: Proceedings of the National Conference on Artificial Intelligence. Morgan Kaufmann, San Mateo (1987)
22. Stoian, G., Popirlan, C.I.: A proposal for an enhanced mobile agent architecture (EMA). In: Annals of the University of Craiova, Mathematics and Computer Science Series, vol. 37(1), pp. 71–79 (2010)
23. Tandareanu, N., Popirlan, C.I.: A Mobile Agents Approach for Knowledge Bases Processing. In: Samarati, P., Yung, M., Martinelli, F., Ardagna, C.A. (eds.) ISC 2009. LNCS, vol. 5735, pp. 27–32. Springer, Heidelberg (2009)
24. Popirlan, C.I.: Knowledge Processing in Contact Centers using a Multi-Agent Architecture. WSEAS Transactions On Computers 9(11), 1318–1327 (2010)
25. Popirlan, C.I., Stefanescu, L.: Mobile Agents System for Intelligent Data Analysis. In: Proceedings of WSEAS Applied Computing Conference (ACC 2009), Athens, Greece, pp. 663–668 (2009)
26. Popirlan, C.I., Dupac, M.: An Optimal Path Algorithm for Autonomous Searching Robots. In: Annals of University of Craiova, Mathematics and Computer Science Series, vol. 36(1), pp. 37–48 (2009)
27. Decker, K., Lesser, V., Whitehair, R.: Extending a blackboard architecture for approximate processing. Journal of Real-Time Systems 2, 47–70 (1990)

Golden Ratio (Sectiona Aurea) in Markovian Ants AI Hybrid

Ilija Tanackov[1], Gordan Stojić[1], Jovan Tepić[1], Milan Kostelac[2],
Feta Sinani[3], and Siniša Sremac[1]

[1] University of Novi Sad, Faculty of Technical Sciences,
Trg Dositeja Obradovića 6, 21000 Novi Sad, Serbia
ilijat@uns.ac.rs
[2] University of of Zagreb, Faculty of Mechanical Engineering and Naval Architecture,
Ivana Lučića 5, 10000 Zagreb, Croatia
[3] Ministry of Transport and Communications,
St. Crvena Skopska Opstina 4, 1000 Skopje, Republic of Macedonia

Abstract. The exponential pheromone signal of the AI hybrid of Markovian Ant Queuing System - MAQS, is divided into the spatial and deposit pheromone fractions which have the identical values. A new hybrid is formed. The convolution of two new exponential signals has the Erlang distribution. Introducing the inter-state in the process of markovization the Erlang Queuing Ant System - EQAS, is solved. Comparison of the average distance between artificial ants in MAQS and EAQS gave particular numerical specificity. The average distances are in φ equilibrium. Constant φ is a famous constant of the Golden ratio.

Keywords: Golden ratio, queuing system.

1 Introduction

Many phenomena in complex systems cannot be successfully analysed by using analytic models. These are, above all, phenomena with a great number of agents which are mutually dependent on interactions. An idea for developing a model, which can solve complex problems of combinatorial optimisation, was inspired by the social insects' collective behaviour. The basic elements of biological ant colony sensory systems, which were applied while developing an ant system (AS) metaheuristic method, are the deposited pheromone trail from contact chemosensory communication – τ (gustation) and visualisation from a videosensory ant communication – η (visibility vector). These ants' sensory system characteristics were used for creating a AS transitory probability $p_{ij}^{k}(t)$ network [1],

$$
p_{ij}^{k}(t) = \begin{cases} \dfrac{\tau_{ij}(t)^{\alpha}\eta_{ij}{}^{\beta}}{\sum_{j \in \Omega_i^k(t)}\tau_{ij}(t)^{\alpha}\eta_{ij}{}^{\beta}}, & j \in \Omega_i^k(t) \\ \\ 0, & otherwise \end{cases}
$$

A. Bouchachia (Ed.): ICAIS 2011, LNAI 6943, pp. 356–367, 2011.

where $\Omega_i^k(t)$ is the set of feasible nodes to be visited by ant k (the set of feasible nodes is updated for each ant after every move), α and β are parameters representing the relative importance of the trail intensity and the visibility.

In accordance to the real biological characteristics of a pheromone, in a discreet period of time, pheromone evaporation and depositing on the route $\tau_{ij}(t) \leftarrow \rho\tau_{ij}(t) + \Delta\tau_{ij}$ is defined, where ρ is the coefficient ($0<\rho<1$) such that ($1-\rho$) represent evaporation of the trail within every iteration. Visualisation is counter-proportional to the Euclidean distance between nods, $\eta_{ij} = 1/d_{ij}$, d_{ij} is the Euclidean distance between nod i and nod j. The basic principle of the artificial ants' route choice is shown on Fig. 1.

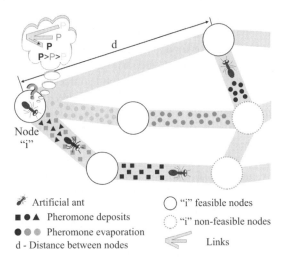

Fig. 1. Ant system, basic logic of pheromone usage

Deposited pheromone trail has a dominant role in the AS method. The existence of pheromones and evaporation are the main memory features that classify the AS method in the area of Swarm Intelligence methods of artificial intelligence.

Visualisation have not memory characteristic and it is alternative in case of complete evaporation of the deposited pheromones. Absolute evaporation of pheromones ($\rho=1$) or calibration of chemosensory and videosensory communications parameters ($\alpha=0 \wedge \beta=1$) reduce AS to the methods of network programming. Due to these circumstances, the visualization is of secondary importance.

Regardless of the conceptual differences between the mathematical formalization of chemosensory and videosensory communication, it is proved that at the regular calibration of parameters the AS algorithm always converges [2].

The outstanding results achieved by the mathematical method inspired by collective behavior of decentralized, self-organized ant systems [3, 4], have justified the previous researches at the real ant colonies and initiated the new ones. The greatest interest was in the field of chemosensory pheromone communication of ants.

Seven different pheromones were found in ants *Monomorium pharaonis*. Trail pheromones are deposited on surfaces using an extruded stinger. Ants can deposit different pheromone types through the same stinger. Each pheromone gland has separate tanks and the control of different pheromones deposit through the same stinger is done by using sphincters [5].

While searching for food, ants *M. pharaonis* use at least three pheromone types - one attractive longlasting pheromone, and two short-lived pheromones, one attractive and one repellent. Attractive and repellent short-lived pheromones have approximately the same evaporation speed. However, the repellent pheromone is deposited in almost two times bigger amount, hence the repellent pheromone effect lasts for 78 minutes, while the attractive pheromone effect lasts for 33 minutes [6]. The repellent pheromone function is a part of a chemical strategy which rejects other colonies' ants while searching for food [7]. Pheromones may have the two-component characteristics [8]. Attractive pheromone deposit varies depending on the food quality [5]. Due to this, ants selected the better of two food sources in 14 out of 18 trails [9]. Evaporation of pheromones can be affected by humidity, temperature, light [10], airflow [11], different substrates [12], etc.

The use of visual landmark recognition by two dimensional renioptic views is proven in ants [13]. This result partialy justifies the application of a visualization in the AS metaheuristic method. Invasive experiments on an ant colony *M. pharaonis* [14] completely exclude the Euclidean visualization. Changing the direction of motion of an ant in a column causes the hysteresis of the pheromone signal, which is successively passed through a column of ants without contacts.

The golden ratio constant [15] $\varphi = (1 + \sqrt{5})/2 = 1{,}6180339887...$, probably the oldest mathematical constant, has not been considered in recent mathematical history. Probably the reason is the wide usage of the Golden ratio in so–called "esoteric sciences". There is a well known fact that the basic symbol of esoteric, the pentagram, is closely connected to the Golden ratio. However, in modern science, an attitude towards the Golden ratio is changing very quickly. The Golden ratio has a revolutionary importance for development in modern science.

In quantum mechanics, El Nashie is a follower of the Golden Ratio and shows in his works [16] that the Golden Ratio plays an outstanding role in physical researches. El Nashie's theory will lead to Nobel Prize if experimentally verified. New partially experimental results [17] confirm the correctness of his theories. After quantum, the golden ratio constant was established in chemical reactions [18, 19], as an individual value, and systematically, in linear and exponential combinations of the golden ratio constant. DNA [20, 21] complied with the golden ratio after the atom compliance with the golden ratio, and it was also transferred to other complex biological structures. The old observation about *phyllotaxis* plants was confirmed [22, 23], then it was expanded to others, non–*phyllotaxis* species of plants [24]. The function of the golden ratio constant was established in human brain research [25]. Alongside DNA structure, we get to the golden ratio constant research in human facial proportions and facial attractiveness assessment [26, 27]. Butusov's resonance theory of the Solar system [28] based on the golden ratio, discovers the importance of this constant beyond the Earth, and takes us to the universe [29, 30, 31].

The concept of artificial intelligence, at the moment, does not have at its disposal models for emotions and ideas simulation, and their transfer between intelligent agents. Artificial intelligence has not achieved an anologue method for creativity yet, which is one of dominant characteristics of human intelligence. Creativity is, first of all, necessary for the adaptation in a new, not previously learnt system of events. The Golden ratio constant has a significant part in aesthetics and art, in human creativity. Therefore, the existence of the golden section constant in AI methods have a important implication, generally. This paper describes one possible synthesis.

2   Ant Sensory System and Pheromone Convolution

Variations of humidity, temperature, light, air flow, substrate characteristics, the individual pheromone capacities of ants etc, result in stochastic characteristic of pheromone communication in ant columns. Inevitable consequence of the stochastic terms is the information entropy of the pheromone communication channel.

Successful functioning of an ant colony led to the conclusion that individuals in the colonies have excellent capacity of calibration and processing of pheromone signals. Calibration and signal processing are realized by the ant sensor system.

General requirements that should be met by a quality sensor can be defined on the basis of Aristotle's principles of logic [32]: the principle of identity, principle of opposites and the principle of non-existence of the third. According to these principles of logic, high-quality sensor meets the following requirements:

1. Is sensitive to the measured property (the principle of identity)
2. Is insensitive to any other property likely to be encountered in its application (the principle of contradiction)
3. Does not influence the measured property (the principle of non-existence of the third)

However, the best sensor in terms of stochastic dynamics of a signal transmits information entropy on the object of communication. Development of pheromone convolution is based on the assumption that the sensory system of ants is ideal in terms of Aristotelian principles of logic.

The stochastic nature of an individual signal can be significantly reduced by pheromone convolution. In accordance with the terms of the Central Limit Theorem (CLT), the convolution of pheromone signals can stabilize the value of the signal by direct variance reduction. The division of a stochastic pheromone capacity in two smaller individual capacities, the effect predicted by Central limit theorem (CLT) is achieved by convolution synthesis. The existence of deposit and spatial pheromone signal represents the convolution basis.

3 Markovian Ant Queueing System - MAQS

Markovian Ant Queuing system [32] is a hybrid of the AS artificial intelligence and the continuous time Markov processes. The basis of the AS is the pheromone communication of subsequent ants and the basis of Markov processes is the exponential propagation of a pheromone signal.

Among all continuous probability distributions with support $[0,\infty)$ and mean M, the exponential distribution with $M=1/\xi$ has the largest entropy. In this condition pheromone signal provide minimal informational cues. Entropy level for exponential distribution is $H(E(\xi))=1-\ln(\xi)$. The choice of exponential distribution is justified by a great number of undesirable factors which cause the largest entropy of a pheromone signal (humidity, temperature, light, airflow, different substrates, etc.). The derived hybrid represents the synthesis of a memory system (AS) and a memoryless system (exponential distribution).

MAQS proceeds from the assumption that the value of pheromone signal is a random variable of exponential distribution $f(d)=\xi e^{-\xi d}$ with d distance from the signal source and the intensity ξ, $\xi \geq 0$. Let the speed of the anterior ant be random and constant, and the speed of the consecutive ant proportional to the value of the received signal. If we express the distance between two consecutive ants by an integer variable X_l of the exponential function of pheromone signal $f(d)$, $X_d=INT(\xi e^{-\xi d})$, then the distance probability between the two consecutive ants equals $P(X_d)$. The probability of a unit distance X_d equals the exponential distribution integral in an interval $(d, d+1)$.

$$P(X_d)=p_d=\int_d^{d+1}\xi e^{-\xi d}d(d)=e^{-d\xi}-e^{-(d+1)\xi}=\frac{1}{e^{d\xi}}-\frac{1}{e^{\xi}e^{d\xi}}=\frac{1}{e^{d\xi}}\left(\frac{e^{\xi}-1}{e^{\xi}}\right)$$

The distance between the ants is measured by the state of the queuing system. Each state of the system corresponds to an integer unit of length. The transition intensities (1) that meet the requirements of movement of the successive ants depending on the intensity of the received signals have the following solution (Fig. 2.):

$$\alpha=\frac{\dfrac{e^{\xi}-1}{e^{(k+1)\xi}\cdot e^{\xi}}}{\dfrac{e^{\xi}-1}{e^{k\xi}\cdot e^{\xi}}+\dfrac{e^{\xi}-1}{e^{(k+1)\xi}\cdot e^{\xi}}}=\frac{1}{e^{\xi}+1},$$

$$\beta=\frac{\dfrac{e^{\xi}-1}{e^{k\xi}\cdot e^{\xi}}}{\dfrac{e^{\xi}-1}{e^{k\xi}\cdot e^{\xi}}+\dfrac{e^{\xi}-1}{e^{(k+1)\xi}\cdot e^{\xi}}}=\frac{e^{\xi}}{e^{\xi}+1}$$

$$(1)$$

MAQS is (Fig. 3)

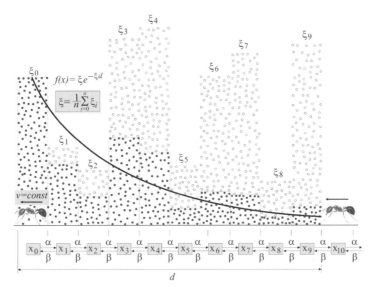

Fig. 2. Exponential distribution of spatial pheromone signal in MAQS, pheromone symbols: active pheromone (●) and evaporated pheromone (○)

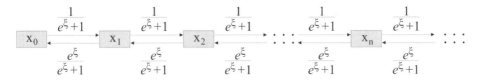

Fig. 3. Markovian ant queueing system - MAQS

If the intensity of the pheromone signal spreading is exponential to ξ parameter, then the analogy of the average distance between two ants equals the number of clients in the system, which amounts to:

$$\sum_{k=0}^{\infty} k p_k = 0\left(1 - \frac{1}{e^{\xi}}\right) + 1\left(\frac{1}{e^{\xi}} - \frac{1}{e^{2\xi}}\right) + \ldots + k\left(\frac{1}{e^{k\xi}} - \frac{1}{e^{(k+1)\xi}}\right) + \ldots = \sum_{k=1}^{\infty}\left(\frac{1}{e^{\xi}}\right) = \frac{1}{e^{\xi} - 1} \quad (2)$$

4   Erlang Ant Queueing System - EAQS

The convolution of ants' basic pheromone capacity can be realised by diffusing one part of the basic odorant (pheromone) on a trail. The source of the odorant is an ant moving across a surface. If the odorant intensity equals ξ, its disposal causes the decomposition of the basic intensity into spatial pheromone intensity λ and deposit pheromone intensity μ. Thereby, $\xi = \lambda + \mu$ condition has been satisfied (Fig. 4).

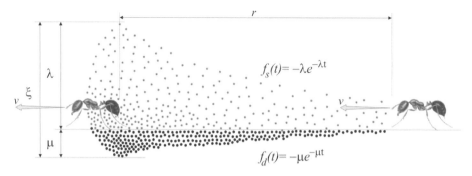

Fig. 4. Indirect decomposition of the basic signal odorant into spatial and deposit fractions of the dual pheromone signal: spatial fraction (●) and deposit fraction (●)

If an exponential pheromone signal, which has capacity ξ from MAQS is divided into two equal parts, $\xi=\lambda+\mu$ (Fig 4.), two new signals are got. Their nature is determined by the nature of the basic signal which is exponentially distributed. As the exponential distribution has maximal entropy among all distributions $H(\xi)=1-ln(\xi)$, distribution of new pheromone signal can't lower the individual uncertainty of new pheromone sygnals. Because of that, $f_s(t)=\lambda e^{-\lambda t}$ is a exponential spatial pheromone signal, and $f_d(t)=\mu e^{-\mu t}$ is a exponential deposit pheromone signal,

In a special case, when spatial and deposit pheromone fraction capacities are the same $\xi=2\chi$, $\chi=\lambda=\mu$, convolution of exponential spatial fraction and exponential deposit fraction has the Erlang distribution. The structure of the new AI hybrid, Erlang Ant Queuing System, EAQS is (Fig. 5.):

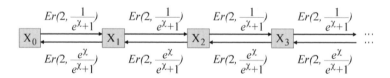

Fig. 5. The structure of Erlang Ant Queueing Sistem, EAQS

Mass Handling System of the Erlang transition intensity between states is not Markovian and it does not handle with the direct analytical solutions. Applying decomposition of the Erlang distribution we have the exponential composition in a queuing system, again. Queuing system is Markovian system, again (Fig. 6):

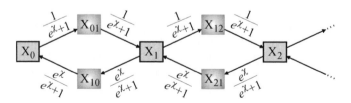

Fig. 6. EAQS with identical spatial and deposit pheromone fractions

Differential equations of EAQS in stationary regime are:

$$p_0' = 0 \Leftrightarrow -\frac{1}{e^{\chi}+1}p_0 + \frac{e^{\chi}}{e^{\chi}+1}p_{10} = 0 \rightarrow p_{10} = \frac{1}{e^{\chi}}p_0$$

$$p_{01}' = 0 \Leftrightarrow \frac{1}{e^{\chi}+1}p_0 - \frac{1}{e^{\chi}+1}p_{01} = 0 \rightarrow p_{01} = p_0$$

$$p_{10}' = 0 \Leftrightarrow \frac{e^{\chi}}{e^{\chi}+1}p_1 - \frac{e^{\chi}}{e^{\chi}+1}p_{10} = 0 \rightarrow p_1 = p_{10} = \frac{1}{e^{\chi}}p_0$$

$$p_1' = 0 \Leftrightarrow \frac{1}{e^{\chi}+1}p_{01} - \frac{1}{e^{\chi}+1}p_1 - \frac{e^{\chi}}{e^{\chi}+1}p_1 + \frac{e^{\chi}}{e^{\chi}+1}p_{21} = 0 \Leftrightarrow$$

$$\Leftrightarrow \frac{1}{e^{\chi}+1}p_0 - \frac{1}{e^{\chi}+1}\frac{1}{e^{\chi}}p_0 - \frac{e^{\chi}}{e^{\chi}+1}\frac{1}{e^{\chi}}p_0 + \frac{e^{\chi}}{e^{\chi}+1}p_{21} = 0 \Leftrightarrow$$

$$\Leftrightarrow -\frac{1}{e^{\chi}+1}\frac{1}{e^{\chi}}p_0 + \frac{e^{\chi}}{e^{\chi}+1}p_{21} = 0 \rightarrow p_{21} = \frac{1}{e^{2\chi}}p_0$$

$$p_{12}' = 0 \Leftrightarrow \frac{1}{e^{\chi}+1}p_1 - \frac{1}{e^{\chi}+1}p_{12} = 0 \rightarrow p_{12} = p_1 = \frac{1}{e^{\chi}}p_0$$

$$p_{21}' = 0 \Leftrightarrow \frac{e^{\chi}}{e^{\chi}+1}p_2 - \frac{e^{\chi}}{e^{\chi}+1}p_{21} = 0 \rightarrow p_2 = p_{21} = \frac{1}{e^{2\chi}}p_0$$

$$p_2' = 0 \Leftrightarrow \frac{1}{e^{\chi}+1}p_{12} - \frac{1}{e^{\chi}+1}p_2 - \frac{e^{\chi}}{e^{\chi}+1}p_2 + \frac{e^{\chi}}{e^{\chi}+1}p_{32} = 0 \Leftrightarrow$$

$$\Leftrightarrow \frac{1}{e^{\chi}+1}\frac{1}{e^{\chi}}p_0 - \frac{1}{e^{\chi}+1}\frac{1}{e^{2\chi}}p_0 - \frac{e^{\chi}}{e^{\chi}+1}\frac{1}{e^{2\chi}}p_0 + \frac{e^{\chi}}{e^{\chi}+1}p_{32} = 0 \Leftrightarrow$$

$$\Leftrightarrow -\frac{1}{e^{\chi}+1}\frac{1}{e^{2\chi}}p_0 + \frac{e^{\chi}}{e^{\chi}+1}p_{32} = 0 \rightarrow p_{32} = \frac{1}{e^{3\chi}}p_0$$

$p_0 = p_{01}$ and for each $k>1$: $p_{k-1\,k} = p_k = p_{k\,k+1}$, $p_k = \frac{1}{e^{k\chi}}p_0$.

We get the probability p_0 from the basic equation $\sum_{i=0}^{\infty} p_i = 1$:

$$2p_0 + 3p_1 + 3p_2 + 3p_3 + \ldots = 1 \Leftrightarrow \left(\sum_{k=0}^{\infty} 3p_i\right) - p_0 = 1 \Leftrightarrow \left(\sum_{k=0}^{\infty} 3p_0\frac{1}{e^{k\chi}}\right) - p_0 = 1 \Leftrightarrow$$

$$\Leftrightarrow 3p_0\left(\sum_{k=0}^{\infty}\left(\frac{1}{e^{\chi}}\right)^k\right) - p_0 = 1 \Leftrightarrow 3p_0\frac{1}{1 - \frac{1}{e^{\chi}}} - p_0 = 1 \Leftrightarrow p_0\frac{3e^{\chi}}{e^{\chi}-1} - p_0 = 1 \Leftrightarrow$$

$$\Leftrightarrow p_0\frac{3e^{\chi} - e^{\chi} + 1}{e^{\chi}-1} = 1 \Leftrightarrow p_0\frac{2e^{\chi}+1}{e^{\chi}-1} = 1 \Leftrightarrow p_0 = \frac{e^{\chi}-1}{2e^{\chi}+1}$$

Probabilities for a convolution system of the EAQS are:

$$p_k = \frac{1}{e^{k\chi}} \frac{e^{\chi}-1}{2e^{\chi}+1}, \quad k \in [0,\infty) \tag{3}$$

The average number of clients in EAQS (with convolution of equal pheromone fractions) is:

$$\sum_{k=0}^{\infty} k p_k = \sum_{k=0}^{\infty} \frac{k}{e^{k\chi}} \frac{e^{\chi}-1}{2e^{\chi}+1} = \frac{e^{\chi}-1}{2e^{\chi}+1} \sum_{k=0}^{\infty} \frac{k}{e^{k\chi}} = \frac{e^{\chi}-1}{2e^{\chi}+1} \frac{e^{\chi}}{\left(e^{\chi}-1\right)^2} \tag{4}$$

$$\sum_{k=0}^{\infty} k p_k = \frac{e^{\chi}}{2e^{2\chi}-e^{\chi}-1} \tag{5}$$

In relation to the total pheromone capacity $\xi=2\chi$, the average number of clients of the EAQS is:

$$\sum_{k=0}^{\infty} k p_k = \frac{e^{\frac{\xi}{2}}}{2e^{\xi}-e^{\frac{\xi}{2}}-1} \tag{6}$$

5 Golden Ratio Equilibrium

In Markovian Ant Queuing System (MAQS), the average number of clients (6) is equal to the average distance between ants (2). Comparison of singular and convolutional average distance between ants provides following ratios:

$$\frac{e^{\frac{\xi}{2}}}{2e^{\xi}-e^{\frac{\xi}{2}}-1} = \frac{1}{e^{\xi}-1} \Leftrightarrow 2e^{\xi}-e^{\frac{\xi}{2}}-1 = e^{\frac{3\xi}{2}}-e^{\frac{\xi}{2}} \Leftrightarrow e^{\frac{3\xi}{2}}-2e^{\xi}+1=0 \tag{7}$$

Replacing $e^{\frac{\xi}{2}} = x$ we get the cubic equation with solutions

$$x^3 - 2x^2 + 1 = \left(x^2-x-1\right)\cdot(x-1)=0, \; x_1 = \frac{1-\sqrt{5}}{2}, \; x_2 = 1, \; x_3 = \frac{1+\sqrt{5}}{2} \tag{8}$$

Real solutions for roots are 1 and $\left(1+\sqrt{5}\right)/2$. The solution 1 for value $\xi=0$ shows the total absence of pheromone emission. It cannot be classified in AS. The only acceptable solution is $\left(1+\sqrt{5}\right)/2$. Value $\left(1+\sqrt{5}\right)/2$ is a famous irrational mathematical constant of Golden ratio with spetial properties $\varphi^n = \varphi^{n-1} + \varphi^{n-2}$,

The average distances of singular and convolutional systems are in equilibrium when the parameter value is $e^{\frac{\xi}{2}} = \varphi \Leftrightarrow \xi = 2\ln\varphi$. Equilibrium of the singular and convolution average distance between ants is equal to φ^{-1} (note, $\varphi^2 = 1+\varphi$):

$$\frac{1}{e^{\xi}-1} = \frac{1}{\varphi^2-1} = \frac{1}{\varphi} = \frac{\varphi}{\varphi^2} = \frac{\varphi}{2\varphi^2-\varphi^2} = \frac{\varphi}{2\varphi^2-\varphi-1} = \frac{e^{\frac{\xi}{2}}}{2e^{\xi}-e^{\frac{\xi}{2}}-1} \equiv \varphi^{-1} = \varphi-1$$

Generally, if the pheromone capacity value is equal to the Golden section constant, the distance between the ants is the in the singular and the convolution system is the same. This is the point of **Golden ratio equilibrium.**

6 Conclusion

Each inspiration by the natural phenomena of the living world has undergone an unbiased test of evolution. One of the basic conditions of evolution is precisely the possibility of adaptation of plant or animal species to new conditions of the environment. Evolutionary survival is the guarantor of the correctness of natural models.

The basis of Markov systems is a natural number e, and the basis of the Ant Systems is the collective behavior of ants, social animals. Both methods are basically inspired by natural phenomena. Therefore, the appearance of $\varphi = 1.6180339...$, constant of creation, the golden section in the observed hybrid is not a big surprise.

Various conclusions may be drawn from the obtained solution. The most important relates to all real systems that can be described by queuing systems with Kendall's notation $M/M/1/\infty/FIFO$. If the intensity of the customer services in the system is conditional random variable of the arrival rate, and an exponent equals $\xi=2\ln\varphi$, then MAQS (Fig. 3) transforms into a queuing system with equilibrium (Fig. 7).

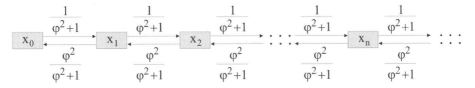

Fig. 7. Markovian ant queueing system with equilibrium – MAQS^{+eq}

MAQS^{+eq} has a unique feature that the fraction of arrival rate exponent intermediate state of the system remains constant. This system gets ρ utilization factor (or "traffic intensity" the mean fraction of time that the server is busy), that in accordance with Pollaczek-Khinchin formula implements mean queuing delay F_q:

$$\rho = \frac{\frac{1}{\varphi^2+1}}{\frac{\varphi^2}{\varphi^2+1}} = \frac{1}{\varphi^2} = 1 - \frac{1}{\varphi}, \quad F_q = (\varphi^2+1)\frac{\frac{1}{\varphi^2}}{1-\frac{1}{\varphi^2}} = \frac{\varphi^2+1}{\varphi}$$

which means that the value of Feller's paradox constant is the fraction of the golden ratio constant. These facts have important implications for any real system that can be modeled as M/M/1/∞/FIFO.

This work is the first finding of Golden ratio constant in the artificial intelligence. The role of the constant φ is implicit, in the natural logarithm function lnφ. But, this is not a first promotion of lnφ value. The constant lnφ also plays a key role in relations of Fibonacci and Lucas consecutive numbers that at Kepler's proof converge to the golden ratio constant and Rikati hyperbolic functions [31]. In this coincidence points is the significance of the results and possible application of Golden ratio constant in AI methods.

Acknowledgment. The study is the part of the investigations realised with the scope of the Project No. 36012/2011 financially supported by the Ministry of Science and Technological Development of the Republic of Serbia.

References

1. Teodorović, D.: Swarm intelligence systems for transportation engineering: Principles and applications. Transportation Research Part C: Emerging Technologies 16(6), 651–667 (2008)
2. Badr, A., Fahmy, A.: A proof of convergence for Ant algorithms. Information Sciences 160(1-4), 267–279 (2004)
3. Dorigo, M., Socha, K.: An introduction to Ant Colony Optimisation. In: González, T.F. (ed.) Handbook of approximation algorithms and metaheurististics. Chapman & Hall/CRC Computer and Information Science Series. Taylor & Francis Group, USA (2007)
4. Teodorović, D., Lučić, P.: The fuzzy ant system for the vehicle routing problem when demand at nodes is uncertain. International Journal on Artificial Intelligence Tools 16(5), 751–770 (2007)
5. Jackson, D., Chaline, N.: Moduluation of pheromone trail strength with food quality in Pharaon's ant, Monomorium pharaonis. Animal Behaviour 74(3), 463–470 (2007)
6. Robinson, E.J.H., Green, K.E., Jenner, E.A., Holcombe, M., Ratnieks, F.L.W.: Decay rates of attractive and repellent pheromones in an ant foraging trail network. Insectes Sociaux 55(1), 246–251 (2008)
7. Hölldobler, B., Morgan, E.D., Oldham, N.J., Liebig, J.: Recruitment pheromone in the harvester ant genus Pogonomyrmex. Journal of Insect Physiology 47(4-5), 369–374 (2001)
8. Sillam-Dussès, D., Kalinová, B., Jiroš, P., Březinová, A., Cvačka, J., Hanus, R., Šobotník, J., Bordereau, C., Valterová, I.: Identification by GC-EAD of the two-component trail-following pheromone of Prorhinotermes simplex. Journal of Insect Physiology 55(8), 751–757 (2009)
9. Sumpter, D.J.T., Beekman, M.: From nonlinearity to optimality: Pheromone trail foraging by ants. Animal Behaviour 66(2), 273–280 (2003)
10. Depickère, S., Fresneau, D., Deneubourg, J.L.: Effect of social and environmental factors on ant aggregation: A general response? Journal of Insect Physiology 54(9), 1349–1355 (2008)
11. Garnier, G., Gautrais, J., Theraulaz, G.: The biological principles of swarm intelligence. Swarm Intelligence 1, 3–31 (2007)

12. Jeanson, R., Ratnieks, F.L.W., Deneubourg, J.L.: Pheromone trail decay rates on different substrates in the Pharaoh's ant, Monomorium pharaonis. Physiological Entomology 28(3), 192–198 (2008)
13. Niven, J.E.: Invertebrate Memory: Wide-Eyed Ants Retrieve Visual Snapshots. Current Biology 17(3), 85–87 (2007)
14. Tanackov, I., Simić, D., Mihaljev-Martinov, J., Stojić, G., Sremac, S.: The Spatial Pheromone Signal for Ant Colony Optimisation. In: Corchado, E., Yin, H. (eds.) IDEAL 2009. LNCS, vol. 5788, pp. 400–407. Springer, Heidelberg (2009)
15. Stakhov, A.: Fundamentals of a new kind of mathematics, based on the Golden Section. Chaos, Solitons & Fractals 27, 1124–1146 (2006)
16. El Nashie, M.S.: Is quantum space a random cantor set with a golden mean dimension at the core? Chaos, Solitons & Fractals 4, 177–179 (1994)
17. Coldea, R., Tennant, D.A., Wheeler, E.M., Wawrzynska, E., Prabhakaran, D., Telling, M., Habicht, K., Smeibidl, P., Kiefer, K.: Quantum Criticality in an Ising Chain: Experimental Evidence for Emergent E_8. Science 327, 177–180 (2010)
18. Yablonsky, G.S., Constales, D., Marin, G.B.: Coincidences in chemical kinetics: Surprising news about simple reactions. Chemical Engineering Science 65, 6065–6076 (2010)
19. Heyrovska, R.: Dependences of molar volumes in solids, partial molal and hydrated ionic volumes of alkali halides on covalent and ionic radii and the golden ratio. Chemical Physics Letters 436, 287–293 (2007)
20. Yamagishi, M.E.B., Shimabukuro, A.I.: Nucleotide Frequencies in Human Genome and Fibonacci Numbers. Bulletin of Mathematical Biology 70, 643–653 (2008)
21. Perez, J.C.: Codon populations in single-stranded whole human genome DNA Are fractal and fine-tuned by the Golden Ratio 1.618. Interdisciplinary Sciences: Computational Life Sciences 2, 228–240 (2010)
22. Mathai, A.M., Davis, A.D.: Constructing the sunflower head. Mathematical Biosciences 20, 117–133 (1974)
23. Ridley, J.N.: Packing efficiency in sunflower heads. Mathematical Biosciences 5, 129–139 (1982)
24. Lanling, Z.L., Wang, G.: Modeling golden section in plants. Progress in Natural Science 19, 255–260 (2009)
25. Pletzer, B., Kerschbaum, H., Klimesch, W.: When frequencies never synchronize: The golden mean and the resting EEG. Brain Research 1335, 91–102 (2010)
26. Schmid, K., Marx, D., Samal, A.: Computation of a face attractiveness index based on neoclassical canons, symmetry, and golden ratios. Pattern Recognition 41, 2710–2717 (2008)
27. Mizumoto, Y., Deguchi, T., Kelvin, W.C.F.: Assessment of facial golden proportions among young Japanese women. American Journal of Orthodontics and Dentofacial Orthopedics 136, 168–174 (2009)
28. Butusov, K.P.: The Golden Section in the solar system. Problemy Issledovania Vselennoy 7, 475–500 (1978)
29. Stakhov, A., Rozin, B.: The "golden" hyperbolic models of Universe. Chaos, Solitons & Fractals 34(2), 159–171 (2007)
30. Leonardo, D.G., Sigalotti, L.D.G., Mejias, A.: The golden ratio in special relativity. Chaos, Solitons & Fractals 30, 521–524 (2006)
31. Stakhov, A., Rozin, B.: On a new class of hyperbolic functions. Chaos, Solitons & Fractals 23, 379–389 (2005)
32. Tanackov, I., Simić, D., Sremac, S., Tepić, J., Kocić-Tanackov, S.: Markovian Ants in a Queuing System. In: Graña Romay, M., Corchado, E., Garcia Sebastian, M.T. (eds.) HAIS 2010. LNCS, vol. 6076, pp. 32–39. Springer, Heidelberg (2010)

A Memetic Algorithm for Routing in Urban Public Transportation Networks

Jolanta Koszelew and Krzysztof Ostrowski

Faculty of Computer Science, Bialystok University of Technology
{j.koszelew,k.ostrowski}@pb.edu.pl

Abstract. This paper presents a new memetic algorithm, which solves bi-criteria version of Routing Problem in Urban Public Transportation Networks. Our solution returns a set of routes, containing at most k quasi-optimal paths with the earliest arrival in the first instance and with minimal number of transfers in the second. The method was implemented and tested on the real-life public transportation network of Warsaw city in Poland. This network was completed with walk links and therefore resultant routes are more practical. Effectiveness of the described solution was compared in two aspects: time complexity and quality of results, with another three algorithms for considered problem. Computational experiments clearly show the memetic algorithm be highly competitive with comparable ones, yielding new improved solutions in the most cases of tested source/destination specifications.

Keywords: memetic algorithm, Bus Routing Problem, bi-criteria optimization, time-dependent model.

1 Introduction

A public transportation route planner is a kind of Intelligent Transportation Systems (ITS) and provide information about available public transport journeys. Users of such system determine source and destination point of the travel, the start time, their preferences and system returns as a result, information about optimal routes. In practice, public transport users preferences may be various, but the most important of them are: the earliest arrival and the minimal number of transfers (changes of vehicles). Finding routes with minimal number of changes is not a difficult problem, but generating routes with minimal time of realization, on the base of dynamic timetables, is much more complexity task. Generally, the Routing Problem in Urban Transportation Networks often shortly named Bus Routing Problem (BRP) constitutes a multi-criteria time-dependent routing and planning problem [11], providing a user with many alternative itineraries for a given urban journey.

The shortest path problem is a core model that lies at the heart of network optimization. It assumes that weight link in traditional network is static, but is not true in many fields of ITS. The optimal path problems in variable-time network break through the limit of traditional shortest path problems and become foundation theory in ITS. The new real problems make the optimal path

A. Bouchachia (Ed.): ICAIS 2011, LNAI 6943, pp. 368–380, 2011.

computing to be more difficult than finding the shortest paths in networks with static and deterministic links, meanwhile algorithms for a scheduled transportation network are time-dependent.

Moreover, standard algorithms considered graphs with one kind of links (undirected or directed) which have no parallel arcs. Graph which models a public transport network includes two kinds of edges: directed links which represent connections between transport stops and undirected arcs which correspond to walk link between transport stops.

Additionally, each node in a graph which represents a transportation network includes details such as: timetables, coordinates of transport stops, etc. This information is necessarily to determine weights of links during realization of the algorithm.

These three differences between standard shortest path problem and routing problem in public transportation network may result in high time complexity of algorithms which solve this problem.

Many methods has been developed for networks with time-dependent connections but most of them take into consideration a network with only one kind of link, without parallel links and returns only one route. Cooke and Halsey [5] modified Bellman's [2] "single-source with possibly negative weights" algorithm to find the shortest path between any two vertices in a time-dependent network. Dreyfus [7] made a modification to the standard Dijkstra algorithm to cope with the time-dependent shortest path problem. Orda and Rom [15] discussed how to convert the cost of discrete and continuous time networks into a simpler model and still used traditional shortest path algorithms for the time-dependent networks. Chabini [4] presented an algorithm for the problem with discrete time and edge weights are time-dependent. Ahuja [1] proved that finding the general minimum cost path in a time-dependent network is NP-hard and special approximation method must be used to solve this problem.

The new memetic algorithm (MA) for BRP presented in this paper generates k routes with the earliest arrival travel time and the minimal number of transfers in lexicographical order. Like the k-shortest paths algorithm [14], these methods generate multiple "better" paths, the user can have more choices from where he or she can select according own preferences such as total amount of fares, convenience, preferred routes and so on.

The computational performance of proposed method had been tested on the real-life urban public transportation network of Warsaw city in Poland. Results of experiments were also compared with three another methods solving the BRP. Two methods are a bio-inspired algorithm based on populations of agents. The first algorithm realizes an cultural algorithm (CA) [17]. The second method applies an ant colony optimization (ACO)[3]. The third comparable method - Routes Generation Matrix Algorithm (RGMA) [13] applies label-setting strategy with two special meta heuristics based on the minimal number of transfer matrix and the minimal number of bus stops matrix. Computer experiments had shown that MA generates routes better than comparable algorithms and is significantly faster than ACO and CA.

The remainder of this paper consists of five sections. Section 2 includes definition of Bus Routing Problem and description of multi-modal urban public transport network model. In Section 3 authors present each step of MA and illustrates it with simple examples. Section 4 is the comparison of effectiveness of comparable methods in two aspects: computation time and quality of resultant routes. The paper ends the section which also includes the major concluding remark.

2   Network Model and Problem Definition

A public transportation network in our model is represented as a bimodal weighted graph $G = \langle V, C, W \rangle$, where V is a set of nodes, C is a set of directed edges and W is a set of undirected edges. This model is an extended version of the *time-dependent* model for BRP proposed in [16]. The extension rests on adding walk connections. Each node in G corresponds to a certain transport stop (bus, tram or metro stop, etc.), shortly named a stop. We assume that stops are represented with numbers from 1 to n. The directed edge c represents an elementary transport connection. For $c = (l, i, j, t_d, t_a)$ bus line number l (or other means of transport) leaves stop i at time t_d and the immediately next stop of this bus is stop j at time t_a. A set of connections is bimodal because it includes, besides elementary transport connections, elementary walk connections. The undirected edge $w = \{i, j, t\}$ is an elementary walk connection of the set W, if walk time in minutes between i and j stops is not greater than *limit* parameter. The value of *limit* parameter has a big influence on the number of network links (density of graph). The t value for undirected edge $\{i, j, t\}$ is equal to walk time in minutes between i and j stops.

At a stop v is possible to transfer from one bus line to another, from bus to walk or from walk to bus. If we transfer from one bus line to another then such transfer is only possible if the time between the arrival and the departure at that station v is larger than or equal to a given, stop-specific, minimum transfer time, denoted by $transfer(v)$.

Let $P = (c_1, ..., c_r)$ be a sequence of elementary connections (transport or walk). Such a sequence P is called a consistent connection (route) from stop v_1 to stop v_r if it fulfills some consistency conditions:

a.   : departure station of c_{i+1} is the arrival station of c_i ;
b.   : if c_i is an elementary transport connection then the time values correspond to the time values t_d and t_a of c_i respect the transfer times and the time of arrival and departure at c_{i-1} and c_{i+1} stops;
c.   :if c_i is an elementary walk connection and c_{i+1} is an elementary transport connection then the departure time of c_{i+1} is later than the sum of the arrival time of c_{i-1} and the walk time of c_i.

A graph representation of public transportation network is shown in Fig. 1. It is a very simple example of the network which includes only nine stops. We mark for transparency only bus line and walk possibilities of direct connections between each pair of stops in this figure. We show detail description only for one example elementary transport connection (between stops 7 and 9) and one elementary walk connection (between stops 2 and 4). Really, there are four elementary transport connections from 7 to 9 which come out of timetables for stops 7 and 9.

In the real world the number of nodes is equal to 3500 for the city with about 1 million of inhabitants.

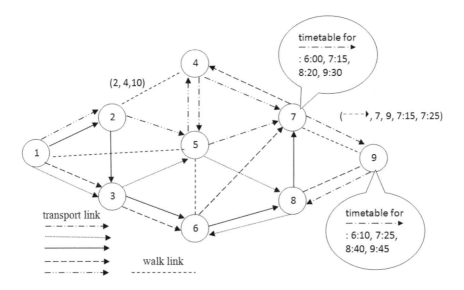

Fig. 1. Graph model a simple transportation network

MA uses graph G as a main o the input parameter. Besides, time-independent version of G is applied in this method. We will call this version *transfers graph* and denote by G_{TR}. $G_{TR} = \langle V, E \rangle$, where V is a set of stops and E is a set of undirected transfer connections. The edge i, j is the transfer connection in G_{TR}, if there is at least one route without transfers between stops i and j. G_{TR} has no weights because we don't consider any time values for connections. We can precompute a transfer graph for given transportation network because this graph is time-independent.

For the timetable-information problems defined below, we are, in addition, given a large, on-line sequence of queries. A query defines a set of valid connections and an optimization criterion (or criteria) on that set of connections. The problem is to find the optimal connection (or a set of optimal connections) with respect to the specific criterion or criteria. In this work, we are concerned with two of the most important criteria, namely, the earliest arrival and the minimum number of transfers, and, consequently, investigate an bi-criteria optimization problem.

Formal definition of our problem is as follows: At the input we have: G - graph of transportation network, G_{TR}- transfer graph of the network, source point of the travel (o), destination point of the travel (d), starting time of the travel $(time_o)$, number of the resultant paths (k), limit for walk links $(limit)$ and the maximal number of transfers $maxtr$. At the output we want to have the set of resultant routes (consistent connections) between stops (o) and d, containing at most k quasi-optimal paths with the earliest arrival and the minimum number of transfers as the two criteria. We find the lexicographically first Pareto-optimal solution (e.g., find among all connections that minimize the earliest arrival the one with minimum number of transfers).

3   Description of MA

Memetic algorithms are evolutionary algorithms[10] that apply a separate local search process to refine individuals (i.e. improve their fitness by hillclimbing)[9]. These methods are inspired by models of adaptation in natural systems that combine evolutionary adaptation of populations of individuals with individual learning within a lifetime. Additionally, memetic algorithms are inspired by Richard Dawkins concept of a meme [6], which represents a unit of cultural evolution that can exhibit local refinement.

MA is based on two key observations: many shortest paths share the same $transfertemplates$ i.e., the sequence of stations where a change of vehicle occurs; direct connections without change of vehicle can be looked up quickly.

3.1   Precomputation Step

Before first running of the MA $transfer\ templates$ - set $TR_{o,d}$ for each pair of o and d stops are determined. A transfer template includes only consecutive transfer stops belongs to route, without time values and number of bus line. We can determine $TR_{o,d}$ sets on the base of the transfer graph G_{TR}. The method for determining $TR_{o,d}$ is defined in [13]. Additionally, the set $TR_{o,d}$ must be divided by separated subsets $TR_{o,d}(i)$ where $i=0..maxtr$. In Fig. 3 transfer templates included in $TR_{1,6}(1)$, for the network presented in Fig. 1 is shown. We can generate routes between o and d very fast using $TR_{o,d}[12]$. The example of transformation templates to routes for the network presented in Fig. 1 are shown in Fig. 2.

During the precomputation step we must also determine a $minimal\ number$ $of\ transfer\ matrix\ Q$. The value of $Q[i,j]$ element i equal to the minimal number of transfers on the routes from stop i to stop j. This matrix is determined on the base of transfer matrix G_{TR} and $maxtr$ value [13] and will be applied in the mutation operator. It's very important that time of realization of precomputation doesn't increase the computation time of MA, because this step is used only one time before first running of the method.

Memetic algorithms as a kind of evolutionary algorithms work on a population of solutions evolves trough the repetitive combination of its individuals. An encoding is said to be indirect if a decoding procedure is necessary to extract

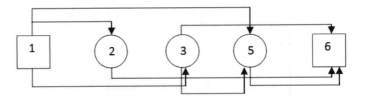

Fig. 2. Transfer templates included in $TR_{1,6}(1)$, for the network presented in Fig. 1

solutions from individuals. In MA we use as individuals time-independent version of consistent connection (route). A time-independent version of consistent connection (route) doesn't include transport time values t_d and t_a for elementary transport connections and a walk time value t forthe the elementary walk connections.A decoding procedure rests on determination of time values for each elementary connections in the individuals. We choose the earliest possible values of t_d and t_a during decoding of course. Time values must satisfied all conditions defined for a consistent connection according to the value of $time_o$ parameter.

3.2   The MA

Using MA routes determination is a multi-stage process involving following steps:

1. **Initialization:** MA starts with generating an initial number of individuals - nP. Individuals are randomly generated as time-independent version of consistent connections with the minimal number of transfers on the base of set $TR_{o,d}(0)$. If after this step the number of individuals is less than nP then we continue generation using templates with one transfer $(TR_{o,d}(1))$, etc. Randomly generated, it does mean that if we have for example the transfer template: $(o, v_1, v_2, ..., v_r, d)$ belonging to $TR_{o,d}(r)$ then we can randomly choose bus lines (walk links) which are common for previous and next stop for each stop in a given transfer template (besides of o and d stops). Note, that the route belonging to the initial population have the least possible number of transfers. However, this does not mean that time-dependent links randomly added to the template will give a route with shortest travel time. The travel time heavily depends from the waiting time at each transfer stop. In Fig.3 individuals generated on the base of the transfer template (1, 5, 6) are presented. The value of nP parameter should be adjusted to the density of G_{TR} graph. The G_{TR} graph density depends on the number of bus lines and the limit for walk links (*limit*). The higher values of these parameters the greater the value of nP. But on the other hand, the higher value of nP, the longer time of realization of each step of MA. The same relationship applies for CA and ACO algorithms. The density of the G_{TR} in the least affect the time of realization of the RGMA. cite Koszelew08. The number of generated individuals after this step may be less than nP. In such situation we generate others individuals with any number of transfers.

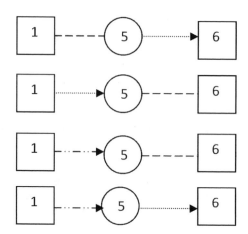

Fig. 3. Example individuals (routes) generated on the base of the transfer template $(1, 5, 6)$, included in $TR_{1,6}(1)$, for the network presented in Fig. 1

2. **Evaluation:** We run decoding procedure for each individuals. Next, we calculate a value of fitness function to evaluate the optimum nature of each route (chromosome). The fitness function should estimate the quality of individuals, according to arrival time of the route and number of transfers lexicographically first Pareto-optimal solution. In each step of improving population participates only nP best individuals. Other individuals are deleted from the population.

3. **Improving population:** After fitness evaluation, the MA starts to improve initial population through ng applications of crossover and mutation. In every generation we first choose with probability pr between crossover and mutation.

   3.1. Crossover: We first select two parent individuals, according to the fitness value: the better an individual is, the bigger chance it has to be chosen. Since chromosomes lengths are different, we presented a new heuristic crossover operator, adjusted to our problem. In the first step we test if crossover can take place. If two parents do not have at least one common bus stop, crossover can not be done and parents remain unchanged. Crossover is implemented in the following way. First we choose one common bus stop, it will be the crossing point. Then we exchange fragments of chromosomes from the crossing point to the end stop in two parent individuals. After crossover, we must correct offspring individuals in two ways. First we eliminate bus stop loops, then we eliminate line loops. The next step is to compute fitness function for these new individuals. Finally, we choose two best individuals from mutated chromosomes and offspring and add them to the population. The example of parents and offspring individuals after crossover operator is shown in Fig. 4.

   3.2. Mutation: We first choose randomly one chromosome (one route). The next step of the mutation operator consists in realization of

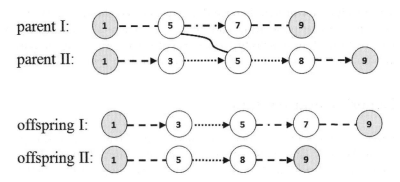

Fig. 4. Example parents and offspring individuals after crossover for network shown in Fig. 1

local search technique (LS) which tries to short cut the route. Let I be randomly chosen chromosome and $I_{TR} = (o, v_1, ..., v_r, d)$ be the transfer template of I. LS searches such pair of stops in I_{TR} for which the number of transfers is greater than minimal. Let o_1 and d_1 be first finding pair of stops in the route I_{TR} with greater than minimal number of transfers. The fragment of I_{TR} from o_1 to d_1 in the chromosome being mutated is substituted by any transfer template contained in TR_{o_1,o_2}. Next, we recalculate new chromosome. Then we compute fitness function for this individual and add it to the population. The example of parent individuals and offsprings after mutation operator is shown in Fig.3 5. To check the minimal number of transfers between stops o_1 and d_1 we use a minimal number transfer matrix Q determined as a result of precomputation step.

5. **Determining results:** k resultant routes are selected from the final population by choosing k routes with the best fitness.

MA applies results of precomputation in the initialization step and the mutation operator. Therefore, initial routes and offsprings individuals after genetic opera-

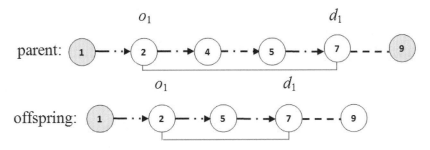

Fig. 5. Example parent and offspring individual after mutation for network shown in Fig. 1

tors have much better fitness than randomly generated chromosomes. Therefore, even for small size of population and number of generations its possible to determine good quality of resultant routes. Small values of nP and ng parameters have a big influence on the reduction of a computation time of the method.

4   Experimental Results

There were a number of computer tests conducted on real data of transportation network in Warsaw city. This network consists of about 4200 stops, connected by about 240 bus, tram and metro lines. Values of common parameters for all comparable algorithms were following: $k = 3$, $limit = 15$, $maxtr = 5$. The value of $limit$ is very important because it influences the density of network. The bigger value of $limit$, the more possibilities of walk links in a network. Density of the network is of a key importance for time-complexity of algorithms. Experiments were made by executing 5 runs for each starting point and destination point. Additional parameters for MA and CA were equal to: $pr = 0.5$, $nP = 30$, $ng = 50$. Experiments have been done with the following parameters settings for ACO: $mCA_{PRIME} = mCA_{SECOND} = 25$, $q_0 = 0.9$, $= 2$, $= 0.25$ (the same for each cast).

We tested three kinds of routes: from the center of the city to the periphery of the city (set CP), routes from the periphery of the city to the center of the city (set PC) and routes from the periphery of the city to the periphery of the city (set PP). Each of these sets includes 30 specification of first (o) and last (d) stops in the route which are difficult cases for each algorithm. First matter is a long distance from o and d (PP set), the second is a high density of the network in o or d localization (CP and PC sets). Algorithms was tested in a computer equipped with an Intel core2 Duo T7300, 2 GHz and 2 GB RAM.

Selected results of tests for 10 chosen specifications of o and d for each examined set of routes, generated by MA, CA, ACO and RGMA, are presented in Tab. 1, Tab. 2 and Tab. 3. For each algorithm we show in these tabels: o and d specification (longitude, latitude), distance between o and d (by car in km), the minimal travel-time for k resultant routes (MA-t,CA-t, ACO-t, RGMA-t), the number of transfers for the route with the minimal travel-time (MA-tr,CA-tr, ACO-tr, RGMA-tr).

All results presented in above tables are confirmation of good quality of routes of MA because the values of travel-time for the best and worst route are less or equal for other comparable method. Generally, only in three case of tested routes the travel-time was worse for MA than for comparable solutions and always the number of transfers for resultant best routes for MA was not greater than for the best route of other algorithms.

The last experiment was focused on comparison of time complexity of algorithms. The results are presented in Fig. 6.In this experiment we tested examples of routes with a minimal number of stops, between 5 and 60. On the horizontal axis there are points representing the minimal number of stops on a route. These values were computed as a result of standard BFS graph search method

Table 1. The results for routes from set $P-C$; $time_o = 7{:}30$; $o =(52.077130, 21.100000)$

d-destination stop	$o-d$	MA-t	CA-t	ACO-t	RGMA-t	MA-tr	CA-tr	ACO-tr	RGMA-tr
(52.219720, 21.025290)	20.0	57	57	59	61	2	2	2	2
(52.222660, 21.016650)	20.6	59	62	63	71	2	2	2	2
(52.216490, 21.005660)	20.8	60	60	62	66	1	3	1	1
(52.229380, 21.002720)	23.6	64	64	66	69	1	2	1	1
(52.217030, 20.981810)	23.9	75	79	80	81	3	3	3	3
(52.236880, 21.016820)	22.7	62	62	66	64	2	2	2	2
(52.232310, 20.976720)	25.6	70	82	78	80	2	3	3	3
(52.244670, 20.965750)	27.0	71	71	79	81	3	3	3	3
(52.234960, 21.006930)	25.2	60	65	67	69	2	2	2	2
(52.233180, 21.002520)	24.3	71	71	73	73	3	3	3	3

Table 2. The results for routes from set $C-P$; $time_o=15{:}30$; $o=(52.222740, 21.004780)$

d-destination stop	$o-d$	MA-t	CA-t	ACO-t	RGMA-t	MA-tr	CA-tr	ACO-tr	RGMA-tr
(52.233690, 20.981700)	22.0	104	104	112	124	3	3	4	4
(52.412200, 20.942090)	26.7	80	82	83	97	3	3	3	3
(52.139660, 20.902150)	12.4	64	64	84	88	2	3	4	4
(52.237870, 20.996560)	13.2.9	86	103	86	88	3	3	3	3
(52.153050, 21.219420)	21.8	81	81	81	84	2	2	3	3
(52.359440, 21.135300)	19.3	63	63	64	63	2	2	2	2
(52.436880, 21.022030)	31.1	72	75	78	83	2	3	2	2
(52.192100, 20.949140)	24.1	35	35	37	44	2	3	3	2
(52.329730, 20.883180)	33.0	67	67	73	84	3	3	3	3
(52.223640, 21.139390)	11.1	60	66	68	71	3	3	2	3

Table 3. The results for routes from set $P-P$; $time_o=7{:}30$; $o=(52.358160, 21.133850)$

d-destination stop	$o-d$	MA-t	CA-t	ACO-t	RGMA-t	MA-tr	CA-tr	ACO-tr	RGMA-tr
(52.049060, 20.783810)	48.5	76	76	88	91	3	3	4	4
(52.412200, 20.942090)	18.3	100	117	137	149	4	4	4	4
(52.139660, 20.902150)	33.6	103	103	123	138	5	5	5	5
(52.153050, 21.219420)	26.6	99	99	149	181	3	3	4	5
(52.232030, 20.993190)	24.2	69	79	80	81	3	3	3	3
(52.436880, 21.022030)	14.4	92	96	108	111	3	3	4	4
(52.223640, 21.139390)	18.0	70	77	84	93	1	2	2	4
(52.054840, 20.924700)	42.3	75	75	78	81	4	4	5	5
(52.329730, 20.883180)	29.1	105	105	106	120	3	5	4	4
(52.303200, 20.777510)	29.5	82	82	87	96	3	3	4	4

and they are correlated with difficulty of the route. On the vertical axis there is marked time of execution. Each possible route with a given number of the minimal number of stops was tested by each algorithm at starting time at 7:30 a.m., weekday. The executing time of algorithms was averaged over every tested routes. We can see that MA performs in significantly shorter time than ACO and

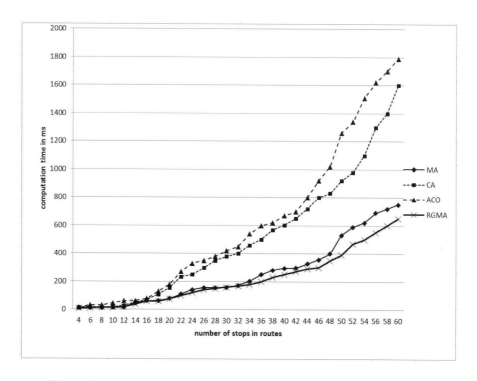

Fig. 6. The comparison of execution time of MA, CA, ACO and RGMA

CA and comparable with RGMA, especially for routes with minimal number of stops not greater than 46.

5   Conclusions

We believe that use of knowledge about public transportation network and local search technique in algorithms which are solving BRP is an idea with a great potential. Computer experiments have shown that MA performs much better than comparable methods based on another artificial intelligence strategy such as ant colony optimization or cultural algorithms. MA applies transform templates which are also used in RGMA. This method is based on label-setting strategy and don't use population and randomization. Therefore, RGMA works on strongly limited space of cases. MA as a population algorithm works on much greater set of cases and performs much better than RGMA. On the other hand population based algorithms has worse time-complexity than methods which try improved only one individual. Though MA returns high quality results even for small size of population ($nP = 30$) and a small number of generations ($ng = 50$). It's possible by applies transfers templates in the initialization step of MA and in the mutation operator.

Future work will be concentrated on testing MA on the transportation network for bigger metropolises or regions with number of stops exceeding 5000. If tests show poor performance of MA the new heuristics must be added to the algorithm. The proposal of improvement which can be considered includes to the algorithm information about geographic location of start and destination stops. Obvoius directions for future research is also make the precomputation faster applies parallel realization or/and cloud computing technique for this step.

Acknowledgments. This research was supported by S/WI/1/11.

References

1. Ahuja, R.K., Orlin, J.B., Pallotino, S., Scutella, M.G.: Dynamic shortest path minimizing travel times and costs. Networks 41(4), 197–205 (2003)
2. Bellman, R.E.: On a Routing Problem. Journal Quarterly of Applied Mathematics 16, 87–90 (1958)
3. Boryczka, U., Boryczka, M.: Multi-cast ant colony system for the bus routing problem. Applied Optimization 86, 91–125 (2004)
4. Chabini, I.: Discrete dynamic shortest path problems in transportation applications. Complexity and Algorithms With Optimal Run Time, Journal Transportation Research Records, 170–175 (1998)
5. Cooke, K.L., Halsey, E.: The shortest route through a network with time-dependent intermodal transit times. Journal Math. Anal. Appl. 14, 493–498 (1996)
6. Dawkins, R.: The Selfish Gene. Clarendon Press, Oxford (1976)
7. Dreyfus, S.E.: An Appraisal of Some Shortest-path Algorithms. Journal Operations Research 17, 395–412 (1969)
8. Galves-Fernandez, C., Khadraoui, D.: Remainder: Distributed Aproach for Solving Time-Dependent Problems in Multimodal Transport Networks. Advanced in Operation Research (2009); doi:10.1016/j.cie.2010.05.018
9. Chi-Keong, G., Yew-Soon, O., Kay Chen, T.: Multi-Objective Memetic Algorithms. SCI, vol. 171. Springer, Heidelberg (2007)
10. Goldberg, D.E.: Genetic algorithms and their applications. WNT, Warsaw (1995)
11. Hansen, P.: Bicriterion path problems. In: Multicriteria decision making: theory and applications. Lecture Notes in Economics and Mathematical Systems, vol. 177, pp. 236–245 (1980)
12. Koszelew, J.: Approximation method to route generation in public transportation network. Polish Journal of Enviromental Studies 17(4C), 418–422 (2008)
13. Piwonska, A., Koszelew, J.: Evolutionary algorithms find routes in public transport network with optimal time of realization. In: Mikulski, J. (ed.) TST 2010. CCIS, vol. 104, pp. 194–201. Springer, Heidelberg (2010)
14. Lawler, E.L.: A procedure for computing the K best solutions to discrete optimization problems and its application to the shortest path problem. Management Science 18, 401–405 (1972)

15. Orda, A., Rom, R.: Shortest path and minimum - delay algorithms in networks with time-dependent edge-length. Journal Assoc. Computer Mach. 37(3), 607–625 (1990)
16. Pyrga, E., Schultz, F., Wagner, D., Zaroliagis, C.D.: Efficient models for timetable inforamtion in public transformation systems. Journal of Experimental Algorithms 12 (2007)
17. Reyes, L.C., Ochoa, C.A., Santilln, C.G., Hernndez, P., Fuerte, M.V.: A Cultural Algorithm for the Urban Public Transportation. In: Corchado, E., Graña Romay, M., Manhaes Savio, A. (eds.) HAIS 2010. LNCS (LNAI), vol. 6077, pp. 135–142. Springer, Heidelberg (2010)

A PDDE-Based Order Scheduling Optimization with Raw Material Uncertainty

Wai-Keung Wong[1], Sunney Yung-Sun Leung[1], and Xianhui Zeng[1,2]

[1] Institute of Textiles and Clothing, The Hong Kong Polytechnic University, Hong Kong
[2] College of Informaton Science and Technology, Donghua University, Shanghai, China
{tcwongca,tcleungs,tcxhzeng}@inet.polyu.edu.hk

Abstract. An adaptive order scheduling system is of great importance for the successful implementation of production planning in dynamic make-to-order production environment where a variety of unexpected disruptions is usually inevitable. This paper investigated the scheduling problem with uncertain arrival of raw materials and limited production capacity. A Pareto discrete differential evolution (PDDE) approach is proposed to generate the approximate optimum scheduling solution with stochastic arrival of raw materials. The PDDE algorithm adopts Pareto selection strategy to improve adaptability of the PDDE algorithm upon evolving towards the global optimal solution and integrates the stochastic simulation model and utility function into the fitness evaluation of the individuals. The experimental results demonstrate that the proposed PDDE optimization model outperforms the industrial practice and has self-adaptation and fitness capacity to responsively self-adjust upon the uncertain arrival of raw material.

Keywords: Order scheduling, uncertain arrival of raw materials, make-to-order (MTO), Pareto discrete differential evolution (PDDE), optimization.

1 Introduction

In today's manufacturing, keeping up with supply and demand is challenging as shortening of products' life cycle and popularity of customized products. More and more manufacturers have shifted from the conventional mass production to a make-to-order (MTO) production mode since small batch production jobs or small customer orders have become the trend of product production [1]. The MTO production system is a kind of dynamically changing systems where a variety of unexpected disruptions is usually inevitable, such as rush orders are accepted, raw materials are in shortage, due dates are changed. It is nearly impossible to predict the requirements of customer orders since they are in general independent from each other [2]. Thus, the key performance indicator for a successful production is on-time delivery due to the uniqueness of the products [3]. An adaptive order scheduling system is of great importance to ensure on-time delivery for the MTO production.

The MTO production is flexible and complicated due to the variety of products, which leads to new problems emerging for the MTO production scheduling. First,

A. Bouchachia (Ed.): ICAIS 2011, LNAI 6943, pp. 381–392, 2011.
© Springer-Verlag Berlin Heidelberg 2011

order selection becomes increasingly important due to production capacity limitation with certain periods, such as peak period. The selection criteria may involve production capacity, trade-off between the revenue and the cost, focusing on particular types of customers, etc. Second, the production cannot be started until the customer orders are received. Thus, stocking enough raw materials is nearly impossible before the orders release due to the uniqueness of the products in MTO production. The production capacity and raw material availability should be jointly considered for the MTO production scheduling. Third, order shifting and order partition are two common ways to improve manufacturing flexibility and production efficiency in MTO production. Order shifting means that an assembly line performs several orders by switching the jobs among them. Order partition occurs when one order is assigned to several assembly lines at different shop floors. It is evident that determining the suitable combinations of order shifting and order partition for MTO production is a NP-hard problem.

Most of previous studies on order scheduling are based on the deterministic estimation of order arrival, raw materials supplies, processing time of each production process [1, 4]. In most real-world MTO environments, availability of raw materials is the crucial factor that affects the adaptability of the order scheduling system. Shortage of materials can lead to not only increasing machine idle time, but also failing to deliver orders at due dates. It is clearly difficult to realize an optimized order scheduling in real-life production environment without considering the arrival of raw materials. The uncertain arrival of raw materials even makes order scheduling problem more complicated and difficult.

This paper will investigate the order scheduling problem with the uncertain arrival of raw materials and limited production capacity for MTO production. The uncertain arrival time of raw materials is considered as a random variable and the multistage arrival of the raw materials is explored. A multi-objective optimization model is derived and the Pareto discrete differential evolution (PDDE) algorithm is proposed to obtain the approximate optimum solution for the order scheduling problem.

2   Problem Formulation

Whether or not the order can be processed in MTO production is determined by production capacity and raw material availability. The raw materials requirement is uncertain due to the fact that the unexpected events occur frequently: rush orders arrive, customer orders are canceled, deliveries are changed, due dates are changed, etc. In this study, a stochastic model of arrival of raw materials is considered based on the circumstance of each order requiring one type of raw material. It is necessary to determine order's production according to arrival of the raw materials and to take assignment decision on how many quantities of raw material is to be used for one order. The objective of order scheduling we explored is to maximize the possibility of meeting the due dates of all orders, with the minimum cost under the stochastic arrival of raw materials.

Suppose that there are s shop floors, each has n assembly lines. L_{kl} denotes the lth assembly line in shop floor S_k ($1 \leq k \leq s$). Let $O=\{O_1,...,O_m\}$ be the set of customer orders. Each order has a due date TD_i, size S_i ($i \in O$), and requires one type of raw material. Assume that $M=\{M_1,\ldots,M_J\}$ is the set of J different types of raw materials. Let $q_{j,i}$ be the amount of the raw materials M_j required by order O_i for making one piece of the corresponding product. $Q_j(t)$ is denoted as the amount of raw material M_j available at time t, and $R_j(t)$ the amount of raw material M_j arrived at time t. For an arbitrary schedule S, the following constraints should be satisfied.

(1) Within a finite production time horizon [0, T], the supply of raw materials is exactly sufficient to accomplish all orders, i.e.,

$$\sum_{t=0}^{T} R_j(t) \geq \sum_{i=1}^{m} S_i \cdot q_{j,i}, \quad \forall j \in M \tag{1}$$

(2) Let X_{ikl} be decision variable indicating if order O_i assigned to assembly line L_{kl} At any time t, if X_{ikl} is equal to 1, assembly line L_{kl} cannot perform O_i until the raw material available is sufficient to complete O_i at least one day, i.e.

$$Q_j(t) \geq C_{ikl} \cdot q_{j,i}, \quad \forall j \in M \tag{2}$$

where C_{ikl} is production capacity of assembly line L_{kl} for performing order O_i at one day. In the case that several orders requires the same type of raw material, the inequalities (2) should be satisfied under each order in turn by adjusting $Q_j(t)$.
(3) Each order should be assigned to at least one assembly line that can process it, i.e.,

$$\sum_{kl} C_{ikl} \cdot X_{ikl} > 0, \quad \forall i \in O \tag{3}$$

In the MTO industries, one of the most important objectives is to meet the due dates of customer orders. Since the arrival of raw materials is uncertain, the production for the corresponding orders is also uncertain which finally results in the uncertain completion time of each production orders. This makes it difficult to evaluate directly the degree of the due dates met. To overcome this difficulty, the completion time satisfaction level for O_i with completion time TC_i, denoted by $SL(TC_i)$, is defined as

$$SL(TC_i) = \begin{cases} (TC_i - T_l)/(T_e - T_l) & T_l < TC_i \leq T_e \\ 1 & T_e < TC_i \leq TD_i \\ (TC_i - T_h)/(TD_i - T_h) & TD_i < TC_i \leq T_h \\ 0 & otherwise \end{cases} \tag{4}$$

Based on formulation (4) and probability theory, the total performance of the order to meet the due date, denoted by $CTSL$, is defined as the expectation of the completion time satisfaction level which is formulated as follow,

$$CTSL = \frac{1}{m} \sum_{i=1,\ldots,m} \int_0^\infty f(TC_i) \cdot SL(TC_i) d(TC_i)) \tag{5}$$

where TC_i is the actual complete time of Order O_i, $f(TC_i)$ is its probability density function. So, the first objective function of the order scheduling problem is to maximize the completion time satisfaction level of all orders, which is expressed as,

Objective 1: maximize the complete time satisfaction level *CTSL* of all orders

$$\max CTSL(\sum_{kl} L_{kl},\ \sum_{i=1,...,m} O_i,\ \sum_{j=1,...J} M_j)$$

$$= \max(\frac{1}{m} \sum_{i=1,...,m} \int_0^\infty f(TC_i) \cdot SL(TC_i) d(TC_i))$$

$$= \min(1 - \frac{1}{m} \sum_{i=1,...,m} \int_0^\infty f(TC_i) \cdot SL(TC_i) d(TC_i)) \qquad (6)$$

The second and third objective functions of the addressed problem are thus to minimize the cost *COS* produced by order shifting and the cost *COP* by order partition respectively. The *COS* is expressed as,

Objective 2: minimize the cost of order shifting

$$\min COS(\sum_{kl} L_{kl},\ \sum_{i=1,...,m} O_i,\ \sum_{j=1,...J} M_j) = \min(E(\sum_{i=1,...,m kl}\sum(CS_i \cdot X_{ikl} \cdot TST_{ikl})) \qquad (7)$$

where CS_i is the cost of order setup for shifting of order O_i, TST_{ikl} is the setup times of order O_i on assembly line L_{kl} of shop floor S_k. $E(\cdot)$ denotes the expectation of a random variable.

For order partition, the cost should be produced when an order is assigned to the assembly lines owned by two or above shop-floors. The *COP* is expressed as,

Objective 3: minimize the cost of order partition

$$\min COP(\sum_{kl} L_{kl},\ \sum_{i=1,...,m} O_i,\ \sum_{j=1,...J} M_j) = \min(E(\sum_{i=1,...,m}(CP_i \cdot TSH_i))) \qquad (8)$$

where CP_i is the cost of order partition for order O_i, TSH_i is the number of shop floors that order O_i is assigned to, which is defined as

$$TSH_i = (\sum_{k=1,..,s} sign(\sum_{l=1,...,n} X_{ikl})) \qquad (9)$$

where $sign(x)=1$ if $x>0$, otherwise $sign(x)=0$.

3   PDDE Algorithm for Order Scheduling of MTO Production

The order scheduling for MTO production planning is a combinational optimization problem, which is NP-hard since the number of its possible solutions grows exponentially with the number of assembly lines, customer orders and raw materials. The classical optimization techniques are very difficult to solve such a problem. Recently, another kind of evolutionary algorithm, differential evolution (DE), has been proven to be very powerful and efficient in finding heuristic solutions from a large range of applications [5,6]. Lampinen and Storn [7] demonstrated that DE was more accurate than several optimization methods including genetic algorithms, simulated annealing and evolution programming. Based on this, DE is adapted in this research. Since the order scheduling problem of MTO production planning is a discrete multi-objective optimization problem. The real-value operators and greedy selection of DE should be extended to handle discrete space and multi-objective optimization of order scheduling. In this study, an improved Pareto discrete differential evolution (PDDE) algorithm, which adopts discrete-value arithmetic operators and modified double-set Pareto selection strategy, is proposed to solve the addressed order scheduling problem.

3.1 Representation

Consider the order scheduling problem with 5 orders to be assigned to 7 assembly lines in 3 shop floors, each order should be processed by at least one assembly line and each assembly line can perform zero or multiple orders in the production. The vector representation of one of the feasible solutions is illustrated in Fig. 1.

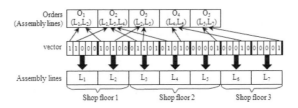

Fig. 1. Sample of the discrete-value vector representation for order scheduling problem

In Fig. 1, the vector is composed of seven sub-vectors, which corresponds to the 7-dimensional parameter. The length of each sub-vector is the same and equal to the number of the orders. The 0 or 1 value of the elements in the sub-vector represents the assigning/un-assigning status of each order to the corresponding assembly line. So in Fig. 1, the assembly line L_1 performs O_1 and O_2, assembly line L_2 does the O_1 and O_3, and so on. It should be noted that the 0-1 discrete-values of the vector make the convention operators of DE inoperable. So, the new operators for the discrete-values are proposed, which are described as follow.

3.2 Mutation

During the Gth generation, the mutation operator based on *DE/rand/*1 method for each target individual $X_{i,G}$ ($i=1,2,...,NP$) is defined as,

$$V_{i,G+1} = X_{r_1,G} + F \cdot (X_{r_2,G} - X_{r_3,G}), \quad r_1 \neq r_2 \neq r_3 \neq i, \tag{10}$$

where r_1, r_2 and r_3 are uniform rand values taken from $\{1,2,...,NP\}$, $V_{i,G+1}$ is a new generated mutant vector and NP is the population size. Clearly, the mutation operator cannot be applied directly for the discrete-value vector representation. This research extended the arithmetic operators to handle the discrete-value vector representation. The modified subtraction and addition operators are described as follows.

Definition 1: Subtraction operator between two individuals
    The subtraction of the sub-vectors is defined as below,

$$C_{ki} - C_{kj} = \begin{cases} 1 & C_{ki} = 1 \text{ and } C_{kj} = 0 \\ 0 & otherwise \end{cases} \tag{11}$$

where C_{ki} is the kth component of the sub-vectors of the individual i, and C_{kj} is the kth component of the sub-vectors of the individual j. Based on formulation (11), the subtraction operator of two individuals can be easily accomplished. Fig. 2 is an example of the subtraction operator between two individuals, $X_{r_2,G}$ and $X_{r_3,G}$.

Fig. 2. Example of the subtraction operator between two individuals

Definition 2: Addition operator of two individuals

The addition of the sub-vectors is defined as below,

$$C_{ki}+C_{kj} = \begin{cases} 0 & C_{ki}=0 \ and \ C_{kj}=0 \\ 1 & otherwise \end{cases} \tag{12}$$

Fig. 3 is an example of the addition operator between two individuals, $X_{r_1,G}$ and $D_{i,G}$.

Fig. 3. Example of the addition operator between two individuals

According to the above Definitions 1 and 2, the mutation operator can be implemented upon the proposed discrete-valued vector representation.

3.3 Crossover

Crossover operator is used to increase the diversity of the population. The conventional crossover operators are required to be extended to the discrete-valued vector correspondingly. Based on the crossover operator, the trial individual $U_{i,G+1}$ is yielded by mixing the target individual $X_{i,G}$ with the mutant individual $V_{i,G+1}$ using the following scheme,

$$U_{i,G+1}^{j} = \begin{cases} V_{i,G+1}^{j} & if \ rand(j) \le P_c \\ X_{i,G}^{j} & otherwise \end{cases} \tag{13}$$

where $rand(j)$ is a uniform random number between [0,1], j denotes the sub-vector index of the individual. $U_{i,G+1}^{j}$, $V_{i,G+1}^{j}$ and $X_{i,G}^{j}$ are the jth sub-vector of $U_{i,G+1}$, and $X_{i,G}$ respectively. P_c is a predetermined crossover constant between [0,1], which is an important parameter to control population diversity.

3.4 Performance Evaluation and Fitness

A stochastic simulation model is developed to represent dynamically the production system behavior, taking into account the main features of the production practical. The detailed process flow of the simulation model can be outlined as follows.

Step 1. Input the production status, such as the number of assembly lines, orders information, capacity of each assembly line. Then initialize the production states and the performance statistics.

Step 2. Determine the priority of the orders according to the production requirement.

Step 3. If the arrival planning of the raw material is uncertain, acquire its concrete arrival planning using the probability method. Then generate arrival timetable of the raw materials according to the arrival planning.

Step 4. Based on the priority, each order is routed to the appropriate assembly line with the concrete time respectively.

Step 5. Collect production state and compute the scheduling performance, namely the values of three objective functions.

Step 6. If the material arrival planning is uncertain, repeat the Step 3 and step 5 until the predefined times and output the performance statistics, else output the scheduling performance directly. And stop.

Once obtaining the values of three object functions, they can be regarded as the fitness value of the individual. Since these values are conflicting and incommensurable, the utility function is defined to combine multiple performance objectives into one overall utility value, fitness $(\bar{x})$, which is defined as,

$$U_i(f_i(\bar{x})) = U_i(p_i) = \begin{cases} 1 & p_i \le a \\ \dfrac{u-1}{b-a} \cdot p_i + \dfrac{b-a \cdot u}{b-a} & a < p_i \le b \\ \dfrac{u}{b-c} \cdot p_i - \dfrac{c \cdot u}{b-c} & b < p_i \le c \\ 0 & p_i > c \end{cases} \tag{14}$$

where U_i is the utility function of performance objective f_i, and a, b, c, and u are parameters of U_i. Thus, the fitness value fitness can be defined as

$$fitness(\bar{x}) = \omega_1 \cdot U_1(f_1(\bar{x})) + \omega_2 \cdot U_2(f_2(\bar{x})) + \omega_3 \cdot U_3(f_3(\bar{x})) \tag{15}$$

where $\omega_1, \omega_2, \omega_3$ are the relative weights placed upon the utility values $U_1(f_1(\bar{x}))$ and $U_2(f_2(\bar{x}))$ and $U_3(f_3(\bar{x}))$ respectively and $\omega_1 + \omega_2 + \omega_3 = 1$.

3.5 Selection

Based on the Pareto optimality of the multi-objective problem, a double-set Pareto selection is proposed to improve the diversity of the population and keep the fast speed of the population evolving towards a good solution. The detailed procedure of the new selection strategy is described as follows.

Step 1. According to the performance objectives and fitness value of the newly-generated trial individual $U_{i,G+1}$, check whether $U_{i,G+1}$ is dominated by at least one individual in P_{po}. If yes, insert $U_{i,G+1}$ into P_{so} and go to step 4; otherwise continue.

Step 2. Find all the individuals in P_{po} which are dominated by $U_{i,G+1}$. If found, remove all the dominated individuals from P_{po} and insert them into P_{so}.

Step 3. Insert $U_{i,G+1}$ into P_{po}. If the size of P_{po} is bigger than half of the population size, move the individual with the smallest fitness value from P_{po} to P_{so}.

Step 4. Remove the individual with the smallest utility value in P_{so} and stop.

The advantages of the above selection strategy are twofold. First, the new individual will be retained based on Pareto optimality even if it has a smaller fitness value. Thus, the individual with part of outstanding features will be retained, while will increase the diversity of the population effectively. Second, the fitness value is used to determine the retaining or discarding of the individuals when too many Pareto optimal solutions exist. The larger the fitness value of the individual is, the higher possibility the individual is retained in the next generation. This ensures the quick convergence speed and the ability of evolving towards the global optimal solution.

4   Experimental Results and Discussion

A real-life order scheduling problem for apparel industry, where the MTO production mode is widely adopted with the popularity of fast fashion, is used to validate the feasibility and effectiveness of the proposed method (PDDE). In apparel manufacturing, the sewing operation is the most critical and complicated process which is always the bottleneck of the apparel production process. An unsuitable order scheduling of apparel production may incur low production efficiency. In this section, the proposed PDDE is utilized for this order scheduling problem and compared with the practical method from industrial practice. A series of experiments were conducted and two out of these experiments are highlighted in this section.

4.1   Experimental Data

The investigated factory consists of four shop floors and each shop floor has two or three assembly lines. During a period of time, several orders are arranged to be processed in the factory simultaneously. The relevant configurations for the orders and the assembly lines are shown in Table 1.

In Table 1, the capacity data are acquired by trial production which is commonly used in apparel manufacturing. Orders O_3 and O_5 cannot be processed by shop floor 3 and shop floor 1 respectively since the corresponding data are not set. The values in columns 'Arrival date' and 'Due date' are the relative days from the beginning of scheduling. For example, the value '-15' in the column of 'arrival date' and the row of 'O_1' represents that the arrival date of O_1 is 15 days before the beginning of scheduling. The column of "material quantity" represents the amount of the raw material is required for making one piece of the corresponding product. The value '4' in column of 'material quantity' and the row of 'O_1' means that the 4 units of raw materials are required for one piece of the product. The column of the cost of setup represents the cost of time and labors for machine setup and production preparing in re-beginning to process a new order. The final column of 'partition' is the cost used in order management when one order is divided and processed in several shop floors.

Table 1. Orders and assembly lines configurations for experiments

Order no.	Capacities of assembly lines for processing each order in one day									Characteristics of Order						
	Shop floor 1		Shop floor 2			Shop floor 3		Shop floor 4		Order size	Arriva l date	Due date	Raw material		Cost	
	Line 1	Line 2	Line 1	Line 2	Line 3	Line 1	Line 2	Line 1	Line 2				type	quantity	setup	partition
O_1	50	65	75	70	45	65	55	85	60	10000	-15	80	1	4	10	5
O_2	25	30	35	32	26	30	28	38	26	5000	-6	65	2	5	8	6
O_3	85	90	100	90	80	/	/	105	90	8000	-2	75	2	3	4	10
O_4	45	50	55	52	45	65	60	80	62	6500	0	55	3	4	10	6
O_5	/	/	90	85	65	80	70	85	75	6000	10	60	4	2	6	7

Two experiments were conducted to evaluate the performance of the PDDE-based scheduling model. The difference of the two experiments is that the order O_5 is not scheduled in Experiment 1, but is scheduled in Experiment 2. The main consideration about this is to investigate the scheduling performance of the PDDE algorithm under the uncertain orders. Meanwhile, in order to evaluate the effects of uncertainty arrival of raw materials, 5 cases about arrival of raw materials are presented for each experiment. The detailed data for arrival dates and quantities of various types of materials are shown in Table 2. In this paper, the uncertainty of arrival of all raw materials is represented as a rand variable with the normal probability distribution.

Table 2. The arrival dates and quantities of various types of materials for different cases

		Arrival dates and quantities of the materials								
		Type 1		Type 2		Type 3			Type 4		
Case 1	Time	0		0		0			0		
	quantity	40000		49000		26000			12000		
Case 2	Time	0	10	10	20	5	15	25	12	20	30
	quantity	10000	30000	25000	24000	10000	10000	6000	5000	4000	3000
Case 3	Time	$N(0,2)$*		$N(10,2)$		$N(5,2)$			$N(12,2)$		
	quantity	40000		49000		26000			12000		
Case 4	Time	$N(0,2)$	$N(10,2)$	$N(10,2)$	$N(20,2)$	$N(5,2)$	$N(15,2)$	$N(25,2)$	$N(12,2)$	$N(20,2)$	$N(30,2)$
	quantity	10000	30000	25000	24000	10000	10000	6000	5000	4000	3000
Case 5	Time	$N(0,4)$	$N(10,4)$	$N(10,4)$	$N(20,4)$	$N(5,4)$	$N(15,4)$	$N(25,4)$	$N(12,4)$	$N(20,4)$	$N(30,4)$
	quantity	10000	30000	25000	24000	10000	10000	6000	5000	4000	3000

*$N(0,2)$ represents the normal probability distribution with mean 0 and standard deviation 2.

4.2 Results Analysis

Table 3 shows the optimized order scheduling solutions for all cases of the two experiments generated by the proposed algorithm M1. It can be seen that only one solution for all cases of each experiment is derived by the industrial practice M2 method since the stochastic arrival dates of the raw materials is not considered in M2, namely, the supplies of all raw materials are assumed to arrive at one time at the beginning of scheduling.

Table 3. The order scheduling solutions for all cases of the two experiments

No.	Methods	Case no.	Shop floor 1		Shop floor 2			Shop floor 3		Shop floor 4	
			Line 1	Line 2	Line 1	Line 2	Line 3	Line 1	Line 2	Line 1	Line 2
Experiment 1	M1	Case 1	O_2	O_2	O_1	O_1	/	O_4	O_4	O_3	O_2,O_3
		Case 2	O_3	O_3,O_4	O_2	O_2	O_2	O_4	O_4	O_1	O_1
		Case 3	O_3	O_3	O_1	O_1	O_2	O_2	O_2	O_4	O_2,O_4
		Case 4	O_3	O_1	O_2,O_3	O_2,O_3	O_2,O_3	O_4	O_4	O_1	O_4
		Case 5	O_3	O_3	O_1	O_1	O_2	O_2	O_2	O_4	O_2,O_4
	M2	-	O_3	O_3	O_2	O_2	O_2	O_4	O_4	O_1	O_1
Experiment 2	M1	Case 1	O_2	O_2	O_3,O_5	O_3,O_5	O_2,O_3	O_4	O_4	O_1	O_1
		Case 2	O_3	O_1	O_2	O_1,O_2	O_5	O_1,O_4	O_1,O_2	O_3,O_4	O_3,O_5
		Case 3	O_2	O_1	O_2,O_3	O_3,O_5	O_3,O_5	O_1	O_4	O_3,O_4	O_2
		Case 4	O_2,O_3	O_3	O_1,O_2,O_5	O_1,O_2,O_5	O_2	O_2,O_4	O_2,O_4	O_1	O_1,O_4
		Case 5	O_2,O_3	O_2	O_2,O_3,O_5	O_1,O_3,O_5	O_2	O_1	O_1	O_3,O_4	O_3,O_4
	M2	-	O_2	O_2	O_3,O_5	O_3,O_5	O_2,O_3	O_4	O_4	O_1	O_1

M1-Proposed method, M2-Industrial Practice

Two key findings can be found from Table 3. First, by comparing the solutions in Experiment 1 with the one in Experiment 2, it can be seen that the order scheduling is more complex in Experiment 2 than in Experiment 1 as there are one more order in Experiment 2 than that in Experiment 1. Clearly, the production tasks (number of orders) have impact on the order scheduling. Second, there are no same solution which exists in any case of experiments 1 and 2 respectively. It indicates that the details of arrival of raw materials are very important to the order scheduling. Based on the order scheduling solutions, the performance comparison results of all cases of the two experiments are shown in Table 4.

Considering the order scheduling results of case 1 of Experiment 1 shown in Table 4, the over performance of the proposed method is slightly inferior to the result of the industrial practice. The reason is that the proposed method uses one less assembly line than the practical method as shown from Table 5. It verifies that the proposed method generates the scheduling result from the viewpoint of the global optimization. Further, comparing the performance of all cases in Experiment 1 with the corresponding ones in Experiment 2, the values of overall performance in Experiment 1 are all better than the ones in Experiment 2. It shows that more orders

Table 4. The performance comparison for all cases of the two experiments

	Case no.	Methods	Overall performance		Completion time satisfaction level			Cost of order setup		Cost of order partition	
			Mean	Standard deviation	Mean	Standard deviation	P(=1)*	Mean	Standard deviation	Mean	Standard deviation
Experiment 1	Case 1	M1	0.984	/	1.0	/	100%	72	/	6	/
		M2	0.990	/	1.0	/	100%	72	/	0	/
	Case 2	M1	0.975	/	1.0	/	100%	86	/	6	/
		M2	0.94	/	0.94	/	0%	72	/	0	/
	Case 3	M1	0.977	0.0061	0.9972	0.0069	81.87%	80.02	1.31	11.93	0.65
		M2	0.974	0.0128	0.9821	0.0146	24.78%	72	0	0	0
	Case 4	M1	0.954	0.0107	0.9875	0.0156	45.26%	90	0	21	0
		M2	0.942	0.0096	0.9414	0.0134	0%	72	0	0	0
	Case 5	M1	0.956	0.0186	0.9785	0.0221	31.62%	85.34	8.95	11.07	2.18
		M2	0.937	0.0201	0.9363	0.0264	0.05%	72	0	0	0
Experiment 2	Case 1	M1	0.979	/	1.0	/	100%	96	/	6	/
		M2	0.979	/	1.0	/	100%	96	/	6	/
	Case 2	M1	0.967	/	1.0	/	100%	102	/	29	/
		M2	0.845	/	0.827	/	0%	98	/	6	/
	Case 3	M1	0.9563	0.0057	0.9919	0.0103	48.61%	114.60	4.71	27	0
		M2	0.9015	0.02	0.8973	0.0273	0%	94.04	3.44	6	0
	Case 4	M1	0.9150	0.0160	0.9893	0.0186	63.21%	186.55	12.50	22.96	0.50
		M2	0.8528	0.0161	0.8359	0.0206	0%	97.07	4.03	6	0
	Case 5	M1	0.9223	0.0204	0.9681	0.0253	13.79%	139.09	9.15	26.51	4.98
		M2	0.8527	0.0289	0.8347	0.0377	0%	95.67	4.58	6	0

* P(=1) represents the probability that the completion time satisfaction level equals to 1

may produce more extra cost on the order setup and partition, which can be neglected in the global optimization of order scheduling.

Three prominent findings can be observed in Table 4. First, the proposed method outperformed the practical method which can be reflected by achieving the higher overall performance value especially in the case that the arrival dates of raw material are uncertain. The solutions generated by the practical method have worst performance in the case of the stochastic arrival dates of the raw material. Second, the uncertain arrival of raw materials makes the performance of the order scheduling worse. For example, under the deterministic arrival dates of the raw materials in cases 1 and 2 of each experiment, the probabilities that the completion time satisfaction level equals to 1 can always reach 100%. However in the cases of uncertain arrival of raw materials, the probabilities that the completion time satisfaction level equals to 1 are smaller than 100% in the solutions generated by both the proposed method and the practice method. It shows that arrival of the raw materials is a crucial factor to make the order scheduling. Third, the uncertainty arrival of raw materials increases the uncertainty of the objective functions of order scheduling. For example, as the standard deviation value of the probability distribution of arrival of raw materials varies from 2 in case 4 to 4 in case 5, the diversity of the probability distribution of the completion time satisfaction level spreads out over a larger range of values.

Moreover, the probability that the completion time satisfaction level equals to 1 decrease from 45.26% in case 4 to 31.62% in case 5 in Experiment 1, from 63.21% in case 4 to 13.79 in case 5 in Experiment 2.

5   Conclusions

This paper investigated the order scheduling problem for MTO production planning with uncertain arrival of raw materials. The mathematical model for the problem has been formulated. A PDDE-based optimization algorithm was proposed to solve the order scheduling problem. Two modified operators, the subtraction and addition operators are introduced to extend the arithmetic operators for real-values to handle the discrete-value vector representation. According to Pareto optimality of the multi-objective problem, a double-set scheme of the population is proposed to maintain the Pareto optimal individuals in the population. The double-set Pareto selection strategy are developed to not only improve effectively the diversity of the population and but also keep the population evolving towards a good solution.

Experiments based on a real-life order scheduling problem of apparel industry have been conducted to validate the feasibility and effectiveness of the proposed algorithm. The experimental results show that firstly, the proposed method substantially outperforms the practical method; secondly, the uncertain arrival of raw materials makes the performance of the order scheduling solutions worse and increases the uncertainty of the objective functions of order scheduling.

Acknowledgements. The authors would like to thank the financial support from The Hong Kong Research Institute of Textiles and Apparel for this project (Project no.:ITP/047/09TP).

References

1. Huang, S.M., Lu, M.S., Wan, G.H.: Integrated order selection and production scheduling under MTO strategy. Int. J. Prod. Res. 49, 4085–4101 (2011)
2. Easton, F.F., Moodie, D.R.: Pricing and lead time decisions for make-to-order firms with contingent orders. Eur. J. Oper. Res. 116, 305–318 (1999)
3. Hendry, L.C., Kingsman, B.G.: Production Planning Systems and Their Applicability to Make-to-Order Companies. Eur. J. Oper. Res. 40, 1–15 (1989)
4. Yin, N., Wang, X.Y.: Single-machine scheduling with controllable processing times and learning effect. Int. J. Adv. Manuf. Technol. 54, 743–748 (2011)
5. Price, K., Storn, R.M., Lampinen, J.A.: Differential evolution - a practical approach to global optimization. Springer, Heidelberg (2005)
6. Chakraborty, U.: Advances in differential evolution. Springer, Heidelberg (2008)
7. Lampinen, J., Storn, R.: Differential Evolution. In: Onwubolu, G.C., Babu, B. (eds.) New Optimization Techniques in Engineering, pp. 123–166. Springer, Heidelberg (2004)
8. Zhou, A., Qu, B.Y., Li, H., Zhao, S.Z., Suganthan, P.N., Zhang, Q.: Multiobjective evolutionary algorithms: A survey of the state of the art. Swarm and Evolutionary Computation 1, 32–49 (2011)

Evolutionary Discrete Firefly Algorithm for Travelling Salesman Problem

Gilang Kusuma Jati and Suyanto

The faculty of Informatics - Telkom Institute of Technology, Jl. Telekomunikasi No. 1 Terusan
Buah Batu, Bandung 40257, West Java, Indonesia
gilang.kusuma@live.com, suy@ittelkom.ac.id

Abstract. This paper addresses how to apply firefly algorithm (FA) for travelling salesman problem (TSP). Two schemes are studied, i.e. discrete distance between two fireflies and the movement scheme. Computer simulation shows that the simple form of FA without combination with other methods performs very well to solve some TSP instances, but it can be trapped into local optimum solutions for some other instances.

Keywords: evolutionary firefly algorithm, travelling salesman problem, discrete distance, movement scheme.

1 Introduction

Traveling Salesman Problem (TSP) is one of the most intensively studied problems all round the world. TSP is although looking very simple problem but it is an important problem of the classical optimization problems that are difficult to solve conventionally. Basically in this problem a salesman needs to visit each city one time and returns back to the city from the start point of travelling. Exact completion on this issue will involve algorithms that require seeking the possibility of all the existing solutions so this problem is also belonging to the class of "NP-Complete" problems. As a result, execution time complexity of this algorithm will be exponential to the size of the input given.

It is very hard to accurately solve TSP. Many methods, which belong to evolutionary computations, have been proposed to solve TSP. Some of them are: Memetic algorithm proposed by Luciana Buriol [1], discrete fuzzy PSO by N. Salmani Niasar [3], genetic algorithm combined with ant colony system by Marcin L. Pilat [4], improved bee colony optimization with frequency-based pruning by Li-Pei Wong [11], and an advanced method called heterogeneous selection evolutionary algorithm (HeSEA) proposed by Huai-Kuang Tsai [10]. Those researchers proposed methods that are combinations of a metaheuristic algorithm with a local search or other metaheuristic algorithms. In [1], [3], [4], and [11], the researchers focused on small TSP with hundreds of cities (nodes). Generally, accuracies of the methods are very high where the produced solutions are very close to the known optimum solutions. In [10], the researchers focused on large TSP with thousands of cities. The method they proposed, called HeSEA, is capable of solving a TSP with up to 3,038

A. Bouchachia (Ed.): ICAIS 2011, LNAI 6943, pp. 393–403, 2011.

cities with deviation of 0% compare to the known optimum solution. It also solved a TSP of 13,509 cities with deviation only 0.74 %.

Firefly algorithm (FA) is one of the nature-inspired metaheuristic algorithms developed by Xin-She Yang [7], originally designed to solve continues optimization problem [2], [8]. However, FA can be discretized to solve a permutation problem, such as flow shop scheduling problems [5]. In this research, evolutionary discrete FA (EDFA) is proposed to solve TSP. Two schemes are studied, i.e. discrete distance between two fireflies and the movement scheme. This study is focused on the simple form of FA without combination with any other method. Some TSP instances studied here are the small ones with up to 666 cities. However, some ideas to improve the FA also slightly discussed at the end of this paper, but no deep analysis.

2 Evolutionary Discrete Firefly Algorithm

Nature-inspired methodologies are among the most powerful algorithms for optimization problems. FA is a novel nature-inspired algorithm inspired by social behavior of fireflies. Firefly is one of the most special, captivating and fascinating creature in the nature. There are about two thousand firefly species, and most fireflies produce short and rhythmic flashes. The rate and the rhythmic flash, and the amount of time form part of the signal system which brings both sexes together. Therefore, the main part of a firefly's flash is to act as a signal system to attract other fireflies. By idealizing some of the flashing characteristics of fireflies, firefly-inspired algorithm was presented by Xin-She Yang [7]. Firefly-inspired algorithm uses the following three idealized rules: 1) all fireflies are unisex which means that they are attracted to other fireflies regardless of their sex; 2) the degree of the attractiveness of a firefly is proportion to its brightness, thus for any two flashing fireflies, the less brighter one will move towards the brighter one and the more brightness means the less distance between two fireflies. If there is no brighter one than a particular firefly, it will move randomly; and 3) the brightness of a firefly is determined by the value of the objective function [7]. For a maximization problem, the brightness can be proportional to the value of the objective function. Other forms of brightness can be defined in a similar way to the fitness function in genetic algorithms [8].

Based on [8], FA is very efficient in finding the global optima with high success rates. Simulation by Xin-She Yang shows that FA is superior to both PSO and GA in terms of both efficiency and success rate [8]. Lukasik and Zak also study FA for continuous constrained optimization task. Their experiment demonstrates the efficiency of FA [2]. These facts give inspiration to investigate how optimum FA in solving TSP. The challenges are how to design discrete distance between two fireflies and how they move for coordination.

2.1 The Representation of Firefly

A solution representation for the TSP is a permutation representation as illustrated by Figure 1. Here, a firefly represents one solution. It is just like a chromosome that represents an individual in genetic algorithm. In this representation, an element of array represents a city (node) and the index represents the order of a tour.

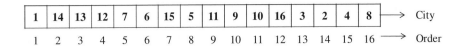

Fig. 1. The permutation representation of a solution

2.2 Distance

In continuous optimization problem, distance between two fireflies is simply calculated using Euclidian distance. For TSP, distance between any two fireflies i and firefly j can be defined as the number of different arc between them. In Figure 2, three arcs 12-7, 6-15, and 5-11 in firefly i do not exist in firefly j. Hence, the number of different arcs between firefly i and firefly j is three. Then, the distance between two fireflies is calculated using formula

$$r = \frac{A}{N} \times 10, \qquad (1)$$

where r is the distance between any two fireflies, A is the total number of different arcs between two fireflies, and N is number of cities. The formula scales r in the interval $[0, 10]$ as r will be used in attractiveness calculation.

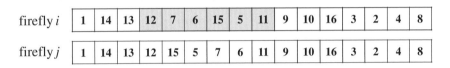

Fig. 2. The distance between two fireflies i and j is defined as the number of different arcs between them

2.3 Attractiveness

In the original FA, the main form of attractiveness function $\beta(r)$ can be any monotonic decreasing function

$$\beta(r) = \beta_0 e^{-\gamma r^2}, \qquad (2)$$

where r is the distance between two fireflies, β_0 is the attractiveness at $r = 0$, and γ is a fixed light absorption coefficient. This scheme is completely adopted by EDFA.

2.4 Light Absorption

In essence, light absorption coefficient γ characterizes the variation of attractiveness value of firefly. Its value is very important in determining the speed of convergence and how the FA behaves. In theory, $\gamma \in [0, \infty)$, but in practice γ is determined by the characteristics of the problem to be optimized.

In condition where $\gamma \to 0$, the attractiveness will be constant and $\beta = \beta_0$. In this case, the attractiveness of a firefly will not decrease when viewed by another. If $\gamma \to$

∞, this means the value of attractiveness of a firefly is close to zero when viewed by another firefly. It is equivalent to cases where the fireflies fly in a very foggy region randomly. No other fireflies can be seen, and each firefly roams in a completely random way. Therefore, this corresponds to the completely random search method.

The coefficient γ functions to determine how much light intensity changes to the attractiveness of a firefly. In this research, γ is in the interval [0.01, 0.15] so that the attractiveness of a firefly viewed by the others will follow the Figure 3.

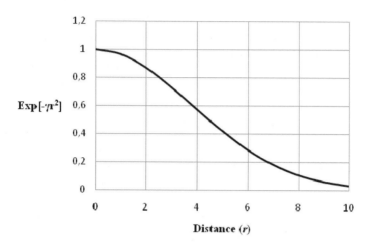

Fig. 3. The correlation of distance and attractiveness

2.5 Movement

The movement of a firefly i attracted to another brighter (more attractive) firefly j is determined by

$$x_i = random(2, r_{ij}),   (3)$$

where r_{ij} is distance between firefly i and j. The length of movement of a firefly will be randomly selected from 2 to r_{ij}. When a firefly moves, existing solutions in the firefly is changed. Since the representation of firefly is a permutation representation, then we use Inversion Mutation to represent the movement. With inversion mutation, the path that has been formed can be maintained so the good path formed previously is not damaged.

Actually, firefly in EDFA has no direction to move. Hence, it moves using Evolution Strategies (ES) concept. Each firefly will move using inversion mutation for m times. First, index on the chromosome will be selected randomly, after it carried an inversion mutation. In other words, each firefly will have m new solutions. After n fireflies move and produce n x m new solutions, then n best fireflies will be selected as the new population.

2.6 EDFA Scheme

The scheme of EDFA is illustrated by the following pseudo code. First, each firefly generates an initial solution randomly. For each firefly, find the brightest or the most attractive firefly. If there is a brighter firefly, then the less bright firefly will move towards the brighter one and if there is no brighter one than a particular firefly, it will move randomly. When a firefly moves, existing solution produced by the firefly is changed. Each firefly move as much as m times. So, there will be $(m \times n) + 1$ fireflies at the end of iteration since only the best firefly will be included in selection process for the next iteration. Then, n best fireflies will be chosen based on an objective function for the next iteration. This condition will continue until the maximum iteration is reached.

Input:
Objective function $f(x)$, $x = (x_1,... x_d)^T$ *{cost function}*
Initialize a population of fireflies x_i $(i = 1, 2, ..., n)$
Define light absorption coefficient γ and number of moves m *{parameters}*
Output:
$x_{i\,min}$
begin
    for $i = 1$ **to** n **do**
        x_i ⬚ Generate_Initial_Solution
    endfor
    repeat
        for $i = 1$ **to** n **do**
            x_j ⬚ Find_Attractive_Firefly(x_i)
            if ($x_j \neq null$) **then**
                Move_Firefly(x_i, x_j) for m times   *{move firefly i towards j}*
            else
                Move_Random(x_i) for m times   *{firefly i move randomly}*
          endif
        endfor
        Select n brightest fireflies from $(m \times n) + 1$
    until *stop condition true*
end

---

3 Results and Discussions

In this study, EDFA is applied for 7 TSP instances downloaded from TSPLIB [6]. Table 1 lists the problem names, numbers of cities, and the lengths of the optimal tour. In [6], the types of TSP instances are Euclidian distances. A TSP instance provides some cities with their coordinates. The number in the name of an instance represents the number of provided cities. For example, ulysses16 provides 16 cities with their coordinates. The problem is what the best tour to visit the 16 cities, according to their Euclidian distances, with a condition where each city should be visited only once.

Table 1. Summary of 7 TSPs taken from TSPLIB: problem names, number of cities (nodes) and the length of the optimal tour

Problem names	Number of cities	Length of the optimal tour
ulysses16	16	6859
ulysses22	22	7013
gr202	202	40160
tsp225	225	3845
a280	280	2578
pcb442	442	50778
gr666	666	294358

3.1 Firefly Population

Population size (n) critically determine the computation time. Here, EDFA is tested using various population sizes on problem gr202 to investigate its correlation with number of trials needed by EDFA to get the optimum solution. Figure 4 represents the correlation of the population size with the average trials to reach the optimum solution (with accuracy of 100%). Average trial decreases when the population size is increased from 5, 10 and 15. But, the average trial increases when the population size is 20 or more. Large population does not guarantee that firefly will reach best solution more quickly. According to Figure 4, the best population size is 15.

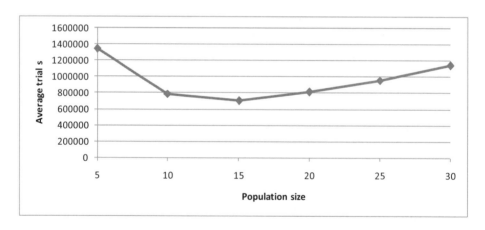

Fig. 4. Correlation of the population size and the average trials needed by EDFA to get the optimum solution

The number of population size determines the number of solutions in each generation. In finding the solution, a firefly with less bright light will follow another one with brighter light (better solution). But, in one generation there could be some fireflies having the same solutions so that the movement of a firefly does not generate better solution.

3.2 Effects of Light Absorption

Light absorption (γ) does not critically determine the computation time. Various values of light absorption were tested on problem gr202 to evaluate its correlation with number of trials needed by EDFA to get the optimum solution. Figure 5 illustrates the relationship between the population size and the average trials to get the optimum solution. Any light absorption, from 0.01 to 0.15, gives quite similar average trials. Thus, the light absorption does not significantly affect the average trials of EDFA.

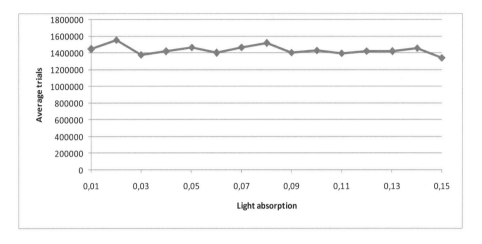

Fig. 5. Correlation of the light absorption and the average trials needed by EDFA to get the optimum solution

3.3 Number of Moves

In EDFA, fireflies have no direction to move. Hence, fireflies move based on a way like in evolution strategies concept. As default, each firefly will make the process of inversion mutation for 8 times. Based on the previous result, the best average trials for problem gr202 can be reached when the population size is 15 and the number of moves is 8. Thus, the total number of moves for each generation is 120. Various numbers of moves, illustrated by Table 2, are tested on problem gr202 to evaluate its correlation with number of trials needed by EDFA to get the optimum solution. The simulation is run for 30 times for each number of moves to get the average trials.

The results show that, in the beginning, the average trials decrease as the number of moves increase. But, when the number of move is 12 or above, the average trials increase. According to Table 2 and Figure 6, the best number of moves is 11 with population size is 11. This setting parameter means that on each generation there will be 11 fireflies and each fireflies move 11 times. The other number of moves, in the interval of 7 and 10, are considerable as the results are quite similar.

Table 2. Results of EDFA applied to gr202 with total trials around 120 in one generation

Problem name	Number of moves	Population size	Total moves per generation	Average trials
gr202	4	30	120	1,342,200
	5	24	120	1,070,808
	6	20	120	854,568
	7	17	119	717,974
	8	15	120	704,232
	9	13	117	656,405
	10	12	120	630,096
	11	**11**	**121**	**586,898**
	12	10	120	694,920
	13	9	117	763,261
	14	9	126	681,609
	15	8	120	662,808

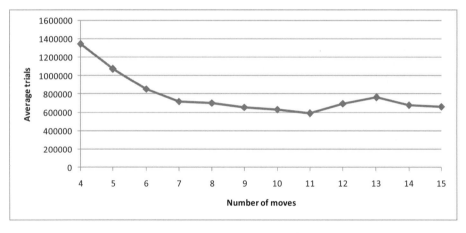

Fig. 6. The correlation of the number of moves with the average trials needed by EDFA to reach the known optimum solution

3.4 Performance of EDFA

EDFA is examined to solve 7 TSP instances to see its performance. In this research, EDFA uses population size of 15 fireflies and the number of light absorption is 0.03. Using those parameters, EDFA are examined using 7 TSP instances. Table 3 shows the worst, best and average accuracy for the 7 instances. The accuracy is calculated by a formula in Equation (4). EDFA always get the best solution for ulysses16, ulysses22, gr202 and gr666 for every runs. However, EDFA is not optimal for three instances: tsp225, a280 and pcb442.

$$r = \frac{best\ solution\ known}{best\ solution\ found} \times 100\% \tag{4}$$

Table 3. Results of EDFA applied to 7 TSP instances, 30 runs for each instance

| Problem | Best solution | | Accuracy (%) | | Average time |
names	known	Worst	Best	Average	(second)
ulysses16	6859	100.000	100.204	**100.119**	0.416
ulysses22	7013	100.000	100.211	**100.207**	6.590
gr202	40160	100.000	100.653	**100.474**	51.167
tsp225	3845	87.758	89.065	88.332	412.274
a280	2578	87.995	89.668	88.297	691.886
pcb442	50778	87.556	89.457	88.505	3404.211
gr666	294358	100	100.356	**100.033**	393.025

3.5 Comparison of EDFA with Memetic Algorithm

Various studies show that Memetic algorithm can find 76% optimal solution for travelling salesman problem [1]. Now the EDFA will be compared to Memetic algorithm for 7 TSP instances. EDFA, implemented using visual C# .Net, is run 30 times. The results are summarized in Table 4.

Table 4. The comparison between EDFA with Memetic algorithm

| Problem | EDFA | Memetic algorithm (k=5%) |
names	Opt/Runs	Opt/ Runs
ulysses16	30/30	30/30
ulysses22	30/30	30/30
gr202	**30/30**	29/30
tsp225	00/30	**02/30**
a280	00/30	**19/30**
pcb442	00/30	**30/30**
gr666	**30/30**	03/30

The Opt/Runs means how many times the algorithm reach the known optimum solution from the total number of runs. For example, 19/30 represents the algorithm reach the known optimum solution for 19 times from 30 runs. In the table, EDFA performed slightly better for gr202 and significantly better for gr666 instance than Memetic algorithm. But, for three TSP instances, tsp225, a280 and pcb442, EDFA performed much worse, where it never reached the known optimum solution. Even, according to Table 3, it reached solutions with low accuracies, only 88%, from the known optimum solutions. This shows that EDFA can be trapped into local optimum solutions for some instances.

3.6 Some Ideas to Improve EDFA

In order to solve TSP, we can improve EDFA by giving direction to the fireflies. Direction can be formed by dividing the TSP instance problem into multiple sub partitions. Each sub partitions can be considered as the direction. We can divide the problem using various ways. The easiest way to divide is based on the coordinates, by X or Y axis. Figure 7 showed TSP instance divided into two sub partitions by Y axis. Another way is to use K-mean to divides the problem into multiple sub-partitions.

Then solves each sub partition separately, and finally use the partial solution to produce a complete tour.

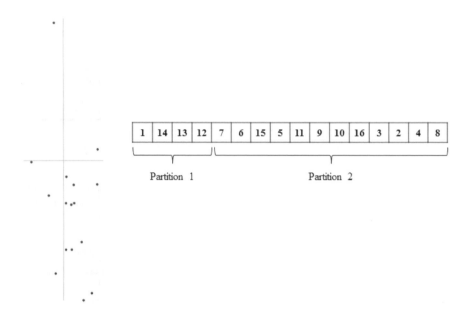

Fig. 7. TSP instance ulysses16 divide into two sub partitions by Y axis

In EDFA, the partition has a role in the movement of fireflies ïïWhen a firefly i is attracted to another brighter (more attractive) firefly j, it calculates the long of the steps should be taken for each partition. Here, a partition can be seen as a dimension in a vector. If there are two partitions, then a firefly can, for example, do a long movement for the first partition and short movement for the second one. Hence, the firefly seems to have a direction of movement. However, the number of partition can be more than two. If a TSP instance has thousands of cities and the cities are distributed into 10 clusters, then the instance is better to divide into 10 partitions. Hence, a firefly can be seen as an object that moves in 10 dimensional vector spaces with a long of step and a direction.

EDFA could be combined with other methods such as Greedy and Lin Kernighan (LK). Greedy works simply by growing Hamiltonian cycle in the graph in which it is necessary that each vertex should be visited only once. Greedy can create this Hamiltonian cycle by first picking the shortest edge and then add this shortest edge to the tour until all the cities are included in the tour. Greedy can repeat this whole procedure until all cities be the part of the Hamiltonian cycle. Greedy can create better tour for initialization of fireflies. LK is one of the best algorithms of TSP which generates an optimal solution for the TSP. LK is the most powerful heuristic. It works as follows. First, it removes an edge from the current tour, and tries to add edges with the other cities in such a way that will create the new shortest tour. In EDFA, LK can also be used to update each partial solution (partition).

4 Conclusion

The proposed method, EDFA, has been successfully implemented to solve TSP. The simulation results indicate that EDFA performs very well for some TSP instances compare to Memetic algorithm. But, it can be trapped into local optimum solutions for some instances since it does not have a direction to do a movement. For improvement, it could be combined with other techniques such as greedy search for the initialization of firefly population or Lin Kernighan algorithm to update each partial solution in a partition and to further improvement of the tour.

Acknowledgments. We would like to thank to Dr Xin-She Yang in Cambridge University for the suggestions and comments on the initial manuscript and our colleagues in Telkom Institute of Technology (IT Telkom) for the advices and motivations.

References

1. Luciana, B., França, P.M., Pablo, M.: A New Memetic Algorithm for the Asymmetric Traveling Salesman Problem. Journal of Heuristics 10(5), 483–506 (2004)
2. Lukasik, S., Żak, S.: Firefly algorithm for Continuous Constrained Optimisation Tasks. Systems Research Institute, Polish. Academy of Sciences, pp. 1–10 (2010)
3. Niasar, N.S., Shanbezade, J., Perdam, M.M.: Discrete Fuzzy Particle Swarm Optimization for Solving Travelling Salesman Problem. In: Proceedingsof International Conference on Information and Financial Engineering, pp. 162–165 (2009)
4. Pilat, M.L., White, T.: Using Genetic Algorithms to Optimize ACS-TSP. In: Dorigo, M., Di Caro, G.A., Sampels, M. (eds.) Ant Algorithms 2002. LNCS, vol. 2463, pp. 12–14. Springer, Heidelberg (2002)
5. Sayadi, M.K.: A Discrete Meta-Heuristic With Local Search for Makespan Minimization in Permutation Flow Shop Scheduling Problems. International Journal of Industrial Engineering Computation 1(1), 1–10 (2010)
6. TSPLIB95: Ruprecht - Karls - Universitat Heildelberg (2011), http://www.iwr.uini-heidelberg.de/groups/comopt/software/TSPLIB95/
7. Yang, X.S.: Nature-inspired Metaheuristic Algorithm. Luniver Press (2008)
8. Yang, X.S.: Firefly Algorithms for Multimodal Optimization. In: Watanabe, O., Zeugmann, T. (eds.) SAGA 2009. LNCS, vol. 5792, pp. 169–178. Springer, Heidelberg (2009)
9. Yang, X.S.: Engineering Optimization: An Introduction with Metaheuristic Applications. Wiley, Chichester (2010)
10. Tsai, H., Yang, J., Tsai, Y., Kao, C.: An Evolutionary Algorithm for Large Traveling Salesman Problems. IEEE Transactions on Systems, Man, and Cybernetics, Part B, 1718–1729 (2004)
11. Wong, L., Chong, C.S.: An Efficient Bee Colony Optimization Algorithm for Travelling Salesman Problem Using Frequency-Based Pruning. In: Proceedings of 7th IEEE International Conference on Industrial Informatics, pp. 775–782 (2009)

Robust Optimization by Means of Vegetative Reproduction

Jorge Maturana* and Fernando Vergara

Instituto de Informática, Universidad Austral de Chile
jorge.maturana@inf.uach.cl
http://www.inf.uach.cl

Abstract. In the last half century, computer science has witnessed the appearance of nature-inspired methods for the resolution of complex optimization problems, which are hardly solved by traditional optimization methods. Metaheuristics like evolutionary algorithms or swarm intelligence have been successfully applied to a wide range of both theoretical and practical problems.

This article presents a new optimization method based in reproduction mechanics of plant clonal colonies. These systems are composed of a set of clones, interconnected and spatially spread over a geographical area. In this new metaheuristic, called *Clonal Colony Optimization* (CCO), problem solutions are associated to clones, that are subject to evolutionary cycles that adaptively reconfigure the geographical covering over the search space of the problem. Solutions coded in this manner would be more robust that those obtained using independent individuals.

Keywords: bio-inspired metaheuristics, robustness, multi-objective optimization, adaptive organization.

1 Introduction

Mathematics and computer science have a long history dealing with optimization problems. Finding a good configuration of control variables of a phenomenon contributes to save time, money and resources. However, in many occasions people do not have total control over variables. Consider for instance the problem of finding a schedule for a manufacturing process where tasks depend on just-in-time reception of parts. If a part fails to arrive at time, schedule must be adapted to avoid an excessive negative effect over total completion time. In this kind of problems, is not enough to find a single good solution (i.e., a schedule), but also to find one that would be resilient to unexpected changes in input variables, what is known as *robustness*. Robustness in search landscapes can be seen as zones where the objective function (total completion time in our example) does not change much when some of the input variables change to a nearby value.

Many optimization methods nowadays are purely quality-driven, i.e., they select a good solution in spite of its associated risks. In order to find a compromise

---

* Corresponding author. This research was founded by Project DID UACh S-2010-50.

A. Bouchachia (Ed.): ICAIS 2011, LNAI 6943, pp. 404–415, 2011.

between quality and robustness, it is necessary to include this criteria in the search process. Methods that do this often involve high computational costs.

This paper presents an optimization method inspired from plant clonal colonies, i.e., a linked, geographically spread set of plants, that adapts its structure and share nutrients among their nodes in order to maximise the life expectancy of the whole colony. Wealthier plants support poorer ones that explore new zones, thus a colony has specialized individuals to either explore or exploit the search space. The result of the search process is a Pareto-optimal set of solutions according to both objectives, namely quality and robustness.

This paper is organized as follows. Sec. 2 discusses solution stability, Sec. 3 outlines basic plant physiology and related models, Sec. 4 recalls several algorithmic methods inspired in nature, Sec. 5 presents the details of our approach while Sec. 6 offers its numerical validation, to finally draw conclusions and present paths for further research in Sec. 7.

2   Problem Stability

Optimization algorithms often deal with the standard formulation of optimization problems: Given a set of variables X, a set of constraints C and an objective function $F(x), x \in X$, the goal is to find values for variables in x that either minimise or maximise $F(x)$. Despite this simple formulation, some problems appear when tackling real-world problems [1]. Variables could undergo unexpected variation because of external events, the measure of F could be noisy, variable over time, or too expensive to be measured directly. We will focus on robustness of solutions, i.e., the sensitivity of the objective function to changes in variables. The challenge of producing robust solutions can be addressed in two different ways [2], either by adapting the obtained solution according to ulterior changes in the environment or by including mechanisms to deliver a robust solution at the end of the search. The first approach implicates a further refinement of the solution when a change in conditions is detected. This refinement takes as input either the original optimum or a set of diverse-good solutions to accelerate the search for a new suitable optimum.

On the other hand, finding a robust optimal solution before knowing the sources of later changes can be done in several ways [1]. A first method, *explicit averaging*, uses Monte Carlo integration, i.e., obtain the average value of a number of randomly sampled disturbances around the solutions evaluated during the search. Another alternative is *implicit averaging*, that happens when population is increased in size, since a large number of individuals close to the interesting zones of the search space is evaluated repetitively. A third method is to consider optimum quality and its variability as separate objectives, in a multi-objective approach. This method, same as explicit averaging, requires to sample the surroundings of solutions to assess their robustness.

Note that these three approaches requires an extra effort: either to increase the number of solutions or the number of evaluations over and near them. This raises computational cost. This paper presents a method that aims to obtain robust solutions without the extra cost in evaluations.

3   Plant Physiology and Reproduction

3.1   Plant Feed, Growth and Reproduction

Plants are living beings that develop complex dynamic mechanisms to adapt to their environment. In order to survive and reproduce, they need several resources, being the most essential ones water, light and nutrients from soil. A geographical placement that bring access to these resources will considerably increase their chances of survive. Unlike animals, plants cannot change their placement in search of better conditions, but they can adapt their physical processes to adjust themselves to current circumstances and orient their growth towards the direction that improves their access to resources.

Plants usually exhibit several reproduction mechanisms. Asexual reproduction (also known as *vegetative reproduction*), create clones of the plant, i.e., a new individual with the same genotypic configuration, by means of cellular division. Although several plants produce unconnected new individuals through asexual reproduction, some others maintain a physical link with their offspring, configuring a *clonal colony*, where each plant (called *ramet*) solidarizes to some point with their neighbours by exchanging resources, extending the geographical coverage of the whole colony, and therefore improving access to distant resources.

Two main forms of vegetative reproduction exist, *stolons* and *rhizomes* (Fig. 1). Stolons are aerial specialized shots that generate a new ramet connected to the colony when good conditions are found. Rhizomes are similar to stolons, except that they grow underground and emerge to create a new ramet.

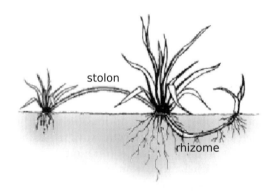

Fig. 1. Vegetative reproduction: stolons and rhizomes

A number of trade-offs are observed in clonal colonies. Given that resources are limited, the colony must "decide" the extent of colonization and its topology. A wider colony will require more energy to transport resources between ramets, so if resources are scarce, the cost of transport could become excessive. A complex relationship exists between ramets, depending on its physiology (genetically determined), the distance between them and the abundance of resources: if the distance is small and the resources scarce, ramets will compete to gain access to them. If the distance is larger, collaboration will benefit ramets, but if it is too large, transport costs became excessive. Finally, the colony must decide, specially when resources become scarce, whether to expand its geographical coverage, or let less efficient ramets die.

Clonal colonies have developed a distributed strategy to assure their survival under difficult conditions. Their geographical deployment and collaborative sharing of resources allows to explore new –sometimes poor-resourced– zones as a collective investment to find better but distant places.

3.2   Biological Models

In botanical studies, several models have been proposed to characterize the geographical spreading of clonal colonies, mainly for descriptive purposes. [3] present an agent-based model to simulate reef development. A toroidal grid that represents seabed is randomly initialized with a number of agents (plants). At every time step, agents apply some development rules to decide in which direction (surrounding cells) the plant will develop. In the short term, results agree with previous models and extrapolation of field studies, providing a parsimonious model for the development of reef topology.

Not all models use a 2D, grid-based platform to characterize plant spreading. [4] presents a 3D simulation model to characterize rhizome growth of an aggressive invasive weed in UK. The model uses *correlated random walk* (CRW) to model the orientation of the rhizome development. Unlike simple random walk, the orientation of rhizomes in CRW is correlated with previous orientation. The model starts from a point and in each time step extends the plant to obtain a 3D simulation of its propagation. The model adjust well to field data, but does not take in consideration soil resources that could orientate the growth of rhizomes in some particular direction.

Even though most studies in biology deal with specific species, there are some theoretical research aiming to develop models to characterize a generic relationship between ramets in a clonal colony. Starting from the evidence obtained in previous studies, indicating that ramets of clonal plants can specialize in collecting some specific resource (light, water), [5] develops an optimal allocation model for clonal systems. This specialization is analogous to specialization units of a multiplant enterprise, where each unit focuses on what it does better and later exchange goods with other units for mutual benefit. The model is developed for a single 2-ramet system, linked by a stolon. A series of variables are defined, and the values of root-shoot ratios that maximizes overall plant performance are found. Despite the comprehensiveness of the model, it is purely theoretical, obtaining, for example, solutions where a full specialization is observed. This situation would be rarely found in nature, since the risk of stolon fragmentation would cause the death of both ramets due to their absolute co-dependence.

4   Nature-Inspired Optimization Methods

In the last 50 years, nature has been a source of inspiration for computer science. Many approaches have been successfully applied to solve complex problems, that traditional optimization methods cannot afford. In this context, *Evolutionary Computation* is an umbrella term for a group of metaheuristics inspired in the evolutionary process. Typically, an *Evolutionary Algorithm* (EA) [6] maintains a set of individuals, where each one encodes a solution to the problem. The variables of the problem constitute the genotype of the individual, that is scored according to how it fits to the objective function. Evolution is done by both combining individuals genotypes, and mutating them randomly, together with a selection process biased to the best individuals. Several variants of this general approach can be found, including Genetic Algorithms, Evolutionary Strategies, Genetic Programming, Estimation of distribution algorithms, Differential Evolution and Memetic Algorithms.

Another example of biological-inspired optimization methods is *Swarm Intelligence* [7], that simulates the emergent behaviour in a group of animals. This category includes *Ant Colony Optimization* (ACO), that mimics the process of path construction observed in ants, and *Particle Swarm Optimization* (PSO), inspired by animal group movement such as bird flocks.

Another method inspired by nature are *Artificial Immune Systems* (AIS) [8], composed of a diverse set of metaheuristics inspired by human immune systems, that attack external threatening organisms (*antigens*), taking care of not attacking own cells. Opposed to evolutionary computation, there is not a common structure that frame different algorithms in this field.

Plant ecology presents several aspects that are of interest to computer science. One of them is the colonization of alien species when they are introduced artificially in a new environment [9]. Some methods have been developed in this context. [10] presents an optimization algorithm inspired in weed colonization by seeds, called *Invasive Weed Optimization*, taking some elements from Evolutionary algorithms and Simulated Annealing. Problem solutions are encoded as plants, that are randomly distributed in the search space. At each generation, each plant produces an amount of seeds proportional to its fitness, calculated linearly between threshold values. Seeds are placed to a Normal-distributed distance of its parent, with a standard deviation that decreases as the search goes on. Since the system is assumed to have a limited capacity, a fixed number of plants can be alive at the end of the generation.

Asexual reproduction principles have been also used in optimization method. [11] proposes a single-solution optimization method called *Asexual Reproduction Optimization*, where the individual encodes an array of variables of the problem. At each time step, the individual is mutated and both the original and the new individuals (named *Larva*) are merged according to a probability to create a new one, and replaces the original individual if it is better.

Most of aforementioned methods use plant genes to encode problem solutions, making them similar to Genetic Algorithms. In spite of the several methods inspired from plant reproduction that has been proposed so far, none of them

–to our knowledge– has used the adaptive mechanisms and the geographical distribution of clonal colonies as a conceptual working basis.

5   Clonal Colony Optimization

Our goal is to develop an adaptive metaheuristic to find robust solutions without incurring in extra computational cost to evaluate the robustness of candidate solutions. This is done by mimicking the collaborative scheme of clonal colonies.

Roughly speaking, CCO maintains a set of candidate solutions, called *plants*, grouped by links between them, forming *colonies*. Several colonies are spread throughout the search space, here called *yard*. Plants in a colony are connected by one-to-one links, in a parent-children relationship (colonies start growing from a single plant that arrives to its position as a seed). Plants are evaluated individually with a *fitness* function, whose value increases as the encoded solution fits the goal of the problem to solve. Besides individual fitness values, the colony holds the colony average value of fitnesses, that is used to evaluate the viability of the colony. To control the excessive growth of the number of plants in the yard (with the consequent computation cost), the yard has a maximum number of plants that can hold, named *carrying capacity*. Each colony, in turn, has its own carrying capacity.

Colonies undergo several processes that constitute the basic structure of CCO (see the algorithm below). Initially, colonies of one plant only are randomly *seed* in the yard. Then, a development cycle starts, including *purging* plants (biased toward low quality ones), *extending* the colony by adding new plants, and *splitting* colonies when the distance between linked individuals become excessive. At every generation the carrying capacity of the yard is *reallocated* among colonies. Once the optimization process is done, the final step is to *distill* a set of solutions with the best trade-off of quality and robustness.

```
Program CCO()
  Seed colonies randomly in the yard
  while(stop condition is not satisfied)
    ForEach(Colony c in the yard)
      Purge(c)
      Extend(c)
      Split(c)
    Reallocate()
  Distill(solutions in the yard)
```

5.1   Required Elements and Design Choices

CCO requires the definition of some aspects. These elements and the particular choices taken during this work are shown below.

Encoding. Variables of the problem to solve must be encoded. This encoding can be directly the decision variables of the mathematical formulation, or a custom mapping, same as all metaheuristics do. In the work presented here, we used an array of real numbers $x = (x_1, \ldots x_n), x_i \in \Re, i = 1 \ldots n$.

Fitness function. A fitness function must be defined. As its name says, the value of this function expresses the fitness of the plant to their environment, so its value rises as the quality of the plant increases.

Distance measure. When extending a colony, the new plant must be somewhat near to its parent, and when splitting a link, the distance of the plants in both extremes must be large. Therefore, its is necessary to define a measure of distance between individuals. This definition is closely related with the concept of neighbourhood used by most metaheuristics. According to our real number encoding, we use an euclidean distance, $d(x, y) = \left(\sum_{i=1}^{n}(x_i - y_i)^2\right)^{1/2}$

Transport model. Wealthy plants in the colony share nutrients (here expressed as fitness) with weaker ones, in order to support exploration of the yard. The degree of this share must be defined. Here we use a single schema: let f_i be the individual fitness of the plant i, and $\bar{f}$ the mean fitness of the colony. A new fitness value –called *transported fitness, f_i^t*– is assigned to plant i obtained by means of the expression $f_i^t = f_i - s \cdot (f_i - \bar{f})$, where $0 \leqslant s \leqslant 1$ is a sharing constant with value 0.3.

Operators definition. Specific definitions of the operators defined above must be provided, namely:

Seed. In the absence of knowledge about the search space, the natural choice is to initialise colonies randomly, as done in this study. However, other methods could be also used to accelerate convergence towards optima.

Purge. Several alternatives may be used to select the plant to purge. Options like choosing the absolute worst, tournament-based or random-choose are the most straightforward ones. In this study we delete the plant that, being created at least 4 generations ago, has the worst fitness value. if more than one plant fulfil this criteria, the one with the higher number of connections is chosen.

Extend. Several methods may be used to select the plant that will generate the offspring. Here we consider fitness proportional. Having chosen the parent, the position of the offspring is yet to be determined. As stated before, the new plant should be close to its parent, but not *too* close. Given our real-number encoding, we take every variable of the plant and add a value obtained from the distribution shown in figure 2, being X_i the range of the i-th variable and $0 < \delta < 1$ a multiplier factor.

Split. When distance between plants become excessive, colony splits. Several considerations can be taken here, such as flux through this link, how autonomous or large is the colony at both ends, or plants age at each side, to avoid killing young buds. In this work we split a colony if a link between two plants is longer that $\frac{3}{2} \cdot \left(\sum_{i=1}^{n}(\delta X_i)^2\right)^{1/2}$ and there are at least 3 plants at each side.

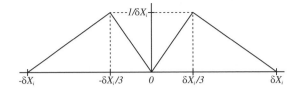

Fig. 2. Probability distribution function used to *Extend* colonies

Reallocate. Yard carrying capacity could be reallocated to implement competition among colonies. Here, for simplicity, carrying capacity is equally assigned to all colonies, so it is updated only when a colony splits.

Distill. The identification of solutions both robust and of good quality is done at the end of the search process, in order to provide the user with concrete results to its problem. This supposes that the result of the search is not a single solution but a set of solutions belonging to the Pareto front. In this work, the most central plant of each colony is chosen to representate it. The criteria to choose it is to minimize the sum of square distances to other plants of the same colony. For all representatives, both their quality and robustness is considered to calculate the Pareto front. Plant quality corresponds to its fitness while robustness is calculated as A_c/σ_c^2 where A_c is the minimum area in the domain that contains the plants (i.e., the extension of the colony in the search space) and σ_c^2 is the variance of fitness values of the plants in the colony (i.e., how of heterogeneous is the quality inside the colony).

CCO takes a couple of elements from existing approaches, namely the variable encoding as entities placement, as done in Particle Swarm Optimization, and the use of a population, as in several mataheuristics. However, there are some novelties that distinguishes it from the rest. In CCO, individuals (ramets) do not encode all aspects we are interested in, since they do not hold information about robusteness. Therefore, we can distinguish two semantic levels: ramets encode problem variables, while colonies encode robustness of the ramets inside them. Cooperation between ramets inside colonies is another new aspect, both exploration and exploitation roles cohabit inside the colony, allowing exploration if strong ramets support weak ones.

6   Numerical Validation

In order to check the viability of our approach, experiments have been carried out in several problems with different landscape properties. We want to verify the convergence of the colonies towards the optimal zones, with different trade-off between quality and robustness. The result of the search is therefore the Pareto-optimal set for these two objectives. Given that our focus is to "see" how the colonies evolve, we have used 2D functions to plot the yard. We have considered positive-value, maximization variations of two standard test functions: Sphere (unimodal) and Ackley (multimodal), along with a tailored function, here named *Yurt*, that is a tunable function producing a set of yurt-shaped protuberances with different heigh, amplitude and slope.

Figure 3 shows the convergence of 5 colonies in standard test functions (Sphere and Ackley) towards the optimal value $-(0,0)$ for both functions– and different values of δ. Yard carrying capacity is 50. In general, we can notice that colonies do tend to approach to optimal areas, regardless of the ruggedness of the landscape, but quite depending on the value of δ. This parameter determines how far a new plant can be from its parent, thus related to the average size of the colony. It also determines the displacement speed of the colony across the search space, therefore its ability to explore. If δ is too small, the colony will move slowly and eventually being trapped in local optima. On the contrary, a large value of δ produces a fast exploration of the search space, but difficult a fine convergence to the global optimum at the end of the search. It seems that a value of δ ranging from 0.1 or 0.3 at the beginning to 0.05 at the end could be beneficial. Since any plant can have offspring in any possible sense, some colonies look tortuous. An "escape form barycenter" method could be included, but it could prevent a further exploration of interesting zones inside the area already covered by the colony.

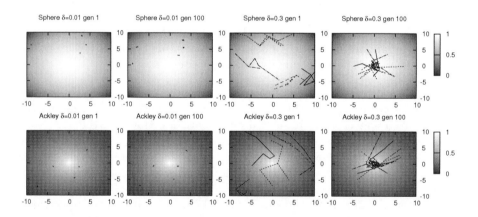

Fig. 3. Evolution of colonies using standard test functions, at the beginning and at the middle search, with different values of δ

In order to study the behaviour of the colonies in search spaces with different levels of robustness, we use a fitness landscape with two plateaux of the same quality but different extension. The evolution of the search is shown in the first row of figure 4. Black circles in the last plot show the location of Pareto-optimal points after 300 generations, with $\delta = 0.1$. The colonies found the two optimal zones, but the *Distill* operator identified the wider one as Pareto-optimal (Similar results were obtained in several runs of the algorithm). Figure 4 (below) shows a

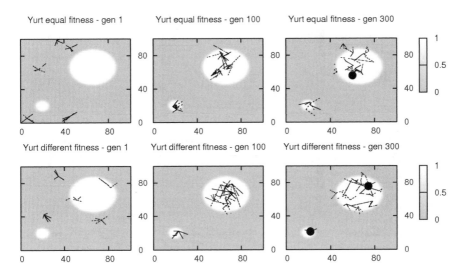

Fig. 4. Placement of colonies in two optimal zones of (a) equal quality and (b) different trade-off of quality and robustness

similar experiment, but this time the narrower zone has a better fitness that the wider one. In this case, two Pareto-optimal points are found, one in each zone.

Figure 5 presents two random-generated Yurt fitness landscapes with different levels of rugosity. We have added Pareto-dominated peaks in order to analyse where the algorithm is converging. The first column shows the placement of colonies after 300 generations.

Note that carrying capacity of the yard and rules of splitting limits the number of colonies in the yard, reason why we have raised carrying capacity up to 200 plants. It is expected that problems with sparse and steep optimal values produce higher colony fragmentation, since different parts of the colony will climb up by separate peaks, leaving an intermediate uninteresting set of plants that will die. This phenomenon can be appreciated in the second column, showing a lower level of fragmentation for simpler landscapes, when compared with the rugged ones. Fragmentation shows the ability of CCO to self adapt colonies partition in face of multimodal problems. Nevertheless, some peaks are covered by more than one colony, implicating a misuse of search resources. Even though this phenomenon also occurs in other metaheuristics, a model that considers concurrent access to resources (as two plants competing for nutrients from soil) could be implemented to purge an entire colony when this happens. Given that colonies define a covering area, overlapping colonies are easier to detect than overlapping individuals.

To provide a basis of comparison, we used a genetic algorithm that encodes pairs (x, y), and operates with arithmetic recombination, gaussian mutation, and tournament selection to pick both breeders and survivors. 200 individuals were evolved during 300 generations. The third column shows the percentage

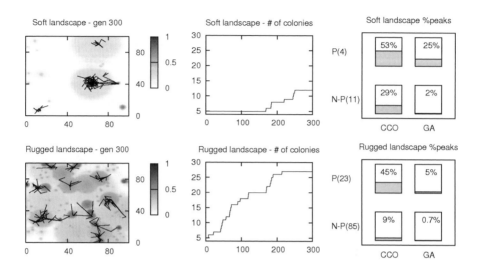

Fig. 5. Final placement of colonies in soft and rugged fitness landscapes, evolution of the number of colonies, and covering of landscape peaks

of Pareto-dominant (P) and non Pareto-dominant (N-P) peaks –concurrently– covered in generation 300 by both CCO and GA. These are average values over 30 runs. The total number of peaks in the landscape are marked in the ordinate axis. The cooperative approach of CCO contributes to keep a higher diversity level during the search, which in turn helps to distribute the search over several optima with different trade-offs of quality and robustness.

7 Conclusions

This article has presented a method inspired from clonal colonies to identify robust results in optimization problems, called *Clonal Colony Optimization*. Some botanical models have been reviewed in order to identify the main aspects in the development of clonal colonies, as well as some existing metaheuristics inspired from plants. Existing methods assess robustness by repetitively measuring fitness in the proximity of each solution, what increases computational cost. In our approach, the fact that a group of solutions is packed together, provides a measure of robustness without additional cost. The fact that solutions are evaluated only once make this approach interesting for problems in which evaluation function is costly.

Tests over a series of problems with different fitness landscapes have been done, in order to validate the method. Some parameters appear to have a great influence over the performance, such as δ and the yard carrying capacity.

Given the novelty of this approach, there are plenty of future work paths. Some of these include scale search spaces to higher dimensions, and using encodings different than those in $\Re^n$. Different design choices can be tried: besides the ones outlined in Sec. 5.1, incorporating a competition mechanism could be beneficial to better explore the search space. A comparison with other techniques is also needed in order to clearly asses differences in computational cost and results. In order to deal with dynamic landscapes, it may be necessary to include an operator to delete an entire colony. This would allow to react rapidly to sudden changes, reassigning resources to exploaration, maybe seeding the freed carrying capacity. Finally, a self adaptive mechanism for crucial parameters such as δ could be further studied.

References

1. Jin, Y., Branke, J.: Evolutionary optimization in uncertain environments–a survey. IEEE Trans.on Evol.Comp. 9(3), 303–317 (2005)
2. Bui, L.T., Michalewicz, Z., Parkinson, E., Abello, M.B.: Adaptation in Dynamic Environments: A Case Study in Mission Planning. IEEE Trans.on Evol. Comp (2010) (accepted)
3. Kendrick, G.A., Marbā, N., Duarte, C.M.: Modelling formation of complex topography by the seagrass Posidonia oceanica. In: Estuarine, Coastal and Shelf Science, vol. 65(4), pp. 717–725. Elsevier, Amsterdam (2005)
4. Smith, J.M.D., Ward, J.P., Child, L.E., Owen, M.R.: A simulation model of Rhizome networks for Fallopia japonica (Japanese Knotweed) in the United Kingdom. In: Ecological Modelling, vol. 200(3-4), pp. 421–432. Elsevier, Amsterdam (2007)
5. Stuefer, J.F., During, H.J., Schieving, F.: A model on optimal root-shoot allocation and water transport in clonal plants. In: Ecological Modelling, vol. 111(2-3), pp. 171–186. Elsevier, Amsterdam (1998)
6. Eiben, A.E., Smith, J.E.: Introduction to Evolutionary Computing. Springer, Heidelberg (2003)
7. Blum, C., Merkle, D.: Swarm Intelligence: Introduction and Applications. Springer, Heidelberg (2010)
8. Dasgupta, D., Nino, F.: Immunological Computation: Theory and Applications. Auerbach Publications (2008)
9. Pyšek, P., Richardson, D.M.: Invasive plants. In: Encyclopedia of Ecology: Ecological Engineering, vol. 3, pp. 2011–2020 (2008)
10. Mehrabian, A.R., Lucas, C.: A novel numerical optimization algorithm inspired from weed colonization. In: Ecological Informatics, vol. 1(4), pp. 355–366. Elsevier, Amsterdam (2006)
11. Farasat, A., Menhaj, M.B., Mansouri, T., Moghadam, M.R.S.: ARO: A new model-free optimization algorithm inspired from asexual reproduction. Applied Soft Computing 10(4), 1284–1292 (2010)

Discrete Particle Swarm Optimization for TSP: Theoretical Results and Experimental Evaluations

Matthias Hoffmann, Moritz Mühlenthaler, Sabine Helwig, and Rolf Wanka

Department of Computer Science, University of Erlangen-Nuremberg, Germany
Matthias.Hoffmann@informatik.stud.uni-erlangen.de,
{muehlenthaler,sabine.helwig,rwanka}@cs.fau.de

Abstract. Particle swarm optimization (PSO) is a nature-inspired technique originally designed for solving *continuous* optimization problems. There already exist several approaches that use PSO also as basis for solving *discrete* optimization problems, in particular the Traveling Salesperson Problem (TSP). In this paper, (i) we present the first theoretical analysis of a discrete PSO algorithm for TSP which also provides insight into the convergence behavior of the swarm. In particular, we prove that the popular choice of using "sequences of transpositions" as the difference between tours tends to decrease the convergence rate. (ii) In the light of this observation, we present a new notion of difference between tours based on "edge exchanges" and a new method to combine differences by computing their "centroid." This leads to a more PSO-like behavior of the algorithm and avoids the observed slow down effect. (iii) Then, we investigate implementations of our methods and compare them with previous implementations showing the competitiveness of our new approaches.

1 Introduction

The problem. Particle Swarm Optimization (PSO) is a popular metaheuristic designed for solving optimization problems on *continuous* domains. It was introduced by Kennedy and Eberhard [11,5] and has since then been applied successfully to a wide range of optimization problems. Since the structure of the PSO algorithm is relatively simple, PSO has to some extent been open for theoretical studies of the swarm behavior. Clerk and Kennedy [4], Trelea [17], and Jiang et al. [9] provide analyses of the convergence behavior of particle swarms, which offer some insights on how to select the swarm parameters, and the initial behavior of a swarm has been analyzed in [8]. Inspired by the performance of PSO on continuous optimization problems, several approaches have also been proposed for applying PSO to discrete problems, such as function optimization on binary domains [12], scheduling problems [1], and the Traveling Salesperson Problem (TSP) [2,18,6,14,15,19].

The TSP is one of the classical problems in discrete optimization. A wealth of methods specifically tailored for solving TSP has been developed and math-

A. Bouchachia (Ed.): ICAIS 2011, LNAI 6943, pp. 416–427, 2011.

ematically and experimentally investigated. A comprehensive overview of this line of research can be found in [7].

But the TSP is also well suited to be approached by (meta-)heuristic methods like PSO. For discrete PSO, new interpretations of "movement" and "velocity" are necessary. The first approach to adapting the PSO scheme to TSP is due to Clerc [2,3]. However, it turns out that this discrete PSO (DPSO) by itself is not as successful as the original PSO for continuous problems. Consequently, subsequent approaches to solving TSP by PSO typically rely on downstream optimization techniques such as k-OPT [15,14] and Lin-Kernighan [6] applied after one PSO iteration to improve the quality of the solution obtained by PSO. Unfortunately, whereas these hybrid algorithms are evaluated experimentally by being run on benchmark instances, they are hard to analyze mathematically, and so far, no theoretical insights were gained about the particles' behavior in discrete PSO at all. In fact, the downstream optimization even conceals the performance of plain DPSO.

Our contribution. In this paper, we present the first theoretical analysis of the discrete PSO algorithms of Clerc [2] and Wang et al. [18], which, to some extent, also applies to the approach of Shi et al. [14]. In particular, we provide for the first time theoretical evidence for why the convergence behavior of these DPSO algorithms for the TSP is quite different from what we would expect from the classical PSO for continuous problems. The key insight is that in later stages of the optimization process, the particles are not likely to converge towards the best solution found so far. In fact, we prove that the distance to the best solution even remains more or less constant.

In the light of the theoretical findings, we then propose a novel interpretation of "particle motion" avoiding the convergence problem mentioned above. Our method is similar to computing the midpoint of a discrete line. Additionally, we introduce a new representation of the "velocity" of a particle, which is based on exchanging edges in a potential solution of a TSP instance. We evaluate our proposed DPSO with respect to seven instances from the TSPlib [13] with 52 to 105 cities. In these experimental evaluations, our focus is on the DPSO performance of different velocity representations because we are in this context mainly interested in the performance of the plain DPSO approaches without subsequent local improvement phases. Our results indicate that the combination of the midpoint-based particle motion with the edge-exchange operator outperforms the other operators as well as those methods which suffer from the identified convergence problem.

In order to also compare our DPSO to the previous approaches which use in the PSO iterations additional local improvement heuristics, we hybridize our DPSO iteration with a 2-OPT local optimization applied to the global attractor. Here, we make two observations: The first one is that better performance of the plain DPSO results in a better performance of the hybridized DPSO. And second, for the first time it is clearly documented that the huge performance gains (that is achieved when using local optimization in comparison to the plain DPSO) indicate that the quality of the solutions found by the DPSO algorithms with local optimization is almost completely determined by the quality of the local optimization. In the previous work [14,18,19], it is not differentiated between the contribution of the PSO and the additional local improvement methods.

The remainder of this paper is organized as follows. In Sec. 2, we provide relevant background information on TSP and PSO. Sec. 3 contains our theoretical analysis of the particle convergence behavior of discrete PSOs for permutation problems. In Sec. 4, we propose the new discrete PSO for the TSP which uses a centroid-based approach for the particle movement. Sec. 5 provides the experimental results which indicate that our proposed approach outperforms other discrete PSOs for the TSP.

2   Preliminaries

2.1   The Traveling Salesperson Problem

The Traveling Salesperson Problem (TSP) is a classical combinatorial optimization problem. An instance $I = (n, \text{dist})$ of the TSP with n cities $\{1, \ldots, n\}$ consists of the distances between each pair of cities, given as an $n \times n$-integer matrix 'dist'. The task is to find a tour with minimum length visiting each city exactly once, including the way back to the initial city. A tour is given as a permutation π of the cities $\{1, \ldots, n\}$, where $\pi(i)$ denotes the ith visited city. Hence the set of optimal solutions of an instance $I = (n, \text{dist})$ is

$$\operatorname*{argmin}_{\pi \in S_n} \left(\text{dist}_{\pi(n), \pi(1)} + \sum_{1 \le i < n} \text{dist}_{\pi(i), \pi(i+1)} \right) ,$$

where S_n is the symmetric group on $\{1, \ldots, n\}$ with the usual composition $\circ$ as group operation. The operation $\circ$ is used for exploring the search space. Note that in this formulation the search space consists of *all* elements of S_n, so one specific cycle of length n is represented by many permutations. The advantage of using all elements of S_n for the proposed discrete PSO is that the particles can move around freely in the search space without the danger of encountering permutations which do not correspond to a valid tour. The decision variant of TSP ("given an integer L, is there a tour in I of length at most L?") is NP-hard and hence, TSP can presumably not be solved exactly in polynomial time.

2.2   (Discrete) Particle Swarm Optimization

Introduced by Kennedy and Eberhard [11,5], particle swarm optimization (PSO) is a population-based metaheuristic that uses a swarm of potential solutions called particles to cooperatively solve optimization problems. Typically, the search space of a problem instance is an n-dimensional rectangle $\mathcal{B} \subseteq \mathbb{R}^n$, and the objective function (often also called fitness function) is of the form $f : \mathbb{R}^n \to \mathbb{R}$. PSO works in *iterations*. In iteration t, each particle i has a *position* $\boldsymbol{x}_i^{(t)} \in \mathcal{B}$ and a *velocity* $\boldsymbol{v}_i^{(t)} \in \mathbb{R}^n$. While moving through the search space, the particles evaluate f at $\boldsymbol{x}_i^{(t)}$. Each particle remembers its best position $\boldsymbol{p}_i$ so far (called local attractor) and the best position p_{glob} of all particles in the swarm so far (called global attractor). In iteration t, the position and velocity of each particle is updated according to the following *movement equations*:

$$v_i^{(t+1)} = a \cdot v_i^{(t)} + r_{\text{loc}} \cdot b_{\text{loc}} \cdot (p_i - x_i^{(t)}) + r_{\text{glob}} \cdot b_{\text{glob}} \cdot (p_{\text{glob}} - x_i^{(t)}) \quad (1)$$

$$x_i^{(t+1)} = x_i^{(t)} + v_i^{(t+1)}. \quad (2)$$

The parameters $a, b_{\text{loc}}, b_{\text{glob}} \in \mathbb{R}$ are constant weights which can be selected by the user. The *inertia* a adjusts the relative importance of the inertia of the particles, and the so-called *acceleration coefficients* b_{loc} and b_{glob} determine the influence of the local and the global attractor, resp. In every iteration, r_{loc} and r_{glob} are drawn uniformly at random from $[0, 1]$. Particles exchange information about the search space exclusively via the global attractor p_{glob}. $p_i - x_i^{(t)}$ is the *local attraction* exerted by the local attractor on particle i, and $p_{\text{glob}} - x_i^{(t)}$ is the *global attraction* exerted by the global attractor.

The PSO algorithm was originally designed for solving optimization problems on continuous domains. Inspired by the success and conceptual simplicity of PSO, several approaches have been proposed to adapt the PSO dynamics to discrete problems including the TSP [2,6,15,14]. In order to adapt PSO's movement equations (1) and (2) to the discrete domain of the TSP, Clerk suggests in [2] the following modifications (or new interpretations) of the terms involved:

- The particle's *position* $x_i^{(t)}$ is a permutation π of the cities, i.e., $\pi = (c_{i_1} c_{i_2} \ldots c_{i_n})$ which corresponds to the tour $c_{i_1} \to c_{i_2} \to \cdots \to c_{i_n} \to c_{i_1}$.
- The *difference* $x - y$ between two positions x and y (also called the attraction of x to y) is represented by a shortest sequence of transpositions $T = t_1, \ldots, t_k$ such that $y \circ T = x$. Transposition $t = (c_m c_r)$ exchanges the two cities c_m and c_r in a given round-trip.
- The *length* of a difference is the length of the sequence T of transpositions.
- The *multiplication* $s \cdot T$ of a difference $T = t_1, \ldots, t_k$ with a scalar s, $0 < s \le 1$, is defined as $t_1, \ldots, t_{\lceil s \cdot k \rceil}$. For $s = 0$, $s \cdot T = \emptyset$. Here, we omit the cases $s > 1$ and $s < 0$ since they do not occur in our proposed PSO.
- The *addition* $T_1 + T_2$ of differences $T_1 = t_1^1, \ldots, t_k^1$ and $T_1 = t_1^2, \ldots, t_l^2$ is defined as $T_1 + T_2 = t_1^1, \ldots, t_k^1, t_1^2, \ldots, t_l^2$.
- The *addition of a difference and a position* is defined as applying the transpositions of the difference to the position.

A small example is presented after the proof of Theorem 1.

In [2], [18] and [14], the difference between two positions x and y in the search space is represented as a list of transpositions that transform round-trip x into round-trip y. In [6], this representation is restricted to adjacent transpositions. In our new approach in Sec. 4, we replace the transposition by a representation which successively exchanges two *edges* in a round-trip. Hence, the difference of two positions x and y is a sequence of edge exchanges of minimal length which transforms x into y.

3   Theoretical Analysis

In this section, we prove that under certain conditions the previously developed variants of DPSO mentioned in Sec. 2 behave counterintuitively when compared to the classical continuous PSO since the convergence rate in DPSO is slowed down. More specifically, we show that transpositions which occur both in the local attraction and in the global attraction cancel each other and prevent the particle from moving closer to the global and local attractor. This is quite different from the behavior observed in continuous PSO where common components in these attractions even result in an amplified attractive force.

The phenomenon that the local and the global attraction in previous approaches have a lot of transpositions in common in the later stages of the optimization process can be observed experimentally. Evaluating the two attractions $p_i - x_i^{(t)}$ and $p_{\text{glob}} - x_i^{(t)}$ for sample runs (see Fig. 1), we see that (in this example) on average about 30% of the transpositions occur in both attractions. Summing the particles in the right half of the bins in Fig. 1, we can conclude that for roughly 20% of the particles, more than a half of the transpositions are shared by the two attractions. We analyzed the DPSO methods from [2,18] that use transpositions for representing distances between particles in what we call the *Long Term Discrete PSO* model (LTD). In this model, we assume that the following four conditions hold:

- Differences between positions are represented by sequences of transpositions.
- $p_i = p_{\text{glob}} =: p$, for all particles i.
- $a = 0$
- r_{loc} and r_{glob} are uniformly distributed.

When the full swarm converges to a common best solution p, all local and global attractors are identical. If $p_i = p_{\text{glob}}$ for a certain particle, then it has visited the

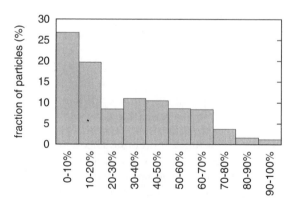

Fig. 1. Similarity of local and global attraction on Clerc's DPSO [2], averaged over 100 runs on the TSP instance berlin52, considering all particles in iterations 990 to 1000

global attractor at least once. We assume the inertia a of the particles being 0 since in our experiments, the performance of the PSO algorithm even becomes worse if the inertia weight is set to a higher value. r_{loc} and r_{glob} are quite often uniformly distributed in practice. This assumption is also made in the mathematical analysis in [17].

For Theorem 1, we assume $b_{loc} = b_{glob}$, which allows for a closed and simple representation. After its proof, we deal with the more general case which can be analyzed analogously and present a small example.

Theorem 1. *Let* $s \in [0, 1]$, *and let* $b_{loc} = b_{glob} = b$. *The probability that in the LTD model a certain particle reduces its distance to* p *in an iteration by a factor of at least* $b \cdot s$, *is* $(1 - s)^2$.

Proof. As $a = 0$, the two movement equations (1) and (2) can be reduced to one:

$$x_i^{(t+1)} = x_i^{(t)} + r_{loc} \cdot b \cdot (p - x_i^{(t)}) + r_{glob} \cdot b \cdot (p - x_i^{(t)})$$

Let d be the number of transpositions in the attraction $(p - x_i^{(t)})$. Since we multiply the difference with $r_{loc} \cdot b$ and $r_{glob} \cdot b$, resp., we apply the first $r_{loc} \cdot b \cdot d$ and then the first $r_{glob} \cdot b \cdot d$ transpositions to $x_i^{(t)}$. Both differences have a common part consisting of the first $\min(r_{loc}, r_{glob}) \cdot b \cdot d$ transpositions.

By applying the first $r_{loc} \cdot b \cdot d$ transpositions, for each transposition an element of $x_i^{(t)}$ reaches the place that it also has in p. However, when applying the transpositions of the second difference, the common part of both differences is applied twice and the elements of the permutation that were already at the right place move now to another place. To bring the elements back to the original place we have to apply the inverse of the common part. Since the inverse of the common part has exactly the same number of transpositions as the common part, the distance to p is only reduced by the transpositions that are not common in both differences and so are only applied once.

The number of the transpositions that are applied only once is $|r_{loc} - r_{glob}| \cdot b \cdot d$. Only these transpositions contribute to the convergence towards p because the other transpositions move the particle further away from p when they are applied a second time. Therefore, we call transpositions that are applied only once "effective transpositions."

The probability that the fraction of effective transposition is at least $b \cdot s$ is, is given by

$$P\left(\frac{|r_{loc} - r_{glob}| \cdot b \cdot d}{d} \geq b \cdot s \right) = P(|r_{loc} - r_{glob}| \geq s) \ .$$

Since r_{loc} and r_{glob} are uniformly distributed, we may conclude (see also Fig. 2 choosing $b_{loc} = b_{glob} = b$): $P(|r_{loc} - r_{glob}| \geq s) = (1 - s)^2$ □

If $b_{\text{loc}} \neq b_{\text{glob}}$, we analogously get the following expression for the probability q_s of the fraction of effective transpositions being larger than s:

$$q_s = \mathrm{P}(|r_{\text{loc}} \cdot b_{\text{loc}} - r_{\text{glob}} \cdot b_{\text{glob}}| \geq s)$$

$$= \mathrm{P}\left(r_{\text{glob}} \leq \frac{b_{\text{loc}} \cdot r_{\text{loc}} - s}{b_{\text{glob}}}\right) + \mathrm{P}\left(r_{\text{glob}} \geq \frac{b_{\text{loc}} \cdot r_{\text{loc}} + s}{b_{\text{glob}}}\right)$$

$$= \int_0^1 \left(\min\left\{1, \max\left\{0, \tfrac{b_{\text{loc}} \cdot r_{\text{loc}} - s}{b_{\text{glob}}}\right\}\right\} + \min\left\{1, \max\left\{0, \tfrac{b_{\text{loc}} \cdot r_{\text{loc}} + s}{b_{\text{glob}}}\right\}\right\}\right) \mathrm{d}r_{\text{loc}}$$

The probability q_s can be visualized like shown in Fig. 2, where q_s amounts to the shaded area.

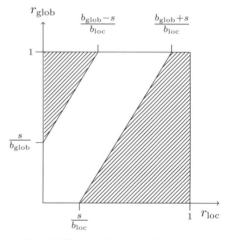

Fig. 2. The shaded area denotes q_s

Consider the following small example. Let $x_i^{(t)} = (1\,5\,2\,7\,3\,9\,4\,6\,8)$ and $p = (1\,2\,3\,4\,5\,6\,7\,8\,9)$. Then $p - x_i^{(t)} = ((2\,3)(3\,5)(4\,7)(6\,8)(8\,9))$. With $b = 0.8$, we have $b \cdot (p - x_i^{(t)}) = ((2\,3)(3\,5)(4\,7)(6\,8))$. With $r_{\text{loc}} = 0.75$ and $r_{\text{glob}} = 0.5$, we get $r_{\text{loc}} \cdot b \cdot (p - x_i^{(t)}) = ((2\,3)(3\,5)(4\,7))$ and $r_{\text{glob}} \cdot b \cdot (p - x_i^{(t)}) = ((2\,3)(3\,5))$, and finally $x_i^{(t+1)} = x_i^{(t)} + r_{\text{loc}} \cdot b \cdot (p - x_i^{(t)}) + r_{\text{glob}} \cdot b \cdot (p - x_i^{(t)}) = (1\,5\,2\,4\,3\,9\,7\,6\,8)$.

The transposition $(4\,7)$ is the only effective transposition. By Theorem 1, the probability that the particle reduces its distance to p by at least 25% is $(1 - 0.3125)^2 \approx 0.47$.

Our analysis directly applies to Clerc's DPSO [2]. The algorithm proposed by Wang et al. [18] works a bit different with respect to the scaling of the attractions. In [18], Wang et al. proposed to scale the attractions by $b_{\text{loc}}, b_{\text{glob}} \in [0, 1]$ keeping each transposition with probability b_{loc} and b_{glob}, resp., in the attraction. So in the LTD model, the movement equations (1) and (2) reduce to

$$x_i^{(t+1)} = x_i^{(t)} + b_{\text{glob}} \cdot (p - x_i^{(t)}) + b_{\text{loc}} \cdot (p - x_i^{(t)}) \ .$$

A transposition becomes an effective transposition if it is kept in exactly one of the two attractions. Therefore, effective transpositions occur with probability $b_{\text{loc}} \cdot (1 - b_{\text{glob}}) + b_{\text{glob}} \cdot (1 - b_{\text{loc}}) = b_{\text{loc}} + b_{\text{glob}} - 2b_{\text{glob}} \cdot b_{\text{loc}}$. This is also the expected value of the fraction of effective transpositions.

The coefficients b_{loc} and b_{glob} are intended to adjust the weight of the local and the global attractor. Intuitively, if the attractors should exert a large influence on the particles, b_{loc} and b_{glob} are set to 1. This works fine in the classical PSO for continuous problems. In the discrete case however, whenever the LTD model applies, the local and global attractions do not pull the particles closer to the attractors at all.

4   A New DPSO for the TSP

4.1   Centroid-Based Particle Movement: A New Interpretation of "Addition"

As described in Sec. 2.2, concatenation is used in [2] and [18] as "addition" of differences, i. e., attractions. In Sec. 3, we showed that this approach has the disadvantage that after some time the expected progress becomes considerably slow. Now we propose a new method of combining the attractions that avoids this disadvantage.

Instead of composing two attractions to a long list of operators, we look at the destinations, which are the points the different weighted attractions lead to, and compute the centroid of those destinations. In our approach, we use no inertia (i. e., we set $a = 0$), but only the attraction to the local and to the global attractor, each weighted in accordance with equation (1). Since we have only two attractors, the centroid can be calculated easily by computing the difference between the destinations, scaling them by one half and adding the result to the first destination. The PSO movement equations can now be expressed with the destination points of the attraction to the local attractor, to the global attractor and a random velocity:

$$d_{\text{loc}} = x_i^{(t)} + r_{\text{loc}} \cdot b_{\text{loc}} \cdot (p_i - x_i^{(t)})$$
$$d_{\text{glob}} = x_i^{(t)} + r_{\text{glob}} \cdot b_{\text{glob}} \cdot (p_{\text{glob}} - x_i^{(t)})$$
$$v_{\text{rand}} = r_{\text{rand}} \cdot b_{\text{rand}} \cdot (p_{\text{rand}} - x_i^{(t)})$$
$$x_i^{(t+1)} = d_{\text{glob}} + \tfrac{1}{2} \cdot (d_{\text{loc}} - d_{\text{glob}}) + v_{\text{rand}}$$

The random movement in the end ensures that the swarm does not converge too fast. A graphical, "continuous" representation is depicted in Fig. 3.

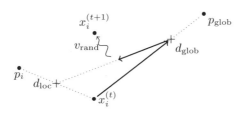

Fig. 3. Centroid-based particle movement

The advantage of this model is that it takes the spatial structure of the search space into account. Since the centroid is the mean of the destinations, our factors b_{loc} and b_{glob} can be transferred easily to the classical PSO by dividing them by 2.

4.2   Edge Recombination: A New Interpretation of "Velocity"

In [2], [18] and [14], the difference between two positions b and a in the search space, i. e., the velocity or the attraction of b to a is expressed as a list of transpositions that transforms one sequence of cities into the other. Here, we propose a new method that is based on edge exchanges. Edge exchanges are a common technique used in local search methods for the TSP [7]. The idea is to improve a solution by exchanging crossing edges, which results in a shorter tour. For an example, see the transformations from Figures 4(a) to (c).

A generalization of this operation is the edge recombination operator. Given a list $\ell = (c_1 c_2 \ldots c_n)$ of cities representing a round-trip, the edge recombination operator $\mathrm{edgeR}(i, j)$ inverts the sequence of cities between indices i and j:

$$\ell \circ \mathrm{edgeR}(i, j) = (c_1 \ldots c_{i-1} \; \underline{c_j \; c_{j-1} \; c_{j-2} \ldots c_{i+2} \; c_{i+1} \; c_i} \; c_{j+1} \ldots c_n)$$

In our approach, we use this operator to express the difference between two particles b and a. Instead of a list of transpositions, the difference (or velocity, or attraction) is now a list of edge recombination operators that yields b if the operators are applied to a.

For example, the difference between $a = (1\ 2\ 6\ 5\ 3\ 4)$ and $b = (1\ 2\ 3\ 4\ 5\ 6)$ is $b - a = (\mathrm{edgeR}(5, 6)\ \mathrm{edgeR}(3, 6))$ (see Fig. 4).

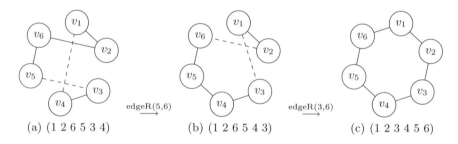

(a) (1 2 6 5 3 4) $\xrightarrow{\mathrm{edgeR}(5,6)}$ (b) (1 2 6 5 4 3) $\xrightarrow{\mathrm{edgeR}(3,6)}$ (c) (1 2 3 4 5 6)

Fig. 4. Visualization of two edge recombinations

The problem of finding the minimum number of edge exchanges that is needed to transform one permutation into the other is NP-complete [16]. Therefore, we use in our experiments the simple and fast approximation algorithm GETLISTOFEDGEEXCHANGES from [10] that is similar to the algorithm that finds the minimum number of transpositions. The solution found by the approximation algorithm GETLISTOFEDGEEXCHANGES has in the worst case $\frac{1}{2}(n-1)$ times more edge exchanges than the optimal solution [10].

5   Experimental Results

In our experiments, we have compared our new approaches to the previous existing ones. We have on purpose initially not done any local optimization between

Table 1. Comparison of different distance representations and movement types without local optimization (left) and with an additional 2-OPT-based local optimization of the global attractor (right)

Move type	Composition	Centroid	Centroid	Centroid	Composition	Centroid	Centroid	Centroid
Distance Repr.	Transposition	Adj. Transposition	Transposition	edgeR	Transposition	Adj. Transposition	Transposition	edgeR
Problem								
berlin52	**104.6%**	**194.6%**	**70.5%**	**22.5%**	**24.2%**	**186,2%**	**8,2%**	**7.0%**
(7542)	18780	23193	15103	10233	10333	23181	8964	8614
	15431.9	22216.8	12862.3	9240.4	9368.1	14692.9	8157.6	8071.5
	±1046.8	±531.6	±863.0	±410.8	±362.6	±1539.6	±241.5	±187.0
	12588	20755	10977	8259	8877	14369	7542	7708
pr76	**220.9%**	**317.7%**	**156.5%**	**88.9%**	**56.9%**	**229.1%**	**5.8%**	**4.7%**
(108159)	416630	468479	347091	249993	19479	460894	128969	122794
	347107.5	451771.6	277404.3	204322.5	169716.3	356021.9	114454.6	113311.6
	±18966.6	±6919.1	±21902.2	±19535.6	±8340.2	±76522.9	±3516.6	±2518.3
	304195	431144	228652	158676	149895	195103	109669	109543
gr96	**310.3%**	**430.4%**	**220.8%**	**128.5%**	**82.9%**	**368.1%**	**9.7%**	**6.3%**
(55209)	251167	302477	204837	149542	121949	299384	63962	63846
	226531.6	292815.8	177107.8	126126.1	100986.2	258421.8	60576.6	58716.1
	±9631.1	±4398.8	±14565.0	±8618.0	±5929.8	±38302.9	±1785.1	±1511.0
	203617	278382	138255	107835	83344	122110	56085	56393
kroA100	**377.2%**	**529.2%**	**238.0%**	**111.2%**	**85.4%**	**401.9%**	**7.4%**	**5.5%**
(21282)	115730	137761	83682	55383	45010	136703	25009	24195
	101552.2	133913.6	71933.4	44945.0	39464.4	106817.7	22864.25	22472.3
	±4468.6	±2291.3	±4702.6	±3498.7	±1908.0	±23555.6	±620.1	±485.8
	91137	125127	60524	37289	35600	40279	21794	21431
kroC100	**386.7%**	**537.4%**	**256.2%**	**133.9%**	**90.0%**	**435.9%**	**8.2%**	**7.1%**
(20749)	112320	135960	84903	58291	45690	136150	24600	24087
	100988.8	132261.1	73903.8	48538.7	39438.7	111195.0	22440.8	22229.4
	±4189.6	±2107.8	±5234.0	±3093.7	±1834.0	±23114.4	±728.4	±655.7
	90375	125228	63107	41237	33682	42998	20996	21034
kroD100	**364.2%**	**503.1%**	**239.0%**	**127.7%**	**86.1%**	**368.9%**	**7.9%**	**7.1%**
(21294)	106556	131549	83922	58077	47876	130923	25091	23941
	98847.9	128438.0	72194.1	48487.5	39625.9	99852.8	22983.5	22808.7
	±4650.5	±1902.7	±4865.6	±3227.4	±2180.0	±21125.3	±589.7	±512.5
	90347	121195	62665	41828	32814	46429	21860	21665
lin105	**421.8%**	**575.8%**	**305.3%**	**188.5%**	**104.4%**	**475.5%**	**18.0%**	**7.1%**
(14379)	87392	100671	69741	49740	33460	98936	18546	16496
	75032.0	97170.6	58284.6	41484.5	29383.8	82754.7	16968.0	15404.8
	±3967.1	±1506.7	±4905.4	±3041.1	±1734.8	±12847.2	±626.2	±414.9
	67391	92116	48110	34121	25383	48322	15306	14600

two iterations to see the clear impact of exchanging the existing approaches with ours. The swarm we use consists of 100 particles and we use 1000 iterations to optimize the function. Each configuration is run 100 times to compute the mean error and the standard deviation. The entries in Table 1 provide data in the following format:

Problem name	**relative error**
(optimal value)	maximal value found by the algorithm
	mean value ± standard deviation
	best solution found by the algorithm

In Table 1, the left four result columns present our results obtained with the proposed DPSO variants without local optimization. In order to make our results also comparable to other approaches, we have added the local optimization method from Shi et al. in [14]. These results are shown in the right four columns of Table 1. Similarly to our proposed approach, the method of Shi also avoids the convergence problems analyzed in Sec. 3, but seems to result in a smaller relative error.

In every four columns block, the first column shows the results of the method representing differences as transpositions and using a simple composition to combine the differences. The other three columns show the results obtained by the centroid-based method from Sec. 4.1. The centroid-based approach is combined with various representations of differences, namely adjacent transpositions, transpositions and the edge recombinations introduced in Sec. 4.2.

Our centroid-based approach avoids the counter-intuitive convergence behavior explained by the theoretical analysis in Sec. 3. The experiments show that this method is a better choice than the simple composition of differences. Another crucial factor is the choice of the representation of particle velocities. Our experimental results show that transpositions are better than adjacent transpositions and that the proposed edge recombination method performs best. Finally, a comparison between different approaches of discrete PSO can only be significant, if the actual contribution of the PSO algorithm is not obfuscated by an additional local search procedure. This is why we show the results of the pure PSO without local optimization, which can serve as a reference for future DPSO variants for the TSP.

6 Conclusions

In our theoretical analysis of discrete PSO for the TSP we showed that the convergence behavior the convergence behavior differs significantly from what we expect from a PSO for continuous problems. Our analysis can be applied mainly to the DPSO variants of Clerc in [2] and Wang in [18] but can also be extended to the approaches of Shi et al. [14]. The convergence behavior can be observed whenever the local and the global attractor of a particle nearly coincide. If this is the case the transpositions occurring in respective velocities cancel each other out. This slows down the particles and prevents convergence.

We proposed a new model for particle motion which from a theoretical point of view does not suffer from the aforementioned convergence problem. This is backed by our experiments, which show a clear improvement of the DPSO performance with this model. Additionally we introduced a representation for particle velocities, which is based on edge exchanges in a tour. Our evaluation shows that the edge exchange-based representation produces better results than traditional approaches from the literature.

References

1. Anghinolfi, D., Paolucci, M.: A new discrete particle swarm optimization approach for the single-machine total weighted tardiness scheduling problem with sequence-dependent setup times. European Journal of Operational Research 193, 73–85 (2009), doi:10.1016/j.ejor.2007.10.044

2. Clerc, M.: Discrete Particle Swarm Optimization, illustrated by the Traveling Salesman Problem. Website (2000),
   http://clerc.maurice.free.fr/pso/pso_tsp/Discrete_PSO_TSP.zip
3. Clerc, M.: Discrete particle swarm optimization, illustrated by the traveling salesman problem. In: Onwubolu, G.C., Babu, B.V. (eds.) New Optimization Techniques in Engineering. Studies in Fuzziness and Soft Computing, pp. 219–239. Springer, Heidelberg (2004)
4. Clerc, M., Kennedy, J.: The particle swarm – Explosion, stability, and convergence in a multidimensional complex space. IEEE Transactions on Evolutionary Computation 6, 58–73 (2002)
5. Eberhart, R.C., Kennedy, J.: A new optimizer using particle swarm theory. In: Proc. 6th International Symposium on Micro Machine and Human Science, pp. 39–43 (1995)
6. Goldbarg, E.F.G., de Souza, G.R., Goldbarg, M.C.: Particle swarm for the traveling salesman problem. In: Gottlieb, J., Raidl, G.R. (eds.) EvoCOP 2006. LNCS, vol. 3906, pp. 99–110. Springer, Heidelberg (2006)
7. Gutin, G., Punnen, A.P. (eds.): The Traveling Salesman Problem and Its Variations. Combinatorial Optimization, vol. 12. Springer, Heidelberg (2002)
8. Helwig, S., Wanka, R.: Theoretical analysis of initial particle swarm behavior. In: Rudolph, G., Jansen, T., Lucas, S., Poloni, C., Beume, N. (eds.) PPSN 2008. LNCS, vol. 5199, pp. 889–898. Springer, Heidelberg (2008)
9. Jiang, M., Luo, Y.P., Yang, S.Y.: Stochastic convergence analysis and parameter selection of the standard particle swarm optimization algorithm. Inf. Process. Lett. 102, 8–16 (2007)
10. Kececioglu, J., Sankoff, D.: Exact and approximation algorithms for sorting by reversals, with application to genome rearrangement. Algorithmica 13, 180–210 (1995)
11. Kennedy, J., Eberhart, R.C.: Particle swarm optimization. In: Proc. IEEE International Conference on Neural Networks, vol. 4, pp. 1942–1948 (1995)
12. Kennedy, J., Eberhart, R.C.: A discrete binary version of the particle swarm algorithm. In: Proc. IEEE Int. Conf. on Systems, Man, and Cybernetics, vol. 5, pp. 4104–4108 (1997)
13. Reinelt, G.: TSPLIB – A traveling salesman problem library. ORSA Journal on Computing 3(4), 376–384 (1991)
14. Shi, X.H., Liang, Y.C., Lee, H.P., Lu, C., Wang, Q.X.: Particle swarm optimization-based algorithms for TSP and generalized TSP. Inf. Process. Lett. 103, 169–176 (2007)
15. Shi, X.H., Zhou, Y., Wang, L.M., Wang, Q.X., Liang, Y.C.: A discrete particle swarm optimization algorithm for travelling salesman problem. In: Proc. 1st Int. Conf. on Computation Methods (ICCM), vol. 2, pp. 1063–1068 (2004)
16. Solomon, A., Sutcliffe, P., Lister, R.: Sorting circular permutations by reversal. In: Dehne, F., Sack, J.-R., Smid, M. (eds.) WADS 2003. LNCS, vol. 2748, pp. 319–328. Springer, Heidelberg (2003)
17. Trelea, I.C.: The particle swarm optimization algorithm: Convergence analysis and parameter selection. Inf. Process. Lett. 85, 317–325 (2003)
18. Wang, K.P., Huang, L., Zhou, C.G., Pang, W.: Particle swarm optimization for traveling salesman problem. In: Proc. 2nd Int. Conf. on Machine Learning and Cybernetics, vol. 3, pp. 1583–1585 (2003)
19. Zhong, W., Zhang, J., Chen, W.: A novel discrete particle swarm optimization to solve traveling salesman problem. In: Proc. IEEE Congress on Evolutionary Computation (CEC), pp. 3283–3287 (2007)

Author Index